The Dream
That Never Was

Other Books in
The Library of
American Comics

ARCHIE BY BOB MONTANA

BLONDIE BY CHIC YOUNG

BLOOM COUNTY BY BERKELEY BREATHED

BRINGING UP FATHER BY GEORGE McMANUS

CANIFF: A VISUAL BIOGRAPHY
BY DEAN MULLANEY

DICK TRACY BY CHESTER GOULD

THE FAMILY CIRCUS
BY BIL KEANE

FLASH GORDON AND JUNGLE JIM
BY ALEX RAYMOND

GENIUS, ISOLATED:
THE LIFE AND ART OF ALEX TOTH
BY DEAN MULLANEY & BRUCE CANWELL

KING AROO BY JACK KENT

LI'L ABNER BY AL CAPP

LITTLE ORPHAN ANNIE BY HAROLD GRAY

MISS FURY BY TARPÉ MILLS

POLLY AND HER PALS BY CLIFF STERRETT

RIP KIRBY BY ALEX RAYMOND

SCORCHY SMITH AND
THE ART OF NOEL SICKLES

SECRET AGENT CORRIGAN
BY AL WILLIAMSON & ARCHIE GOODWIN

TERRY AND THE PIRATES BY MILTON CANIFF

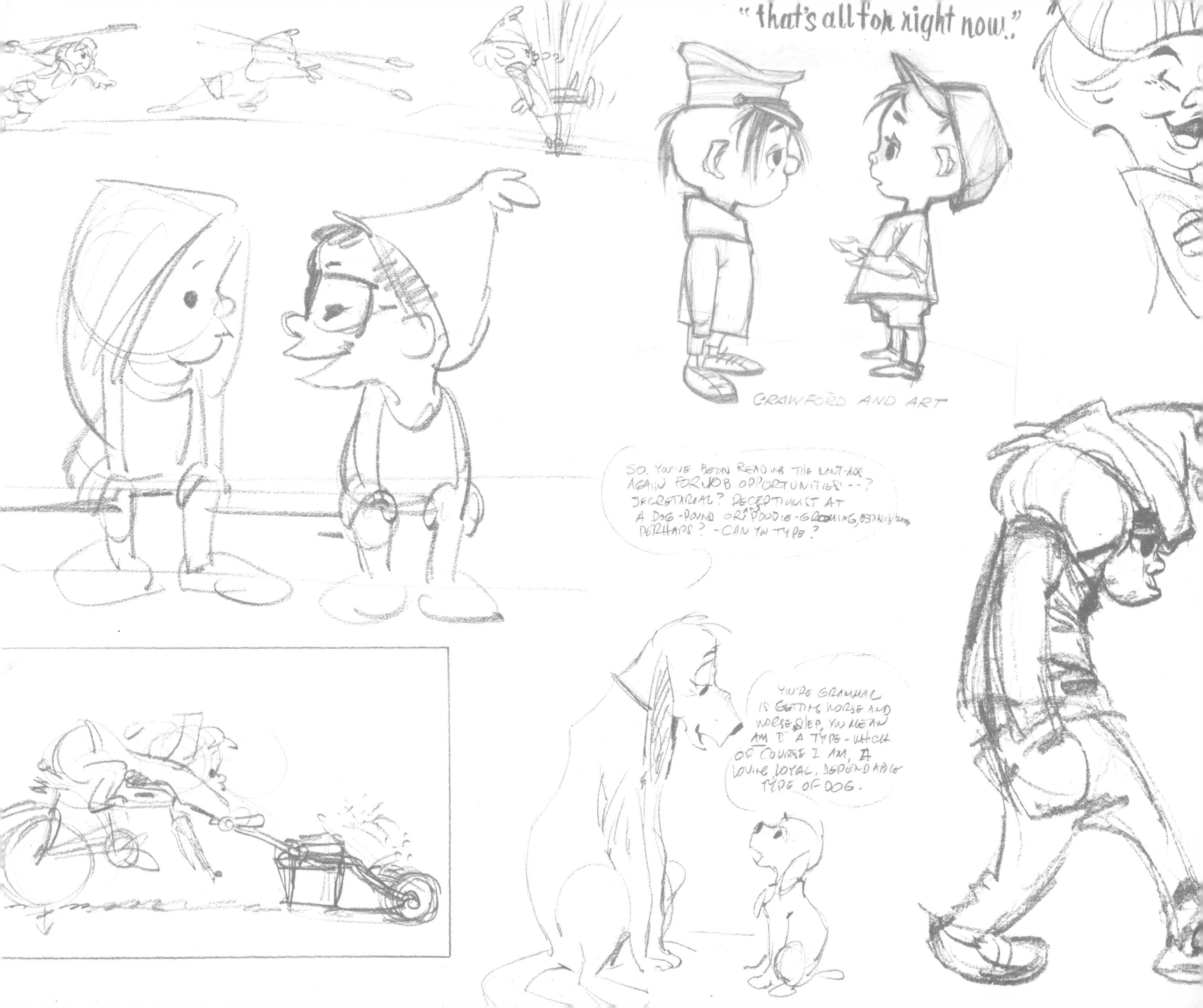
"that's all for right now."
CRAWFORD AND ART
SO, YOU'VE BEEN READING THE WANT-ADS AGAIN FOR JOB OPPORTUNITIES --? SECRETARIAL? RECEPTIONIST AT A DOG-POUND OR AT A POODLE-GROOMING ESTABLISHMENT, PERHAPS? -CAN YOU TYPE?
YOU'RE GRAMMAR IS GETTING WORSE AND WORSE, SKEP. YOU MEAN AM I A TYPE - WHICH OF COURSE I AM, A LOVING LOYAL, DEPENDABLE TYPE OF DOG.

Chuck Jones
The Dream
That Never Was

Edited by Dean Mullaney and Kurtis Findlay
Designed by Lorraine Turner

THE
LIBRARY OF
AMERICAN
COMICS

IDW PUBLISHING
SAN DIEGO, CALIFORNIA

CHUCK JONES

The Dream That Never Was

Edited by DEAN MULLANEY and KURTIS FINDLAY

Designed by LORRAINE TURNER

THE LIBRARY OF AMERICAN COMICS

IDW PUBLISHING
SAN DIEGO, CALIFORNIA

The Dream That Never Was

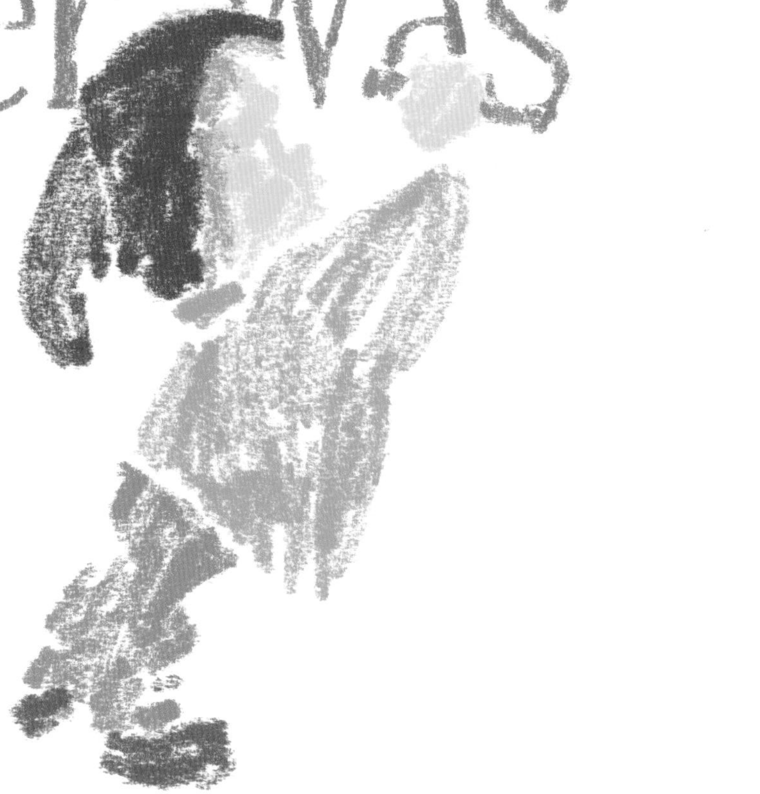

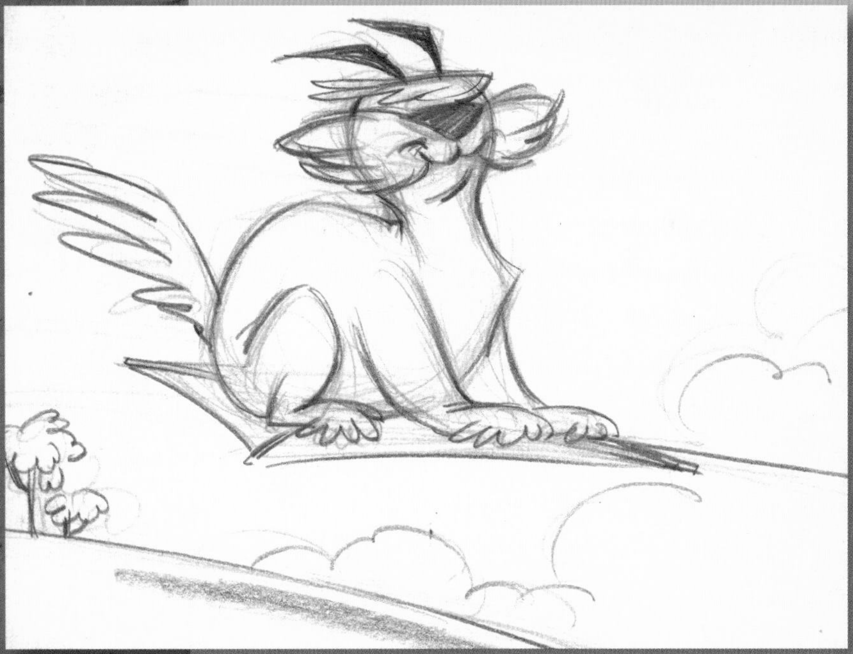

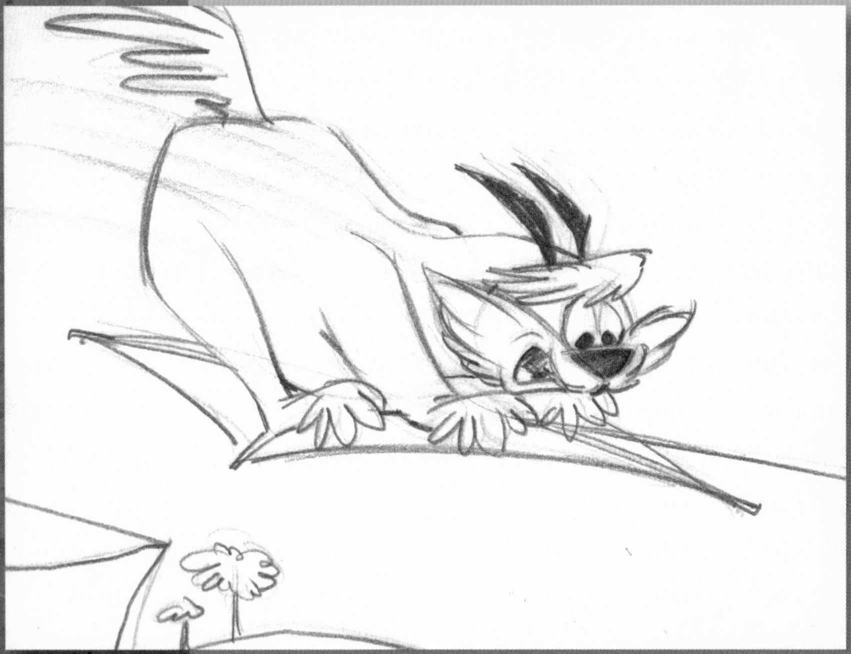

THE LIBRARY OF AMERICAN COMICS
www.libraryofamericancomics.com

EDITED BY Dean Mullaney and Kurtis Findlay
DESIGNED BY Lorraine Turner
ASSOCIATE EDITOR Bruce Canwell

Thanks to Marian Jones, Mark Kausler, Don Michel, Don Morgan, Robert Reed, and Darrell Van Citters for their recollections in interviews with the author; to Linda Jones Clough, Andy Mangels, and Carl Bell for their recollections in letters or emails to the author.

Additional thanks to Rosemary Arioli, Michael Barrier, Jerry Beck, Trung and Fay Duong, the Levitow family, Alan Light, Bill Peckmann, Lisa Timmons, and Steve Tippie.

Special thanks from Kurtis Findlay to "my wife, Katie, whose love and support for me and this project was unmatched."

Art on this page and opposite from *Crawford* storyboards, 1969.

ISBN: 978-1-61377-030-6

First Printing, November 2011

IDW Publishing
a Division of Idea and Design Works, LLC
5080 Santa Fe Street, San Diego, CA 92109
www.idwpublishing.com

IDW Publishing
Ted Adams, Chief Executive Officer/Publisher • Greg Goldstein, Chief Operating Officer
Robbie Robbins, EVP/Sr. Graphic Artist • Chris Ryall, Chief Creative Officer
Matthew Ruzicka, CPA, Chief Financial Officer • Alan Payne, VP of Sales

Distributed by Diamond Book Distributors
1-410-560-7100

CHUCK JONES: THE DREAM THAT NEVER WAS

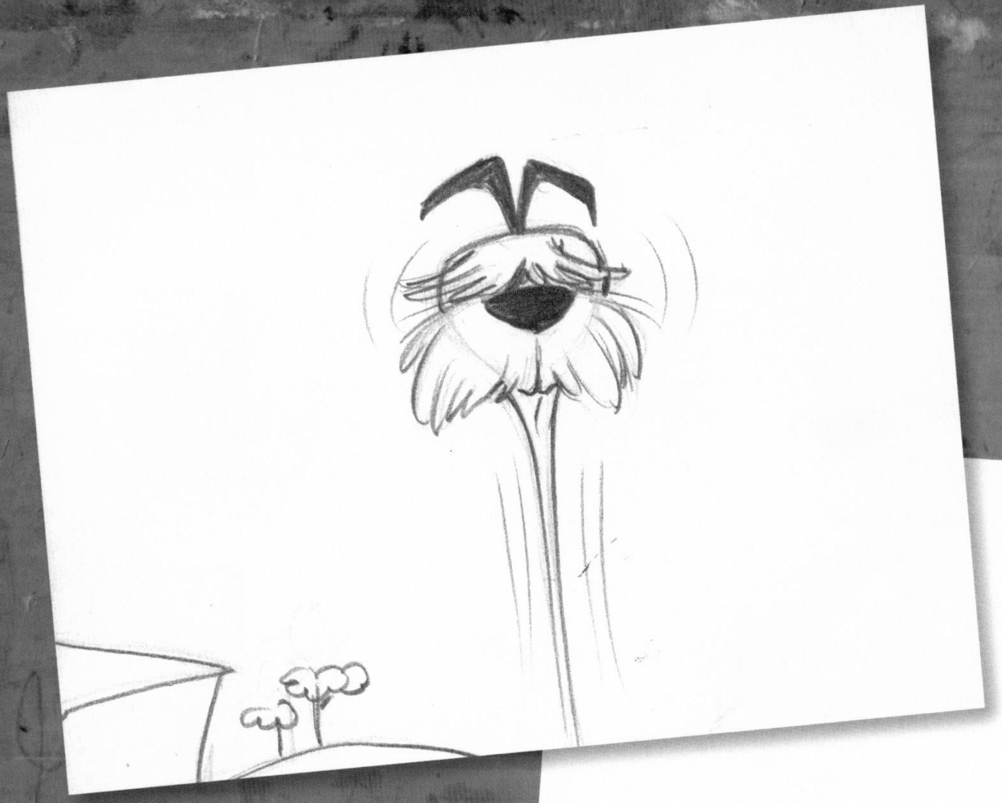
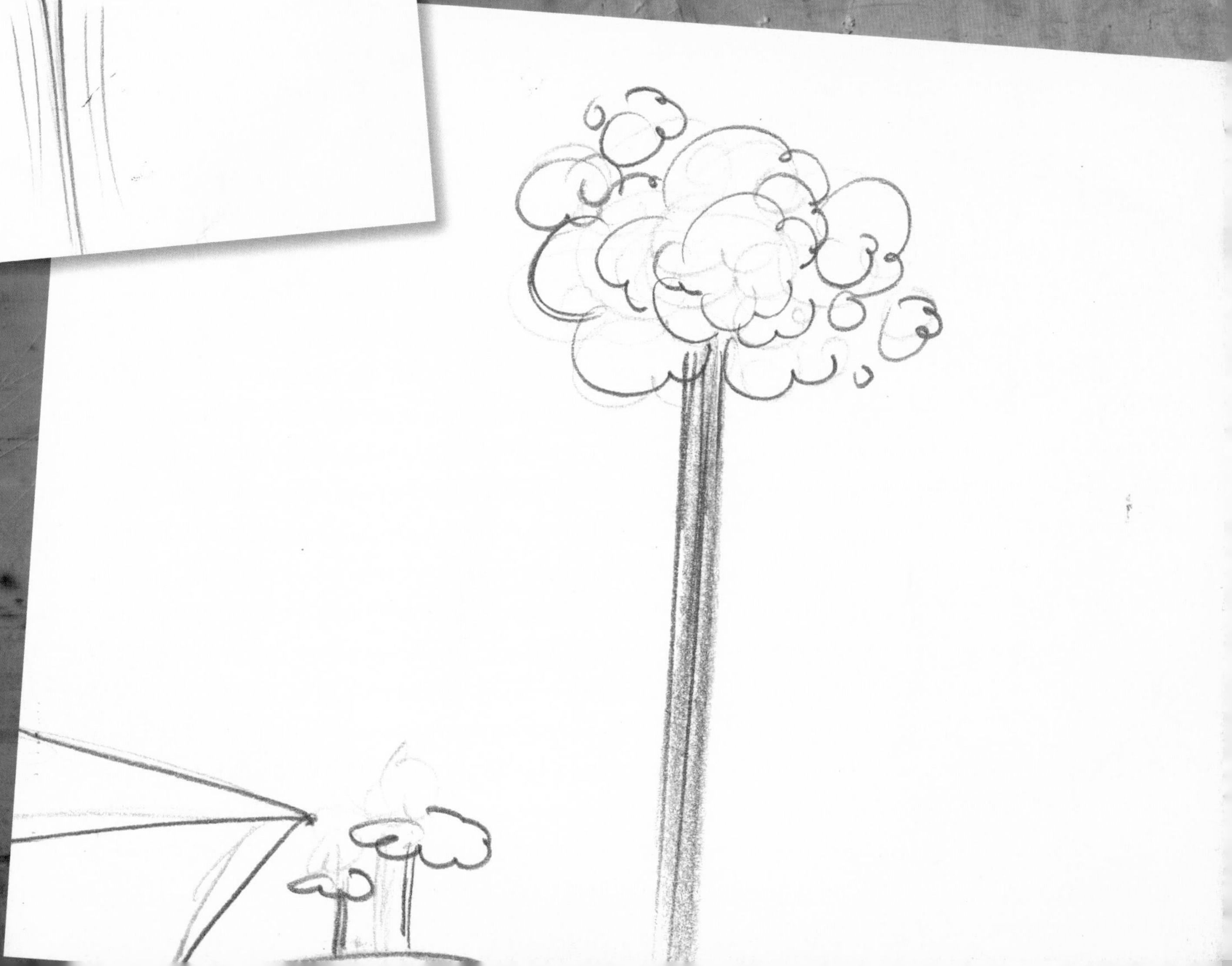

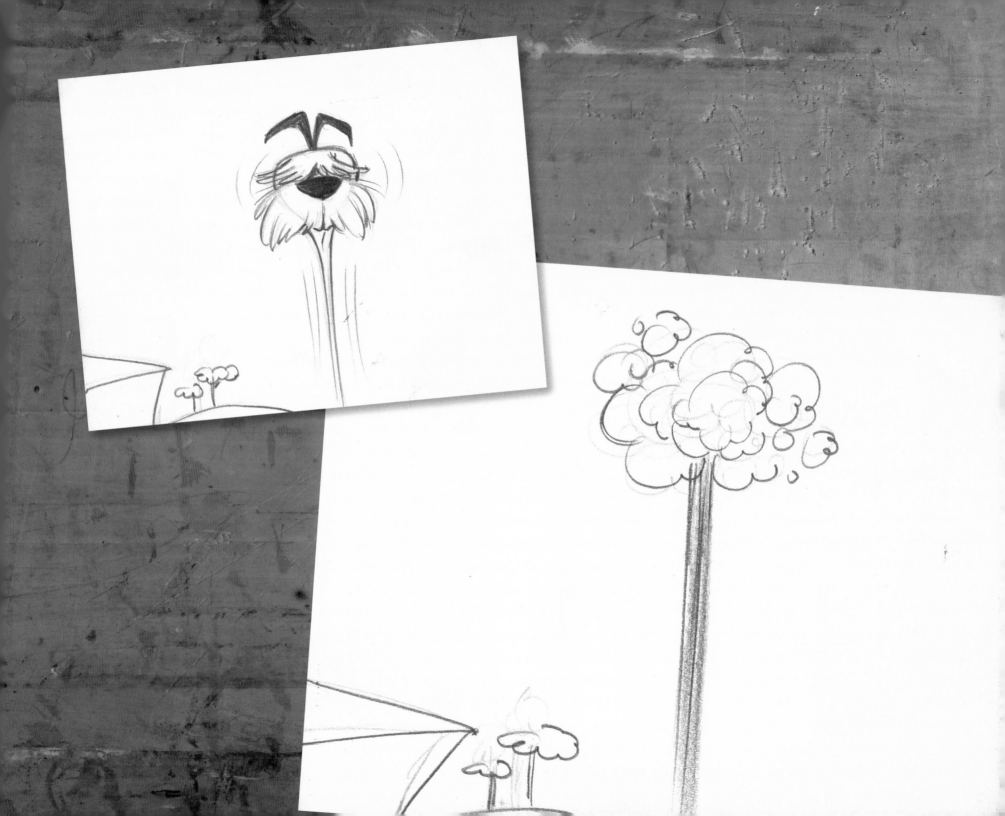

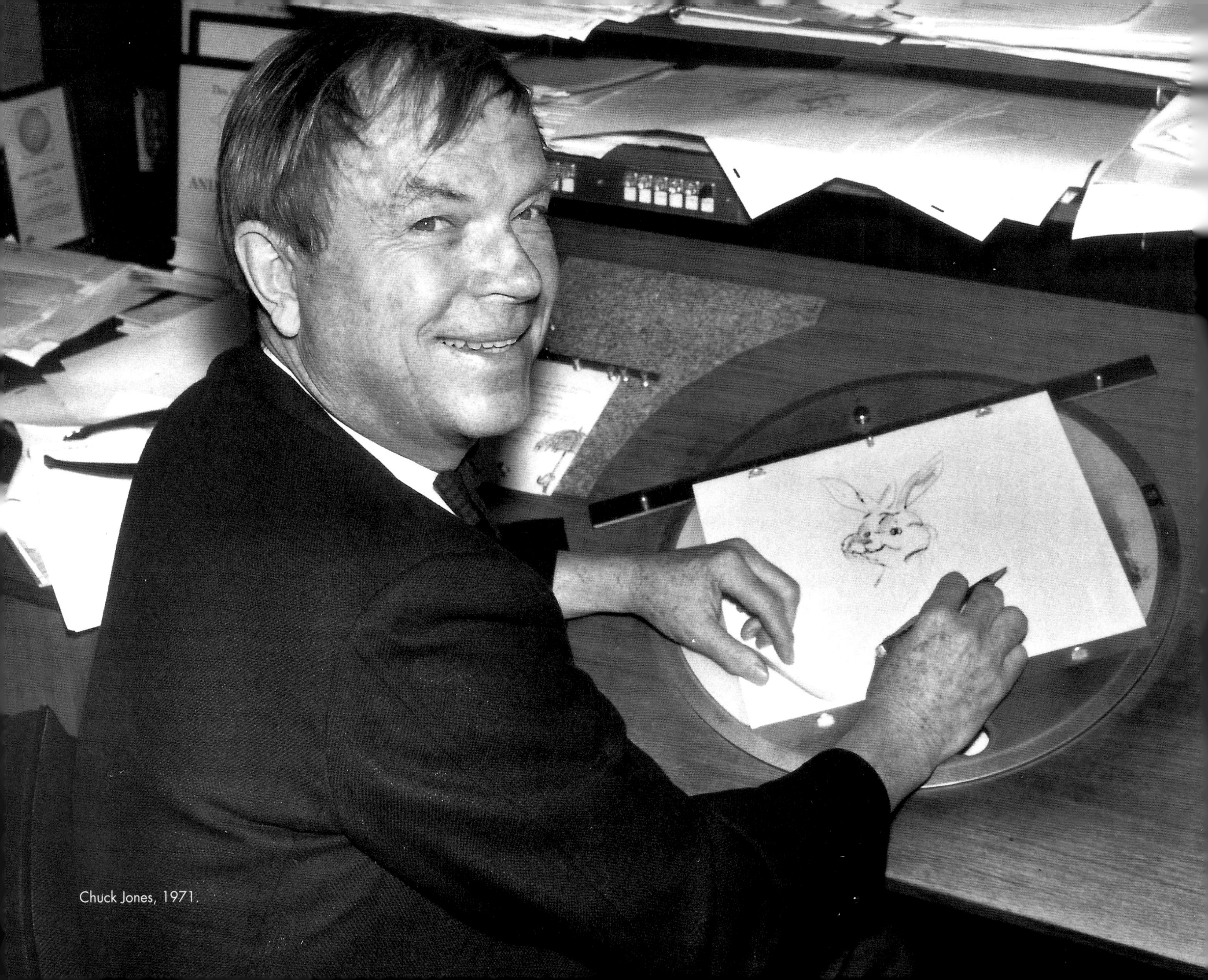

Chuck Jones, 1971.

The Dream That Never Was

Introduction by KURTIS FINDLAY

"…there is a new strip being offered that I'm completely sold on. It's undoubtedly the best comic strip ever offered. In all seriousness and without exaggeration, it's probably the greatest thing to ever happen to newspapers since Gutenberg. Trouble is, I can't seem to convince anyone else of this.

I'm referring to a promo piece that came in the mail a few weeks ago for a new strip to hit the papers in January. Its name: Crawford."

—Tom Crawford, Bemidji (Minnesota) *Pioneer,* December 18, 1977.

On Monday, January 9, 1978, the New York *Daily News* and a mere handful of small newspapers introduced a new strip to their comics sections entitled *Crawford*. Few were as enthusiastic as the editor of the Bemidji *Pioneer* (see quote at right), making *Crawford* only slightly less obscure in 1978 than it is today. (The *Pioneer* didn't end up carrying *Crawford* after all, despite the lobbying from its editorial namesake). The strip lasted only a few months—by May, it was discontinued.

It was not the first newspaper strip to barely get off the ground, and it will hardly be the last. What makes *Crawford* noteworthy is that it was created, written, and drawn by legendary animator Chuck Jones.

In Jones's long and accomplished career, *Crawford* is only a footnote to his more famous creations, yet it offers a fascinating insight to the creative process and dogged determination of the Academy Award-winning director of *Duck Amuck*; *What's Opera, Doc?*; *Dr. Seuss's How the Grinch Stole Christmas*; and many other classics.

Chuck Jones's work is dutifully studied by animation professionals and his career continues to intrigue historians of the medium. So why is it that a comic strip featuring his own creations and signature art style was met with barely a yawn? In the intervening years it has never been mentioned in interviews or biographies and its only reference in Chuck's autobiography, *Chuck Amuck,* is Crawford's name amongst a list of other, better known creations such as the Road Runner & Coyote and Pepé Le Pew. No explanation, no history, no examples, no context…leaving readers to wonder about the mystery that is *Crawford*.

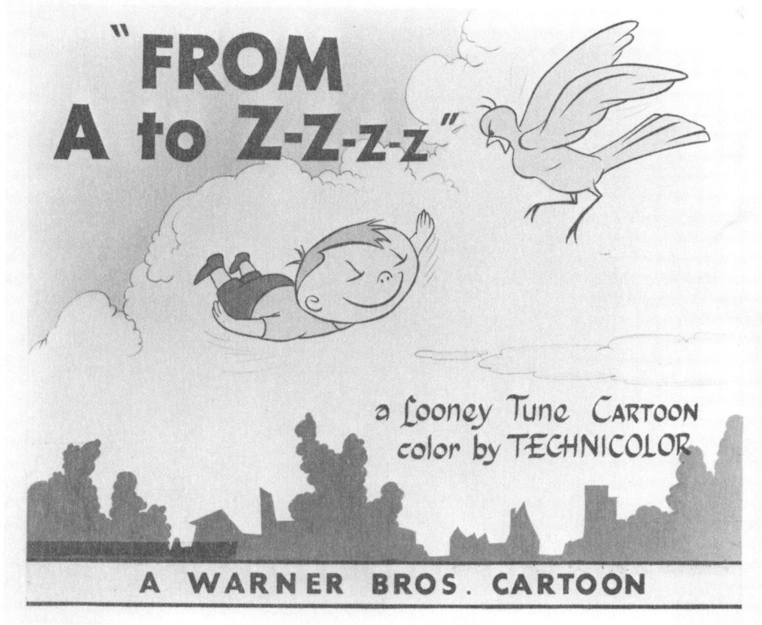
"FROM
A to Z-Z-z-z"
a Looney Tune CARTOON
color by TECHNICOLOR
A WARNER BROS. CARTOON

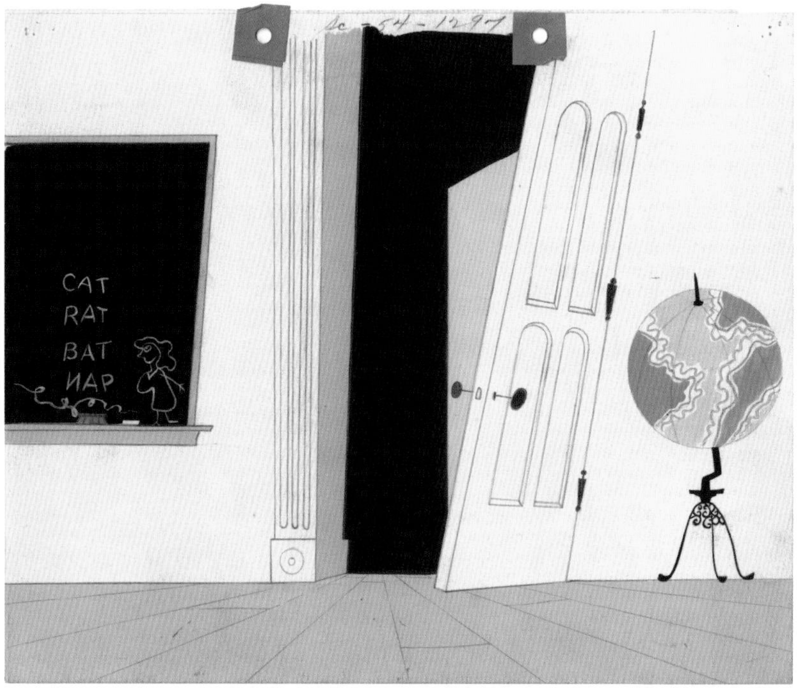
CAT
RAT
BAT
NAP

Crawford's inauspicious debut in America's funny pages, however, isn't where the story begins, nor where it ends. Jones considered Crawford to be a childlike version of himself and the story of *Crawford* is a twenty-seven-year journey in which the character weaved in and out of some of Chuck Jones's most popular cartoons. Crawford was initially conceived for the earliest *Road-Runner* TV series in 1962, but as happened time and time again throughout the 1960s and 1970s, the character ended up on the cutting room floor or was never realized.

When the opportunity arose in 1977 to create a newspaper comic feature, some of Chuck's associates were surprised that he would commit himself to the rigorous and demanding schedule of a daily strip, especially in the midst of running his own animation studio. But Chuck Jones saw it as a means to share one of his most cherished characters with the public, and—deadlines or not—this was his best hope to do it.

• • • • •

Charles Martin Jones was born on September 21, 1912 in Spokane, Washington, although he wasn't to stay there very long, as his family moved to Southern California when he was six months old. At the age of fifteen, rather than finishing high school, Chuck enrolled in the Chouinard Art Institute (now the California Institute of the Arts) in order to nurture his budding talent in drawing and illustration.

In 1931, after attempting a career in commercial art, Chuck found a job as a cel washer for the Ub Iwerks Animation Studio. At the time Iwerks was considered the leading animator in the field. A long-time friend of—and eventual partner with—Walt Disney, he was primarily responsible for most of the early cartoons released by Disney, including Oswald the Rabbit, Mickey Mouse, and *Silly Symphonies*. A falling out over credits resulted in Iwerks leaving to form his own studio in 1930. Chuck worked on the *Flip the Frog* and *Willie Whopper* cartoons and quickly climbed the ranks, eventually becoming an in-betweener (drawing the interstitial movements between the animator's key poses). When Ub Iwerks realized that a lowly cel washer had been promoted to the lofty position of in-betweening, he did not just see to it that Jones was released from the company, he had his secretary do the firing. The firing may have disillusioned Chuck, but it was fortuitous as well, since the secretary happened to be Dorothy Webster, whom Chuck would marry in 1935.

Jones began his association with *Looney Tunes* in 1933, when he was hired at Leon Schlesinger Productions as an assistant animator. Schlesinger's studio was expanding thanks to the popularity of their two cartoon series, *Looney Tunes* and *Merrie Melodies*, distributed by Warner Bros. Pictures. In 1935 Jones was promoted to animator and assigned to a unit under the direction of Fred "Tex" Avery. Over the following few years, in a dilapidated building on the Warner Bros. lot that the animators christened "Termite Terrace," the groundwork was being laid for what would become worldwide pop cultural history.

Opposite: A lobby card and background painting for the first Ralph Phillips cartoon, the Oscar-nominated *From A to Z-Z-Z-Z*; background by Maurice Noble, painted by Philip DeGuard.

Right: Sketches from 1957's *Boyhood Daze*, the second short starring Ralph.

It was not long before Chuck got his chance in the director's chair. When *Looney Tunes* director Frank Tashlin left the studio in 1938, Chuck took over Tashlin's unit and during the next thirty years created many of the most memorable Warner Bros. cartoons, including *Rabbit of Seville; Duck, Rabbit, Duck; One Froggy Evening; Duck Dodgers in the 24½ Century;* and *Rabbit Seasoning*. He earned eight Academy Award nominations for his Warner Bros. films, twice bringing home Oscar. He added his own personal touch to the studio's star performers, most notably shaping the personas of Bugs Bunny and Daffy Duck as they are known today. In addition to creating some of the studio's biggest stars (the aforementioned Pepé Le Pew and Road Runner & Coyote, as well as Marvin the Martian), Jones and his team brought to life several well-regarded but lesser-known characters (Marc Anthony, Hubie and Bertie, and Claude Cat). Beginning with *The Dover Boys of Pimento University* in 1942, his artistic and directorial talents redefined comic timing and stylized graphics in the animation medium.

• • • • •

By the 1950s Leon Schlesinger had sold his interest in the studio and the animation unit was renamed Warner Bros. Cartoons. Chuck Jones and his cohorts were entering what Jerry Beck and Will Friedwald, in the book *Warner Bros. Animation Art*, call their "most fertile period." Jones referred to his team of animators as "artists who firmly believed in the pleasure of their craft and the joy of animation." His team consisted of some of the best talent in the industry, men whose individual gifts fit perfectly under Chuck's direction: Michael Maltese wrote at the top of his game in a career that included work at MGM (*Tom and Jerry*) and Hanna-Barbera (*The Flintstones*); Maurice Noble constructed elaborate and stylized sets and backgrounds that were beautifully painted by Philip DeGuard; and Chuck's animation team—Ken Harris, Ben Washam, Lloyd Vaughan, Richard Thompson, and Abe Levitow—were producing some of the studio's best work.

It was during this time that Chuck Jones created Ralph Phillips, an average boy with an overactive imagination, who can be considered the direct precursor to Crawford. Inspired by the fantastic daydreams of Walter Mitty—as portrayed by Danny Kaye on the big screen—Ralph would frequently escape the boredom of reality by entering his vivid daydreams, much to the chagrin of his teacher or parents.

Warner Bros. released the first of two short films to star Ralph Phillips on October 16, 1954. It was a *Looney Tune* titled *From A to Z-Z-Z-Z* and earned the studio an Academy Award nomination for Best Short Subject. In the film, Ralph's daydreams take him soaring through the air like a bird, galloping through the Wild West, and to the deepest depths of the ocean. He battles Indians, killer sharks, heavyweight champions, and even mathematical equations.

Ralph's second and final Warner Bros. appearance—*Boyhood Daze*, a *Merrie Melody* from 1957—follows a format similar to the first. Sent to his room for hitting a baseball through a glass window, Ralph enters the many worlds of his imagination. This time around he is a famous jungle explorer, a fighter pilot, a criminal in prison, and George Washington. These two short films are notable not only for Ralph Phillips, but also for their incredible array of stylized backdrops. Layout artist Maurice Noble pushed the envelope with the lines, colors, and angles used in Ralph's various dreamscapes.

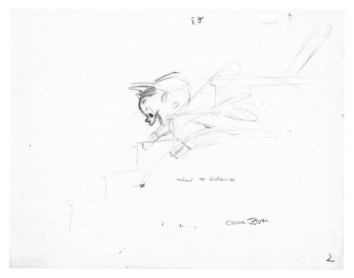

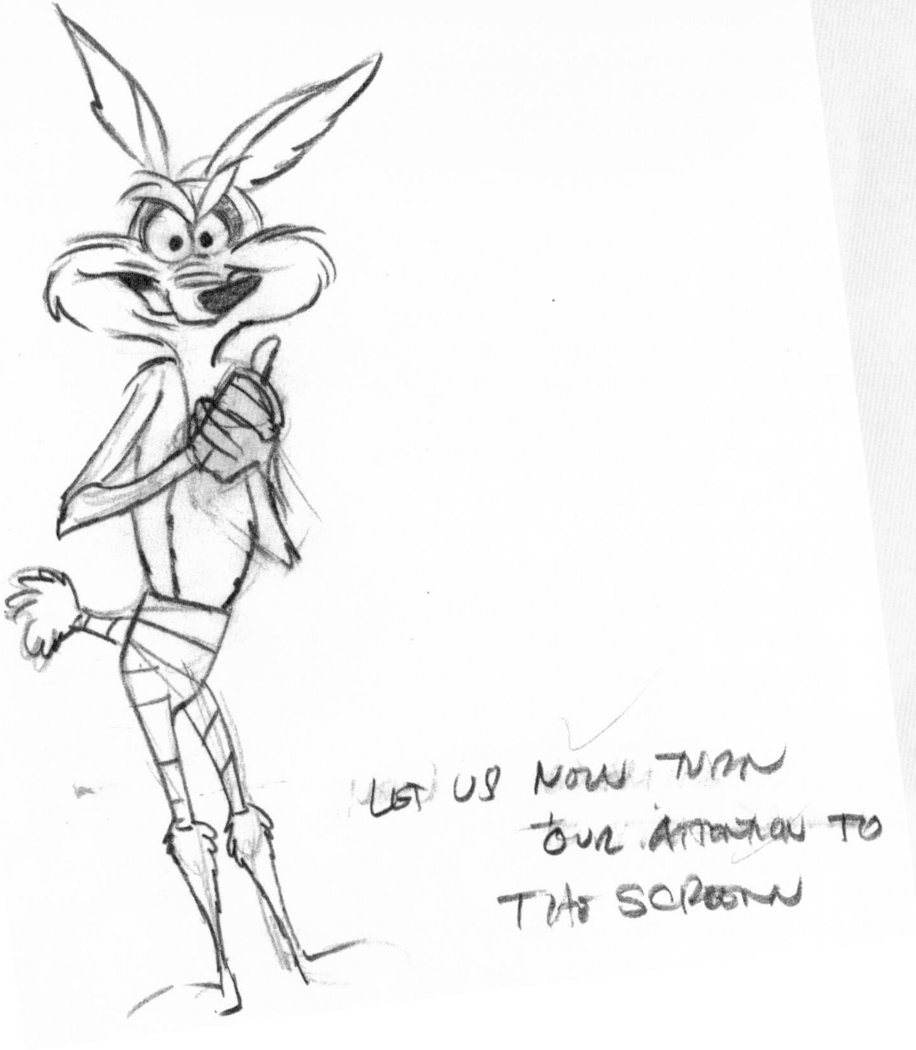
LET US NOW TURN
OUR ATTENTION TO
THAT SCREEN

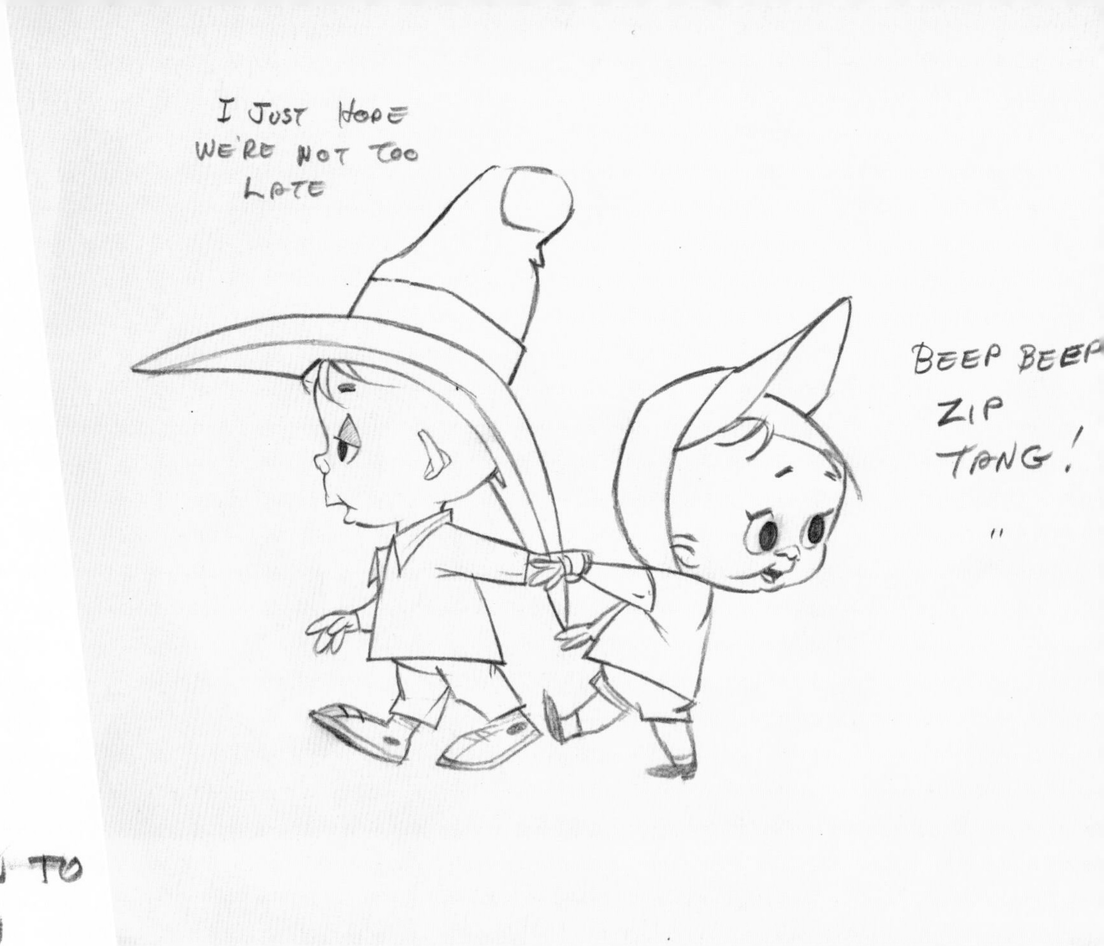
I JUST HOPE
WE'RE NOT TOO
LATE
BEEP BEEP
ZIP
TANG!

"I had no trouble writing dialogue or creating drawings for the Ralph Phillips cartoons, as Ralph is [me] as a child," Chuck Jones recalled. The director often revisited childhood in his filmmaking: it is from a long line of young protagonists such as Sniffles the Mouse, Ralph Phillips, *Phantom Tollbooth's* Milo, and Kipling's Mowgli that we eventually get Crawford, although it would be about two decades after Ralph Phillips before Crawford would reach the public eye.

• • • • •

Warner Bros. found major success bringing *Looney Tunes* to television in 1960 by packaging their theatrical cartoons as part of *The Bugs Bunny Show.* Forty half-hour episodes were ordered, mainly consisting of shorts from the 1950s with newly produced bridging sequences. The final episode would air mid-1961 and Warner Bros. set the ball into motion for a new show for the 1962 season. Chuck Jones's unit produced a pilot for *The Adventures of the Road-Runner,* which was to follow the same structure as *The Bugs Bunny Show*—classic *Looney Tunes* segued with all-new segments. However, for the pilot two new *Road-Runner* episodes were made, making the entire episode new material.

The bridging animation featured Ralph Phillips and his cowboy-hat-wearing older brother, Arnold, watching Wile E. Coyote on television. They are entranced; the television has sucked away their imaginations and they stare at the box with blank expressions. They're not completely mindless, however. Ralph says, "I sometimes think I'm the Road Runner. BEEP! BEEP! ZIP TANG!" and "Sometimes I wish he'd catch him," to which his brother replies, "If he caught him there wouldn't be any more Road Runner. You wouldn't like that, would you?"

This cartoon is a prime example of the multifarious nature of Chuck Jones's art: he

Opposite: Sketches of Wile E. Coyote and Ralph and Arnold Phillips from 1962's *The Adventures of the Road-Runner.*

Below and right: A script page and Chuck's notes about the show's format. The script is the first written reference to the character Crawford.

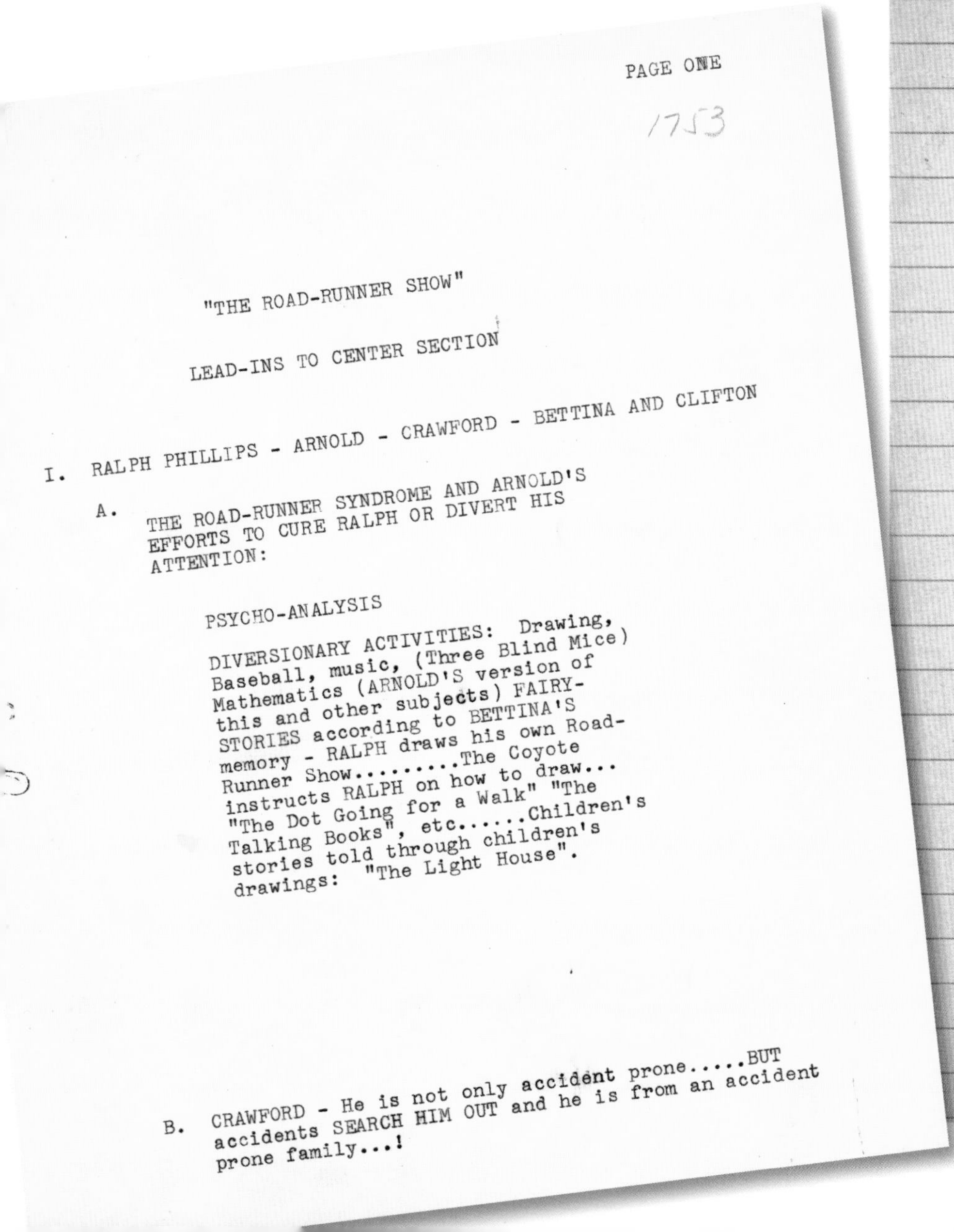

PAGE ONE

1753

"THE ROAD-RUNNER SHOW"

LEAD-INS TO CENTER SECTION

I. RALPH PHILLIPS - ARNOLD - CRAWFORD - BETTINA AND CLIFTON

A. THE ROAD-RUNNER SYNDROME AND ARNOLD'S EFFORTS TO CURE RALPH OR DIVERT HIS ATTENTION:

PSYCHO-ANALYSIS

DIVERSIONARY ACTIVITIES: Drawing, Baseball, music, (Three Blind Mice) Mathematics (ARNOLD'S version of this and other subjects) FAIRY-STORIES according to BETTINA'S memory - RALPH draws his own Road-Runner Show.........The Coyote instructs RALPH on how to draw... "The Dot Going for a Walk" "The Talking Books", etc......Children's stories told through children's drawings: "The Light House".

B. CRAWFORD - He is not only accident prone.....BUT accidents SEARCH HIM OUT and he is from an accident prone family...!

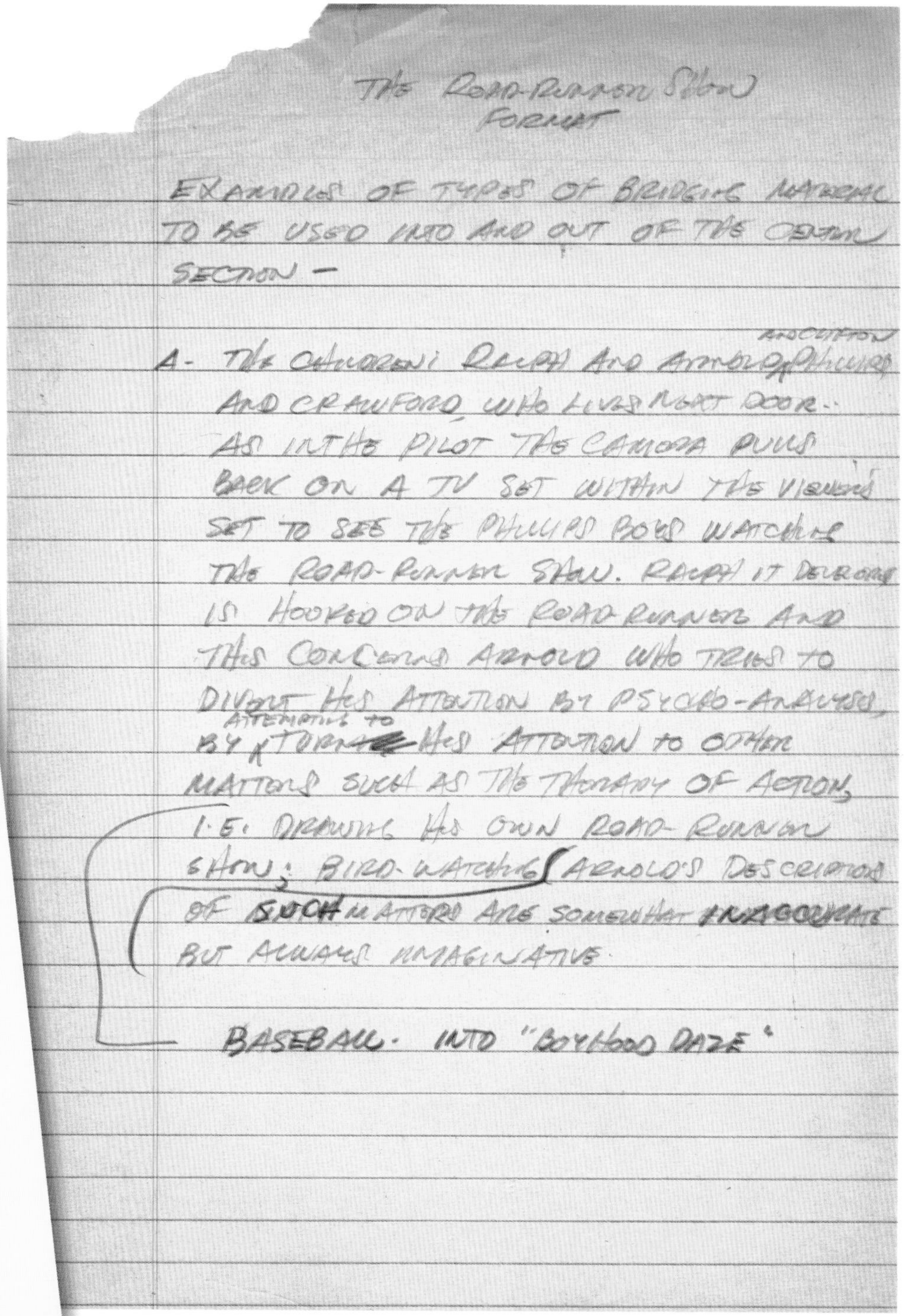

THE ROAD-RUNNER SHOW
FORMAT

EXAMPLES OF TYPES OF BRIDGING MATERIAL TO BE USED INTO AND OUT OF THE CENTER SECTION —

A- THE CHILDREN: RALPH AND ARNOLD PHILLIPS AND CLIFTON AND CRAWFORD, WHO LIVES NEXT DOOR. AS IN THE PILOT THE CAMERA PULLS BACK ON A TV SET WITHIN THE VIEWERS SET TO SEE THE PHILLIPS BOYS WATCHING THE ROAD-RUNNER SHOW. RALPH IT DEVELOPS IS HOOKED ON THE ROAD-RUNNER AND THIS CONCERNS ARNOLD WHO TRIES TO DIVERT HIS ATTENTION BY PSYCHO-ANALYSIS, BY ATTEMPTING TO ~~TURNING~~ HIS ATTENTION TO OTHER MATTERS SUCH AS THE THEORY OF ACTION, I.E. DRAWING HIS OWN ROAD-RUNNER SHOW; BIRD-WATCHING. ARNOLD'S DESCRIPTION OF SUCH MATTERS ARE SOMEWHAT INADEQUATE BUT ALWAYS IMAGINATIVE.

BASEBALL · INTO "BOYHOOD DAZE"

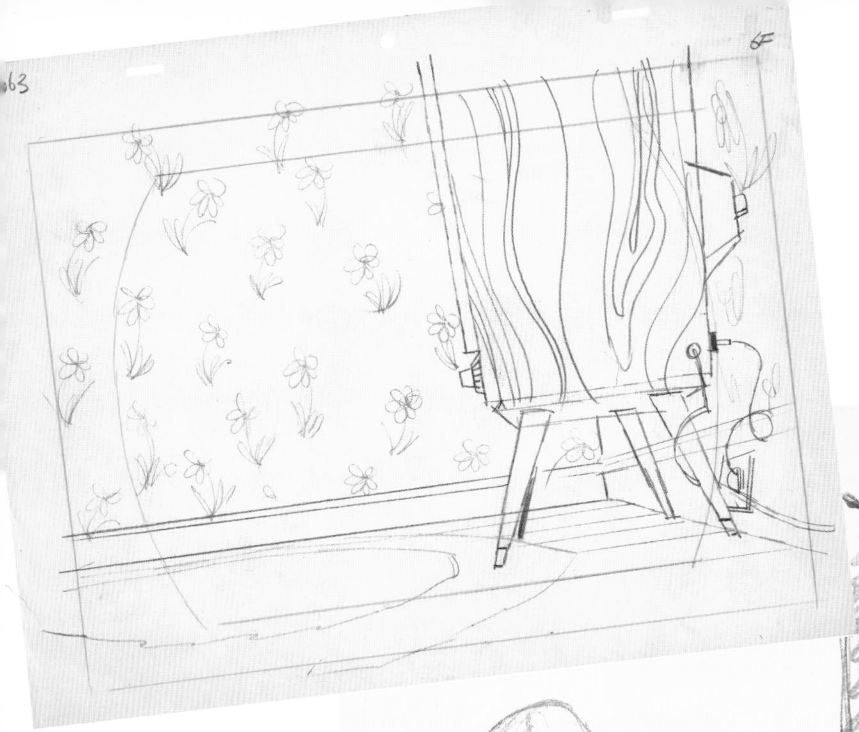

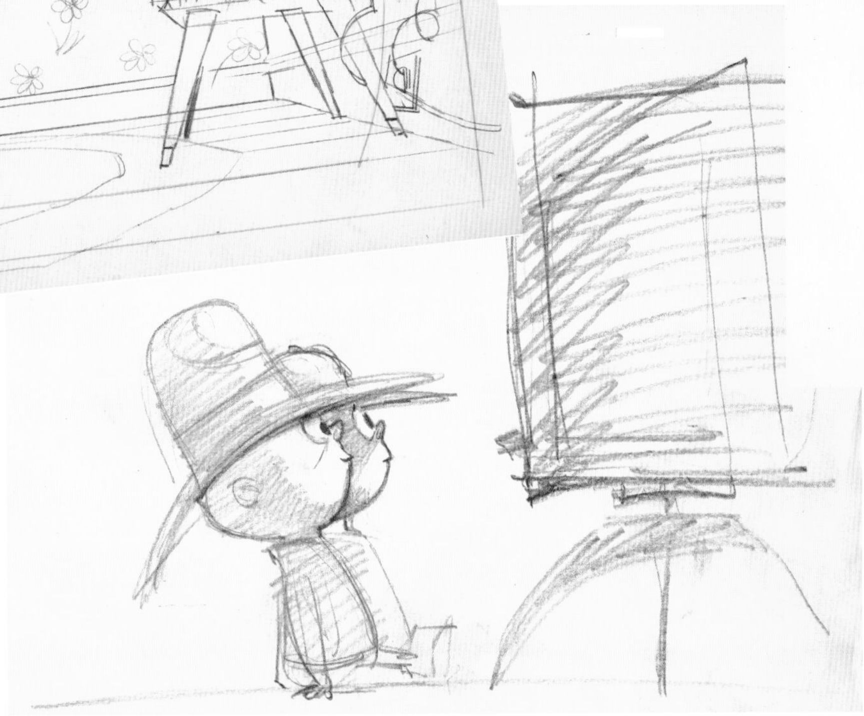

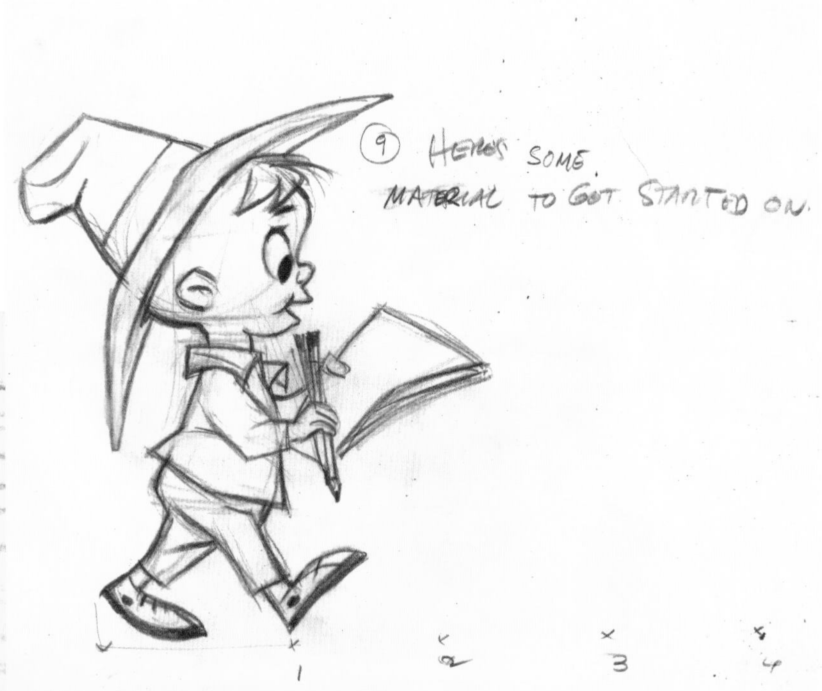
9 HERE'S SOME MATERIAL TO GET STARTED ON.

Both pages: Sketches of the bridging segments for *The Adventures of the Road-Runner*. The top right illustration is by Maurice Noble.

presents the Road Runner and Wile E. Coyote as entertainment on screen while having his passive TV viewers, Ralph and Arnold (though in this introductory sequence, Arnold's name and relationship to Ralph are not stated), act as stand-ins for the audience. It's an approach that he later uses to good effect in the *Crawford* comic strip when Crawford and his friend, Morgan, sit in front of a television contemplating what is being displayed in front of them.

ABC never picked up *The Adventures of the Road-Runner* and Warner Bros. shut down their animation studio in 1963, but not before releasing the twenty-six-minute featurette to theaters. Had the series continued, Ralph Phillips and his brother would have been regular characters. In each episode Ralph would be fixated on the Road Runner while Arnold would try to find ways to distract Ralph from the screen—enticing him into drawing, bird watching, or playing baseball.

Given the chance to develop the series further, Jones planned to add more children: Ralph and Arnold's younger brother, Clifton, an incredibly intelligent infant without the means to communicate; Bettina, a neighboring child who tells fairy tales in her own unique fashion; and finally, their next door neighbor…Crawford. Although not the Crawford that later appeared in the comic strip—Chuck's first portrait describes him as "not only accident prone…BUT accidents SEARCH HIM OUT and he is from an accident prone family…!"

WELL IT'S BEEN GOING ON
SINCE I WAS VERY YOUNG.
BUT IT SORT OF CAME TO
WELL... IT ALL A HEAD

DURING
ARITHMETIC LESSON

YESTERDAY

DISS INTO
PAN OF

SINCE SCHOOL.
ATHOME
RECITING.

Left and opposite: Chuck in his new studio space—Tower Twelve, Inc.—in the Sunset-Vine Tower in Hollywood.

Because ABC didn't greenlight the series, Crawford never became a Warner Bros. property. Therefore, unlike Ralph Phillips, Crawford could travel with Chuck Jones to the next chapter in his life.

• • • • •

In 1962 Chuck was approached by director Abe Levitow, then at United Productions of America (UPA); Abe had started out at Leon Schlesinger Productions at the age of seventeen as an in-betweener under Jones's mentorship. Levitow moved from in-betweener to one of Jones's top animators, eventually directing a few *Looney Tunes* in the late '50s. Fresh from being a key animator on UPA's first animated feature, *1001 Arabian Nights* (starring Mr. Magoo), as well as directing a 1961 series of *Dick Tracy* cartoons, Levitow wanted his former boss's help in developing a second animated feature for the studio.

Together with his wife, Dorothy, Chuck Jones wrote the screenplay for *Gay Pur-ee*, an animated musical featuring the voices of Judy Garland, Robert Goulet, and Red Buttons. Chuck was more than willing to help his former protégé even though he had an exclusive contract with Warner Bros. Jones figured that Warner executives most likely would never notice his name on the production since the film was being distributed by United Artists. He planned to slip under the radar.

In a cruel twist of fate, the deal with UA fell through and Warner Bros. picked up the distribution rights for *Gay Pur-ee*. When Jack Warner found out that Jones had been moonlighting, his contract was promptly terminated. Chuck's almost thirty-year tenure at

the Warner Bros. Cartoon Studios and his having created a goldmine of characters and award-winning cartoons meant nothing to studio mogul Warner, who never really cared about the animation department. "I don't know what the f**k you do," said the Warner brother in a 1943 meeting with Chuck, "all I know is we make Mickey Mouse!" It was 1962, and suddenly Chuck Jones was out on his own, wondering what to do next.

With a lifetime of experience behind him, the fifty-year-old director, along with his business partner, Les Goldman, formed a new animation studio, Tower Twelve, Inc. Occupying the twelfth floor of the Sunset-Vine Tower at 6290 Sunset Boulevard, Chuck's new space had a 360-degree view of Hollywood. "That view…was unmatched," recalls animator Mark Kausler. "You'd go up there and you'd just want to stare out that window all day. I don't know how anybody got any work done." Chuck outfitted the various offices and work areas with solid oak desks and stations and leather upholstered furniture—a far cry from the working conditions of Termite Terrace. He also installed a screening room in the middle of the twelfth floor, where, animator Carl Bell fondly remembers, "he kept a library of his Warner Bros. films in 16mm for screening to the crew, or available to each of us individually. Chuck had the entire floor as a working facility. 'My door is always open,' he said, and meant it."

When the word got out that Jones was starting his own studio—and knowing that Warner Bros. was planning to shut down their animation unit— many of his long-time *Looney Tunes* cohorts jumped ship and rejoined their former leader. Among them were animators Ken Harris, Richard Thompson, Ben Washam, and Tom Ray.

"He had his good buddies with him and it was a happy place to work," remembers Don Morgan, who early in his career was brought to Tower Twelve as a layout artist by his mentor, Abe Levitow. "Everybody wore ties. Chuck wore a bowtie, but the rest of them wore regular ties."

Rented space on the eleventh floor was used to store the vast amount of drawings produced by the artists on the floor above. "When I was there [in 1976] they had Irv Wyner, who was an old Warner Bros. background painter," recalls Darrell Van Citters, now animation director, but originally an errand boy in the building. "He was down there [on the eleventh floor] painting backgrounds on the Road Runner and Coyote stuff for

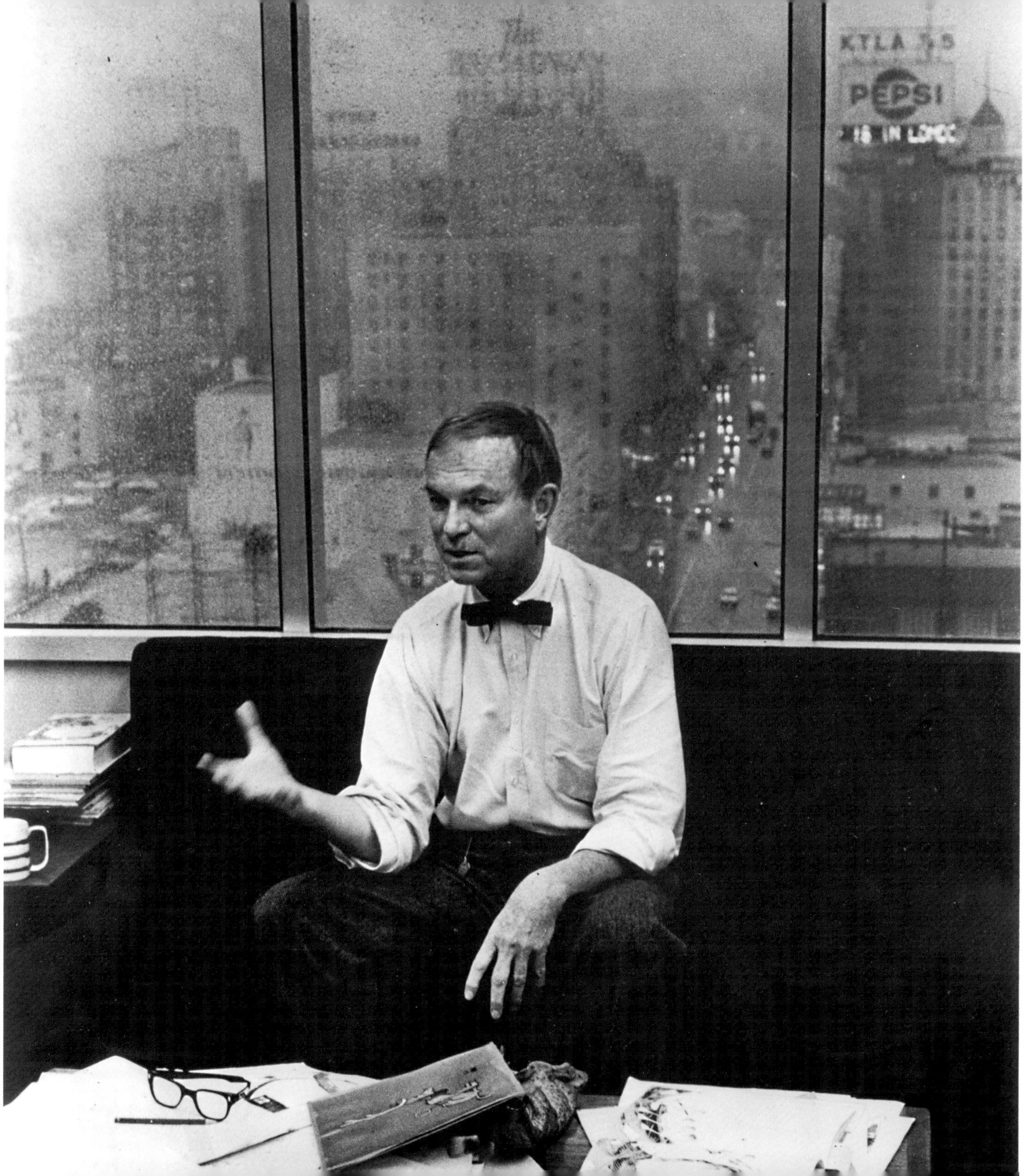
KTLA
PEPSI

DARLING...
(MOTHER'S VOICE IS HEARD.)
TOWER TWELVE
Sunset-Vine Tower
6290 Sunset Boulevard
...NOT WITH DADDY'S..
GIRL SHOOTS A LITTLE BLOB OF SOAP INTO AIR FOR FINAL BIT TO CAKE.
...FOAMY!
MOTHER'S LOUD "FOAMY" CAUSES GIRL INTO STARTLED "TAKE", AND TO LOSE HOLD ON "FOAMY" CAN.
Hollywood 28, Calif.
(END ON ZOOM-IN)
(END)
CAN LANDS ON CAKE, FOLLOWED BY THE BLOB OF SOAP COMING DOWN ON HER HEAD.
TRUCK IN ON CAN FOR MATCH DISSOLVE TO LIVE ACTION.

BRISKLY, HE SQUIRTS "FOAMY" ON DOG.
TOWER TWELVE
MAKING DOG LOOK LIKE A FRENCH POODLE.
JUNIOR...
FATHER'S VOICE IS HEARD...
6290 Sunset Boulevard
Hollywood 28, Calif.
..NOT WITH MY FOAMY!
SWOOSH!
CAT ZIPS AWAY AS BOY LISTENS TO FATHER'S VOICE.

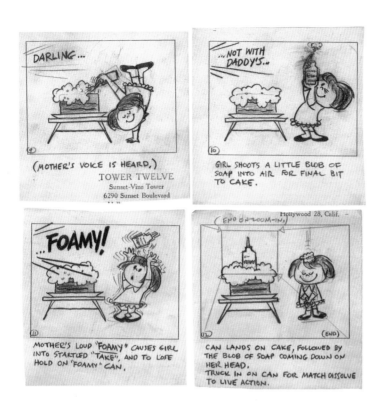

Sesame Street that they were doing. So sometimes I'd go down there for lunch and just listen to him talk a bit, and his various gripes and grudges and stuff like that.... I don't know why he was down there and not on the twelfth floor."

On the top floor of the Sunset-Vine Tower was a swank restaurant and jazz club called Room at the Top (later renamed "Simply Blues"). Chuck and his friends spent many hours in the restaurant reminiscing about the good old days at the Warner Studio. Don Morgan often joined the group for martinis and remembers how "Al Gordon, the manager, treated all of Chuck's boys like honored guests.... We were all official Lodge Members up there."

Chuck kept all production within the walls of Tower Twelve, except for the pencil tests and final color camera—which were done on the MGM lot—and the ink and paint, which was provided by Auril Thompson at her studio near Warners.

The first work Les Goldman secured for the newly formed company was television commercials, including a series of spots for Gillette products. A few featured the company mascot, Sharpie the Parrot, who would sing and dance while explaining the subtleties of Gillette's new line of Super Blue razor blades. One memorable ad for Gillette Foamy shaving cream had two children using shaving cream in unconventional ways. A young boy uses Foamy to shave a dog to look like a French Poodle. He is about to feed Foamy to a cat when his father yells, "Junior! Not with my Foamy!" A little girl then enters the scene and does a pirouette before squirting Foamy on a cake as if it were icing or whipped cream. Her mother yells, "Darling, not with daddy's Foamy!"

UPA also contracted Tower Twelve to produce a commercial for General Electric light bulbs featuring their star character, Mr. Magoo. Other work included a Heineken Beer ad and an animated station identification for CBS. It was a short time later that Jones would get a gig more suited to the caliber of his work. Walter N. Bien, president of SIB Productions, negotiated a deal with MGM to produce a new series of *Tom & Jerry* cartoons. MGM had closed down their animation studio in 1957 and in 1962 was looking to bring glory back to their characters after a season of critically panned *Tom & Jerrys* by UPA director Gene Deitch. Bien assured MGM that he had a fully-capable animation studio to do the work—which he did, run by Lou Scheimer and Hal Sutherland.

For reasons unknown, Bien decided not to use his in-house team and instead contracted with Tower Twelve. Upon discovering this news, Sutherland and Scheimer broke ties with Bien and formed their own studio, Filmation Associates, and went on to become a major force in television animation for the next three decades.

Chuck Jones had previously worked with Walter Bien in 1957 when Jones's Warner

Bros. unit contributed an animated sequence to a Bien-produced episode of *Bell Labs Science*. Chuck agreed to produce the *Tom & Jerry* series and assembled a group of all-stars that closely resembled his old Warner team. Carl Bell explains, "His animation staff was basically his Warner Bros. unit, augmented with [Disney alumni] Don Towsley, whom I assisted, and Hal Ambro, who became a great friend and teacher." Writer Michael Maltese came over from Hanna-Barbera, Philip DeGuard returned to paint backgrounds, and Mel Blanc and June Foray provided the voice work. Les Goldman supervised production and Chuck co-directed with his long-time Warner layout artist, Maurice Noble. Bien was the Executive Producer. The first short, *Pent-House Mouse,* was released on July 27, 1963.

Critics, audiences, and even Chuck himself agreed that while these new cartoons looked better than the other cartoons produced at the time, they were only a shadow of their original counterparts. In a 1971 interview with Joe Adamson, Chuck explained that he "didn't understand [Tom and Jerry] the way Bill [Hanna] and Joe [Barbera] did. I tried to make them like Bill and Joe, tried to think the way they thought, but it didn't work out well, so I just kind of changed the characters to fit my own way of thinking."

Tower Twelve only produced a half-dozen *Tom & Jerrys* when MGM decided that rather than contracting the work out to a third party, they would reinvest in quality animation by restarting an MGM-owned animation studio. So Chuck and Les Goldman sold Tower Twelve to MGM and it was renamed MGM Animation/Visual Arts. Other than the name change, the studio continued to exist as before. They remained on the twelfth floor of the Sunset-Vine building and Chuck and his employees retained their jobs. The buyout didn't include SIB Productions or Walter Bien, who returned to his previous job producing television commercials for Paramount. Once the deal was finalized, Chuck sent his entire staff home for a week, on full salary, with the mandate to "be creative."

Chuck's partnership with MGM presented new opportunities to keep his creative juices flowing. He eventually placed the directing chores for *Tom & Jerry* in the capable hands of Abe Levitow and Ben Washam, among others. Now in charge of MGM Animation/Visual Arts, it was up to Chuck Jones to bring new ideas and projects to the table—for theaters and also for television. *Tom & Jerry* would continue until 1967, a total of thirty-four films, with Chuck directing the occasional episode.

Jones and Levitow also teamed to produce *Off to See the Wizard*—MGM's answer to Disney's *Wonderful World of Color*—which aired on ABC during the 1967-1968 season. The show featured animated *Wizard of Oz*-themed openings and closings sandwiched around MGM's children's programming.

• • • • •

The directors and animators of *Looney Tunes* carried the hilarious tradition of slapstick comedy—a mainstay of the silent era stars Charlie Chaplin, Buster Keaton, and Harold Lloyd—into the thirties, forties, and fifties. While the rest of the cinematic world was turning away from such visual humor, favoring satire and dark comedy in response to the disillusioned post-World War II era, it was with the *Looney Tunes* of the 1950s that Chuck Jones

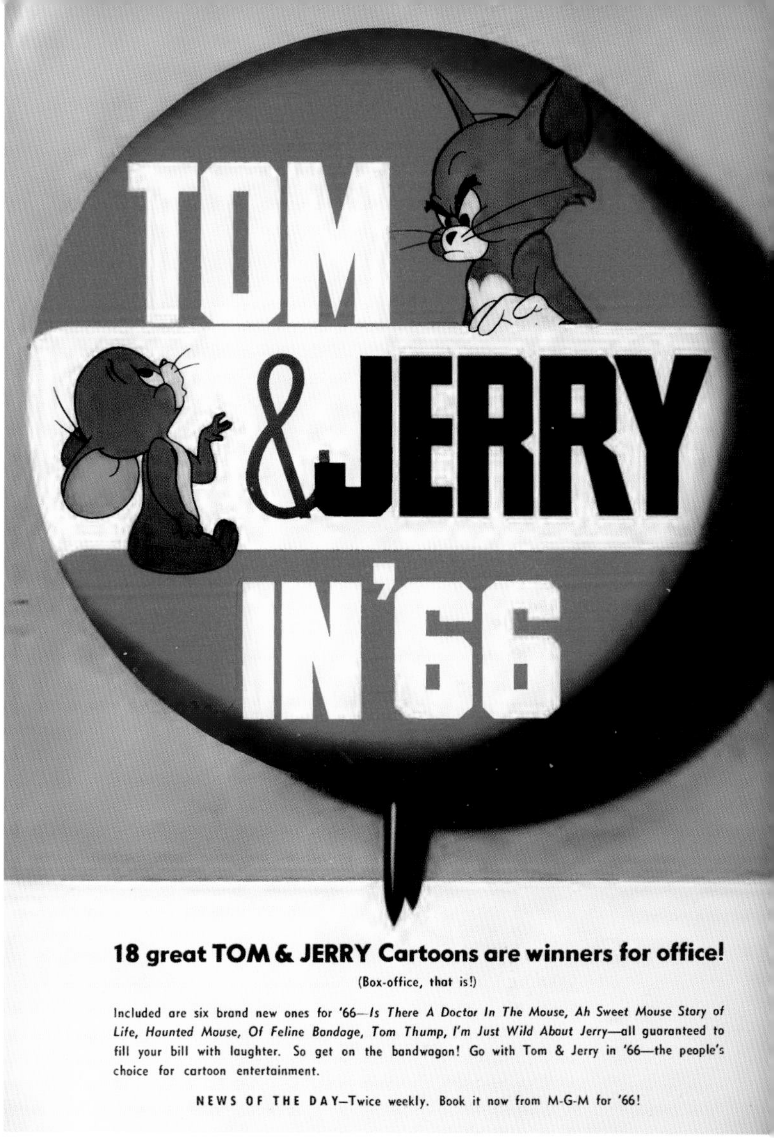

TOM
& JERRY
IN '66
18 great TOM & JERRY Cartoons are winners for office!
(Box-office, that is!)
Included are six brand new ones for '66—*Is There A Doctor In The Mouse, Ah Sweet Mouse Story of Life, Haunted Mouse, Of Feline Bondage, Tom Thump, I'm Just Wild About Jerry*—all guaranteed to fill your bill with laughter. So get on the bandwagon! Go with Tom & Jerry in '66—the people's choice for cartoon entertainment.
NEWS OF THE DAY—Twice weekly. Book it now from M-G-M for '66!

Opposite: Storyboards for a Gillette Foamy shaving cream commercial, early 1960s.

Above: An ad for the *Tom & Jerry* series from *Box Office* magazine, November 1965.

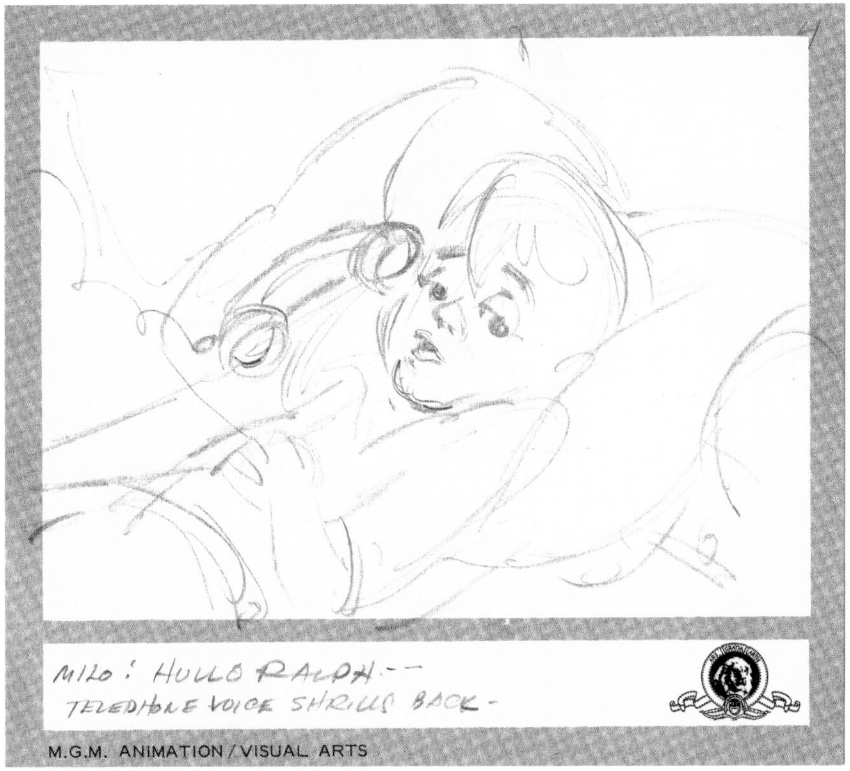
MILO: HULLO RALPH--
TELEPHONE VOICE SHRILLS BACK-
M.G.M. ANIMATION / VISUAL ARTS

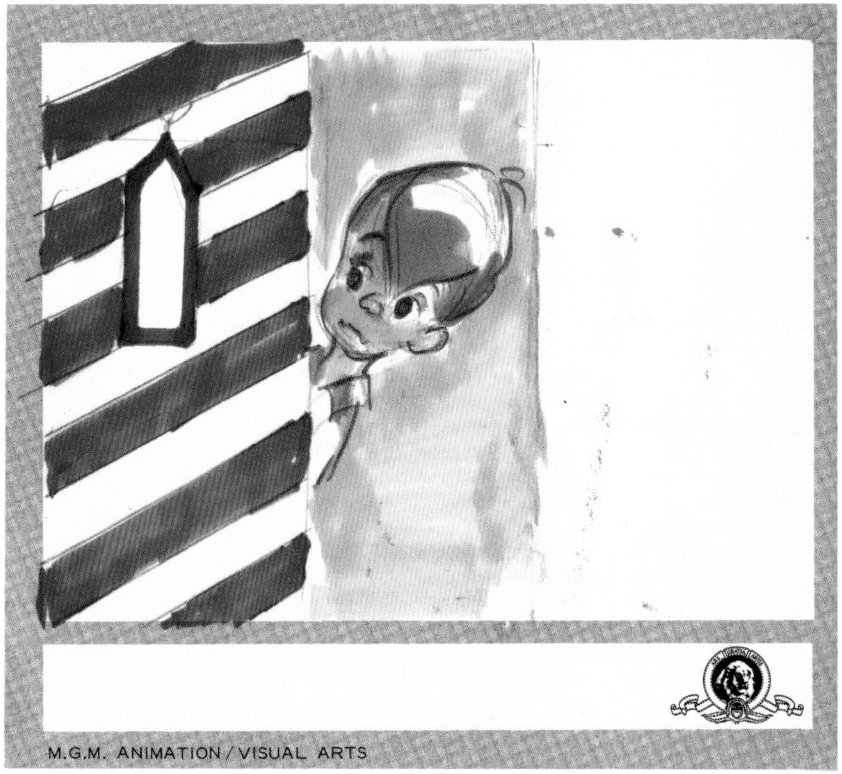
M.G.M. ANIMATION / VISUAL ARTS

perfected his unique blend of slapstick combined with verbal banter and witty one-liners. By the 1960s cartoons began to favor verbal gags over visual, with more emphasis on dialogue and narration. Even Chuck's humor changed during the time he was in charge of MGM Animation/Visual Arts. Having been well-read since he was a child, he loved wordplay and semantics and fancied himself an amateur philosopher, often quoting the works of Mark Twain and Dorothy Parker, his two favorite authors.

Looking past the *Tom & Jerry* series, he picked projects that would play to his love of literature and verbal puns. First on his list was an adaptation of Norton Juster's book, *The Dot and the Line: A Romance in Lower Mathematics.* The ten-minute short film, narrated by Robert Morley, told the tale of a Line who was in love with a Dot but couldn't seem to do anything to get her attention. The film is highly visual, but relies on the narration to set up most of the sight gags. Released to theaters on December 31, 1965, it went on to win the Academy Award for Best Animated Short Film. After the celebrated success of the film, Chuck took out a full-page ad in *Variety* and the *Hollywood Reporter*, crediting every single person who worked on the picture.

Maurice Noble, who co-directed the film with Chuck, drew the storyboards. "When Chuck saw them," said Noble in his biography, *Stepping Into the Picture*, "he basically said to me, 'Juster is just going to flip, he'll be so happy with this'… but Juster was anything but happy when he saw the storyboards and became very angry with the production. Meetings were had; lawyers were involved; changes needed to be made." After all was said and done, Maurice and Chuck still had no idea why Juster was so upset; they continued on as planned and produced an award-winning short film. Juster remains displeased with the film to this day.

Having already secured the rights to another of Juster's books, Chuck began work on his first feature-length film, *The Phantom Tollbooth*, this time without any involvement from the book's author. The ninety-minute feature, co-directed by Abe Levitow, was primarily animated, with live-action scenes at the beginning and the end directed by another *Looney Tunes* alum, David Monahan. The live-action opening introduces the main character, a young boy named Milo, played by *The Munsters*'s Butch Patrick. Milo is in school but boredom has clearly captured his mind. Once class is dismissed Milo walks home, so disinterested in the world that he passes by several interesting scenes without looking up.

Milo shares a common bond with Ralph Phillips—a general apathetic outlook on

Opposite: Storyboards for *The Phantom Tollbooth*, Chuck's first feature-length film.

Below: Butch Patrick, who starred as Milo in *The Phantom Tollbooth*.

Right: Publicity photography of Chuck holding Norton Juster's novel on which the film was based.

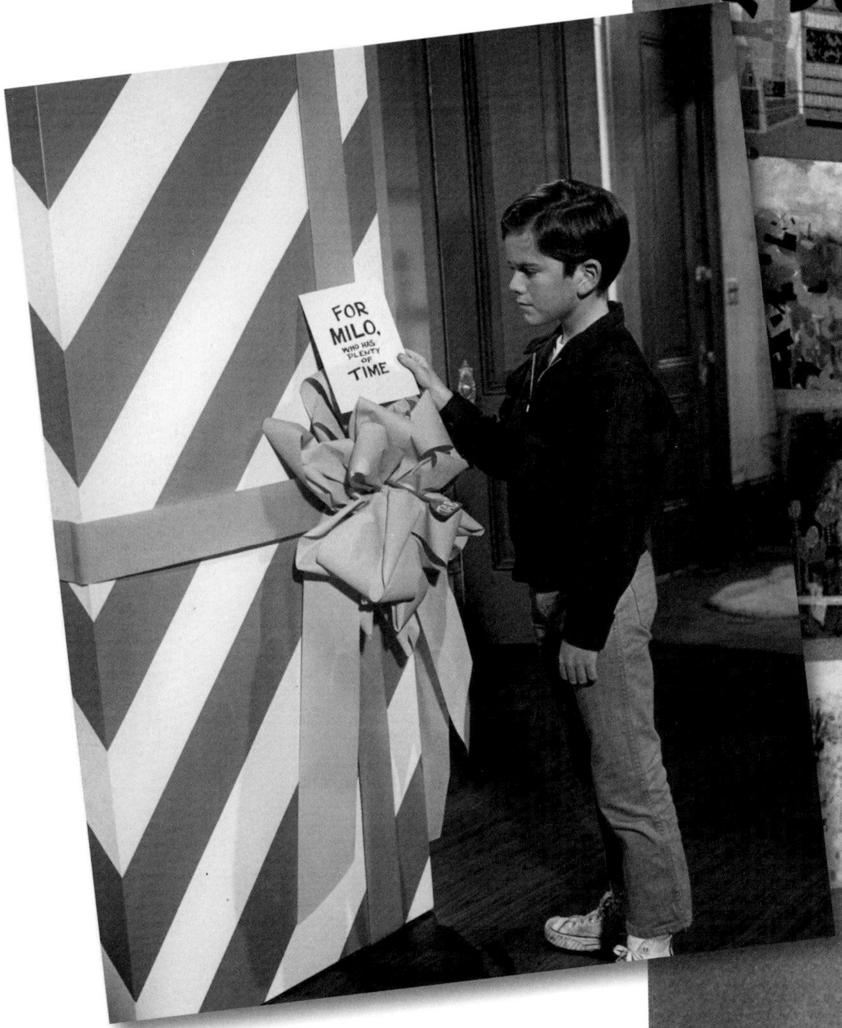
FOR MILO, WHO HAS PLENTY OF TIME

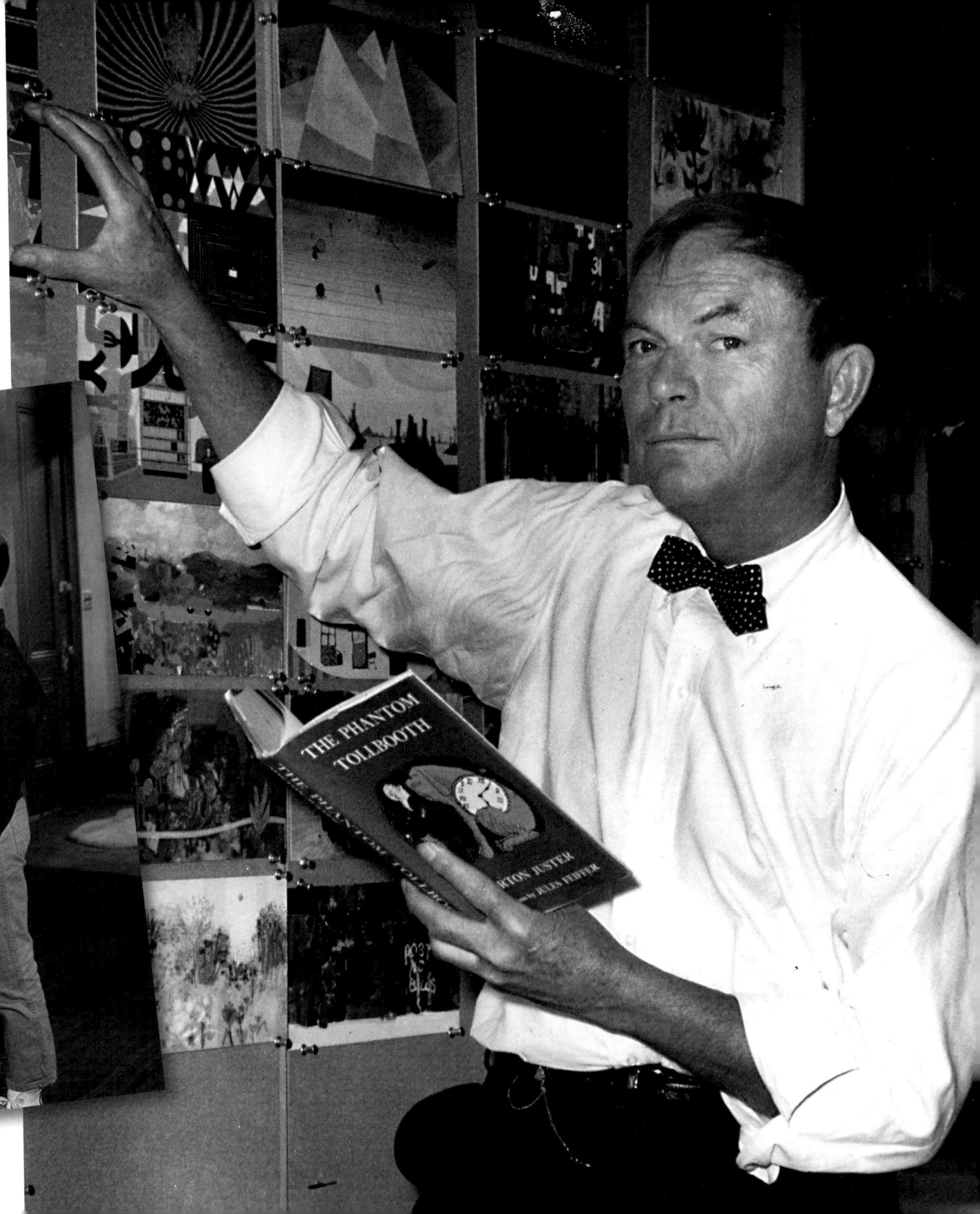
THE PHANTOM TOLLBOOTH

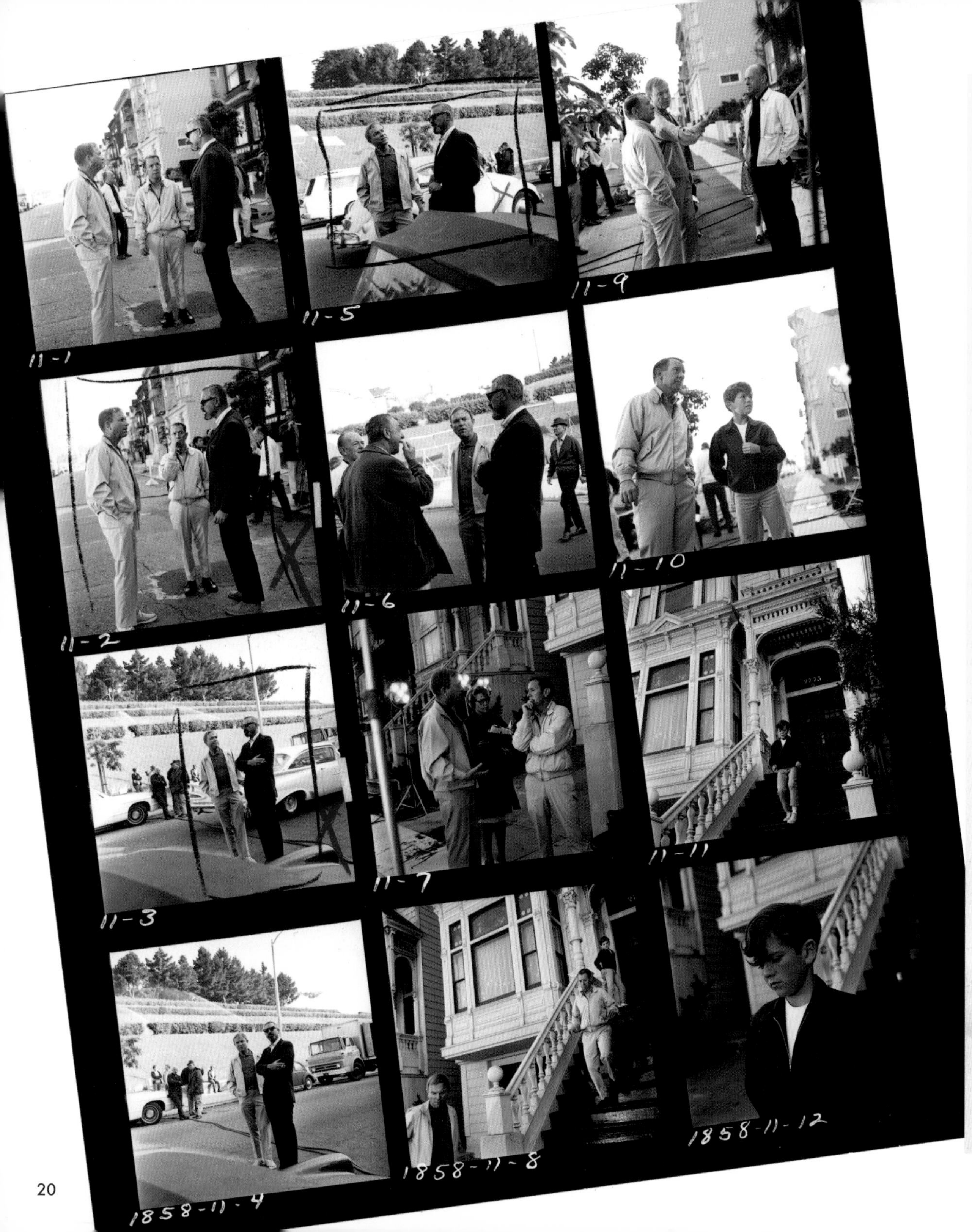
11-1
11-5
11-9
11-2
11-6
11-10
11-3
11-7
11-11
1858-11-4
1858-11-8
1858-11-12

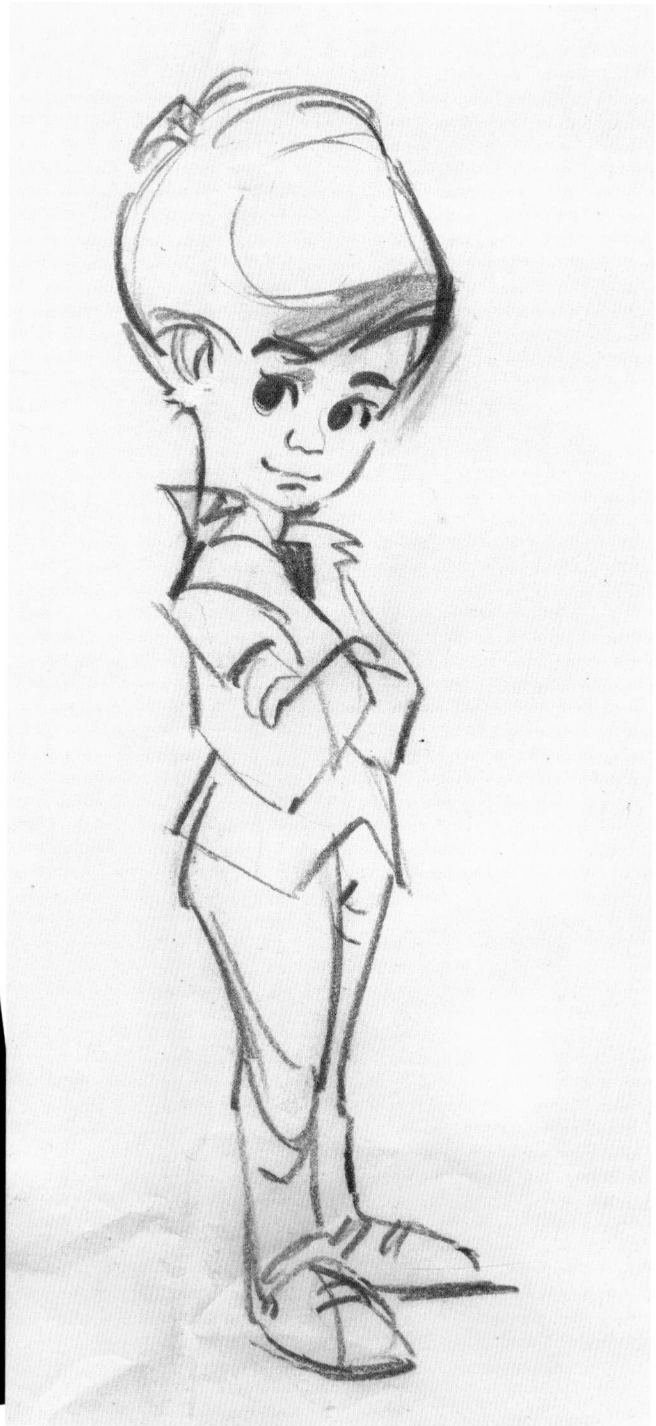

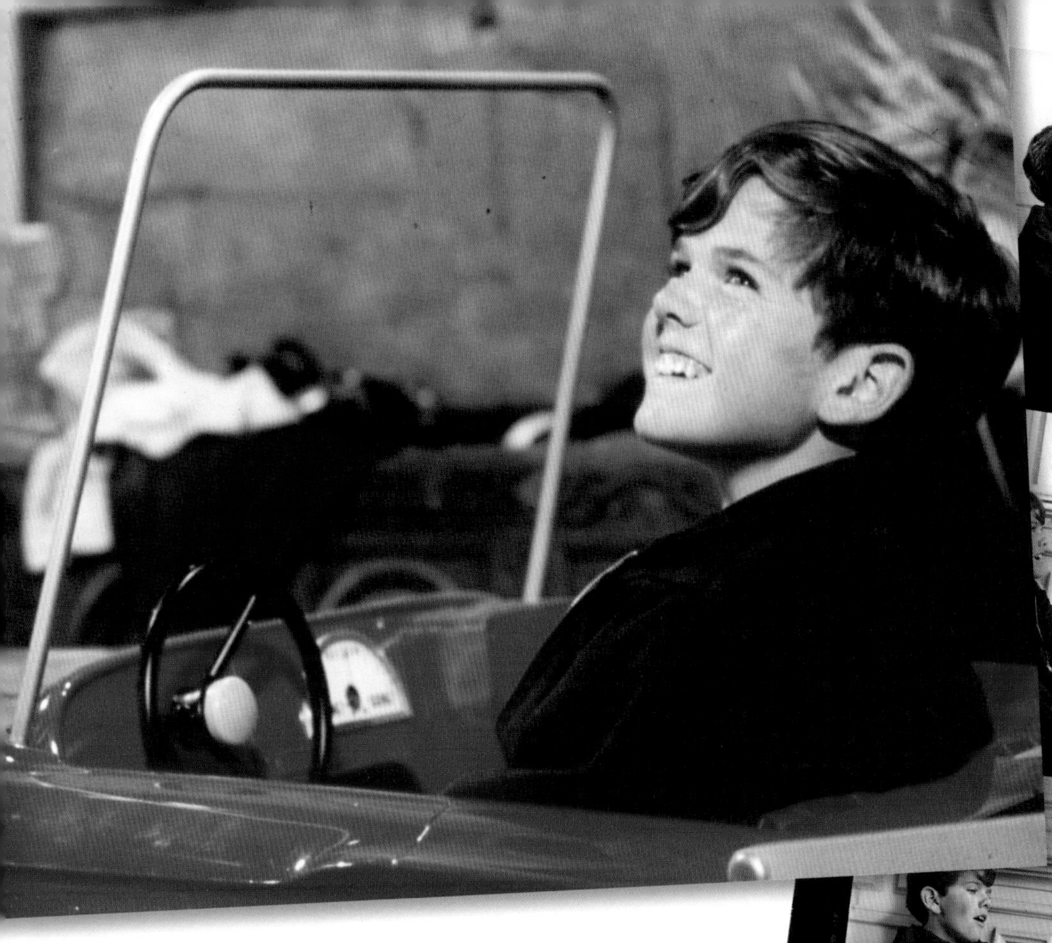

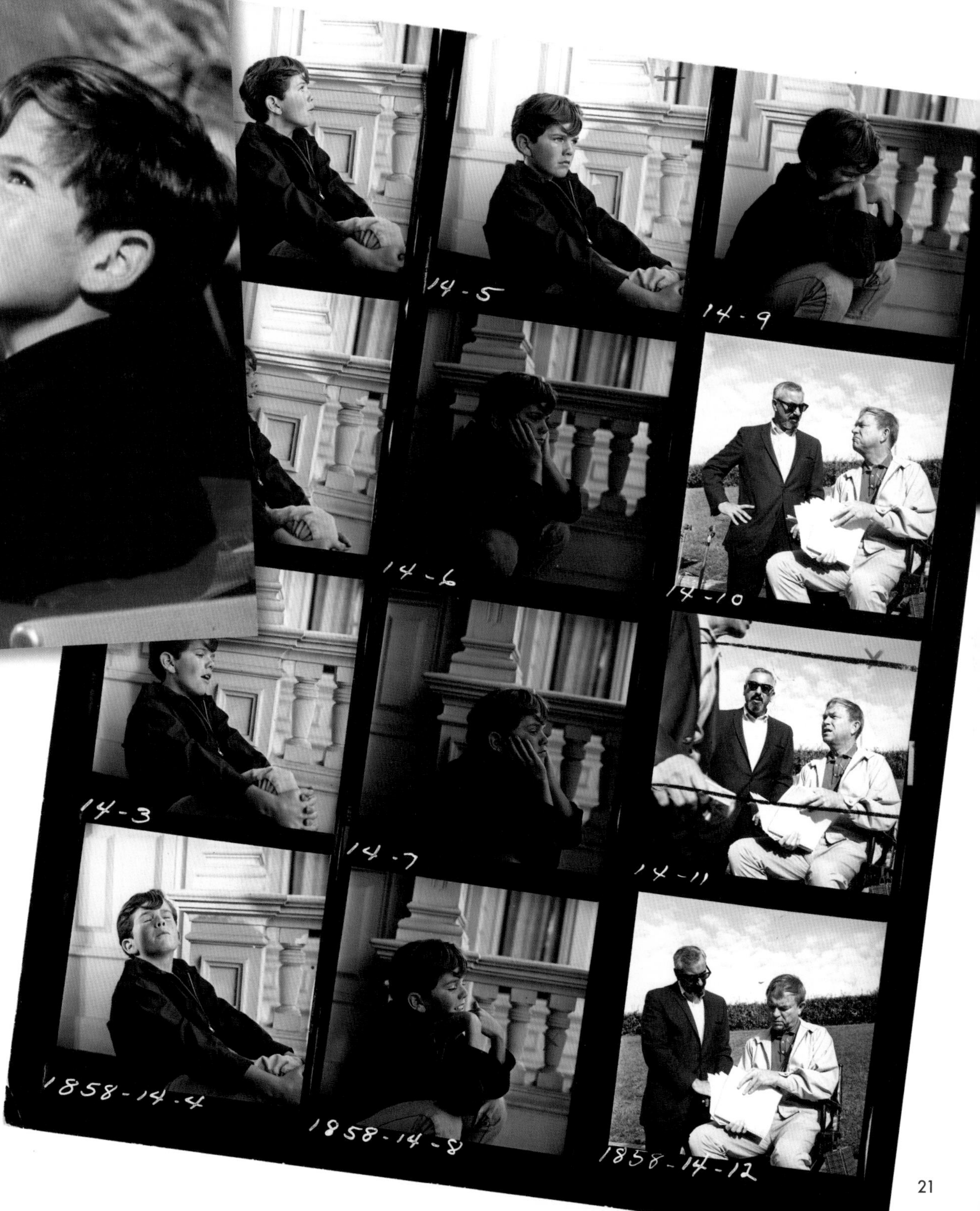
14-5
14-9
14-6
14-10
14-3
14-7
14-11
1858-14-4
1858-14-8
1858-14-12

Opposite right: Character sketch for Milo.

Both pages: Chuck Jones, co-director Abe Levitow, and actor Butch Patrick on the set of *The Phantom Tollbooth*.

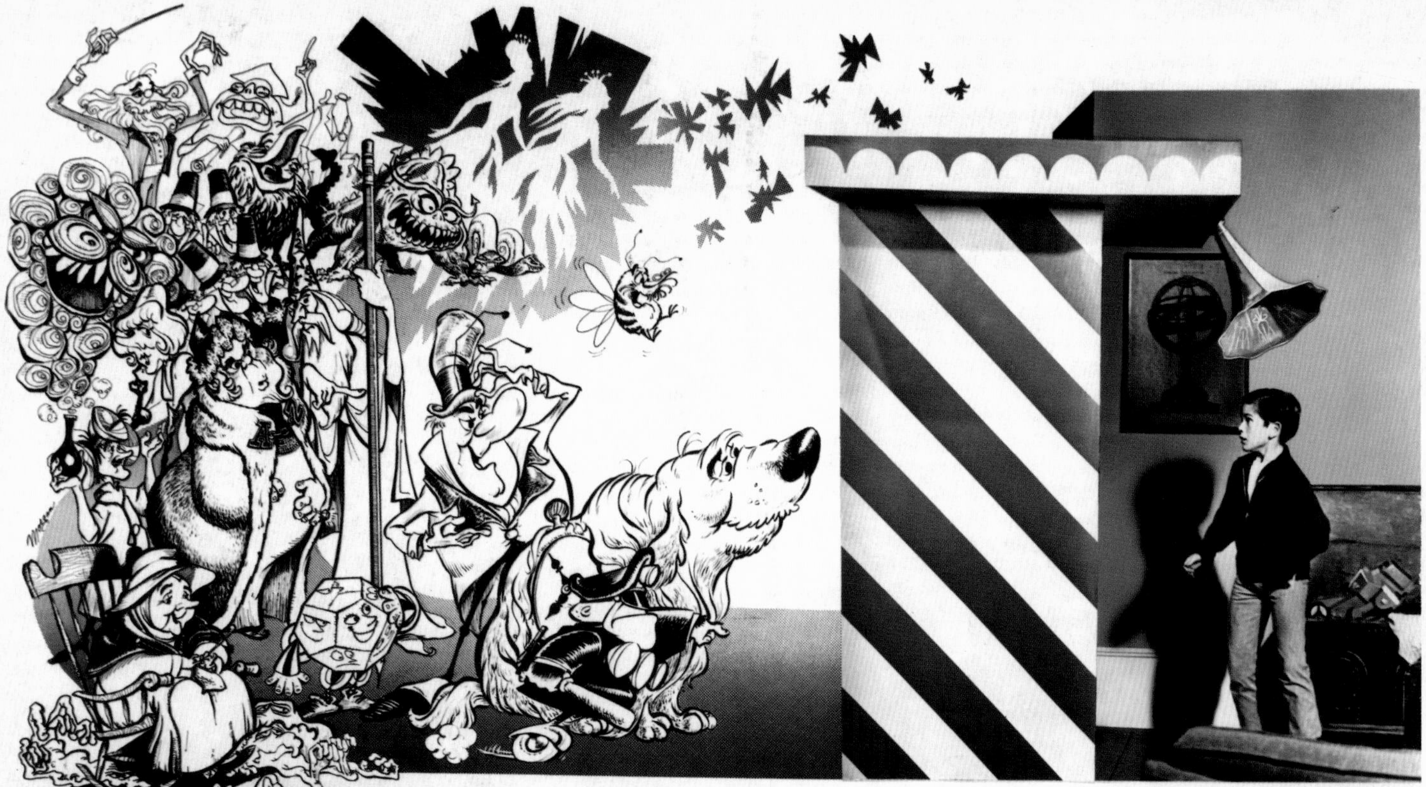

Left: Composite of Butch Patrick entering the animated world beyond the tollbooth.

Opposite: Chuck Jones and co-director Abe Levitow.

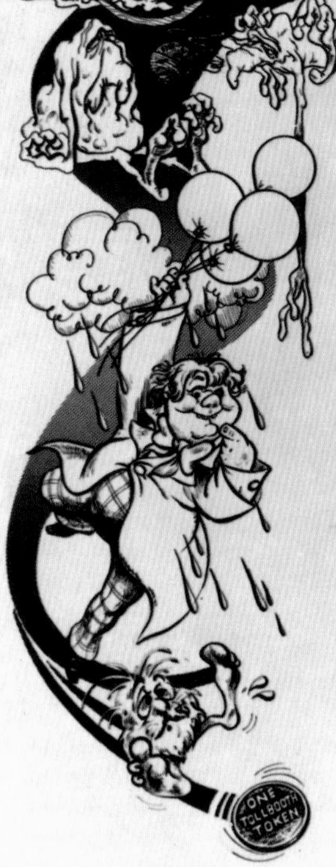
ONE TOLLBOOTH TOKEN

reality. This is a common theme for Chuck, who as a child found school to be tedious and dull; it's also an archetype of many of his characters, eventually manifesting itself in Crawford. Ralph, however, had his incredible imagination to fall back on, where Milo was stuck in his rut until he got help from a Tollbooth.

It is through this magic tollbooth that Milo enters the animated Kingdom of Wisdom, where idioms come to life and puns are built into the natural and manmade geography of its two main cities, Digitopolis and Dictionopolis. Milo learns that the two cites are in dispute over the equality of numbers and letters and that he must rescue the two princesses, Rhyme and Reason, from the Castle in the Air to restore order to their respective cities.

Again, Juster was dissatisfied with Jones's take on his work, calling it drivel. "It was a film I never liked. I don't think they did a good job on it… It was well reviewed, which also made me angry." Critics praised Jones's and Noble's signature design and the near-impossible task of bringing to life a world so highly dependent on wordplay and semantics. Its sophisticated intelligence, coupled with the fact that cartoons are generally thought of as children's fare, could be part of the reason it failed to pack cinemas. In his autobiography, Chuck reduces *Phantom Tollbooth* to a single sentence, "A critical success, a box-office question mark." The film was finished in 1969, but MGM initially debuted it in a small handful of kiddie matinees, delaying a full theatrical release until late 1970. Since then, *Phantom Tollbooth* has been largely forgotten, save for a small cult following.

Aside from the *Tom & Jerrys, The Dot and the Line* is one of only two theatrical short films Chuck Jones produced for MGM. The second is *The Bear That Wasn't*, released on December 31, 1967. *The Bear That Wasn't* is based on the 1946 children's book by another of Chuck's former Termite Terrace co-workers, Frank Tashlin.

Tashlin's book, about a bear who stumbles onto an industrial factory and is convinced by factory workers that he is actually a man, was an instant hit with the public. Animation studios from all over the world, including Disney, were knocking on his door wanting to do an adaptation. Tashlin turned down every one of them, fearing they would fail to do his precious work justice. When Chuck Jones called him, hoping to triumph where so many other studios had failed, Frank agreed to let Chuck and his team do the picture.

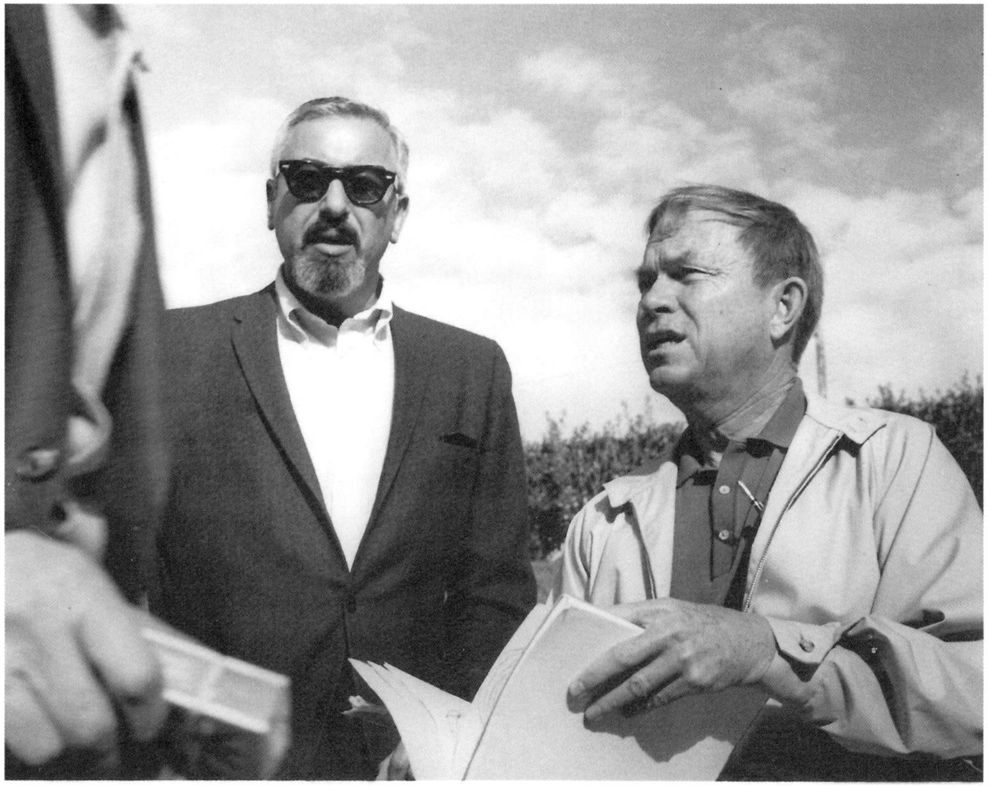

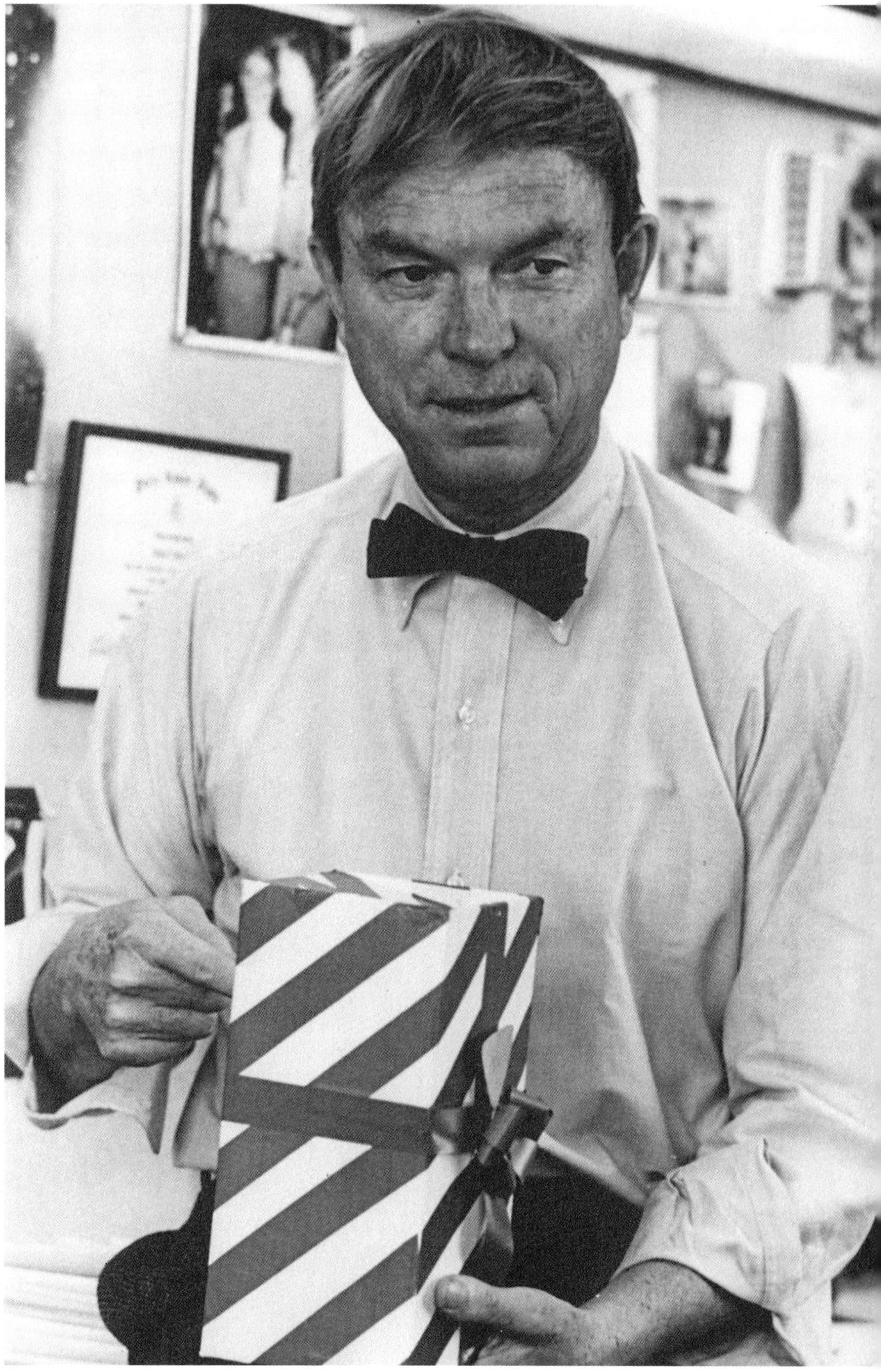

He had liked Chuck's version of *The Dot and the Line*, so he thought his book was in good hands.

Frank Tashlin had no involvement in the production despite having a co-producer credit. Chuck did this as a favor; in case the film won an Academy Award, Frank would get one as well. "Why worry about it," said Frank in a 1971 interview with Michael Barrier. "The guy was gonna take the book and put it on the screen, and he was a very capable man."

When Tashlin saw it in the theater, however, he was very disappointed. He explained, "Up front in the beginning of this thing, when they are telling him he is a man and he is insisting he's a bear, they put a cigarette in his mouth. Now, the picture was destroyed there, because by the acceptance of a cigarette… he was already a man.… Psychologically, the picture was ruined. It stopped working from that point on. So that was a terrible experience." In Frank's mind, "they destroyed the cartoon with one little thing. I saw that, I almost cried. I never talked to Chuck about it; I've never talked to him since. It was a terrible thing."

The Bear That Wasn't marks the final theatrical short from MGM. The studio closed its animation department in 1969.

Tashlin wasn't the only author who was hesitant to see his work on the screen. Ted Geisel, better

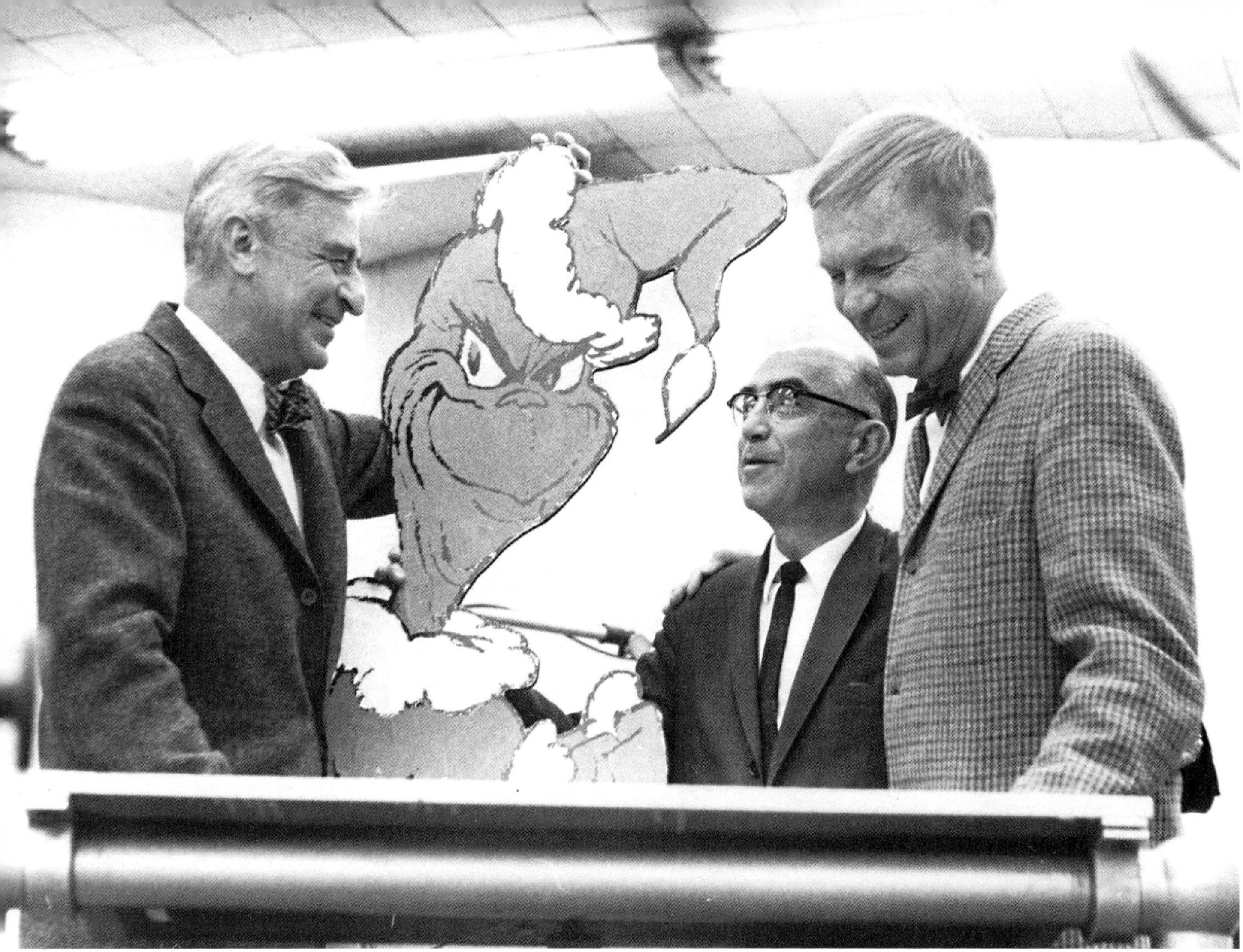

Left: Ted Geisel ("Dr. Seuss"), Les Goldman, and Chuck Jones.

Opposite: Geisel, Boris Karloff, and Jones.

known to the world as Dr. Seuss, also wasn't keen on the idea, especially after his dreadful experience writing the screenplay for Columbia's *The 5,000 Fingers of Dr. T.* Chuck met Ted when they worked together in Frank Capra's U.S. Army Air Force First Motion Picture Unit during World War II: together they made Army training films starring a buffoonish character named Private Snafu. The two remained good friends, regularly exchanging letters after the war. When all other studios' offers were rejected by Ted, Chuck managed to persuade him that it was "time to put Dr. Seuss on television…. We didn't know which book to use, but it was early enough in [1966] that we could get it done for Christmas, so it had to be *The Grinch.*"

Chuck and Ted worked closely together on *Dr. Seuss's How The Grinch Stole Christmas*, writing a screenplay that would fill twenty-two minutes, redesigning the characters to work for animation, and finding voices that could represent Ted's creations, including the inspired choice of Boris Karloff as The Grinch. Making changes for animation was a challenge for Geisel, who had toiled long and hard perfecting the book. At first he accommodated the changes, but as the production went along his book became less and less recognizable to him.

"Ted fought us on backgrounds, and the characters because, again, they were different from the book," said Chuck in the biography, *Mr. Geisel and Dr. Seuss*. "So I really had a 'mano a mano' with him.... When it was finished, Dr. Seuss's agents screamed and yelled—they thought the picture was terrible. And poor Ted Geisel didn't know what to make of it all." Regardless of the disagreements, *Dr. Seuss's How the Grinch Stole Christmas* quickly became a beloved holiday classic, earning consistently high ratings for many decades after its debut on December 18,1966.

While his experience on *The Grinch* was certainly frustrating, it wasn't discouraging enough for Ted Geisel to completely throw in the towel. Chuck proposed the idea of a second television special, this time based on *Horton Hears a Who.* At first Geisel was reluctant, but after overwhelmingly positive reviews of the *The Grinch*, he gave his approval. The two met the same issues working together on *Horton.* Chuck described it as "equally difficult and equally enjoyable." The half-hour special aired on March 19, 1970, a few months after MGM closed down their animation department. Despite their professional differences, Chuck and Ted remained friends for the rest of their lives. Ted Geisel went to DePatie-Freleng Enterprises to produce his next television special, *The Cat in the Hat,* and as a sign of good faith to his friendship with Chuck, he brought Chuck along to help with the storyboards, but ultimately the children's book author was happier during his time with DePatie-Freleng.

The Grinch and *Horton* half-hour television specials were co-produced by MGM-TV and Chuck Jones Enterprises, a production company Chuck set up mainly for legal reasons in 1962 specifically for the production of animation specials for television. MGM Animation/Visual Arts was set up to produce cartoons for theatrical distribution and was fully funded by MGM; the television specials were funded in part by sponsors and networks.

Chuck Jones only produced three television specials while he was the head of MGM Animation/Visual Arts. Sandwiched between the two Seuss specials was *The Pogo Special Birthday Special,* based on the popular comic strip by Walt Kelly. The story follows Pogo the possum and his animal friends as they plan a "family birthday" for their pal Porky Pine. Chuck provided the voices for Porky Pine, Bun Rab, and Basil the Butterfly. Walt Kelly voiced P.T. Bridgeport, Albert the Alligator, and Howland Owl. June Foray and Les Tremaine, two of Jones's regular collaborators, filled out the rest of the cast, the former in the role of Pogo.

"Pogo was a lot easier to animate than the Grinch," said Jones. "The Grinch was basically a two-dimensional character and we had to develop a fully rounded presentation. Pogo, a comic strip star, has been drawn thoroughly from all angles—maybe because Walt himself once worked in animation for Disney."

Kelly worked for Disney Studios from 1936 to 1941 before pursuing a career in comic

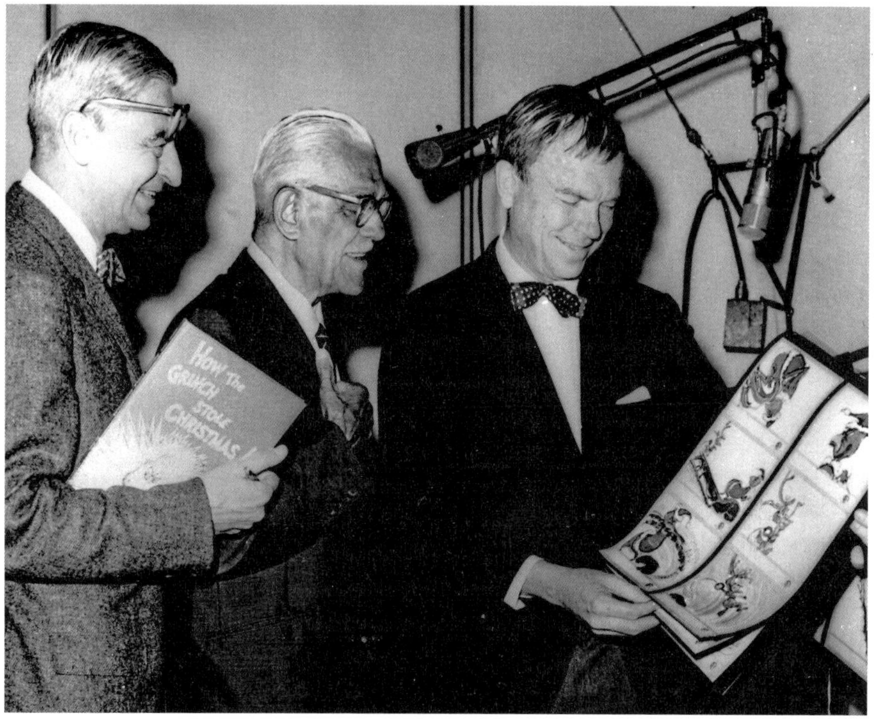

How the Grinch Stole Christmas!

books which led to the *Pogo* newspaper strip. He had been out of the animation industry for thirty years when he partnered with Chuck and was taken aback upon realizing the industry had changed and the quality of television animation wouldn't live up to the great Disney features that he worked on, such as *Snow White* and *Pinocchio.* Walt's widow, Selby Daily Kelly, and author Steve Thompson explained that "Kelly was forced to compromise repeatedly during the production, and was not satisfied with the final result." Disney animator Ward Kimball, a close friend of Walt's, said it was more than just compromise:

"When I had lunch with him at Musso & Frank's," recalled Ward in an interview in *Phi Beta Pogo,* "I asked him, 'How did you ever okay Chuck's *Pogo* story?' He said, 'I didn't.... [Chuck] changed it after our last meeting!' I asked, 'Who okayed giving the little skunk girl a humanized face?' Kelly's face turned red, and he bellowed, 'Waiter! Bring me another bourbon!' Oh, that made him mad."

Selby Kelly and Steve Thompson acknowledge that while the *Pogo* special is "not as good as Kelly would have liked, it is also not as bad as he was afraid it was."

The Idaho State *Journal,* two days before the May 18, 1969 telecast, made a wry observation: "The feature *Albert & Pogo* started in a comic book. It folded. The first newspaper to publish *Pogo* as a strip folded. Now numerous papers are in danger. Today TV trembles. *Pogo* will appear on NBC. NBC squirms." Little did the journalist know that within the next few months it wouldn't be NBC that would see its end, but rather MGM Animation/Visual Arts.

The studio was facing the biggest financial crisis in its history and in 1969 was purchased by Las Vegas mogul Kirk Kerkorian, who was more interested in the studio's retail property than its filmmaking. Kerkorian sold off most of the studio's backlot and all of the costumes and props accumulated during its glory days. MGM Animation/Visual Arts became a downsizing casualty.

When looking back at the films Chuck Jones produced during his time with MGM Animation it is hard to believe that not a single one of them was based on any of Chuck's original ideas. Whether it was his own decision or dictated by MGM executives, the creator of some of the best-known cartoon characters in history worked only on adaptations of popular contemporary material.

"In some ways, these recent projects have been more difficult," said Jones in 1969. "At least they've required more discipline, because we're taking characters that already have identity, and bringing them to life. People know what they look like in a still form, so when they get up and move and talk, they must be logical extensions of what has gone before."

What made the projects more difficult for Chuck's unit was that all of the authors were alive at the time Jones was adapting their work. As is the case with most film adaptations, the mark of the director is heavily felt on the finished product and the essence of the source material is changed to accommodate its translation to another medium. Chuck's experience with Juster, Geisel, Tashlin, and Kelly aside, the director did exactly what he set out to do—create quality cartoons with the fullest animation his budgets would allow and remain as faithful to the source material as possible. The result is some of the best animation to come out of the sixties.

• • • • •

In any studio—animation or live action—it is impossible to produce a movie or television series based on every single idea to come out of its creative minds. Concepts that may seem like terrific ideas often never see the light of day for any number of reasons: the demanding schedules of other productions, staff changes, network executives, and cost, among others. Tower Twelve was no exception. Dozens of concepts, many of which could have been hits in the hands of Chuck Jones, were shelved in their infancy.

Some of the unproduced work during Chuck's MGM years include adaptations of several Dr. Seuss books, including the obscure *Seven Lady Godivas;* a series about canine gangsters called *The Unscratchables;* a Droopy revival called *Trooper Droop,* for which an entire storyboard was produced*;* a *Chronicles of Narnia* animated series; *Gossamer the Flying Turtle; Ponce de Lion and Monsieur Cou-Cou,* which Don Morgan describes as an attempt to "recreate the Coyote and the Road Runner with an African cuckoo and a lion—which wasn't as obvious;" and *The Halloween Tree,* based on a story from Chuck's childhood. This latter project was to be co-produced by Ray Bradbury. The show never materialized, but Bradbury later wrote a short story in 1972 based on their concept and produced an animated half-hour special in 1993 with Hanna-Barbera.

In this graveyard of unproduced TV pilots rests *Crawford,* starring the accident-prone nine-year-old boy with a vivid imagination that Chuck had originally created for the *Adventures of the Road-Runner* series in the early '60s. This would-be animated television series explored the typical crises, triumphs, and problems that accompany growing up. It's a very different Crawford than the laid-back pseudo-intellect who would appear in the 1978 comic.

"Crawford is the New York Mets of boyhood," explained Chuck in his initial draft of the series, circa 1967, a year before the basement-dwelling Mets' "miracle" season, in which they won their first World Series. "I think it is possible to sympathize and to understand him for much the same reasons; both Crawford and the Mets are much more typical of every man, and every boy's frustrations and occasional triumphs than, say, were the New York Yankees' more or less unbroken chain of triumphs, touched only occasionally by the humanity of failure. The Yankees were a picture of perfection, the Mets (and Crawford) are a reflection of life."

There are several reasons to consider Crawford as having evolved from Ralph Phillips,

RICHARD HAYDN

THE "PROFESSOR"

THE UNSCRA...

"CURLEY"

TENNOR LOON

"THE UN·SCRATCHABLES"
(23 SKID·ROW

This page: Production drawings for
The Unscratchables—a parody of the
popular TV show *The Untouchables*—
one of several unproduced series during
Chuck's MGM tenure.

a character that Chuck never had the opportunity to fully explore during his *Looney Tunes* days. Early sketches of Crawford certainly show a passing resemblance between Ralph and him, and some of Chuck's earliest descriptions of Crawford could easily confuse him as Ralph Phillips's doppelganger:

> [Crawford] drifts into his imaginary epic worlds through boredom, lassitude or a kind of intelligent disgruntlement, triggered usually by discouragement with the world around him, and always with a small visual hook from the workaday world: bird into boy; fishbowl into sunken submarine; the "corner" in a school room reserved for a dunce into a corner of a boxing ring.

However, there was versatility to the format of the Crawford concept that allowed Jones to take it in any direction: fantasy, science fiction, moments in history, famous literary worlds, etc. In order to accomplish this, Chuck created several points of view so Crawford could appropriately interact with the different environments. The Daydreamer, as described above, was only one aspect of Crawford's character. Here is Chuck explaining the rest:

Crawford, the Artist:
> His drawings reflect his moods and his reactions to the world around him without reference to prevailing styles in art. His is a kind of mobile Rorschach lab. Our knowledge of his worlds is through his drawings and our animation of them.

Crawford, the Rational Human Being:
> His attitude toward the world is one of absolute reasonableness. Anything and everything is self-explanatory. He explains the self-evidence of all things. Trees have roots to keep them from falling over, leaves to provide shade. The leaves drop off in the fall because shade is not necessary in the winter.

Crawford, the Inventor:
> The boy in the ointment, the mechanic with the bruised thumb in all matters involving nuts, bolts, screws, springs and the leverage principle. Some of Crawford's inventions:
> Small mops to be attached to the backs of each shoe to tidy up after tracked mud.

> A three mile leash to keep your dog from becoming inhibited.
> A fishing line with a small light bulb attached to enable the fish to see the worm while night fishing; a device for injecting tranquilizers into worms so they won't be afraid of the dark, or mind being bait.
> A humane fly-swatter that merely stuns the fly—object—to teach the fly a lesson, if he returns you hit him with a common fly-swatter.

Crawford, the Musician:
> Whose function in life is to practice on the piano. He only practices forty-five minutes a day, but those forty-five minutes always come when anybody else is going some place: swimming, the circus, free ice cream, parades, etc. Crawford can always tell when the interesting things of life are about to occur for then the peremptory off-stage voice beckons him to the inflexible keyboard. His only escape is to drift into fantasies concerned with the music page, and on this field his thoughts wander as the musical notes and symbols become moving creatures: mice and men and other relaxing items.

And finally, of course, just Crawford:
> The hero. The accident-prone, the unfortunate unlucky, rather poignant side of all of us, a man of hope wherewithal, a gallant misfit in a technology determined to destroy him.

Chuck Jones and his wife fine-tuned the proposal so *Crawford* was ready to pitch to MGM. In their 1969 outline every episode of the proposed series was to contain three major segments, each with its own theme and graphic style. Crawford would get a completely new character design in each of these segments to fit the unique style of the world he enters.

A major change to Chuck's original outline was to have the various roles designated to Crawford assigned to different characters.

The Daydreamer, for example, is now Winfield, whose design was lifted from Arnold Philips, the kid in the cowboy hat from *The Adventures of the Road-Runner*.

Another character lifted from the *Road-Runner* pilot is Bettina, also called Angela in some versions, the Rational Human Being. To Bettina, there is no mystery to life—everything to her is crystal clear.

> Potatoes grow in the ground because that is where the iron is, potatoes are heavy because they have iron in them, contrasted to

lettuce that has not, and is not. Lettuce is actually young spinach. Iron is made up of mollycoddles and atom. The atom was named after the first man who was married to Eve.

She imparts her special kind of knowledge to anyone who will listen. This usually ends up being her little brother, Homer,

> …known more familiarly and more often as 'Go Home'. He accepts anyone's viewpoint without question; it is one way of surviving in a world populated by over-sized bureaucrats. He sees no reason to dispute a mad world anyway.

The Scientist is Fenton, also called Albert Dreistein in some of Chuck's notes.

> Fenton's interest in all matters is in the realm of pure science. His explanations that Bettina scrambles so colorfully are lucid, clear and authentic. He is not disturbed by Bettina; he doesn't hear her at all. But, he does disturb Homer, who occasionally has hallucinatory dreams involving both Fenton's and Bettina's explanations of the same subject.

Joe Green picks up the role of the Musician. Chuck's idea was to have Joe drift into a fantasy world where musical notes and symbols come to life while Joe practices the piano. It's a concept he previously explored in *High Note*, a 1960 *Looney Tune*.

Eddie Thompson takes over Crawford's Inventor persona, creating such machines as "a kit containing all the elements necessary to teach a group of ants to emulate the changing of the guards at Buckingham Palace. (There are a few bugs in this.)"

Granville is the Artist, but the character never made it past the outline. No art was found in Jones's files that featured Granville, Eddie, Joe, or Fenton, and none of them show up in any other outlines. Also just an initial thought is Jerome, "the sporting member of the community, the owner of the catcher's glove, the puck, the net."

And finally…Crawford.

> Crawford is, of course, accident prone but he is also frustration prone. If it is possible to be prone-prone, Crawford can manage that too. In any activity in which the normal position is vertical such as skating (roller, ice or board) Crawford's position is horizontal—or prone. In life's great pharmacopoeia

Crawford is the boy in the ointment. But, just as with many other people who seem to get a little more than their share of the dirty end of the stick compensatory events do occur to strengthen the balance.

Narrating each episode is Caulfield, Crawford's older brother who is never seen but is the omniscient voice that tells the audience of Crawford's exploits. His opening line to each episode is always the same:
"I'm worried about Crawford…."

> The voice is that of a 14- or 15-year-old boy, vastly wise in experience, sharp, well educated, the classic older brother, or a normal Holden Caulfield. He is able to deliver any line an adult narrator could deliver without seeming either omnipotent or preachy. Yet he is as certain of his knowledge of child psychology, behaviorism and training as the average parent. He can also reflect Crawford's viewpoint pretty well. After all, he is a recent graduate.

> He can identify Crawford's field of endeavor early in each episode: Kite flying, table tennis, football, kitchen chemist, doghouse architecture, skate boarding, etc., and comment upon successive failures and frustrations much as Robert Benchley did in his memorable shorts.

Jones storyboarded an entire sequence to include in the pitch to MGM (see pages 234-281). It involves Crawford's attempt to fly a kite, which was also a focus in several iterations of his outline. The episode is a quintessential Chuck Jones cartoon, complete with the signature poses, timing, and blackout gags that he first developed in his *Looney Tunes* days. Chuck most likely timed out the sequence to six minutes, the standard length of his classic shorts.

Along with Bettina, Homer, and Winfield, two other characters are in the storyboards: Crawford's unnamed bratty sister and the neighborhood dog, Myopia the Abominable Sheep-dog. Bits and pieces of other *Crawford* storyboards exist, all by unknown artists, making Crawford's kite-flying adventure the best example of what this animated series could have been.

Crawford's neighborhood pals are the focus of only the first six minutes of a twenty-two-minute episode. The purpose of this segment, "Here Comes Crawford," is to instruct the viewer how to accomplish everyday boyhood tasks: how to ride a bicycle; how to build a

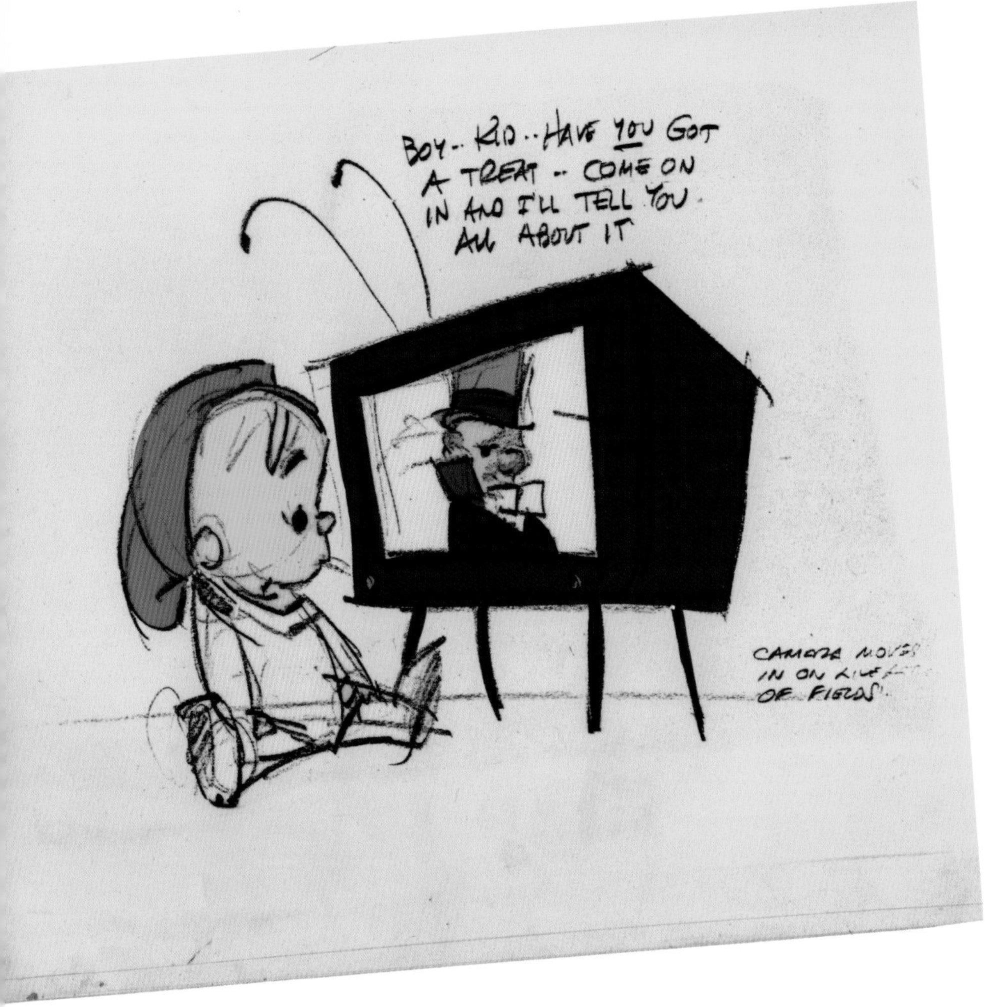
BOY.. KID.. HAVE YOU GOT A TREAT -- COME ON IN AND I'LL TELL YOU ALL ABOUT IT

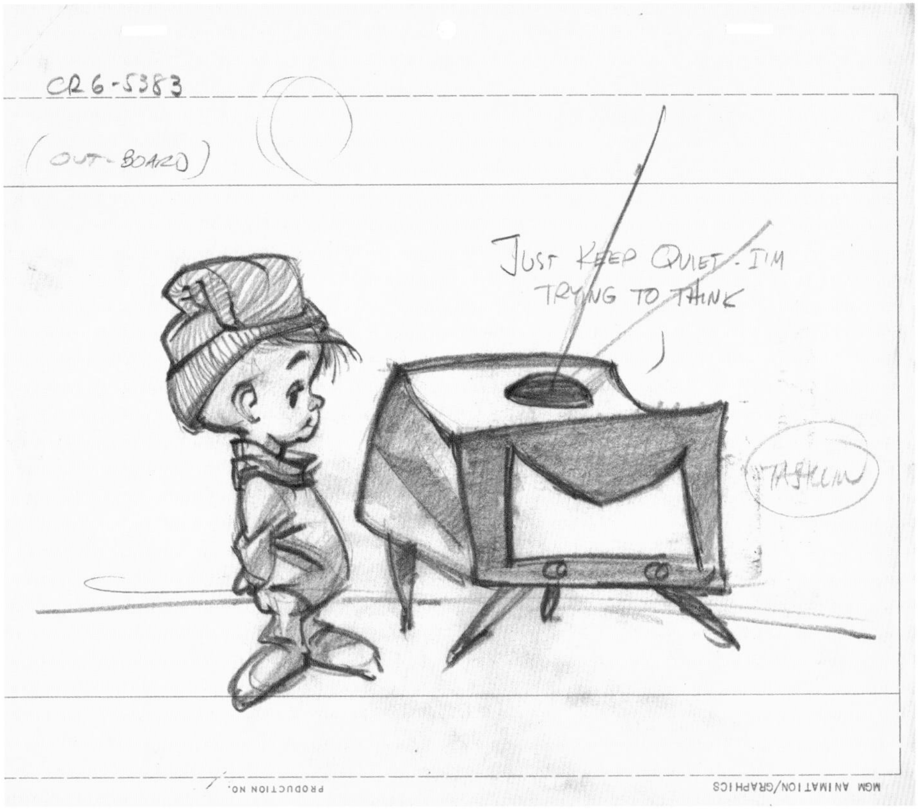
CR6-5383
(OUT-BOARD)
JUST KEEP QUIET - I'M TRYING TO THINK

treehouse; how to ski, skate, and sled; how to trick or treat; how to fly a kite… Given Crawford's clumsy nature, these are actually more like a series of how *not* to's.

The second Crawford segment is *Charlie and Otto.* The plan was for each *Charlie and Otto* episode to begin with Crawford being sent to his room as a result of whatever happened in the *Here Comes Crawford* sequence. Caulfield's narration sets the stage:

> Caulfield: One thing more that worries me about old Crawford… he doesn't mind going to bed. I mean, that's not normal. In my day kids were different. I mean we HATED to go to bed, but my brother can hardly wait to get there, particularly when he's had a bad day.
>
> In our house bedrooms are out of bounds to anybody except the person who lives there…you can only go in if you are invited. Very modern psychology, you know. But it can get out of hand because Crawford never invited ANYBODY in, except in the daytime. It's not that I'm nosey, I don't want to disturb his budding libido or something, but this kid's got troubles, dreams of really weird-o things, makes the nuttiest sounds in his sleep. Listen, and you'll see what I mean.…

From there the viewer follows Crawford into his dream world, where he is greeted by three pieces of household furniture. The dream world, however, is only a springboard for the furniture to take Crawford into other countries, worlds, or situations. Crawford could go anywhere and do anything that his imagination allowed, which also enabled the writers freedom to explore the most unusual ideas, and for the animators to show off their incredible talents.

Jones explains the roles of the furniture in his outline:

> If Crawford's days are sheer Hell, his nights are sheer wonder. No one ever quite knows in watching Crawford's nocturnal adventures whether Charlie, Psyclops, and Otto are actually living furniture, just

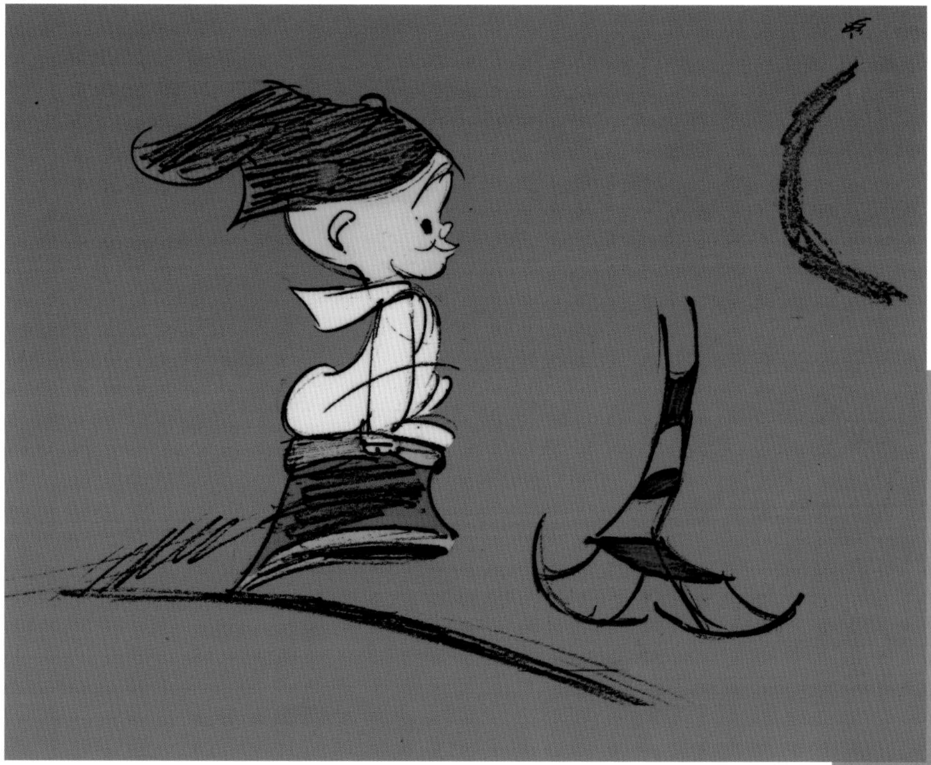

Both pages: Presentation artwork for the "Charlie and Otto" segment of the proposed *Crawford* TV series, circa 1969.

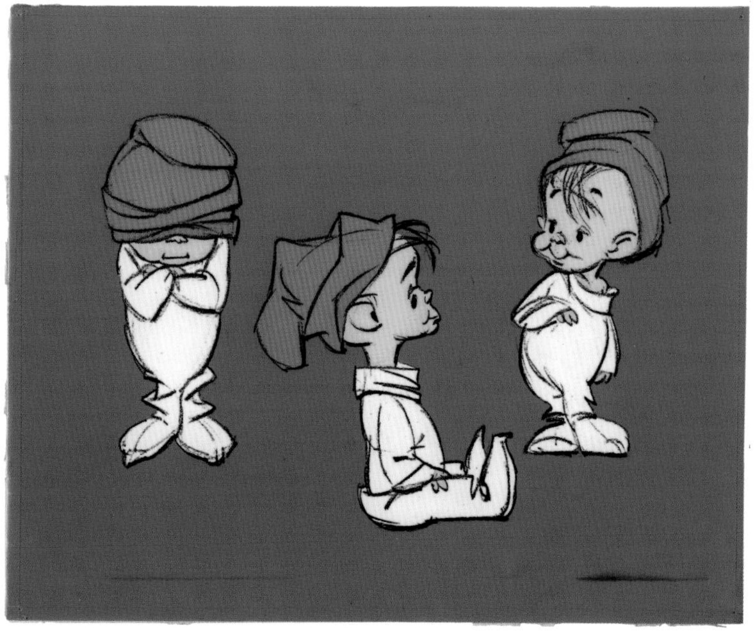

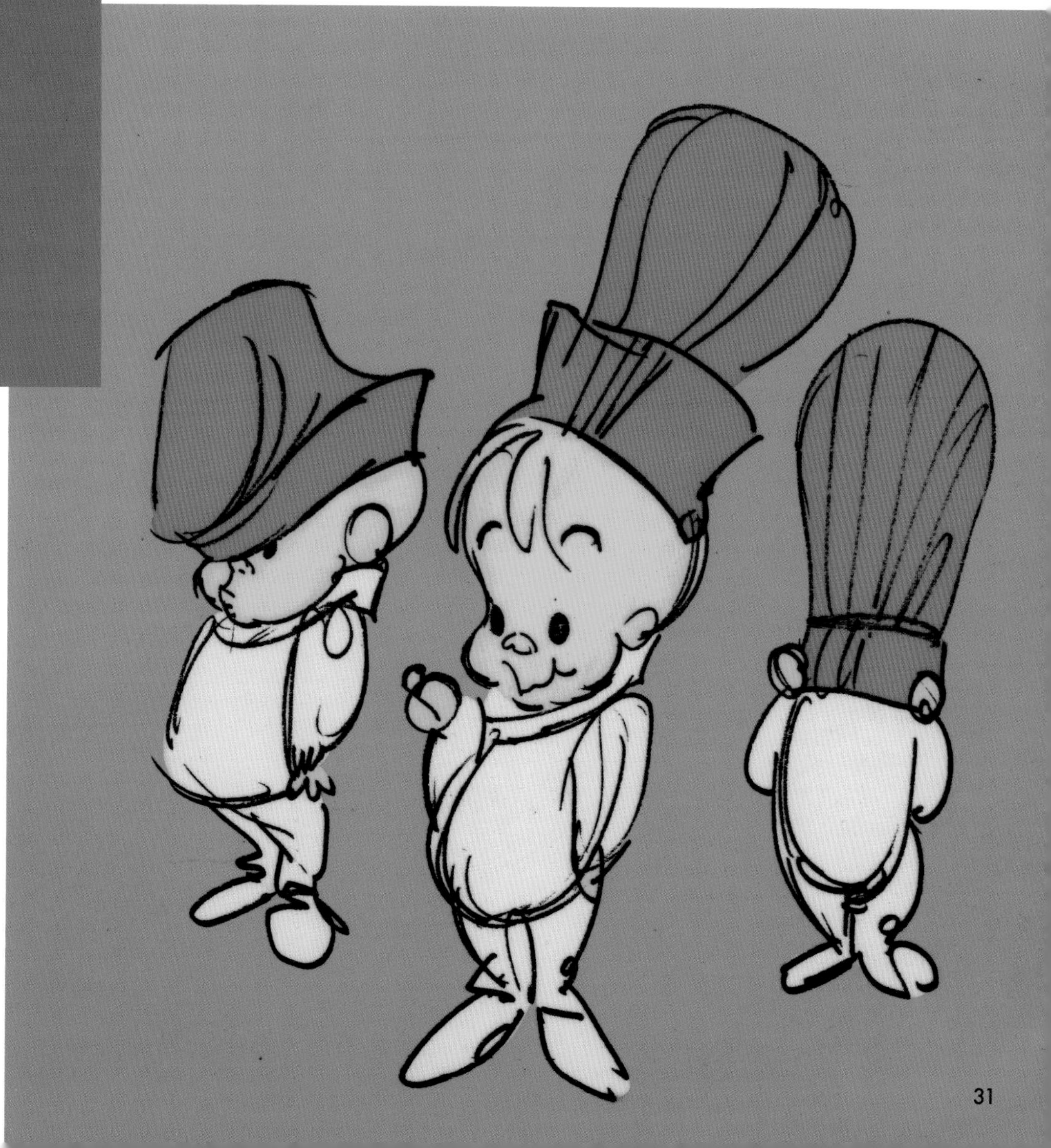

furniture, just Crawford's imagination, or visitors from outer space. (The planet Hepplewhite to be exact.)

But whatever they are they don't take any guff from Crawford. No matter how hideous a day he has had on the hustlings of the playground or schoolroom he gets no pity from the skinny rocking chair (Charlie), the strange half foot-stool, half toad-stool (Otto), or the opinionated TV set (Psyclops) that make up the furnishings of his room. "Pity doesn't cost anything," says Charlie (quoting Mark Twain), "and it isn't worth anything." But, if his furniture is low on sympathy it is high on peculiar behavior.

Charlie is not only a rocking-chair but can be when need be, a "rocket-chair", if only to emphasize a point by taking Crawford to the scene-of-the-action: A ride down the Cuesta bob-sled run in Switzerland for instance, or a race with a small asteroid or a visit behind the scenes of a cash-register factory.

Otto, who is not only over-stuffed but hollow, has the ability to speak to small animals who sound hollow or are over-stuffed: owls, toads, sea anemones etc. His method of transportation is slower but he manages to get Crawford there anyway; if it is a fiddler crab rally at Perth-Amboy or the annual horned-toad june bug fest in Coachella Valley.

Psyclops is a stolid immovable TV set of high pretensions and inordinate pre-conceptions. He believes only in educational TV but "educational" can be anything from "Hansel and Gretel" [told] from the witch's point of view, to the story of the "Three (SCREAM)s". He is the only TV set around that functions solely from memory and he can rack up an old Buster Keaton comedy or a bit from a 1927 newsreel as well as an educational three minutes exploring the possibilities of how it would have been if man had had wheels instead of feet, or the dog, rather than man, had had the brain.

Chuck's vision for the episodes within the TV set was to push the envelope of television animation to places it had never gone before. In some cases the viewer would be placed in the point of view of rather unusual objects, called "What's it like…" Inside a cash register? To be a bullet? To see like a fly? Inside a cow? Considering that networks and corporate sponsors didn't wish to put a lot of money into television animation, one wonders how Chuck thought he could pull off such elaborate set-ups.

Jones never shied away from vocalizing his disdain for the level of animation made for

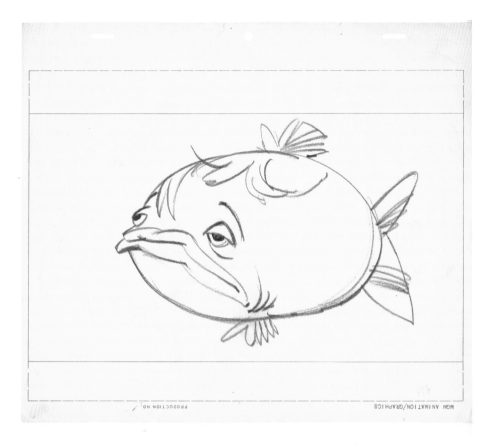

the television industry. "Present cartoon shows, effective as some of them may be, are largely auditory. They are not animated as such. They are a series of more or less held drawings supporting a kind of radio script. They are illustrated narratives….not animation."

Coming from a legacy of "full animation," it is no wonder that Chuck wanted to continue the tradition with his studio. He expressed his policy regarding animation at Tower Twelve:

We believe that what is needed now is a show that can *only* be done in animation, one that *depends* upon animation, one that contains material only possible in animation. i.e. a boy flying or becoming a frog or living with animated books requires him to be an animated character too, but we want his actions to explain *what* he does, not the incessant narrator or the flood of overwhelming dialogue characteristic of today's animated shows. We want the audience to *look* at the screen, not glance at it.

To paraphrase: animation on TV has not been tried and found wanting, it has not been tried. We want to try it.

Pages 32-35: Presentation artwork for the "Fiddler's Green" segment of the proposed *Crawford* TV series, circa 1969.

· · · · ·

The third and final main segment of the show was to be a serial adventure that continued from episode to episode. One of these storylines was a holdover from the shelved *Adventures of the Road-Runner* show: *Don Coyote and Sancho Plazma,* about "a Spanish Hidalgo and his servant, a blood-hound with all the range of facial expression of a Buster Keaton."

Most of these ideas never made it past words on paper, but there is one concept that was further explored in Chuck's 1969 outline. *Fiddler's Green* was meant to be a serialized season-long Crawford adventure. Each *Fiddler's Green* saga would end on a cliffhanger, something that was not standard practice on television in the sixties—especially in a children's cartoon.

Chuck's concept was that a guppy in Crawford's bedroom aquarium sends him to the mysterious world below the surface of the sea—another nod to Crawford's predecessor, Ralph Phillips. The guppy introduces himself as Alfred Lord Grouper, "a fat Charles Laughtonish fish, who speaks only Shakespearean, having once inadvertently swallowed a quarto edition of the Bard bound in leather." The fish takes Crawford to the Cradle of the Deep, "where baby fish of all varieties are nurtured and rocked and swung to and fro in the hammock of the Gulf Streams."

It is here that Crawford meets a host of colorful characters. Heavysides, the Right Whale, "who becomes a kind of pachyderm of the deep to Crawford. He is embarrassed about always being right, but—what are you going to do?" The Cross-Porpoise, "the only unhappy porpoise in the ocean." Crawford makes it his mission to teach the Cross-Porpoise how to smile.

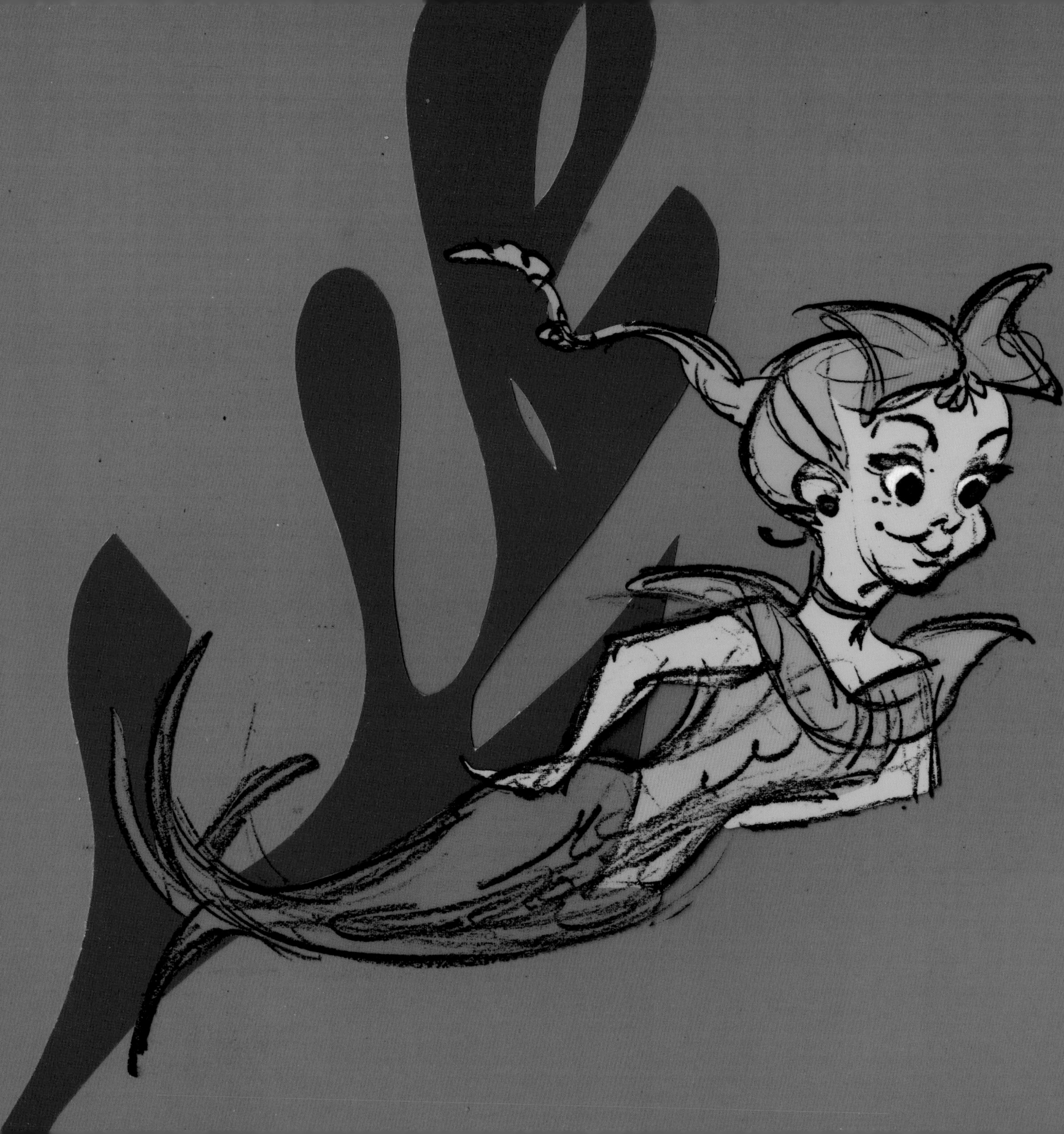

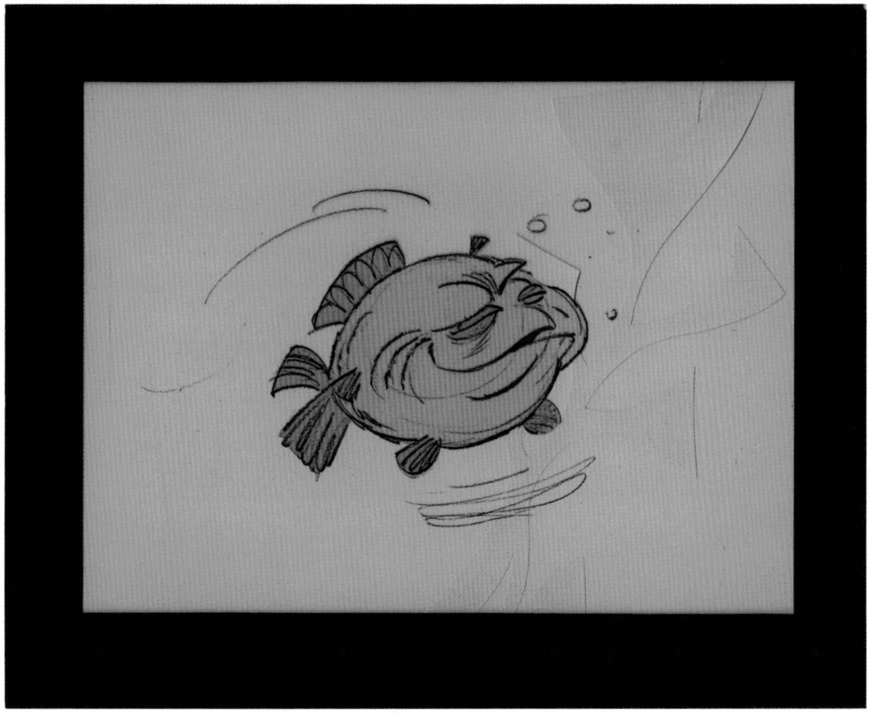

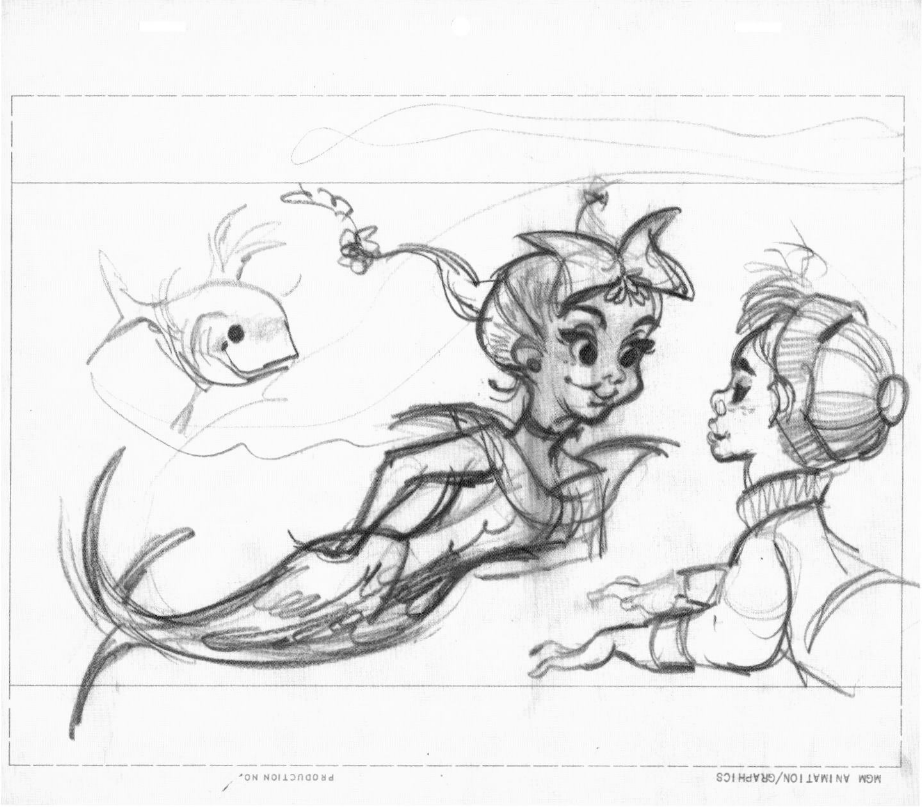

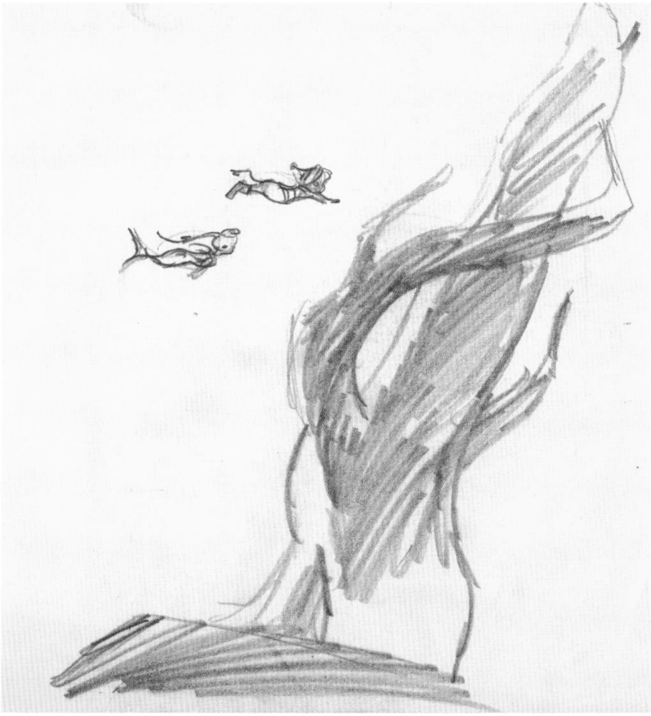

Most important to the story are Melissa Scudder, "daughter of Admiral Fabian Scudder, the keeper of the Eddystone Light" and Annelida, "the mermaid with the sea-fern hair, who share Crawford's great adventures." Together Crawford and Annelida swim to different underwater locales and mystical islands, including Avalon, the island where King Arthur went to gain immortality.

Chuck Jones proposed that Crawford be given a completely different design for each segment of the show. The Crawford in *Fiddler's Green* has body proportions closer to that of a real child, rather than the short and cute stature of Crawford from the *Here Comes Crawford* storyboards. His wardrobe consists of a Jacques Cousteau-style hat and turtleneck, perfect for deep-sea exploration in a cartoon world. This wardrobe would later serve as Crawford's signature outfit in the newspaper strip.

As if the *Crawford* sequences weren't ambitious enough, Chuck envisioned several other recurring segments, many only a minute or two in length, which would be designed in a variety of different graphic styles and interspersed throughout each episode. One segment had children's drawings come to life with experimental animation. Jones collected drawings and material from actual children thinking that "children's drawings accurately reveal their needs and hopes, their dreams and their remarkable sense of color, or drama and their ingenuousness." Another, called "Ted Geisel's World," was drawn in the style of Dr. Seuss, and told in rhyme. In another, a magic paint brush taught the viewer how to draw.

Many other ideas were brainstormed revolving around the human senses, time, genetics, music, and even

Opposite: Chuck and director Richard Williams in London working on *A Christmas Carol, Being a Ghost Story of Christmas,* which won the Academy Award for Best Animated Short in 1972.

visits to other countries done in the style of Tex Avery's *Looney Tunes* travelogues. Spot gags featuring visual puns were used as bumpers to bring the show into and out of commercial breaks.

The *Crawford* animated series was not seriously pursued at this time, although Chuck appeared to have put more thought into it than his other shelved projects. Most likely due to the *Tom & Jerry* series and his other MGM work, as well as his insistence on high-quality animation, Chuck simply didn't have the time to devote to such an ambitious animated series.

After the completion of *Phantom Tollbooth* in 1969, MGM decided to once again close down its animation department. Chuck Jones, now fifty-seven years old, was forced to look in a new direction.

• • • • •

"It used to be said that there were three great influences on a child: home, school, and church. Today, there is a fourth great influence, and you ladies and gentlemen in this room control it," declared Federal Communications Commission (FCC) President Newton N. Minnow in a 1961 address criticizing the National Association of Broadcasters for turning a blind eye to the "vast wasteland" of television programming. "Is there no room on television to teach, to inform, to uplift, to stretch, to enlarge the capacities of our children? Is there no room for programs deepening their understanding of children in other lands? ... Is there no room for reading the great literature of the past, for teaching them the great traditions of freedom? There are some fine children's shows, but they are drowned out in the massive doses of cartoons, violence, and more violence."

Despite having President John F. Kennedy's support, Minnow struggled with getting reforms through Congress and he eventually left the FCC. In 1968 two hundred "housewives and mothers" in Massachusetts formed a grassroots organization called Action for Children's Television (ACT) in part to continue the crusade begun by Minnow and other concerned parents. Among their agendas the women petitioned the FCC for fourteen commercial-free hours of children's programming per week.

Within a couple of years, agitation from ACT and the FCC goaded NBC into creating a new position, a Vice-President in charge of Children's Programming. The other major networks quickly followed and in 1970, ABC hired Chuck Jones in that role. Eager to contribute positively to the medium he thoroughly hated, Chuck spent the next ten months developing new ideas for Saturday morning television. He was quickly disillusioned, concluding that ABC was not really interested in any of his ideas or suggestions. He quipped, "It was like being dancing master at Forest Lawns [cemetery]."

Toward the end of the year, Chuck began work on what would be his only television series, *The Curiosity Shop,* a name that Chuck's wife, Dorothy, borrowed from Dickens. In order to focus completely on *Curiosity Shop,* Chuck stepped down from his role as Vice-President in charge of Children's Programming to executive produce the show; an up-and-coming Michael Eisner took his place almost fifteen years before ascending to the position of chief executive officer of The Walt Disney Company.

Each of the seventeen one-hour *Curiosity Shop* programs featured three or four children as they explore a store filled with gadgets, books, and antiquities. In one corner a treehouse, home to a chimpanzee named Darwin; in another a waterbed for a seal named Eunice. A computer on a desk answered the kids' questions with more questions. One of the walls was filled with animals that talked. An "Elevator to Anywhere" transported the children to destinations all over the world and beyond!

"Children are islands of curiosity in a sea of question marks," said Chuck Jones when talking about *Curiosity Shop,* "Their first word is no; their second word is why. Much more sophisticated is how, which comes later. We get too much involved in how-rope-is-made syndromes in television. Let's first work at getting rid of no and find out why."

At the beginning of each episode the kids would find an object they had never seen before. This led to a number of questions which would be addressed through a series of short segments—a combination of animation, live-action, and puppetry. Chuck used his connections to bring a number of well-known writers to pen their own episodes: Ray Bradbury; Walt Kelly; Mike Marmer and Stan Burns of *The Carol Burnett Show;* gag writer, screenwriter, and lyricist Larry Markes.

Chuck also invited animators from all over the world to contribute segments to his show. George Pal produced one short in his famous stop-motion animation, a sketch in which a group of tools battle a bully blowtorch. The tools eventually overcome the bully when its body is punctured by a tack and drained of its fluid. Other animation groups that contributed included the Croatia-based Zagreb Studios and the National Film Board of Canada. The NFB's Don Arioli was particularly important to the show, storyboarding several episodes. The rest of the animated sequences were conceived by Chuck and animated by Abe Levitow in the Tower Twelve studio offices. One recurring sketch involved a bookworm called Professor Trivia, who was chased by Cou-Cou, a French bird that Chuck

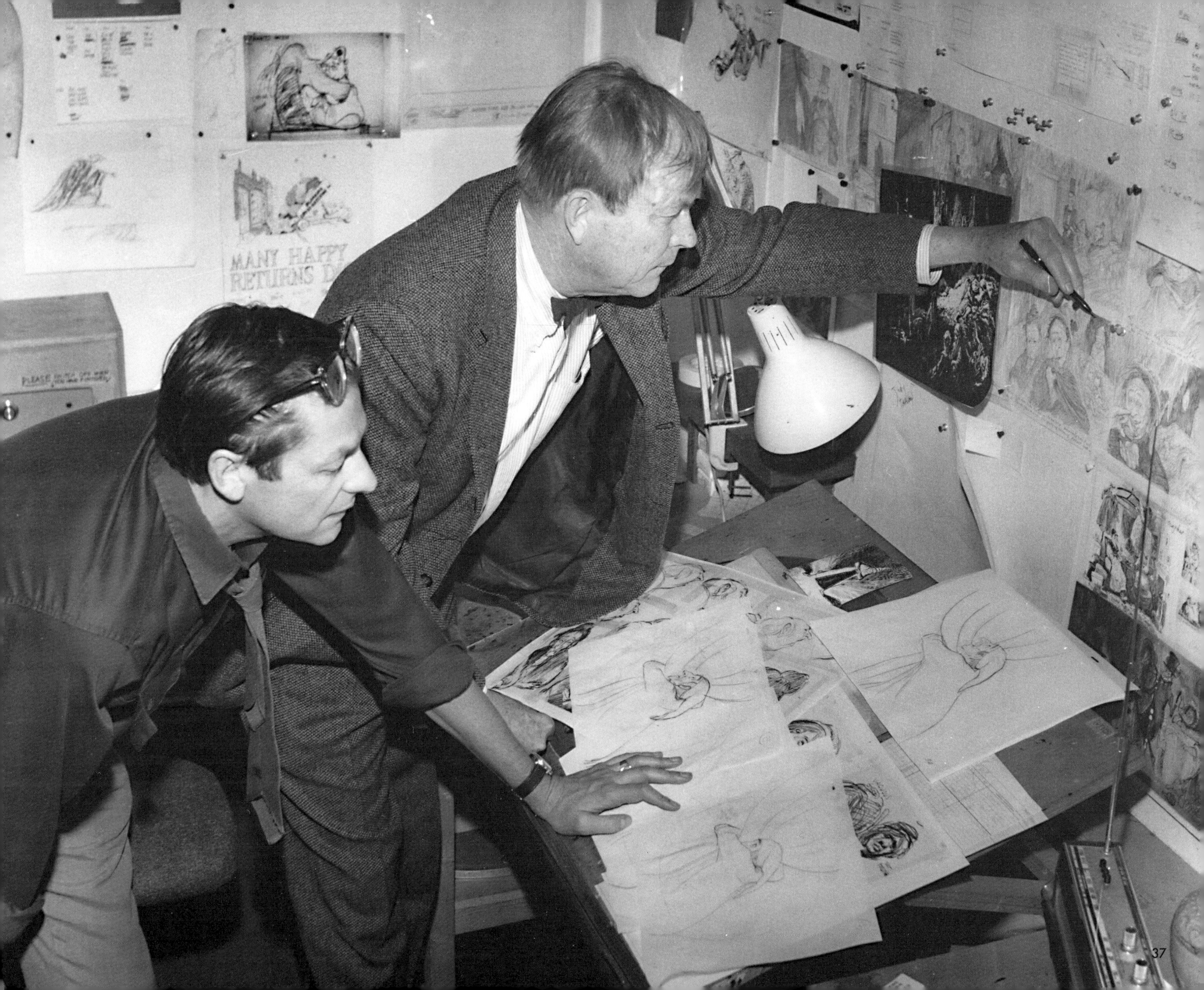
MANY HAPPY
RETURNS D

originally created for his aborted *Ponce de Lion* pilot during the MGM days.

Another of Chuck's ideas was to animate popular newspaper comic strip characters and use them to teach lessons to children. He approached Robert Reed, president of the Chicago Tribune–New York News Syndicate, who arranged to get permissions for various characters. The line-up included Johnny Hart's *B.C.,* Mell Lazarus's *Miss Peach,* Virgil "VIP" Partch's *Big George,* Irving Phillips' *Strange World of Mr. Mum,* and Hank Ketcham's *Dennis the Menace.* Ketcham himself guest-starred in two episodes. Also noteworthy was an animated appearance of Stan and Jan Berenstain's Bear family. For all of these characters, this was their first animated appearance. The relationship with Reed would loom large in *Crawford*'s future.

The Curiosity Shop's format borrowed heavily from the *Crawford* proposal Chuck and Dorothy had developed in 1969. Many of the thirty-second segments that were originally designed for *Crawford* were adapted to fit this show. The transportation to any place no matter how impossible via the Elevator to Anywhere sounds a lot like the way Charlie the Rocket Chair would take Crawford on special journeys. Certain questions in the "What's It Like…" part of *Crawford* were asked by the kids in the shop. Even spot gags originally drawn for *Crawford* made it into *Curiosity Shop.*

The show debuted on September 11, 1971. It was approved by the National Education Association, the largest teachers' organization in America, the first time a weekly television series on a major network would gain such an approval. Network executives were not impressed with the ratings, however, and cancelled the series after only one season. For ABC, an educational show such as this did not provide an adequate revenue stream.

ABC then sent Jones to London to oversee Richard Williams's *A Christmas Carol, Being a Ghost Story of Christmas* TV special. Master animator Ken Harris, one of Chuck's top animators from his Warner unit, had been there for months developing the prime-time special's unique visual aesthetic before his former boss arrived. Chuck said that his job was "to find a sponsor and a network" (which he did earlier, when he was still Director of Children's Programming for ABC), but John Grant, in his book *Masters of Animation,* wrote that Jones was actually called in because Williams was having trouble keeping to his budget and schedule. Soon after Chuck arrived he called on Abe Levitow to join them. When the half-hour special aired on ABC on December 21, 1971, it was critically acclaimed for its chilling, and often downright scary, retelling of the Dickens classic. It was later released to theaters in order to qualify for an Oscar, taking home the 1972 award for Best Animated Short.

Jones maintained a good relationship with ABC after his official work with them was finished; Chuck Jones Enterprises continued to produce a series of TV specials for them.

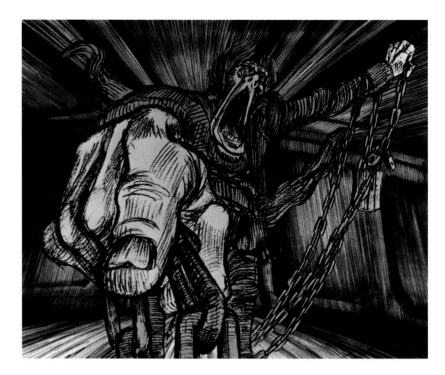

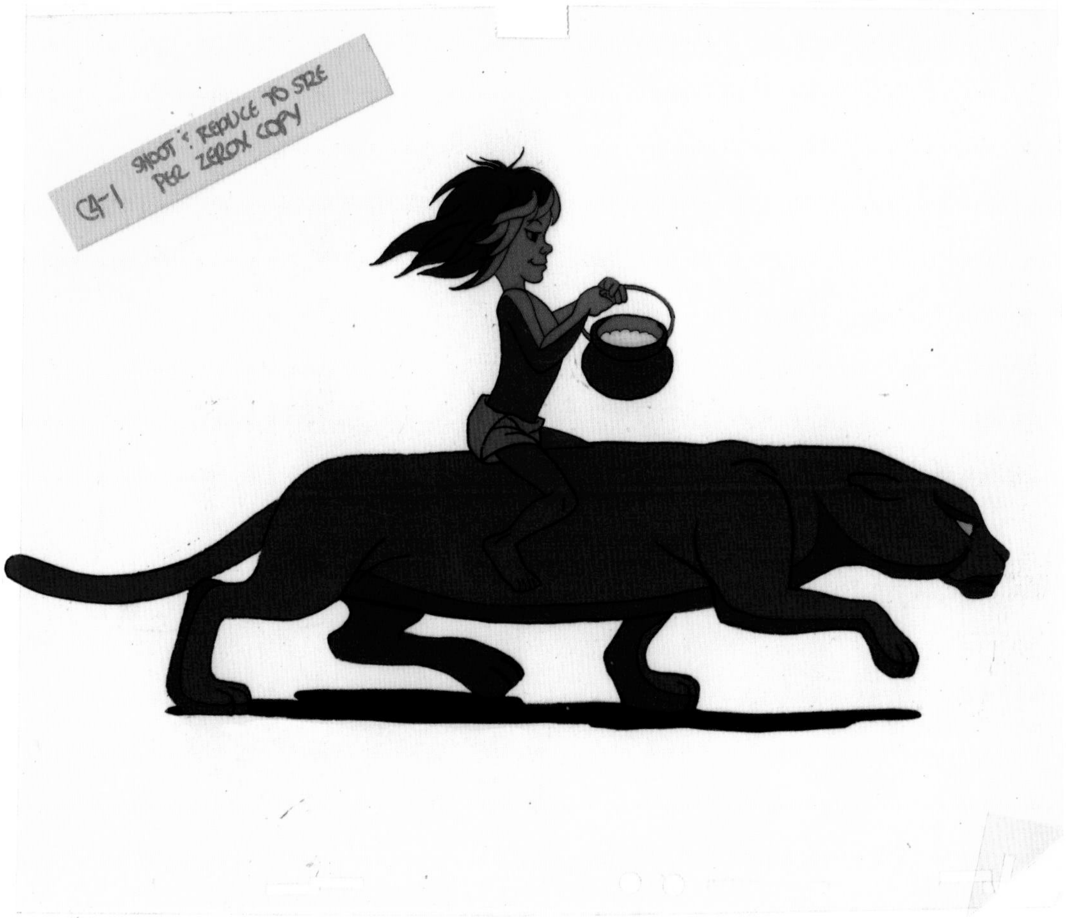
C4-1
SHOOT & REDUCE TO SIZE
PER ZEROX COPY

Opposite: Publicity stills from *A Christmas Carol.*

Left: A cel from *Mowgli's Brothers,* the last of the *Jungle Book* TV specials.

Still working out of his old Tower Twelve office space, Chuck began work on an adaptation of George Selden's 1960 novel, *The Cricket in Times Square,* the story of a cricket whose chirping sounds like a violin virtuoso and who can mimic any song. "Chuck thought his Cricket was perfect," says Mark Kausler. Certainly others also thought well enough of the musical insect, because it was awarded a Golden Eagle Certificate by the Council on International Nontheatrical Events, Inc. (CINE), a Silver Medal at the International Animation Festival, and the Parent's Choice Award for excellence in television programming after its April 23, 1973 premiere.

ABC was impressed with the recognition *Cricket* received and commissioned two sequels. The sequels were not based on Selden's subsequent books, but rather all-new stories, written by Chuck Jones. Work began only a few months after the first *Cricket* special aired, and six months later, *A Very Merry Cricket* premiered on December 14, 1973. Unfortunately, it did not become a Christmas classic like *Grinch.* Jones and his team spent the better part of 1974 working on the subsequent *Yankee Doodle Cricket*, produced as part of ABC's Bicentennial project, first airing on January 16, 1975, and then rebroadcast in July 1976 to coincide with the actual Bicentennial. It was nominated for an Emmy Award.

Congruent to their work on *Yankee Doodle Cricket,* the crew at the Tower began to develop *Rikki-Tikki-Tavi,* the first in what would be a trilogy of television specials based on the stories from Rudyard Kipling's *Jungle Book.* As a tremendous fan of Kipling's literature and disgusted by the song-and-dance version Disney made in 1966, Chuck was determined to create serious stories that fully realized the harshness (and sometimes darkness) of Kipling's jungle and its inhabitants. *Rikki-Tikki-Tavi* debuted on CBS on January 9, 1975. *The White Seal* followed a few months later, on March 24. Finally, *Mowgli's Brothers* aired on February 11, 1976.

Chuck loved to tell the story of how he went to Kipling's daughter to inquire about the pronunciation of the name "Mowgli." As a child, Chuck had always read the name with

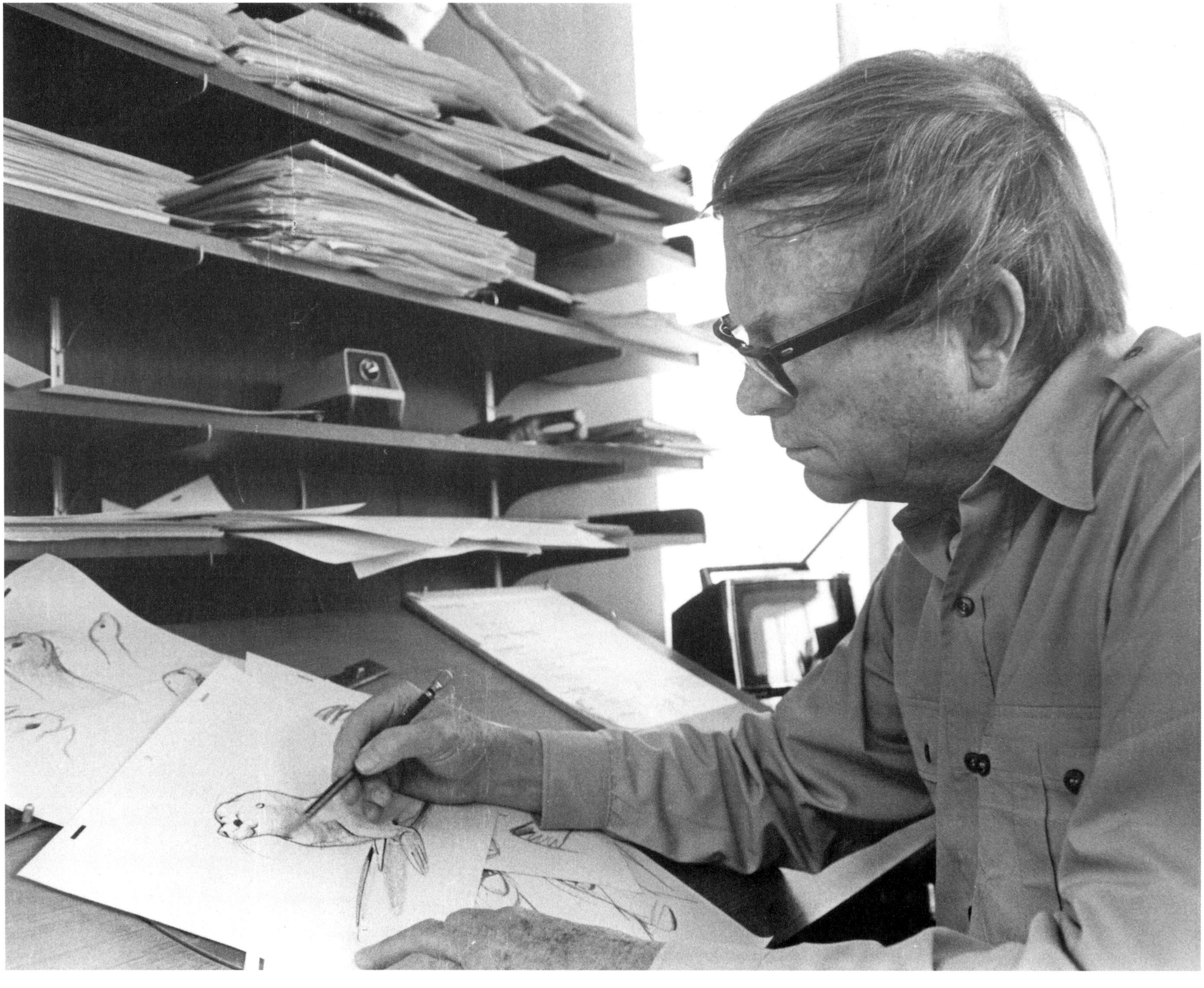

Opposite: Chuck drawing *The White Seal*, the second of his *Jungle Book* TV specials, which aired in March 1975.

Right top: Mowgli hugs Baloo the Bear in this cel from *Mowgli's Brothers*, February 1976.

Right bottom: Mowgli character study.

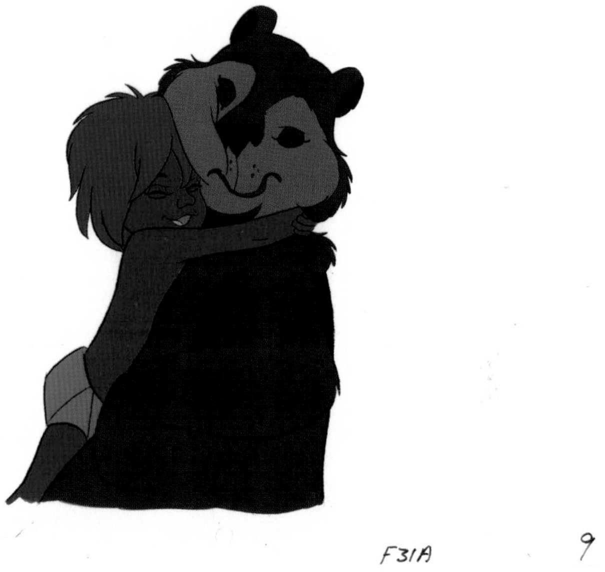
F31A
9

"Mow" rhyming with "cow." In the Disney version, however, the character's name was pronounced with "Mow" sounding like "toe," which caused Chuck to second-guess his pronunciation.

"Before we started our film, I discovered that Kipling's daughter was still alive and called her. In an elegant, British dowager-like voice, she confirmed my pronunciation and added, 'and, I hate Walter Disney.' It was the only time I ever heard anybody call him Walter. In her lifetime, she said nobody ever pronounced anything but Mauwgli."

These three films were among Chuck's favorites, and possibly the furthest from the slapstick comedy that brought him fame at Warner Bros.

• • • • •

In the seventies Chuck Jones had another go at turning *Crawford* into an animated television series, this time with the help of animator, writer, and storyboard artist Don Arioli. The two had remained good friends after *Curiosity Shop* was cancelled. Don had become a freelance writer and artist, working on a number of projects for Chuck.

Arioli had recently written and storyboarded a sex education film for Health and Welfare Canada, telling the story of the birds and the bees from the point of view of Adam and Eve. The concept was rejected, ironically for a sex education film, because it showed full frontal nudity. He reworked the concept, doing away with people and instead using talking sex organs to get the information across. Not surprisingly, *Jimmy Penis and Vicki Vulva* didn't make it past the Health and Welfare department officials either, but the storyboards have become NFB legend. Appreciating the humor and sarcasm in Don's pitch, Chuck Jones offered to help Don circulate *Jimmy Penis* among American educators, but no one picked it up. Don later reworked the story for print and published it in 1987 under the title *Condoms are Safe.*

The exact nature of Arioli's contributions to this later incarnation of *Crawford* may never be fully known. Don Arioli passed away in 2005, but on a wall in his house is a drawing by Chuck Jones with an inscription thanking Don for all he had done. Chuck also acknowledged using many of Don's ideas in the comic strip.

What's clear is that the concept of the show was cleaned up and simplified. The random

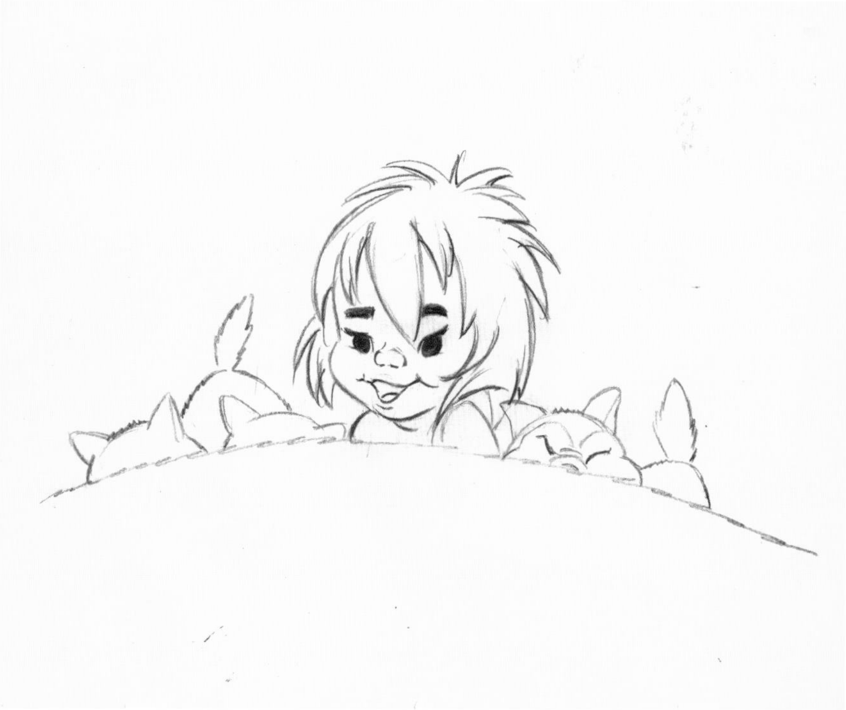

segments were removed, leaving only the three main: Crawford and his friends, Crawford in his room, and the serial adventure. The character of Winfield morphed into the character of Morgan, Crawford's younger, naïve friend, who would later follow Crawford into the comic strip. Interestingly, Morgan's design resembles Crawford's original from 1969, right down to the short stature, army hat, and long sleeves. The idea that Crawford's design would change in each segment was dropped in favor of a consistent look, one that would also follow Crawford into the comic strip. In a letter Jones wrote to his mother in the early seventies, he explained that Crawford's design was based on his grandson, Craig Kausen.

Chuck and Don set out to find a network that would share their enthusiasm, but to no avail. The persistent pair once came close and spent months in negotiations with a major network, only to ultimately be turned down.

"It always throws me when people say 'I think this is a little too original,'" Arioli said in a 1977 interview.

Chuck Jones was eventually reunited with the *Looney Tunes* cast when Warner Bros. approached him to produce a new television special starring Bugs Bunny and Daffy Duck. Jones cast the pair as dueling conductors for an orchestral performance of Camille Saint-Saëns's *Carnival of the Animals*. Chuck Jones Enterprises also produced a few Road Runner & Coyote spots for *Sesame Street*. Soon more *Looney Tunes* specials followed: *A Connecticut Rabbit in King Arthur's Court* (1978), *Daffy Duck's Thanks-for-Giving Special* (1979), *Bugs Bunny's Looney Christmas Tales* (1979), and *Bugs Bunny's Bustin' Out All Over* (1980). Chuck partnered with his old Warner colleague Friz Freleng, head of DePatie-Freleng Enterprises, to produce a few of these specials. Warner Bros. also asked Chuck to devise a plan to release a collection of classic Warner Bros. shorts in a feature-film format. Strung together with all-new animation, Chuck collected several of his best *Looney Tunes* in a package called *The Bugs Bunny/Road Runner Movie* (1979).

Closing out the seventies were two *Raggedy Ann* holiday specials that Jones produced for the Bobbs-Merrill Company, *Raggedy Ann and Andy in the Great Santa Claus Caper* (1978) and *Raggedy Ann and Andy in the Pumpkin Who Couldn't Smile* (1979). Jones created a new character for these specials, a stuffed sheepdog named Raggedy Arthur.

• • • • •

Sometime in the early half of 1977, Chuck Jones and Chicago Tribune–New York News Syndicate president Robert Reed met for lunch at Simply Blues. Interviewed for this book, Reed recalls, "We were doing some animation projects together. He was doing the

Curiosity Shop which had cartoonists like Johnny Hart and others doing work for it. He contacted them through me and we got to know each other after that." Bob Reed always made an attempt to see Chuck when he was on the West Coast.

In the course of their lunch Reed presented Chuck with the opportunity to write and draw his own newspaper strip. The newspaper executive was looking for a kid-focused comic strip that could be his syndicate's answer to United Features's *Peanuts.* He thought that Chuck's creativity, not to mention his name recognition, could be a key advantage. Chuck had just come off several months of unsuccessful negotiations over his *Crawford* television series, and with *Crawford* fresh in mind, he saw the potential of using these characters in a daily newspaper comic strip. Chuck Jones accepted Robert Reed's offer and began adapting his characters to their new environment.

During another one of Bob Reed's visits to California, he was sitting in Chuck's office discussing *Crawford* when he received a call from his office and had a short and slightly frantic conversation with his assistant. When Bob hung up, Chuck asked if there was a problem. Indeed there was: Stan Lynde—creator, writer, and artist on the long-running Western comic strip *Rick O'Shay*—had quit over a contract dispute with the syndicate. Sitting in on this meeting was Chuck's personal assistant, Marian Dern. Chuck thought about it for a second and asked, "How about having her write it?" pointing to Marian, knowing she had a career as a professional writer before working for Chuck Jones Enterprises. After a short question and answer session, Marian agreed. (In 1983 Marian agreed to another of Chuck's proposals when she agreed to be Mrs. Chuck Jones, almost five years after Dorothy passed away.)

"But who could we get to draw it?" asked Bob. Chuck looked around his office and noticed a poster for the 1977 San Diego Comic-Con that one of his employees had put up on the wall. "How about this guy?" he suggested. Chuck didn't know the artist; he just liked the picture and thought it would suit the strip. He contacted the Comic-Con and obtained the contact information for the artist of the poster, Filipino cartoonist Alfredo Alcala. Little did Chuck know that Alcala had just lost a contract and was facing deportation unless he found another job. Chuck's recommendation provided Alfredo with the work he needed to legally stay in the country. Alfredo Alcala, whose career began in 1948 and lasted fifty years, remained one of the most-sought after comics artists until his death in 2000.

Why exactly did Chuck decide to do a comic strip? This was a question asked by more than a few of his friends and coworkers. Was he bored with his job? Was he looking for a new challenge? Did it pay really well? Chuck half-jokingly offered his answer to such questions, saying, "I suppose that many animators/animation directors have buried within

Right: Chuck's note to Don Arioli concerning the newspaper strip.

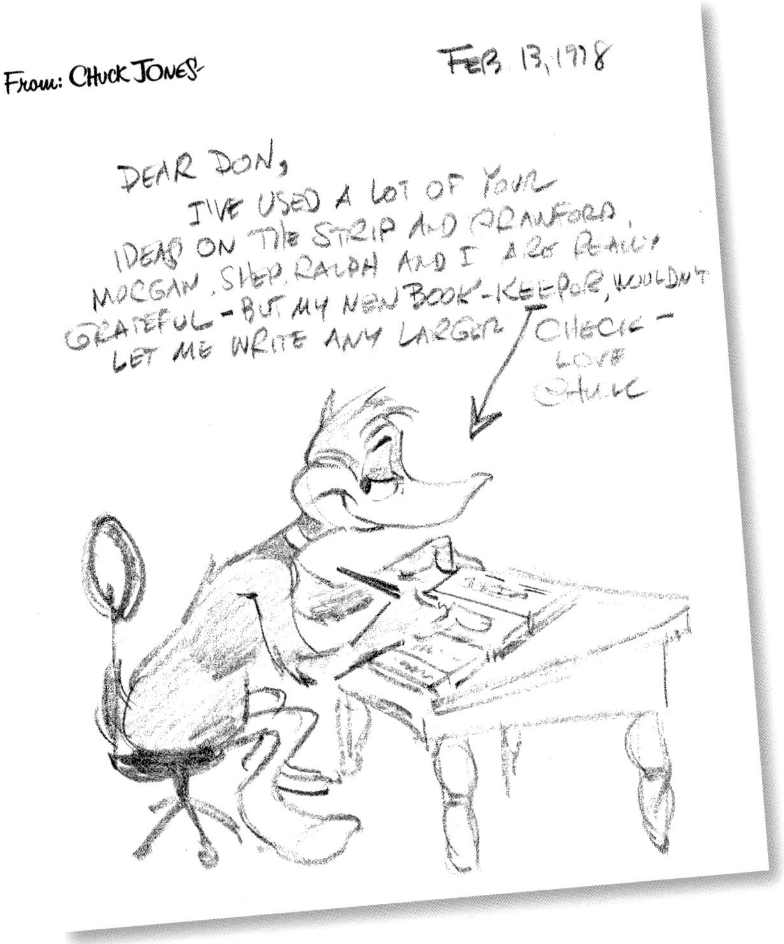
From: CHUCK JONES
FEB 13, 1978
DEAR DON,
I'VE USED A LOT OF YOUR
IDEAS ON THE STRIP AND CRAWFORD.
MORGAN, SHEP, RALPH AND I ARE REALLY
GRATEFUL - BUT MY NEW BOOK-KEEPER, WOULDN'T
LET ME WRITE ANY LARGER
CHECK -
LOVE
CHUCK

them a like desire to leave the four or five thousand drawings necessary for a six-minute animated cartoon to go forth and startle the newspaper world through the four or five boxes of a daily newspaper strip."

Chuck's job as an animation director was to draw the characters in their "extreme" poses—that is, drawing the character at the key moments in their movements that best dictate their actions. Part of what makes a comic strip is a sequence of "extreme poses" in little boxes, not unlike storyboards. A comic strip would also allow Chuck to play with dialogue in a way he never could in animation. Aside from a few instances in *Phantom Tollbooth* and one in the *Pogo Special Birthday Special* involving the word "October" (Chuck reused this gag in *Crawford*), physical manifestations of dialogue are rarely seen in Chuck's cartoons. The dialogue in the word balloons plays an important role in the *Crawford* comic strip, with some week-long stories dwelling on one simple exchange of words.

"As to drawing and writing a strip about children," said Chuck Jones about *Crawford,* "it is quite natural for me to do so. My first directorial effort in animation was about a child cat in *The Night Watchman* in 1938 and I worked through all kinds of children of various animals, including the young of people."

Throughout Chuck's first few years as a director of *Merrie Melodies* and *Looney Tunes,* children were the subjects of several of his films, many of which seem influenced by his own childhood experiences. *The Night Watchman* reflects Chuck's determination to be the man of the house to his siblings—he had one younger brother and two older sisters—while his father, who was a salesman of various trinkets, was often away on business trips. In *Robin Hood Makes Good* (1939) a young squirrel is left role-playing the parts the older two brothers don't want. *Mighty Hunters* (1940) was a near-perfect adaptation of James Swinnerton's *Canyon Kiddies* comic strip and Chuck's first attempt at directing an ensemble of children. In one of Jones's most infamous cartoons, *Angel Puss* (1944), a little African-American boy has a run-in with a mischievous cat. Chuck had a run-in of his own with a cat named Johnson, and *Chuck Amuck* devotes an entire chapter to the influence Johnson had on Chuck's boyhood. In seventeen cartoons, two of Chuck's child characters—Sniffles the Mouse and Inki the Pygmy—experienced the world in a way only children can. These early years are known as Chuck's "Disney years" due to the overly cute characters and storylines obviously inspired by the Disney pictures of the time and by a preference for charm over humor. Around the mid-1940s Chuck's style matured and evolved into the comedy for which he is now famous. The kids took the backseat as Jones started using more of Leon Schlesinger's star performers and creating a few of his own. It wouldn't be until 1954 that Chuck Jones would create his best-known child character, Ralph Phillips.

"I suppose the genesis of Crawford began … in an Academy Award-nominated short called *From A to Z-Z-Z-Z,*" Chuck recalled. "I did not realize it consciously then, but I was beginning to realize what peculiar, marvelous, and unpredictable cubs were those born to human beings."

Children became a focus for his post-Warner Bros. cartoons. Milo, the protagonist in *The Phantom Tollbooth* (1970), must discover his imagination in order to overcome boredom. Chuck's adaptation of Rudyard Kipling's *White Seal* (1975) and *Mowgli's Brothers* (1976) show a seal pup and a man cub proving their self-worth to their disapproving parental figures, who consider them outcasts. While children are not the featured players, *Dr. Seuss's How the Grinch Stole Christmas, Rikki-Tikki-Tavi, A Cricket in Times Square,*

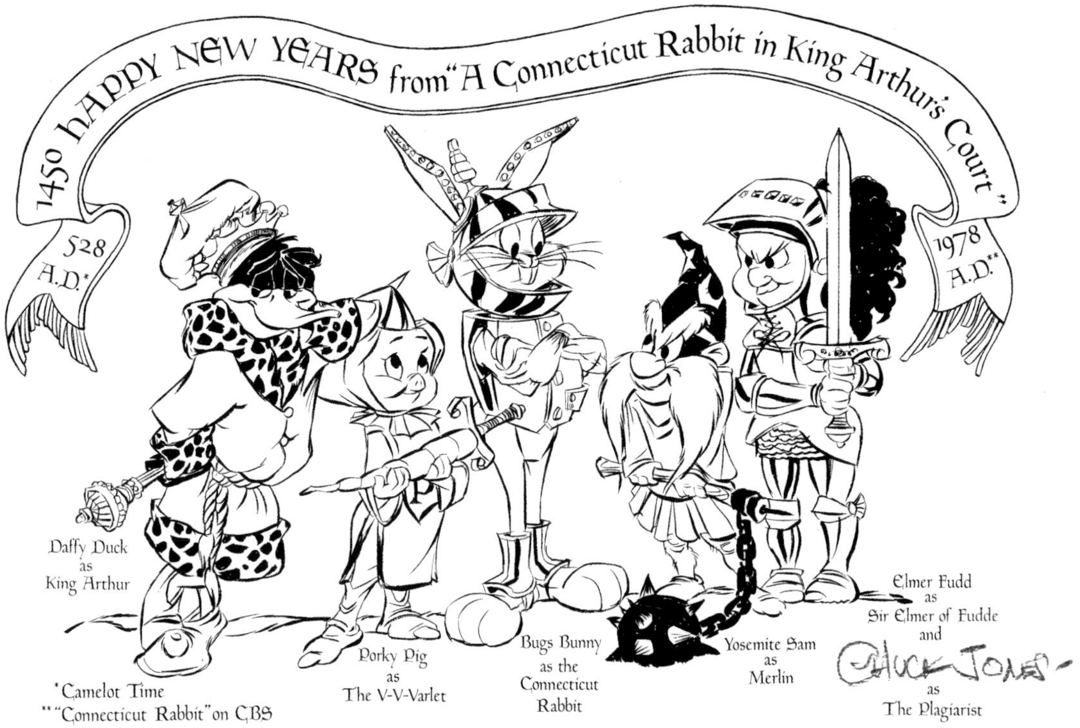
1450 hAPPY NEW YEARS from "A Connecticut Rabbit in King Arthur's Court"
528 A.D.*
1978 A.D.**
Daffy Duck as King Arthur
Porky Pig as The V-V-Varlet
Bugs Bunny as the Connecticut Rabbit
Yosemite Sam as Merlin
Elmer Fudd as Sir Elmer of Fudde and
Chuck Jones as The Plagiarist
*Camelot Time
**"Connecticut Rabbit" on CBS

Left: Chuck's *Looney Tunes* take on Mark Twain's classic novel.

Opposite: Presentation artwork for the last attempt to include Crawford in an animated series proposal in which Chuck was directly involved—1984's *Earth Creatures*.

and the *Raggedy Ann* specials all find the main characters interacting with children in a child's world.

But none of these child characters were as close to Jones as Crawford. And since no network seemed to want him, Chuck Jones set forth into unfamiliar territory, determined to bring Crawford to life one way or another.

This opportunity to produce a *Crawford* comic strip came at a time when Chuck Jones Enterprises was not as busy as they had been in the recent past. Aside from producing some short segments for the *Electric Company,* their workload was fairly light. A deal to make a new *Looney Tunes* television special based on Mark Twain's *A Connecticut Yankee in King Arthur's Court* was in the works, but it would be a few months before that project would commence. Chuck spent a lot of time in his office or the restaurant upstairs redesigning the Crawford character, sketching out gags and preparing for the debut of his new comic strip. He was in regular meetings with Bob Reed and Don Michel, who served as Chuck's editor for *Crawford.*

A start date of November 14, 1977 was set and Chuck spent a good part of the summer writing, drawing, and inking the first few months' worth of strips. It is probable that he wanted to start the strip earlier than November, judging by unpublished summer vacation- and Halloween-themed gags with a 1977 copyright date.

He filled dozens of notepads with possible gags, sketched out in tiny thumbnail versions. Some weeks he planned to have a common theme, others were comprised of stand-alone bits. After he decided which jokes he liked best he roughed out each panel in blue pencil on twelve-field animation paper. He would clean up the image in pencil, then pass it along to Don Foster to cut, paste onto Bristol board, and apply the word balloons.

Foster was the titles man for the Warner Bros. cartoons and had an incredible sense of typography. After Warner Bros. Cartoons closed, Don joined Chuck at MGM and then Chuck Jones Enterprises, where he stayed until work at the Tower waned in the early eighties. "He did really good comic strip lettering," says Don Morgan, who for a time assisted Walt Kelly on *Pogo*. "He did all the title lettering, too….I was pretty good friends with Don and I never saw him draw anything, but he could sure as hell letter." Don not only did Chuck's lettering, but also cleaned up some of Chuck's occasional inking mistakes.

After Don determined that he had enough space for the word balloons, Chuck would ink the strip with a brush. Sometimes Chuck would go back and redraw panels. Norman-Vincent, for example, went through a complete change, which meant that the strips in which he appeared all had to be partially redone.

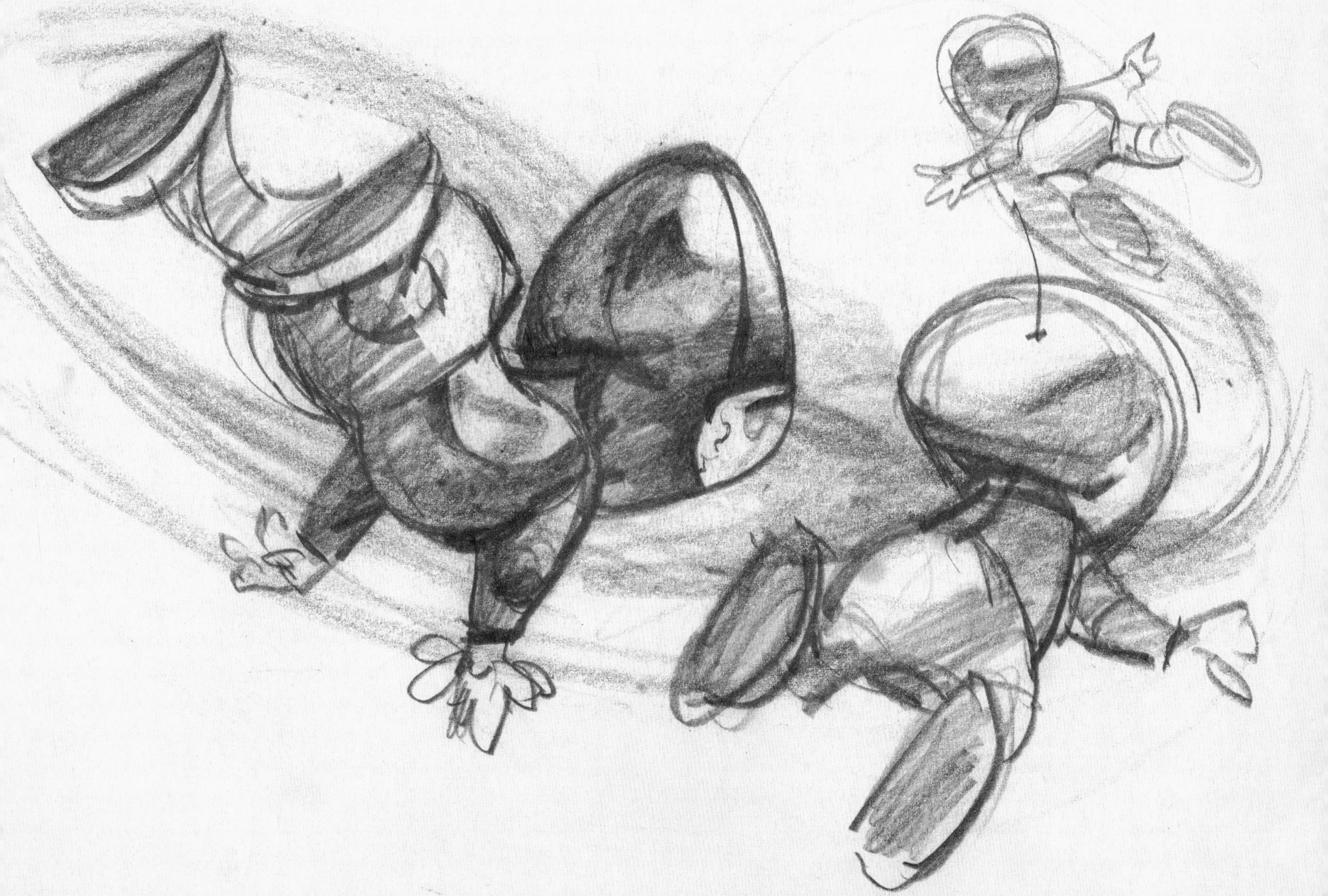

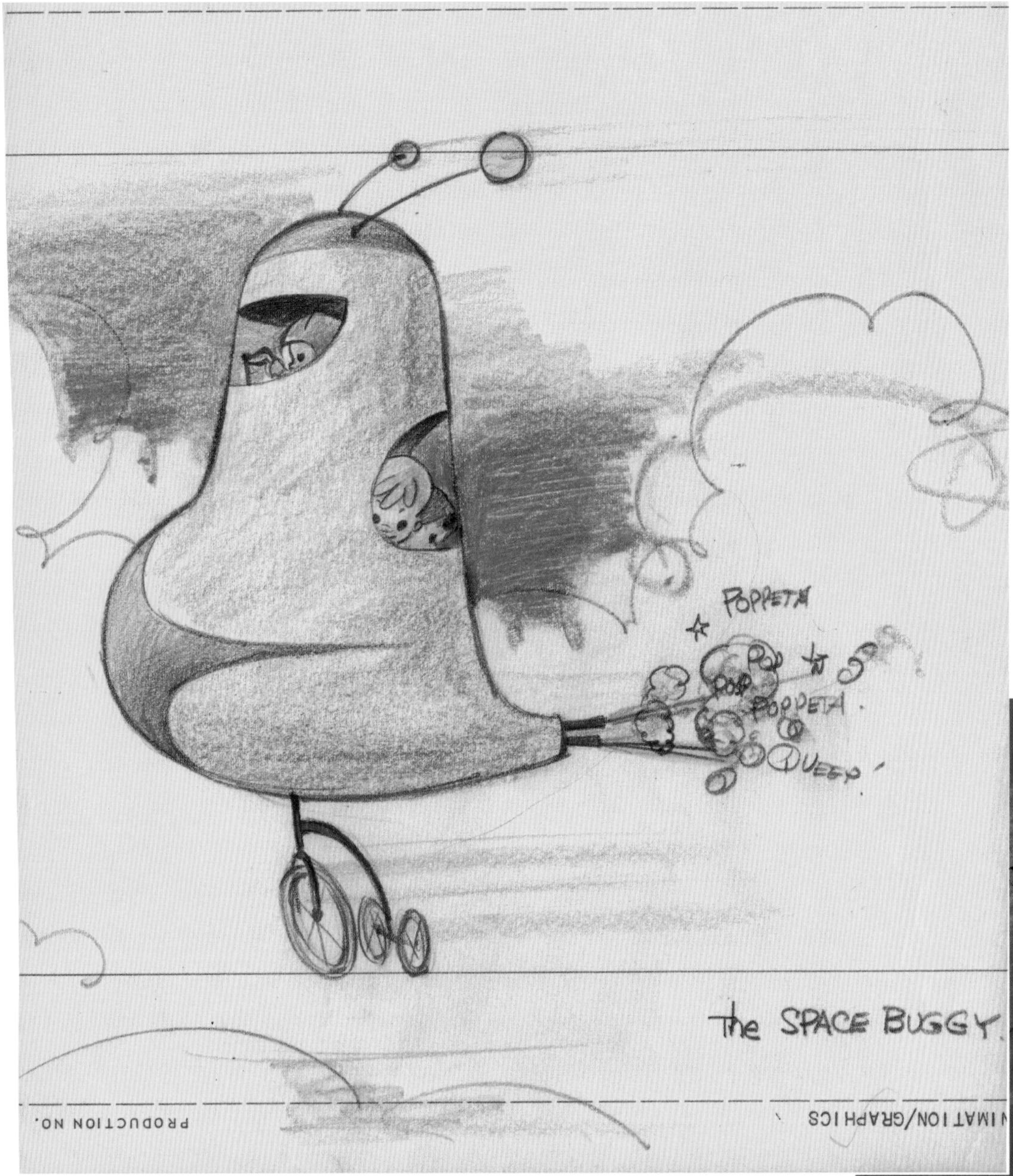
POPPETA
POP
POP
POPPETA
QUEEP'
the SPACE BUGGY.

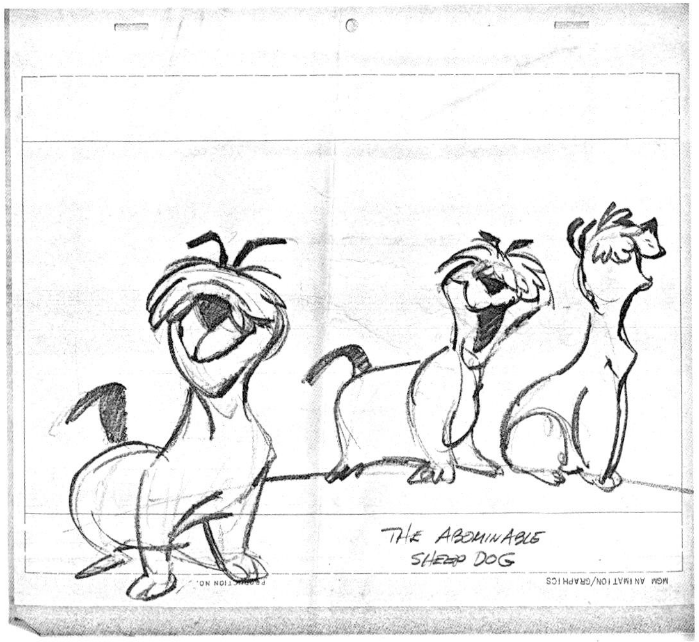
THE ABOMINABLE
SHEEP DOG

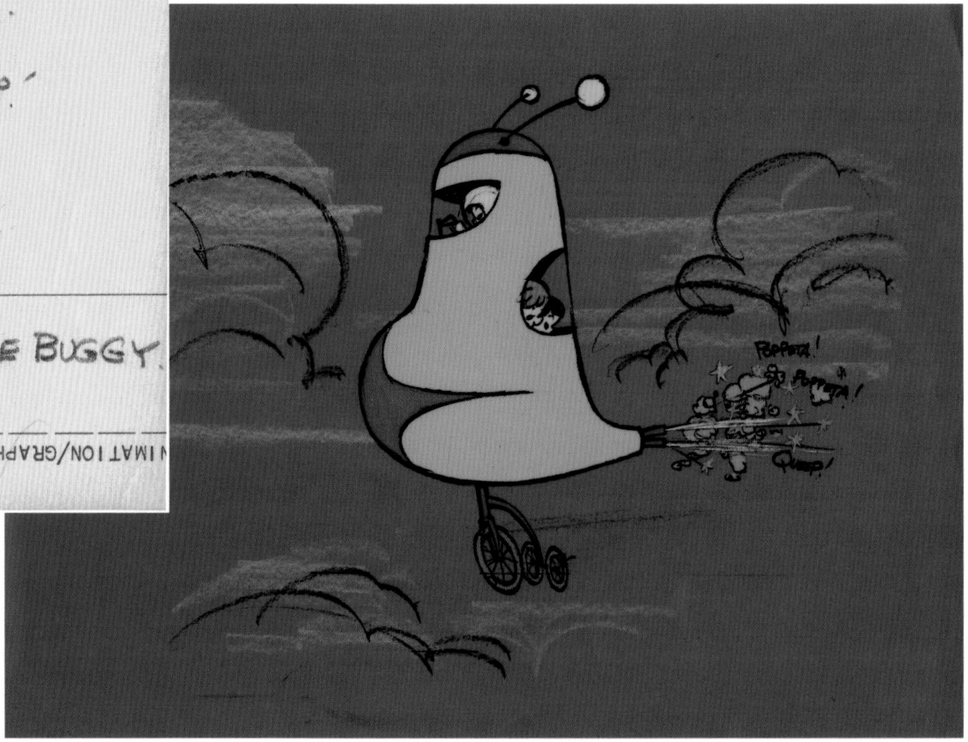
POPPETA!
POPPETA!
QUEEP!

Top right: Sketch from the proposed *Crawford* TV show.

Above, right, and opposite: Presentation and preliminary artwork for *Earth Creatures*.

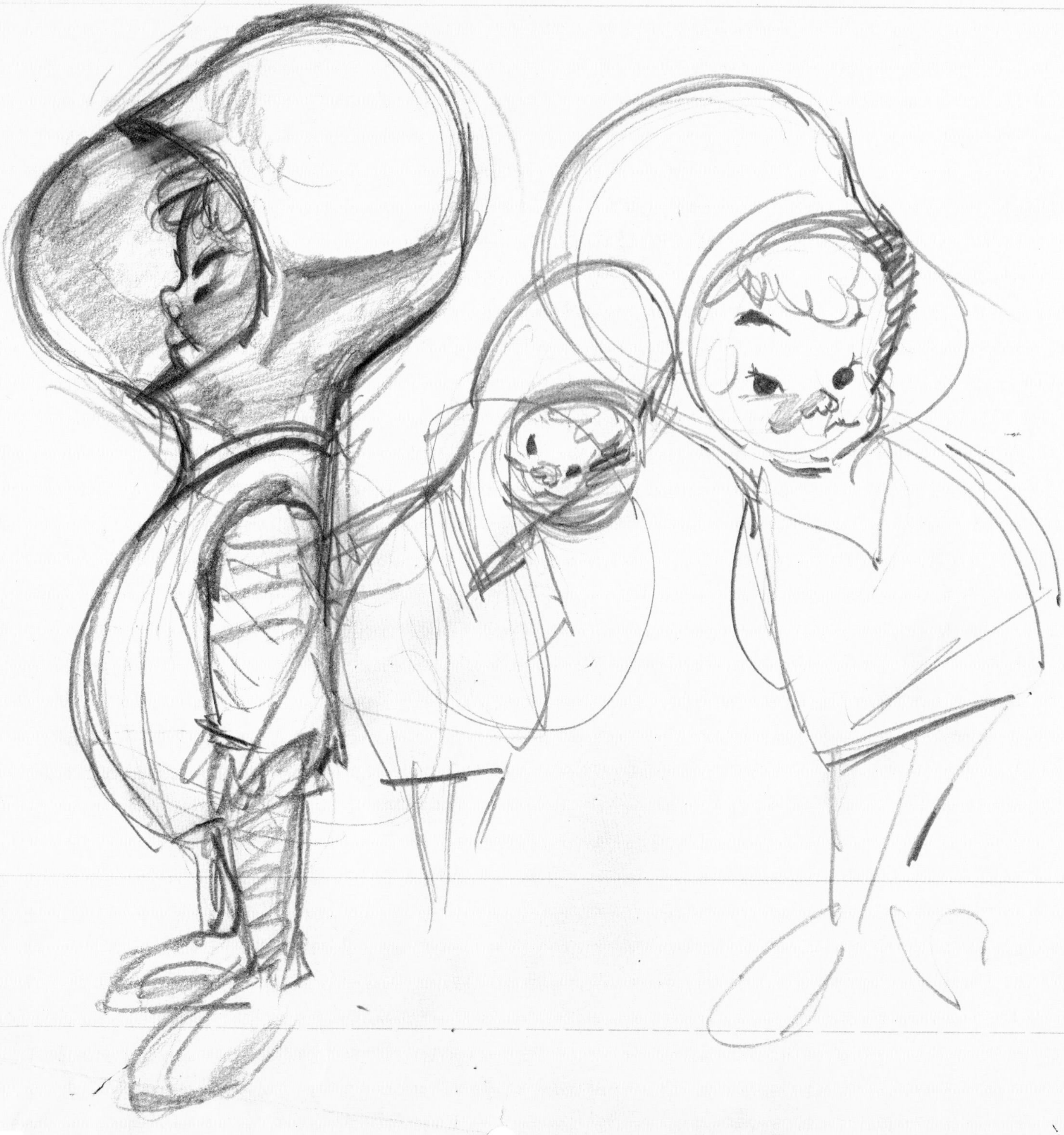

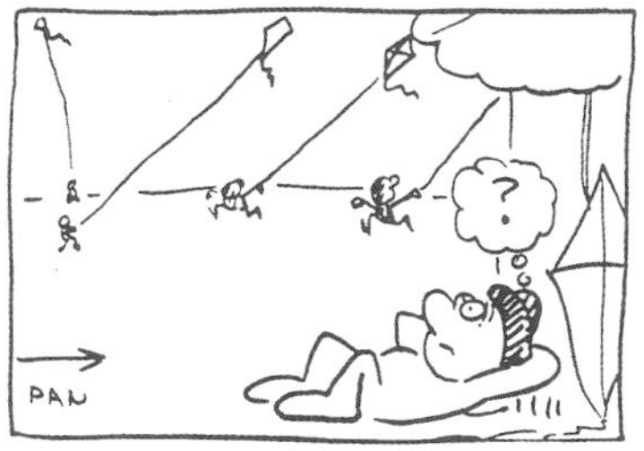
?
PAN

OPEN on exterior shot of kids flying kites. PAN OVER TO CRAWFORD, deep in thought.

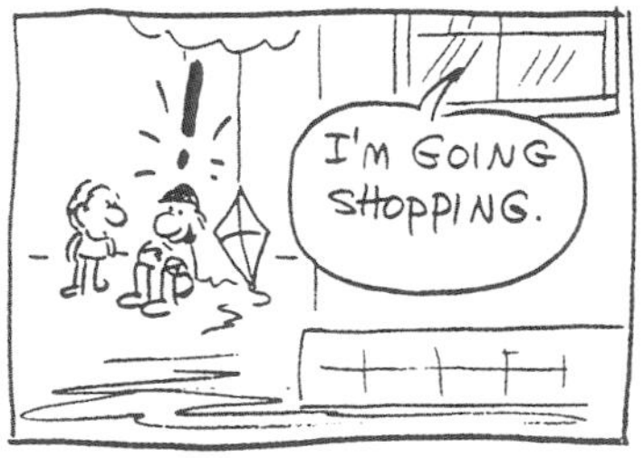
I'M GOING SHOPPING.

CUT TO LONG SHOT, taking in Crawford's kitchen window. We hear his mother say she's taking the car. CRAWFORD reacts.

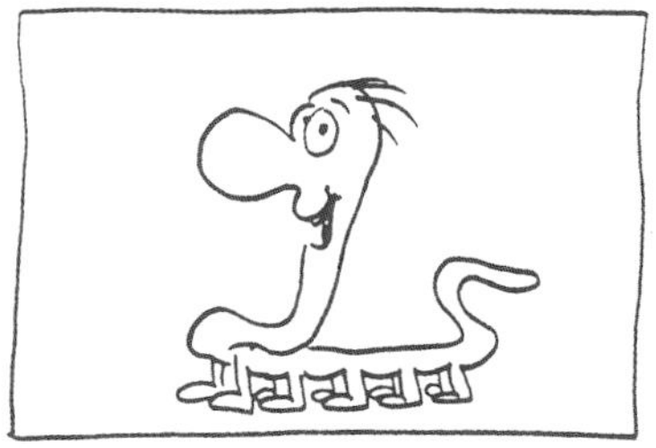

HE IS INTERRUPTED BY THE SNAKERPILLAR, a creature drawn by Crawford. It will interrupt at the drop of a hat if it sees an opportunity to tell a story. Its stories never have anything to do with the theme of the program. Snakerpillar is really an excuse to do nonsense stuff.

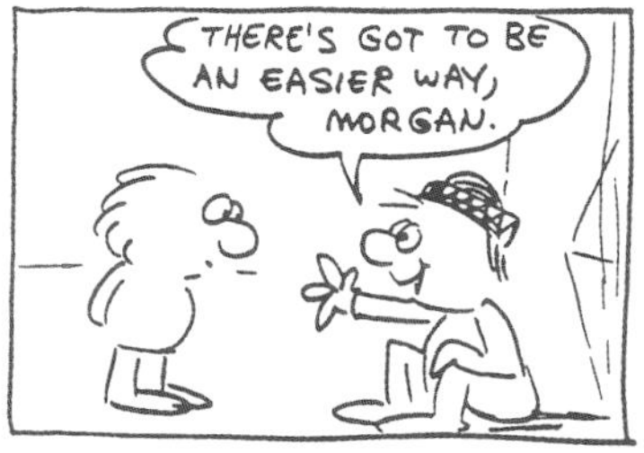
THERE'S GOT TO BE AN EASIER WAY, MORGAN.

MORGAN ENTERS and pesters CRAWFORD to fly his kite before the wind dies. CRAWFORD explains that there must be an easier way to fly a kite than running around wasting "all that energy."

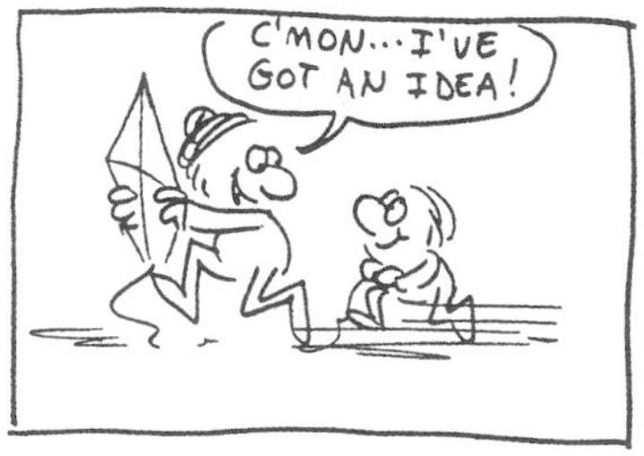
C'MON... I'VE GOT AN IDEA!

CRAWFORD grabs the kite and runs out of frame.

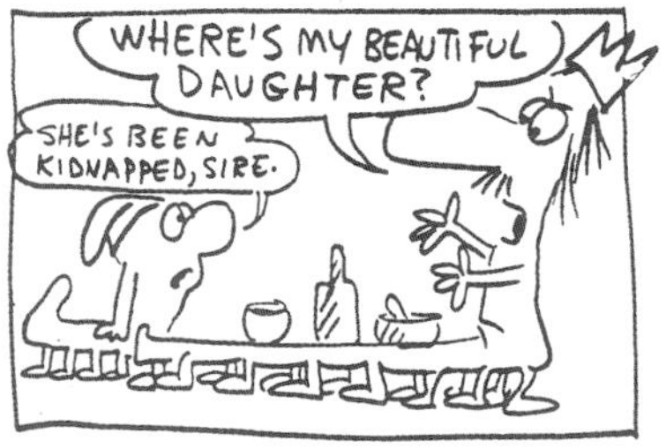
WHERE'S MY BEAUTIFUL DAUGHTER?
SHE'S BEEN KIDNAPPED, SIRE.

One of Snakerpillar's favourite tales is "The Missing Princess." The technique used to illustrate this story will be the "animated" cartoon strip (absurd posing accompanied by animated speech balloons).
Length: Approx. 2:00

For reasons now forgotten by those involved, the start date for the strip was pushed back again, this time to January 9, 1978, causing Thanksgiving- and Christmas-themed gags to go unpublished. In the weeks leading up to *Crawford*'s launch, Chuck and Bob put together a publicity book that introduced newspaper editors all over the country to his family of intellectually minded children, yet few editors decided to add it to their comic pages.

"I think it was a bit too sophisticated for the public and the editors," explains Robert Reed. "Chuck was a brilliant cartoonist and it was a good concept. You can have the best idea in the world, but if the editors don't like it, it will never get off the ground."

The strip also occasionally addressed contemporary culture and politics. One character, Libby, reflected the women's liberation movement that was gaining momentum in the seventies. Another example is a week-long story that has Crawford writing a letter to the Supreme Court demanding that corporal punishment be banned in schools. This refers to the high court's April 1977 ruling to uphold a bill that legalized paddling, or spanking, by teachers or principals in school classrooms. When the strip's start date was pushed to January 1978, the corporal punishment episodes were moved to April 1978. By that time the story was old news, making it seem like Chuck was a bit out of touch with current events.

Animator Mark Kausler remembers working in the Tower at the time: "We thought, here's this plum thing that everybody wants, every cartoonist I know would love to sell a strip and have it in a lot of papers and have it make a lot of money. So here's Chuck, he's got that opportunity at his doorstep and we thought he was extremely casual about it and didn't take it seriously enough."

Dorothy's death in February 1978, shortly after *Crawford* had made its debut, undoubtedly took its toll on the cartoonist.

Chuck's editor, Don Michel, when interviewed for this book, recalls that the strip "had a fairly good start, and it dwindled." He postulates that Chuck's "own creativity did him in.... You'll notice that it changes frequently. That was a weakness and I think it hurt

Opposite: The final—unsuccessful—effort in 1989 to revise and sell the 1969 Crawford concept. These storyboards were drawn by Paul Sabella and Julian Harris from Don Arioli's designs.

him.... [The strips] would come in batches from Chuck, who was in California. We were in New York and I would read them and I would talk to him and I would say, 'That's a whole new character. You can't have continuity in a strip if you keep changing characters.' And he got it, but I think he got it late."

Chuck faced a difficult challenge trying to distill twenty years and many permutations of the character into a few small panels every day. Creating a successful comic strip wasn't as simple as putting together a sequence of extreme poses. By the time he figured out the rhythm of writing for a syndicated strip, many newspapers had already dropped *Crawford.*

Regardless of the reasons, the syndicate pulled the plug after less than five months. The final daily was published on Saturday, May 27, 1978. The Sundays, since they were produced on a different schedule, carried on until July 2nd.

Whatever learning curve Jones experienced adapting to the new medium, one thing is clear: from the very first daily his art was distinct and comfortable, full of the "Chuck-isms" that so identify his work—the emotion conveyed in subtle facial expressions, the way he told entire stories through as few lines as possible, the strong poses, the sideways glances. His penchant for "full animation" can even be found in the static panels of *Crawford.* Except if called for by the gag, each panel shows a shift in the character's posture, a reflection of real life. His art evolved somewhat in the comic strip's short life—this is most noticeable when comparing the way he drew the human figure at the beginning of the strip and at the end. Crawford and Morgan start out as caricatures of human beings, their large heads and stubby legs exaggerated (a reference back to his Ralph Phillips character). By May 1978 Chuck's designs for Morgan and Crawford had morphed into more normally proportioned children.

If Chuck had taken advantage of the opportunity to fully develop the strip's potential, *Crawford* may have had a long and successful run. Despite *Crawford's* brief appearance as a newspaper strip, Chuck was delighted to finally be able to realize this character who had occupied his mind and heart for so many years. It was a journey he undertook completely behind-the-scenes, and Crawford, instead of attaining comic strip immortality, had to settle for a brief fifteen minutes of fame.

• • • • •

Crawford's journey did not end with the comic strip. In 1984 Chuck added Crawford to the cast of an animated show called *Earth Creatures*, another on-again-off-again series he had been trying to sell since 1969. *Earth Creatures* follows the adventures of Terry, a young alien who comes to Earth and befriends a group of children. Together in Terry's Space Buggy they journey around the globe, exploring the variety of life kids experience in different countries and cultures. Very little about Crawford is the same in this show: he gets a new personality and a new design. The only thing that ties him to the Crawford of the comic strip is his name and his red hair. *Earth Creatures* never took off, grounding Crawford once more.

In 1989—twenty-seven years after Chuck first created the unlucky youngster as a side character for the *Adventures of the Road-Runner*—he once again tried to resurrect his *Crawford* television proposal. This time he handed the project over to Don Arioli, who took what had been developed in the seventies and reworked it for a modern audience. Crawford and Morgan remained the protagonists and many of the segments remained intact. In fact, the kite-flying scenario that Chuck storyboarded for the original proposal remained the featured story in the 1989 proposal, this time boarded by Paul Sabella and Julian Harris based on Don's character designs. Names were changed (the TV—Psyclops—was renamed Wutson) and new characters were added (such as the Snakerpillar, who is always willing to tell a story), but the premise and heart of the show were the same.

It remains unproduced...the final iteration of the Chuck Jones dream that never was.

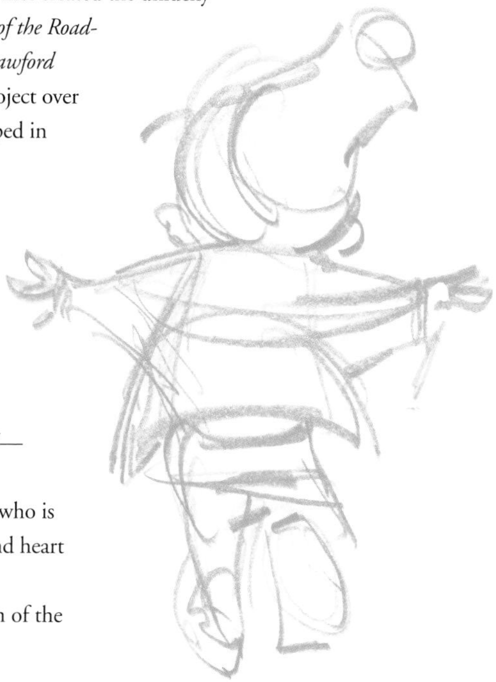

Sketches and character designs

When Chuck Jones began work on *Crawford* in the 1960s he had no idea he would still be developing it a decade later. The character went through many different designs, mainly because it was Chuck's idea to have him embody a different look and personality in the various segments of the proposed 1969 *Crawford* TV series. The following pages include many of those designs, including an African-American rendition.

Crawford's original design is the color image on page 55. For the newspaper strip, the 1969 design was totally scrapped in favor of a more human-like structure; the big-headed, short-stature character designs Chuck used in the 1950s were no longer the approach he took to drawing children in the '70s. Crawford and his friends from the strip bear a closer resemblance to Ralph from *The Pumpkin Who Couldn't Smile* than to Ralph Phillips.

Many of the strip's other cast members went through changes of their own. A lot of Crawford's hand-me-downs, such as the army hat, were given to Morgan. The most notable is Norman-Vincent, who was given a complete make-over. Since the strip never had a chance to fully develop, some characters such as Clifton, Butcher, and Howard never made it into the series, while others such as Sam Dunk only appeared in a week's worth of dailies.

• • • • •

The character descriptions on the following pages were written by Jones for the newspaper strip publicity book. Some of the characters were inspired by real people. Norman-Vincent is a parody of Norman Vincent Peale, the noted minister, motivational speaker, and author of the 1952 bestseller *The Power of Positive Thinking*. Chuck didn't think favorably of Peale or his aphorisms such as, "When life hands you a lemon, make lemonade." If Chuck's least favorite thinker was Norman Vincent Peale, there's no doubt that the smart and pointedly witty Mark Twain was his favorite; he created Mick Twain as the perfect foil for Norman-Vincent. S.I. Hawaii Kaya is a nod to S.I. Hayakawa, the then-Senator of California who was a well-known linguist and semanticist.

—Kurtis Findlay

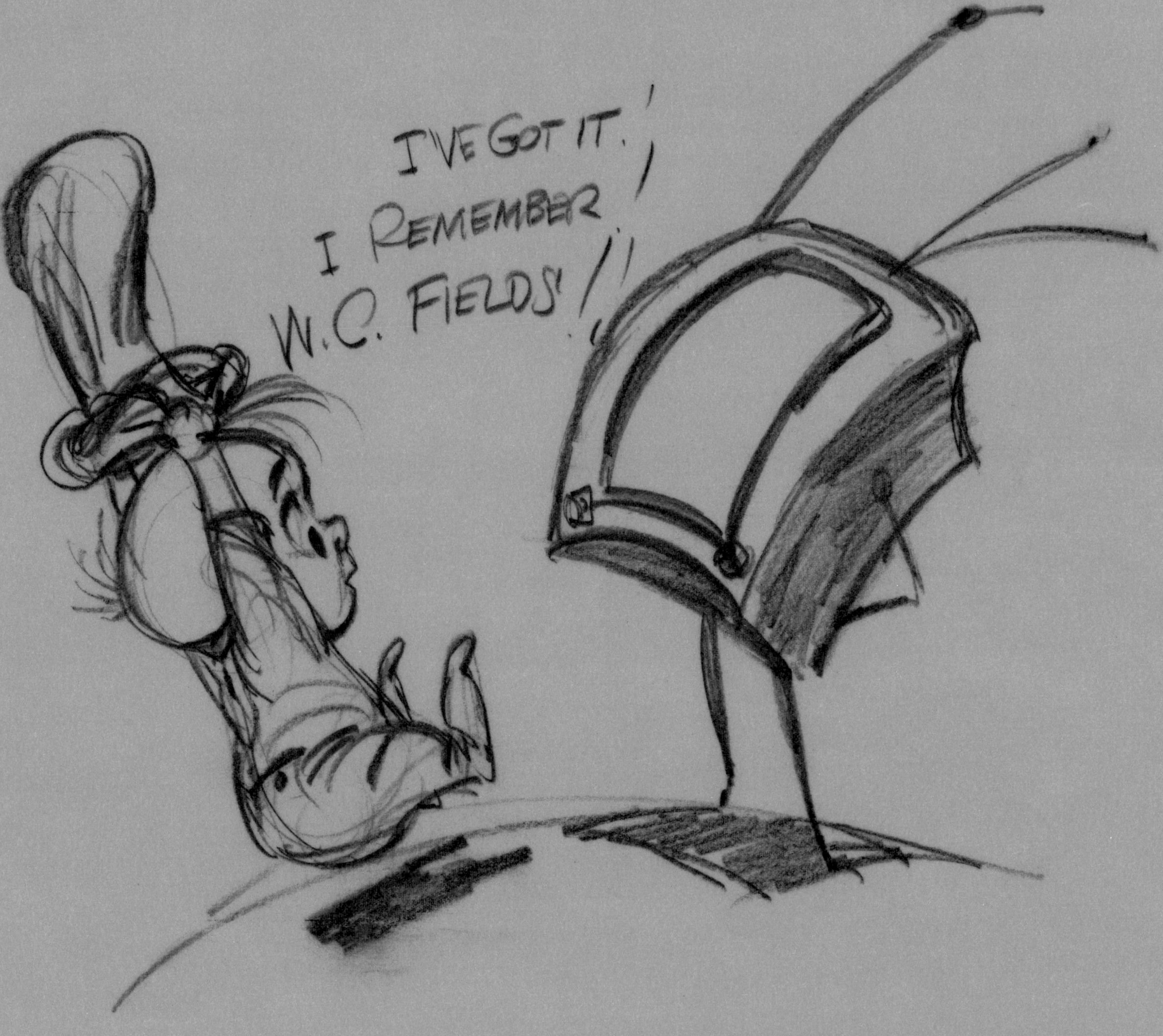
I'VE GOT IT.
I REMEMBER
W.C. FIELDS!

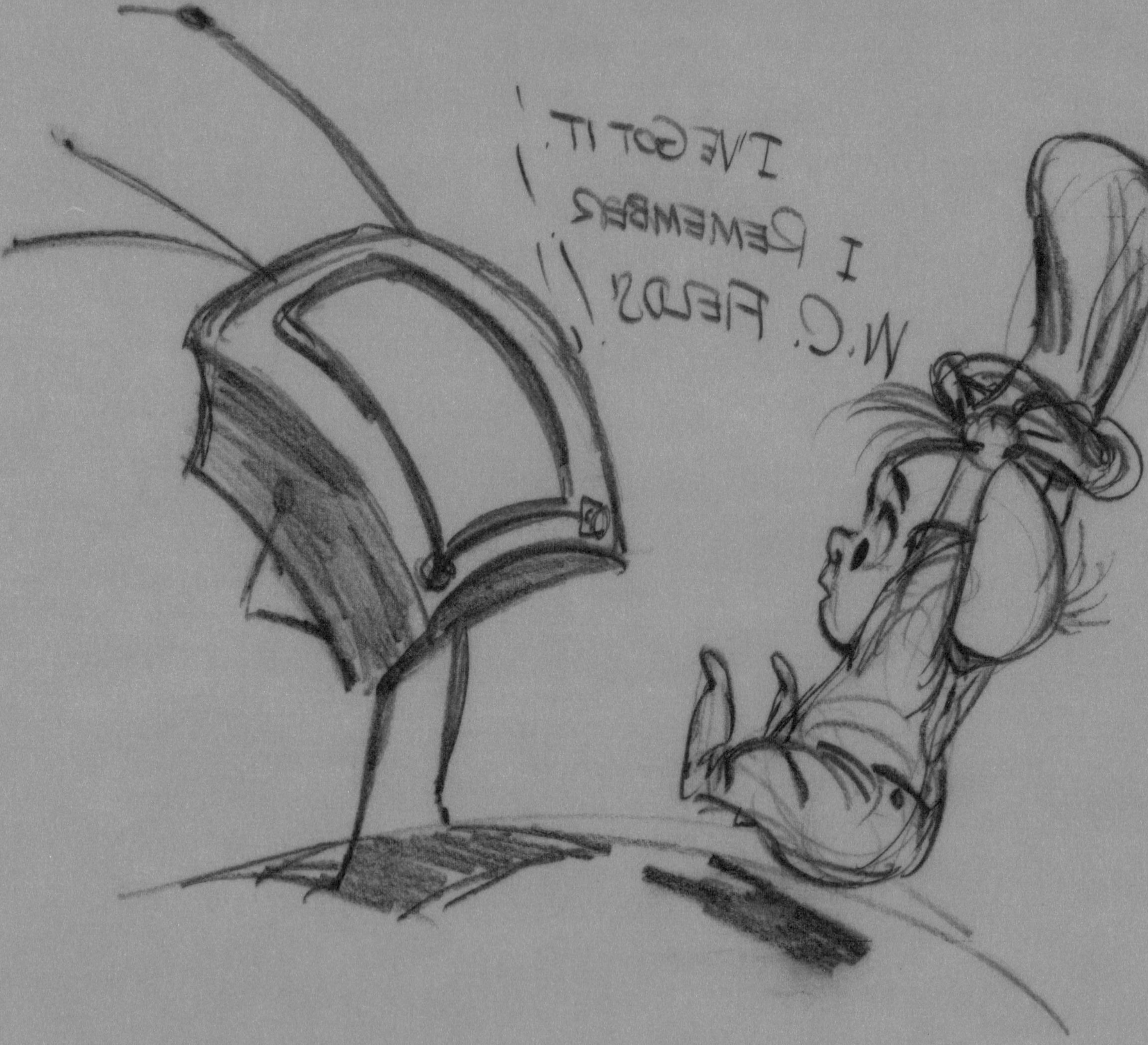
I'VE GOT IT.
I REMEMBER
W.C. FIELDS

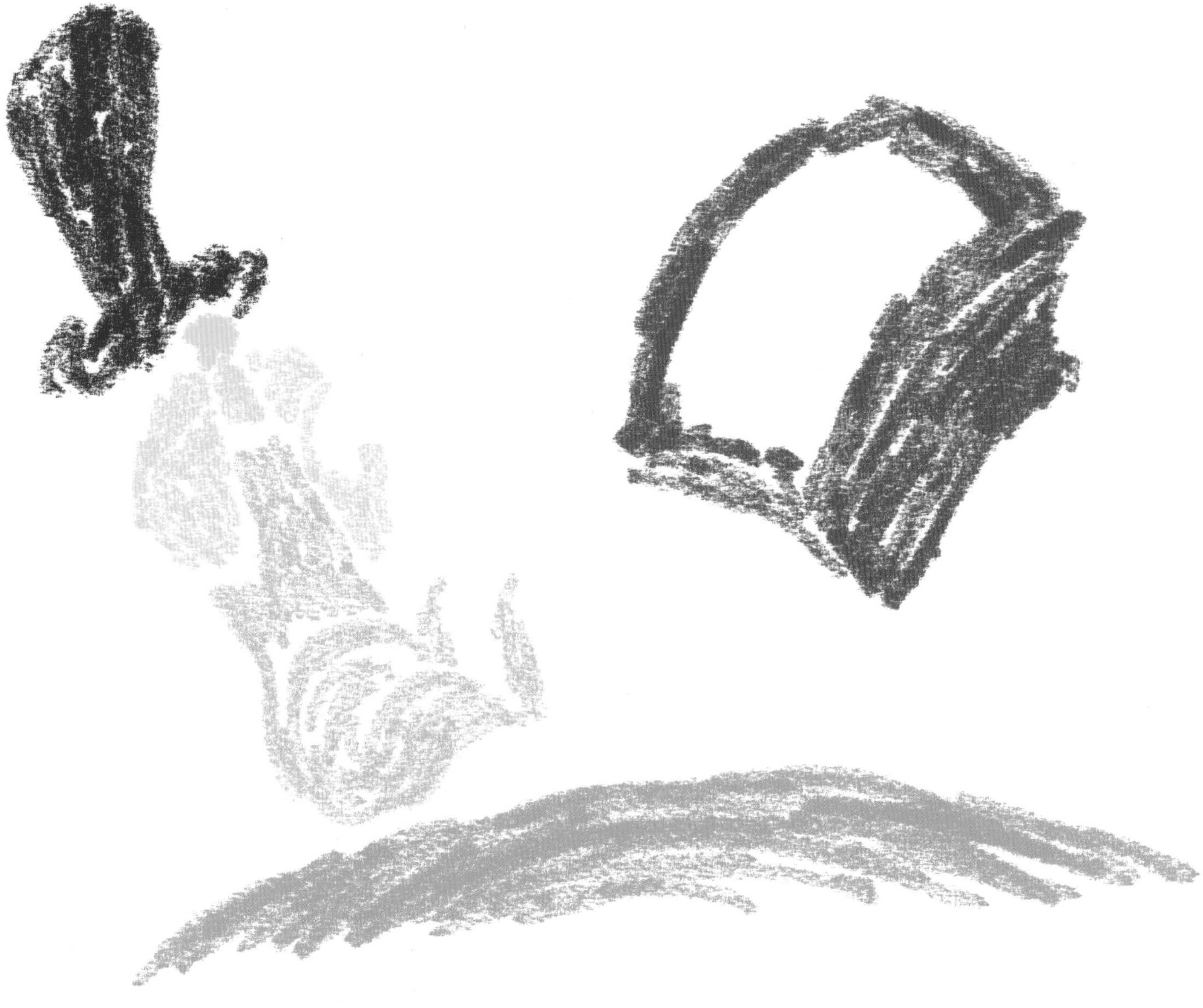

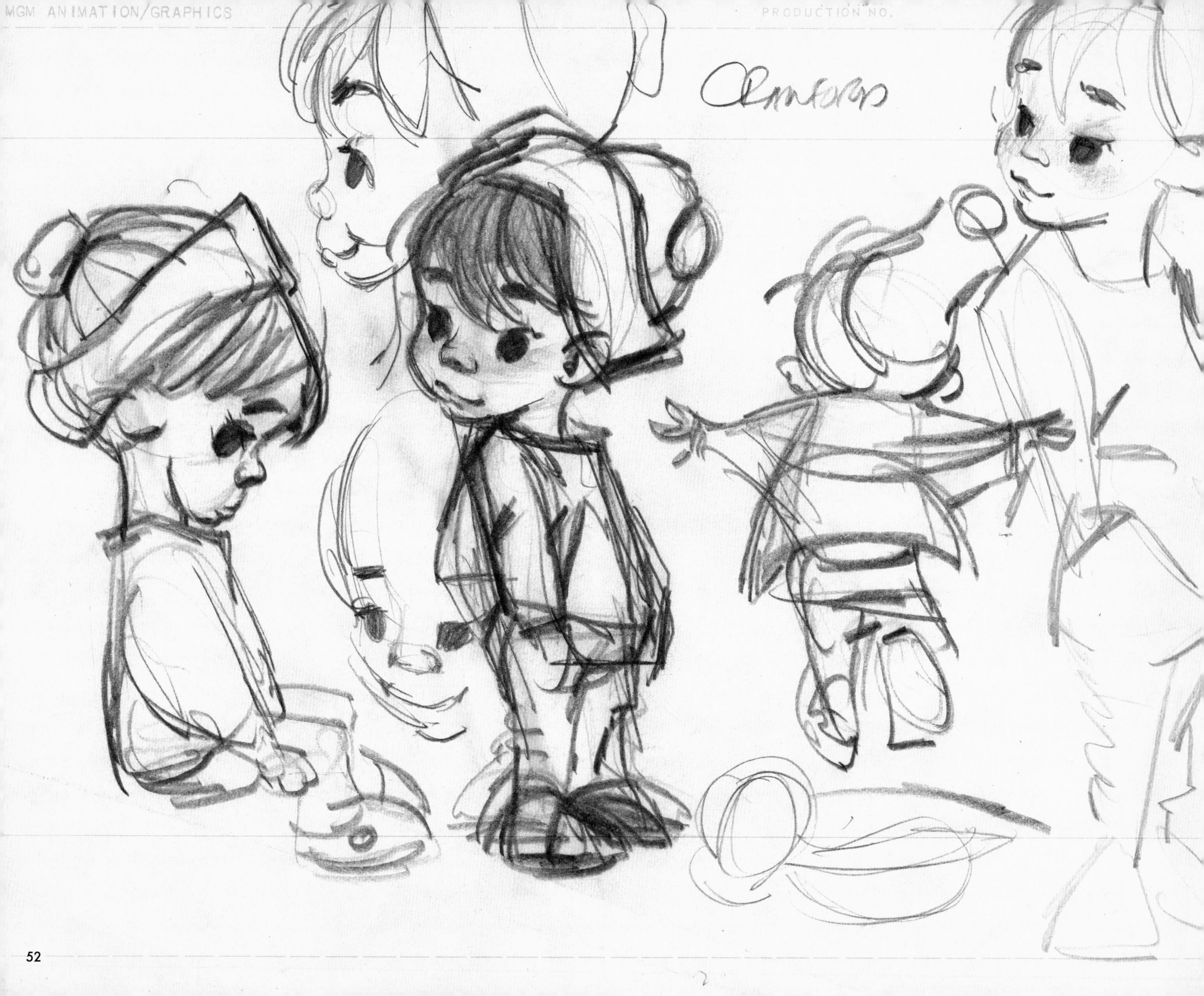
MGM ANIMATION/GRAPHICS
PRODUCTION NO.

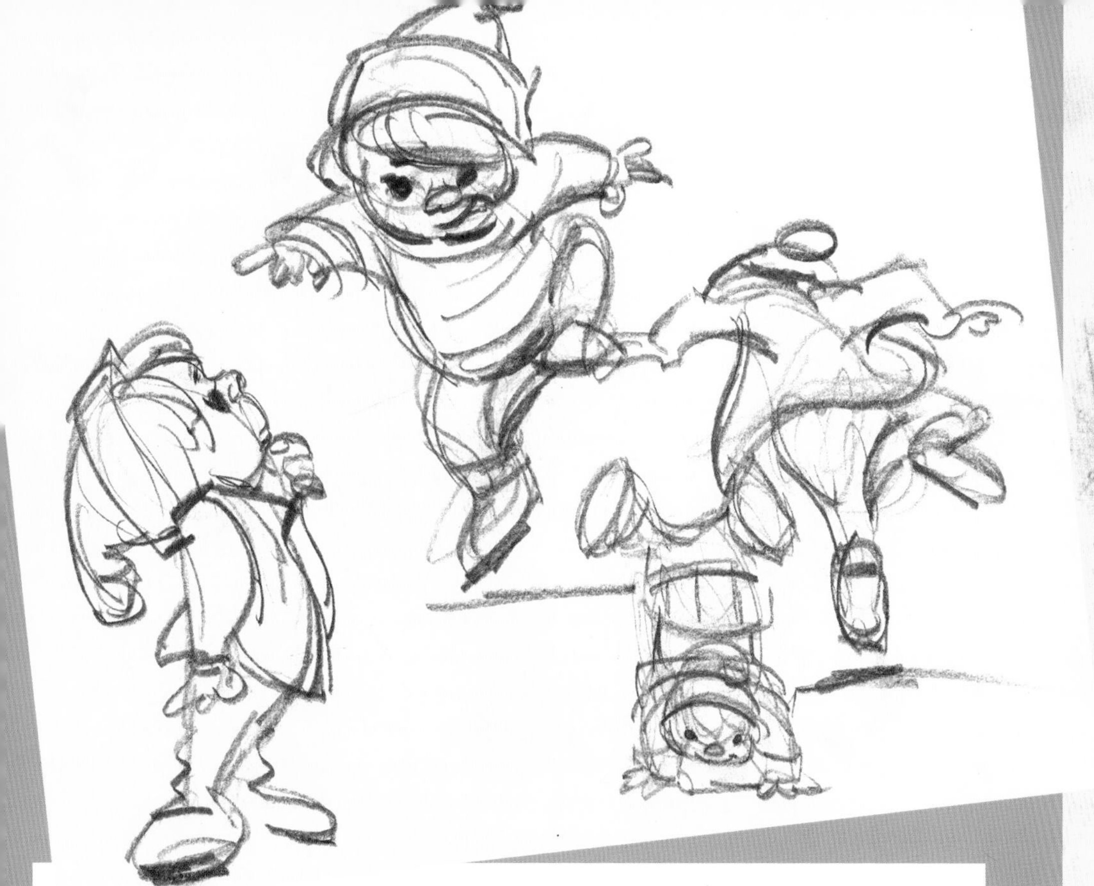

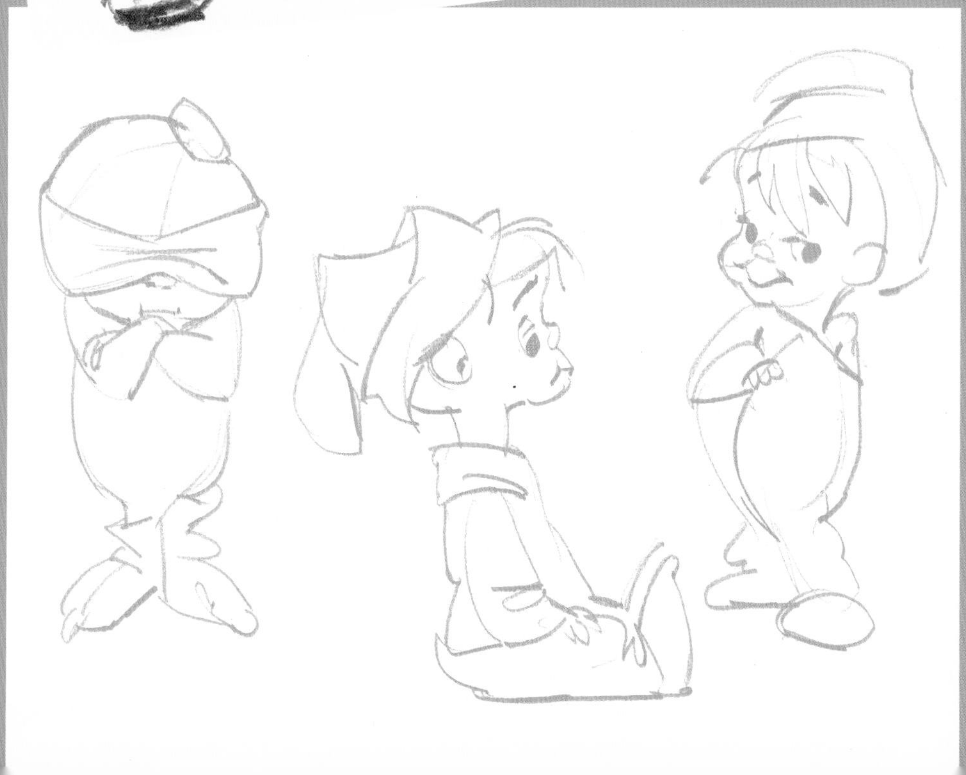

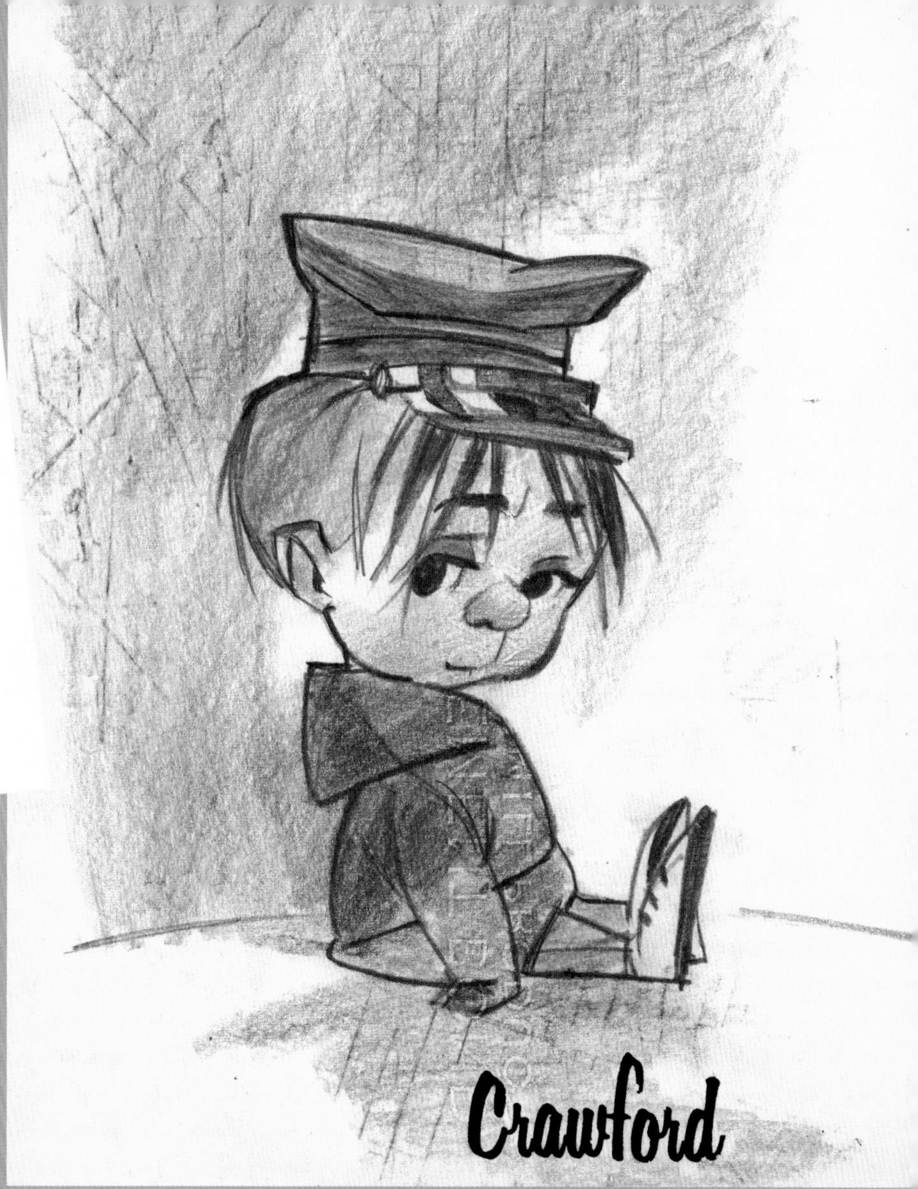
Crawford

CRAWFORD

Crawford has been in my mind's eye for a number of years. His age seems to vary from six to thirteen, a modestly disrupting phenomenon for those who like everything to be tidy. He is the heart of boyhood, an amateur at life, and ordinary as to be unusual. But his boyishness lives beyond his years—he is the baby who puts oatmeal in his left eye, and the middle-aged man who puts his sixth martini in that same eye. He neither wins nor loses; he simply experiments with life and in the process brings us all laughter—and hope.

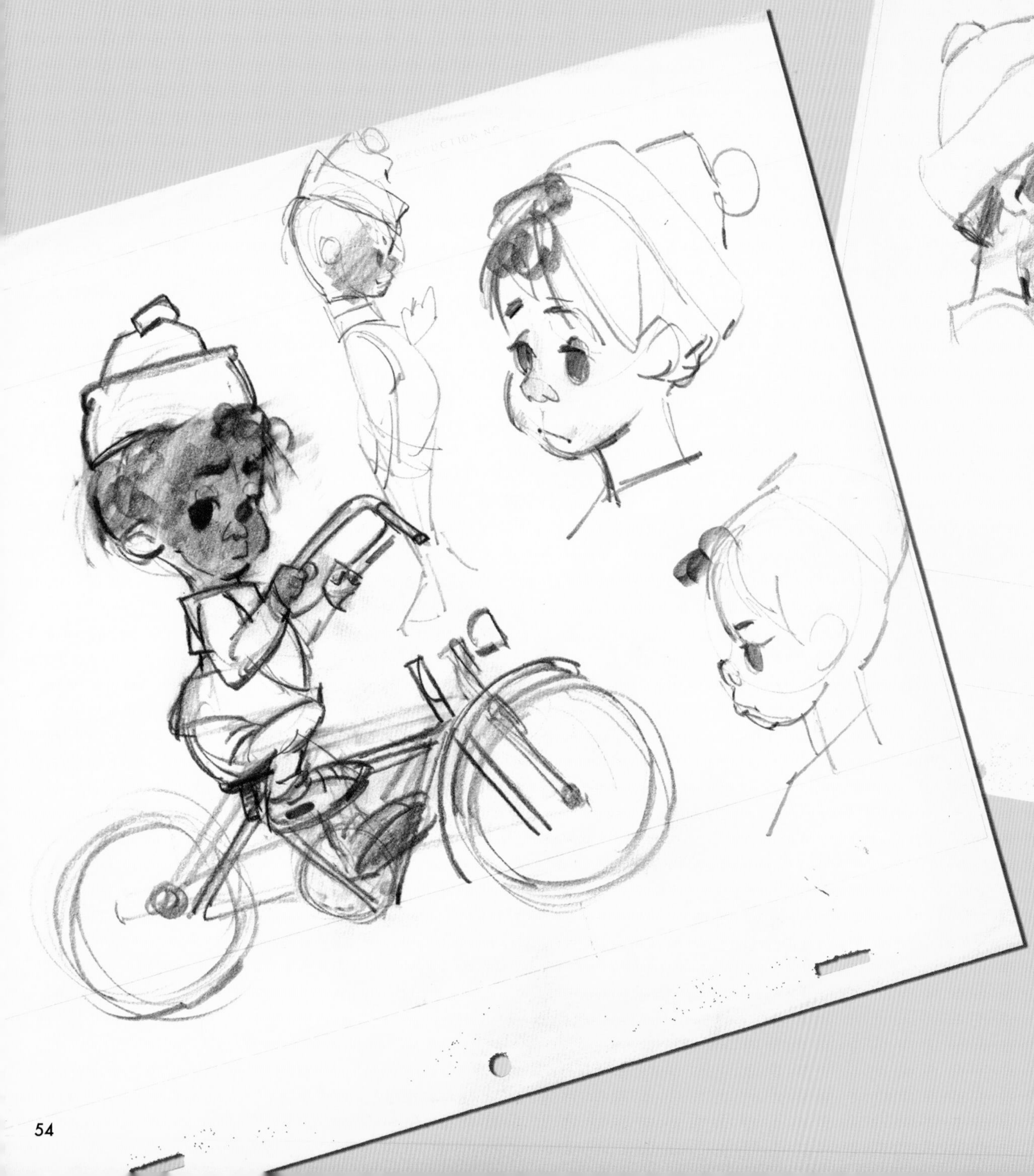
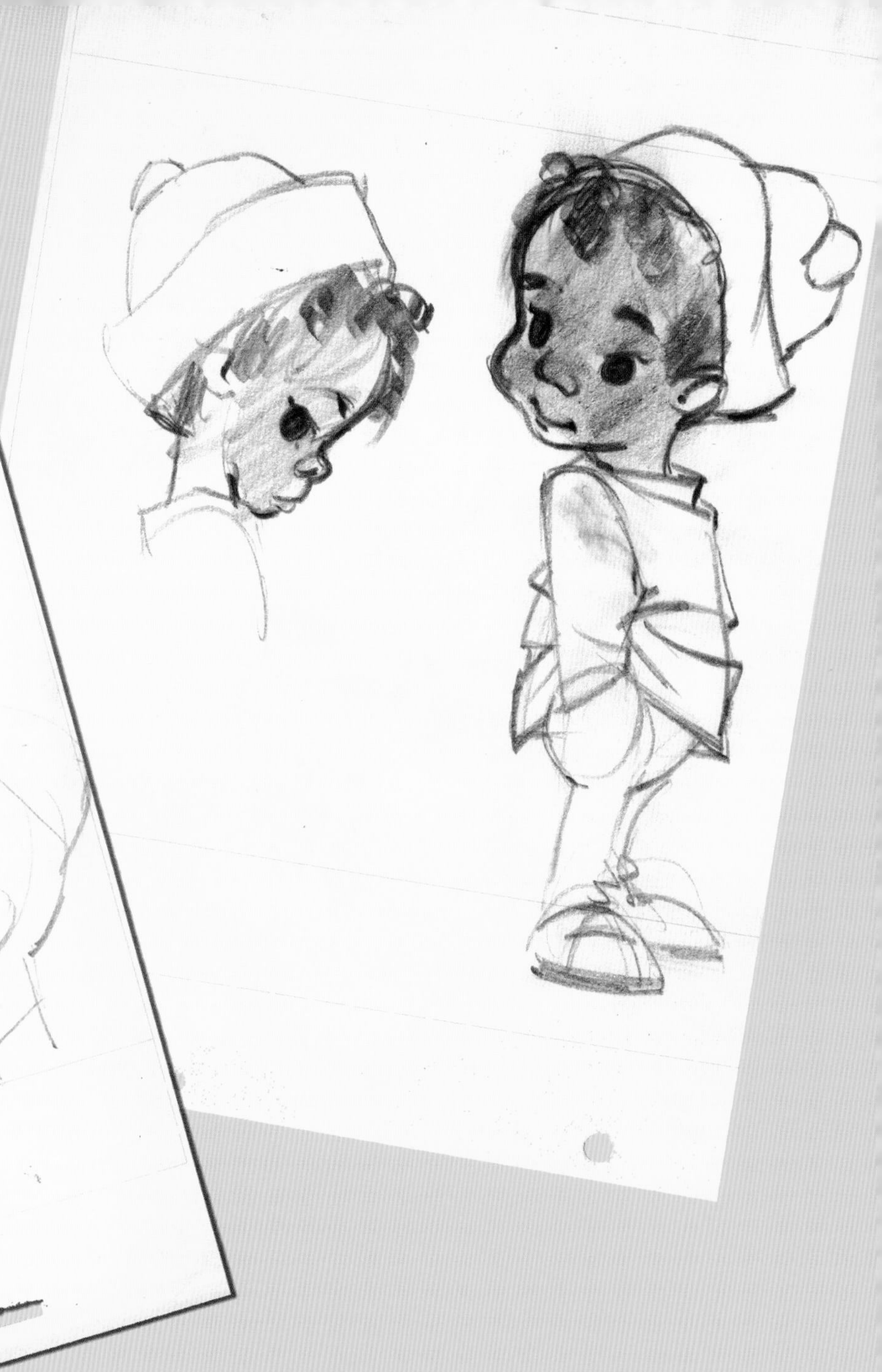

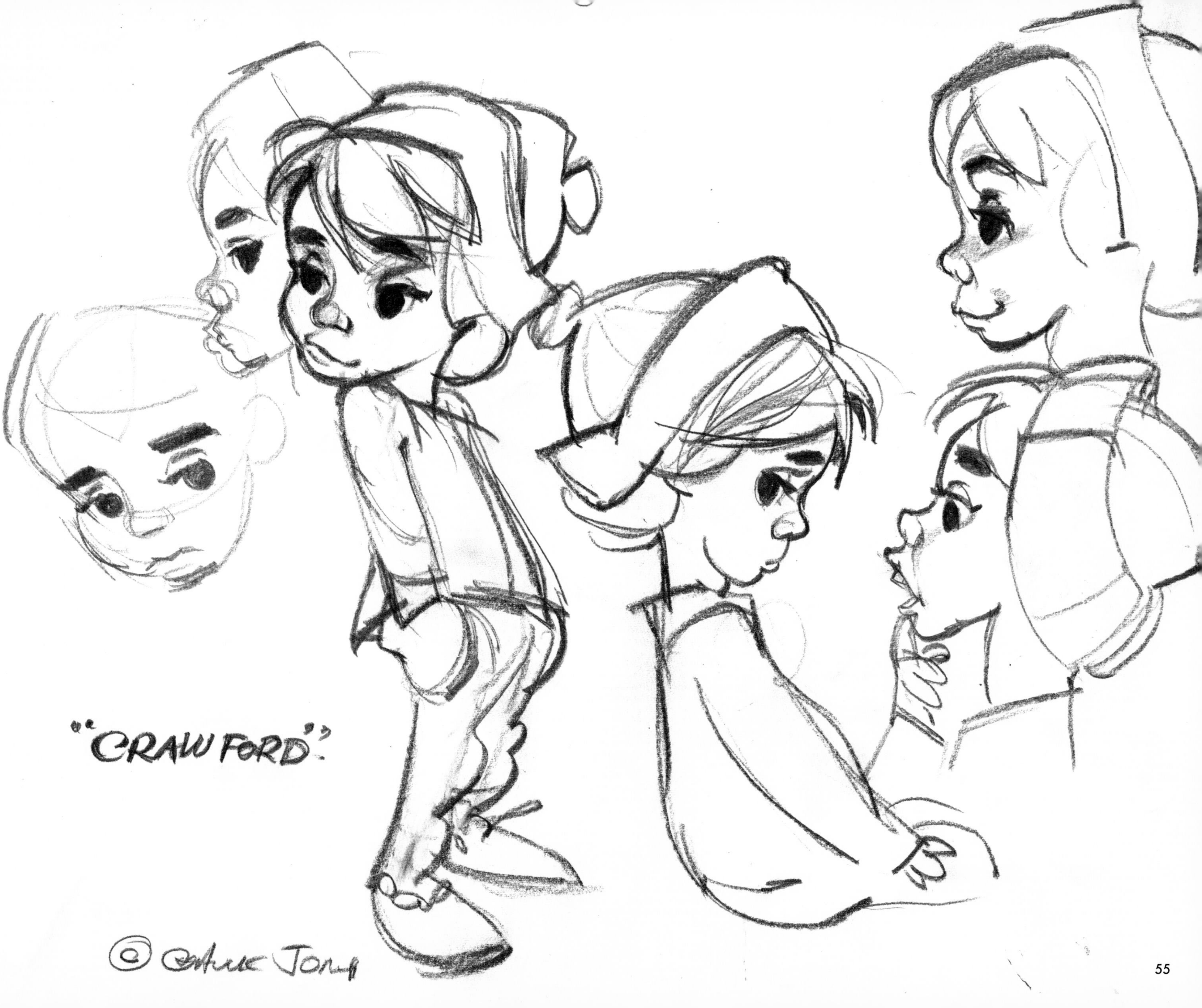
"CRAWFORD"
© Milt Kahl Jones

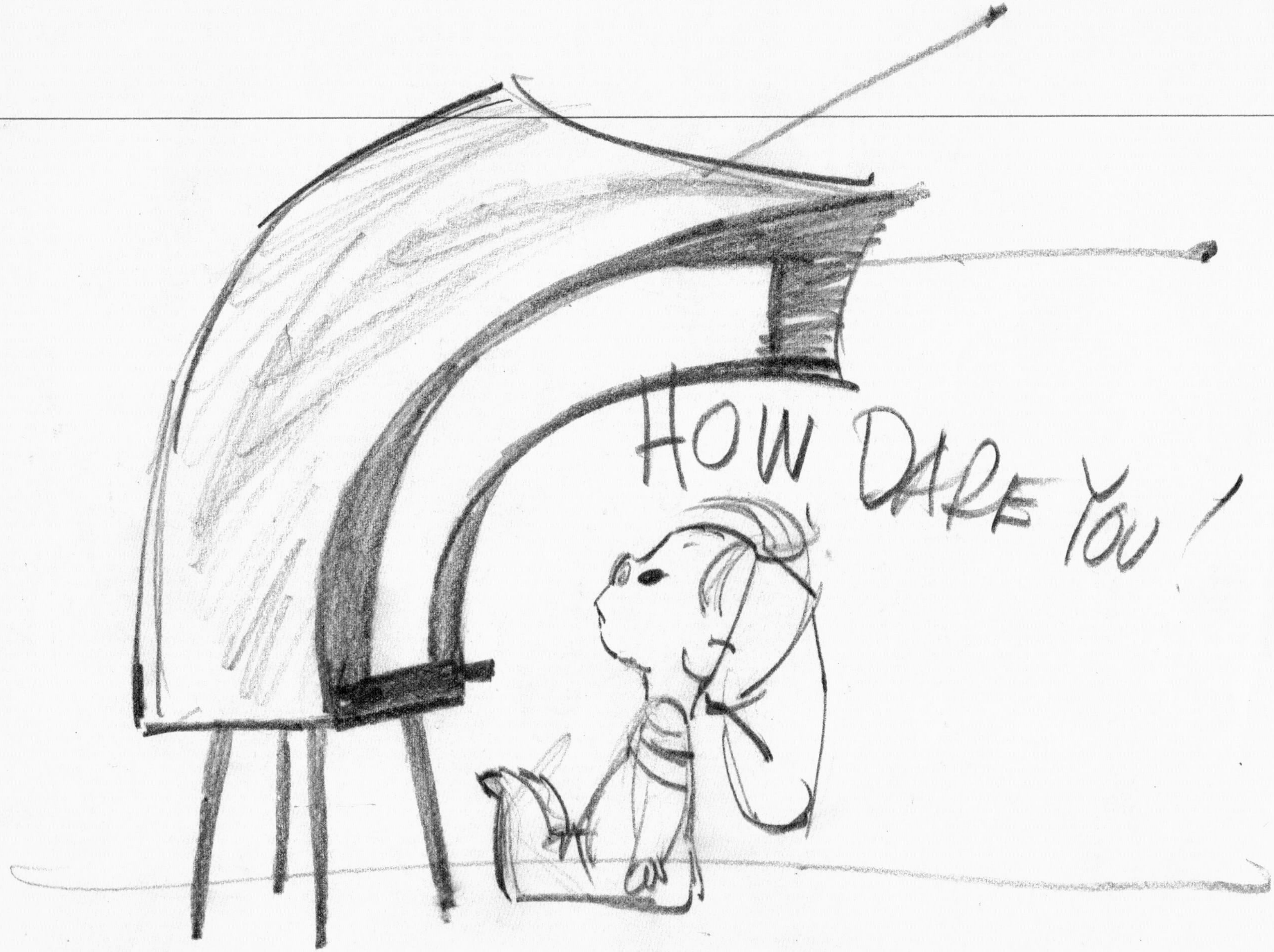
HOW DARE YOU!

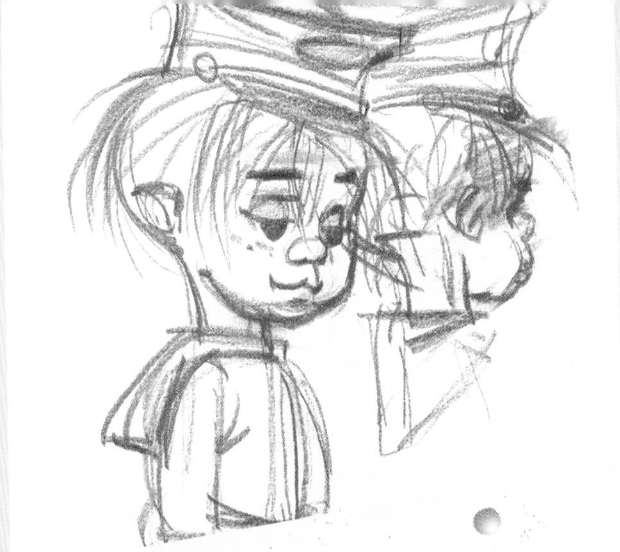

MORGAN

If genius can be identified as a dramatic lapse of memory, Morgan is a genius. He can't remember Crawford's name any more than Einstein could remember his paychecks at Princeton or Wagner whose wife to take home. He is, however, blessed with a memory for facts, especially those considered to be obscure and trivial. He is innocent, unprovocable—and the one who will always be told to stay home.

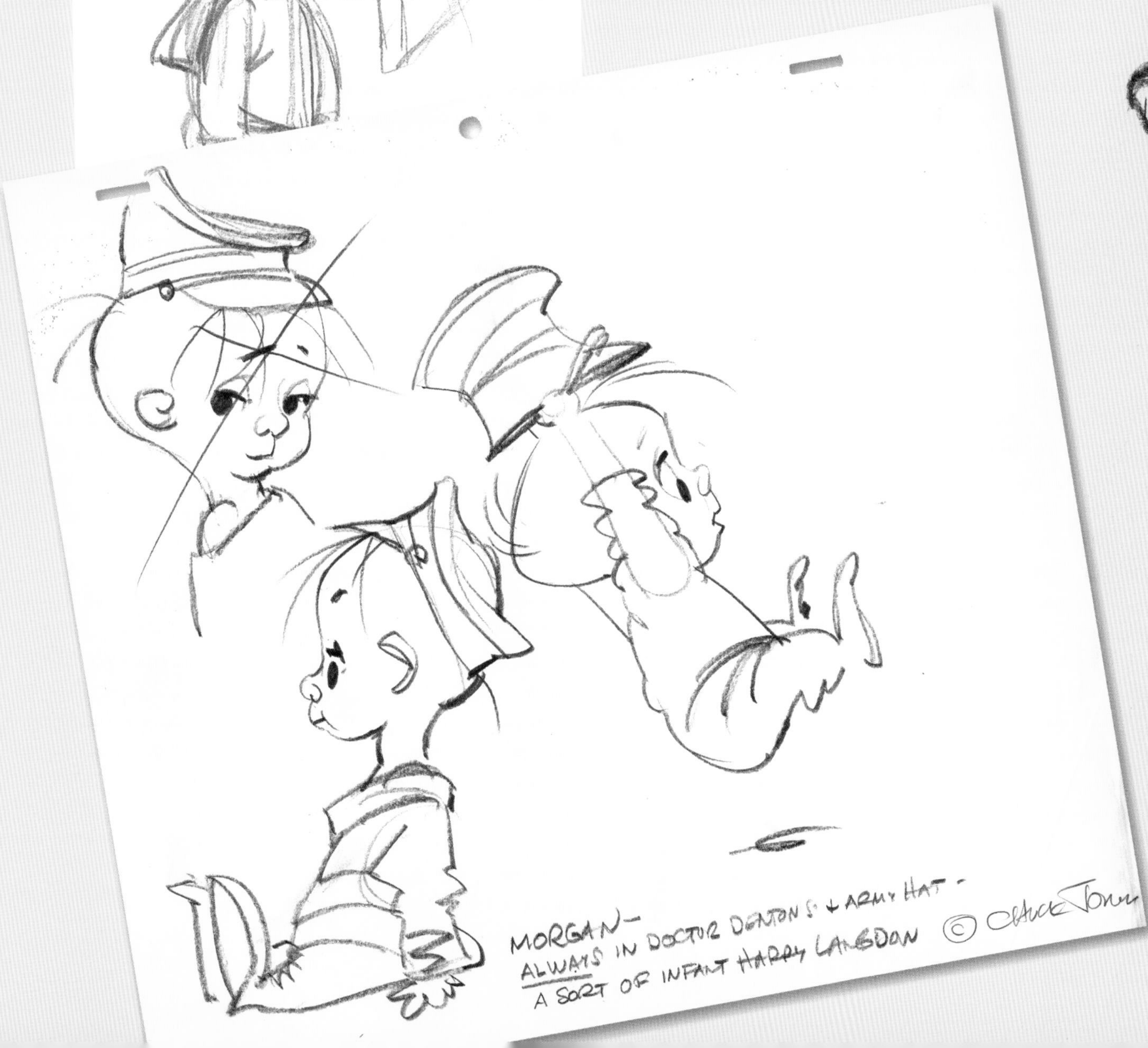
MORGAN—
ALWAYS IN DOCTOR DENTON'S + ARMY HAT -
A SORT OF INFANT HARRY LANGDON
© Chuck Jones

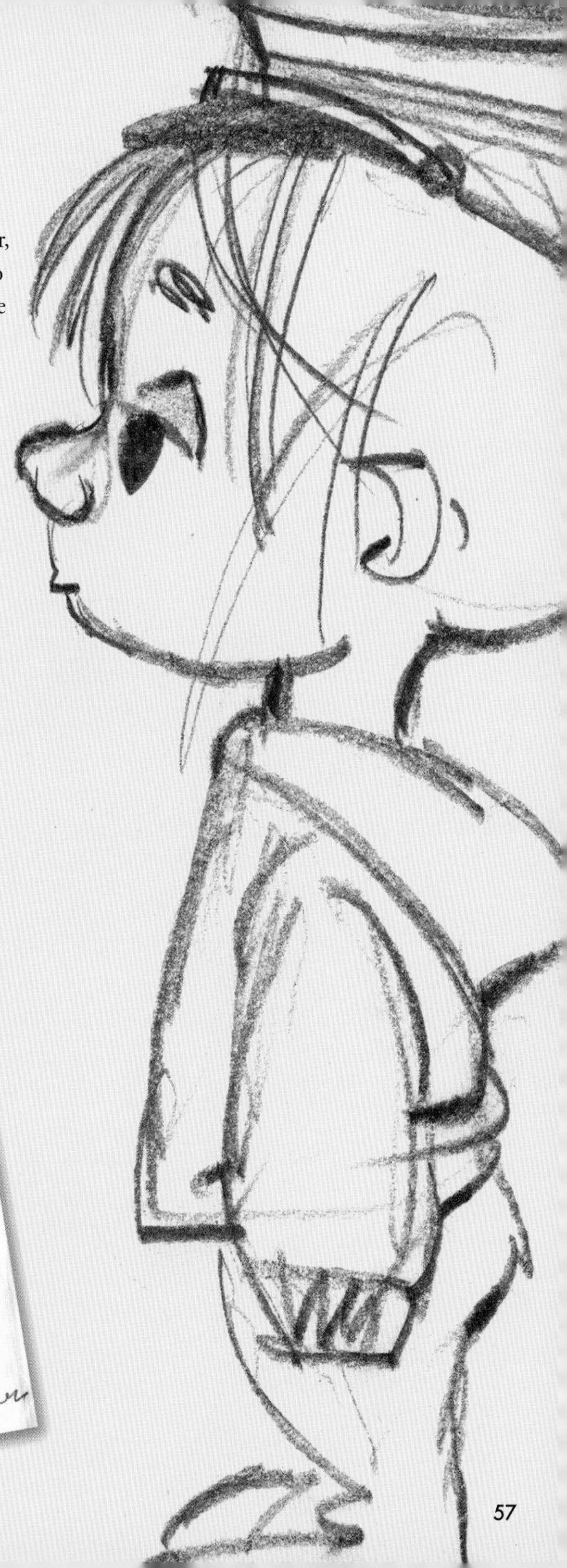

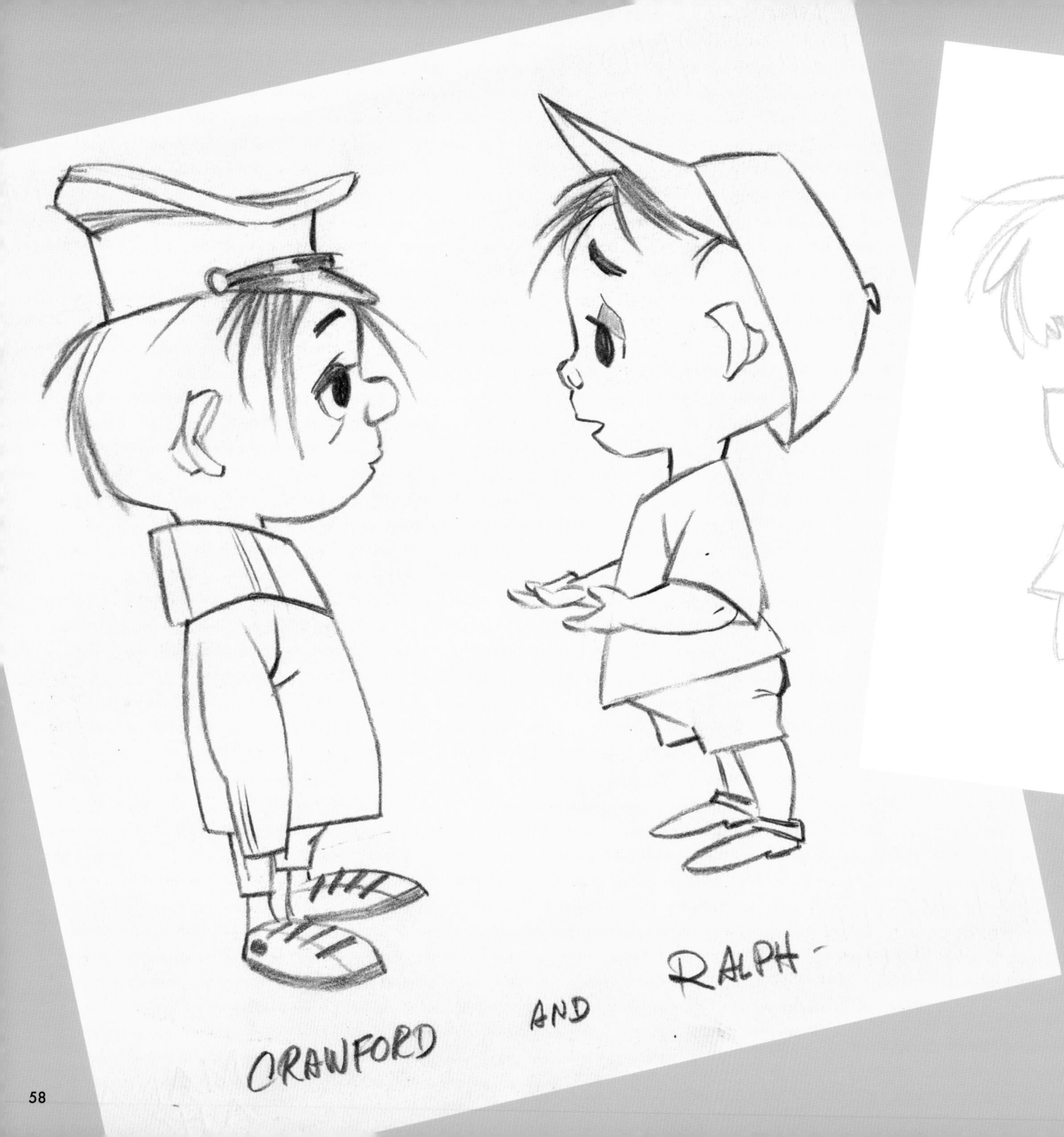
RALPH -
AND
CRAWFORD
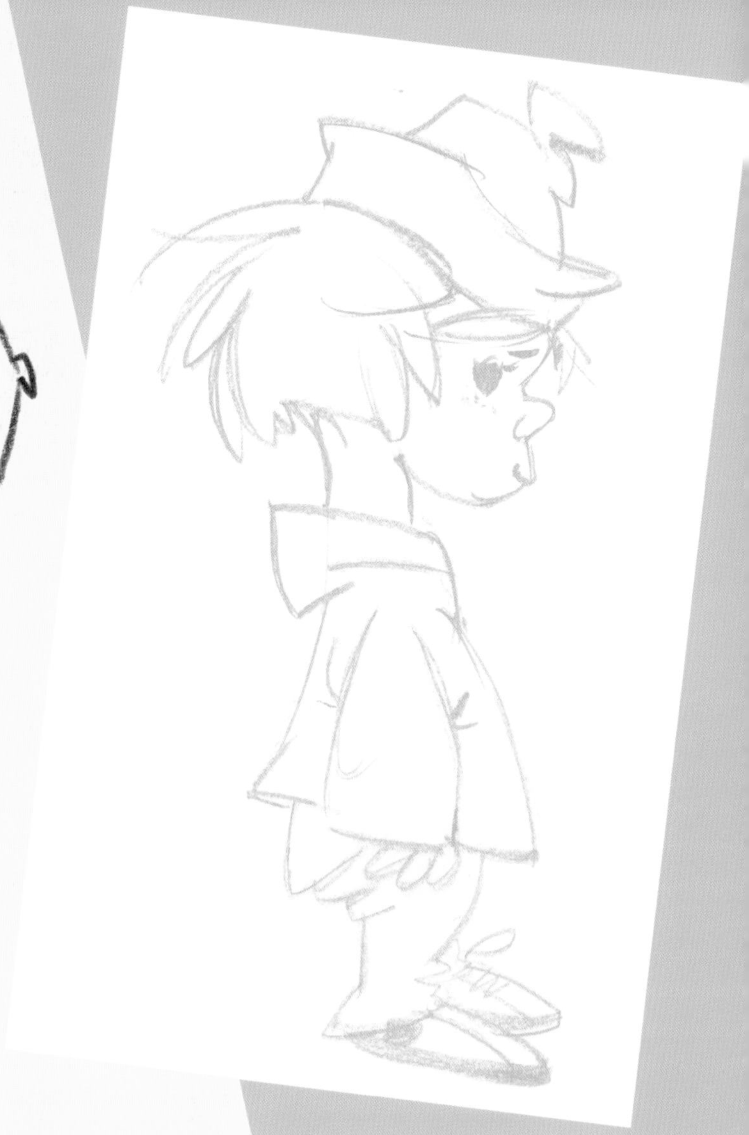

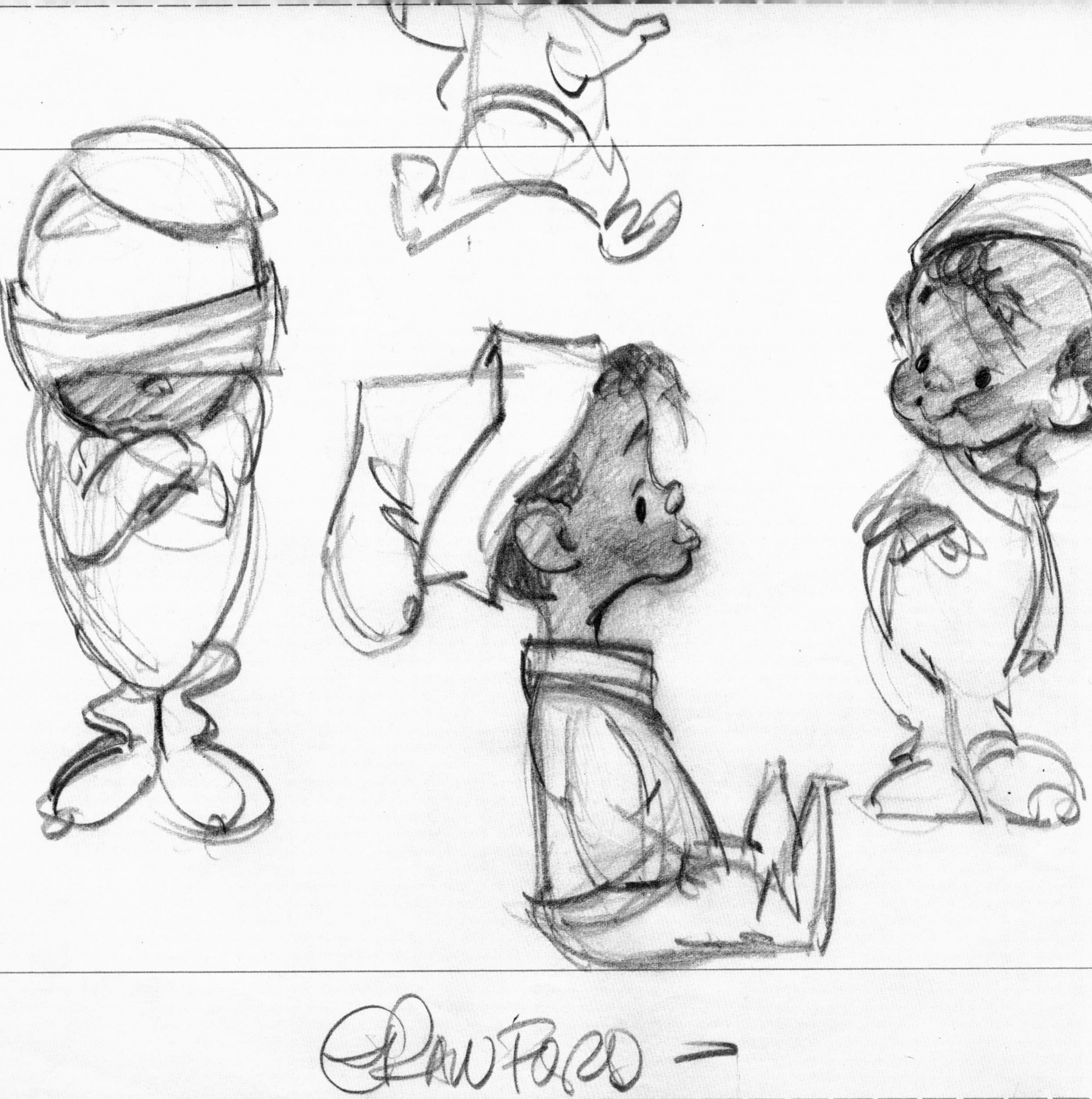
CRAWFORD -

LIBBY

Libby is too young to accurately define the two sexes, but there are times when she is aggressively certain that if there is another one, she is against it. And there are times when she has a strong suspicion that Crawford is not only a member of the opposition but criminally dangerous as well. I must point out that her name is not derived from women's "lib" as you probably thought but rather from Liberty Hamstein, a maternal great-great-grandmother who chained herself to William McKinley for about 14 minutes of protest.

LIBBY   +   MIOK TWAIN

I DUNNO. LOOKS TO ME LIKE FEMININE GONE TO ITS HEAD

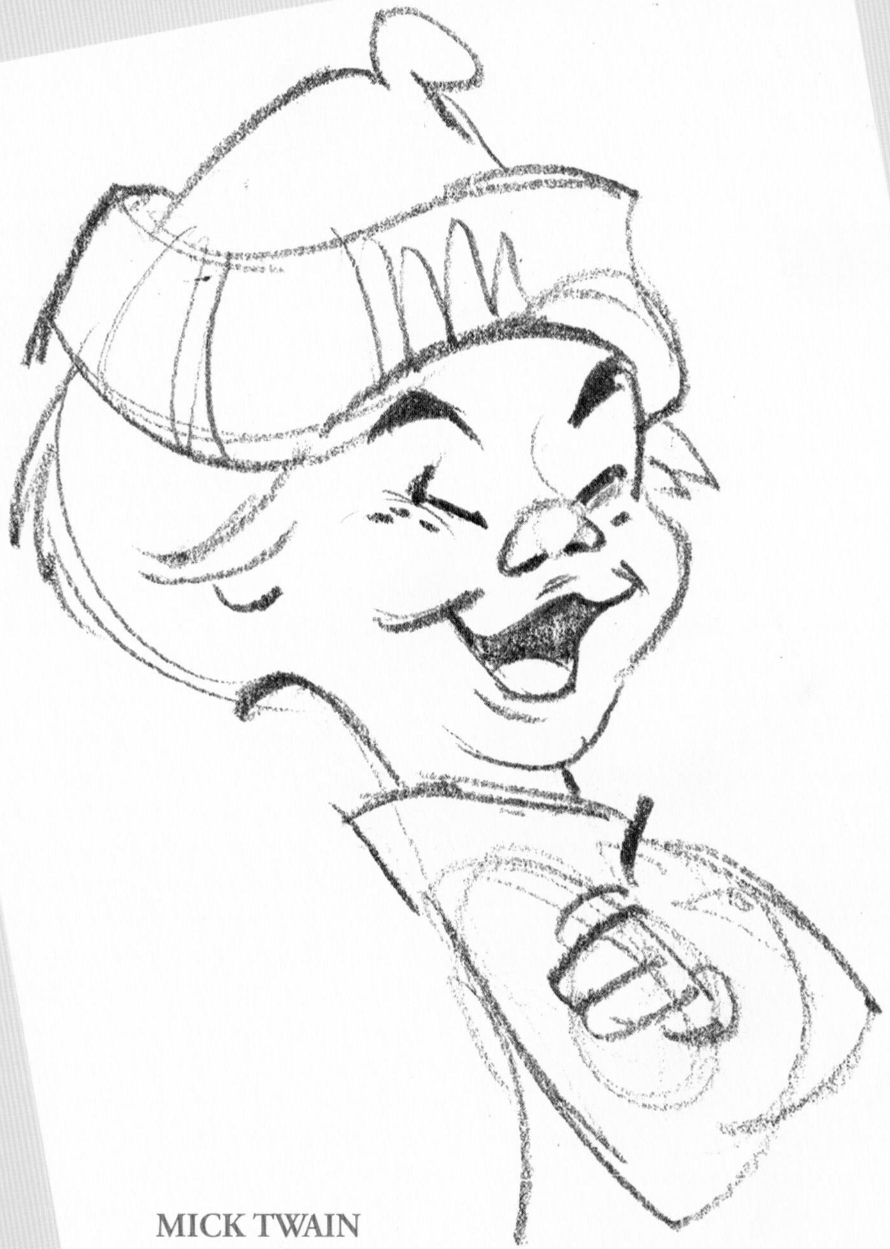

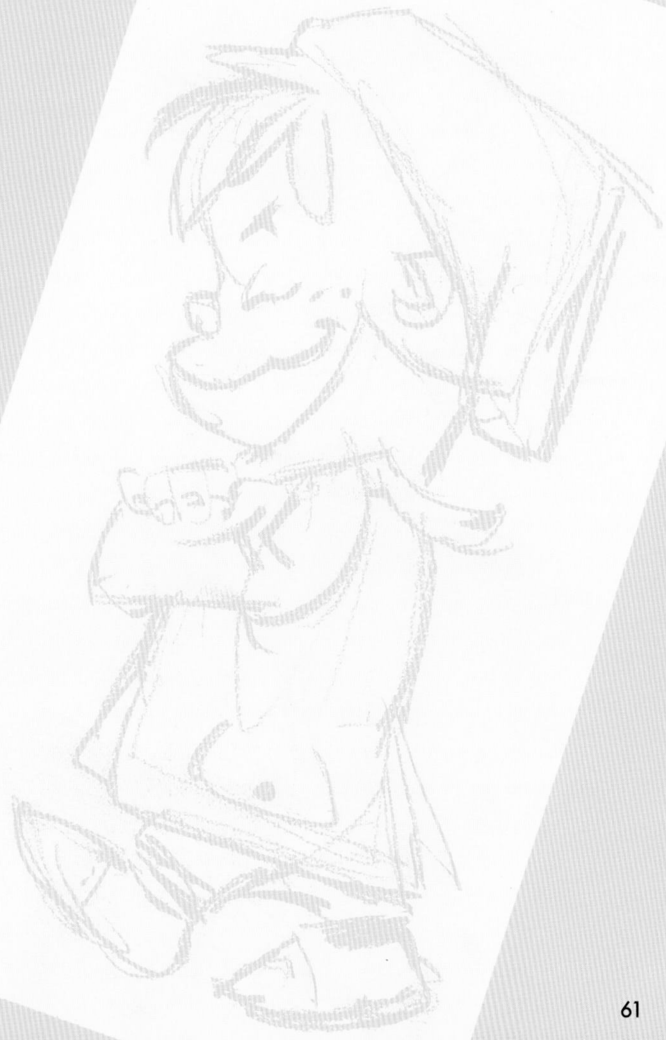

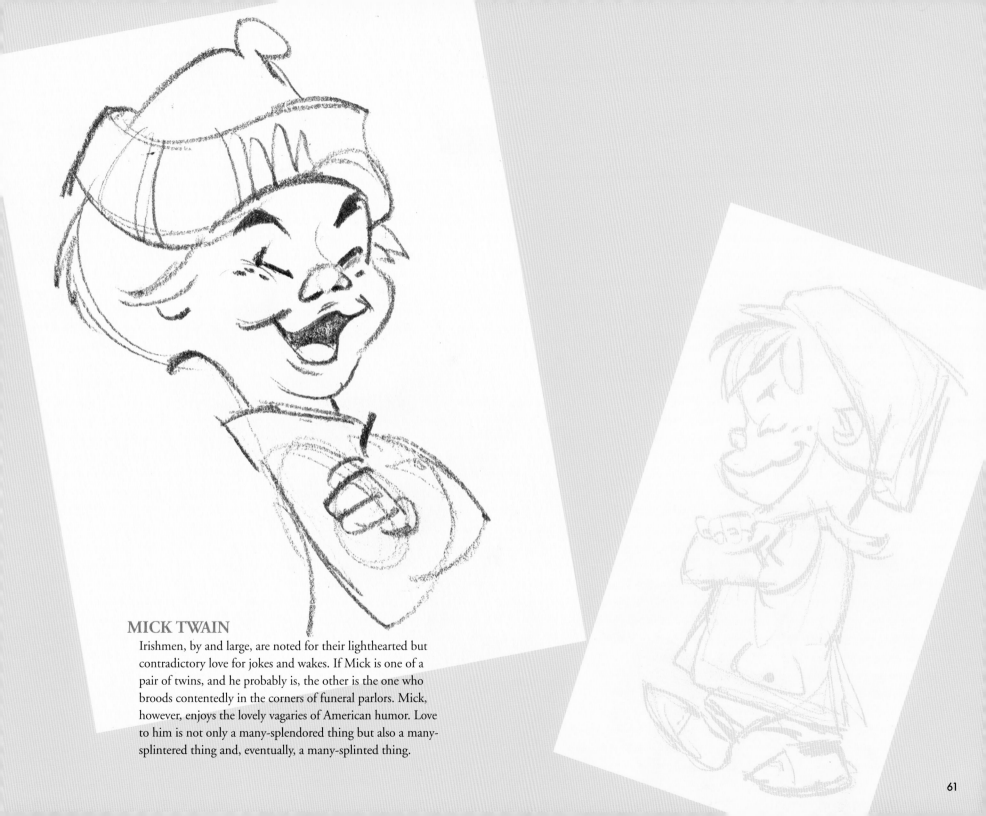

MICK TWAIN

Irishmen, by and large, are noted for their lighthearted but contradictory love for jokes and wakes. If Mick is one of a pair of twins, and he probably is, the other is the one who broods contentedly in the corners of funeral parlors. Mick, however, enjoys the lovely vagaries of American humor. Love to him is not only a many-splendored thing but also a many-splintered thing and, eventually, a many-splinted thing.

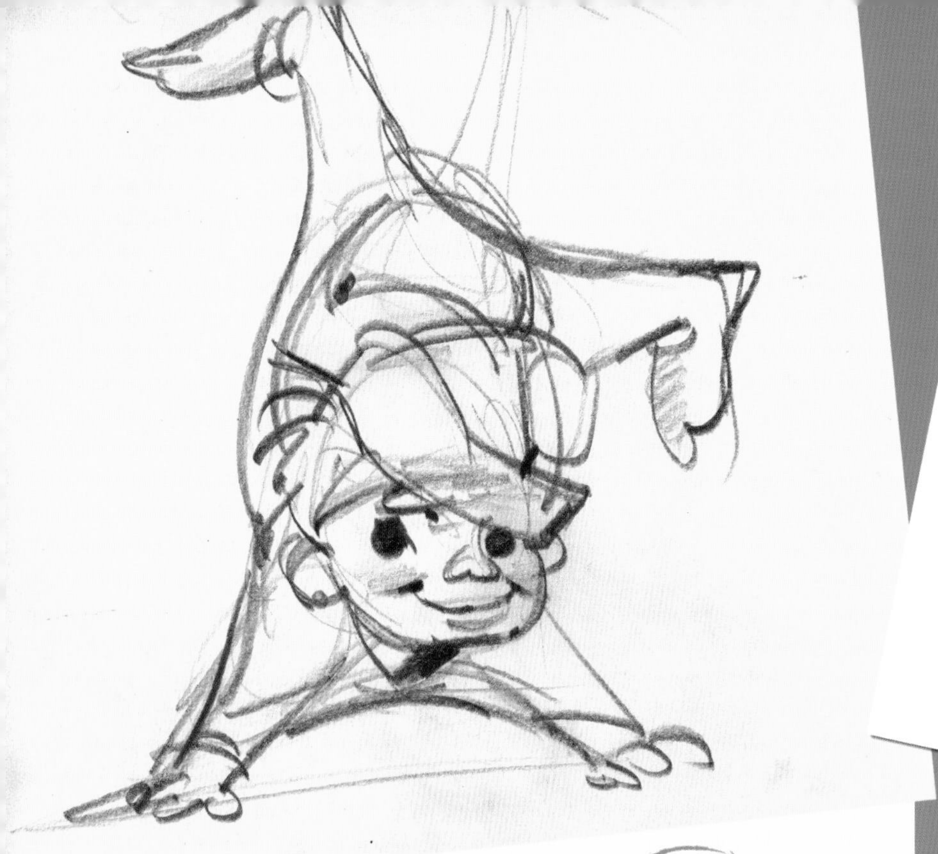

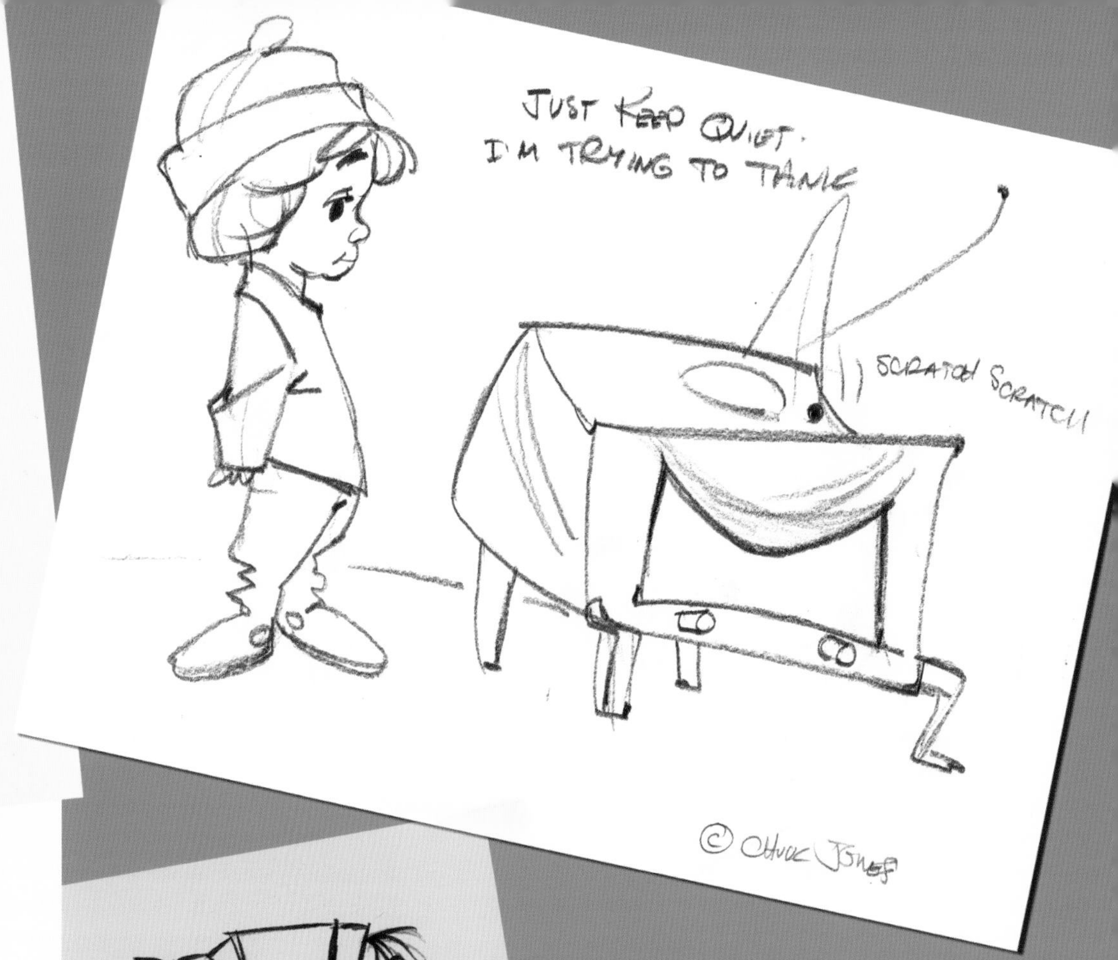
JUST KEEP QUIET.
I'M TRYING TO THINK
SCRATCH SCRATCH
© CHUCK JONES

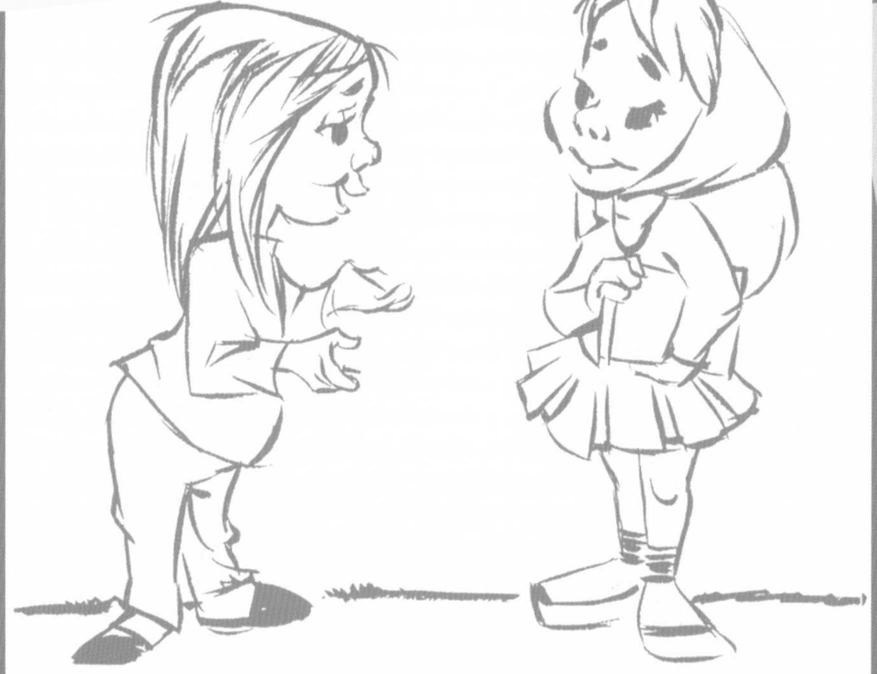

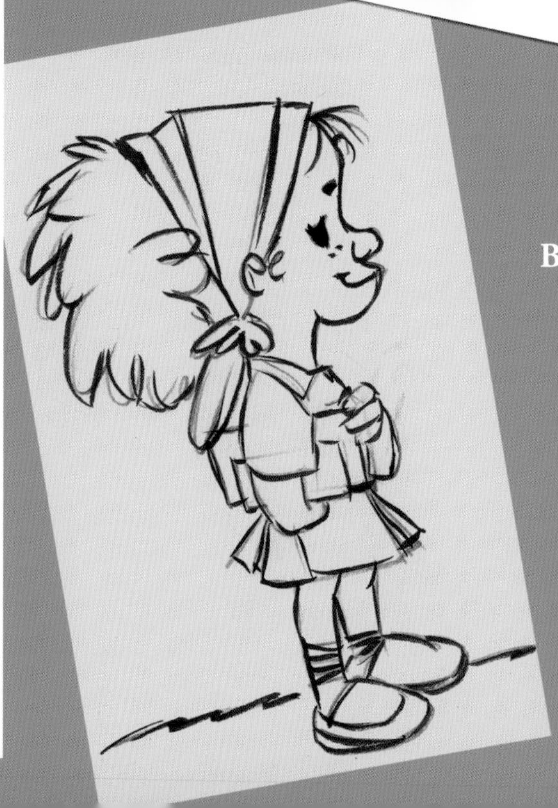

BELLA

No militant feminist she. Although often seen in the company of Libby, Bella suspects that there may be something practical, even useful, about boys. She is a dreamer even when she has no idea what the dream is about, and for her there seems to be a roseate potential in boys, indefinable but worth study. When Bella finds out what all this is about, it is going to be just fine for everybody.

NORMAN-VINCENT

Norman-Vincent is a fountainhead of aphorisms spouted, usually without invitation, from his beloved good book, "A Treasury of Nausea." He is an infant do-gooder who will undoubtedly graduate into writing a "Dear Normy" column, telling others how to cope with vicissitudes he has never encountered.

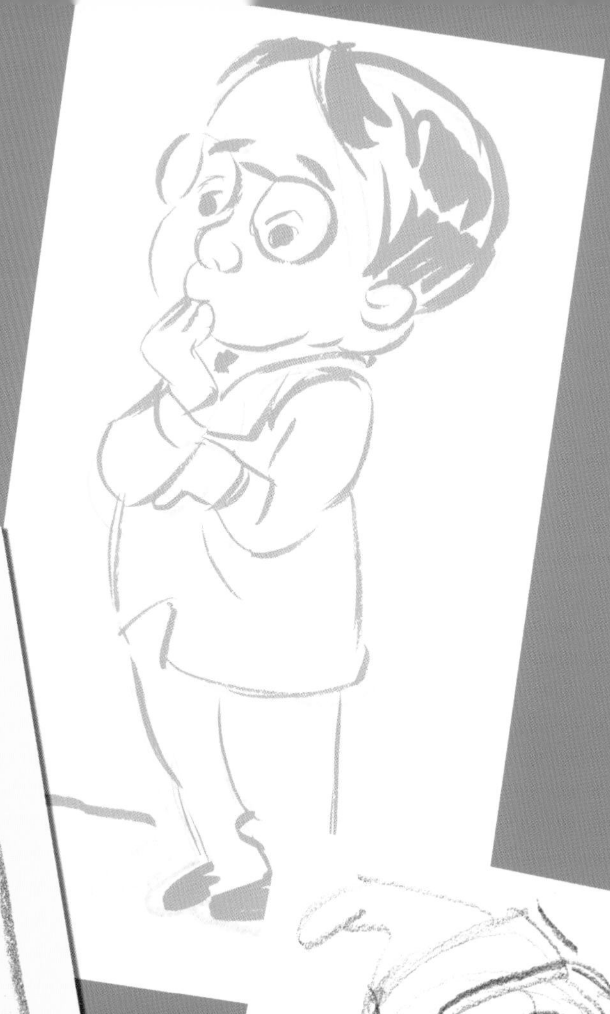

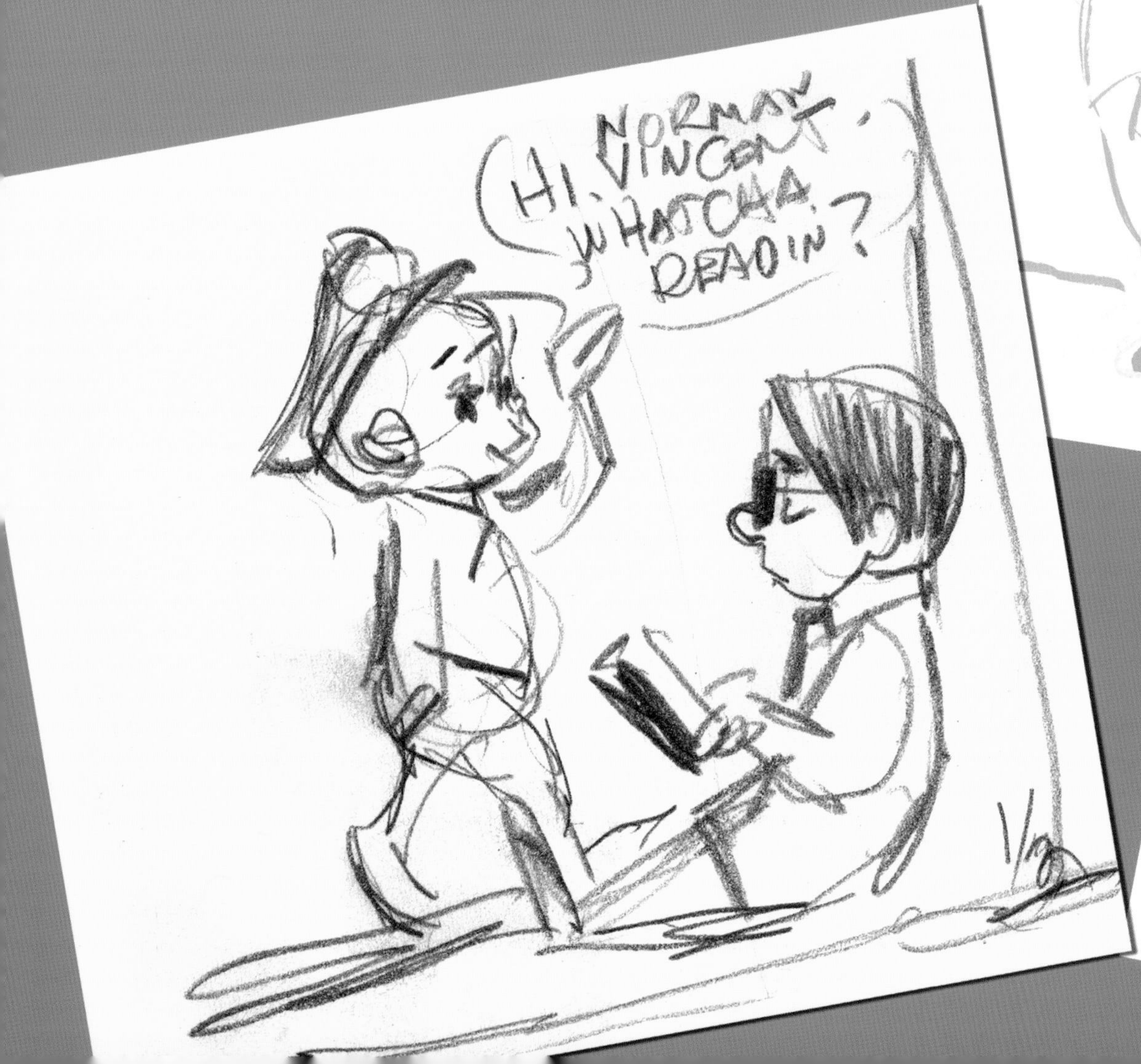
HI, NORMAN VINCENT. WHATCHA READIN?

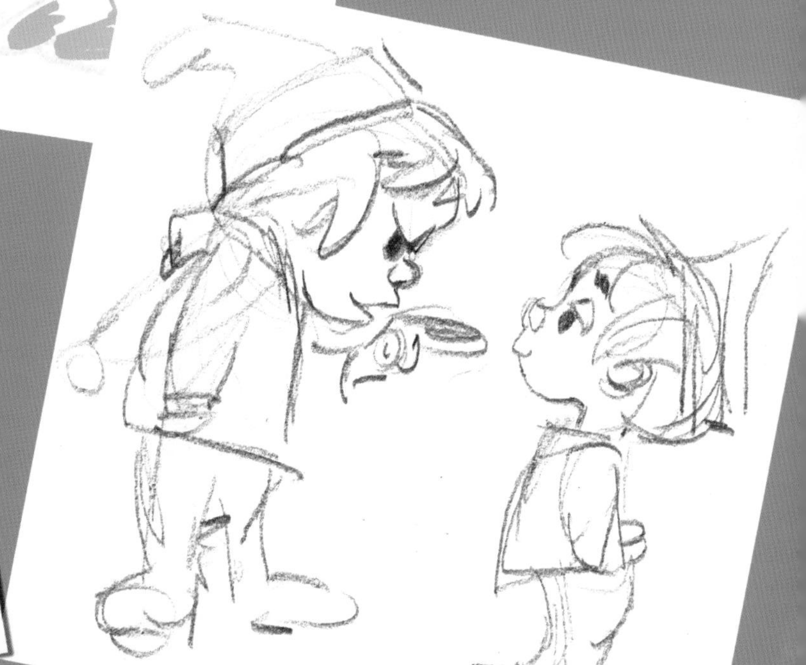

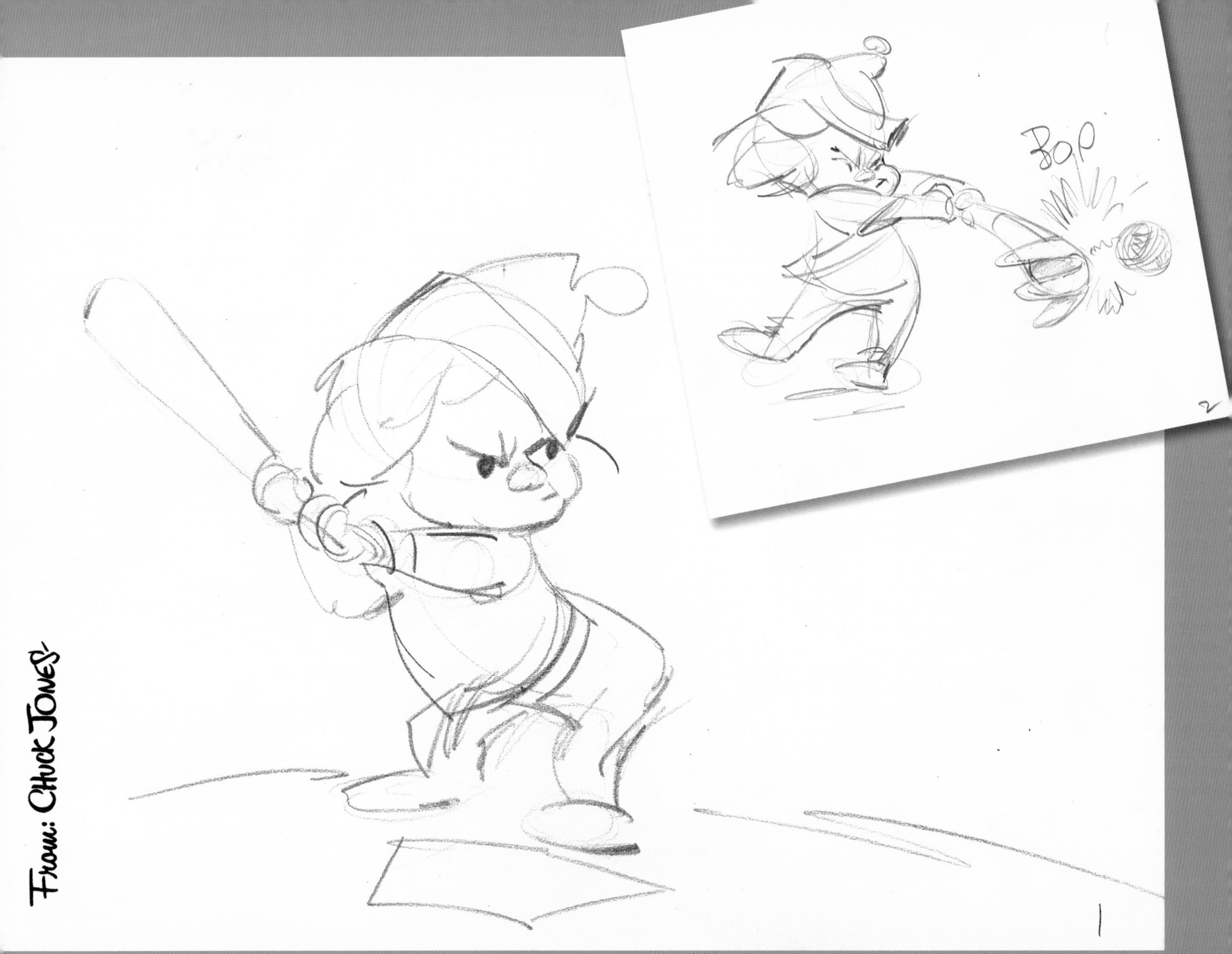
From: Chuck Jones
Bop
2
1

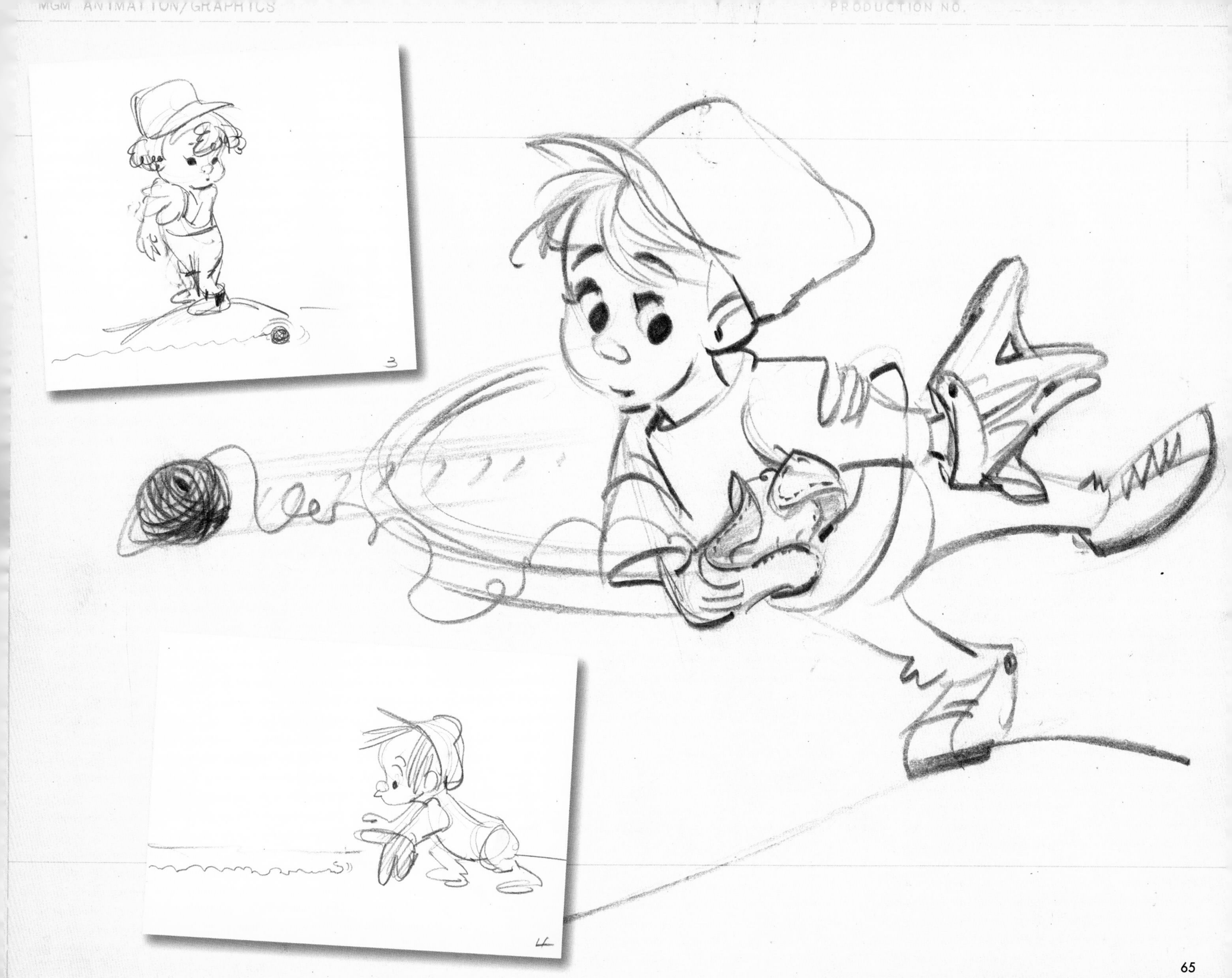
MGM ANIMATION/GRAPHICS
PRODUCTION NO.
3
4

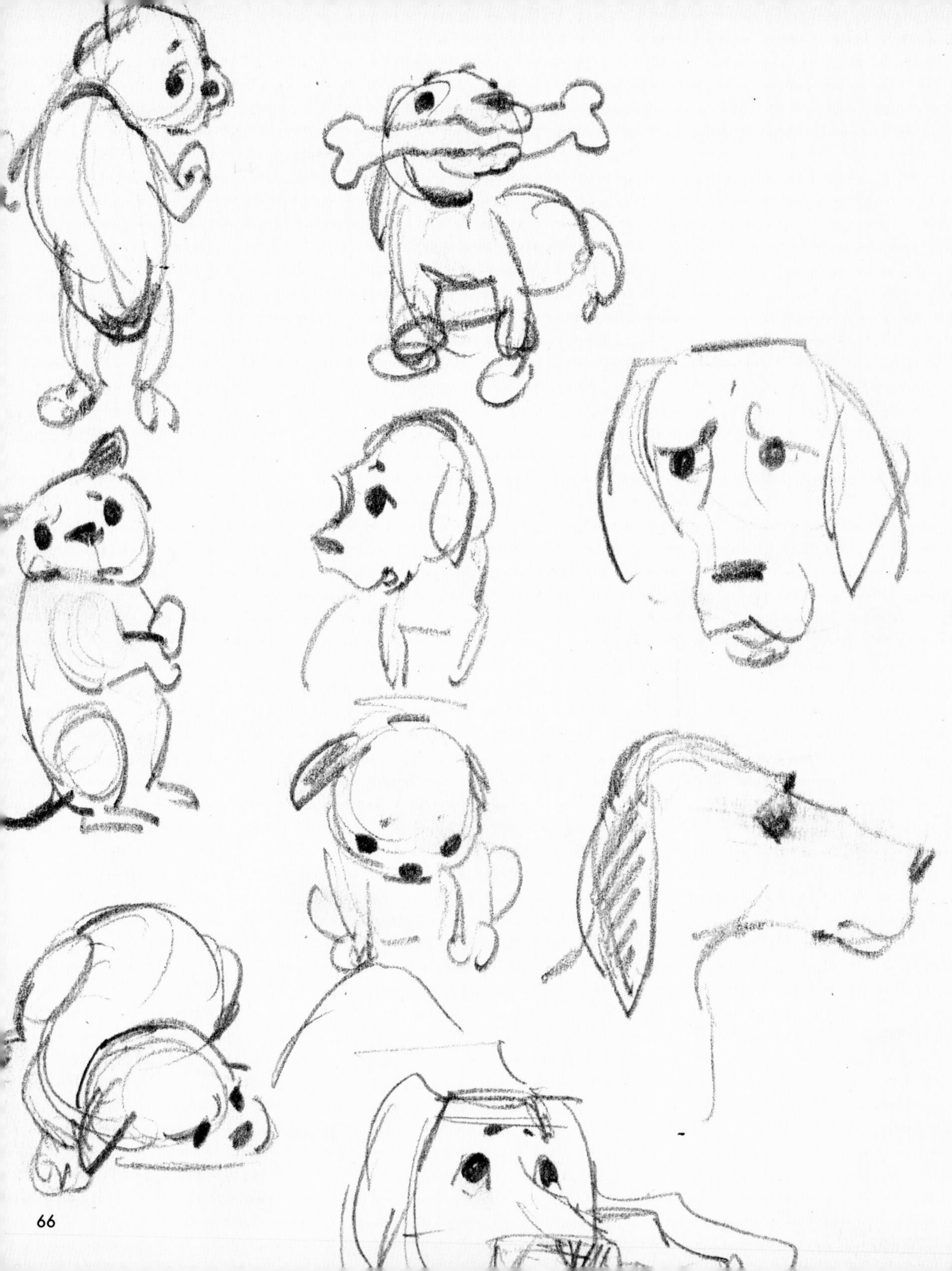

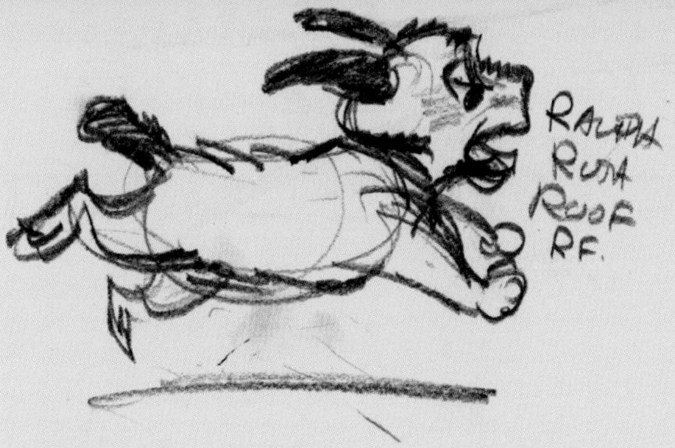
ROOF
RF.

RALF

Ralf is the winter of canine discontent. Too large to pass as a hamster, he once tried on a catsuit in hopes of escape but found that he looked more like a badly stuffed teddy bear rather than a feline. Ralf is the Crawford of dogdom; he hopes to survive but has the uncomfortable feeling that he is going backward through life and may be entering a second puppyhood. The only thing of any size about him in his inferiority complex, and it is towering.

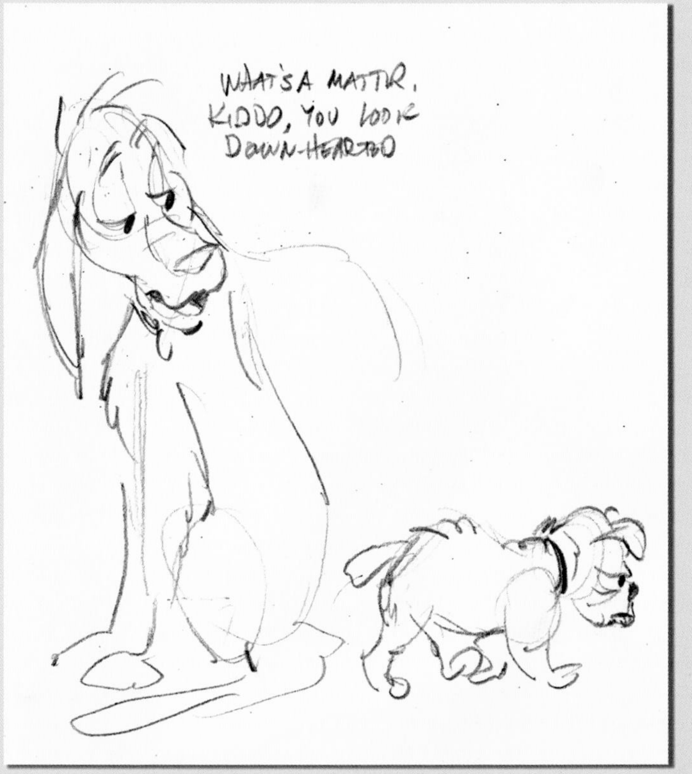
WHAT'S A MATTR, KIDDO, YOU LOOK DOWN-HEARTED

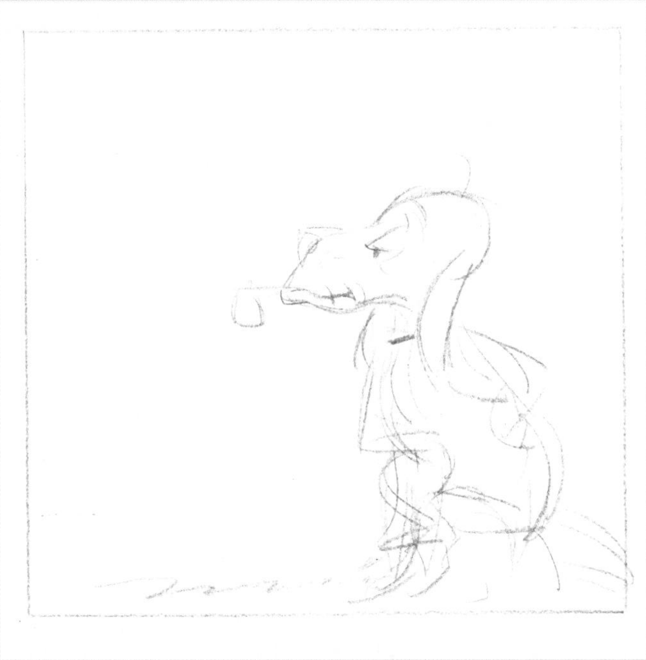

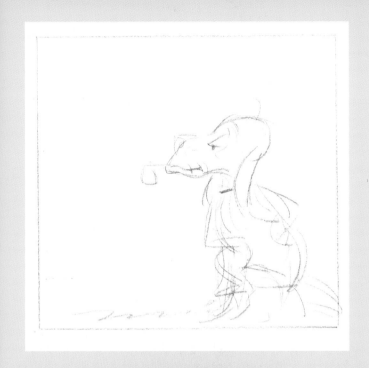

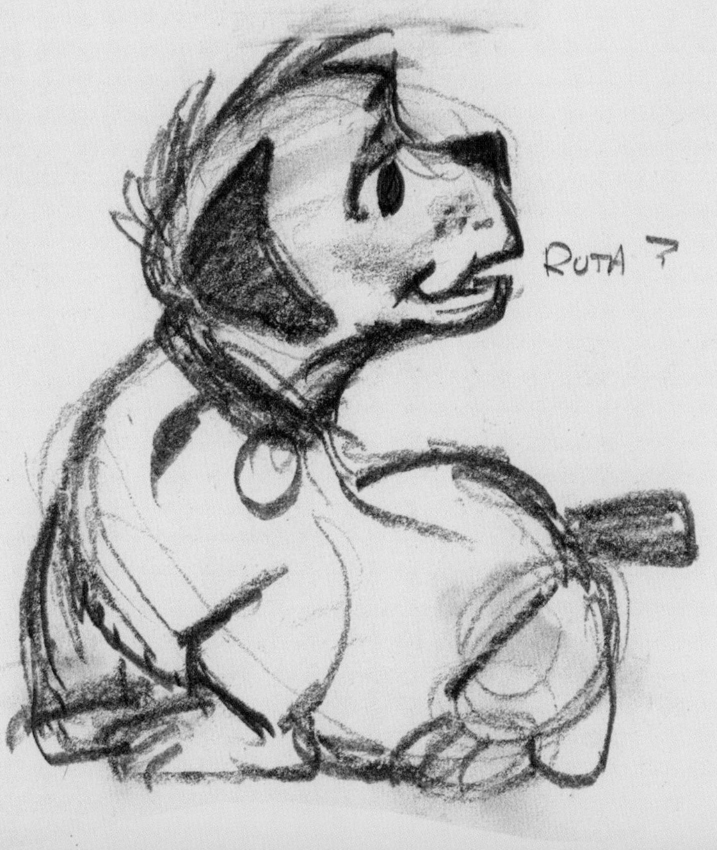
RUTA ?

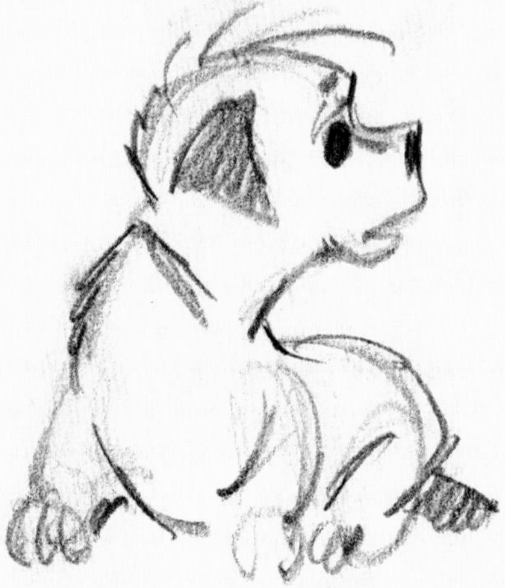

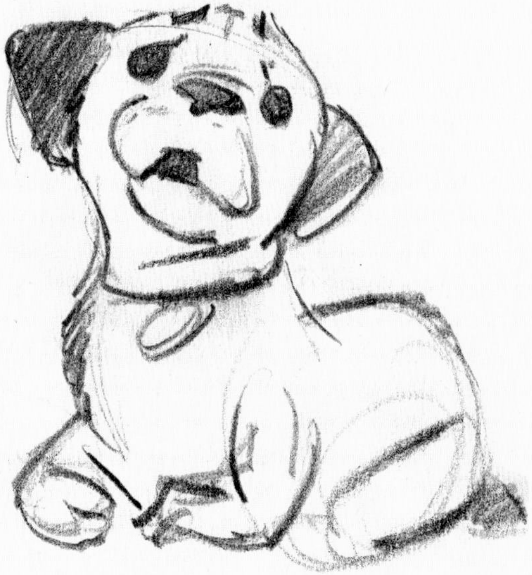

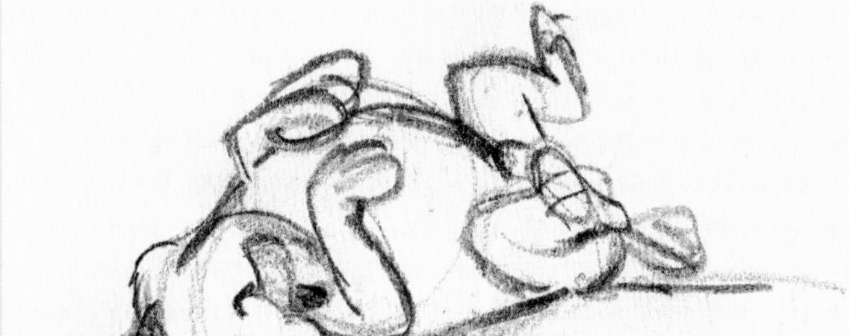

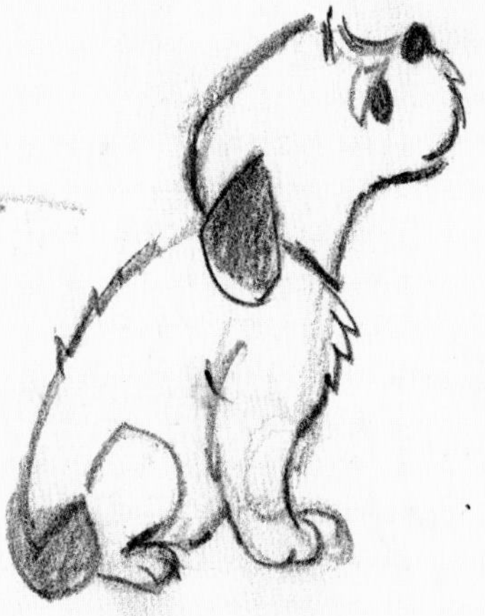

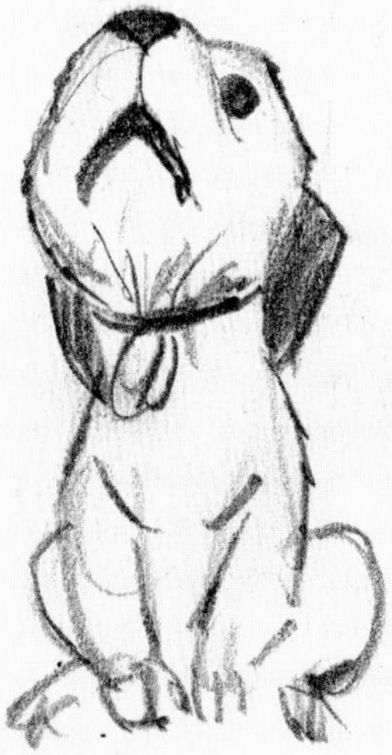

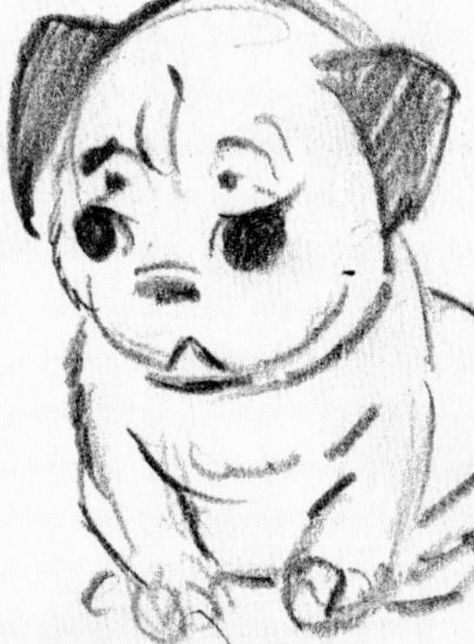

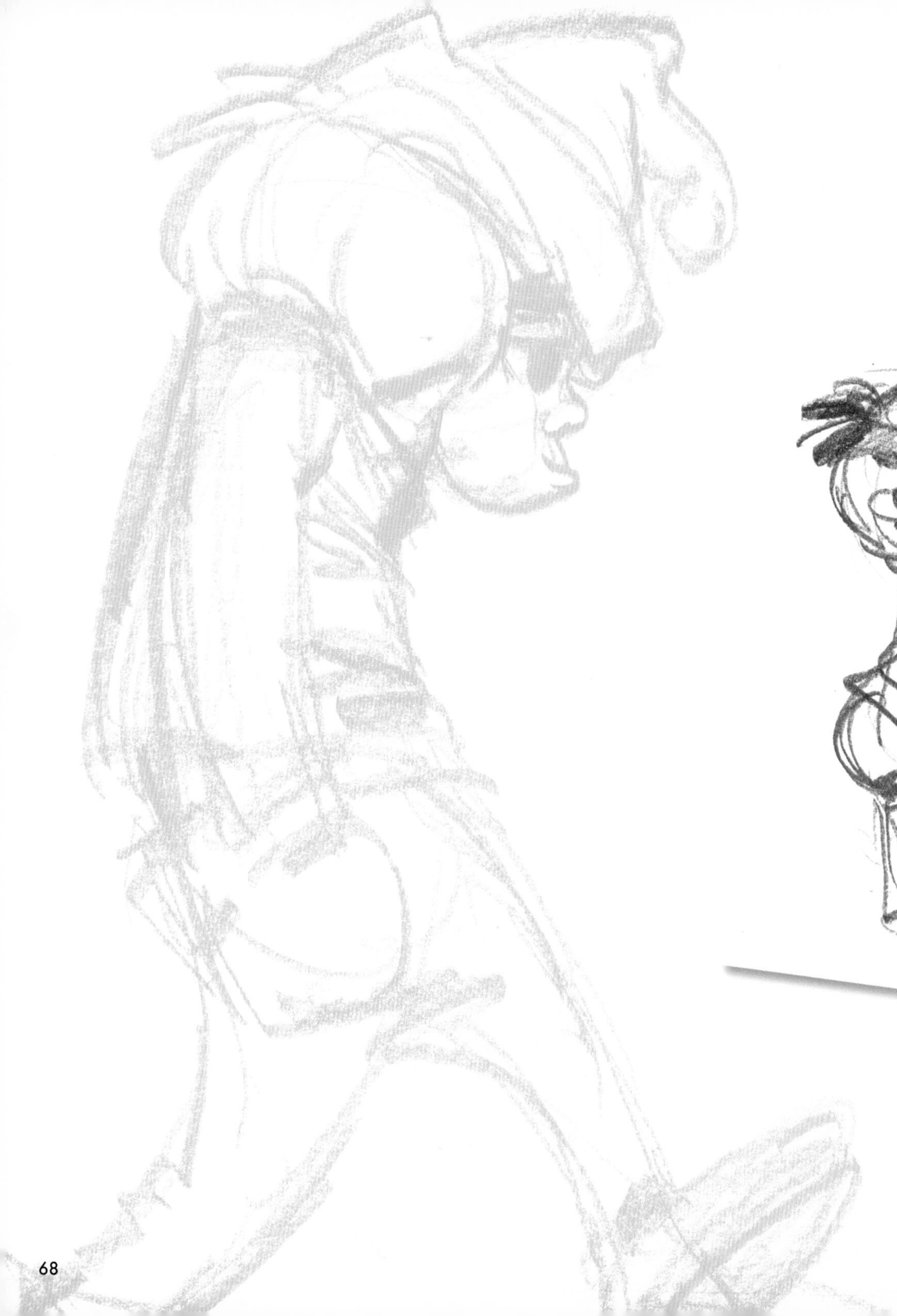

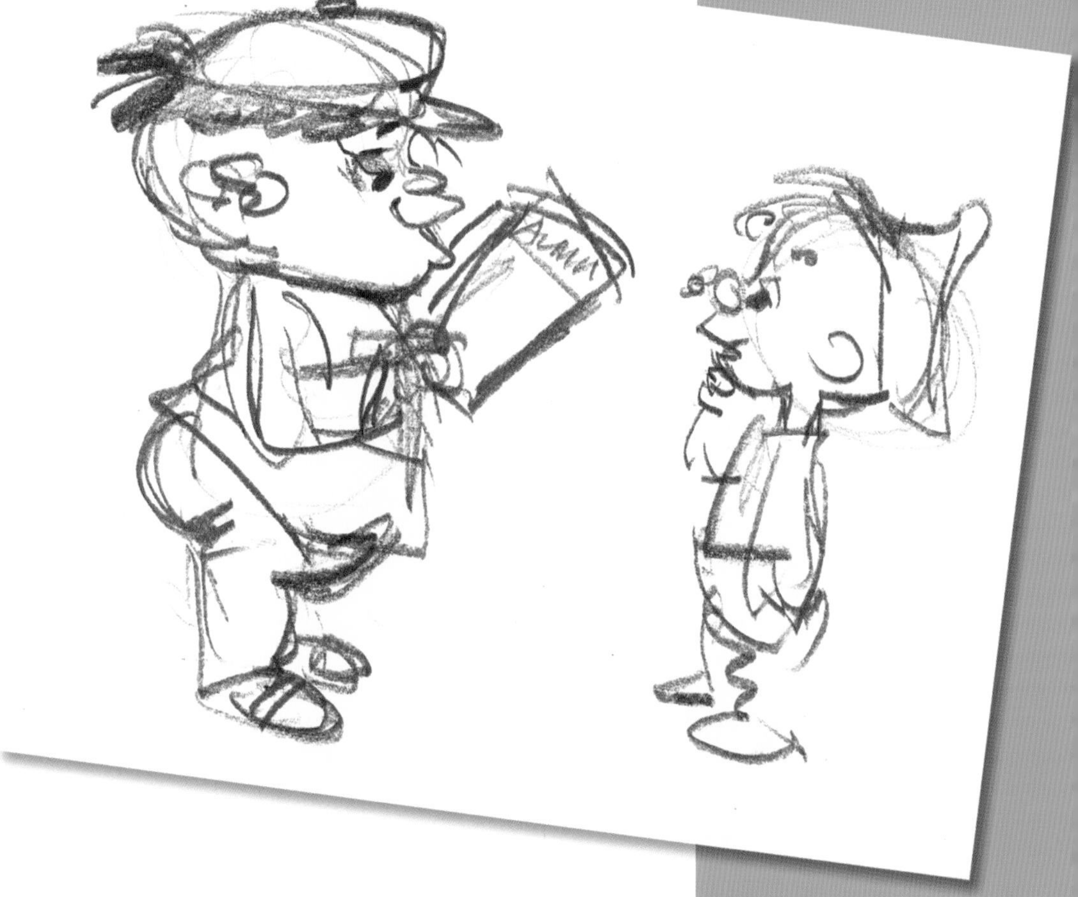

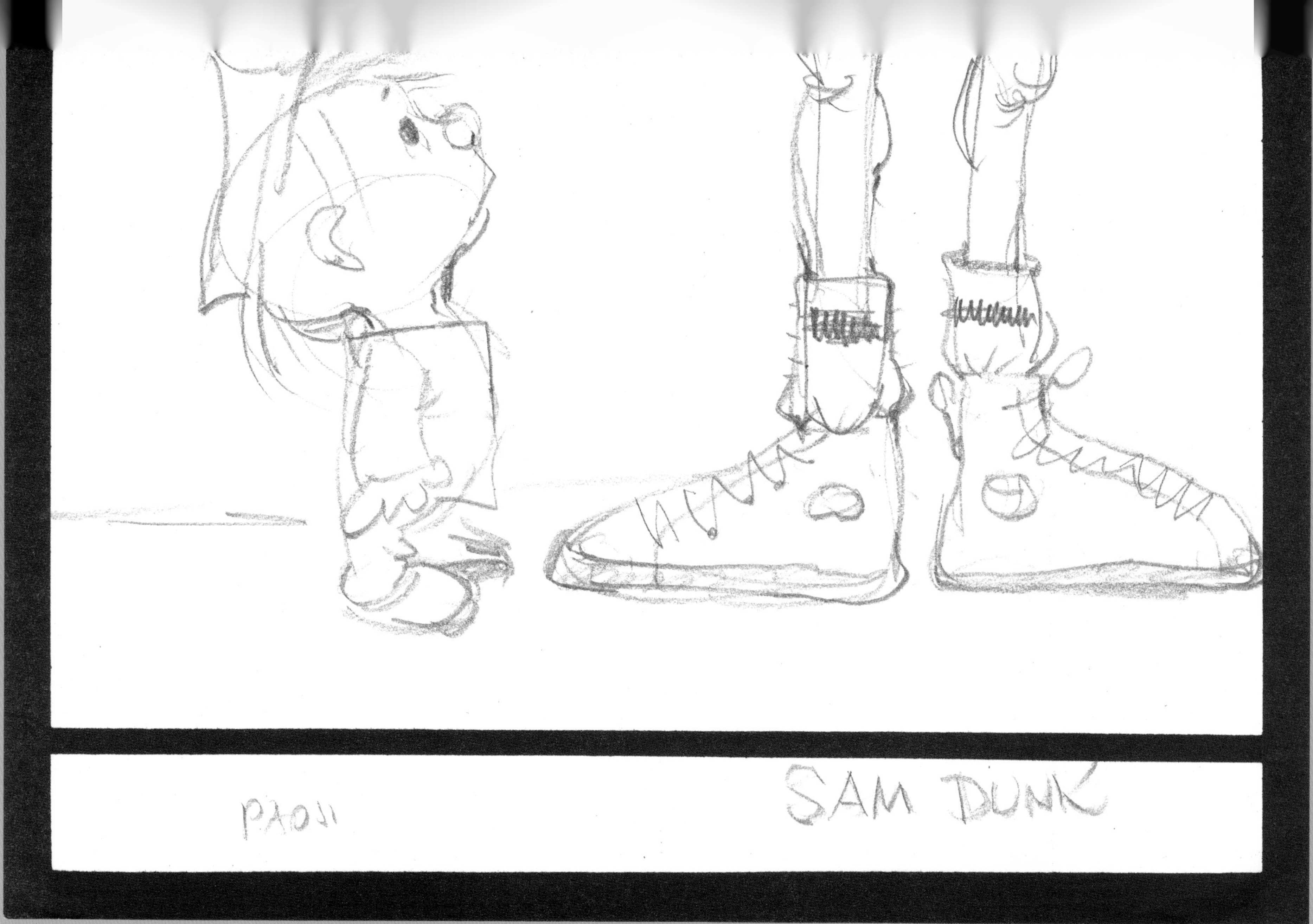
SAM DUNK

SAM DUNK

Many boys have hobbies. In the case of Sam Dunk they are all concentrated into a single pastime, growing. He is eleven but no one is sure whether that is his age in years or height in feet. Sam is more first draft choice than boy, though early scouting reports say that coaches must be prepared to have baskets raised when he enters the game.

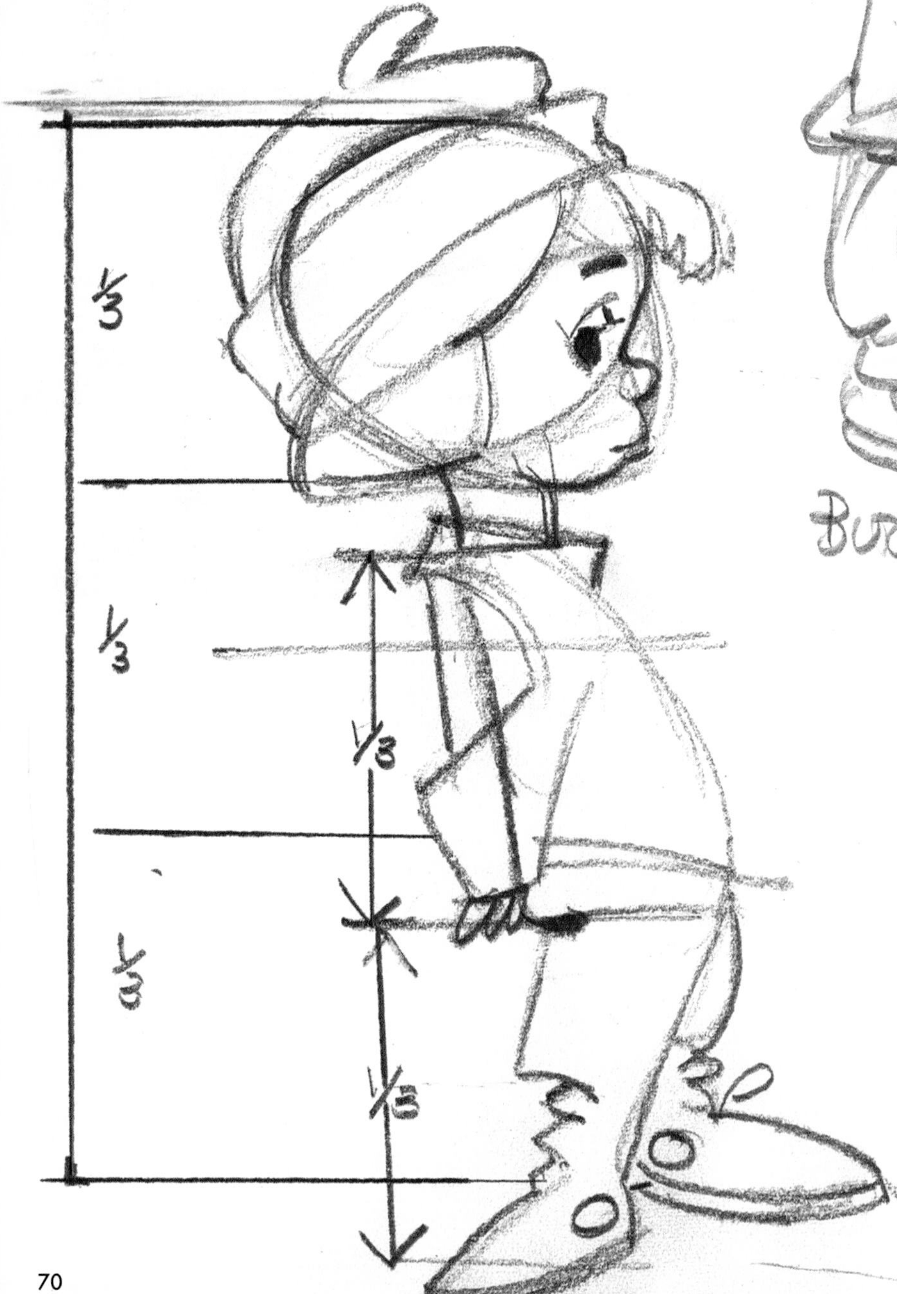
1/3
1/3
1/3
1/3
1/3
1/3

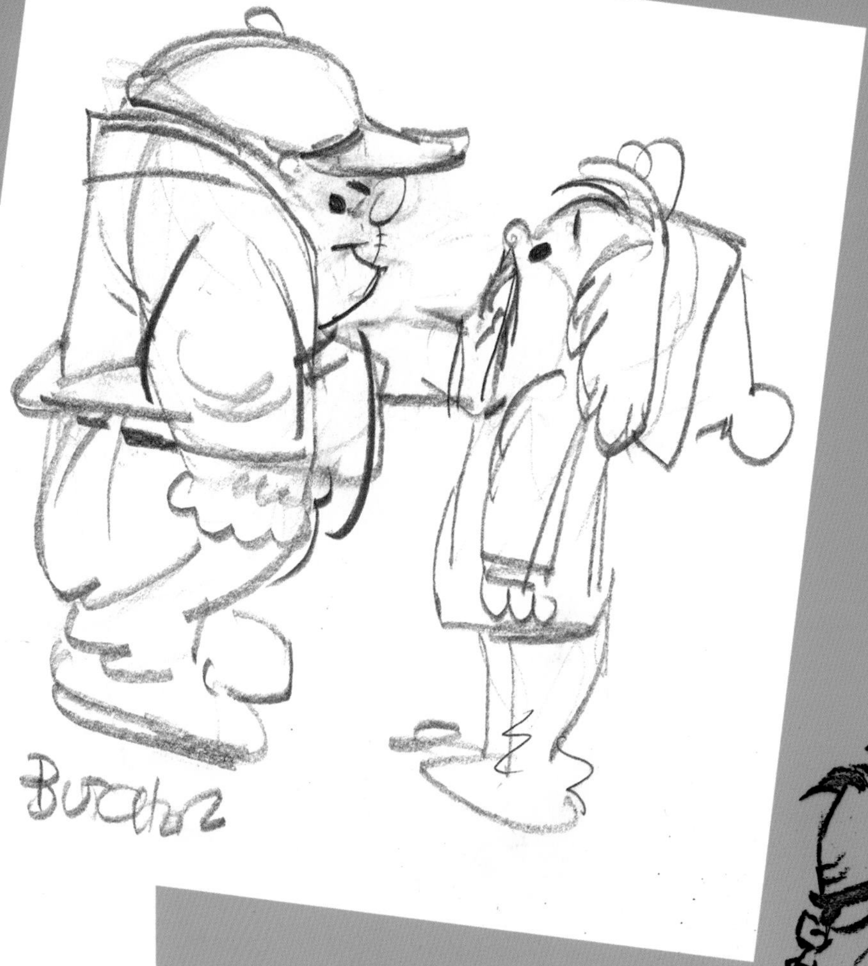
Butcher

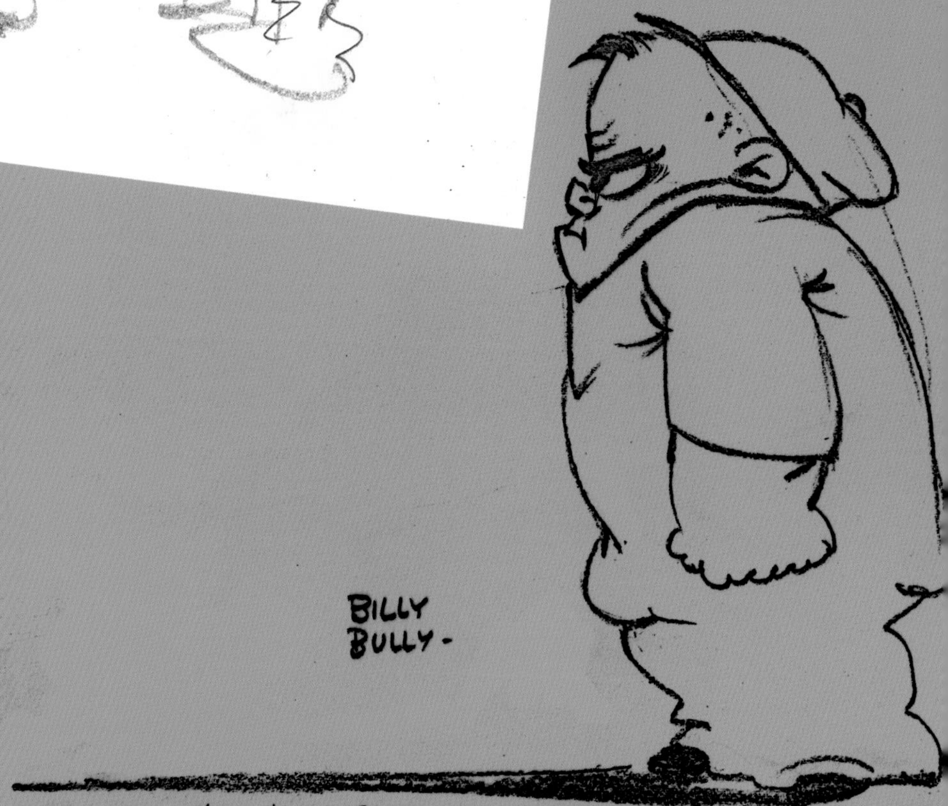
BILLY
BULLY-
HE ALWAYS CASTS A SHADOW.

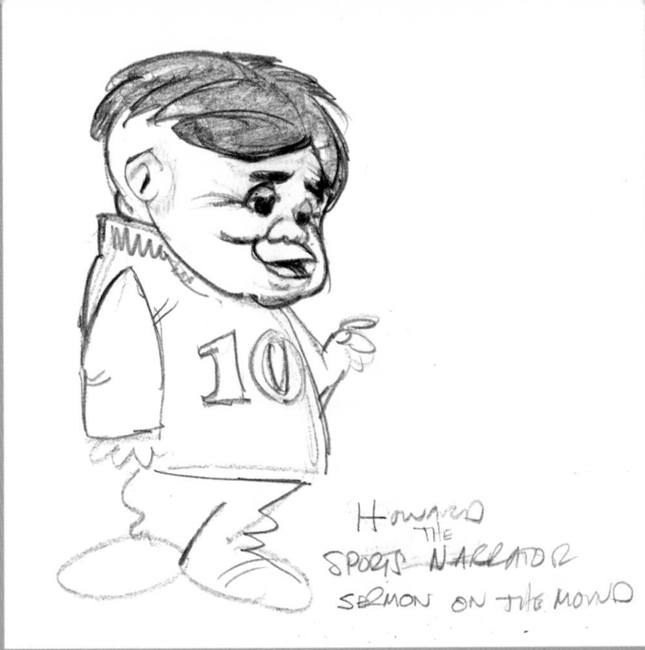
10
HOWARD
THE
SPORTS NARRATOR
SERMON ON THE MOUND

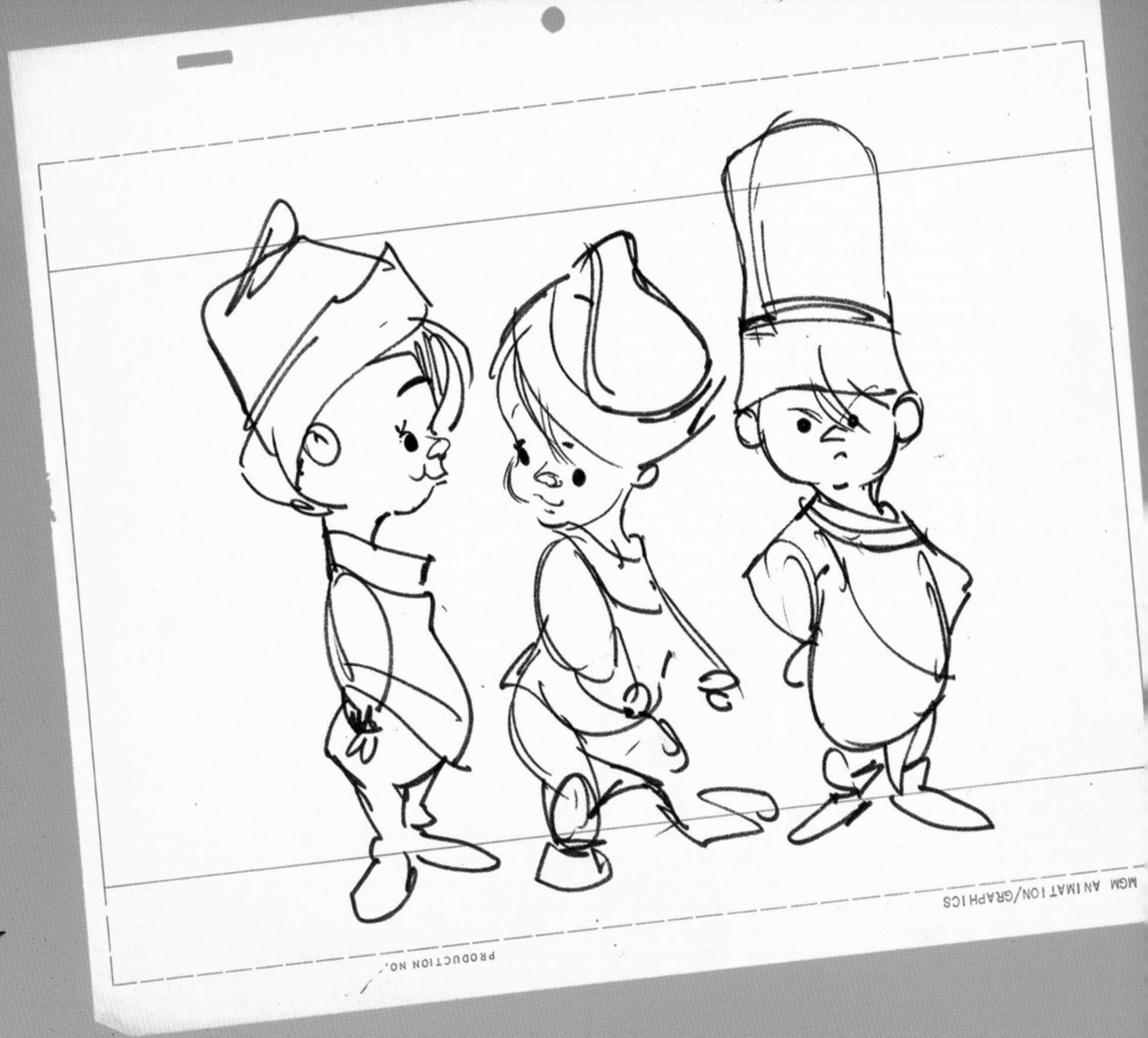
MGM ANIMATION/GRAPHICS
PRODUCTION NO.

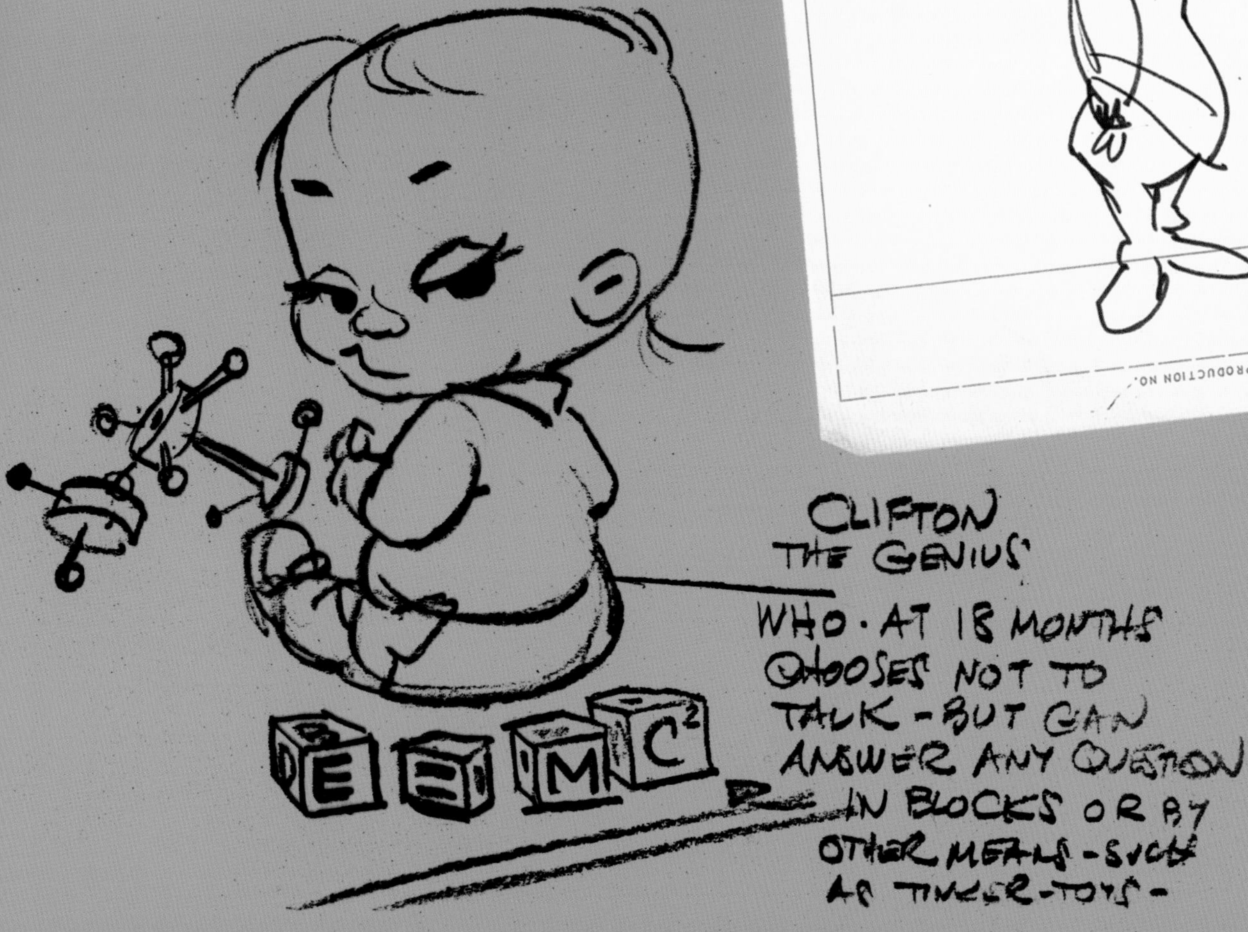
E
E
M
C²
CLIFTON
THE GENIUS
WHO · AT 18 MONTHS
CHOOSES NOT TO
TALK - BUT CAN
ANSWER ANY QUESTION
IN BLOCKS OR BY
OTHER MEANS - SUCH
AS TINKER-TOYS -

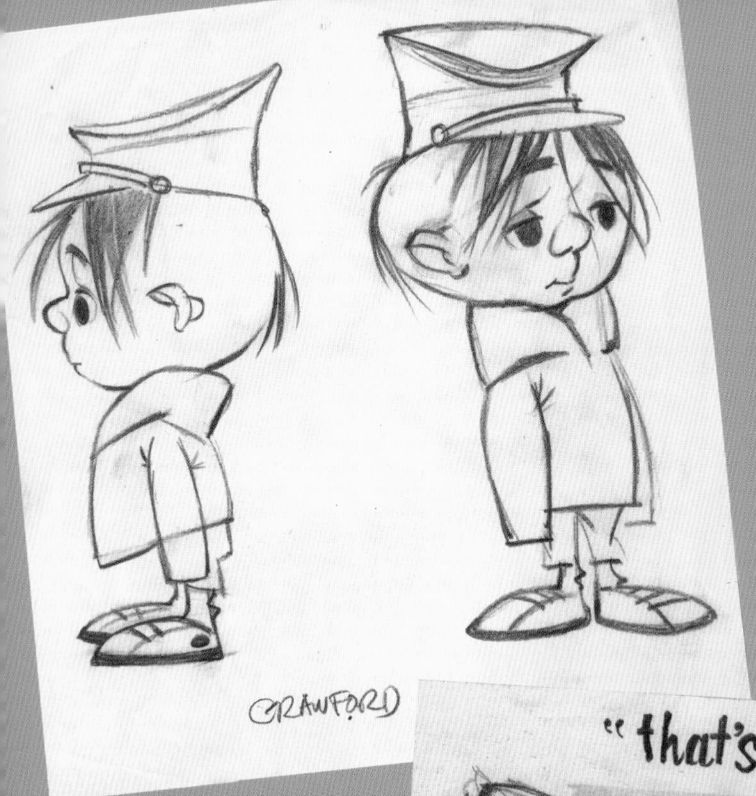
CRAWFORD

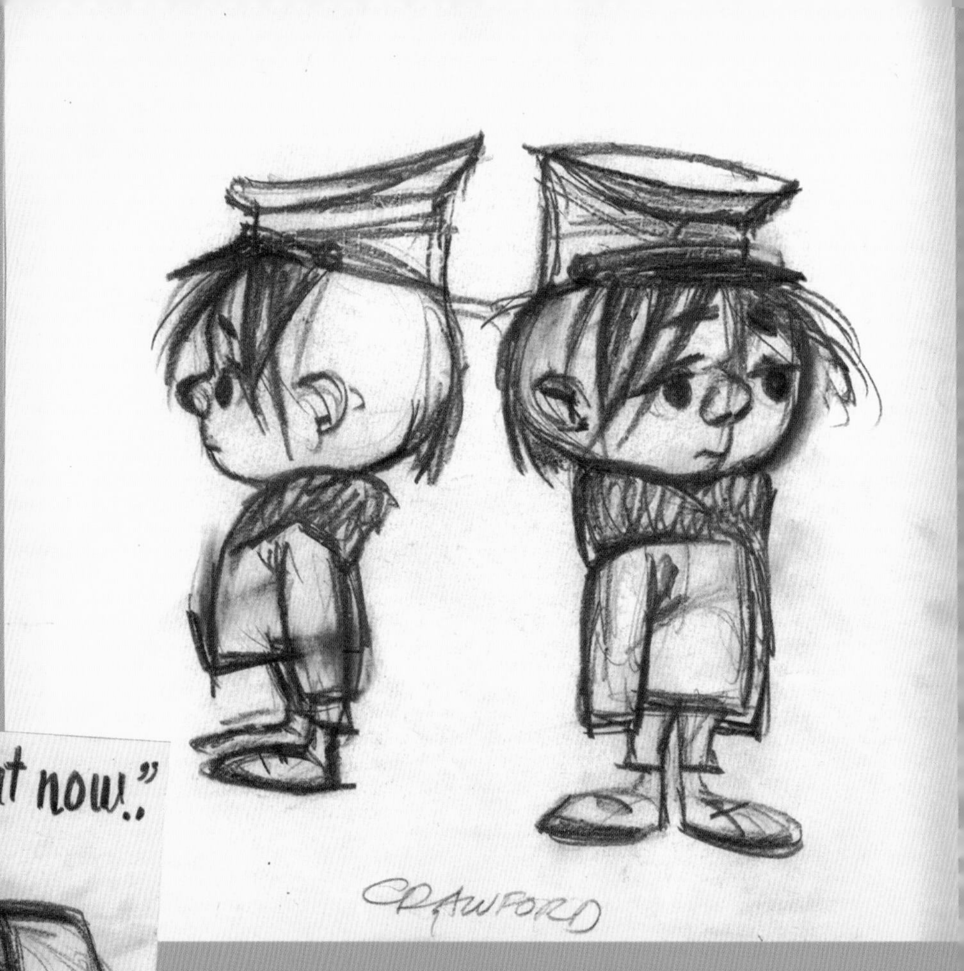
CRAWFORD

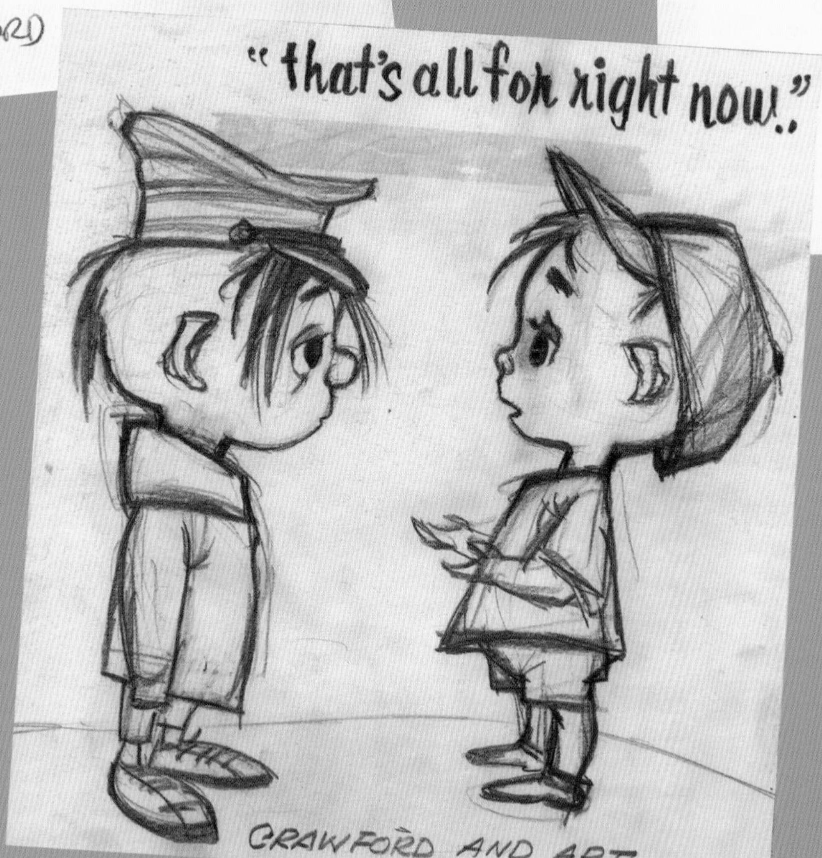
" that's all for right now."
CRAWFORD AND ART

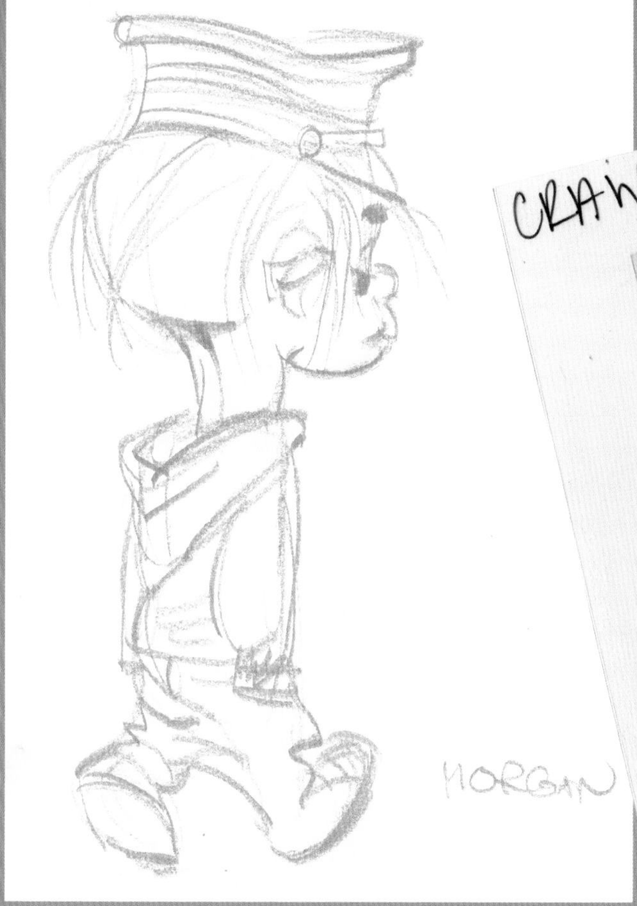
MORGAN

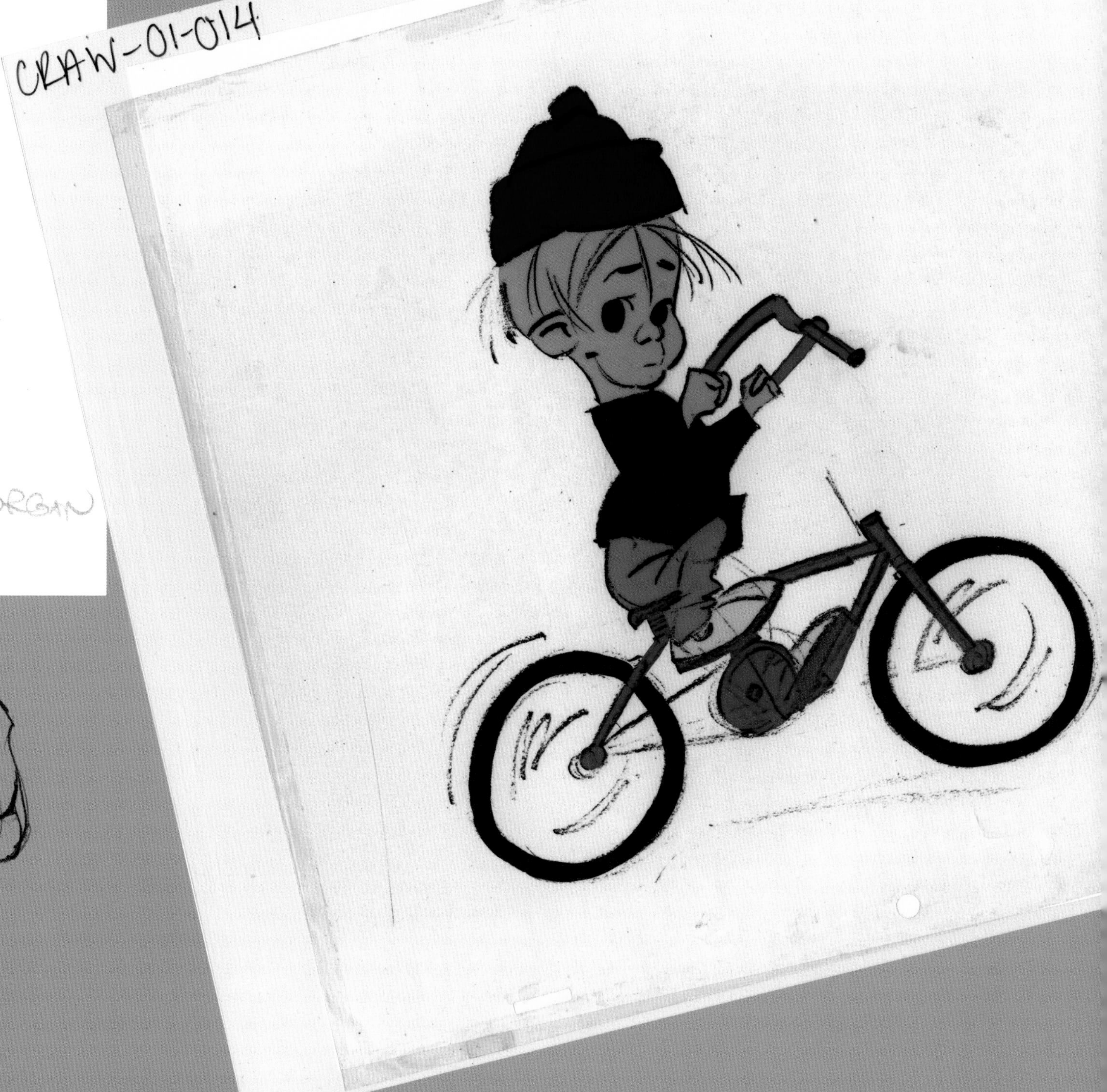
CRAW-01-014

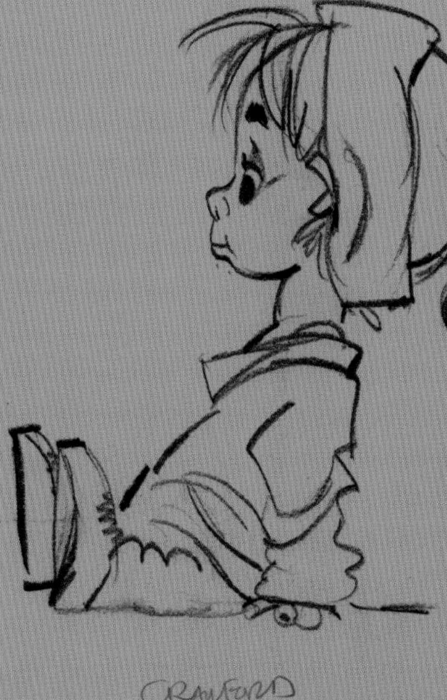
CRAWFORD

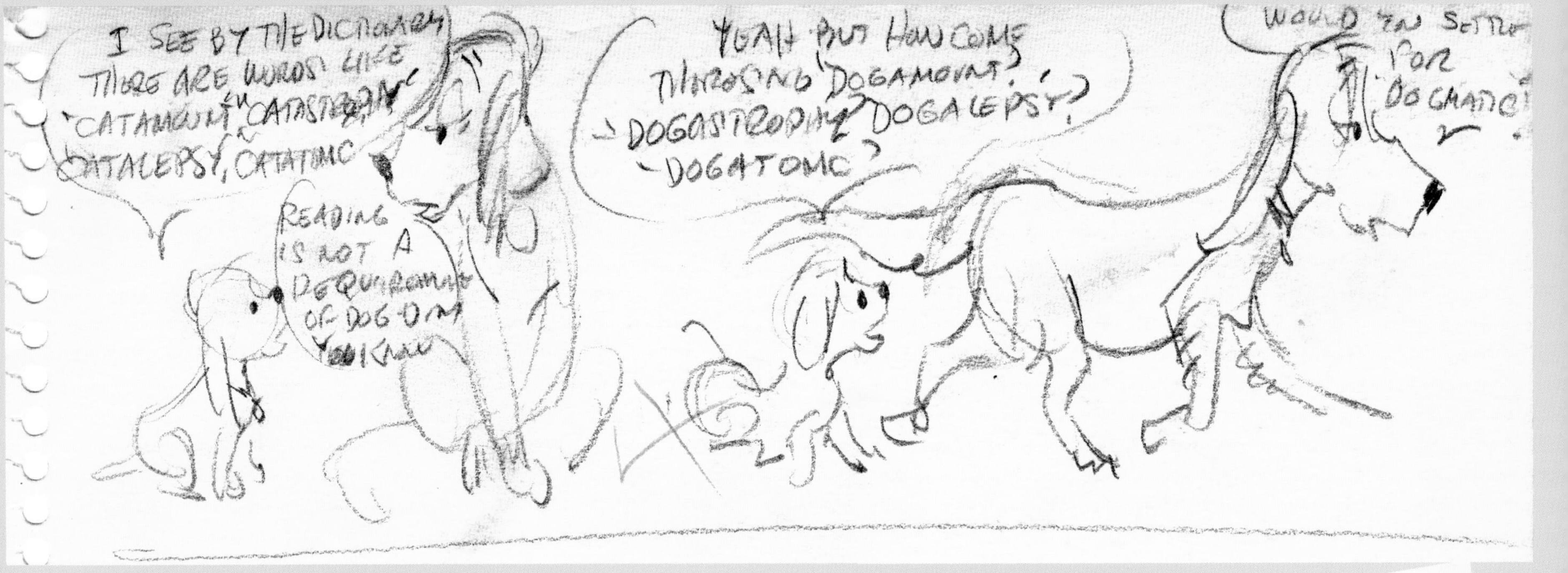
I SEE BY THE DICTIONARY THERE ARE WORDS LIKE "CATAMOUNT," "CATASTROPHIC," "CATALEPSY," "CATATONIC"
READING IS NOT A REQUIREMENT OF DOG-DOM YOU KNOW
YEAH BUT HOW COME THERE'S NO "DOGAMOUNT"? "DOGASTROPHE"? "DOGALEPSY"? "DOGATONIC"?
WOULD 'EN SETTLE FOR DOGMATIC?

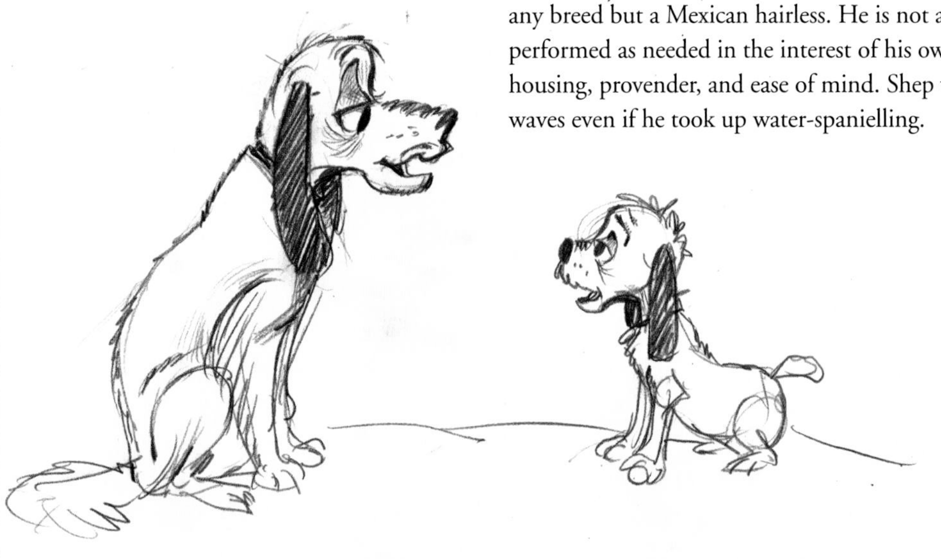

SHEP

Shep is a shepherd because that is what his master wants him to be, but he could—and with alacrity would—be a pointer, a retriever, a Sealyham, smallish St. Bernard, or just about any breed but a Mexican hairless. He is not an actor; he performed as needed in the interest of his own comfort, housing, provender, and ease of mind. Shep wouldn't make waves even if he took up water-spanielling.

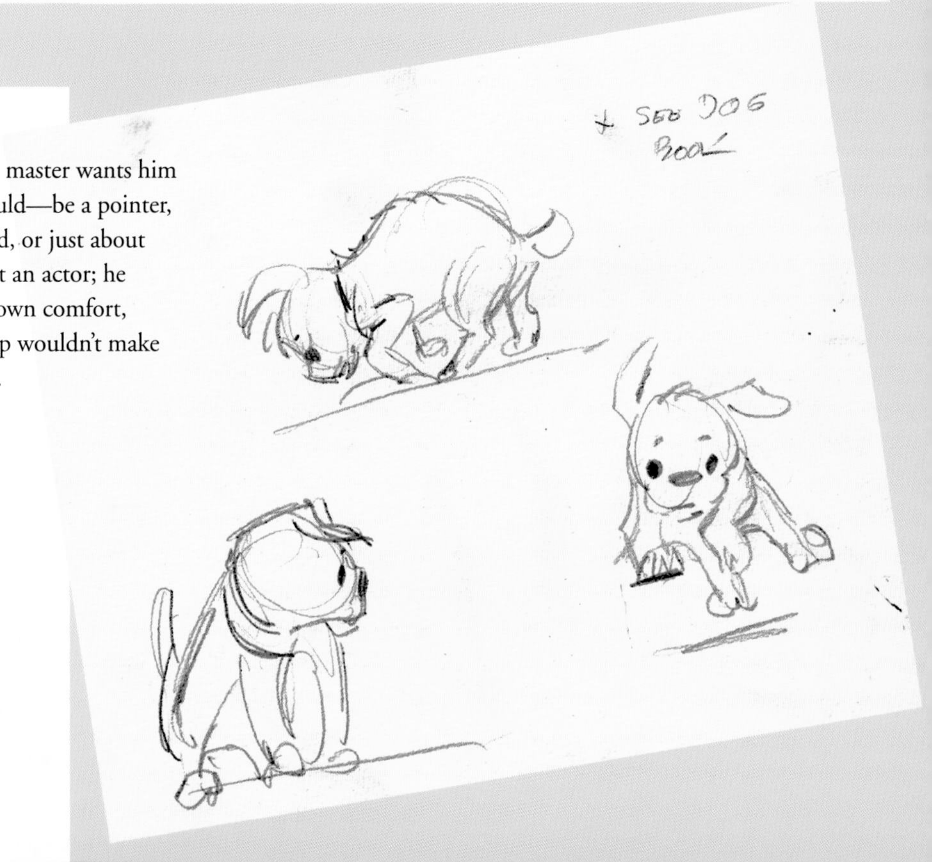
+ SEE DOG BOOK

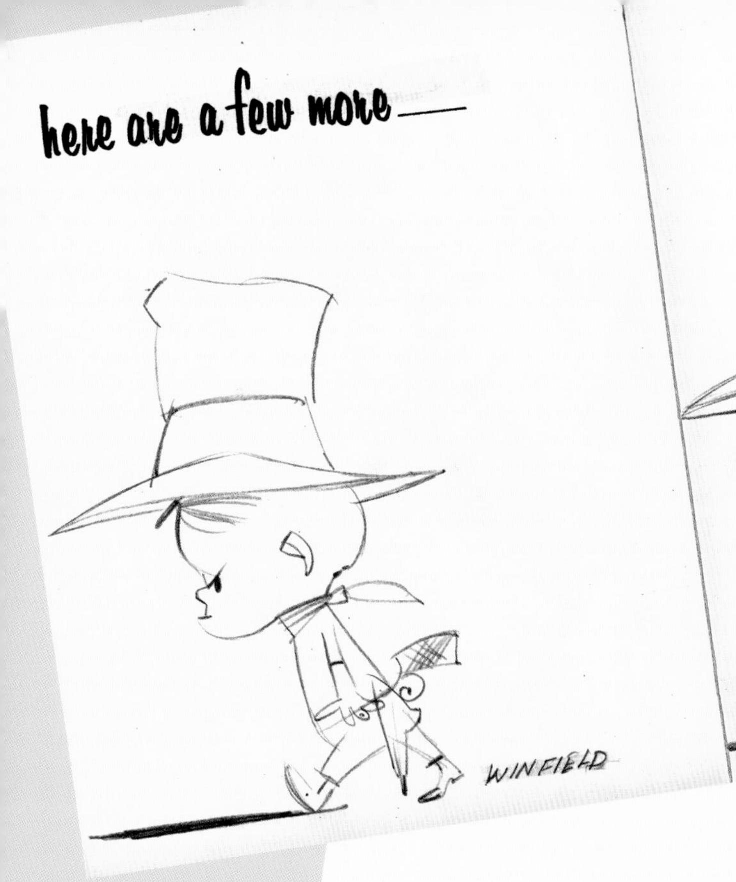
here are a few more —
WINFIELD

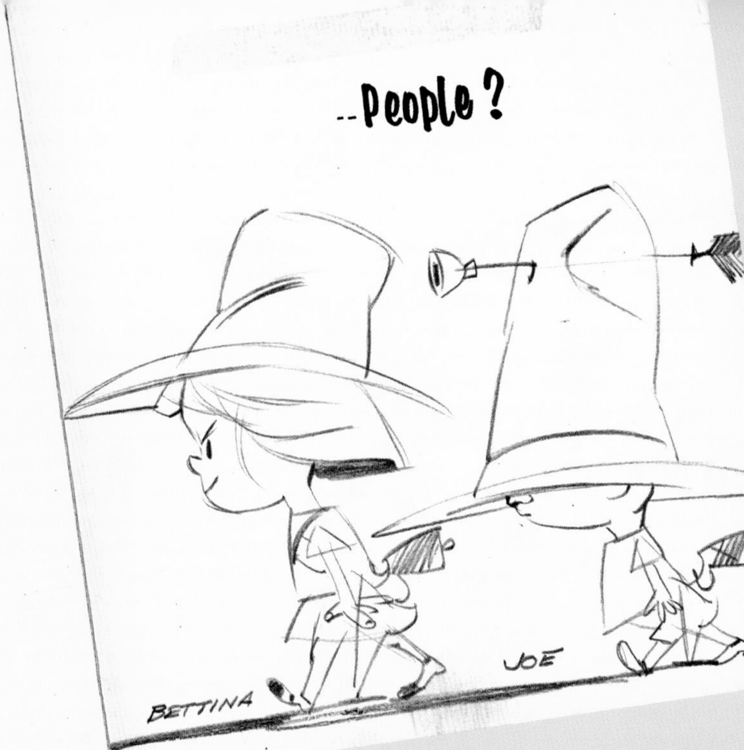
--People ?
BETTINA
JOE

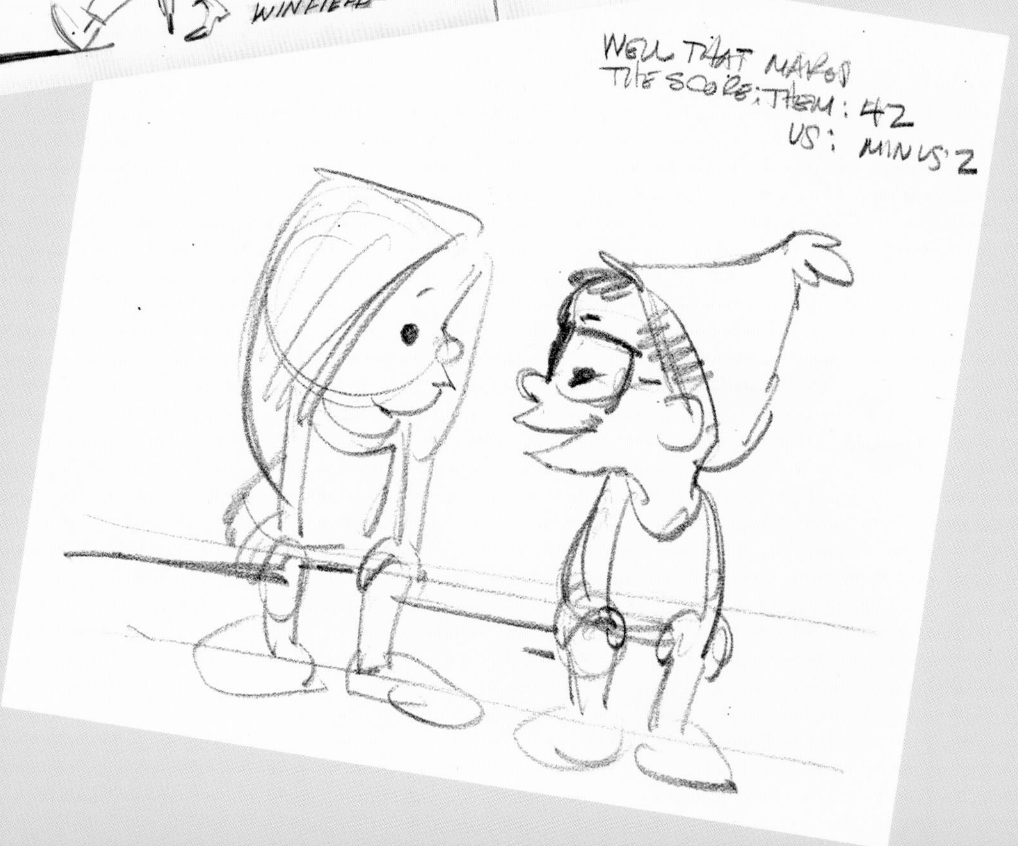
WELL THAT MAKES THE SCORE: THEM: 42
US: MINUS 2

S. I. HAWAII KAWA

Just as a phonetically related senator is serving as a freshman congressman, S.I. Hawaii Kawa is serving as a freshman semanticist. He recognizes the value of words as useful sounds, as surgically effective though bloodless weapons, and—most of all—as self-delighting surprises. The only word he seems not to fully understand is "sleep." He fears that to really know it would mean that he was missing something.

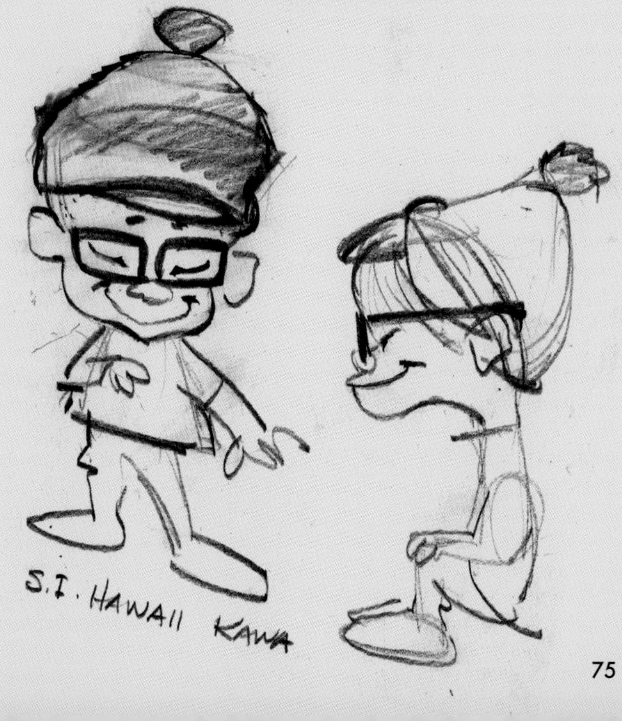
S.I. HAWAII KAWA

CRAW-01-005: CRAW-01-006

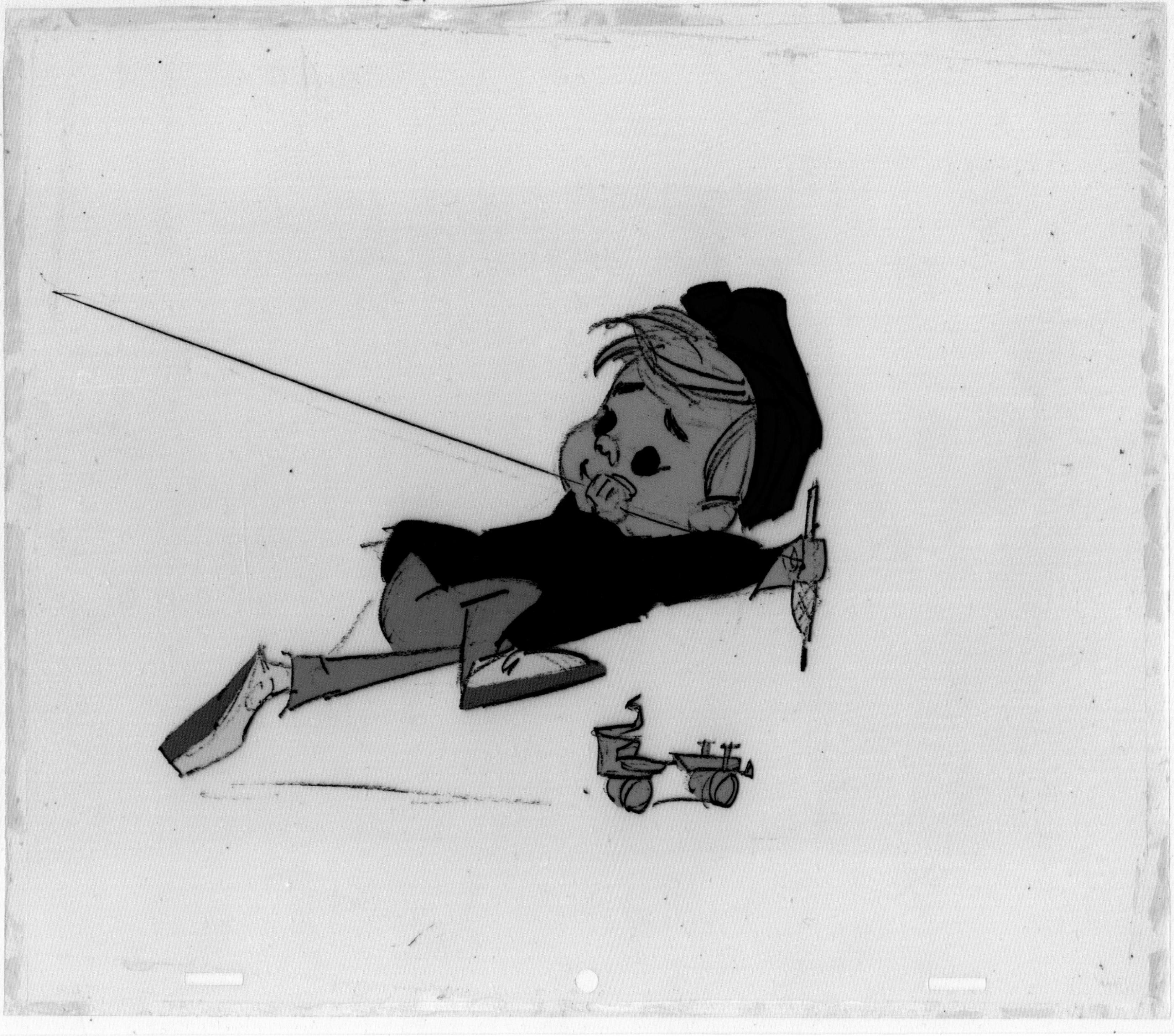

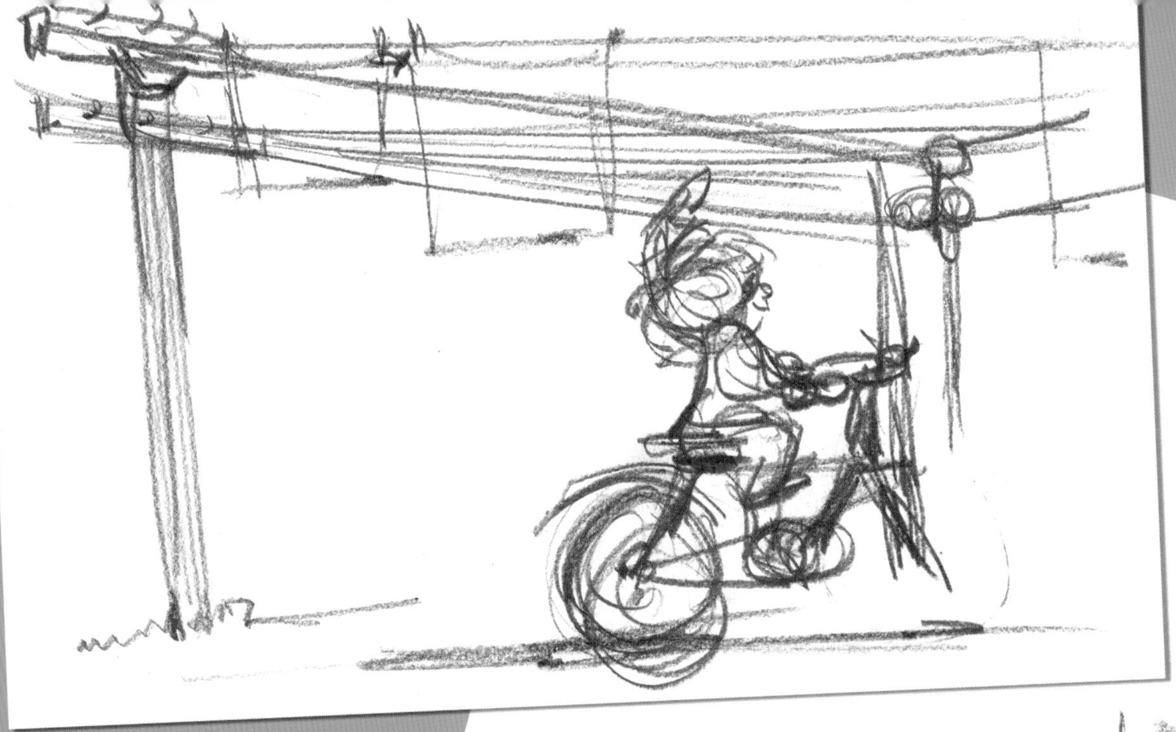

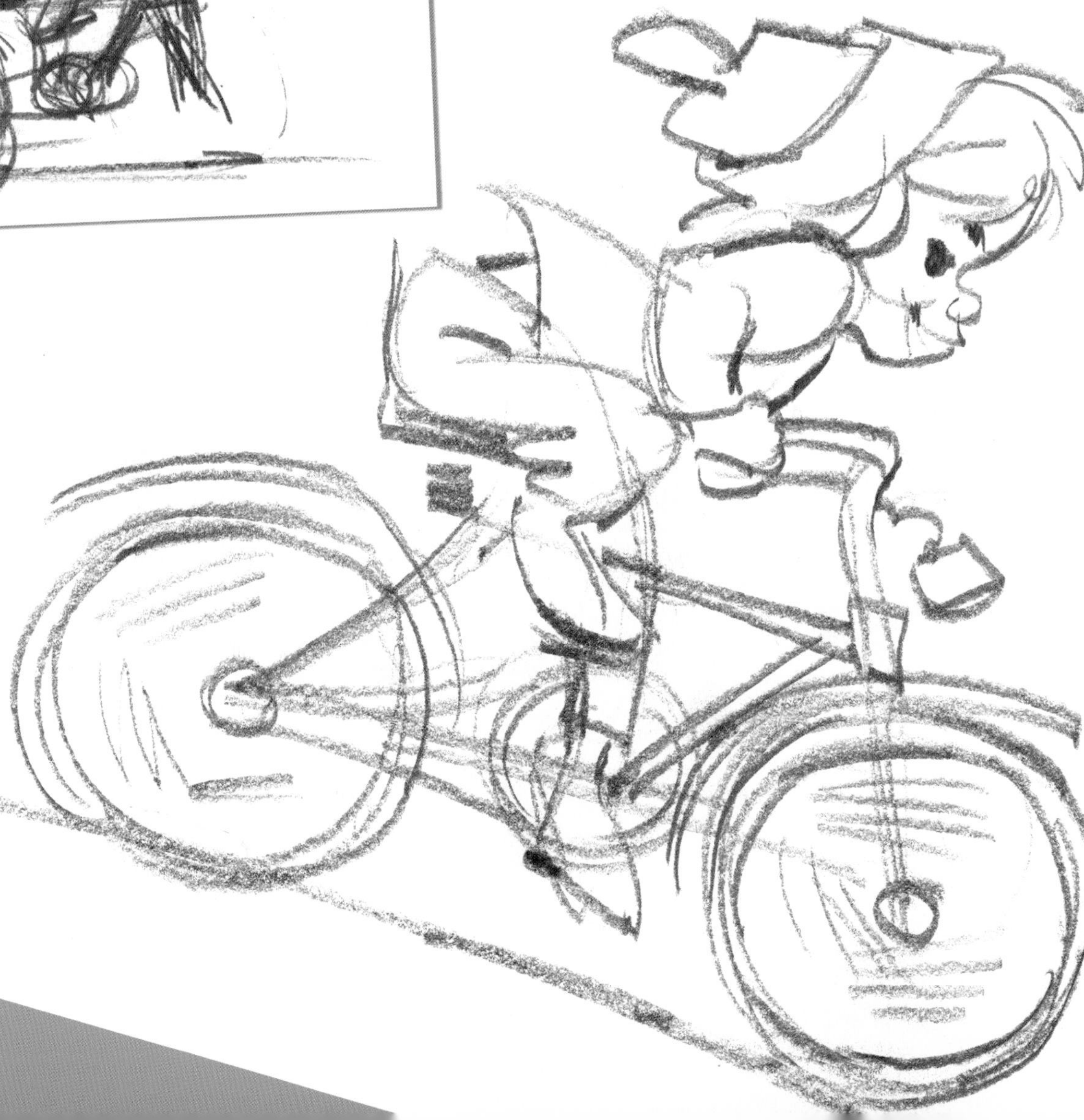

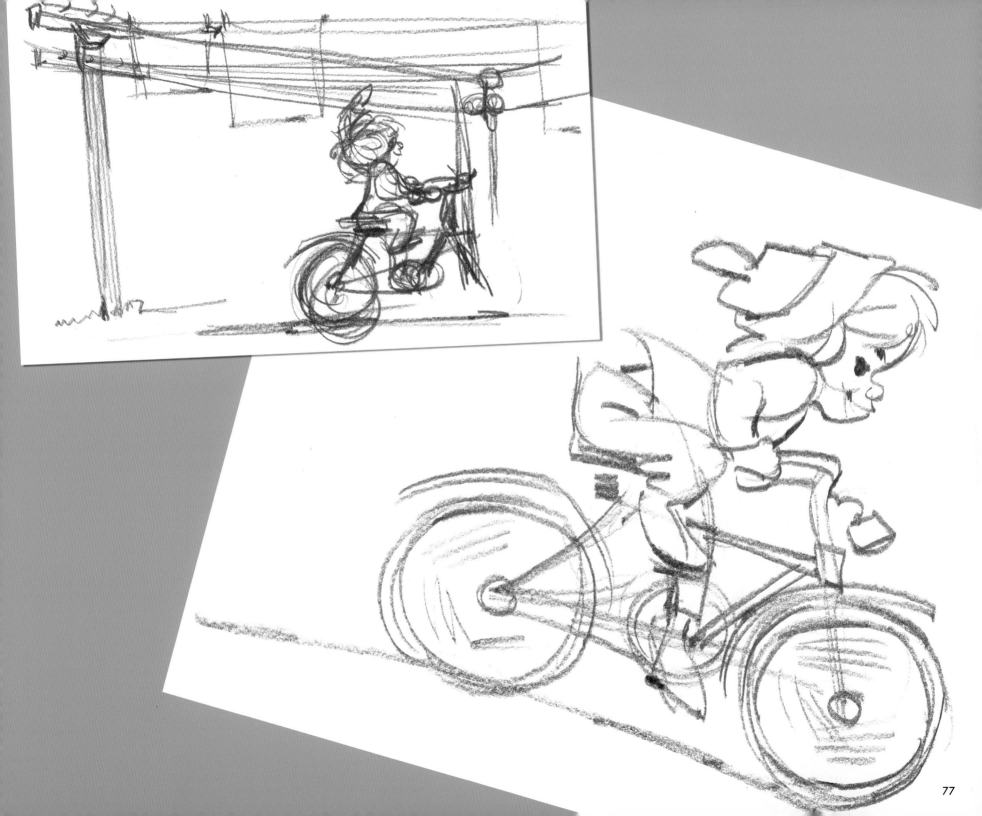

GLORY
STEINEM
MORNING

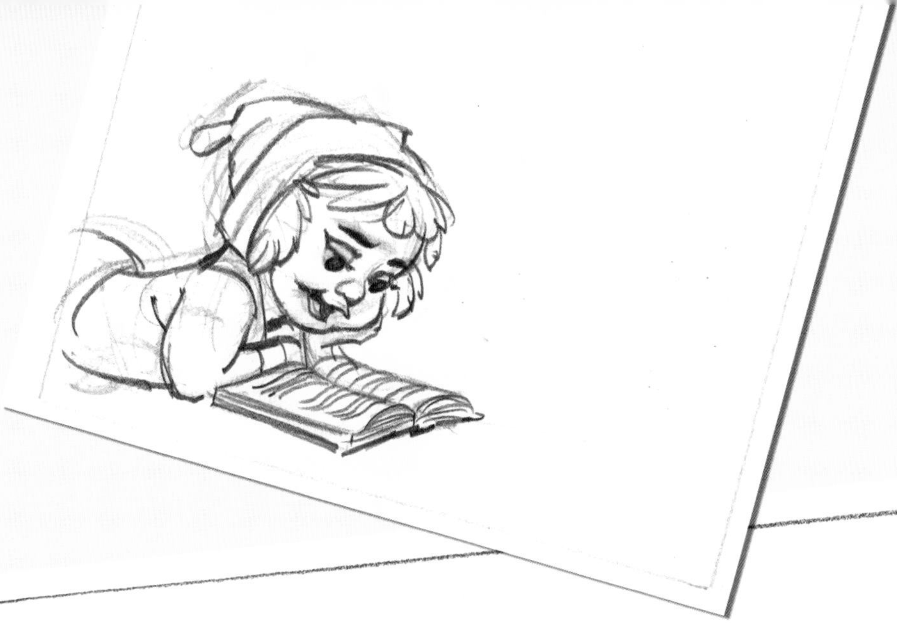

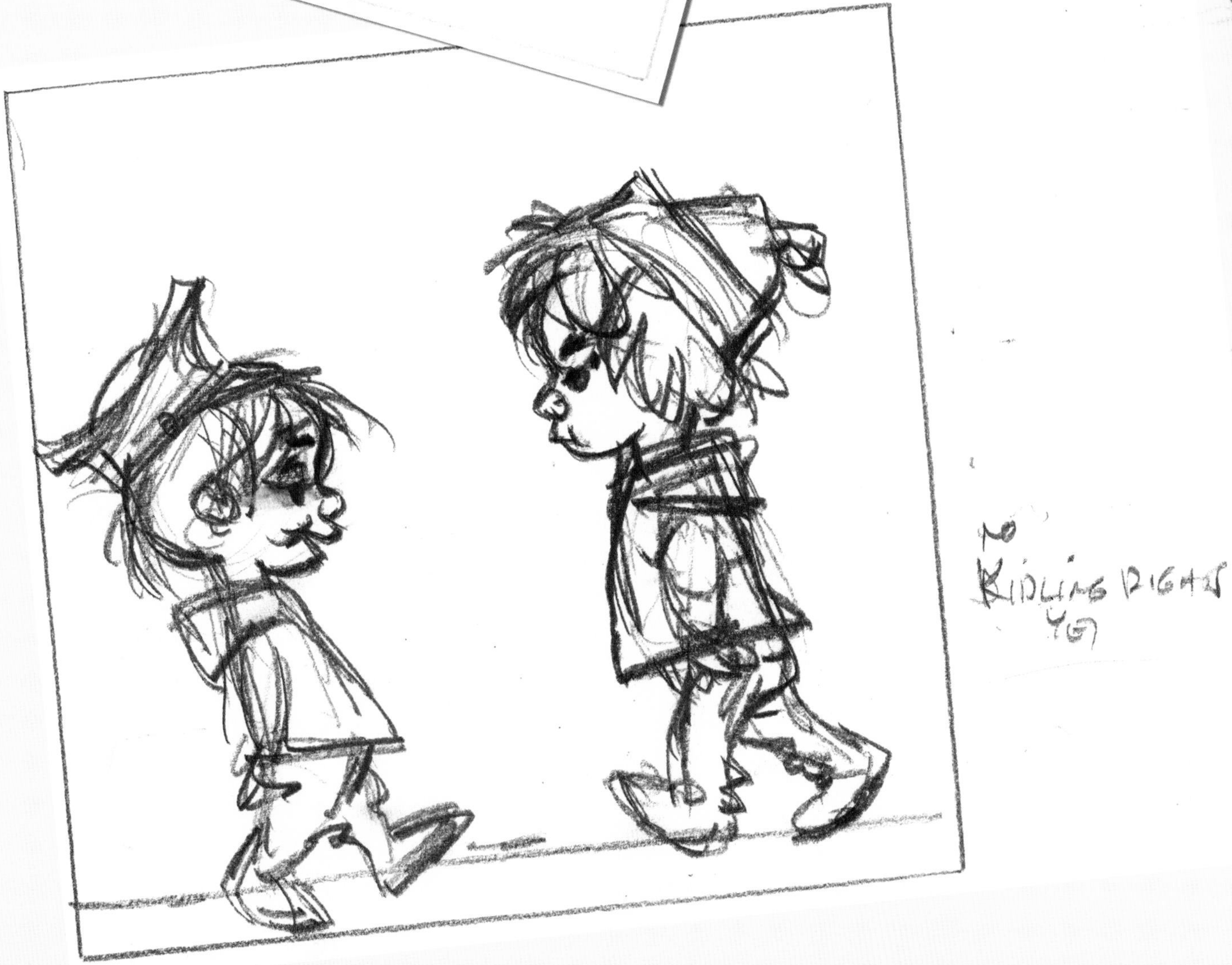

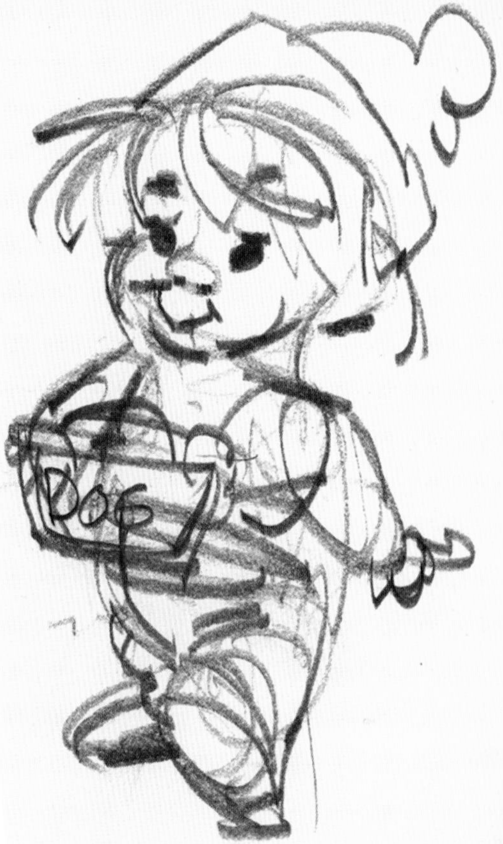
DOG

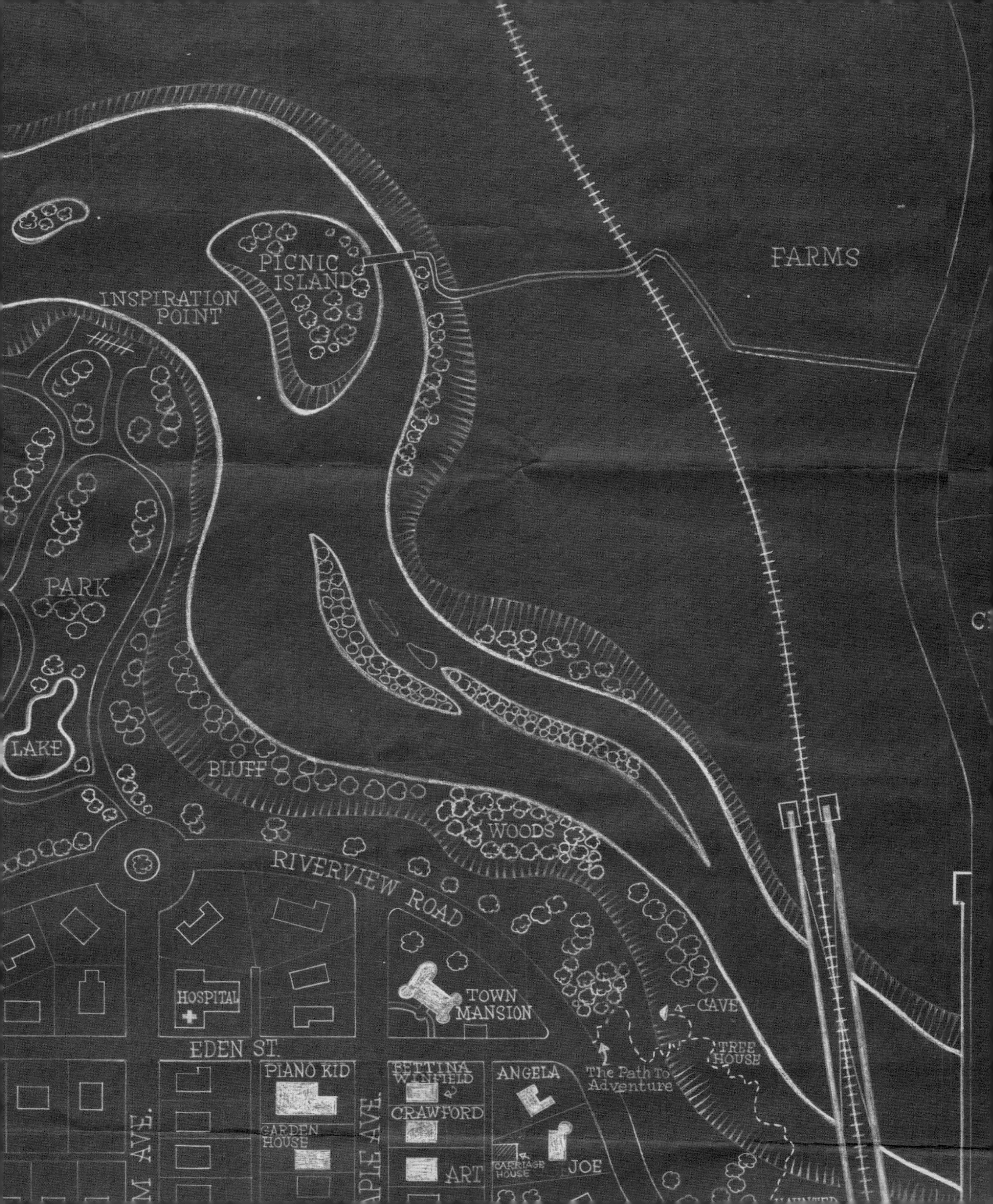
FARMS
PICNIC ISLAND
INSPIRATION POINT
PARK
LAKE
BLUFF
WOODS
RIVERVIEW ROAD
HOSPITAL
TOWN MANSION
CAVE
TREE HOUSE
The Path To Adventure
EDEN ST.
PIANO KID
BETTINA WINFIELD
ANGELA
CRAWFORD
GARDEN HOUSE
ART
CARRIAGE HOUSE
JOE

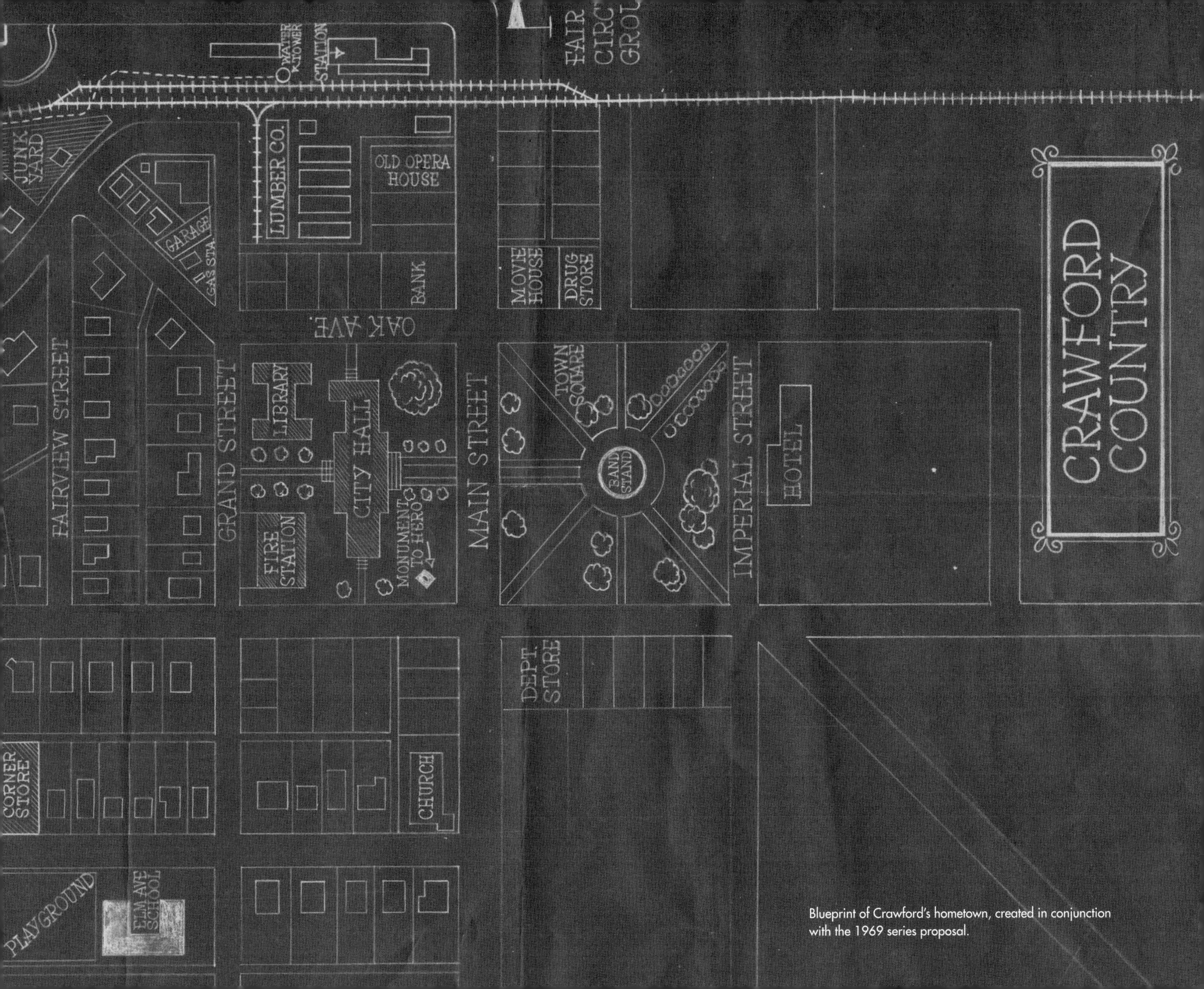
CRAWFORD COUNTRY
WATER TOWER
STATION
JUNK YARD
LUMBER CO.
OLD OPERA HOUSE
GARAGE
GAS STA
BANK
MOVIE HOUSE
DRUG STORE
OAK AVE.
FAIRVIEW STREET
GRAND STREET
LIBRARY
CITY HALL
FIRE STATION
MONUMENT TO HERO
MAIN STREET
TOWN SQUARE
BAND STAND
IMPERIAL STREET
HOTEL
DEPT. STORE
CORNER STORE
CHURCH
PLAYGROUND
ELM AVE SCHOOL

Blueprint of Crawford's hometown, created in conjunction with the 1969 series proposal.

the newspaper strip

Editing a collection of newspaper comics is in one way fairly straightforward: we organize the strips in the order in which they were originally published. *Crawford*, however, presents a unique challenge, in that there are several anomalies in the publication dates. The strip's first week offers a good example—we are introduced to Crawford and Morgan while the gags revolve around Morgan's deliberate inability to remember Crawford's name. The first four dated dailies (January 9-12) follow suit, but the fifth and sixth dailies (January 13-14) are separate throwaway gags. From Chuck Jones's sketches and preliminary roughs we know that the unpublished December 20, 1977 strip and the published February 6, 1978 were originally planned to be part of that first week, as was an unpublished Sunday.

Another example is the Sunday published on February 12, which is the conclusion to a week-long daily sequence about the Supreme Court that wasn't published until the week of April 10…two months later! A third example is when Morgan talks with S.I. Hawaii Kawa in the February 25 daily…yet more than nine weeks afterward, in the May 8 installment, Crawford introduces S.I. to Morgan as the "new kid on the block."

What happened? Why were so many strips printed out of order?

We don't know, but it's likely that the chaos caused by the delay in the series' premiere was a contributing factor. Jones had to throw out holiday strips and other early sequences to accommodate the January 1978 launch. He was playing catch-up before the first strip was published. *Crawford* editor Don Michel also notes that Jones was originating more ideas than he had room for in the confines of a daily strip and tried introducing more characters than he had time to develop.

We know from Jones's notes that he made elaborate thematic plans for the series. His notations and numbering system are guides to his intent, but a greater guide—and one that trumps any other—is his dating of the strips for publication. We have therefore used his notes and the many preliminary drawings and gags to correct the order of only the most obvious errors in the original publication dates; it's not our job to story-edit the series thirty-five years after the fact. Since part of the *Crawford* saga is that the strip did not succeed, it's important to see the series as it was published. We have added and subtracted strips when necessary; some weeks, therefore, will have seven dailies, some five. We've also run Jones's preliminaries on pages contiguous to the printed versions. This keeps the material together and allows readers to easily compare them. We have done the same in the case of alternate versions.

Could the dating confusion have contributed to the series' early demise? It's possible. It's also possible that producing a syndicated strip was not as forthright and easy as Chuck originally thought. Regardless, these strips provide a great insight to the creative process of one of our most treasured cartoonists.

—Dean Mullaney

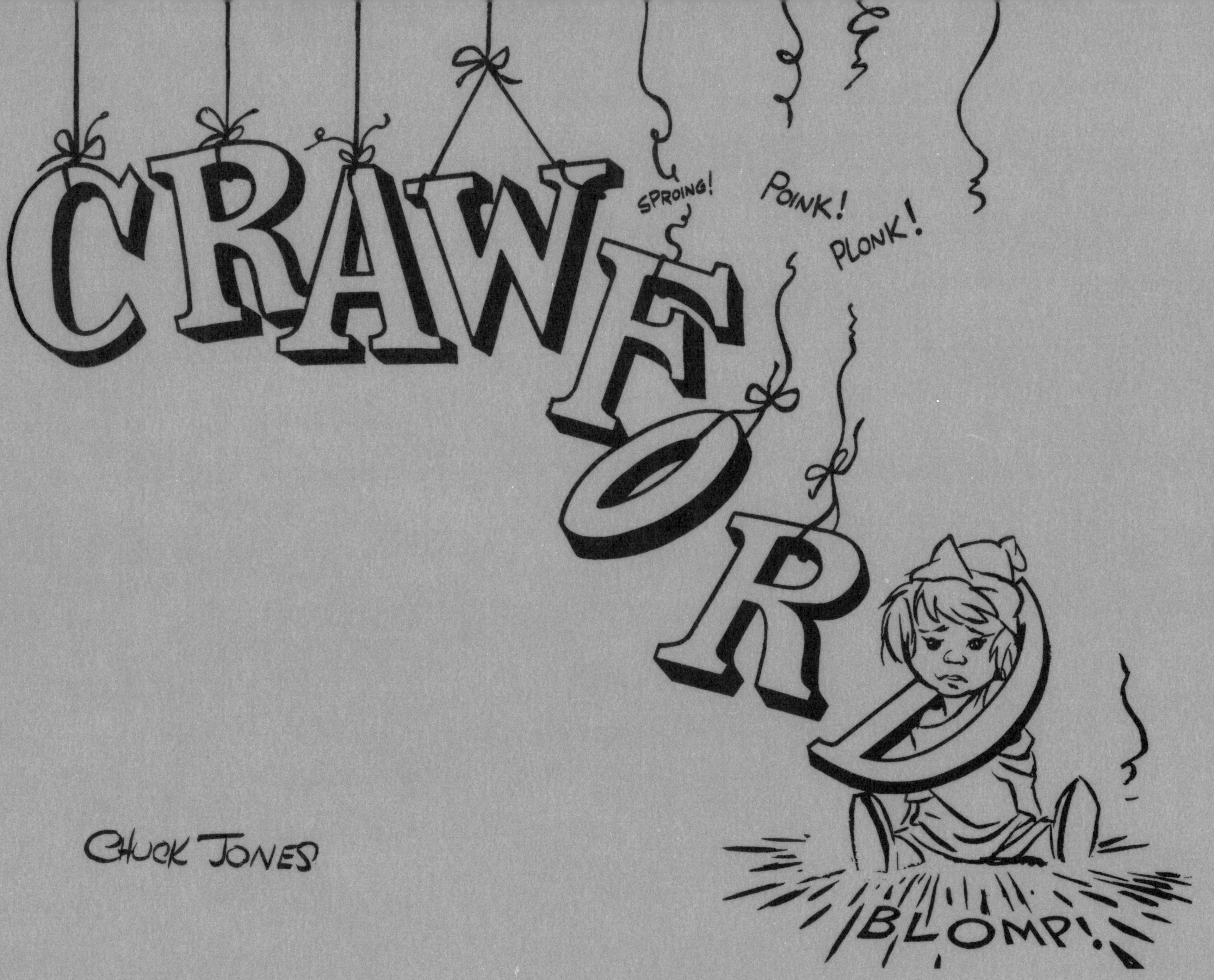
CRAWFORD
SPROING!
POINK!
PLONK!
BLOMP!

CHUCK JONES

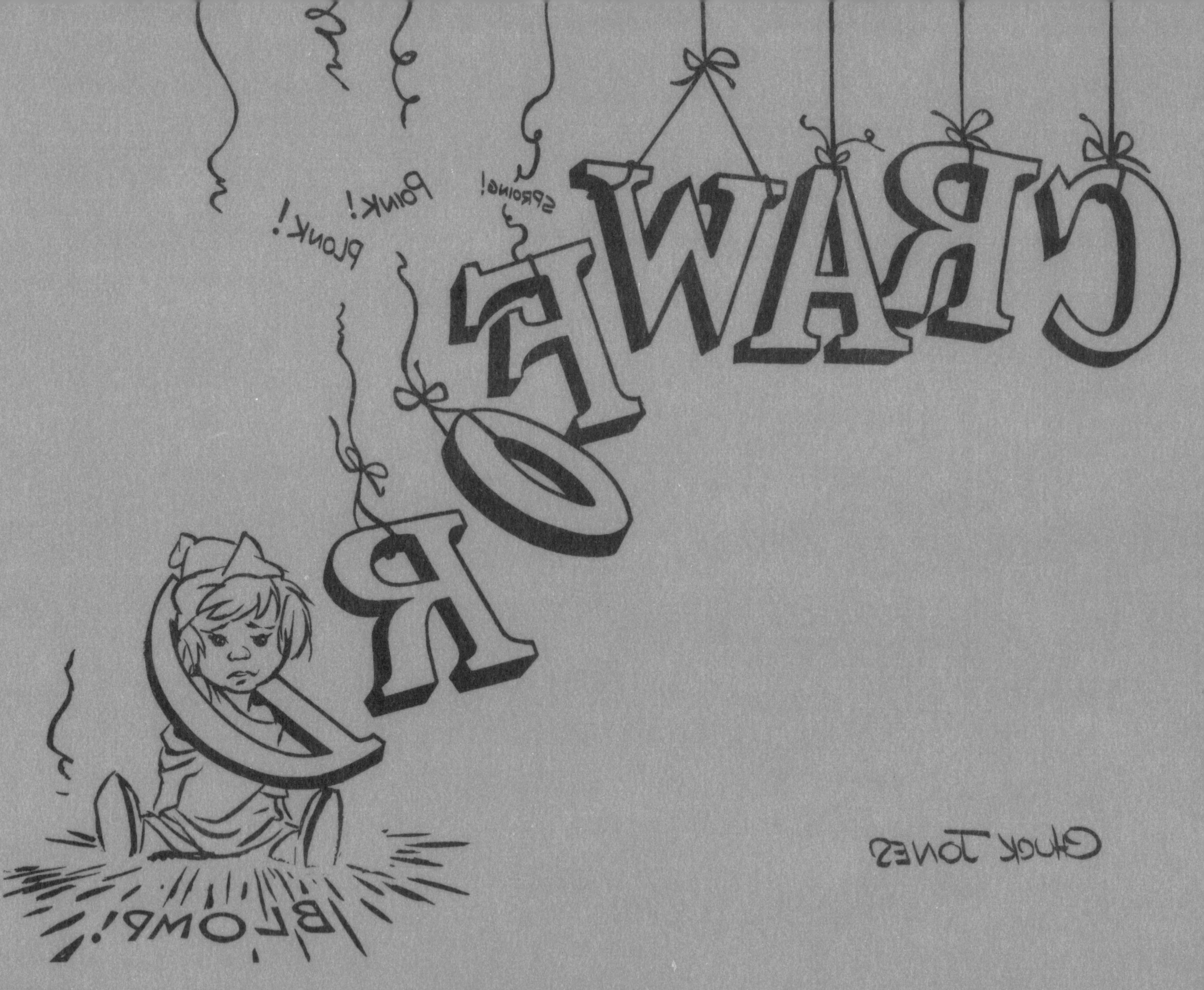

CRAWFORD
SPROING!
POINK!
PLONK!
BLOMP!
Chuck Jones

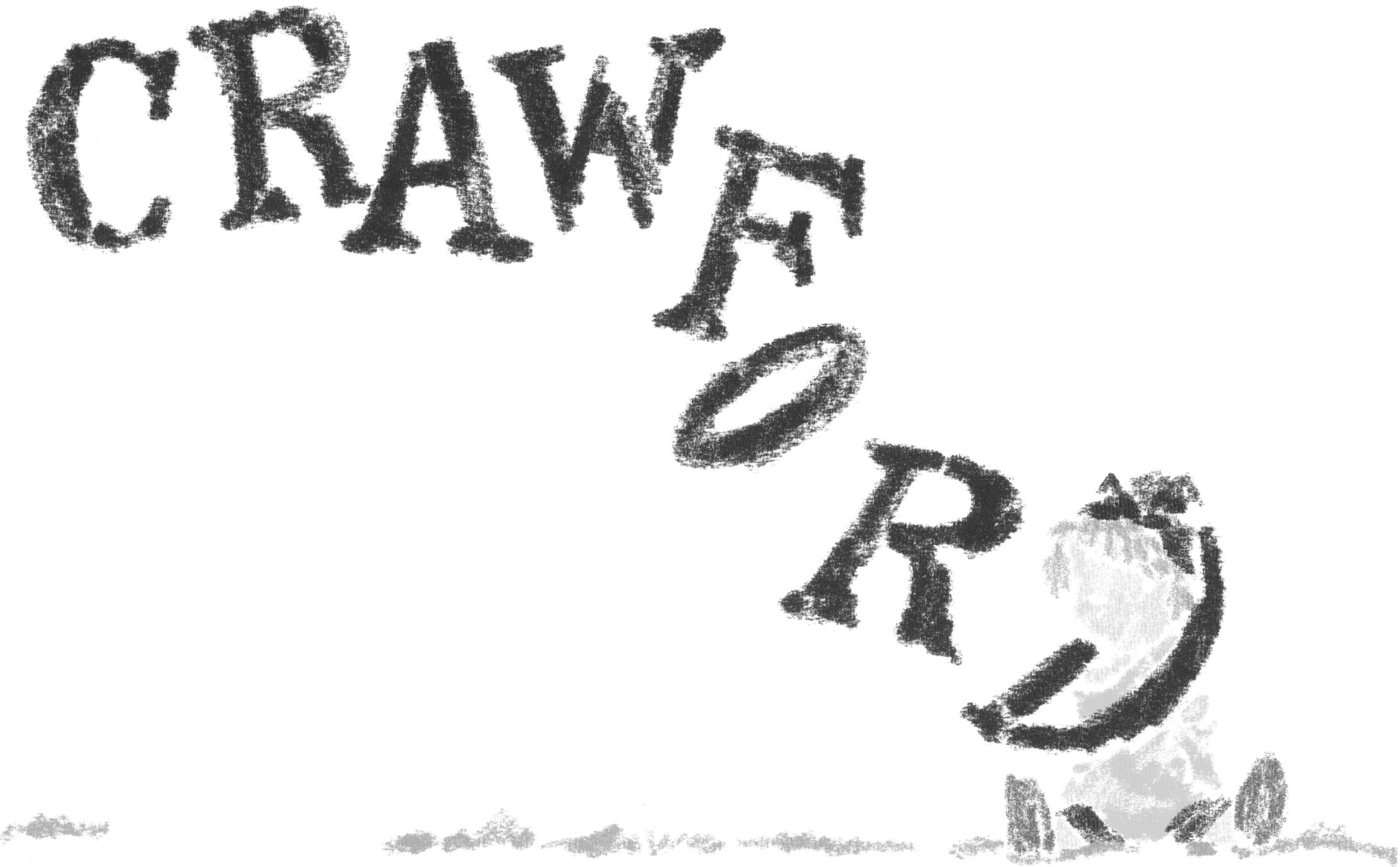
CRAWFORD

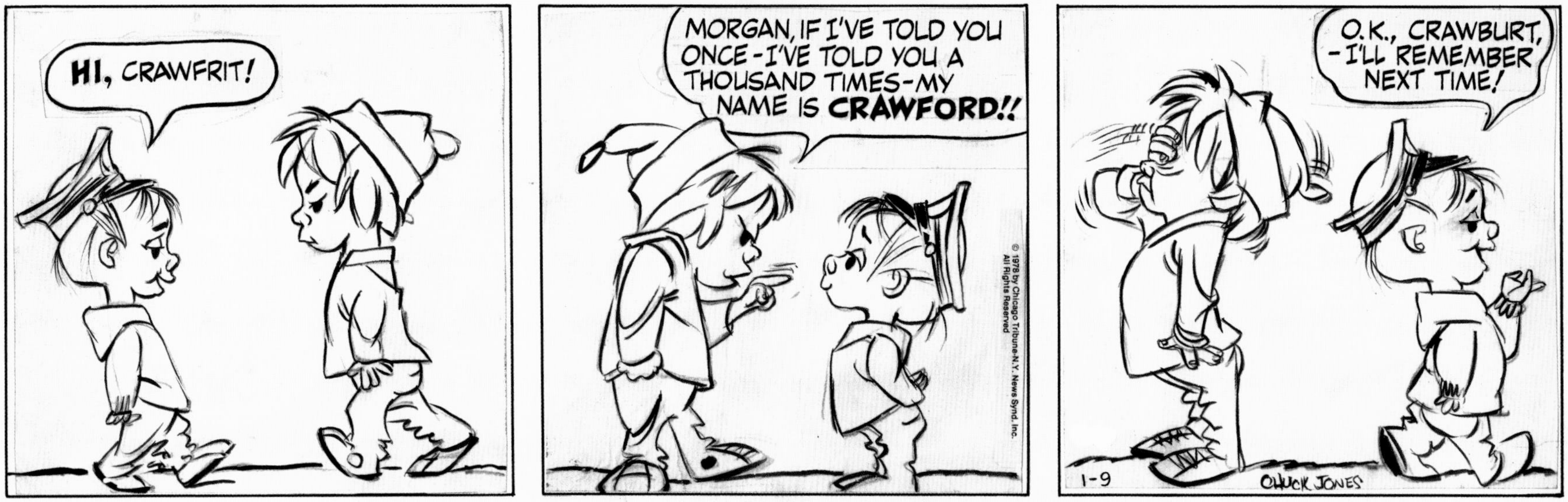
HI, CRAWFRIT!
MORGAN, IF I'VE TOLD YOU ONCE - I'VE TOLD YOU A THOUSAND TIMES - MY NAME IS **CRAWFORD!!**
© 1978 by Chicago Tribune-N.Y. News Synd. Inc.
All Rights Reserved
O.K., CRAWBURT, - I'LL REMEMBER NEXT TIME!
1-9
CHUCK JONES

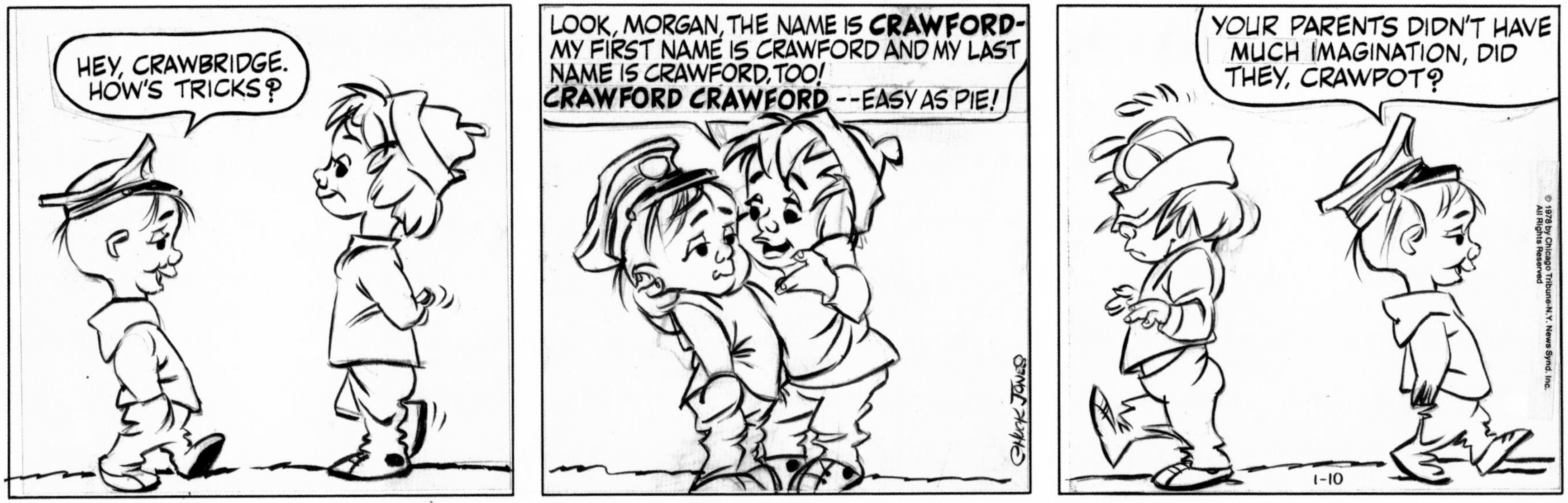
HEY, CRAWBRIDGE. HOW'S TRICKS?
LOOK, MORGAN, THE NAME IS **CRAWFORD** - MY FIRST NAME IS CRAWFORD AND MY LAST NAME IS CRAWFORD, TOO!
CRAWFORD CRAWFORD - - EASY AS PIE!
CHUCK JONES
YOUR PARENTS DIDN'T HAVE MUCH IMAGINATION, DID THEY, CRAWPOT?
© 1978 by Chicago Tribune-N.Y. News Synd. Inc.
All Rights Reserved
1-10

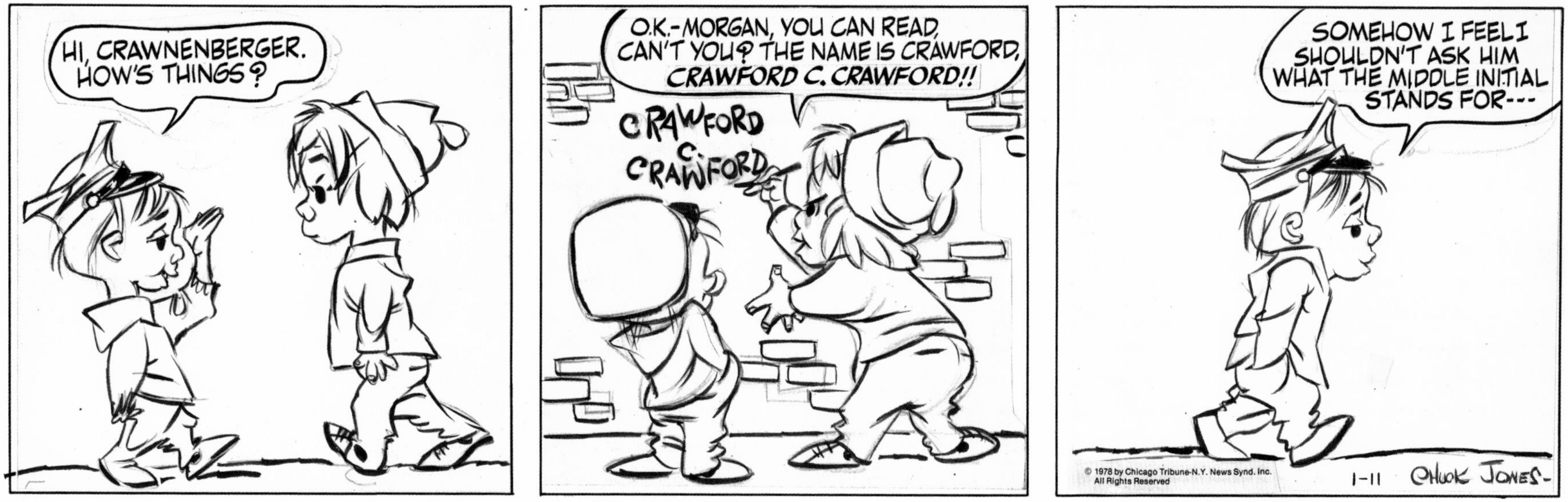
HI, CRAWNENBERGER. HOW'S THINGS?
O.K.-MORGAN, YOU CAN READ, CAN'T YOU? THE NAME IS CRAWFORD, CRAWFORD C. CRAWFORD!!
CRAWFORD C. CRAWFORD
SOMEHOW I FEEL I SHOULDN'T ASK HIM WHAT THE MIDDLE INITIAL STANDS FOR---
© 1978 by Chicago Tribune-N.Y. News Synd. Inc. All Rights Reserved
1-11
CHUCK JONES

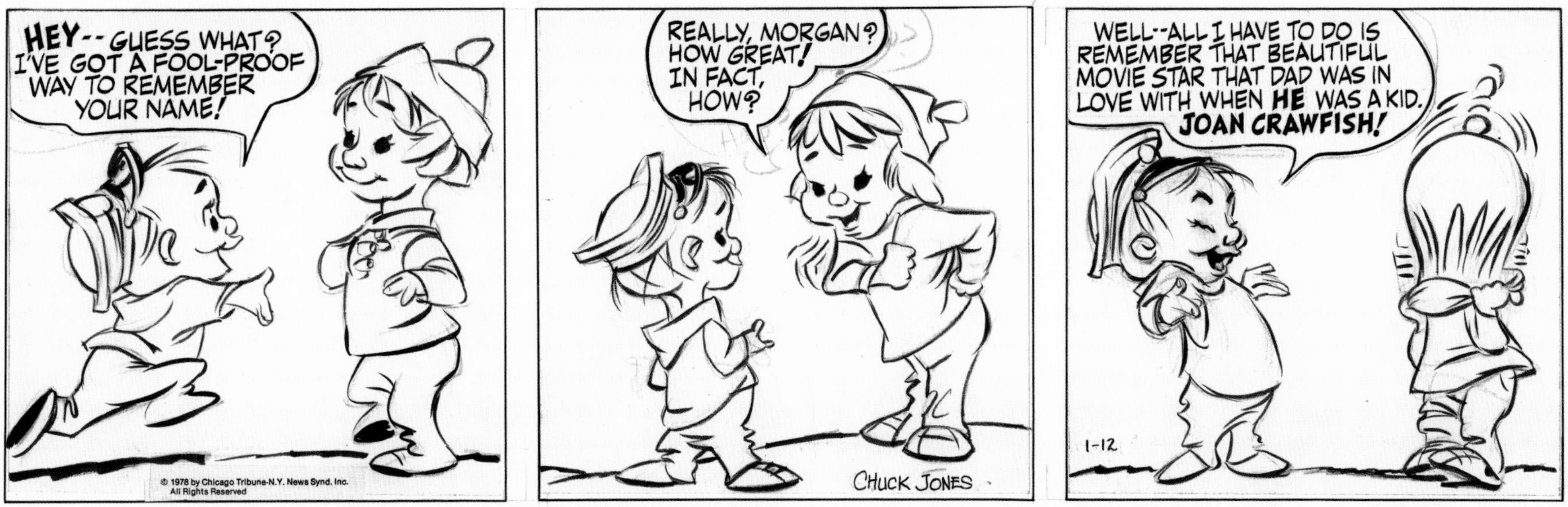
HEY-- GUESS WHAT? I'VE GOT A FOOL-PROOF WAY TO REMEMBER YOUR NAME!
© 1978 by Chicago Tribune-N.Y. News Synd. Inc. All Rights Reserved
REALLY, MORGAN? HOW GREAT! IN FACT, HOW?
CHUCK JONES
WELL--ALL I HAVE TO DO IS REMEMBER THAT BEAUTIFUL MOVIE STAR THAT DAD WAS IN LOVE WITH WHEN HE WAS A KID. JOAN CRAWFISH!
1-12

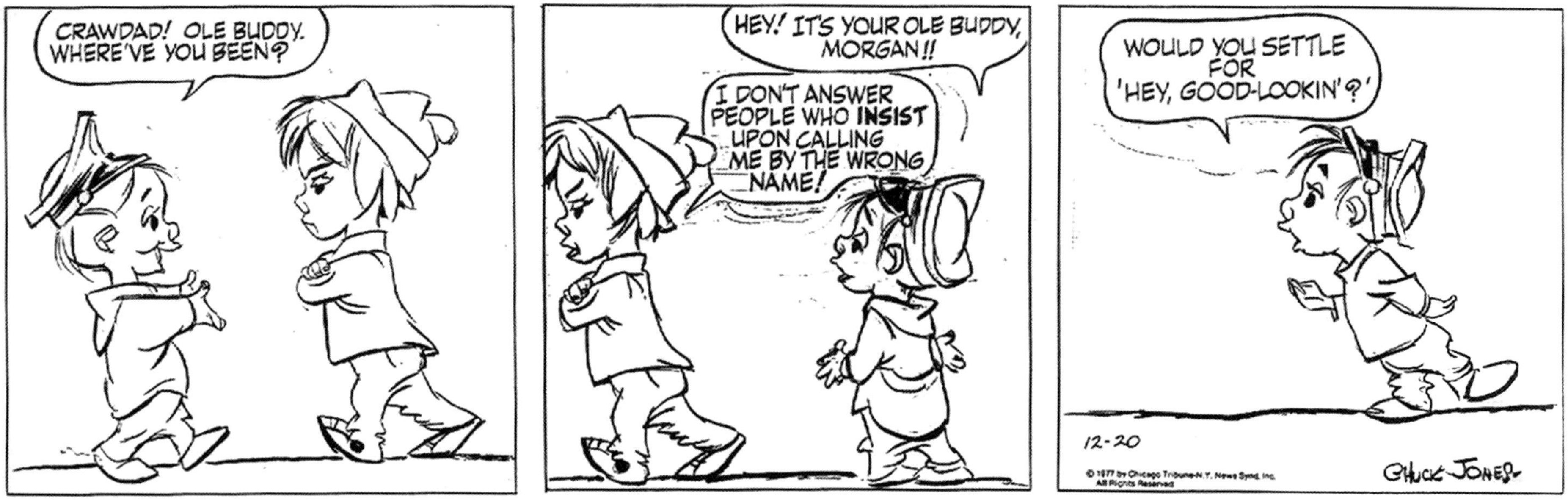
CRAWDAD! OLE BUDDY. WHERE'VE YOU BEEN?
HEY! IT'S YOUR OLE BUDDY, MORGAN!!
I DON'T ANSWER PEOPLE WHO INSIST UPON CALLING ME BY THE WRONG NAME!
WOULD YOU SETTLE FOR 'HEY, GOOD-LOOKIN'?'
12-20

Unpublished daily.

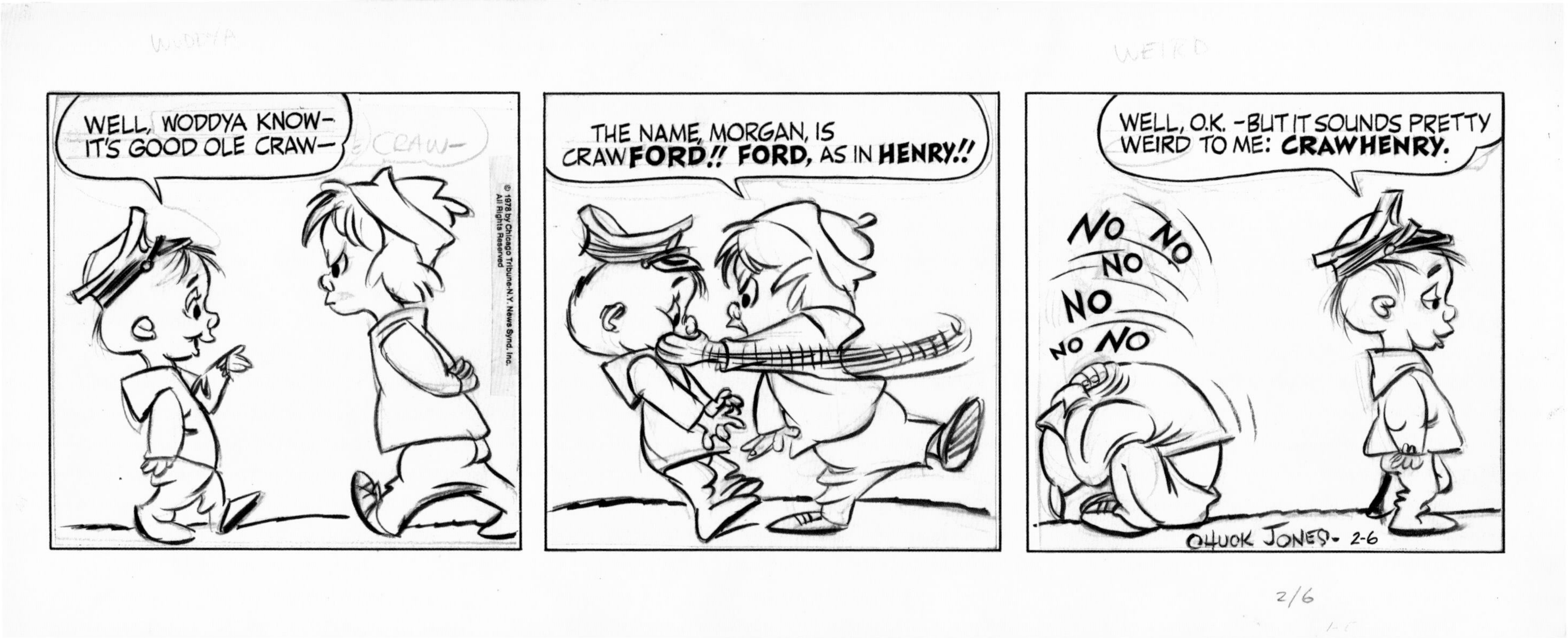
WELL, WODDYA KNOW– IT'S GOOD OLE CRAW–
THE NAME, MORGAN, IS CRAWFORD!! FORD, AS IN HENRY!!
NO NO NO NO NO NO
WELL, O.K. –BUT IT SOUNDS PRETTY WEIRD TO ME: CRAWHENRY.

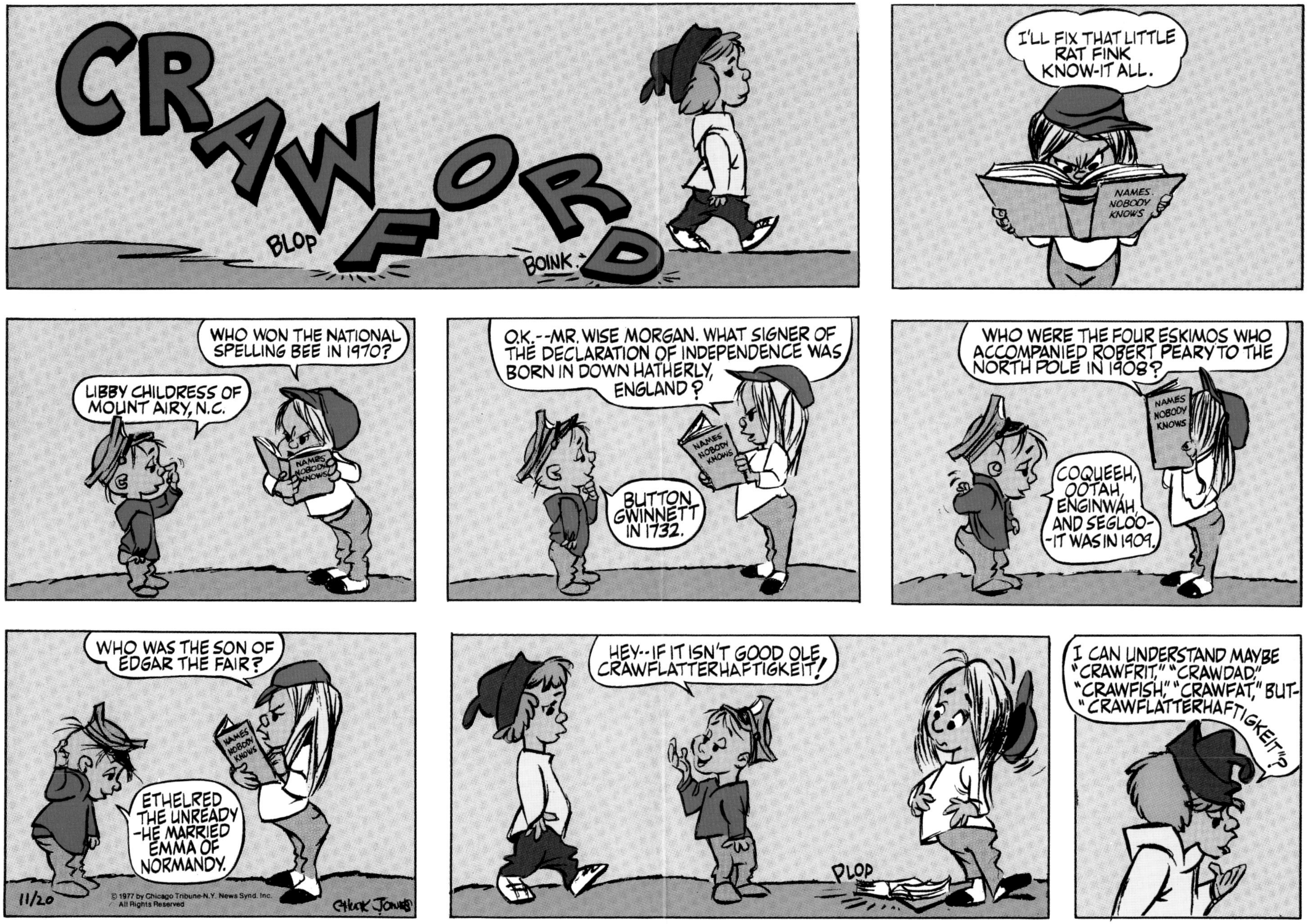
CRAWFORD
BLOP
BOINK
I'LL FIX THAT LITTLE RAT FINK KNOW-IT ALL.
NAMES NOBODY KNOWS
WHO WON THE NATIONAL SPELLING BEE IN 1970?
LIBBY CHILDRESS OF MOUNT AIRY, N.C.
O.K.--MR. WISE MORGAN. WHAT SIGNER OF THE DECLARATION OF INDEPENDENCE WAS BORN IN DOWN HATHERLY, ENGLAND?
BUTTON GWINNETT IN 1732.
WHO WERE THE FOUR ESKIMOS WHO ACCOMPANIED ROBERT PEARY TO THE NORTH POLE IN 1908?
COQUEEH, OOTAH, ENGINWAH, AND SEGLOO--IT WAS IN 1909.
WHO WAS THE SON OF EDGAR THE FAIR?
ETHELRED THE UNREADY -HE MARRIED EMMA OF NORMANDY.
11/20
© 1977 by Chicago Tribune-N.Y. News Synd. Inc. All Rights Reserved
Chuck Jones
HEY--IF IT ISN'T GOOD OLE CRAWFLATTERHAFTIGKEIT!
PLOP
I CAN UNDERSTAND MAYBE "CRAWFRIT," "CRAWDAD," "CRAWFISH," "CRAWFAT," BUT-"CRAWFLATTERHAFTIGKEIT"?

Unpublished Sunday.

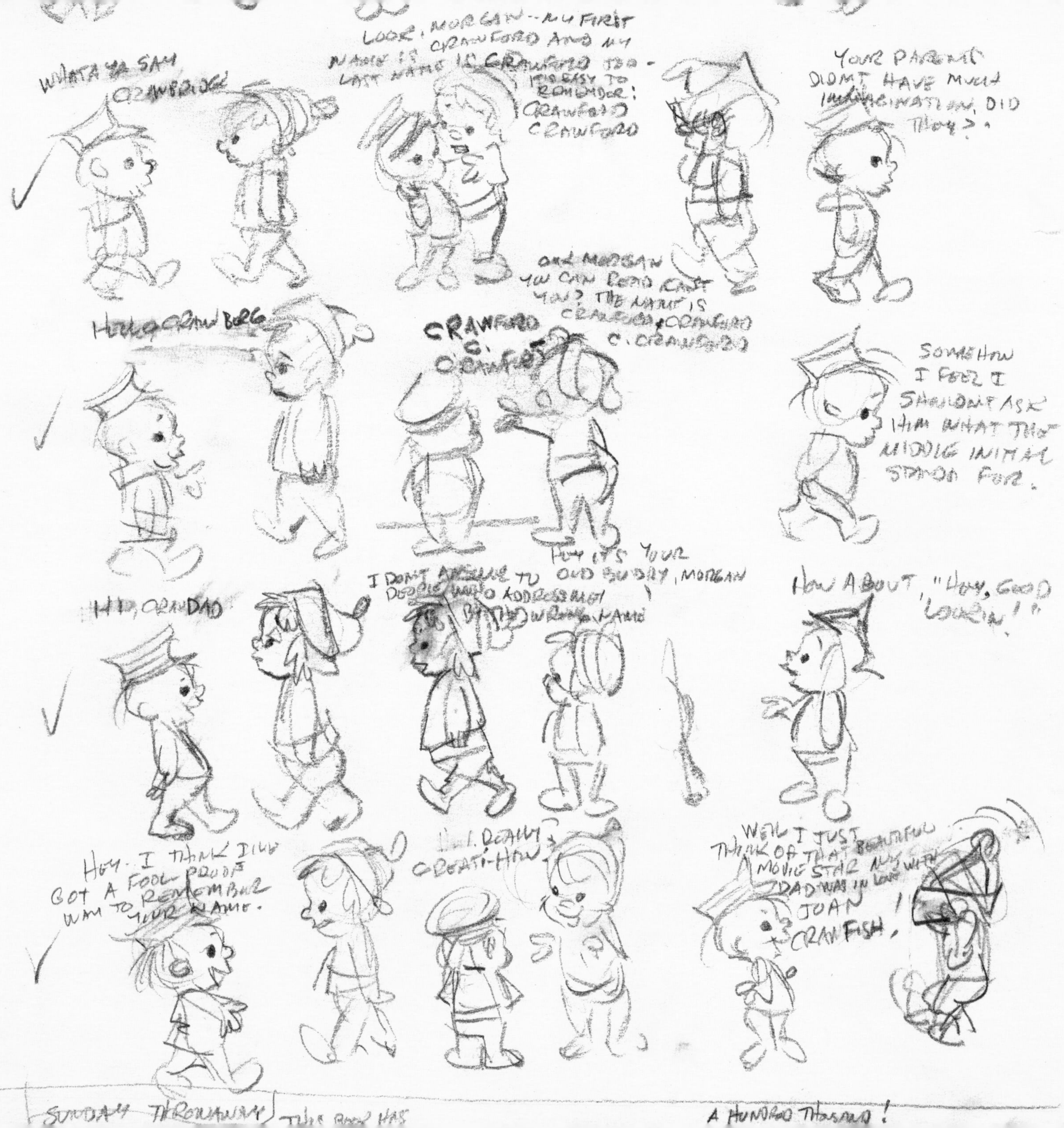
WHATA YA SAY CRAWBRIDGE
LOOK, MORGAN--MY FIRST NAME IS CRAWFORD AND MY LAST NAME IS CRAWFORD TOO - IT'S EASY TO REMEMBER! CRAWFORD CRAWFORD
YOUR PARENTS DIDN'T HAVE MUCH IMAGINATION, DID THEY?
HELLO CRAWBERG
CRAWFORD C. CRAWFORD
OH, MORGAN YOU CAN READ CAN'T YOU? THE NAME IS CRAWFORD C. CRAWFORD
SOMEHOW I FEEL I SHOULDN'T ASK HIM WHAT THE MIDDLE INITIAL STANDS FOR.
HI, CRANDAD
HEY IT'S YOUR OLD BUDDY, MORGAN!
HOW ABOUT, "HEY, GOOD LOOKIN'!"
HEY- I THINK I'VE GOT A FOOL PROOF WAY TO REMEMBER YOUR NAME.
WELL I JUST THINK OF THAT BEAUTIFUL MOVIE STAR MY DAD WAS IN LOVE WITH JOAN CRANFISH!
SUNDAY THROWAWAY
THIS PAGE HAS
A HUNDRED THOUSAND!

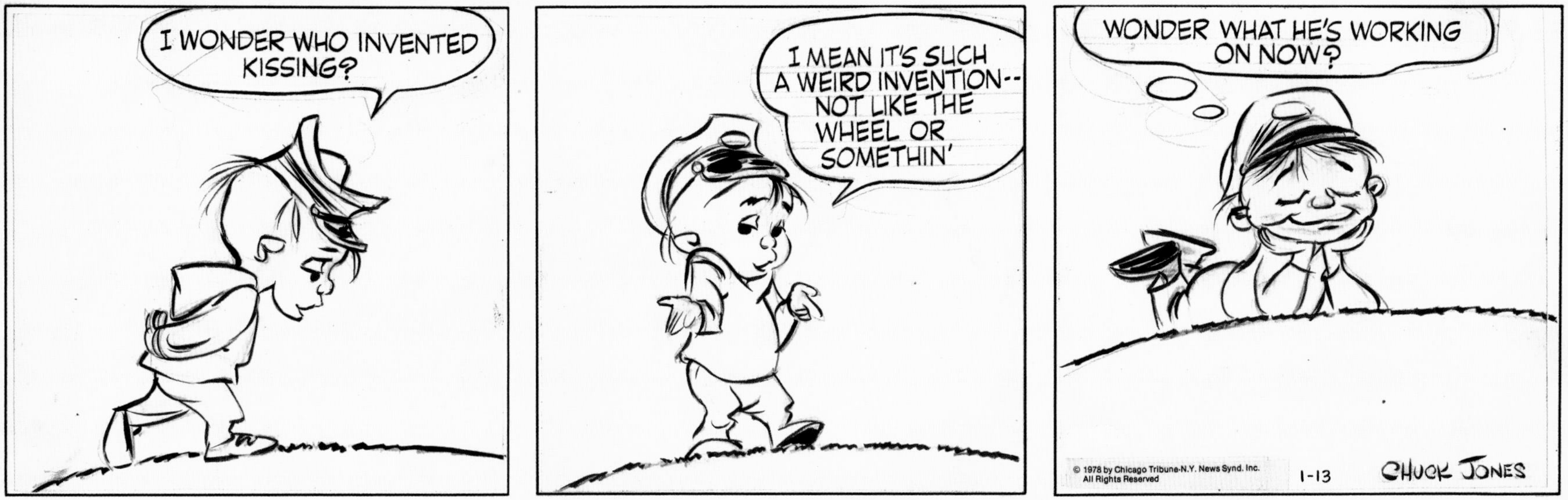
I WONDER WHO INVENTED KISSING?
I MEAN IT'S SUCH A WEIRD INVENTION-- NOT LIKE THE WHEEL OR SOMETHIN'
WONDER WHAT HE'S WORKING ON NOW?
© 1978 by Chicago Tribune-N.Y. News Synd. Inc. All Rights Reserved
1-13
CHUCK JONES

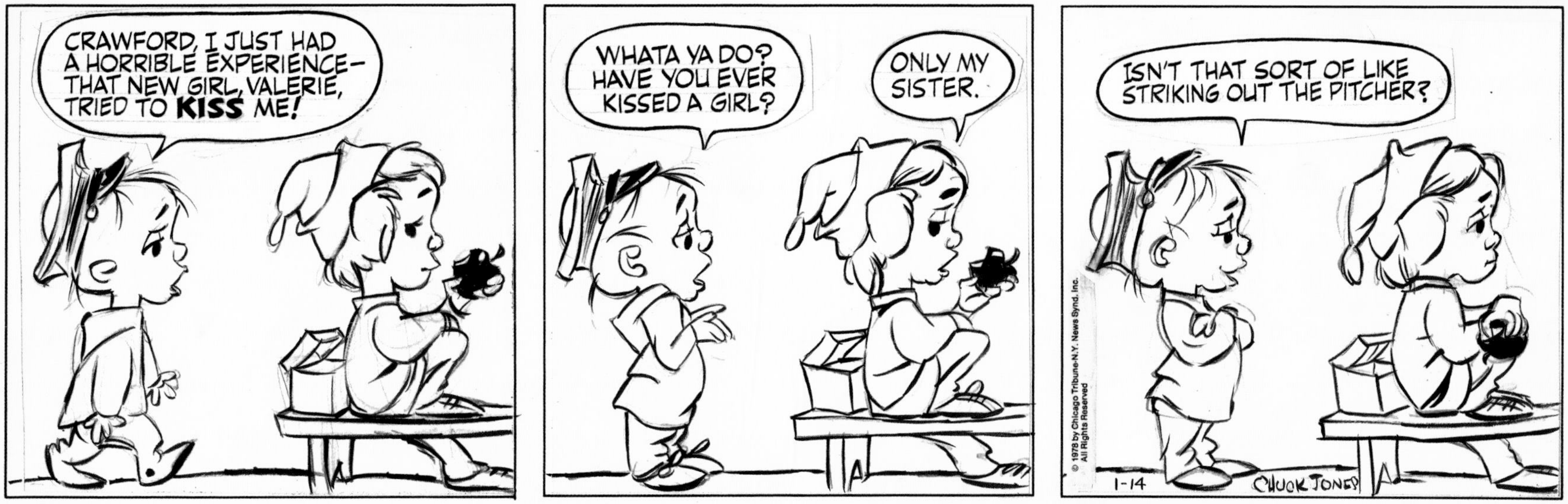
CRAWFORD, I JUST HAD A HORRIBLE EXPERIENCE- THAT NEW GIRL, VALERIE, TRIED TO **KISS** ME!
WHATA YA DO? HAVE YOU EVER KISSED A GIRL?
ONLY MY SISTER.
© 1978 by Chicago Tribune-N.Y. News Synd. Inc. All Rights Reserved
ISN'T THAT SORT OF LIKE STRIKING OUT THE PITCHER?
1-14
CHUCK JONES

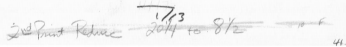

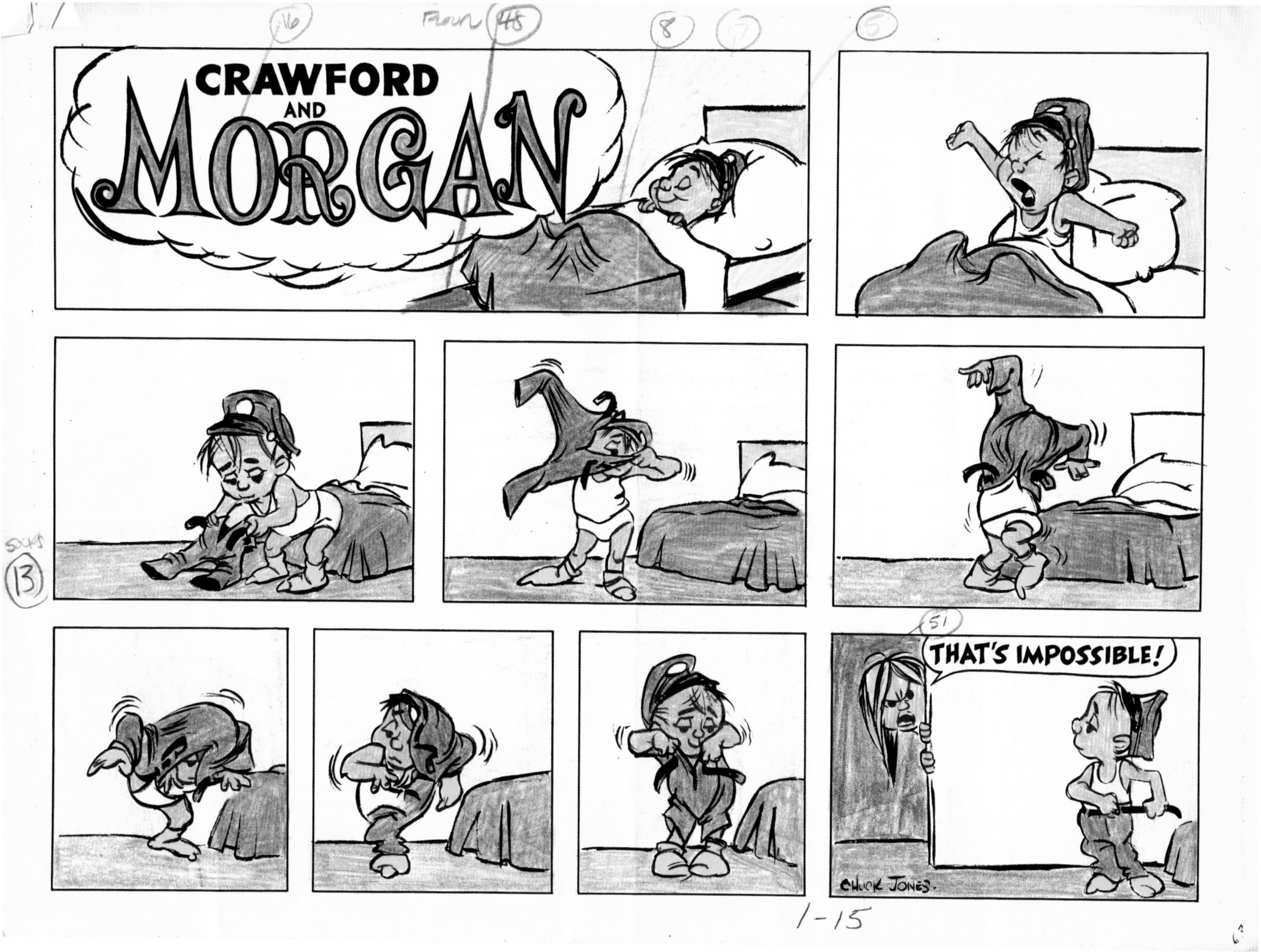
CRAWFORD
AND
MORGAN
THAT'S IMPOSSIBLE!
CHUCK JONES.
1-15

Chuck Jones's color guide for the engravers.

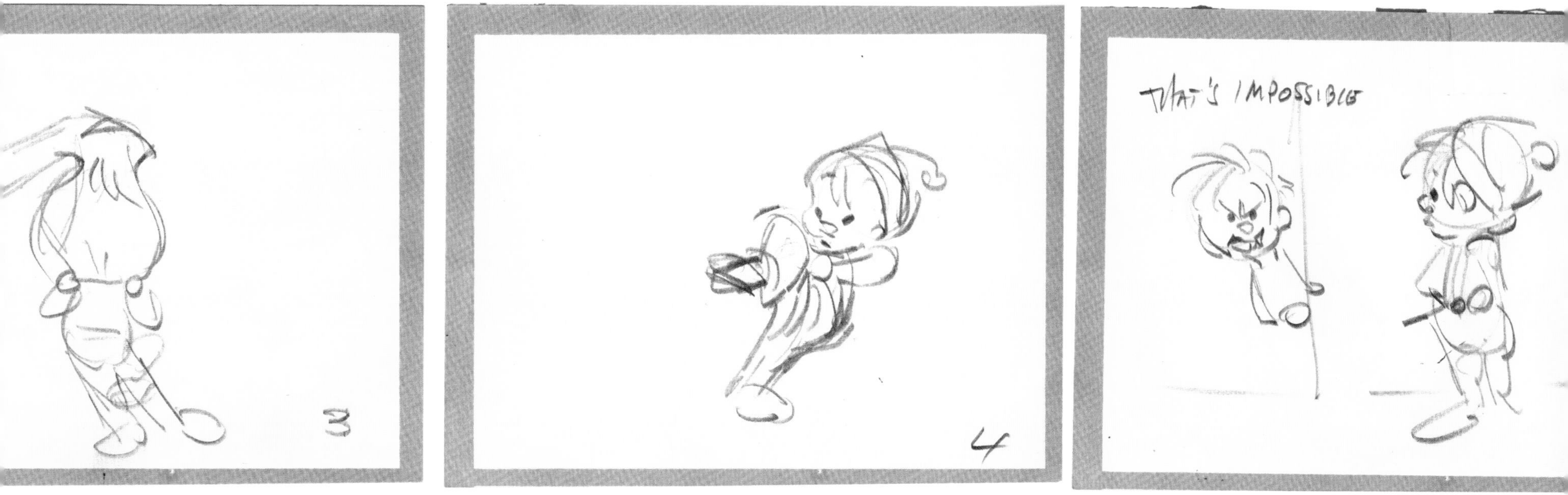
3
4
THAT'S IMPOSSIBLE

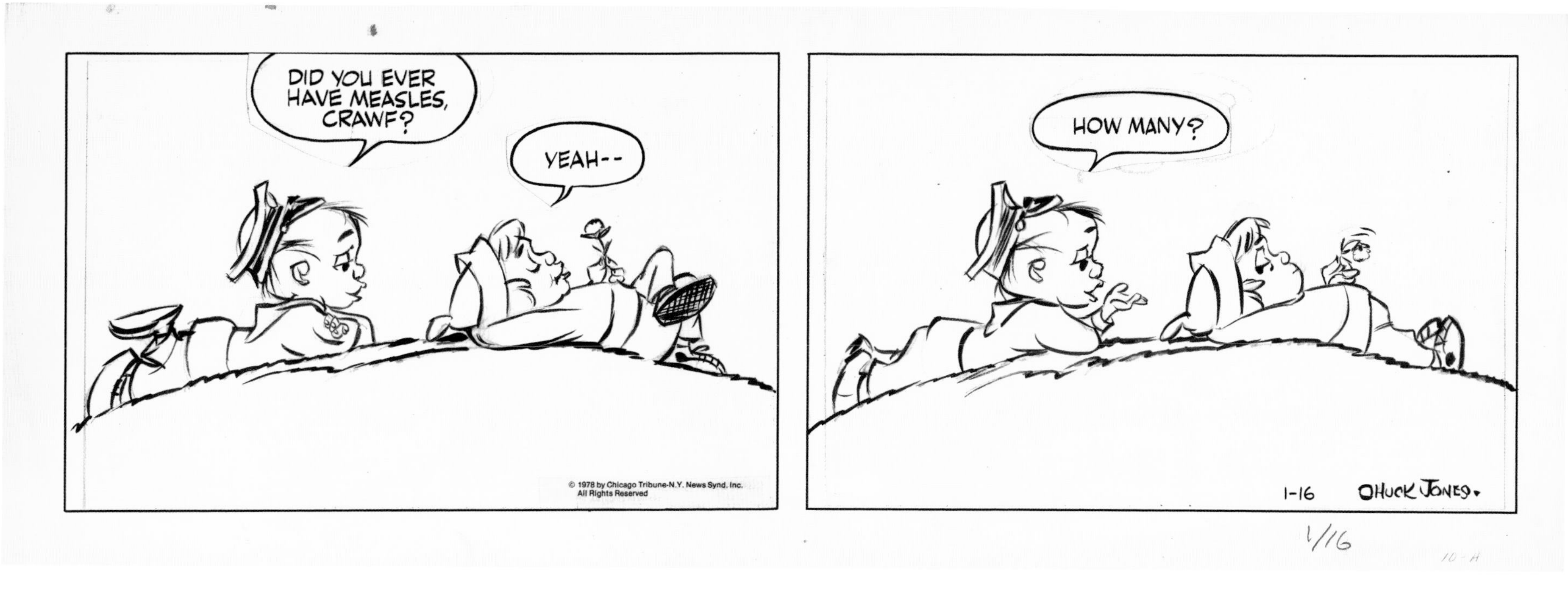
DID YOU EVER HAVE MEASLES, CRAWF?
YEAH--
© 1978 by Chicago Tribune-N.Y. News Synd. Inc. All Rights Reserved
HOW MANY?
1-16
CHUCK JONES
1/16

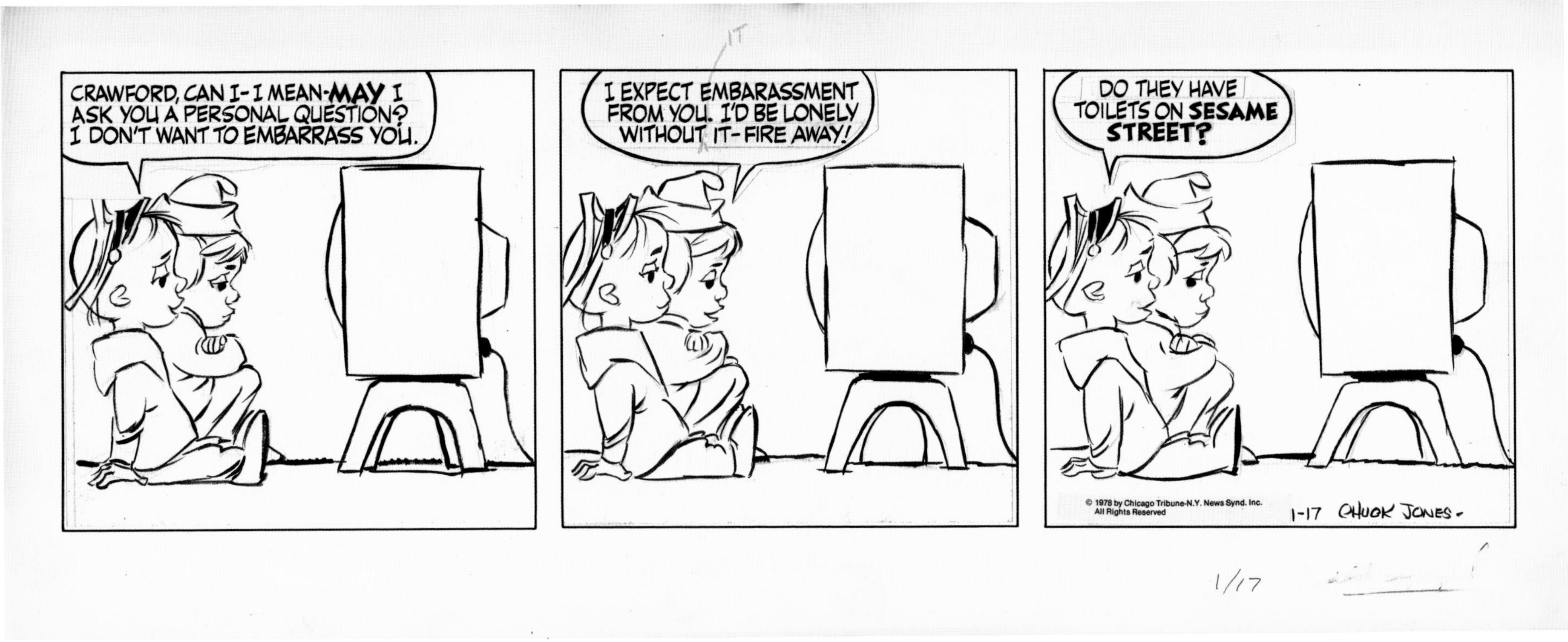
CRAWFORD, CAN I- I MEAN-MAY I ASK YOU A PERSONAL QUESTION? I DON'T WANT TO EMBARRASS YOU.
I EXPECT EMBARASSMENT FROM YOU. I'D BE LONELY WITHOUT IT- FIRE AWAY!
DO THEY HAVE TOILETS ON SESAME STREET?
© 1978 by Chicago Tribune-N.Y. News Synd. Inc. All Rights Reserved
1-17 CHUCK JONES
1/17

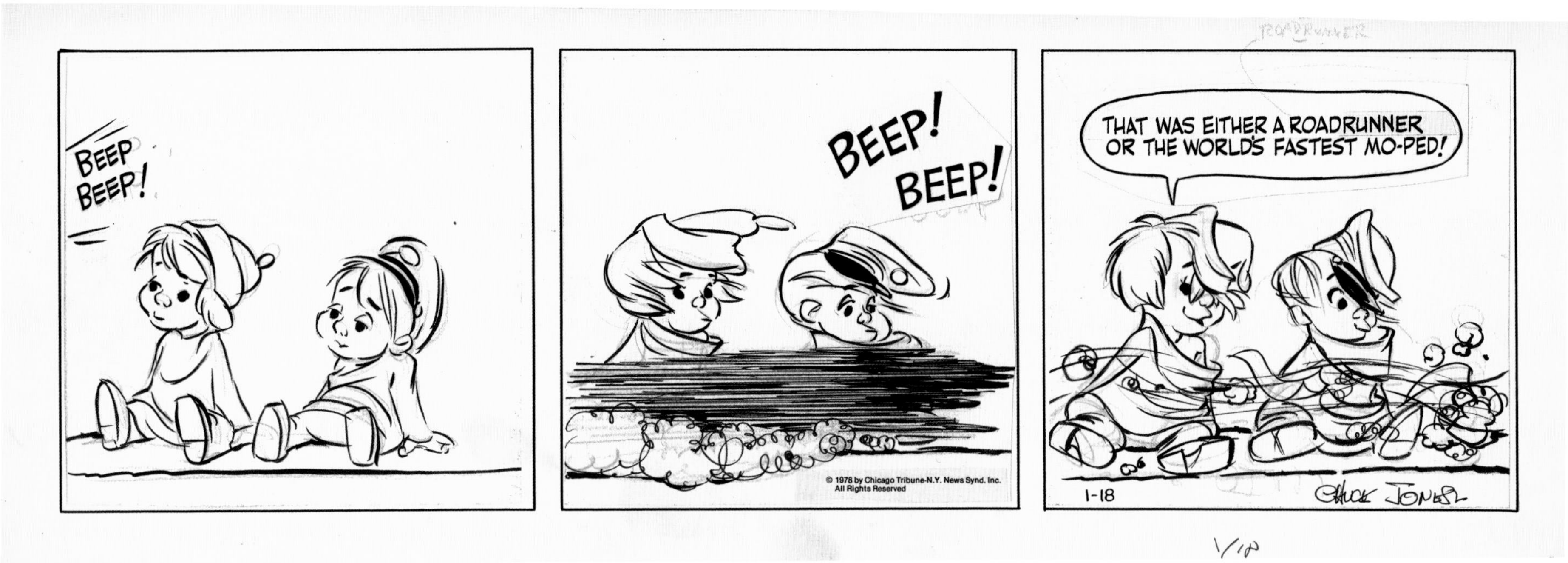
BEEP BEEP!
BEEP! BEEP!
© 1978 by Chicago Tribune-N.Y. News Synd. Inc. All Rights Reserved
THAT WAS EITHER A ROADRUNNER OR THE WORLD'S FASTEST MO-PED!
1-18 CHUCK JONES

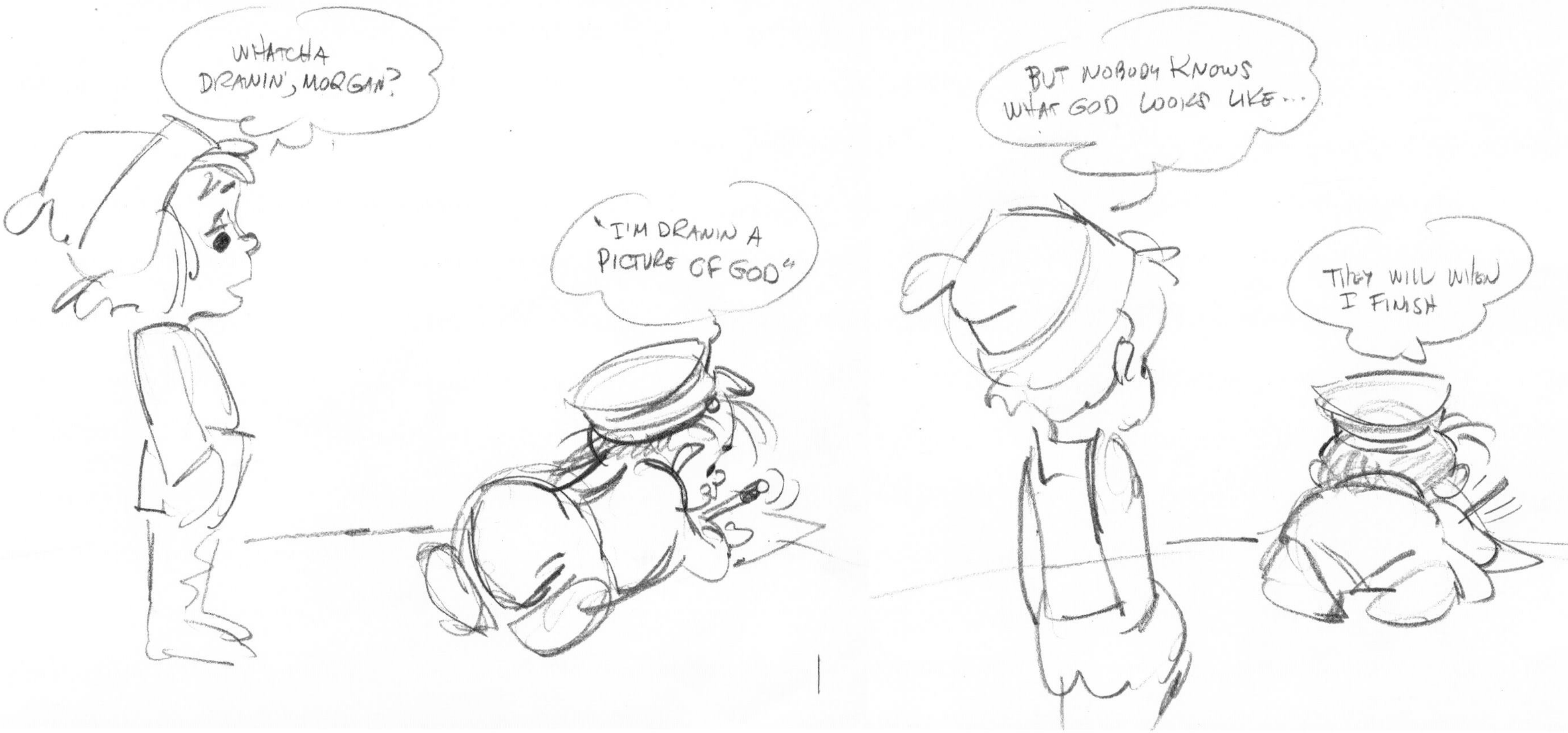
WHATCHA DRAWIN', MORGAN?
"I'M DRAWIN A PICTURE OF GOD"
BUT NOBODY KNOWS WHAT GOD LOOKS LIKE...
THEY WILL WHEN I FINISH

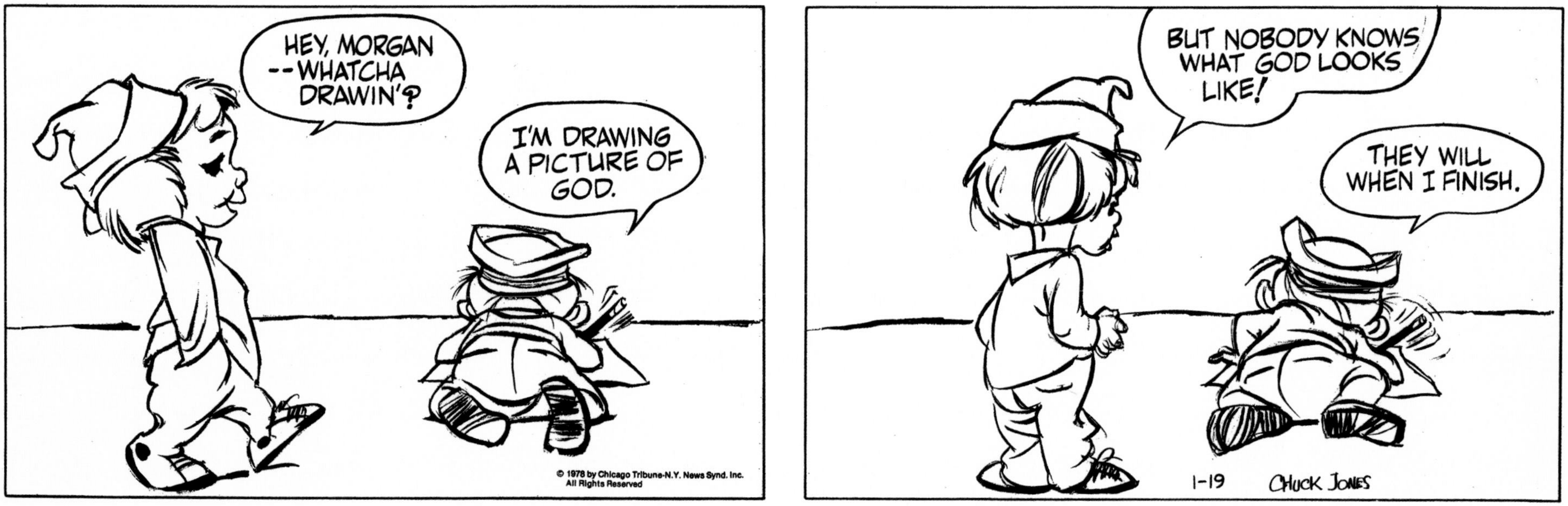
HEY, MORGAN --WHATCHA DRAWIN'?
I'M DRAWING A PICTURE OF GOD.
© 1978 by Chicago Tribune-N.Y. News Synd. Inc. All Rights Reserved
BUT NOBODY KNOWS WHAT GOD LOOKS LIKE!
THEY WILL WHEN I FINISH.
1-19
CHUCK JONES

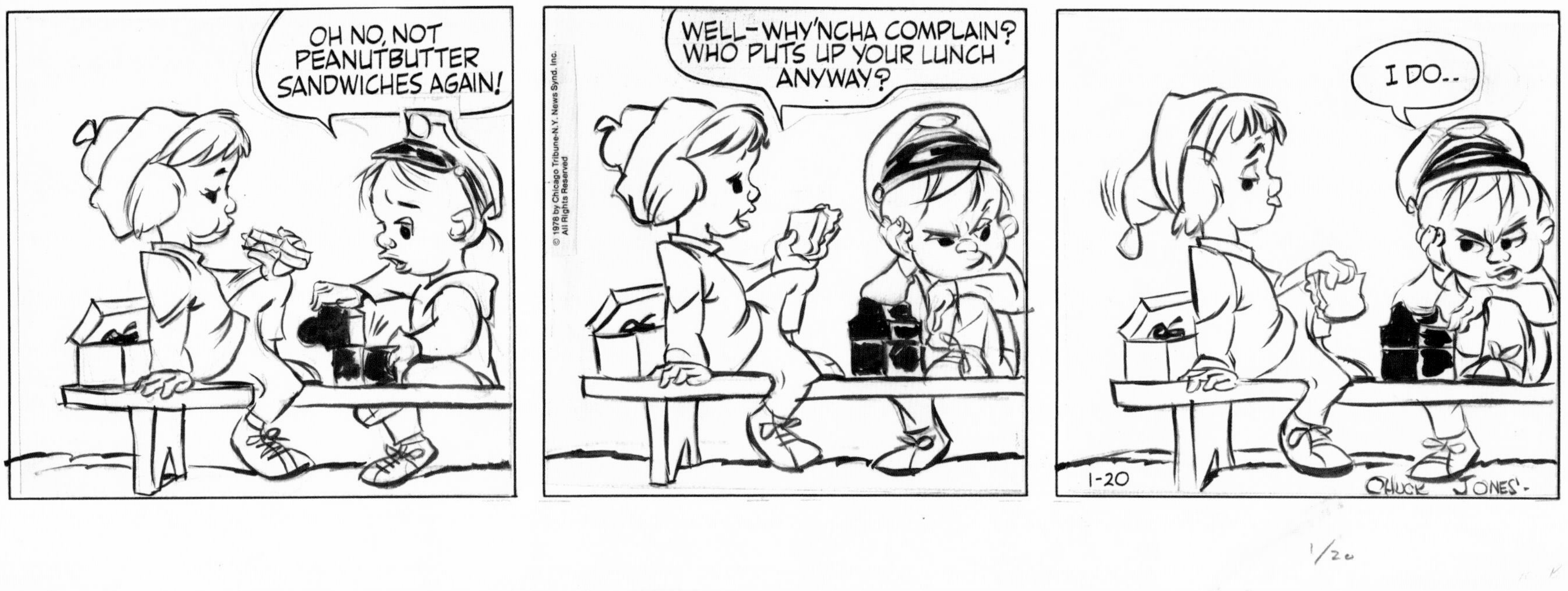
OH NO, NOT PEANUTBUTTER SANDWICHES AGAIN!
© 1978 by Chicago Tribune-N.Y. News Synd. Inc. All Rights Reserved
WELL-WHY'NCHA COMPLAIN? WHO PUTS UP YOUR LUNCH ANYWAY?
I DO..
1-20
CHUCK JONES
1/20

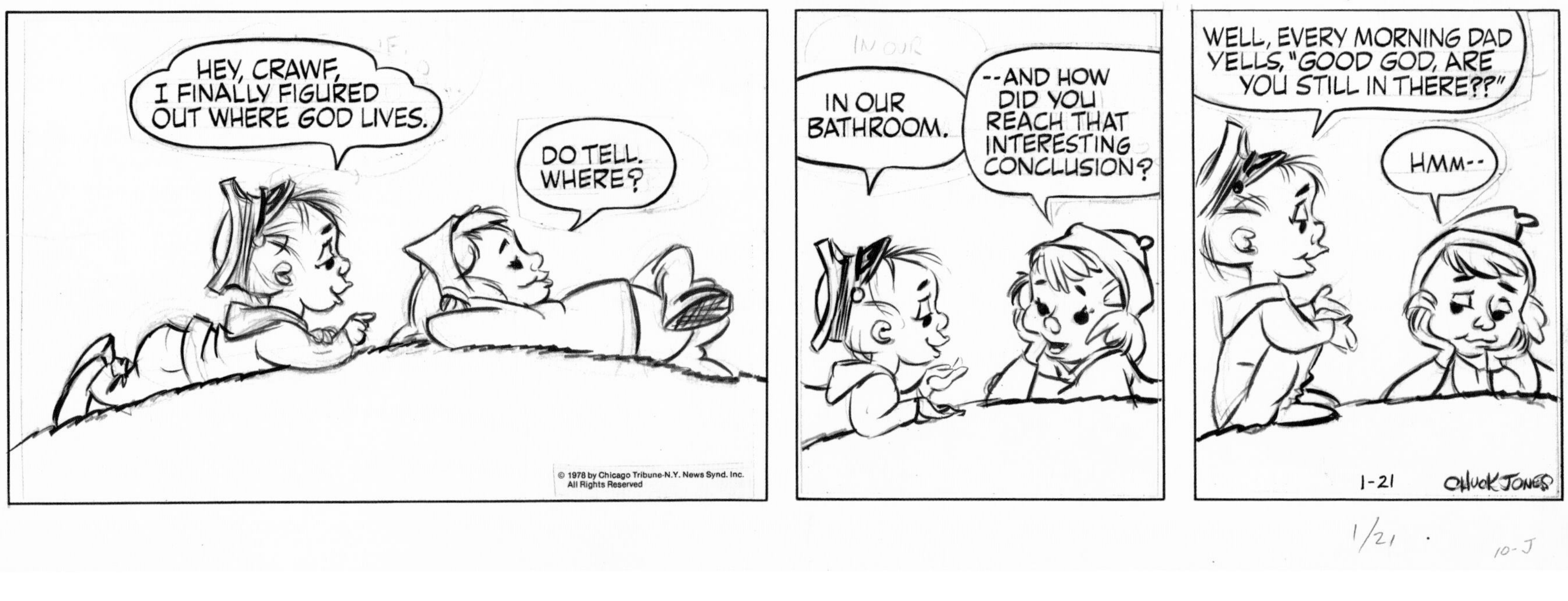
HEY, CRAWF, I FINALLY FIGURED OUT WHERE GOD LIVES.
DO TELL. WHERE?
© 1978 by Chicago Tribune-N.Y. News Synd. Inc. All Rights Reserved
IN OUR BATHROOM.
--AND HOW DID YOU REACH THAT INTERESTING CONCLUSION?
WELL, EVERY MORNING DAD YELLS, "GOOD GOD, ARE YOU STILL IN THERE??"
HMM--
1-21
CHUCK JONES
1/21

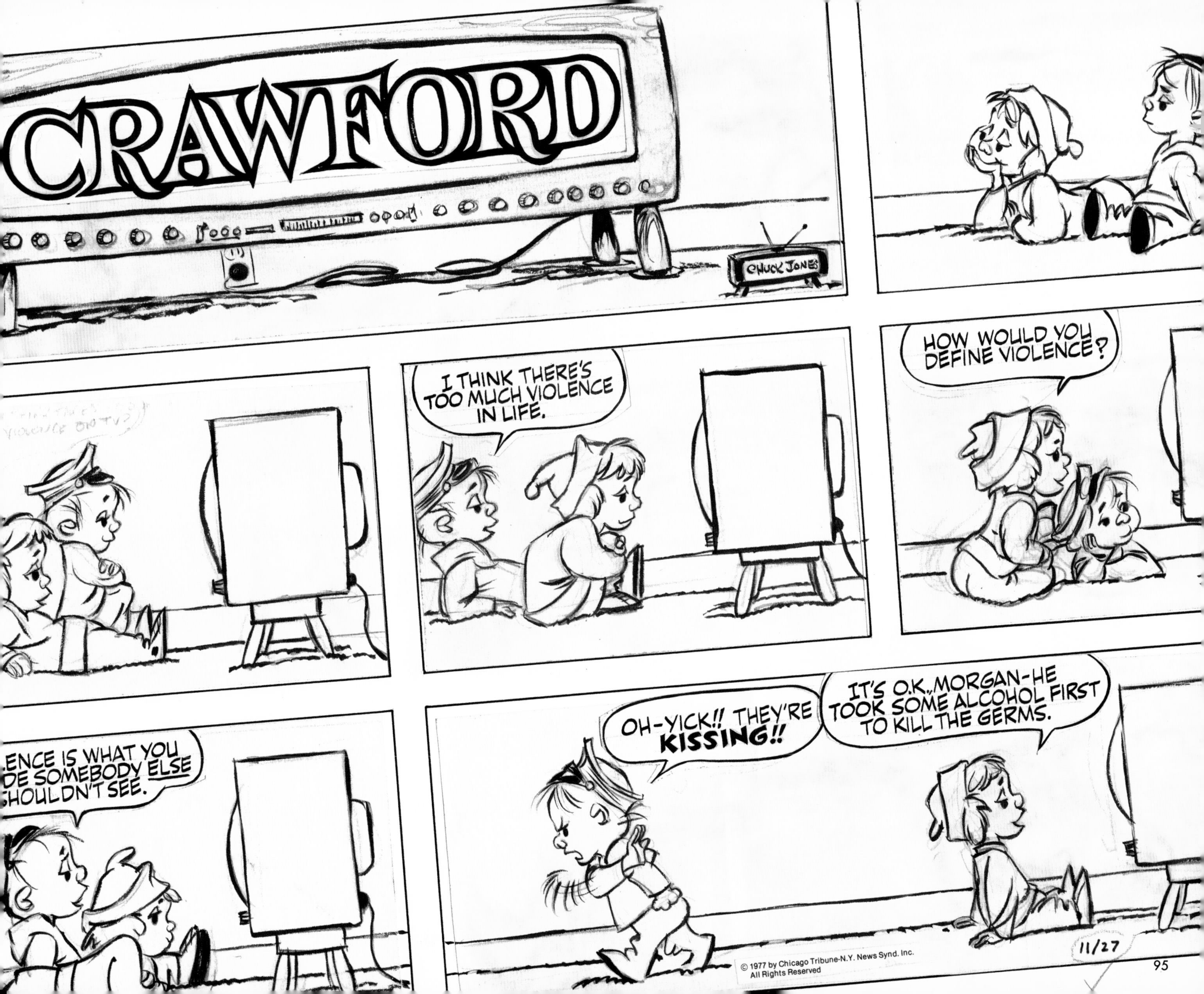

CRAWFORD
CHUCK JONES
I THINK THERE'S TOO MUCH VIOLENCE IN LIFE.
HOW WOULD YOU DEFINE VIOLENCE?
ENCE IS WHAT YOU DE SOMEBODY ELSE SHOULDN'T SEE.
OH-YICK!! THEY'RE **KISSING**!!
IT'S O.K., MORGAN-HE TOOK SOME ALCOHOL FIRST TO KILL THE GERMS.
11/27

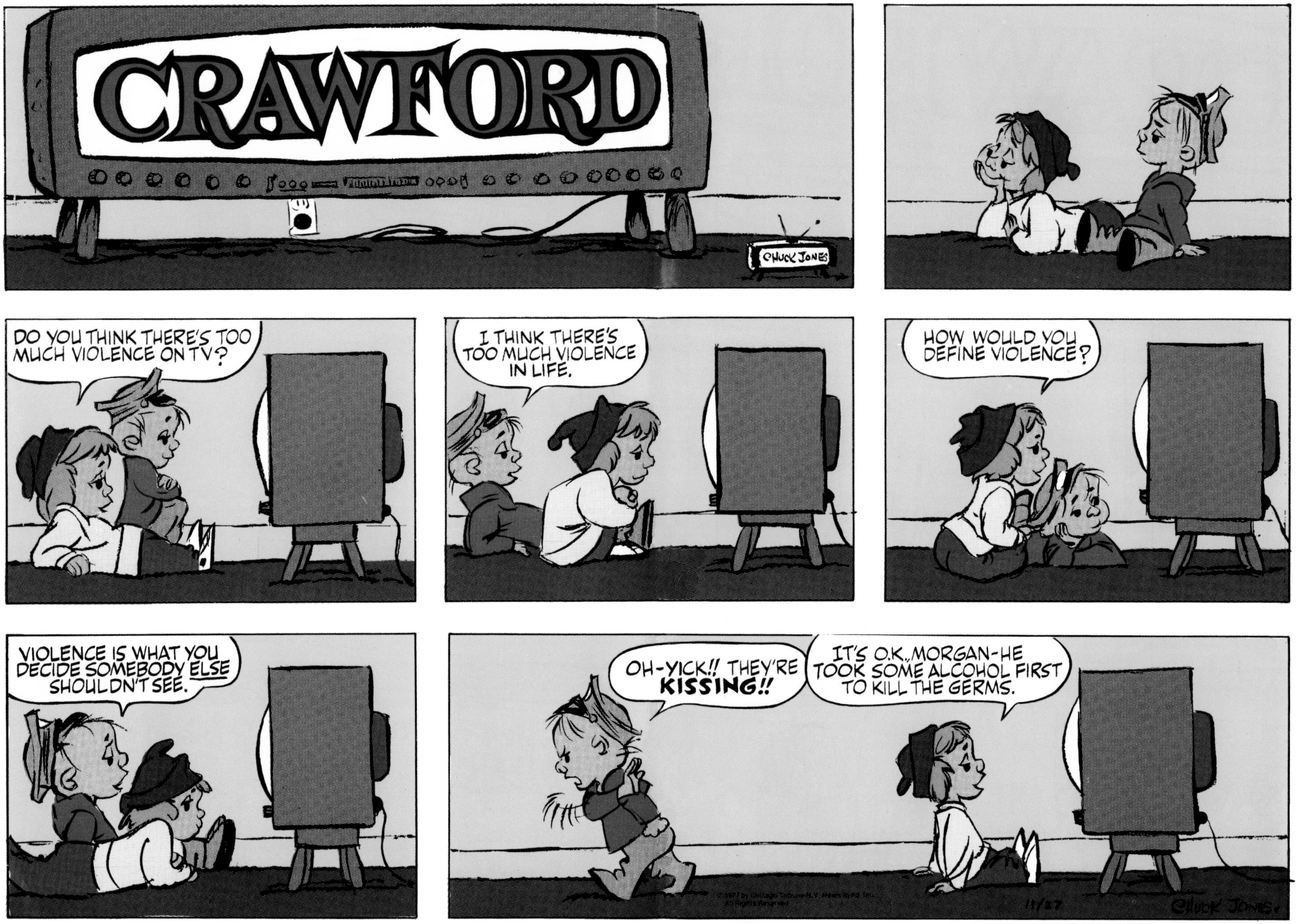
CRAWFORD
CHUCK JONES
DO YOU THINK THERE'S TOO MUCH VIOLENCE ON TV?
I THINK THERE'S TOO MUCH VIOLENCE IN LIFE.
HOW WOULD YOU DEFINE VIOLENCE?
VIOLENCE IS WHAT YOU DECIDE SOMEBODY ELSE SHOULDN'T SEE.
OH-YICK!! THEY'RE KISSING!!
IT'S O.K., MORGAN-HE TOOK SOME ALCOHOL FIRST TO KILL THE GERMS.
CHUCK JONES

Above and previous page: This strip, published on January 22, 1978, was originally slated for November 27, 1977.

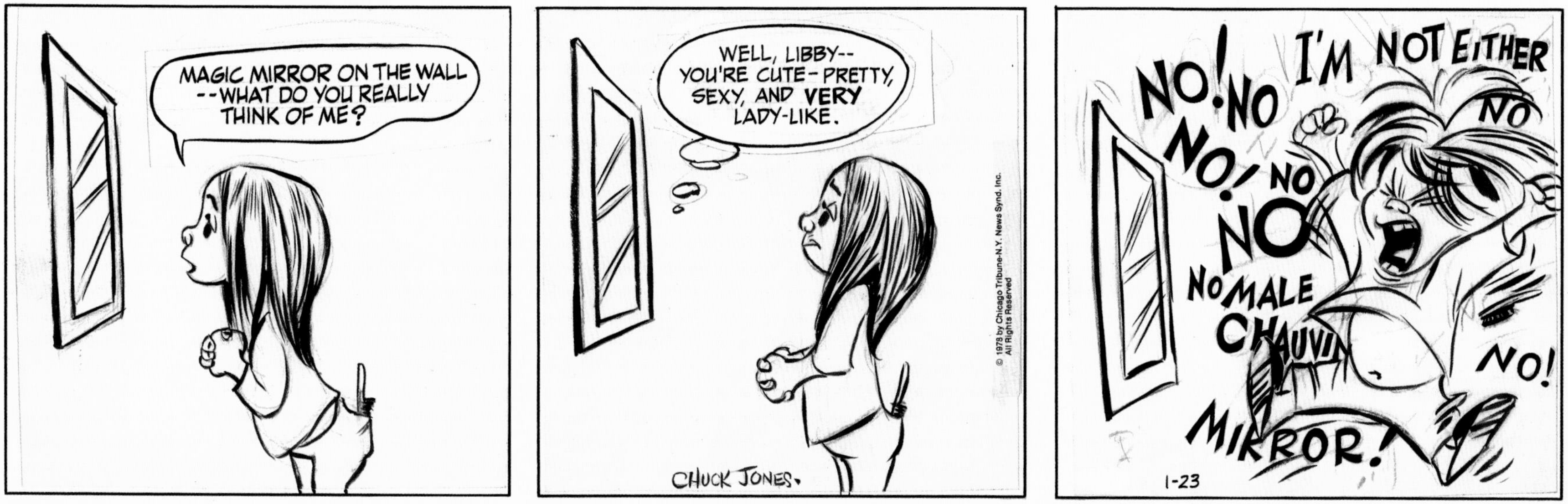
MAGIC MIRROR ON THE WALL --WHAT DO YOU REALLY THINK OF ME?
WELL, LIBBY-- YOU'RE CUTE-PRETTY, SEXY, AND **VERY** LADY-LIKE.
CHUCK JONES.
© 1978 by Chicago Tribune-N.Y. News Synd. Inc. All Rights Reserved
NO! NO I'M NOT EITHER NO
NO! NO NO
NO MALE CHAUVI
NO!
MIRROR!
1-23

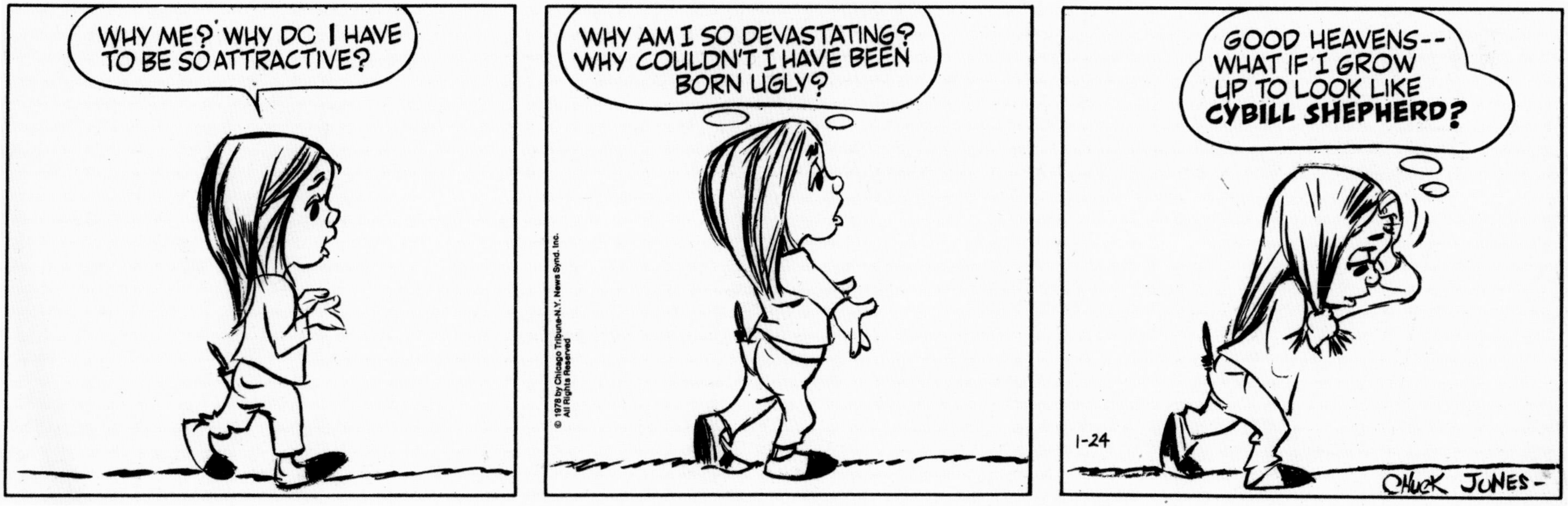
WHY ME? WHY DO I HAVE TO BE SO ATTRACTIVE?
WHY AM I SO DEVASTATING? WHY COULDN'T I HAVE BEEN BORN UGLY?
© 1978 by Chicago Tribune-N.Y. News Synd. Inc. All Rights Reserved
GOOD HEAVENS-- WHAT IF I GROW UP TO LOOK LIKE **CYBILL SHEPHERD?**
1-24
CHUCK JONES-

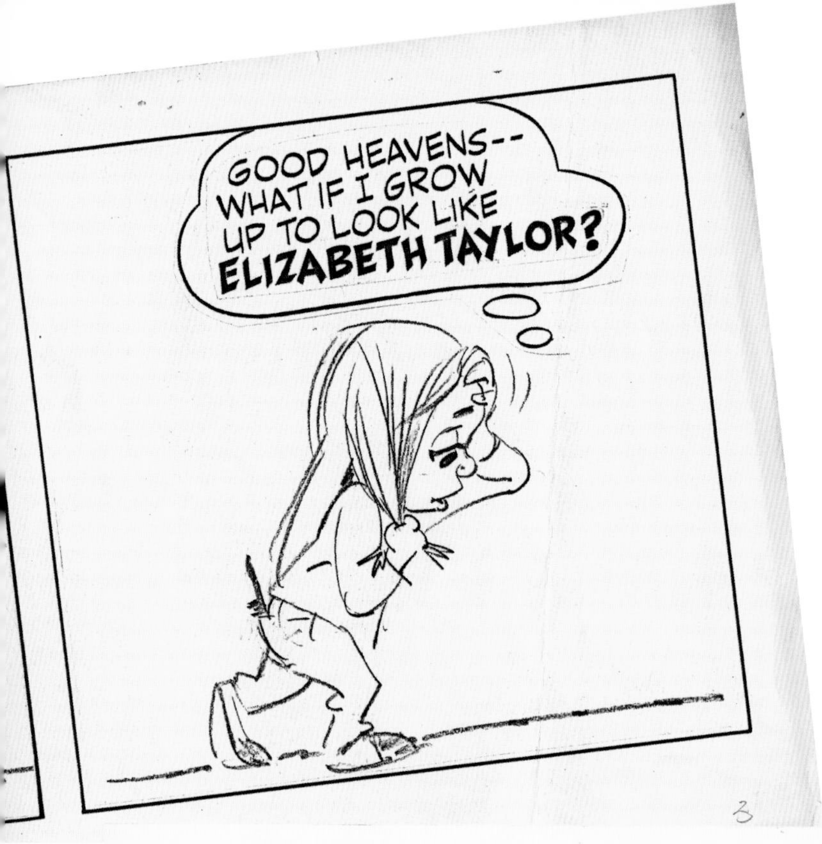
GOOD HEAVENS--
WHAT IF I GROW
UP TO LOOK LIKE
ELIZABETH TAYLOR?
3

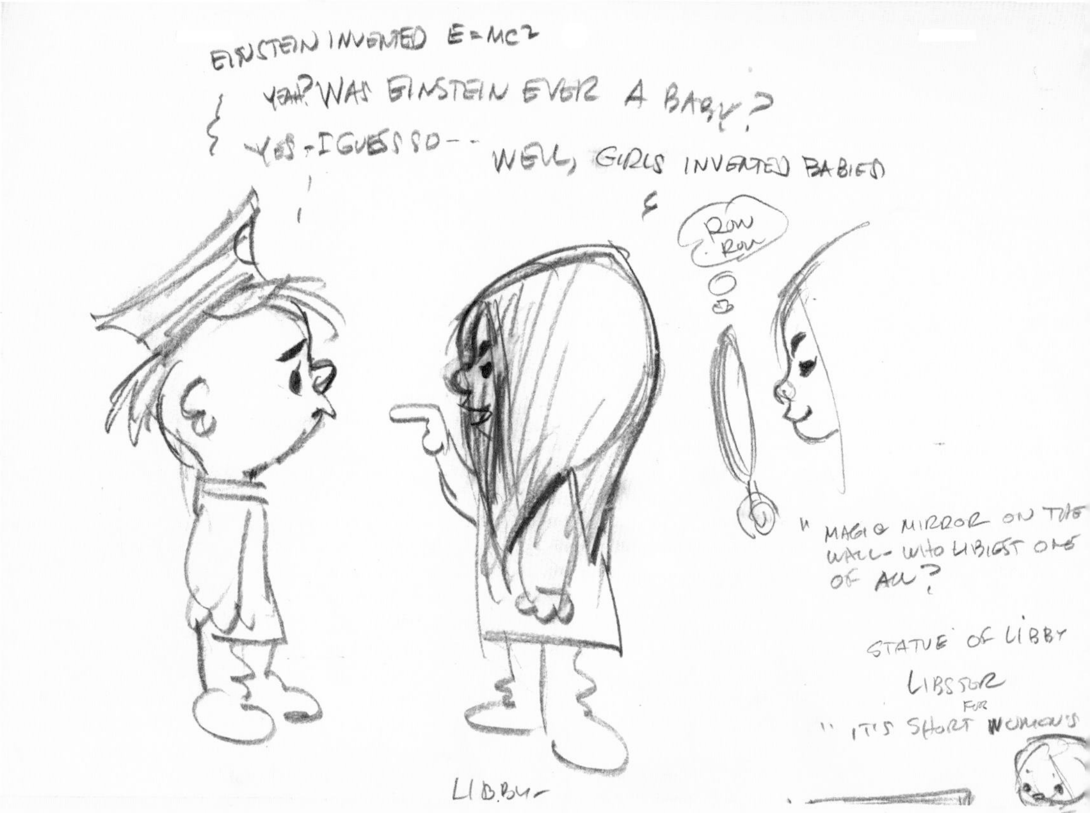
EINSTEIN INVENTED E=MC2
YEAH? WAS EINSTEIN EVER A BABY?
YES-I GUESS SO--
WELL, GIRLS INVENTED BABIES
"MAGIC MIRROR ON THE WALL- WHO LIBBIEST ONE OF ALL?
STATUE OF LIBBY
LIBBY

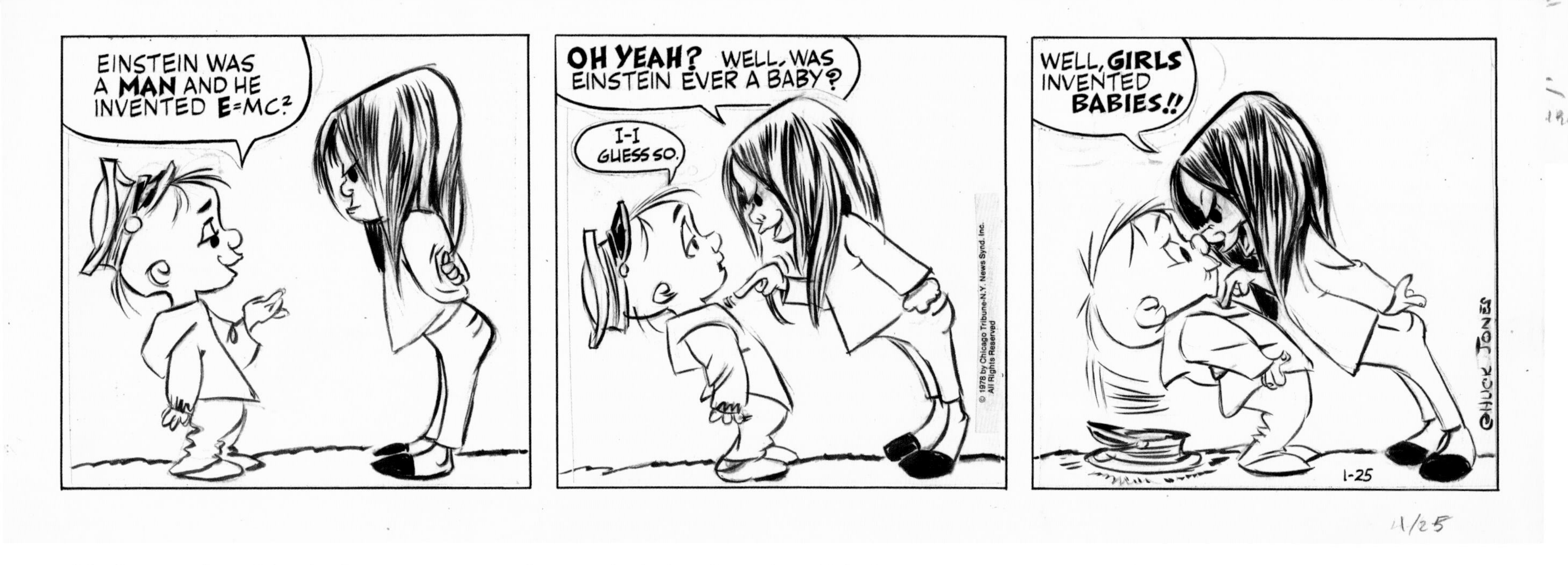
EINSTEIN WAS A MAN AND HE INVENTED E=MC²
OH YEAH? WELL, WAS EINSTEIN EVER A BABY?
I-I GUESS SO.
© 1978 by Chicago Tribune-N.Y. News Synd., Inc. All Rights Reserved
WELL, GIRLS INVENTED BABIES!!
©HUCK JONES
1-25
1/25

Top left: The original punch line for the January 24 strip references Elizabeth Taylor; in the published version Chuck changes the reference to the more topical Cybill Shepherd.

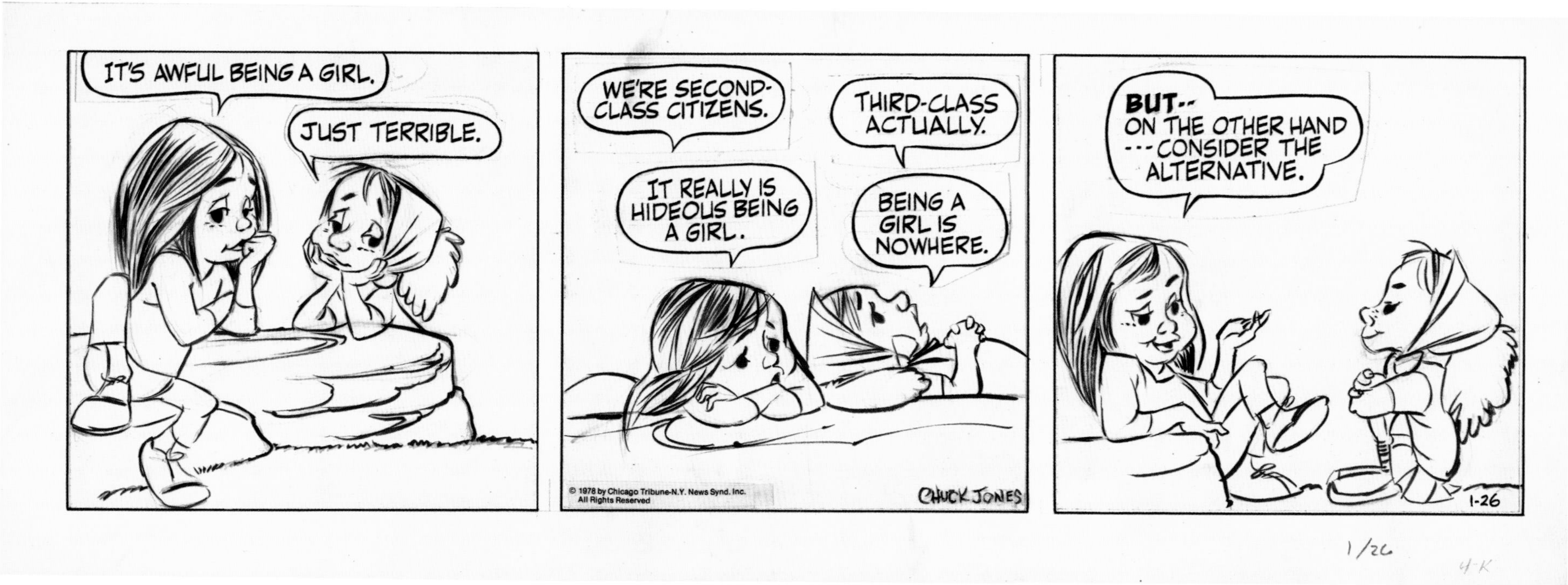
IT'S AWFUL BEING A GIRL.
JUST TERRIBLE.
WE'RE SECOND-CLASS CITIZENS.
THIRD-CLASS ACTUALLY.
IT REALLY IS HIDEOUS BEING A GIRL.
BEING A GIRL IS NOWHERE.
© 1978 by Chicago Tribune-N.Y. News Synd. Inc. All Rights Reserved
CHUCK JONES
BUT-- ON THE OTHER HAND ---CONSIDER THE ALTERNATIVE.
1-26

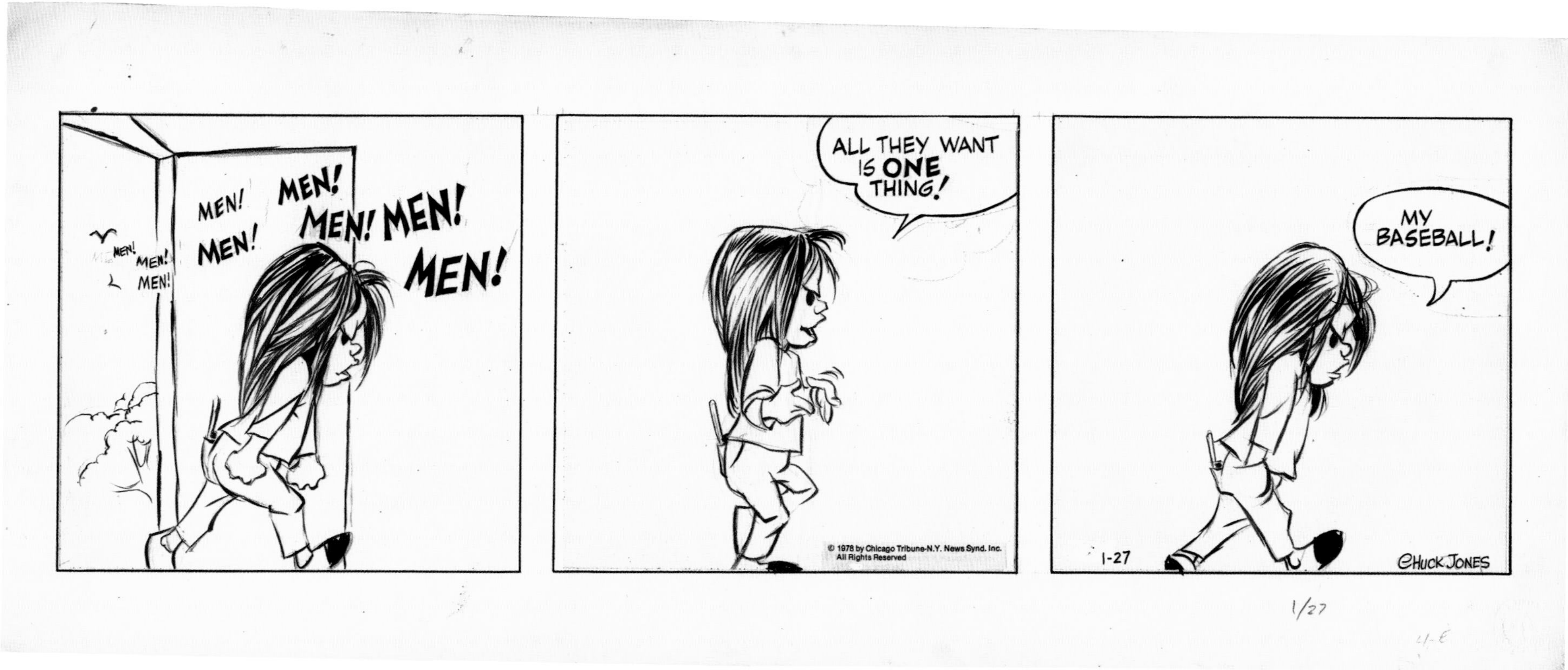
MEN! MEN! MEN!
MEN! MEN! MEN! MEN! MEN! MEN!
ALL THEY WANT IS ONE THING!
© 1978 by Chicago Tribune-N.Y. News Synd. Inc. All Rights Reserved
MY BASEBALL!
1-27
CHUCK JONES

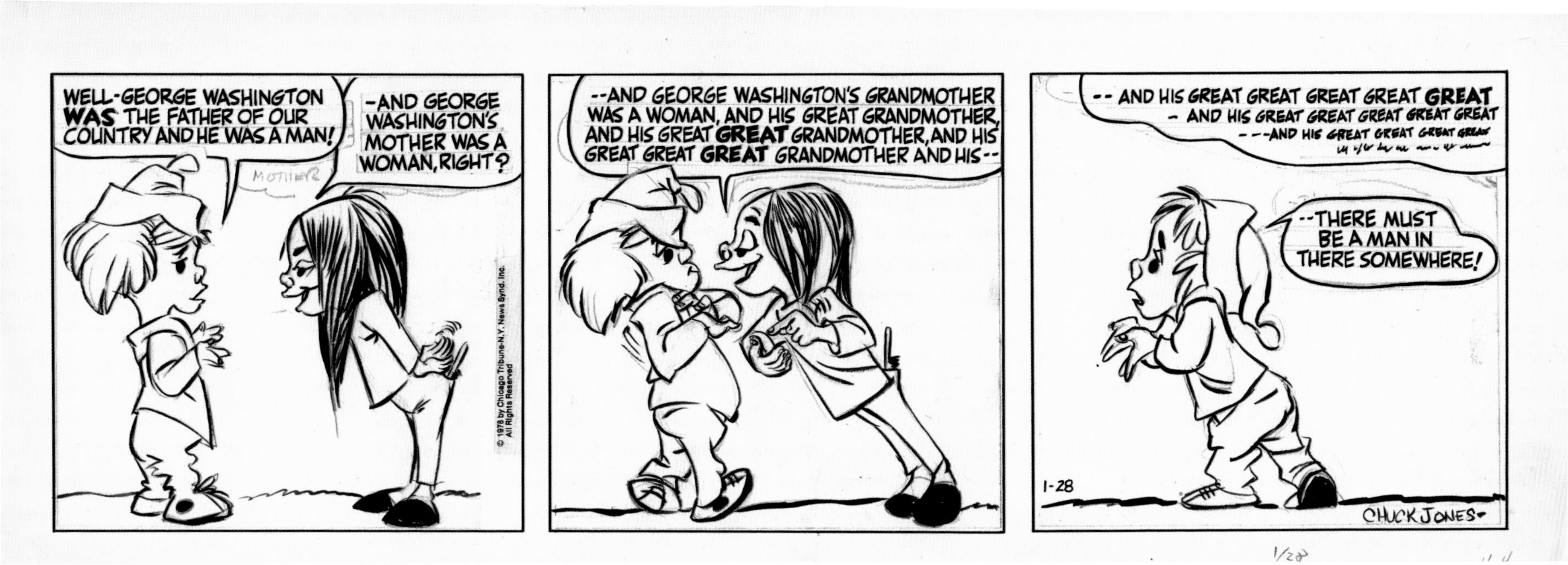
WELL-GEORGE WASHINGTON WAS THE FATHER OF OUR COUNTRY AND HE WAS A MAN!
-AND GEORGE WASHINGTON'S MOTHER WAS A WOMAN, RIGHT?
MOTHER
© 1978 by Chicago Tribune-N.Y. News Synd. Inc. All Rights Reserved
--AND GEORGE WASHINGTON'S GRANDMOTHER WAS A WOMAN, AND HIS GREAT GRANDMOTHER, AND HIS GREAT GREAT GRANDMOTHER, AND HIS GREAT GREAT GREAT GRANDMOTHER AND HIS--
-- AND HIS GREAT GREAT GREAT GREAT GREAT
- AND HIS GREAT GREAT GREAT GREAT GREAT
- --AND HIS GREAT GREAT GREAT GREAT
--THERE MUST BE A MAN IN THERE SOMEWHERE!
1-28
CHUCK JONES
1/28

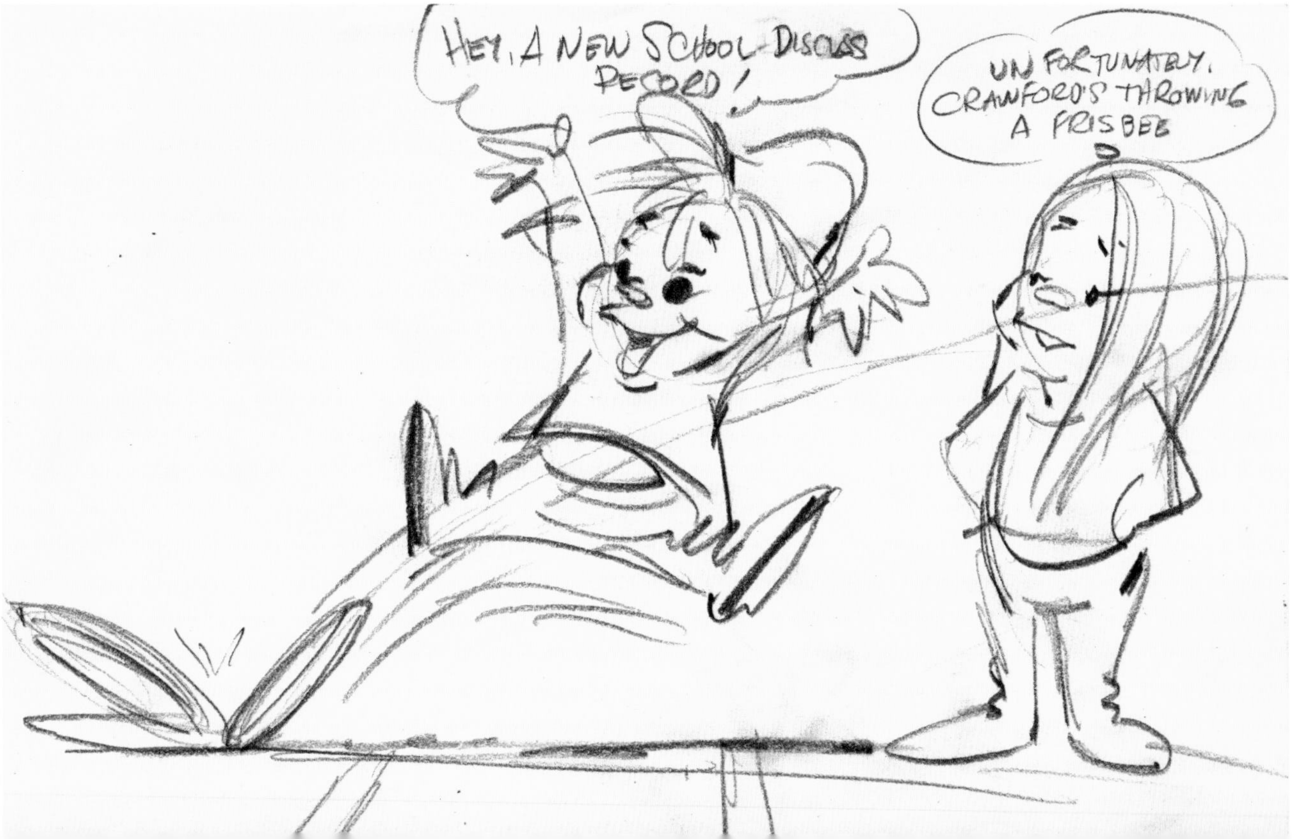
HEY, A NEW SCHOOL DISCUSS RECORD!
UNFORTUNATELY, CRAWFORD'S THROWING A FRISBEE

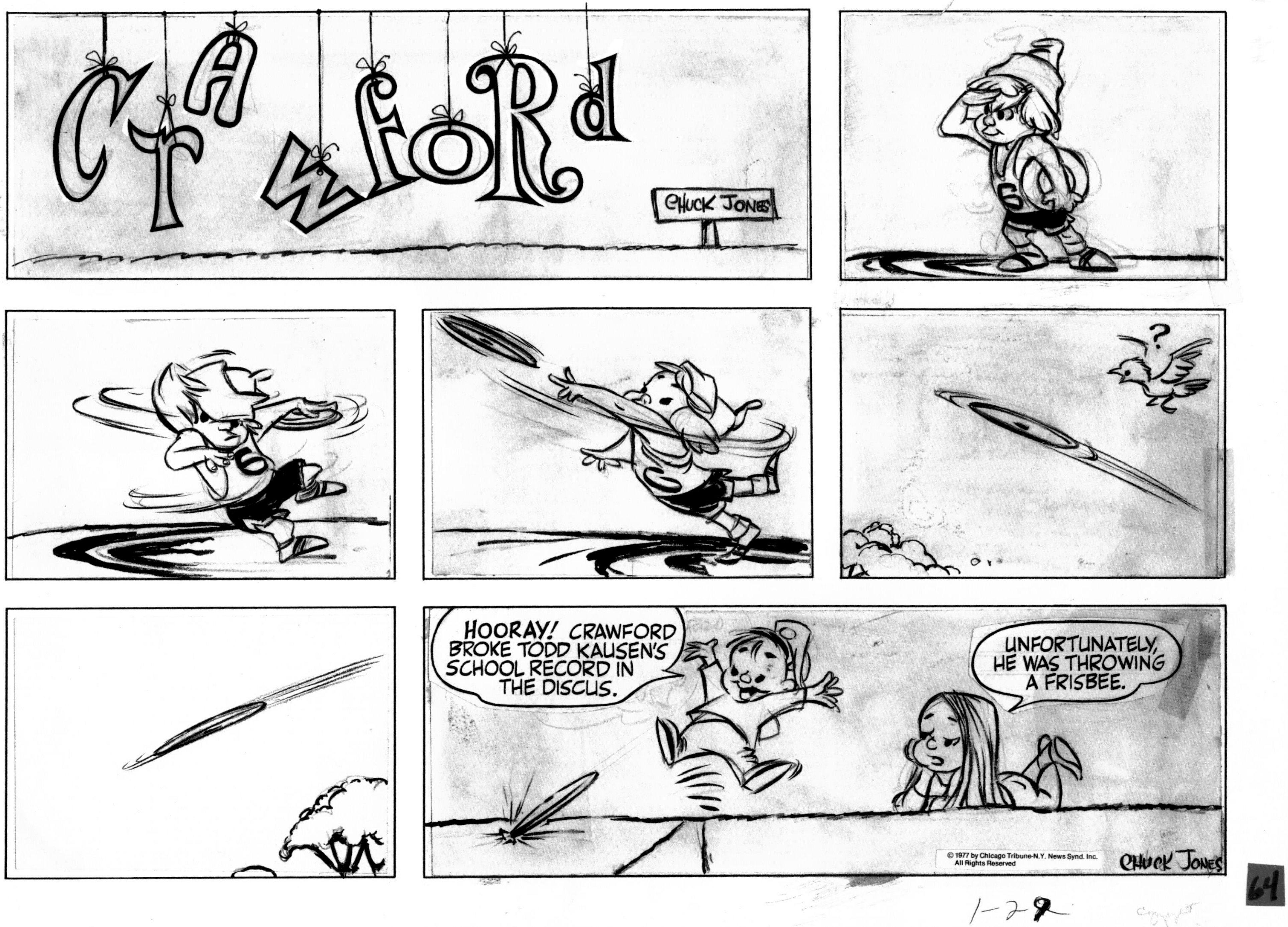
CRAWFORD
CHUCK JONES
?
HOORAY! CRAWFORD BROKE TODD KAUSEN'S SCHOOL RECORD IN THE DISCUS.
UNFORTUNATELY, HE WAS THROWING A FRISBEE.
© 1977 by Chicago Tribune-N.Y. News Synd. Inc. All Rights Reserved
CHUCK JONES
64
1-29

Todd Kausen is one of Chuck Jones's grandsons.

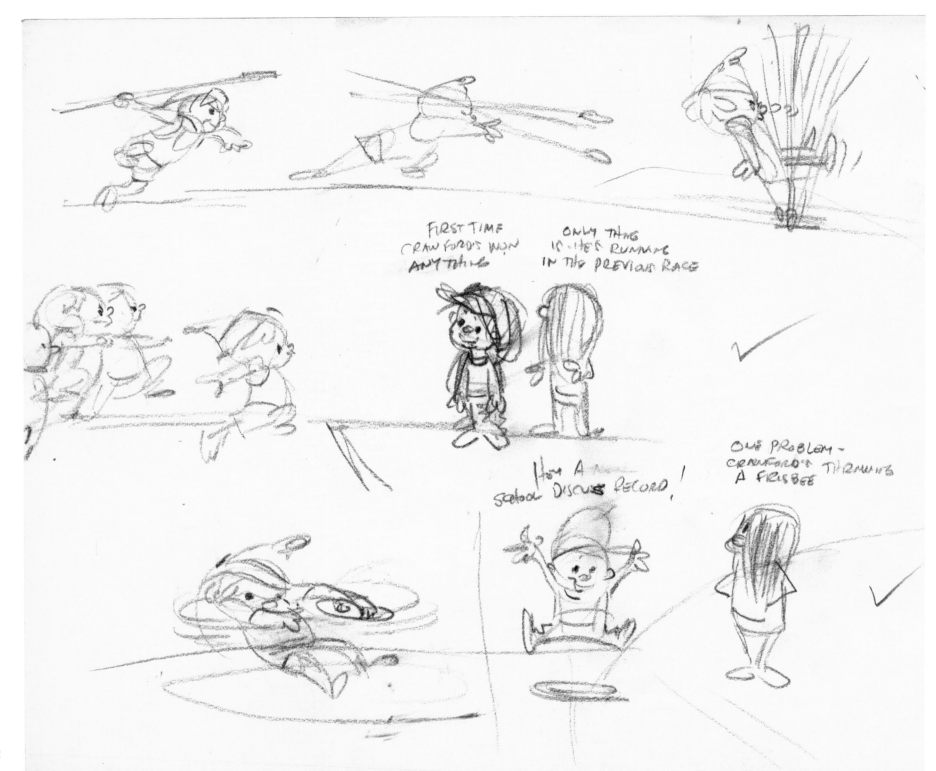

FIRST TIME
CRAWFORD'S WON
ANYTHING

ONLY THING
IS HE'S RUNNING
IN THE PREVIOUS RACE

He's A
School DISCUS RECORD!

ONE PROBLEM -
CRAWFORD'S THROWING
A FRISBEE

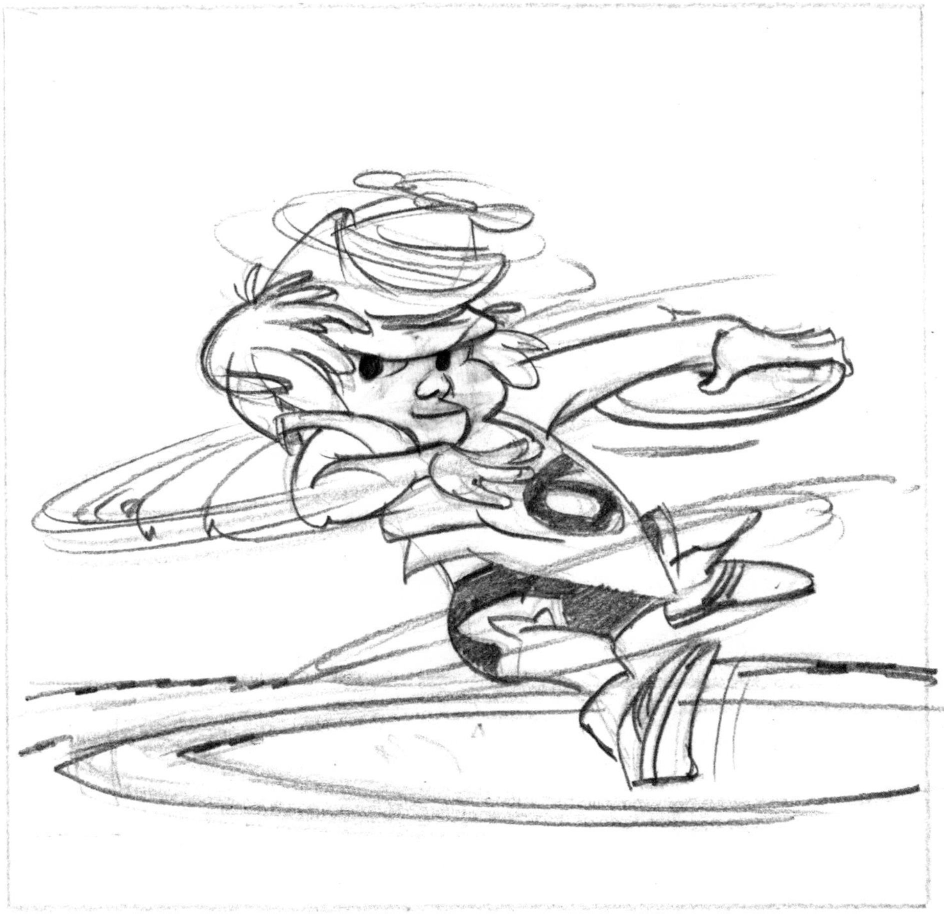

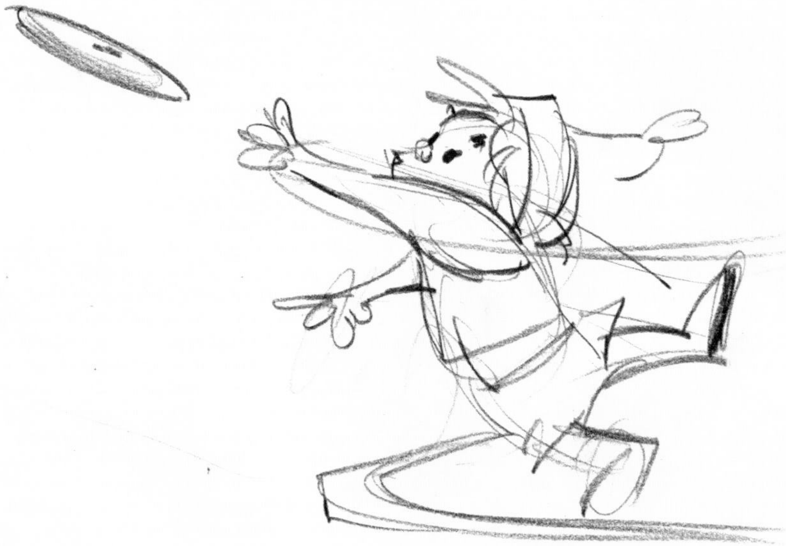

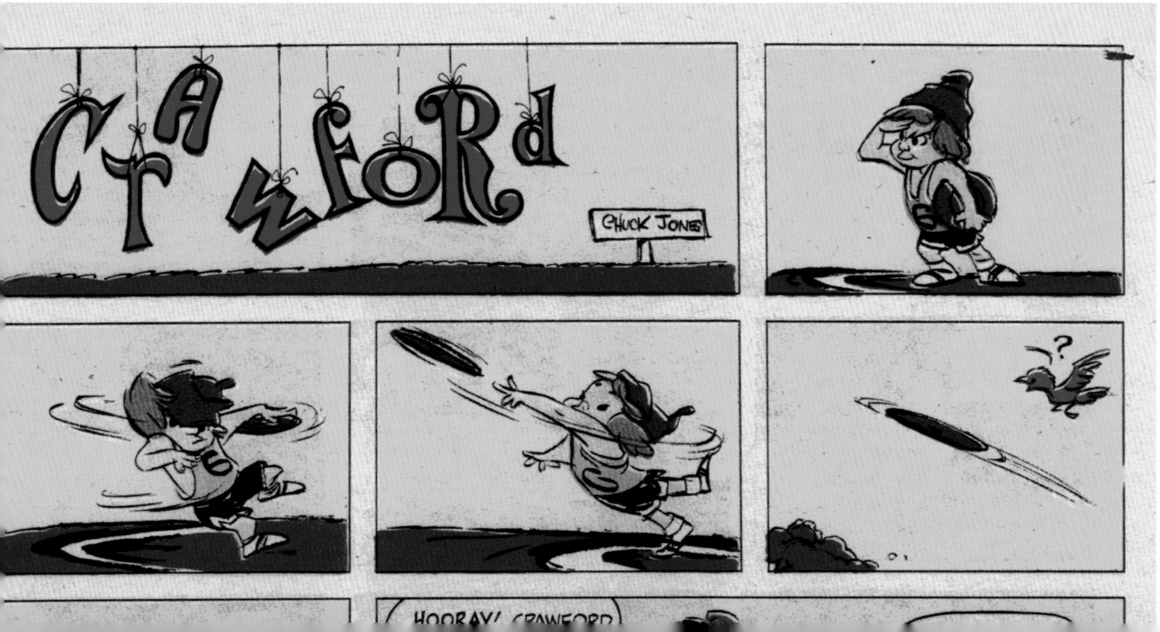
CRAWFORD
CHUCK JONES
?
HOORAY! CRAWFORD

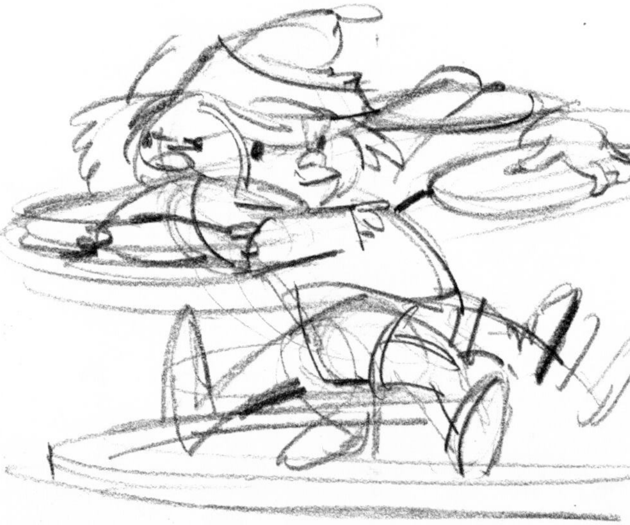

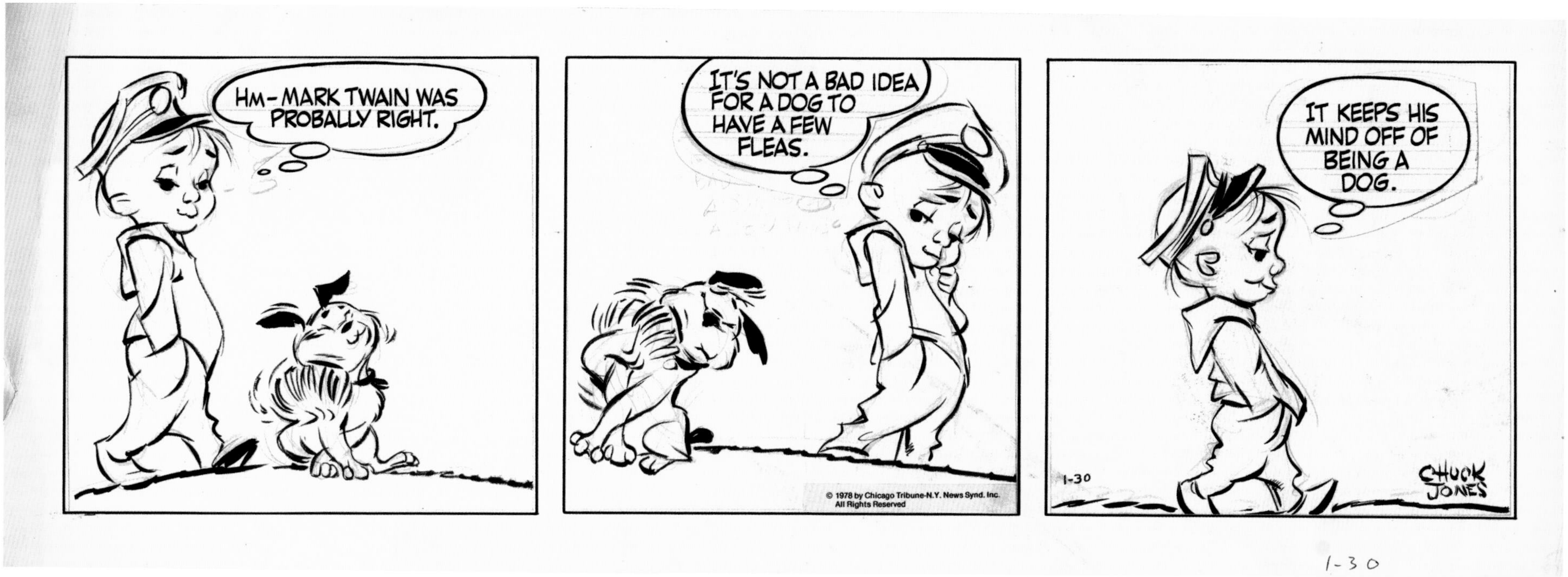
HM-MARK TWAIN WAS PROBALLY RIGHT.
IT'S NOT A BAD IDEA FOR A DOG TO HAVE A FEW FLEAS.
© 1978 by Chicago Tribune-N.Y. News Synd. Inc. All Rights Reserved
IT KEEPS HIS MIND OFF OF BEING A DOG.
1-30
CHUCK JONES
1-30

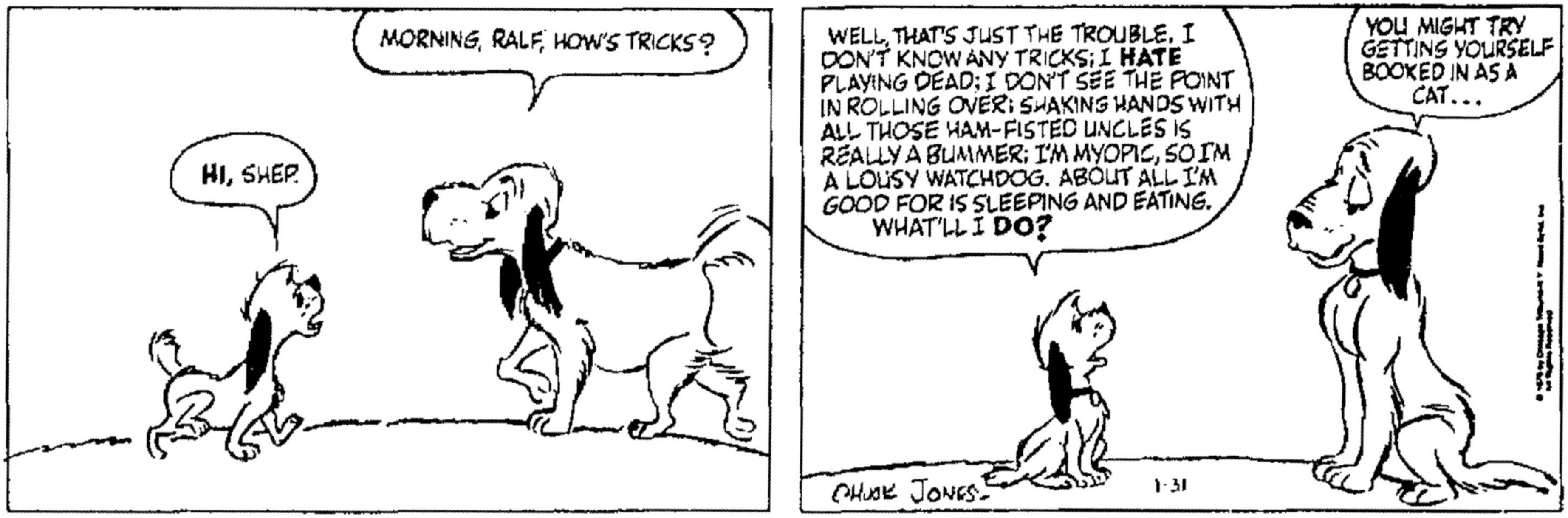
MORNING, RALF, HOW'S TRICKS?
HI, SHEP.
WELL, THAT'S JUST THE TROUBLE. I DON'T KNOW ANY TRICKS; I **HATE** PLAYING DEAD; I DON'T SEE THE POINT IN ROLLING OVER; SHAKING HANDS WITH ALL THOSE HAM-FISTED UNCLES IS REALLY A BUMMER; I'M MYOPIC, SO I'M A LOUSY WATCHDOG. ABOUT ALL I'M GOOD FOR IS SLEEPING AND EATING. WHAT'LL I **DO?**
YOU MIGHT TRY GETTING YOURSELF BOOKED IN AS A CAT...
CHUCK JONES
1-31

One of a handful of strips for which Chuck Jones's files contain no original art or printed version; rather than omit the strip, we print it from a microfilm copy.

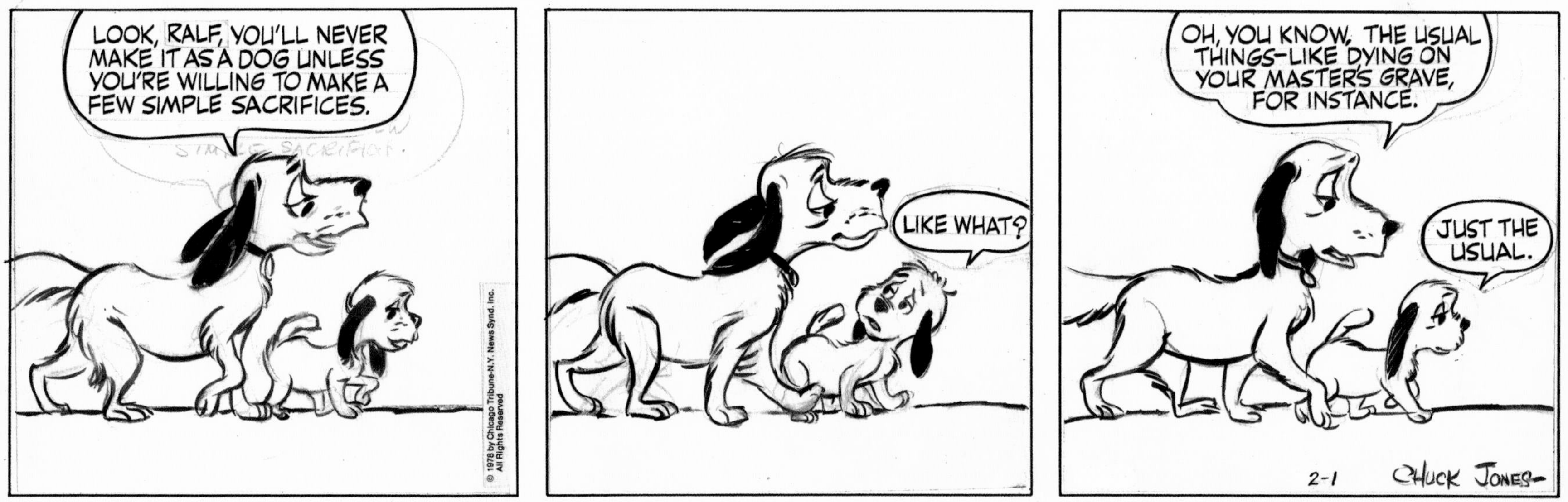
LOOK, RALF, YOU'LL NEVER MAKE IT AS A DOG UNLESS YOU'RE WILLING TO MAKE A FEW SIMPLE SACRIFICES.
© 1978 by Chicago Tribune-N.Y. News Synd. Inc. All Rights Reserved
LIKE WHAT?
OH, YOU KNOW, THE USUAL THINGS–LIKE DYING ON YOUR MASTER'S GRAVE, FOR INSTANCE.
JUST THE USUAL.
2-1
CHUCK JONES

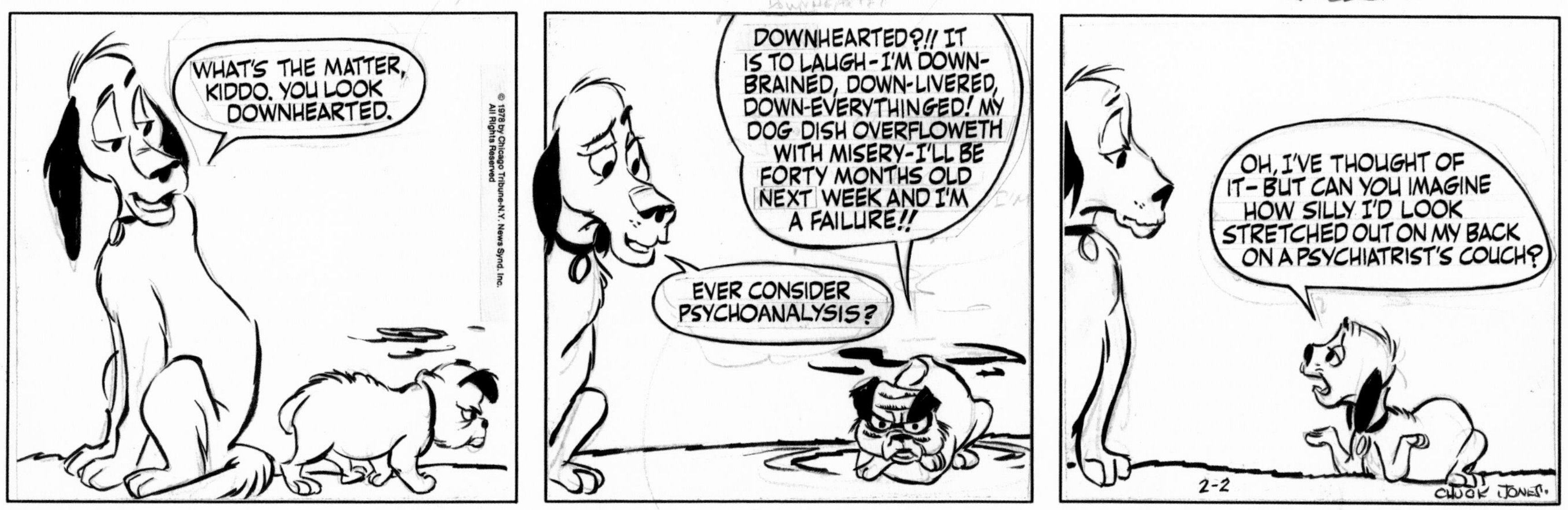
WHAT'S THE MATTER, KIDDO. YOU LOOK DOWNHEARTED.
© 1978 by Chicago Tribune-N.Y. News Synd. Inc. All Rights Reserved
DOWNHEARTED?!! IT IS TO LAUGH-I'M DOWN-BRAINED, DOWN-LIVERED, DOWN-EVERYTHINGED! MY DOG DISH OVERFLOWETH WITH MISERY-I'LL BE FORTY MONTHS OLD NEXT WEEK AND I'M A FAILURE!!
EVER CONSIDER PSYCHOANALYSIS?
OH, I'VE THOUGHT OF IT-BUT CAN YOU IMAGINE HOW SILLY I'D LOOK STRETCHED OUT ON MY BACK ON A PSYCHIATRIST'S COUCH?
2-2
CHUCK JONES

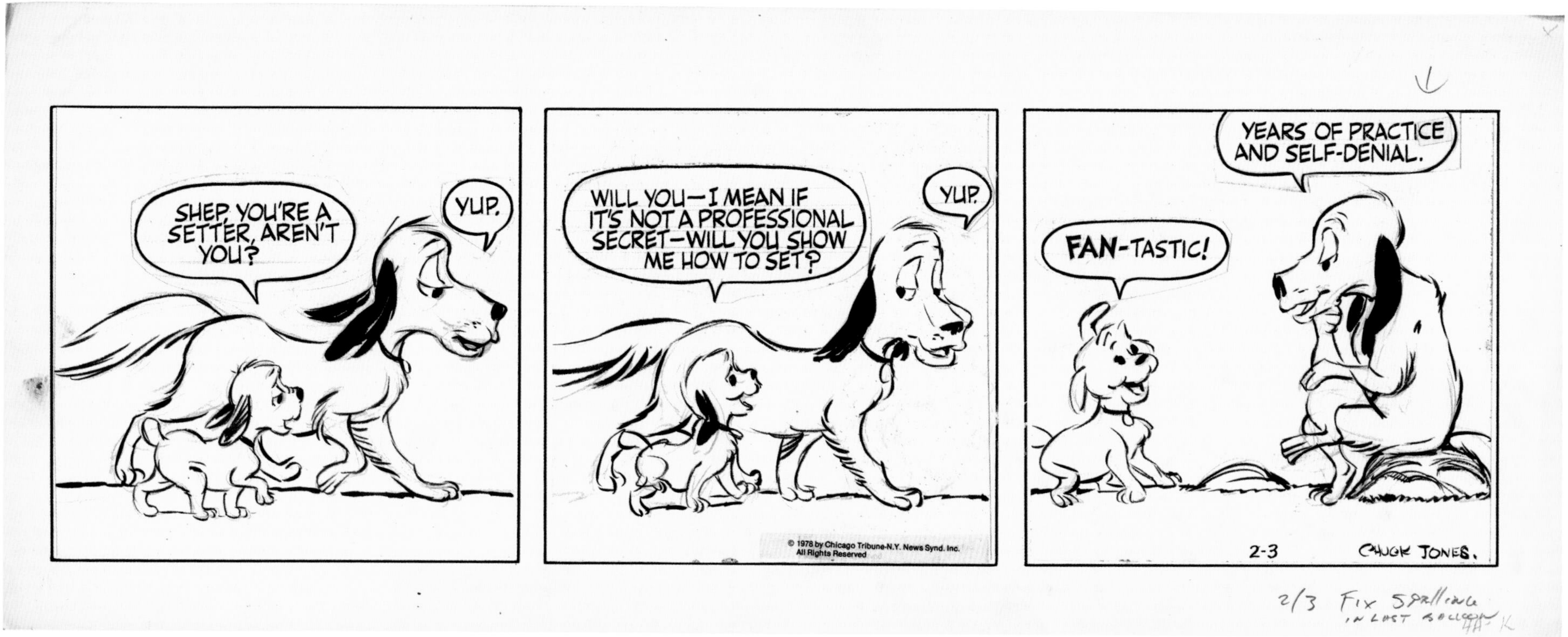
SHEP, YOU'RE A SETTER, AREN'T YOU?
YUP.
WILL YOU—I MEAN IF IT'S NOT A PROFESSIONAL SECRET—WILL YOU SHOW ME HOW TO SET?
YUP.
© 1978 by Chicago Tribune-N.Y. News Synd. Inc. All Rights Reserved
FAN-TASTIC!
YEARS OF PRACTICE AND SELF-DENIAL.
2-3
CHUCK JONES.
2/3 Fix spelling in last balloon

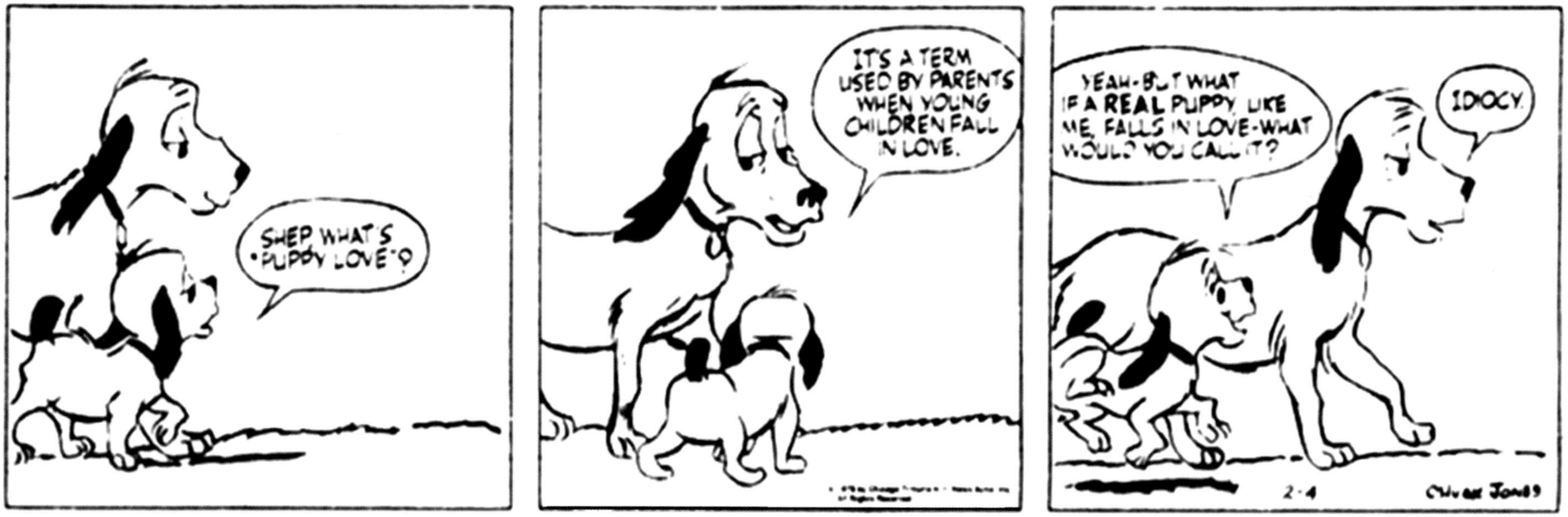
SHEP WHAT'S "PUPPY LOVE"?
IT'S A TERM USED BY PARENTS WHEN YOUNG CHILDREN FALL IN LOVE.
YEAH-BUT WHAT IF A REAL PUPPY, LIKE ME, FALLS IN LOVE-WHAT WOULD YOU CALL IT?
IDIOCY.
2-4
CHUCK JONES

One of a handful of strips for which Chuck Jones's files contain no original art or printed version; rather than omit the strip, we print it from a microfilm copy.

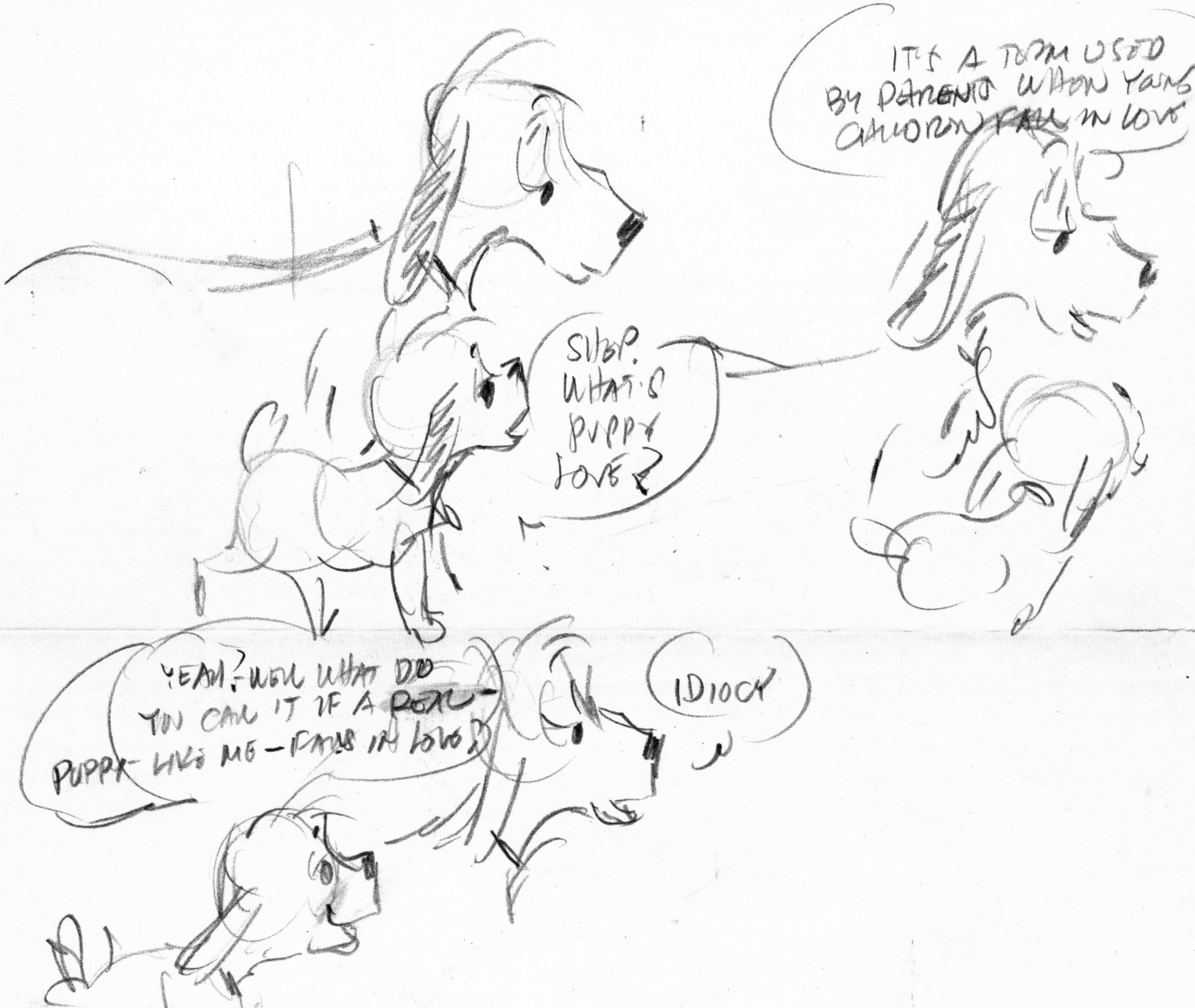
WHAT'S PUPPY LOVE?
IT'S A TERM USED BY PARENTS WHEN YOUNG CHILDREN FALL IN LOVE
YEAH? WELL WHAT DO YOU CALL IT IF A REAL PUPPY LIKE ME — FALLS IN LOVE?
IDIOCY

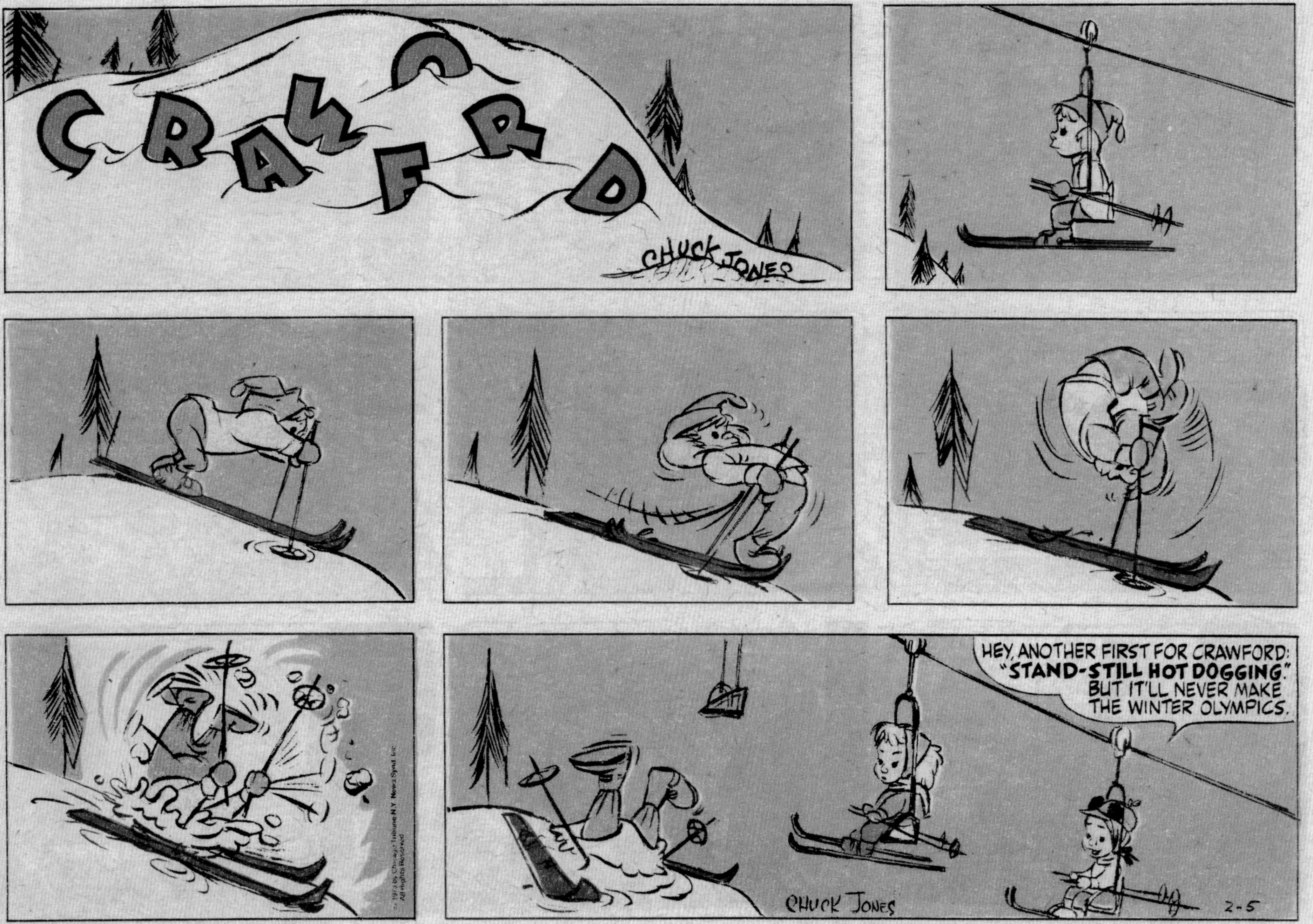
CRAWFORD
CHUCK JONES
© 1973 by Chicago Tribune-N.Y. News Synd. Inc. All Rights Reserved
CHUCK JONES
2-5
HEY, ANOTHER FIRST FOR CRAWFORD: "**STAND-STILL HOT DOGGING**." BUT IT'LL NEVER MAKE THE WINTER OLYMPICS.

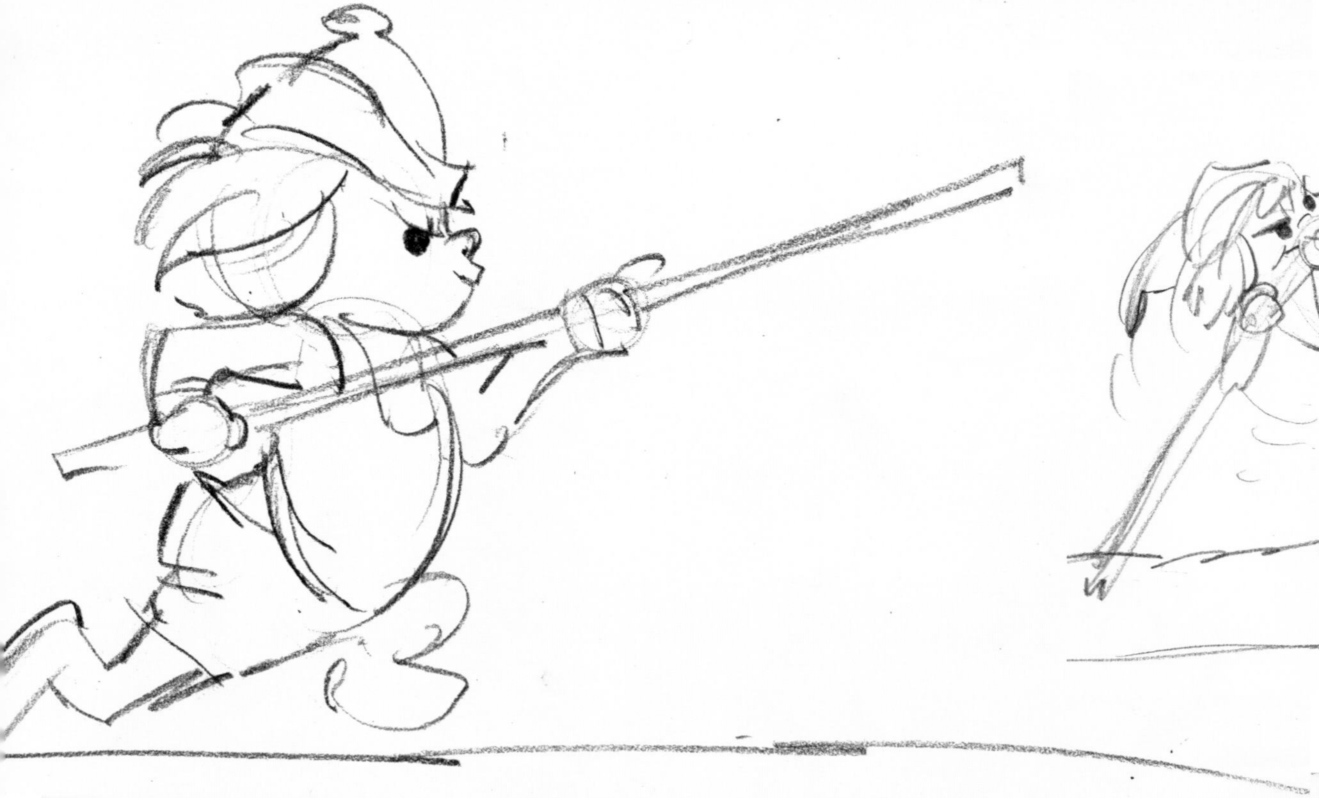

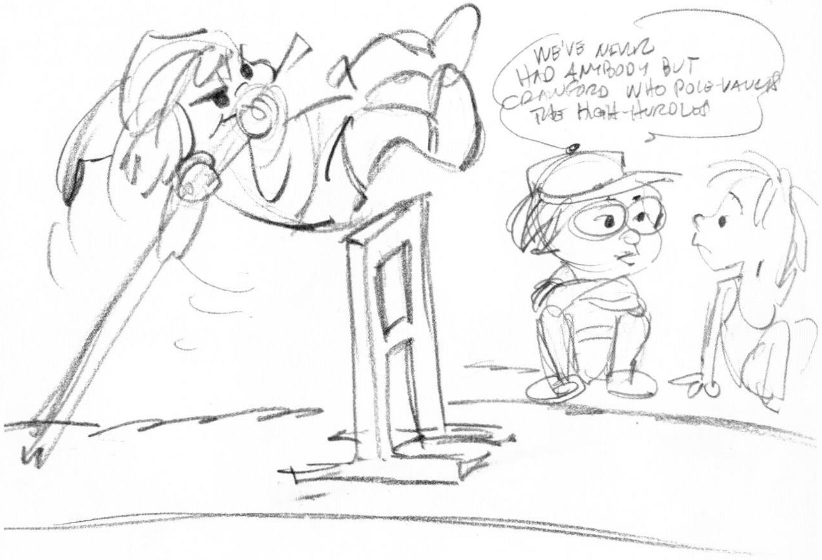
WE'VE NEVER HAD ANYBODY BUT CRAWFORD WHO POLE-VAULTS THE HIGH-HURDLES

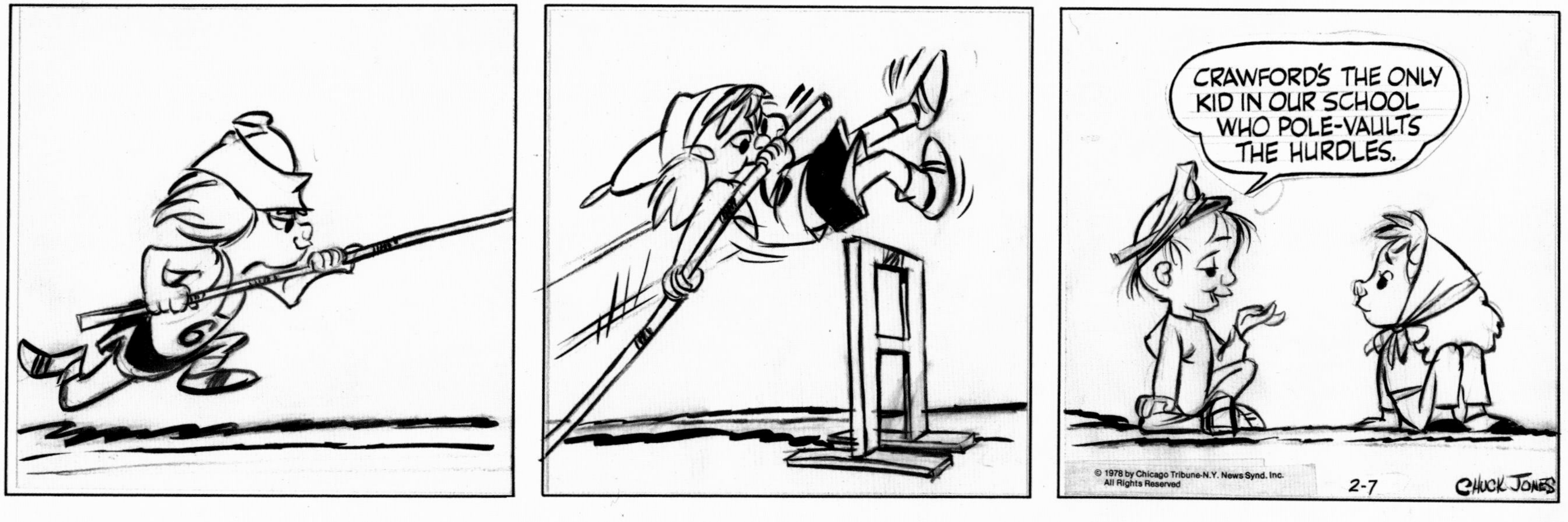
CRAWFORD'S THE ONLY KID IN OUR SCHOOL WHO POLE-VAULTS THE HURDLES.
© 1978 by Chicago Tribune-N.Y. News Synd. Inc. All Rights Reserved
2-7
CHUCK JONES

2/7

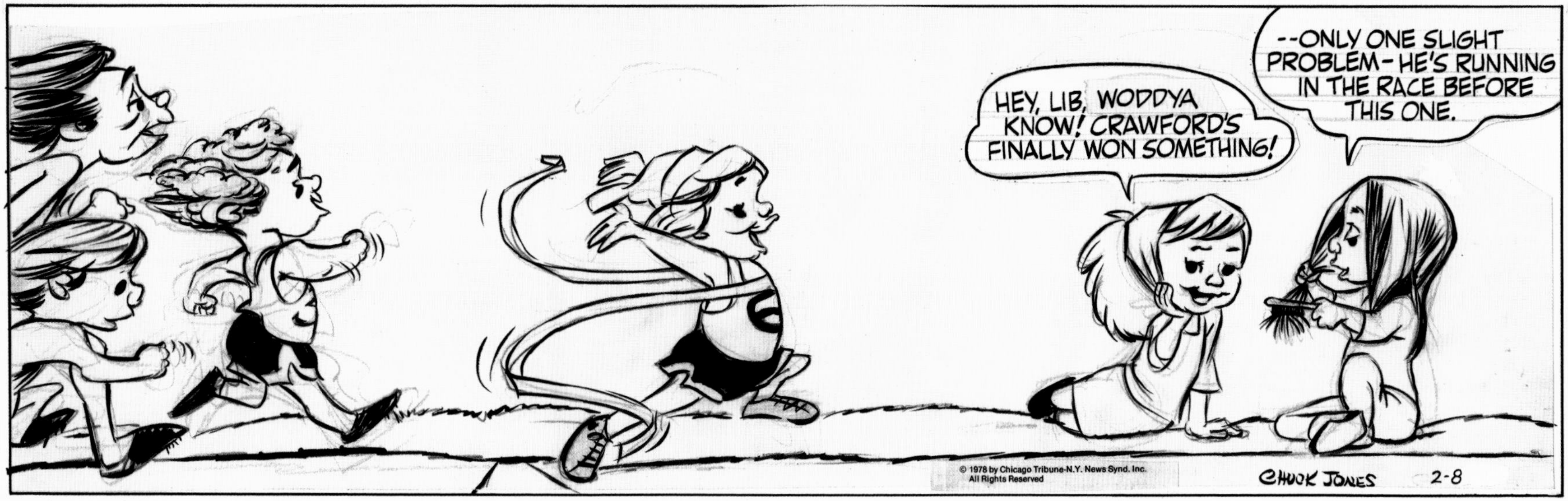
HEY, LIB, WODDYA KNOW! CRAWFORD'S FINALLY WON SOMETHING!
--ONLY ONE SLIGHT PROBLEM-HE'S RUNNING IN THE RACE BEFORE THIS ONE.
© 1978 by Chicago Tribune-N.Y. News Synd. Inc. All Rights Reserved
CHUCK JONES
2-8

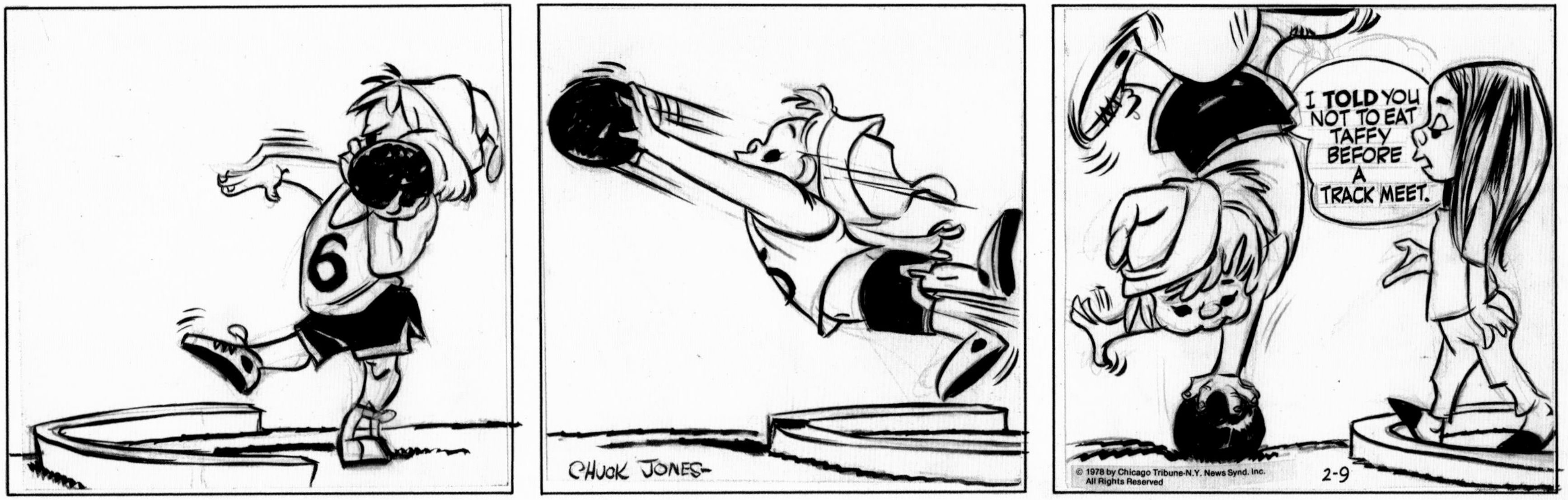
6
CHUCK JONES
I TOLD YOU NOT TO EAT TAFFY BEFORE A TRACK MEET.
© 1978 by Chicago Tribune-N.Y. News Synd. Inc. All Rights Reserved
2-9

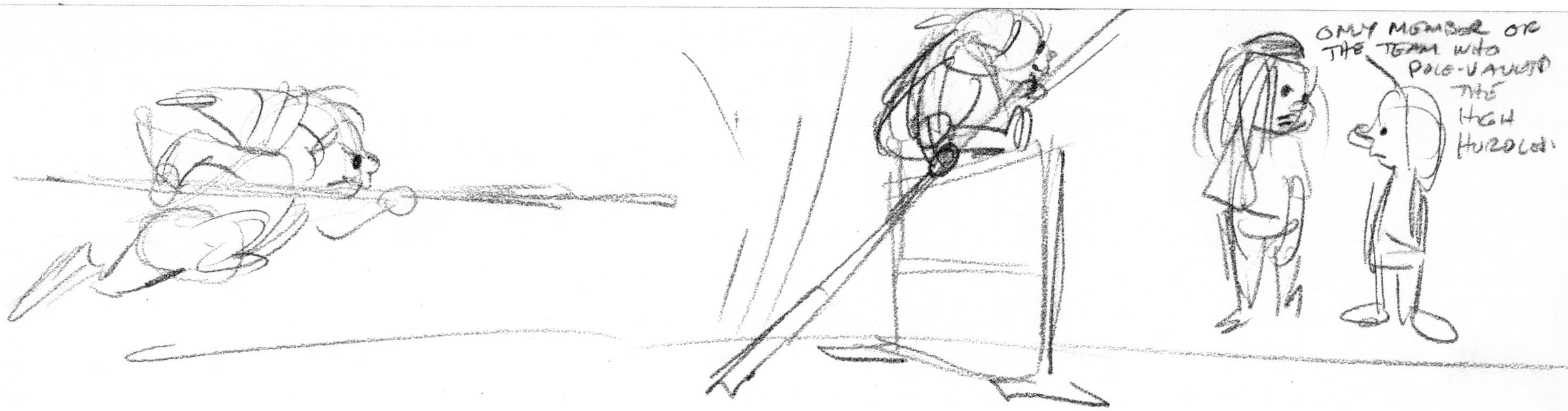
ONLY MEMBER OF THE TEAM WHO POLE-VAULTED THE HIGH HURDLE!

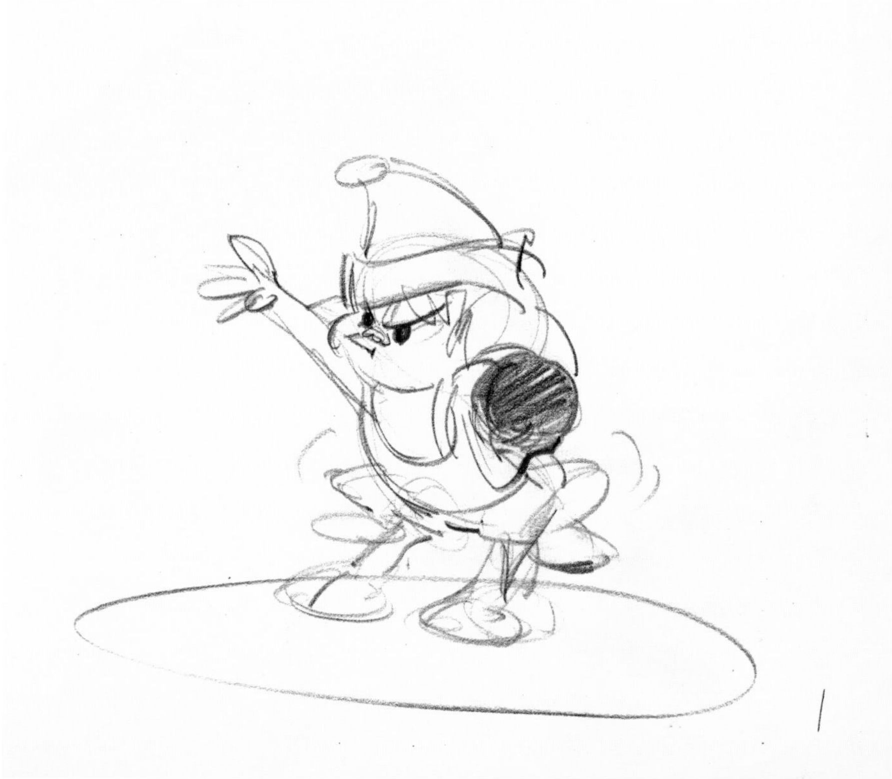

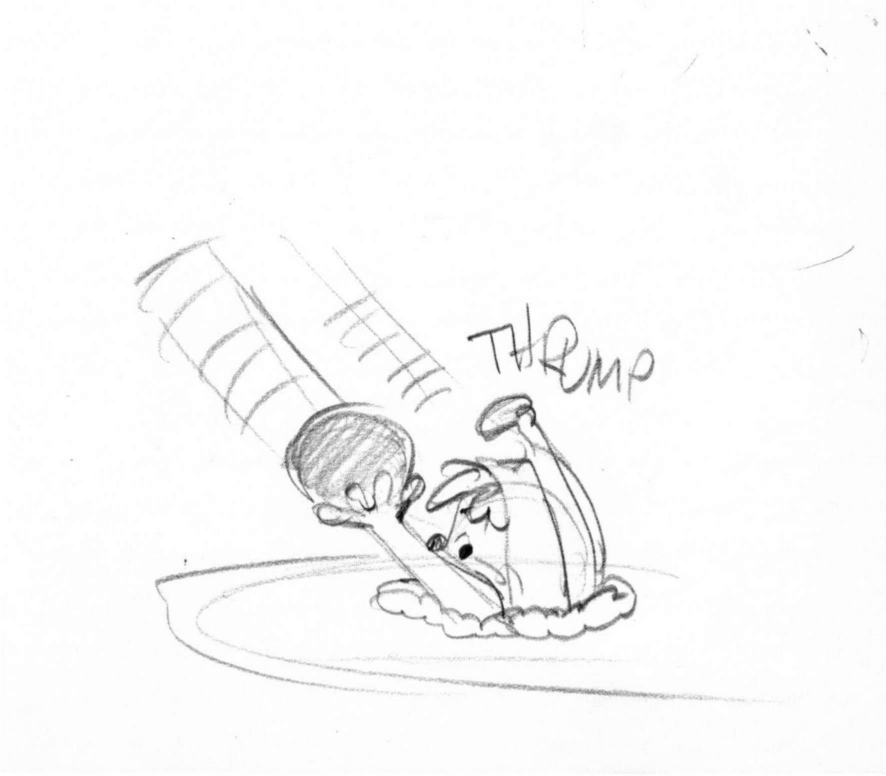
THRUMP

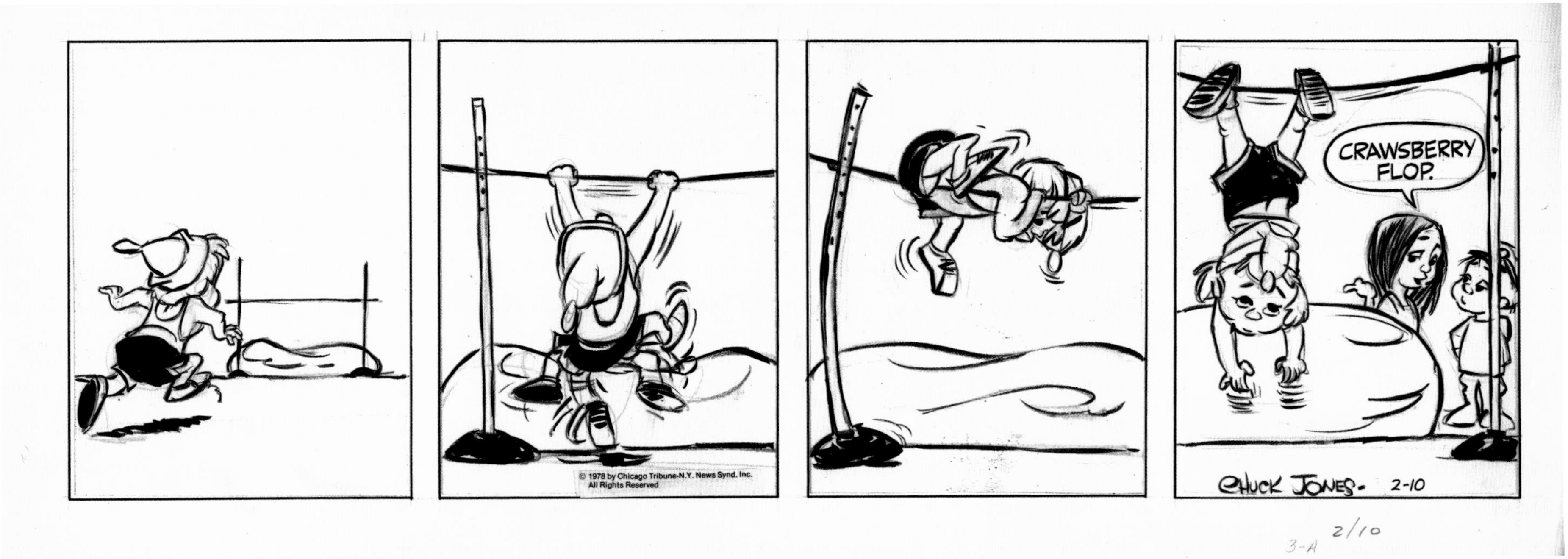
© 1978 by Chicago Tribune-N.Y. News Synd. Inc.
All Rights Reserved
CRAWSBERRY FLOP.
CHUCK JONES 2-10
2/10
3-A

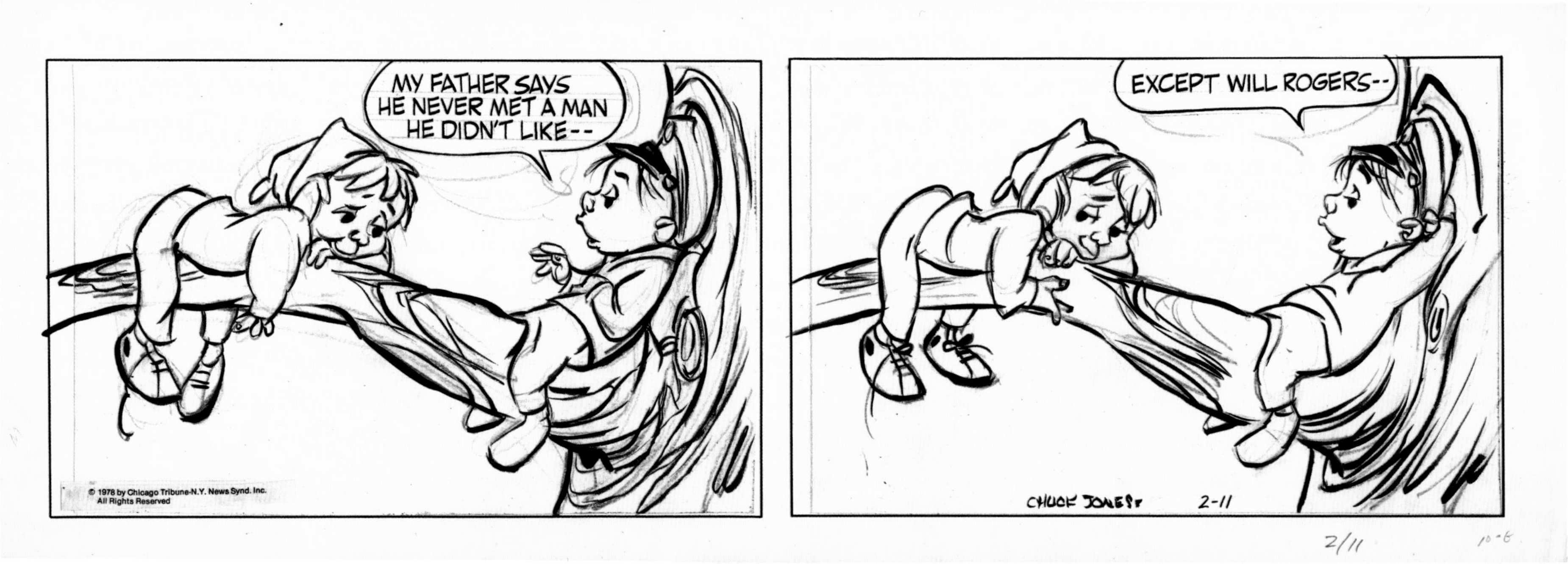
MY FATHER SAYS HE NEVER MET A MAN HE DIDN'T LIKE--
© 1978 by Chicago Tribune-N.Y. News Synd. Inc.
All Rights Reserved
EXCEPT WILL ROGERS--
CHUCK JONES 2-11
2/11

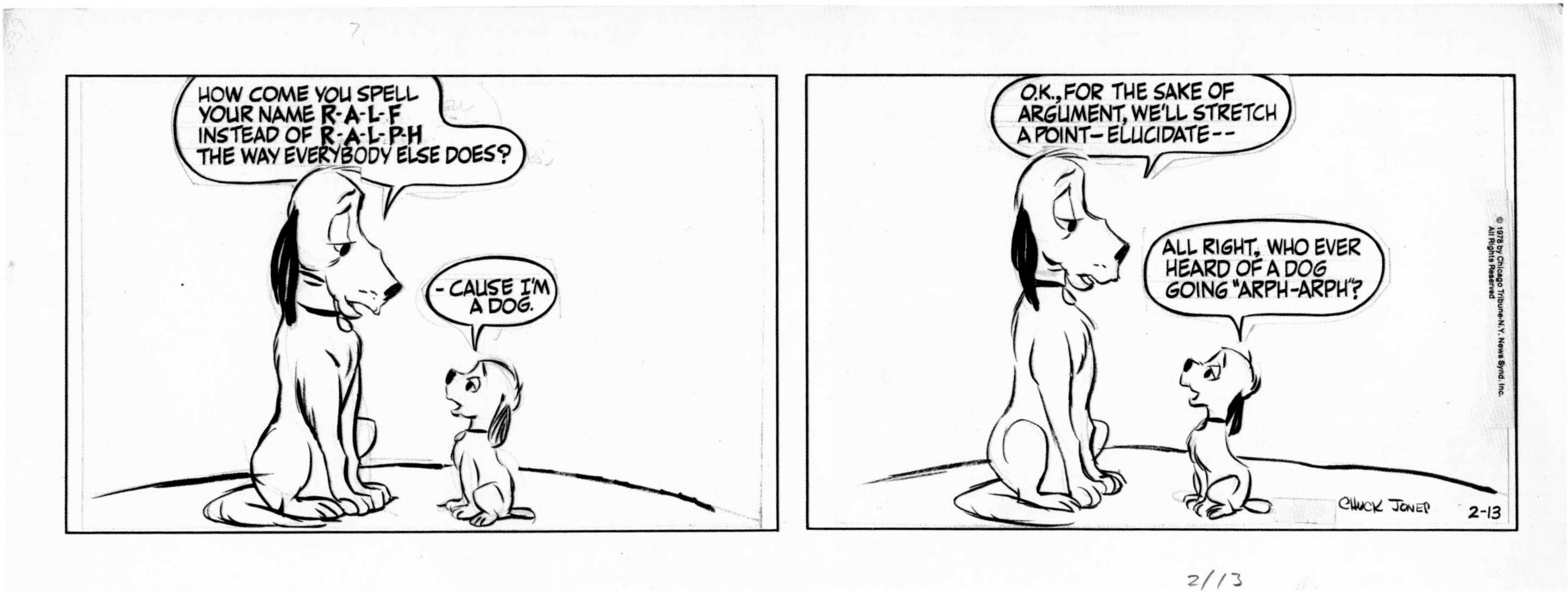
HOW COME YOU SPELL YOUR NAME R-A-L-F INSTEAD OF R-A-L-P-H THE WAY EVERYBODY ELSE DOES?
-CAUSE I'M A DOG.
O.K., FOR THE SAKE OF ARGUMENT, WE'LL STRETCH A POINT—ELUCIDATE--
ALL RIGHT, WHO EVER HEARD OF A DOG GOING "ARPH-ARPH"?
© 1978 by Chicago Tribune-N.Y. News Synd. Inc. All Rights Reserved
CHUCK JONES
2-13
2/13

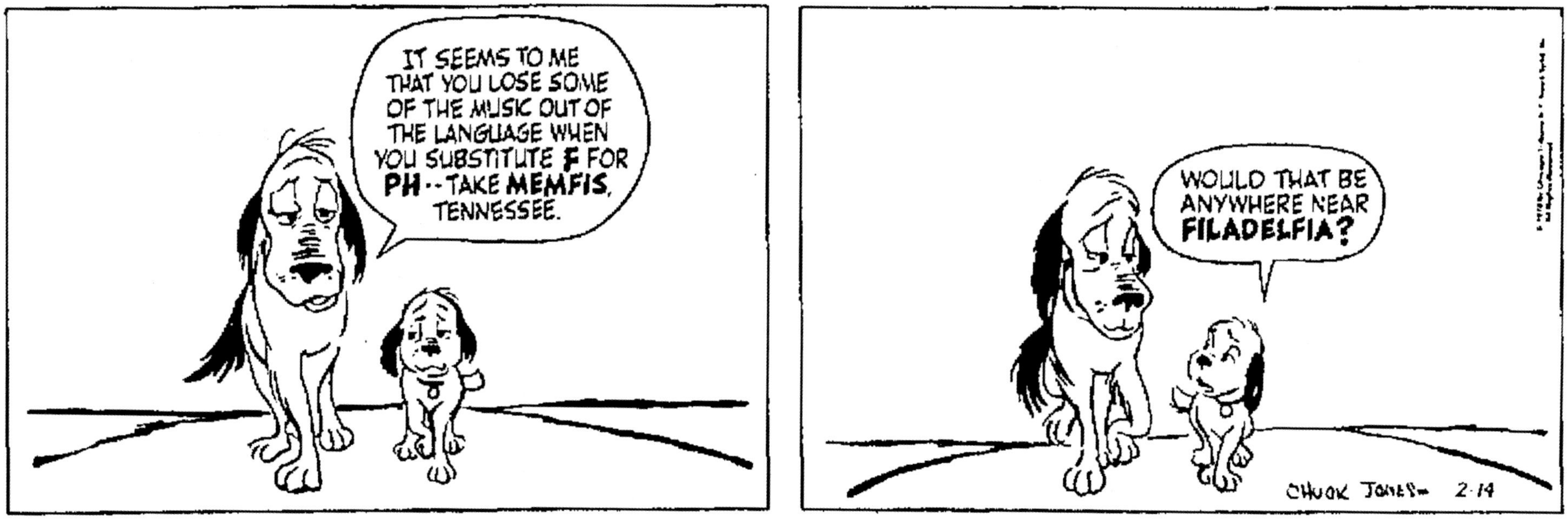
IT SEEMS TO ME THAT YOU LOSE SOME OF THE MUSIC OUT OF THE LANGUAGE WHEN YOU SUBSTITUTE F FOR PH--TAKE MEMFIS, TENNESSEE.
WOULD THAT BE ANYWHERE NEAR FILADELFIA?
CHUCK JONES
2-14

One of a handful of strips for which Chuck Jones's files contain no original art or printed version; rather than omit the strip, we print it from a microfilm copy.

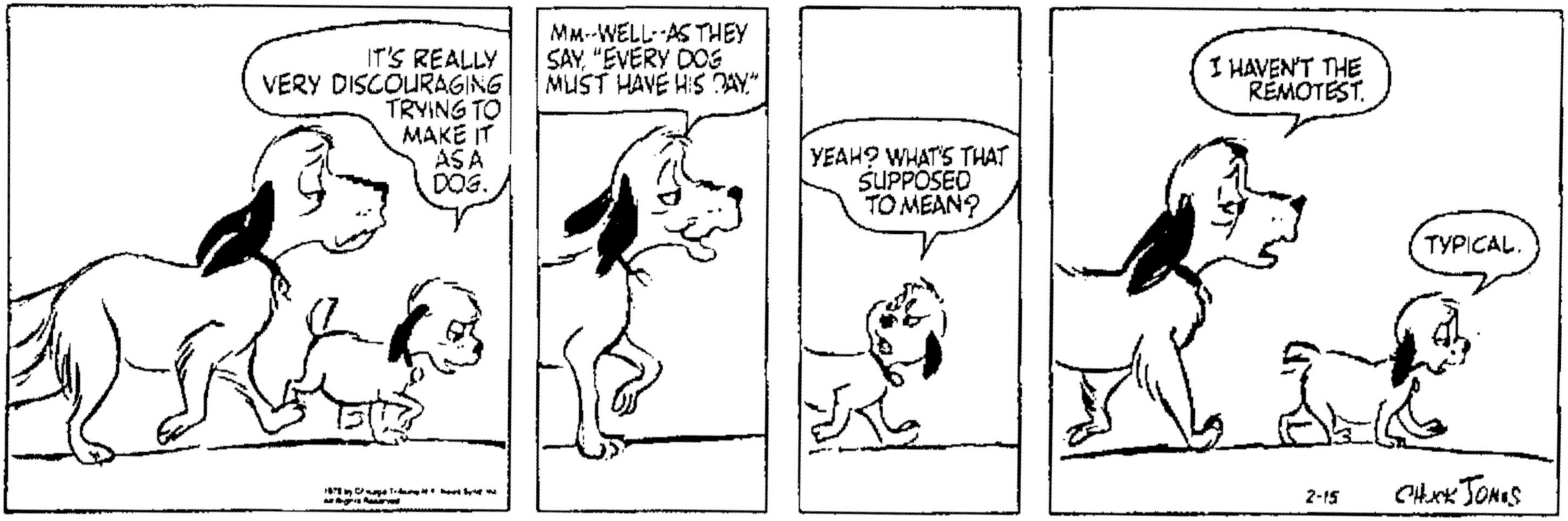
IT'S REALLY VERY DISCOURAGING TRYING TO MAKE IT AS A DOG.
MM--WELL--AS THEY SAY, "EVERY DOG MUST HAVE HIS DAY."
YEAH? WHAT'S THAT SUPPOSED TO MEAN?
I HAVEN'T THE REMOTEST.
TYPICAL.
2-15
CHUCK JONES

One of a handful of strips for which Chuck Jones's files contain no original art or printed version; rather than omit the strip, we print it from a microfilm copy.

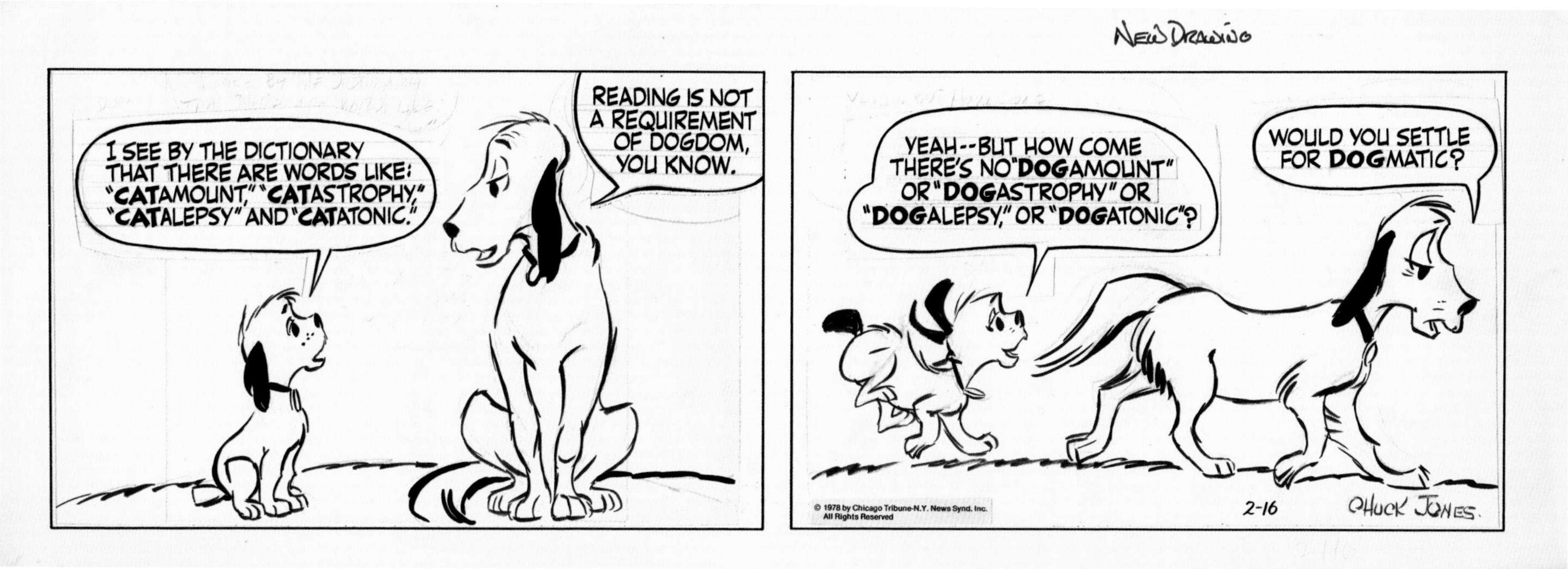
NEW DRAWING
I SEE BY THE DICTIONARY THAT THERE ARE WORDS LIKE: "**CAT**AMOUNT," "**CAT**ASTROPHY," "**CAT**ALEPSY" AND "**CAT**ATONIC."
READING IS NOT A REQUIREMENT OF DOGDOM, YOU KNOW.
YEAH--BUT HOW COME THERE'S NO "**DOG**AMOUNT" OR "**DOG**ASTROPHY" OR "**DOG**ALEPSY," OR "**DOG**ATONIC"?
WOULD YOU SETTLE FOR **DOG**MATIC?
© 1978 by Chicago Tribune-N.Y. News Synd. Inc.
All Rights Reserved
2-16
CHUCK JONES.

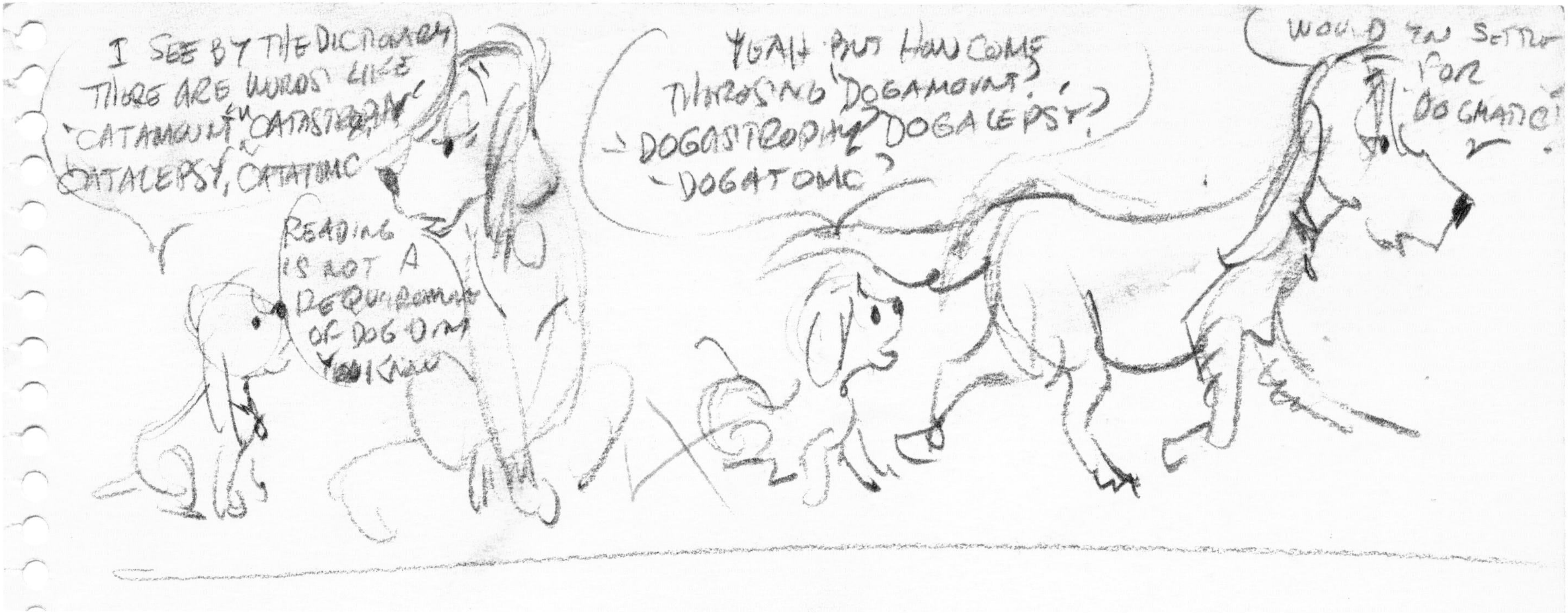
I SEE BY THE DICTIONARY
READING IS NOT A
DOGALEPSY?
DOGATONIC?
FOR DOGMATIC?

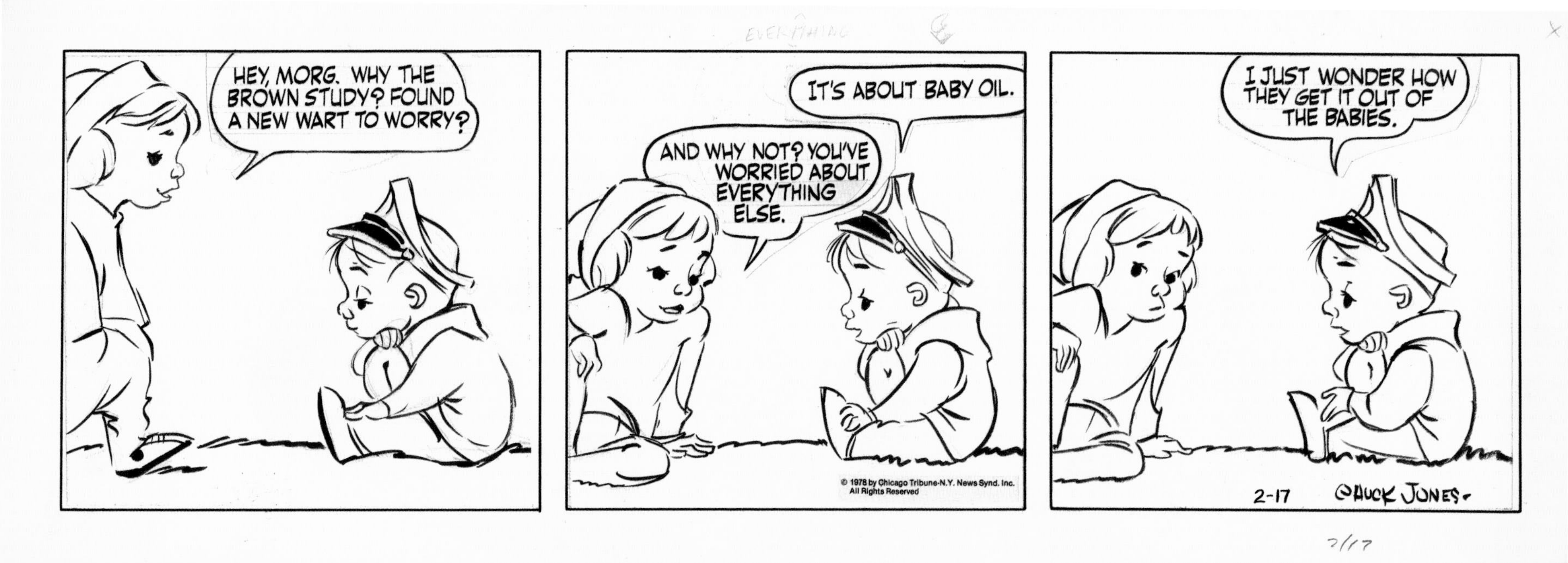
HEY, MORG. WHY THE BROWN STUDY? FOUND A NEW WART TO WORRY?
IT'S ABOUT BABY OIL.
AND WHY NOT? YOU'VE WORRIED ABOUT EVERYTHING ELSE.
I JUST WONDER HOW THEY GET IT OUT OF THE BABIES.
© 1978 by Chicago Tribune-N.Y. News Synd. Inc. All Rights Reserved
2-17
2/17

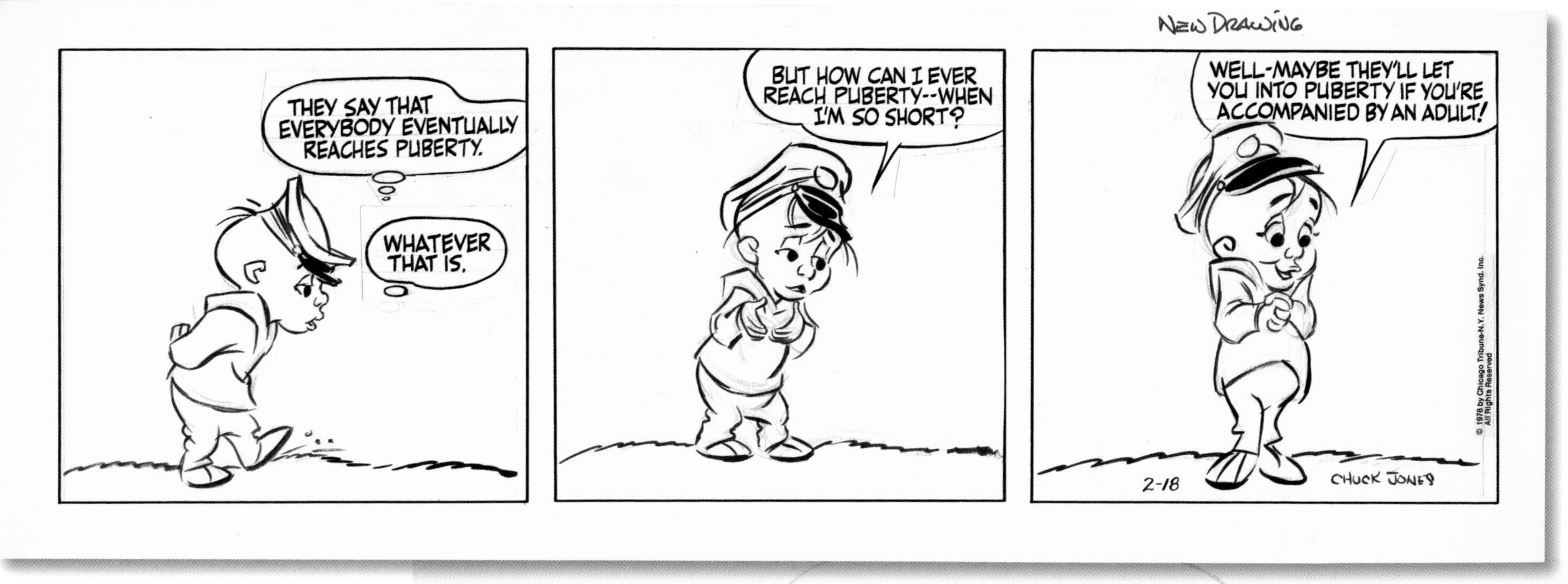
NEW DRAWING
THEY SAY THAT EVERYBODY EVENTUALLY REACHES PUBERTY.
WHATEVER THAT IS.
BUT HOW CAN I EVER REACH PUBERTY--WHEN I'M SO SHORT?
WELL-MAYBE THEY'LL LET YOU INTO PUBERTY IF YOU'RE ACCOMPANIED BY AN ADULT!
© 1978 by Chicago Tribune-N.Y. News Synd. Inc. All Rights Reserved
2-18
CHUCK JONES

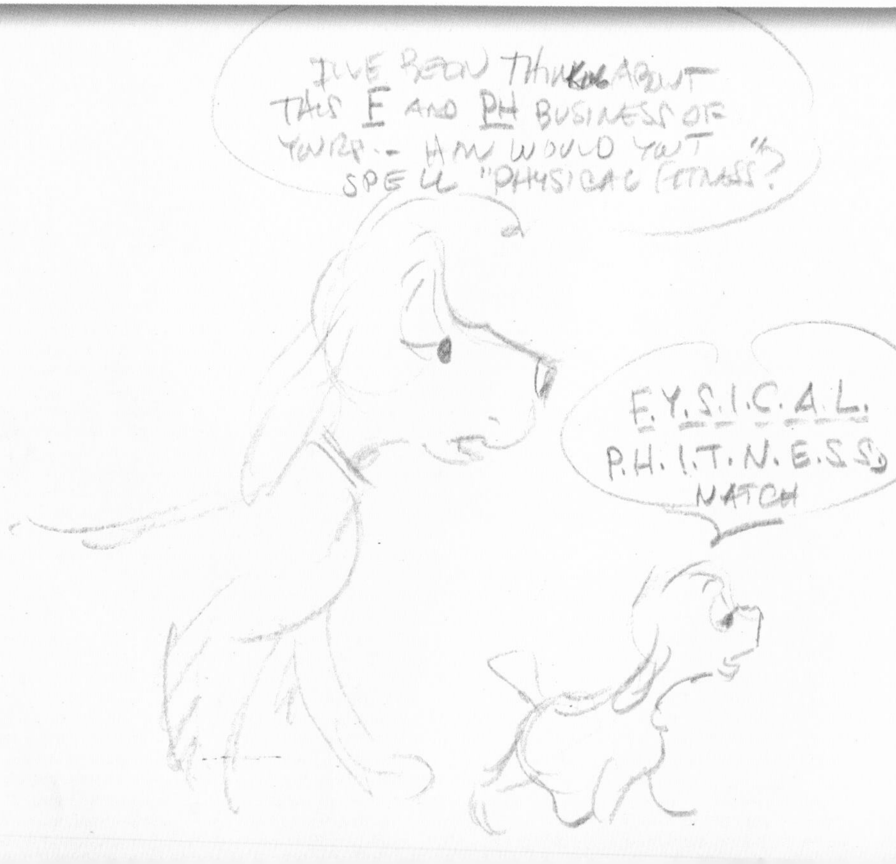
I'VE BEEN THINKING ABOUT THIS F AND PH BUSINESS OF YOURS -- HOW WOULD YOU SPELL "PHYSICAL FITNESS"?
F.Y.S.I.C.A.L. P.H.I.T.N.E.S.S NATCH

2 BOX-6

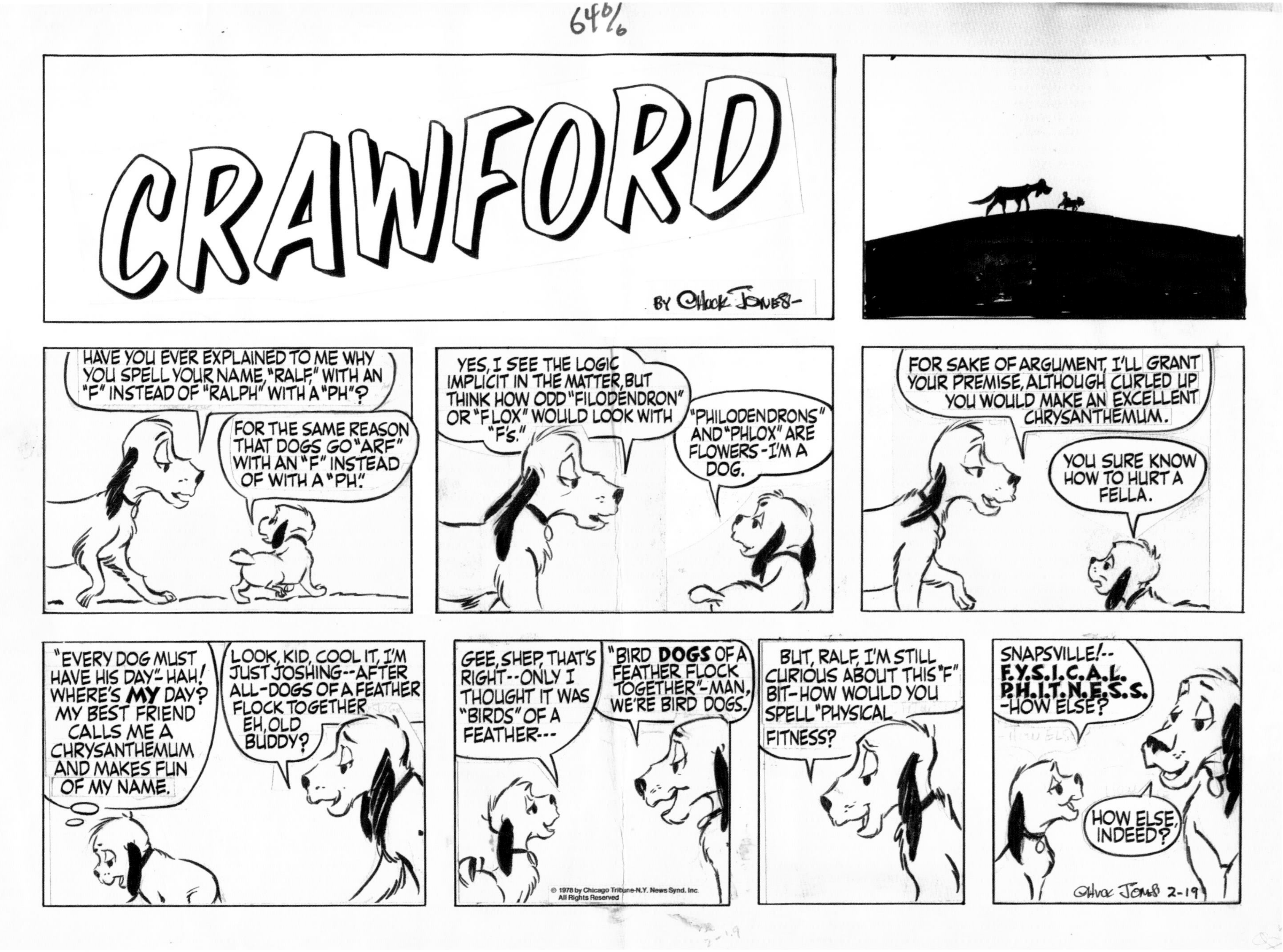

CRAWFORD
BY CHUCK JONES
HAVE YOU EVER EXPLAINED TO ME WHY YOU SPELL YOUR NAME, "RALF," WITH AN "F" INSTEAD OF "RALPH" WITH A "PH"?
FOR THE SAME REASON THAT DOGS GO "ARF" WITH AN "F" INSTEAD OF WITH A "PH."
YES, I SEE THE LOGIC IMPLICIT IN THE MATTER, BUT THINK HOW ODD "FILODENDRON" OR "FLOX" WOULD LOOK WITH "F's."
"PHILODENDRONS" AND "PHLOX" ARE FLOWERS - I'M A DOG.
FOR SAKE OF ARGUMENT, I'LL GRANT YOUR PREMISE, ALTHOUGH CURLED UP YOU WOULD MAKE AN EXCELLENT CHRYSANTHEMUM.
YOU SURE KNOW HOW TO HURT A FELLA.
"EVERY DOG MUST HAVE HIS DAY" - HAH! WHERE'S **MY** DAY? MY BEST FRIEND CALLS ME A CHRYSANTHEMUM AND MAKES FUN OF MY NAME.
LOOK, KID, COOL IT, I'M JUST JOSHING -- AFTER ALL - DOGS OF A FEATHER FLOCK TOGETHER EH, OLD BUDDY?
GEE, SHEP, THAT'S RIGHT -- ONLY I THOUGHT IT WAS "BIRDS" OF A FEATHER---
"BIRD **DOGS** OF A FEATHER FLOCK TOGETHER" - MAN, WE'RE BIRD DOGS.
© 1978 by Chicago Tribune-N.Y. News Synd. Inc. All Rights Reserved
BUT, RALF, I'M STILL CURIOUS ABOUT THIS "F" BIT - HOW WOULD YOU SPELL "PHYSICAL FITNESS"?
SNAPSVILLE! -- **F.Y.S.I.C.A.L. P.H.I.T.N.E.S.S.** - HOW ELSE?
HOW ELSE, INDEED?
CHUCK JONES 2-19

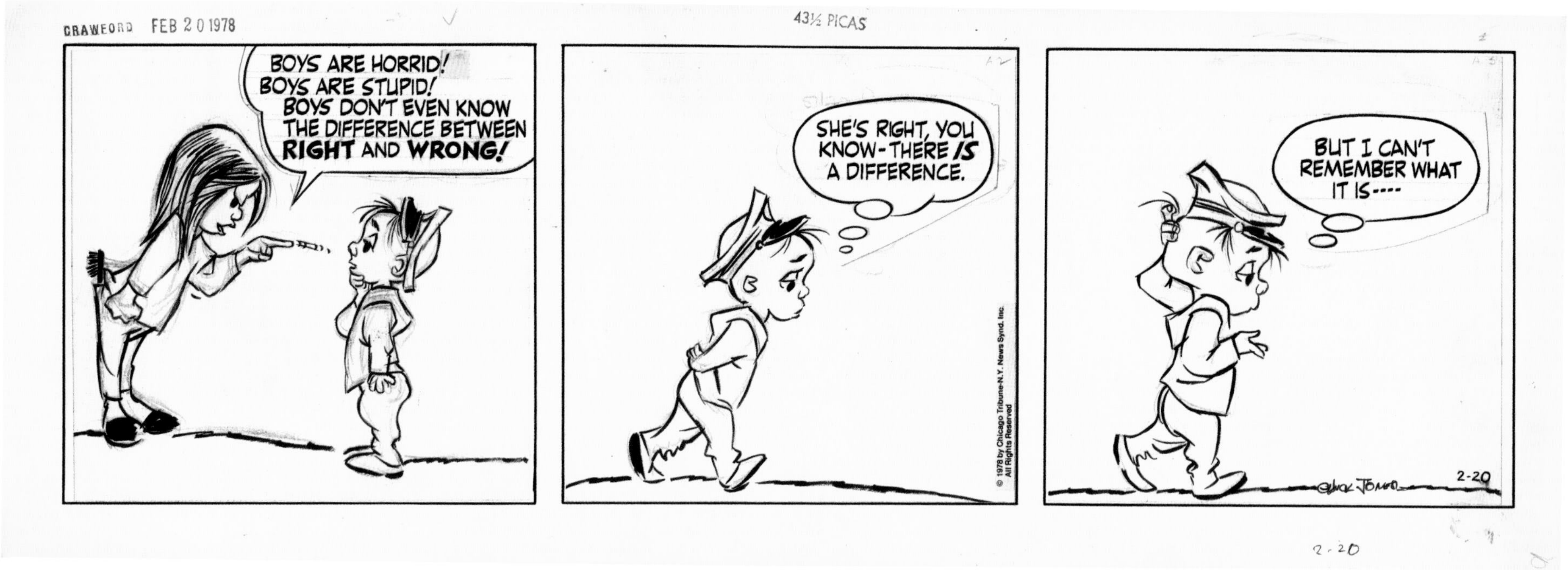
CRAWFORD FEB 20 1978
43½ PICAS
BOYS ARE HORRID! BOYS ARE STUPID! BOYS DON'T EVEN KNOW THE DIFFERENCE BETWEEN **RIGHT** AND **WRONG!**
SHE'S RIGHT, YOU KNOW- THERE *IS* A DIFFERENCE.
© 1978 by Chicago Tribune-N.Y. News Synd. Inc. All Rights Reserved
BUT I CAN'T REMEMBER WHAT IT IS----
2-20
2-20

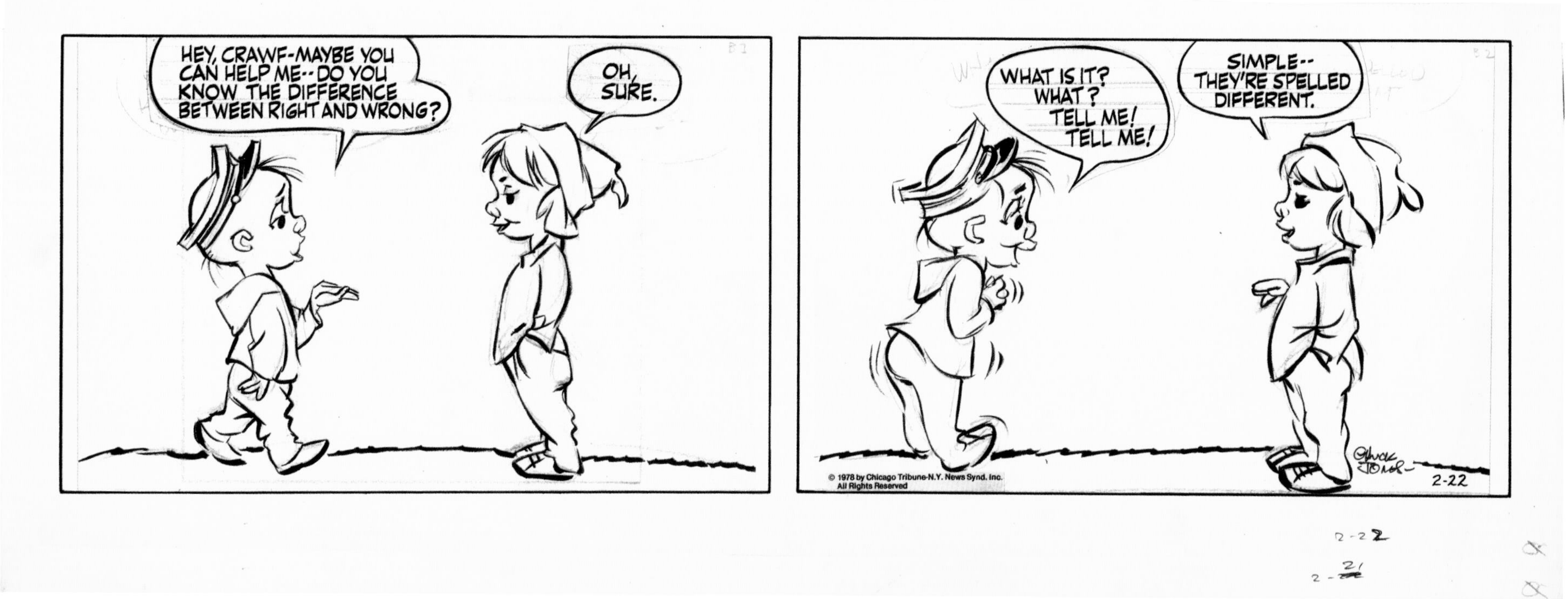
HEY, CRAWF-MAYBE YOU CAN HELP ME--DO YOU KNOW THE DIFFERENCE BETWEEN RIGHT AND WRONG?
OH, SURE.
WHAT IS IT? WHAT? TELL ME! TELL ME!
SIMPLE-- THEY'RE SPELLED DIFFERENT.
© 1978 by Chicago Tribune-N.Y. News Synd. Inc. All Rights Reserved
2-22
2-22

This week's linked gags were dated and printed out of sequence. Jones's notes (see page 120) indicate his intended order.

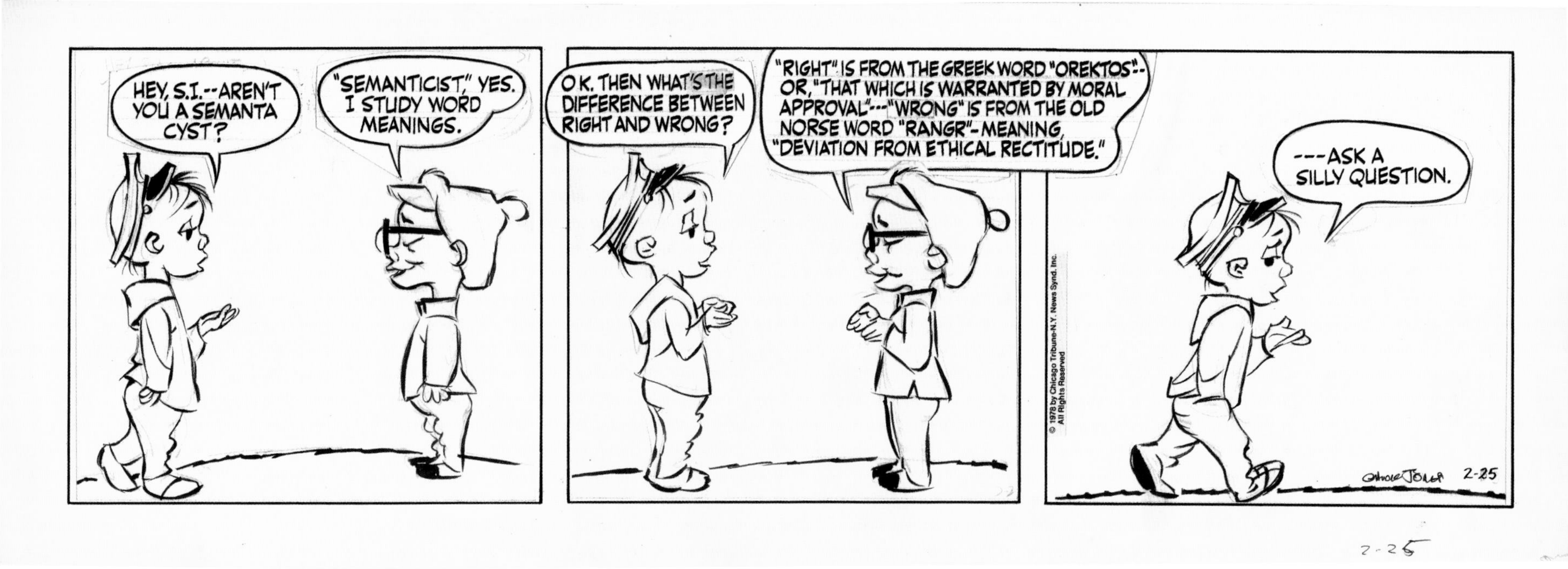
HEY, S.I.--AREN'T YOU A SEMANTA CYST?
"SEMANTICIST," YES. I STUDY WORD MEANINGS.
O K. THEN WHAT'S THE DIFFERENCE BETWEEN RIGHT AND WRONG?
"RIGHT" IS FROM THE GREEK WORD "OREKTOS"-- OR, "THAT WHICH IS WARRANTED BY MORAL APPROVAL"--"WRONG" IS FROM THE OLD NORSE WORD "RANGR"-MEANING, "DEVIATION FROM ETHICAL RECTITUDE."
© 1978 by Chicago Tribune-N.Y. News Synd. Inc. All Rights Reserved
---ASK A SILLY QUESTION.
2-25
2-25

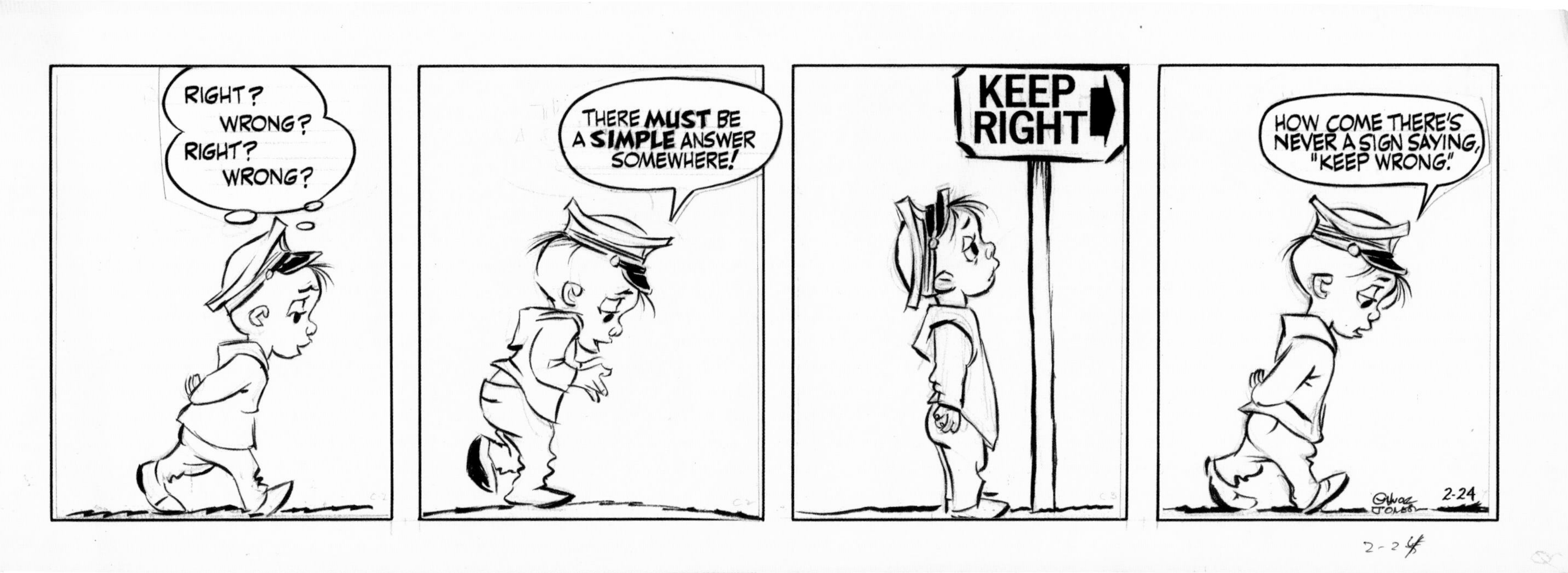
RIGHT? WRONG? RIGHT? WRONG?
THERE MUST BE A SIMPLE ANSWER SOMEWHERE!
KEEP RIGHT
HOW COME THERE'S NEVER A SIGN SAYING, "KEEP WRONG."
2-24

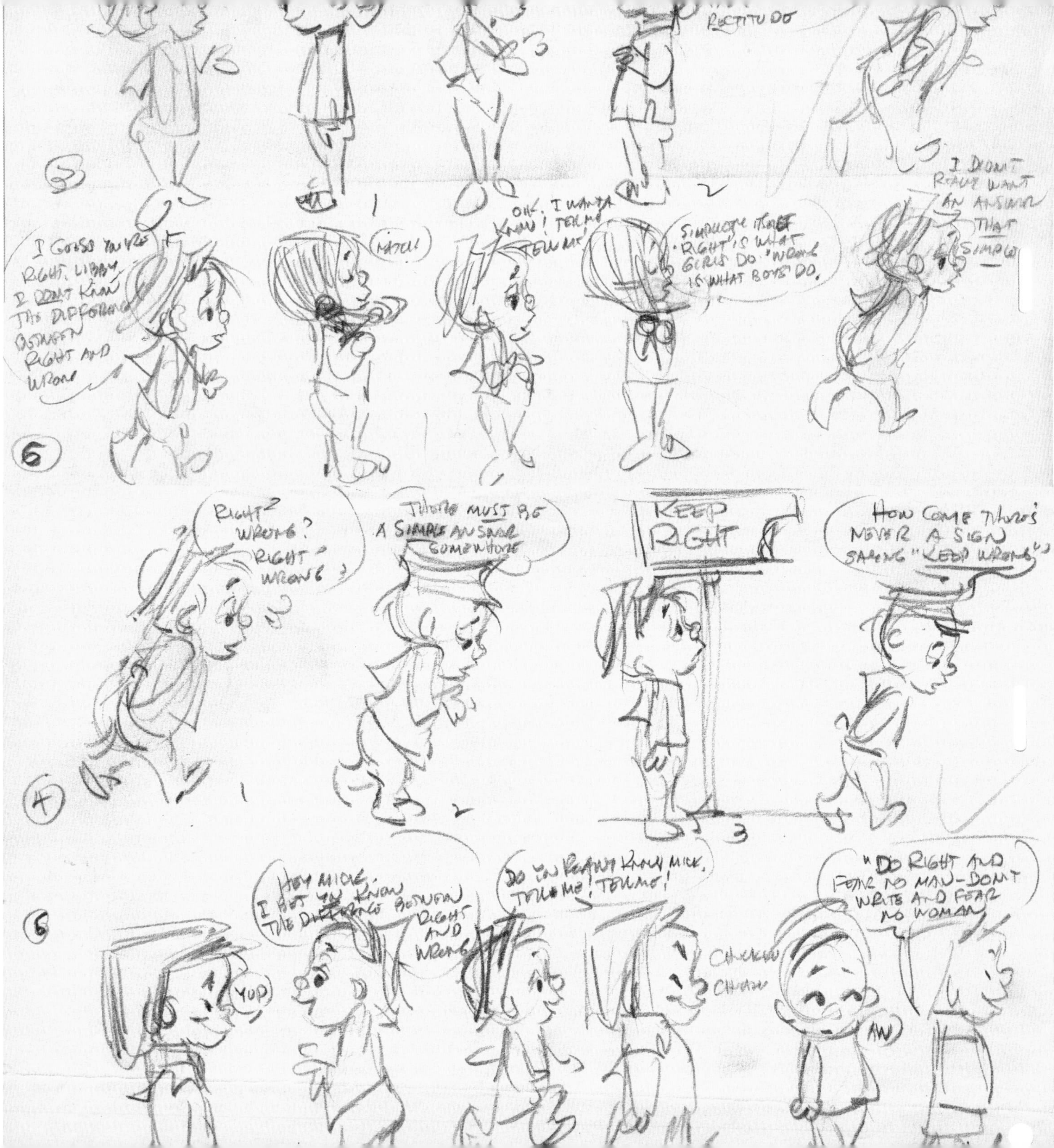

I DON'T REALLY WANT AN ANSWER THAT SIMPLE
I GUESS YOU'RE RIGHT, LIBBY. I DON'T KNOW THE DIFFERENCE BETWEEN RIGHT AND WRONG
OH, I WANNA KNOW! TELL ME TELL ME!
"RIGHT" IS WHAT GIRLS DO "WRONG" IS WHAT BOYS DO.
RIGHT? WRONG? RIGHT? WRONG?
THERE MUST BE A SIMPLE ANSWER SOMEWHERE
KEEP RIGHT
HOW COME THERE'S NEVER A SIGN SAYING "KEEP WRONG"?
HEY MICK, I BET YOU KNOW THE DIFFERENCE BETWEEN RIGHT AND WRONG
YUP
DO YOU REALLY KNOW MICK, TELL ME! TELL ME!
"DO RIGHT AND FEAR NO MAN - DON'T WRITE AND FEAR NO WOMAN"
AW

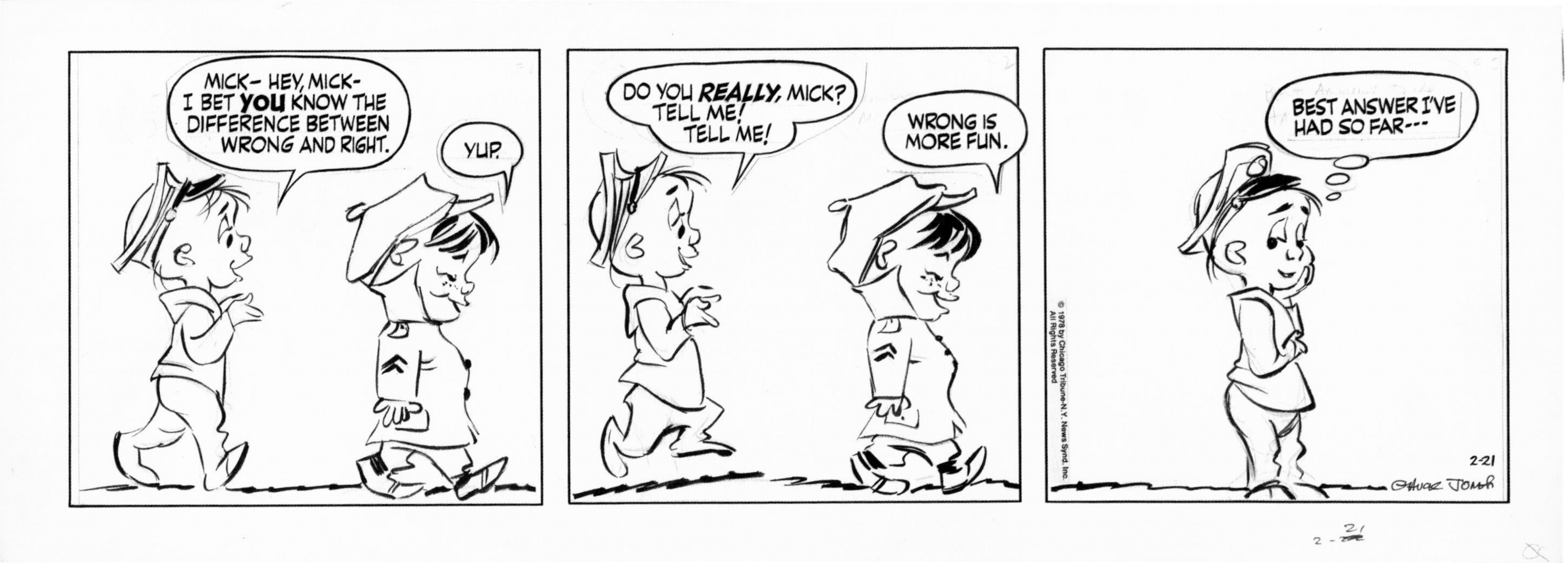
MICK– HEY, MICK– I BET YOU KNOW THE DIFFERENCE BETWEEN WRONG AND RIGHT.
YUP.
DO YOU REALLY, MICK? TELL ME! TELL ME!
WRONG IS MORE FUN.
BEST ANSWER I'VE HAD SO FAR---
© 1978 by Chicago Tribune-N.Y. News Synd. Inc. All Rights Reserved
2-21

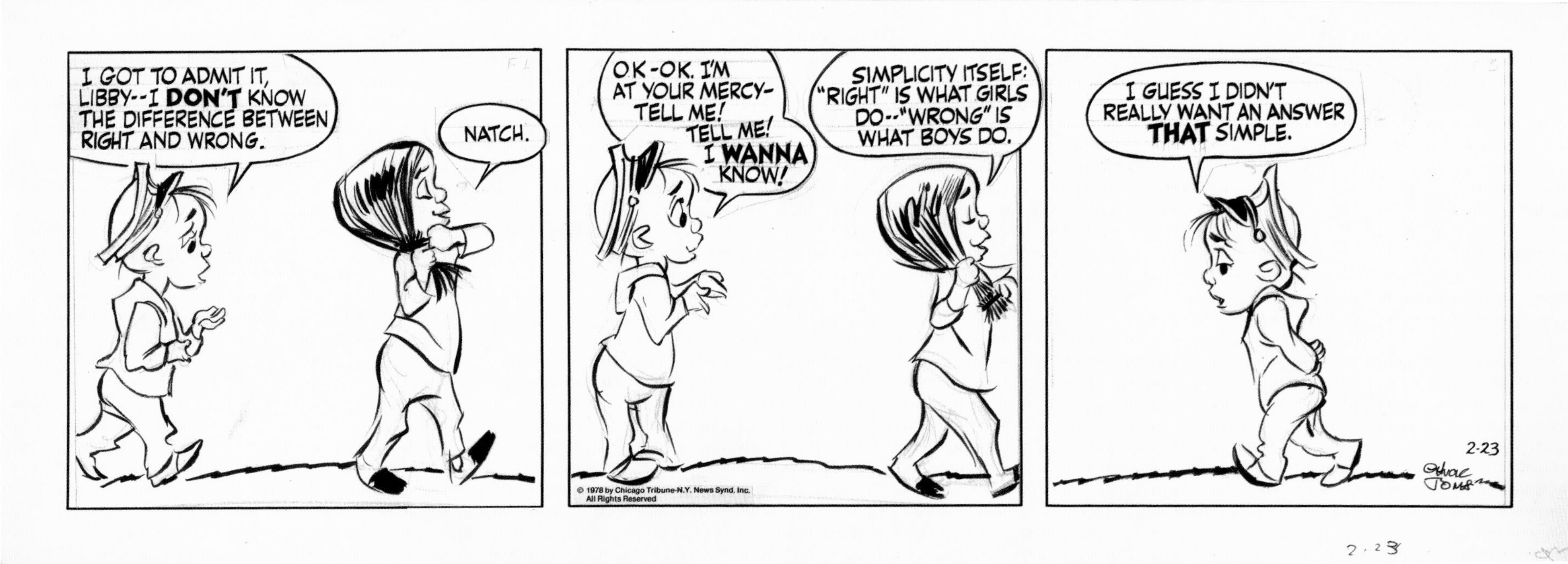
I GOT TO ADMIT IT, LIBBY--I DON'T KNOW THE DIFFERENCE BETWEEN RIGHT AND WRONG.
NATCH.
O.K.-OK. I'M AT YOUR MERCY- TELL ME! TELL ME! I WANNA KNOW!
SIMPLICITY ITSELF: "RIGHT" IS WHAT GIRLS DO--"WRONG" IS WHAT BOYS DO.
I GUESS I DIDN'T REALLY WANT AN ANSWER THAT SIMPLE.
© 1978 by Chicago Tribune-N.Y. News Synd. Inc. All Rights Reserved
2-23

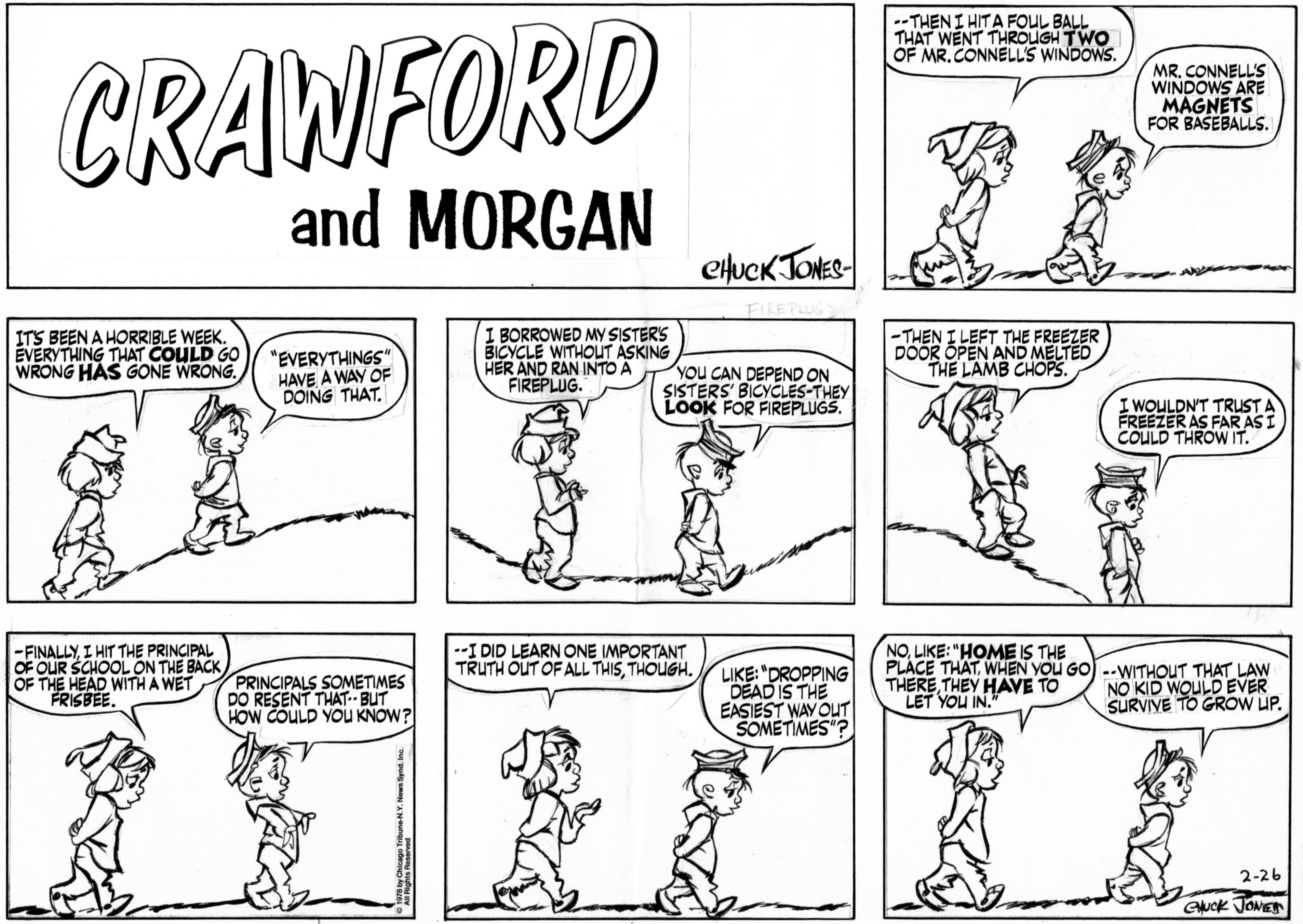
CRAWFORD and MORGAN
CHUCK JONES
--THEN I HIT A FOUL BALL THAT WENT THROUGH TWO OF MR. CONNELL'S WINDOWS.
MR. CONNELL'S WINDOWS ARE MAGNETS FOR BASEBALLS.
IT'S BEEN A HORRIBLE WEEK. EVERYTHING THAT COULD GO WRONG HAS GONE WRONG.
"EVERYTHINGS" HAVE A WAY OF DOING THAT.
I BORROWED MY SISTER'S BICYCLE WITHOUT ASKING HER AND RAN INTO A FIREPLUG.
YOU CAN DEPEND ON SISTERS' BICYCLES-THEY LOOK FOR FIREPLUGS.
-THEN I LEFT THE FREEZER DOOR OPEN AND MELTED THE LAMB CHOPS.
I WOULDN'T TRUST A FREEZER AS FAR AS I COULD THROW IT.
-FINALLY, I HIT THE PRINCIPAL OF OUR SCHOOL ON THE BACK OF THE HEAD WITH A WET FRISBEE.
PRINCIPALS SOMETIMES DO RESENT THAT-- BUT HOW COULD YOU KNOW?
© 1978 by Chicago Tribune-N.Y. News Synd. Inc. All Rights Reserved
--I DID LEARN ONE IMPORTANT TRUTH OUT OF ALL THIS, THOUGH.
LIKE: "DROPPING DEAD IS THE EASIEST WAY OUT SOMETIMES"?
NO, LIKE: "HOME IS THE PLACE THAT, WHEN YOU GO THERE, THEY HAVE TO LET YOU IN."
--WITHOUT THAT LAW NO KID WOULD EVER SURVIVE TO GROW UP.
2-26
CHUCK JONES

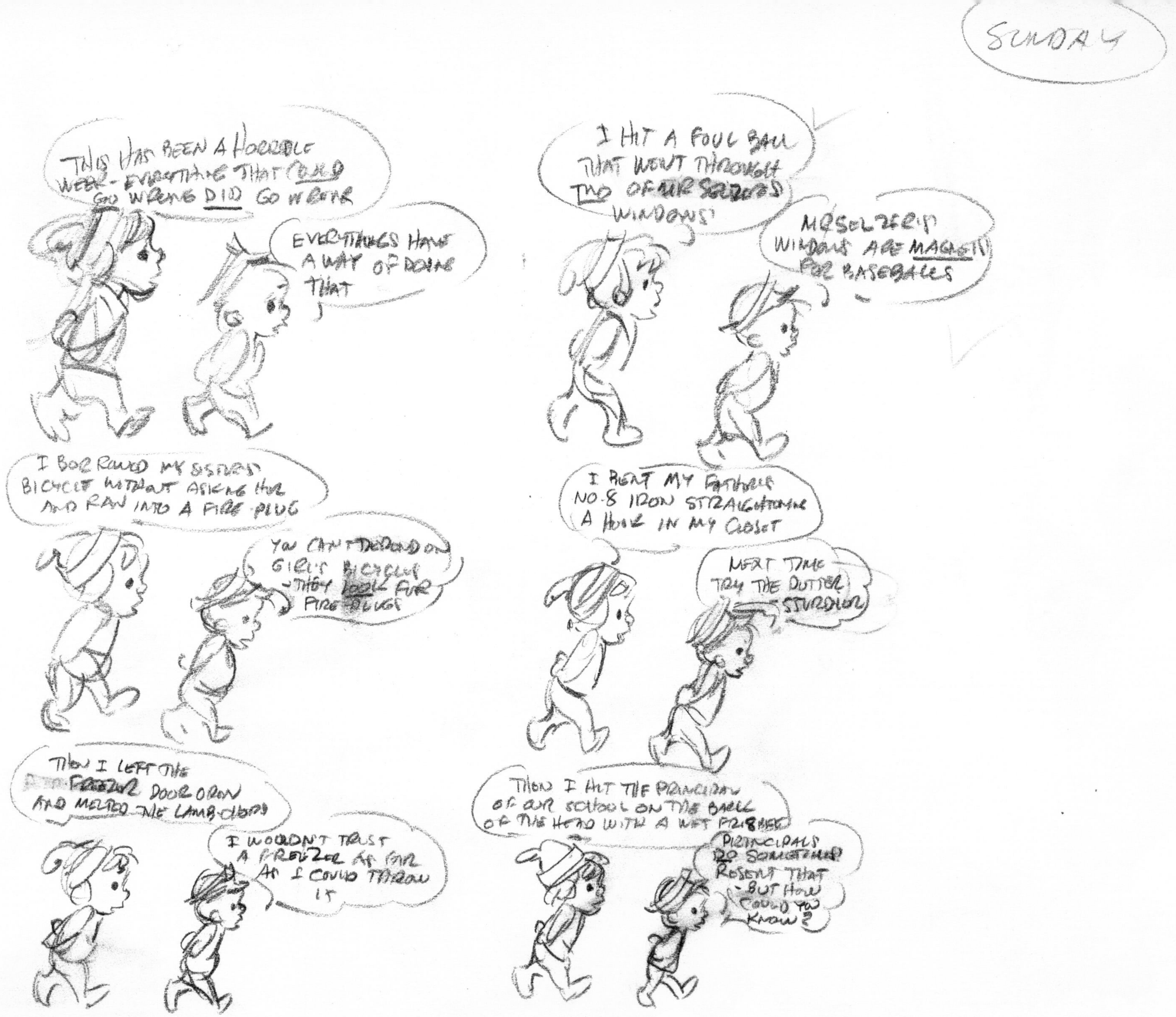
SUNDAY
THIS HAS BEEN A HORRIBLE WEEK - EVERYTHING THAT COULD GO WRONG DID GO WRONG
EVERYTHINGS HAVE A WAY OF DOING THAT
I HIT A FOUL BALL THAT WENT THROUGH TWO OF MR SELZER'S WINDOWS!
MR SELZER'S WINDOWS ARE MAGNETS FOR BASEBALLS
I BORROWED MY SISTER'S BICYCLE WITHOUT ASKING HER AND RAN INTO A FIRE PLUG
YOU CAN'T DEPEND ON GIRL'S BICYCLES - THEY LOOK FOR FIRE PLUGS
I BENT MY FATHER'S NO. 8 IRON STRAIGHTENING A HOOK IN MY CLOSET
NEXT TIME TRY THE BUTTER STIRRER
THEN I LEFT THE FREEZER DOOR OPEN AND MELTED THE LAMB CHOPS
I WOULDN'T TRUST A FREEZER AS FAR AS I COULD THROW IT
THEN I HIT THE PRINCIPAL OF OUR SCHOOL ON THE BACK OF THE HEAD WITH A WET FRISBEE
PRINCIPALS DO SOMETIMES RESENT THAT - BUT HOW COULD YOU KNOW?

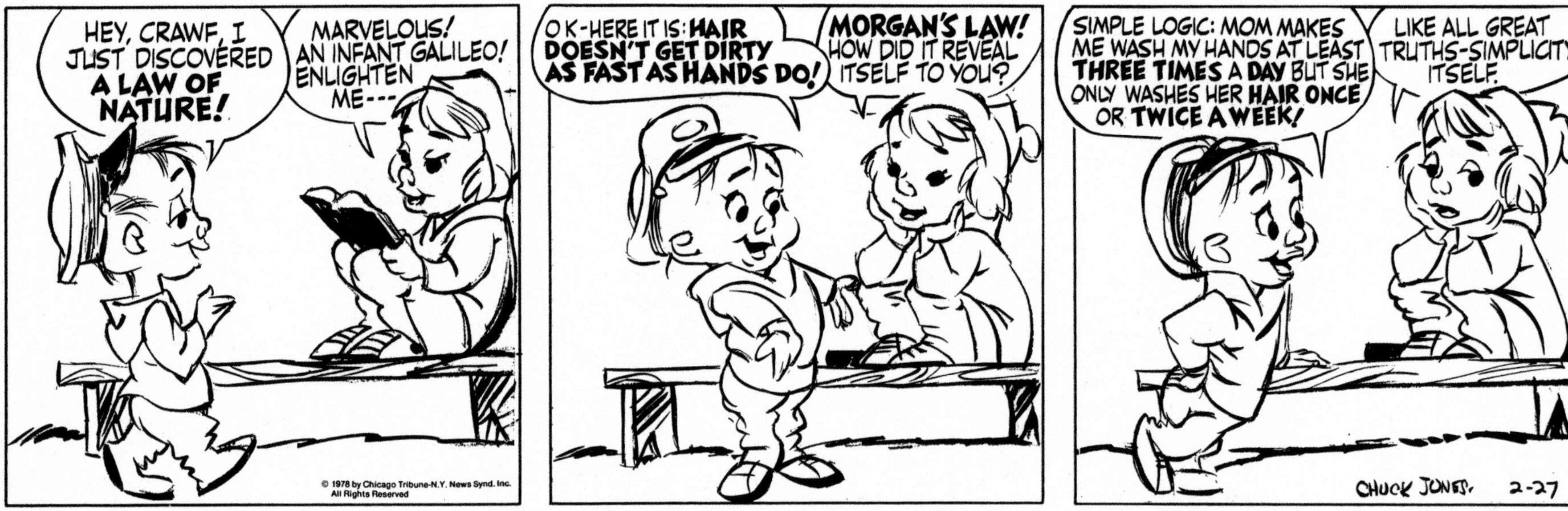

HEY, CRAWF, I JUST DISCOVERED **A LAW OF NATURE!**
MARVELOUS! AN INFANT GALILEO! ENLIGHTEN ME---
O K-HERE IT IS: **HAIR DOESN'T GET DIRTY AS FAST AS HANDS DO!**
MORGAN'S LAW! HOW DID IT REVEAL ITSELF TO YOU?
SIMPLE LOGIC: MOM MAKES ME WASH MY HANDS AT LEAST **THREE TIMES A DAY** BUT SHE ONLY WASHES HER **HAIR ONCE** OR **TWICE A WEEK!**
LIKE ALL GREAT TRUTHS-SIMPLICITY ITSELF.
© 1978 by Chicago Tribune-N.Y. News Synd. Inc. All Rights Reserved
CHUCK JONES. 2-27

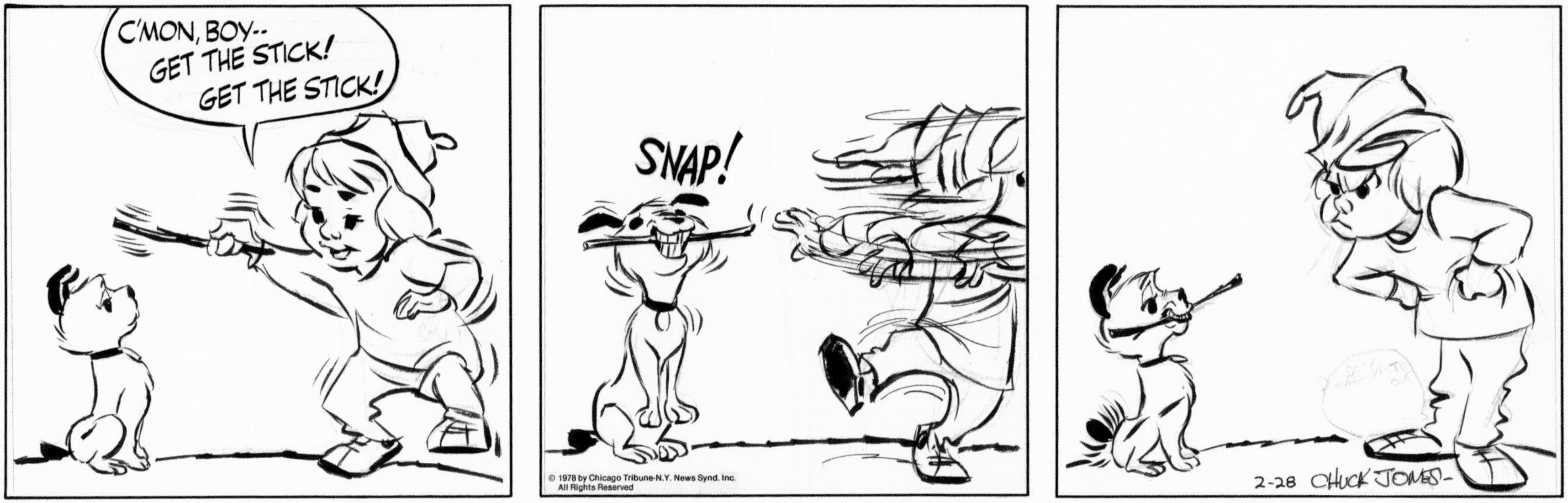

C'MON, BOY.. GET THE STICK! GET THE STICK!
SNAP!
© 1978 by Chicago Tribune-N.Y. News Synd. Inc. All Rights Reserved
2-28 CHUCK JONES-

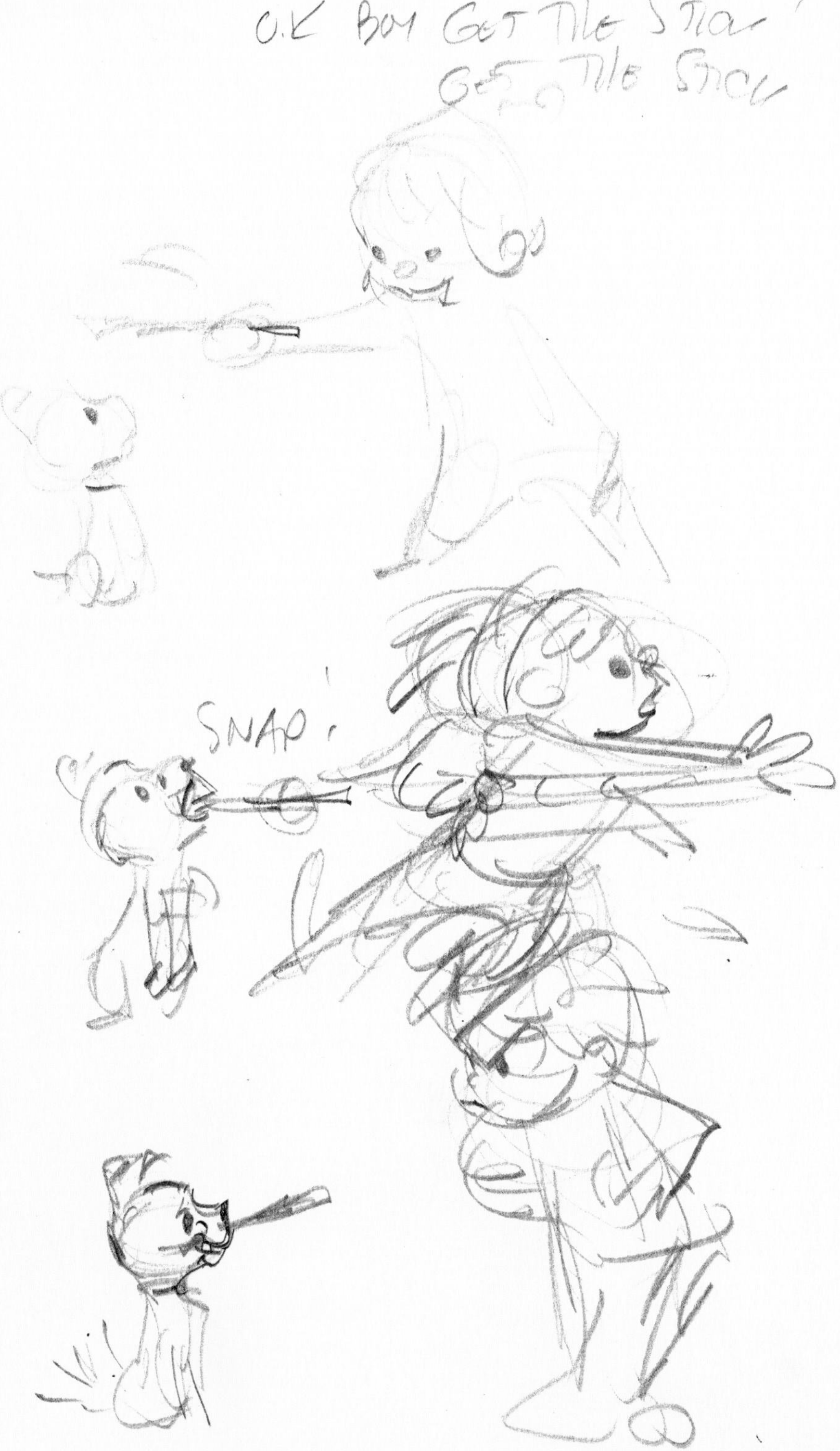
O.K BOY GET THE STICK!
GET THE STICK
SNAP!

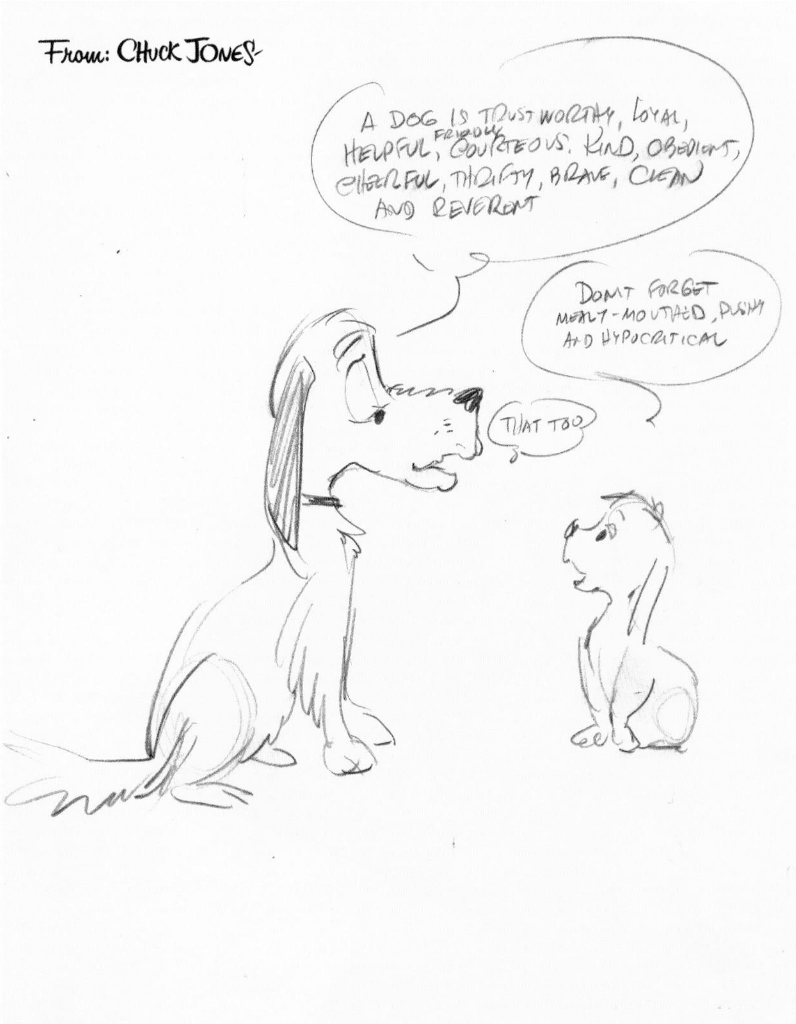
From: CHUCK JONES
A DOG IS TRUSTWORTHY, LOYAL, HELPFUL, FRIENDLY, COURTEOUS, KIND, OBEDIENT, CHEERFUL, THRIFTY, BRAVE, CLEAN AND REVERENT
DONT FORGET MEALY-MOUTHED, PUSHY AND HYPOCRITICAL
THAT TOO

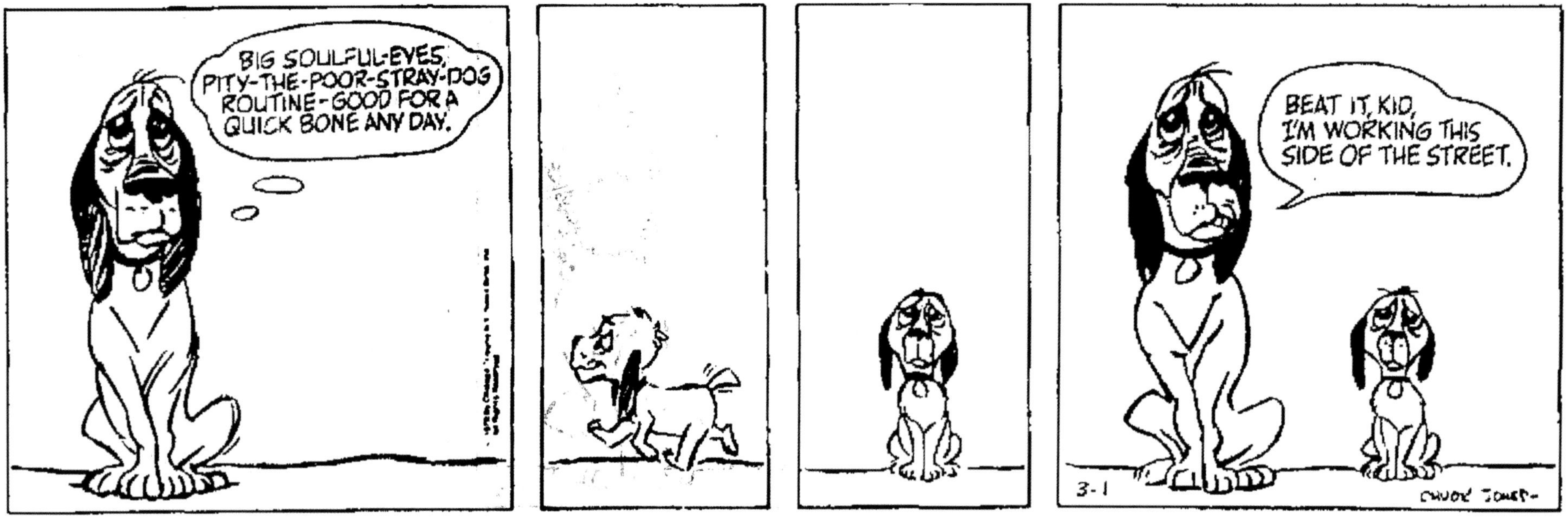

BIG SOULFUL-EYES, PITY-THE-POOR-STRAY-DOG ROUTINE-GOOD FOR A QUICK BONE ANY DAY.
BEAT IT, KID, I'M WORKING THIS SIDE OF THE STREET.
3-1
CHUCK JONES-

One of a handful of strips for which Chuck Jones's files contain no original art or printed version; rather than omit the strip, we print it from a microfilm copy.

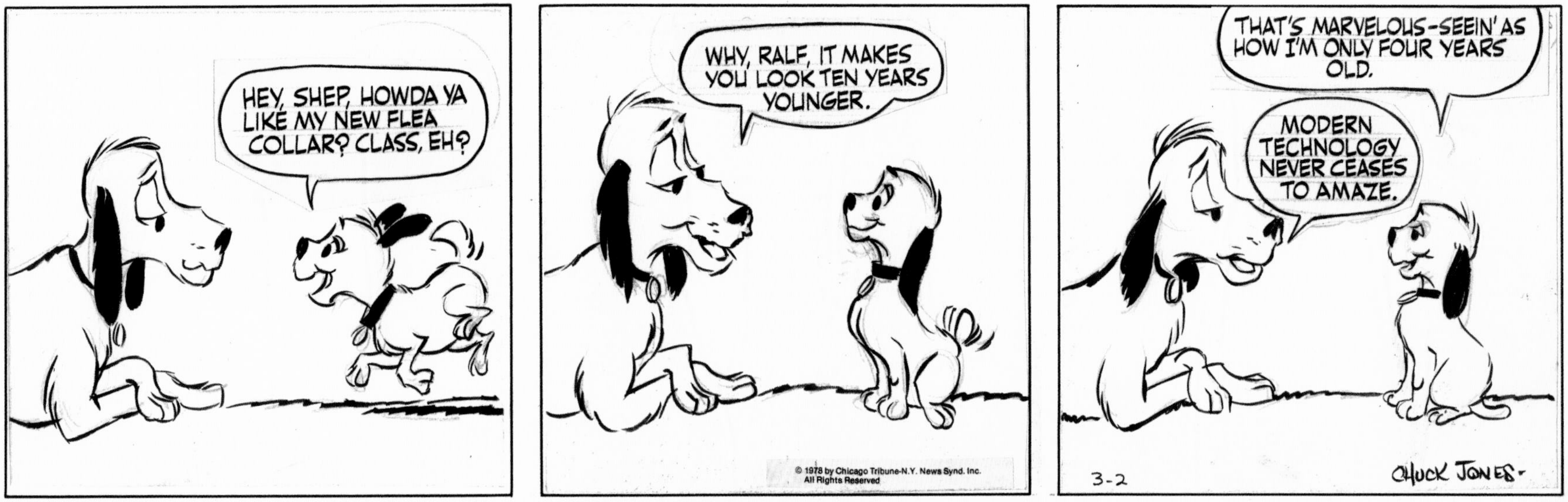

HEY, SHEP, HOWDA YA LIKE MY NEW FLEA COLLAR? CLASS, EH?
WHY, RALF, IT MAKES YOU LOOK TEN YEARS YOUNGER.
© 1978 by Chicago Tribune-N.Y. News Synd. Inc.
All Rights Reserved
THAT'S MARVELOUS-SEEIN' AS HOW I'M ONLY FOUR YEARS OLD.
MODERN TECHNOLOGY NEVER CEASES TO AMAZE.
3-2
CHUCK JONES-

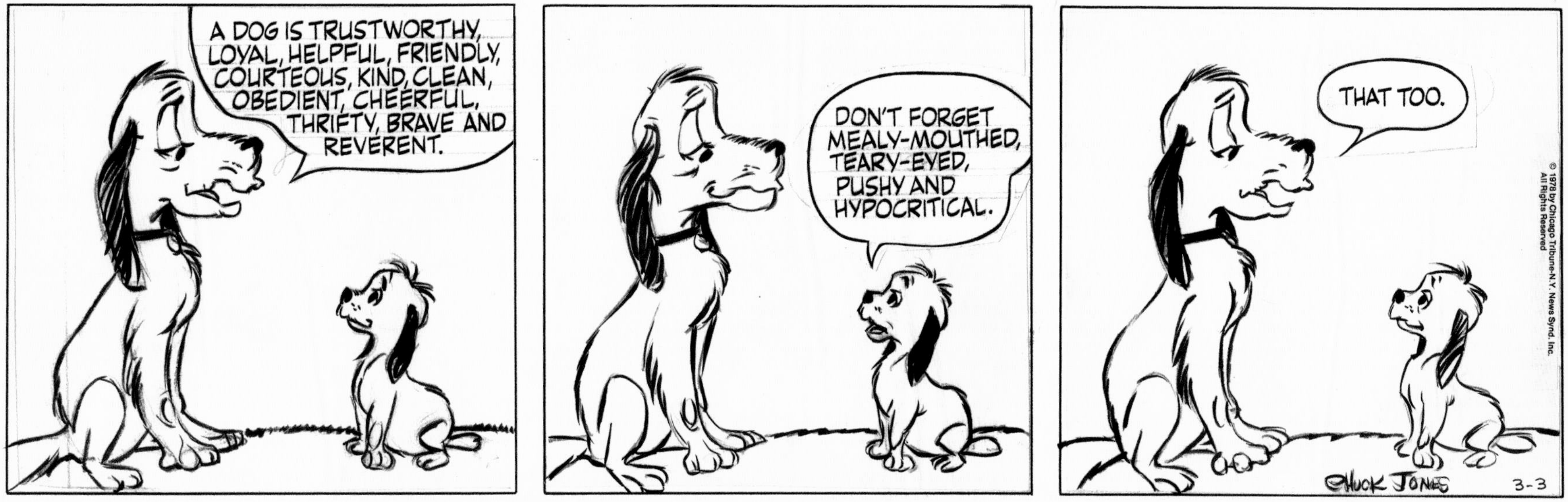
A DOG IS TRUSTWORTHY, LOYAL, HELPFUL, FRIENDLY, COURTEOUS, KIND, CLEAN, OBEDIENT, CHEERFUL, THRIFTY, BRAVE AND REVERENT.
DON'T FORGET MEALY-MOUTHED, TEARY-EYED, PUSHY AND HYPOCRITICAL.
THAT TOO.
© 1978 by Chicago Tribune-N.Y. News Synd. Inc. All Rights Reserved
CHUCK JONES
3-3

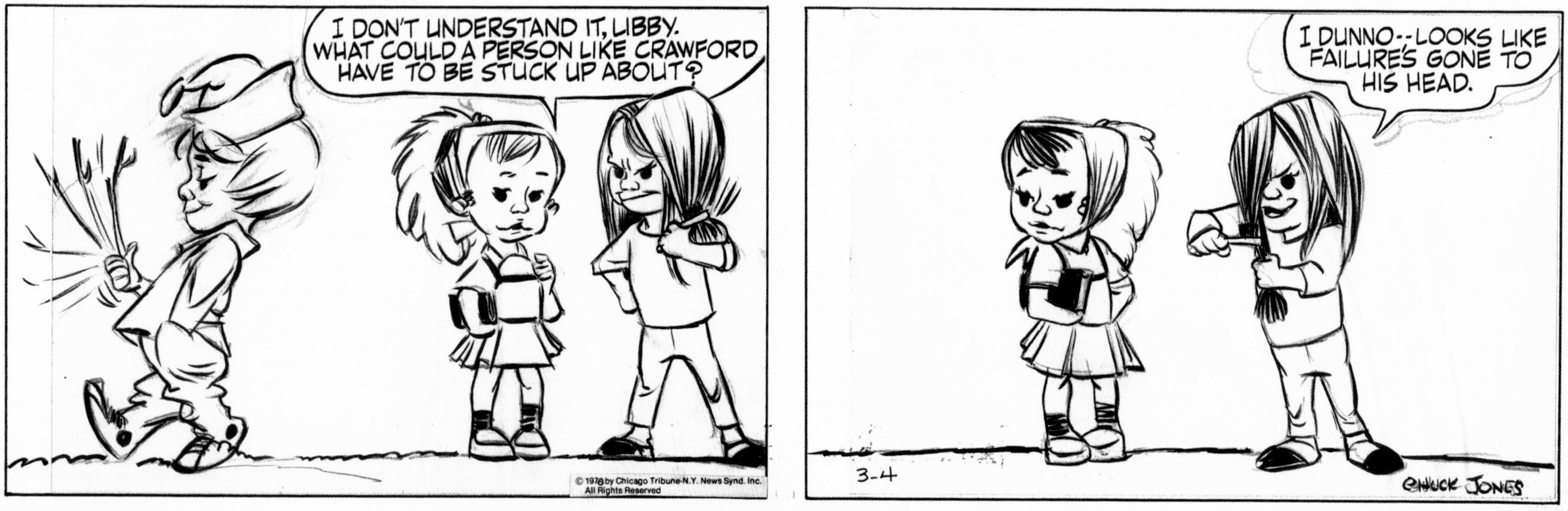
I DON'T UNDERSTAND IT, LIBBY. WHAT COULD A PERSON LIKE CRAWFORD HAVE TO BE STUCK UP ABOUT?
© 1978 by Chicago Tribune-N.Y. News Synd. Inc. All Rights Reserved
I DUNNO--LOOKS LIKE FAILURE'S GONE TO HIS HEAD.
3-4
CHUCK JONES

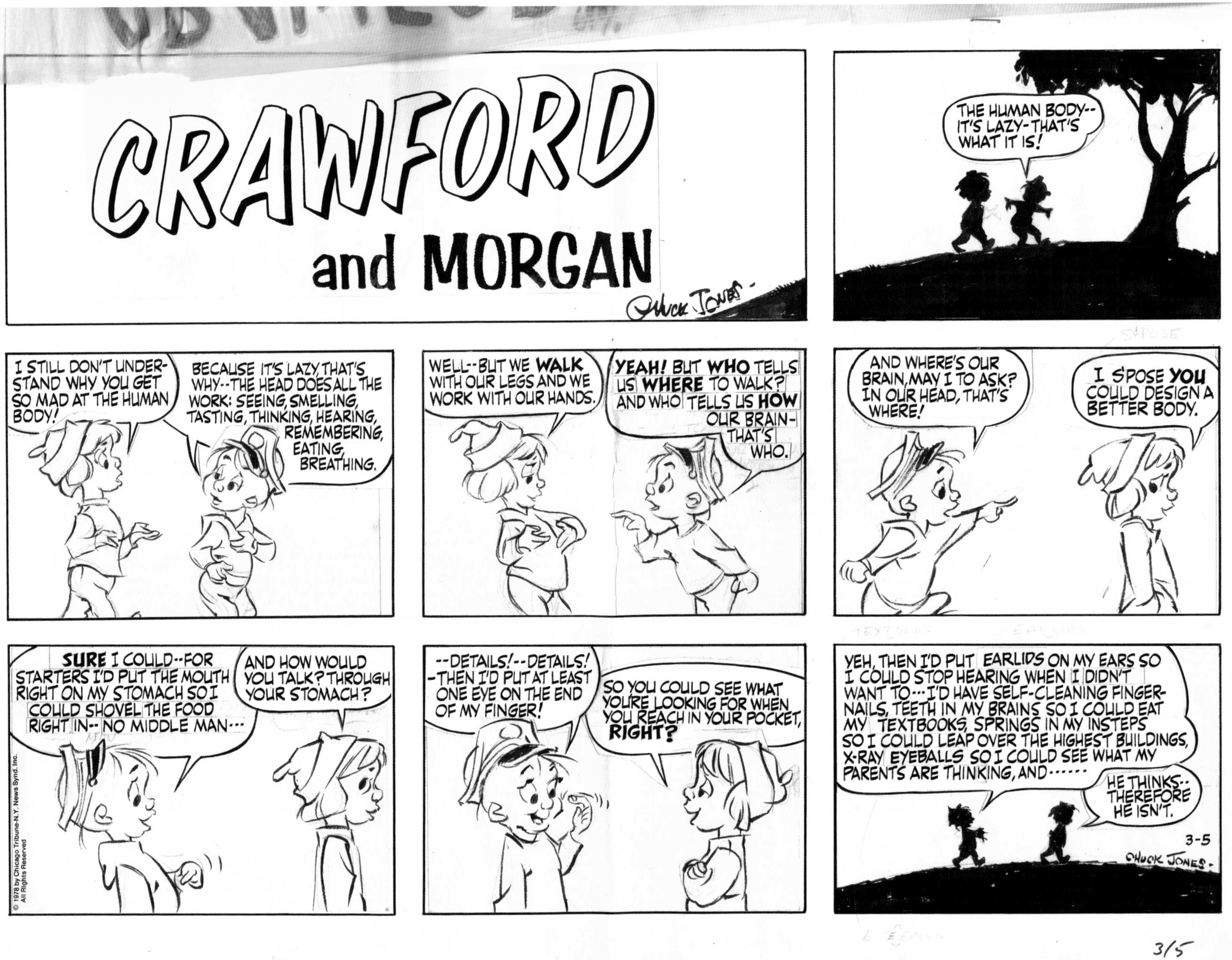
CRAWFORD
and MORGAN
CHUCK JONES
THE HUMAN BODY-- IT'S LAZY-THAT'S WHAT IT IS!
I STILL DON'T UNDERSTAND WHY YOU GET SO MAD AT THE HUMAN BODY!
BECAUSE IT'S LAZY, THAT'S WHY--THE HEAD DOES ALL THE WORK: SEEING, SMELLING, TASTING, THINKING, HEARING, REMEMBERING, EATING, BREATHING.
WELL--BUT WE WALK WITH OUR LEGS AND WE WORK WITH OUR HANDS.
YEAH! BUT WHO TELLS US WHERE TO WALK? AND WHO TELLS US HOW OUR BRAIN-THAT'S WHO.
AND WHERE'S OUR BRAIN, MAY I TO ASK? IN OUR HEAD, THAT'S WHERE!
I S'POSE YOU COULD DESIGN A BETTER BODY.
SURE I COULD--FOR STARTERS I'D PUT THE MOUTH RIGHT ON MY STOMACH SO I COULD SHOVEL THE FOOD RIGHT IN-- NO MIDDLE MAN---
AND HOW WOULD YOU TALK? THROUGH YOUR STOMACH?
--DETAILS!--DETAILS! -THEN I'D PUT AT LEAST ONE EYE ON THE END OF MY FINGER!
SO YOU COULD SEE WHAT YOU'RE LOOKING FOR WHEN YOU REACH IN YOUR POCKET, RIGHT?
YEH, THEN I'D PUT EARLIDS ON MY EARS SO I COULD STOP HEARING WHEN I DIDN'T WANT TO---I'D HAVE SELF-CLEANING FINGER-NAILS, TEETH IN MY BRAINS SO I COULD EAT MY TEXTBOOKS, SPRINGS IN MY INSTEPS SO I COULD LEAP OVER THE HIGHEST BUILDINGS, X-RAY EYEBALLS SO I COULD SEE WHAT MY PARENTS ARE THINKING, AND------
HE THINKS.. THEREFORE HE ISN'T.
3-5
CHUCK JONES
© 1978 by Chicago Tribune-N.Y. News Synd. Inc. All Rights Reserved
3/5

Chuck Jones's color guide for the engravers.

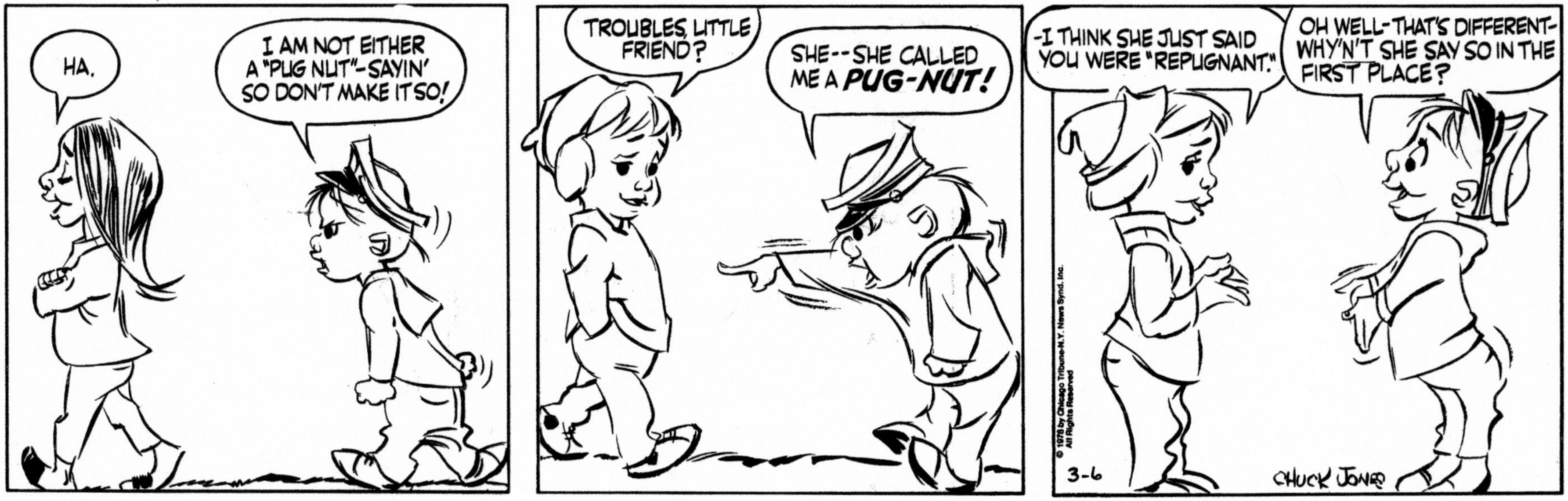
HA.
I AM NOT EITHER A "PUG NUT"-SAYIN' SO DON'T MAKE IT SO!
TROUBLES, LITTLE FRIEND?
SHE--SHE CALLED ME A **PUG-NUT!**
-I THINK SHE JUST SAID YOU WERE "REPUGNANT."
OH WELL-THAT'S DIFFERENT-WHY'N'T SHE SAY SO IN THE FIRST PLACE?
© 1978 by Chicago Tribune-N.Y. News Synd. Inc. All Rights Reserved
3-6
CHUCK JONES

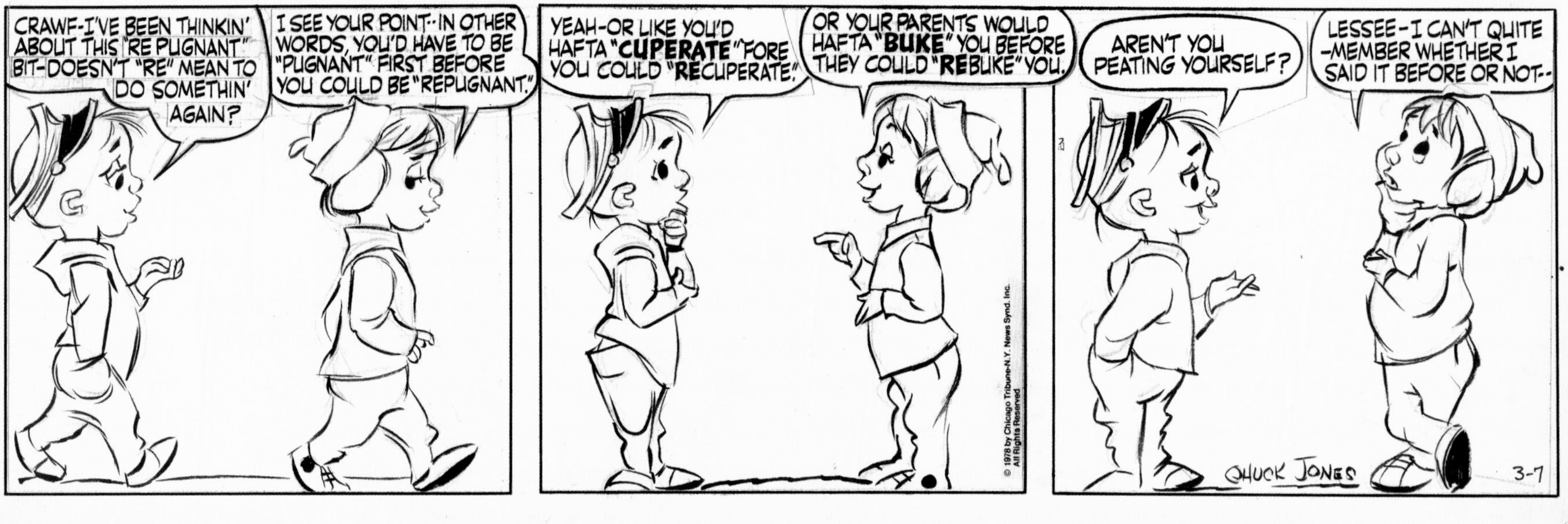
CRAWF-I'VE BEEN THINKIN' ABOUT THIS "RE PUGNANT" BIT-DOESN'T "RE" MEAN TO DO SOMETHIN' AGAIN?
I SEE YOUR POINT--IN OTHER WORDS, YOU'D HAVE TO BE "PUGNANT" FIRST BEFORE YOU COULD BE "REPUGNANT."
YEAH-OR LIKE YOU'D HAFTA "**CUPERATE**" 'FORE YOU COULD "**RE**CUPERATE."
OR YOUR PARENTS WOULD HAFTA "**BUKE**" YOU BEFORE THEY COULD "**RE**BUKE" YOU.
© 1978 by Chicago Tribune-N.Y. News Synd. Inc. All Rights Reserved
AREN'T YOU PEATING YOURSELF?
LESSEE-I CAN'T QUITE -MEMBER WHETHER I SAID IT BEFORE OR NOT--
CHUCK JONES
3-7

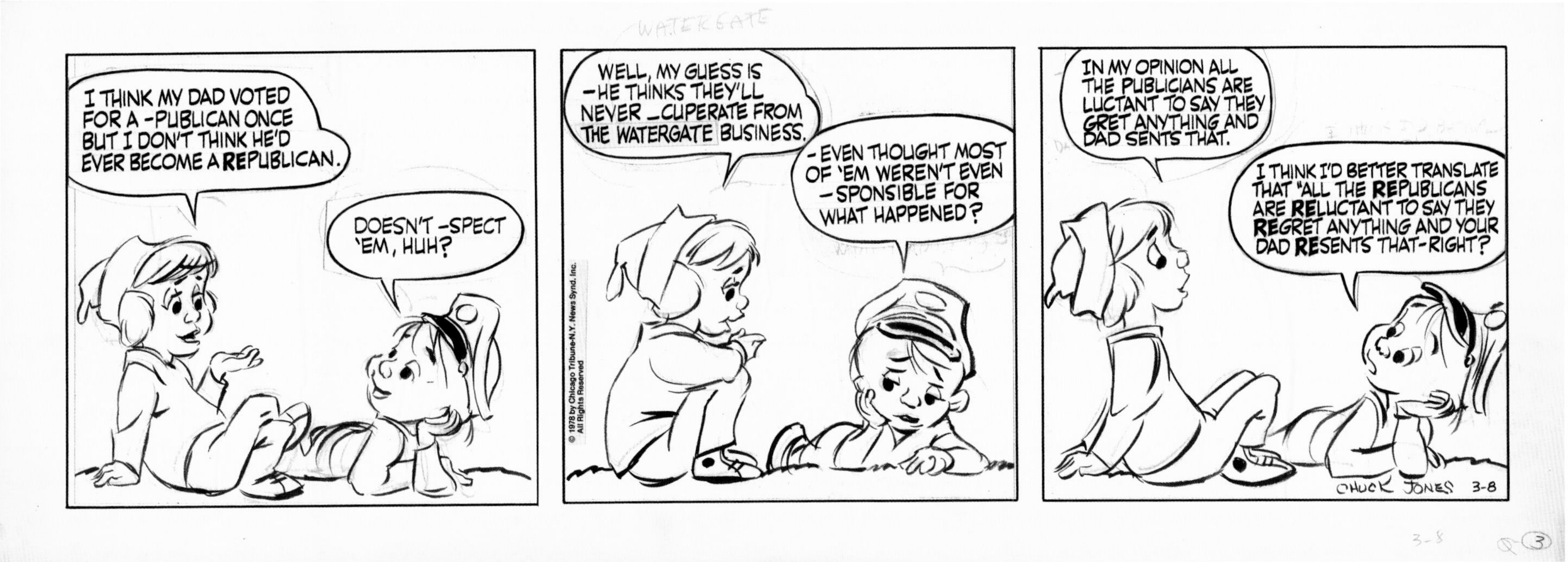
WATERGATE
I THINK MY DAD VOTED FOR A -PUBLICAN ONCE BUT I DON'T THINK HE'D EVER BECOME A REPUBLICAN.
DOESN'T -SPECT 'EM, HUH?
© 1978 by Chicago Tribune-N.Y. News Synd. Inc. All Rights Reserved
WELL, MY GUESS IS -HE THINKS THEY'LL NEVER -CUPERATE FROM THE WATERGATE BUSINESS.
- EVEN THOUGHT MOST OF 'EM WEREN'T EVEN -SPONSIBLE FOR WHAT HAPPENED?
IN MY OPINION ALL THE PUBLICANS ARE LUCTANT TO SAY THEY GRET ANYTHING AND DAD SENTS THAT.
I THINK I'D BETTER TRANSLATE THAT "ALL THE REPUBLICANS ARE RELUCTANT TO SAY THEY REGRET ANYTHING AND YOUR DAD RESENTS THAT-RIGHT?
CHUCK JONES 3-8

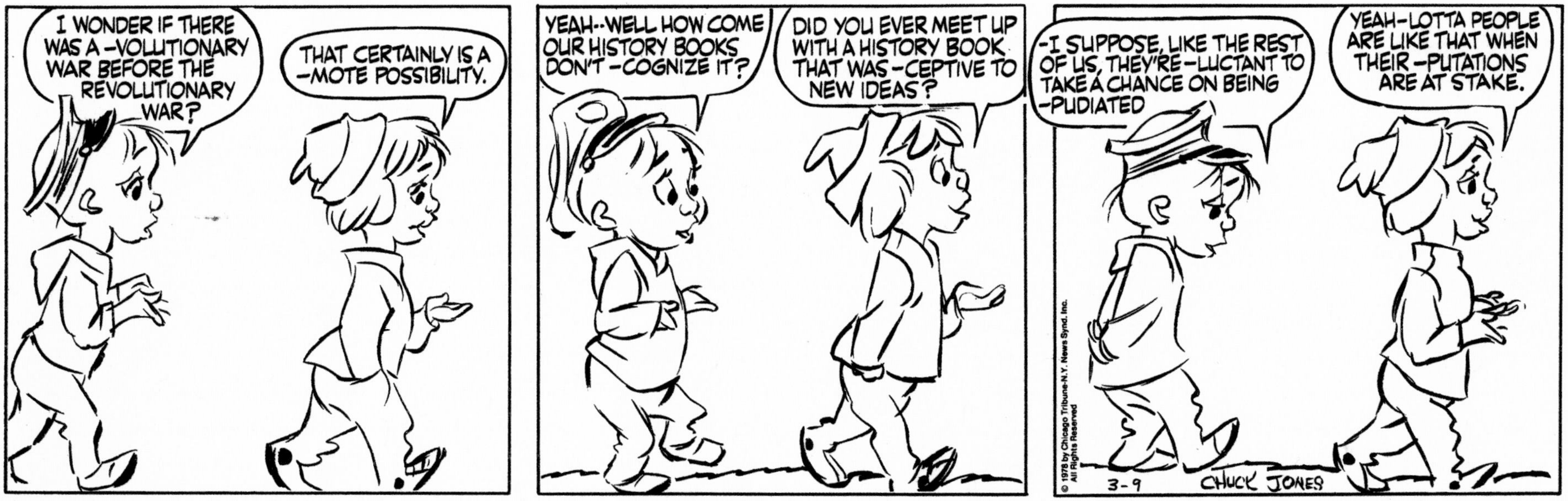
I WONDER IF THERE WAS A -VOLUTIONARY WAR BEFORE THE REVOLUTIONARY WAR?
THAT CERTAINLY IS A -MOTE POSSIBILITY.
YEAH--WELL HOW COME OUR HISTORY BOOKS DON'T -COGNIZE IT?
DID YOU EVER MEET UP WITH A HISTORY BOOK THAT WAS -CEPTIVE TO NEW IDEAS?
-I SUPPOSE, LIKE THE REST OF US, THEY'RE -LUCTANT TO TAKE A CHANCE ON BEING -PUDIATED
YEAH-LOTTA PEOPLE ARE LIKE THAT WHEN THEIR -PUTATIONS ARE AT STAKE.
© 1978 by Chicago Tribune-N.Y. News Synd. Inc. All Rights Reserved
3-9 CHUCK JONES

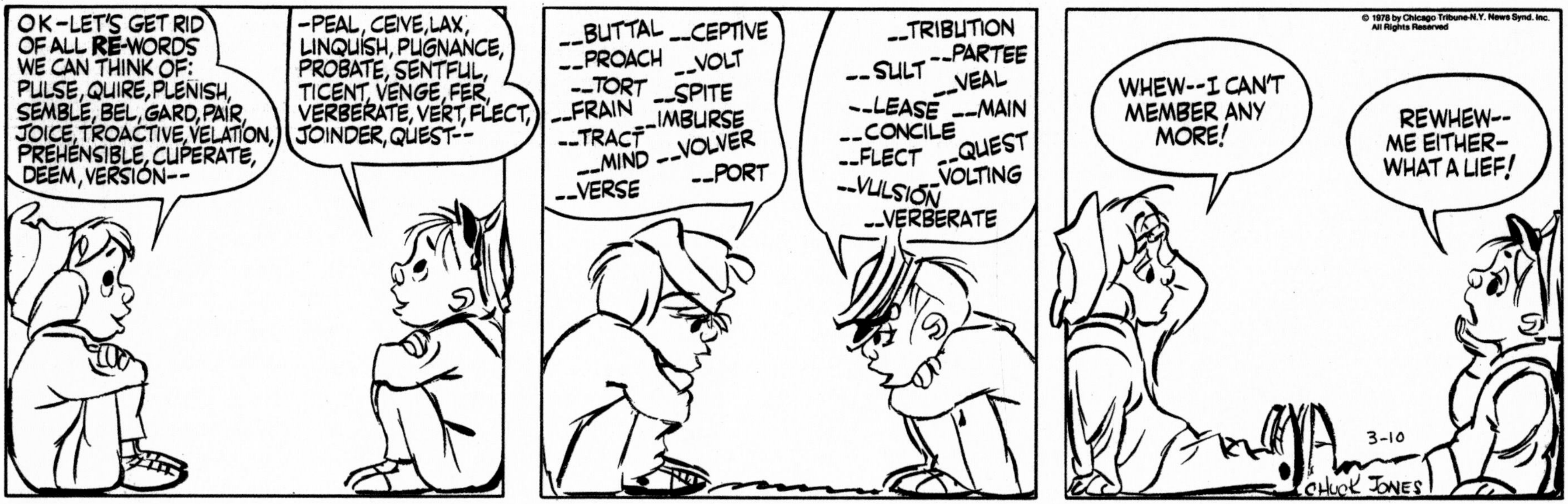
OK–LET'S GET RID OF ALL **RE**-WORDS WE CAN THINK OF: PULSE, QUIRE, PLENISH, SEMBLE, BEL, GARD, PAIR, JOICE, TROACTIVE, VELATION, PREHENSIBLE, CUPERATE, DEEM, VERSION--
–PEAL, CEIVE, LAX, LINQUISH, PUGNANCE, PROBATE, SENTFUL, TICENT, VENGE, FER, VERBERATE, VERT, FLECT, JOINDER, QUEST--
--BUTTAL --CEPTIVE --PROACH --VOLT --TORT --SPITE --FRAIN --IMBURSE --TRACT --VOLVER --MIND --PORT --VERSE
--TRIBUTION --SULT --PARTEE --VEAL --LEASE --MAIN --CONCILE --FLECT --QUEST --VULSION --VOLTING --VERBERATE
© 1978 by Chicago Tribune-N.Y. News Synd. Inc. All Rights Reserved
WHEW--I CAN'T MEMBER ANY MORE!
REWHEW-- ME EITHER– WHAT A LIEF!
3-10
CHUCK JONES

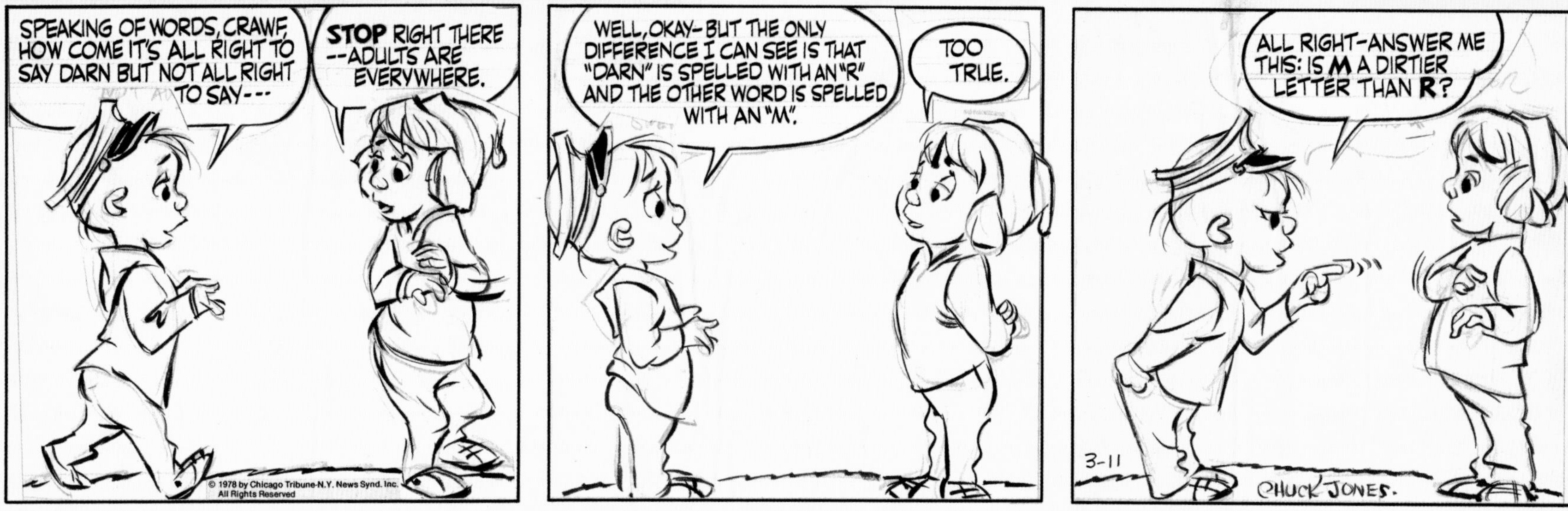
SPEAKING OF WORDS, CRAWF, HOW COME IT'S ALL RIGHT TO SAY DARN BUT NOT ALL RIGHT TO SAY---
STOP RIGHT THERE --ADULTS ARE EVERYWHERE.
© 1978 by Chicago Tribune-N.Y. News Synd. Inc. All Rights Reserved
WELL, OKAY– BUT THE ONLY DIFFERENCE I CAN SEE IS THAT "DARN" IS SPELLED WITH AN "R" AND THE OTHER WORD IS SPELLED WITH AN "M".
TOO TRUE.
ALL RIGHT–ANSWER ME THIS: IS **M** A DIRTIER LETTER THAN **R**?
3-11
CHUCK JONES.

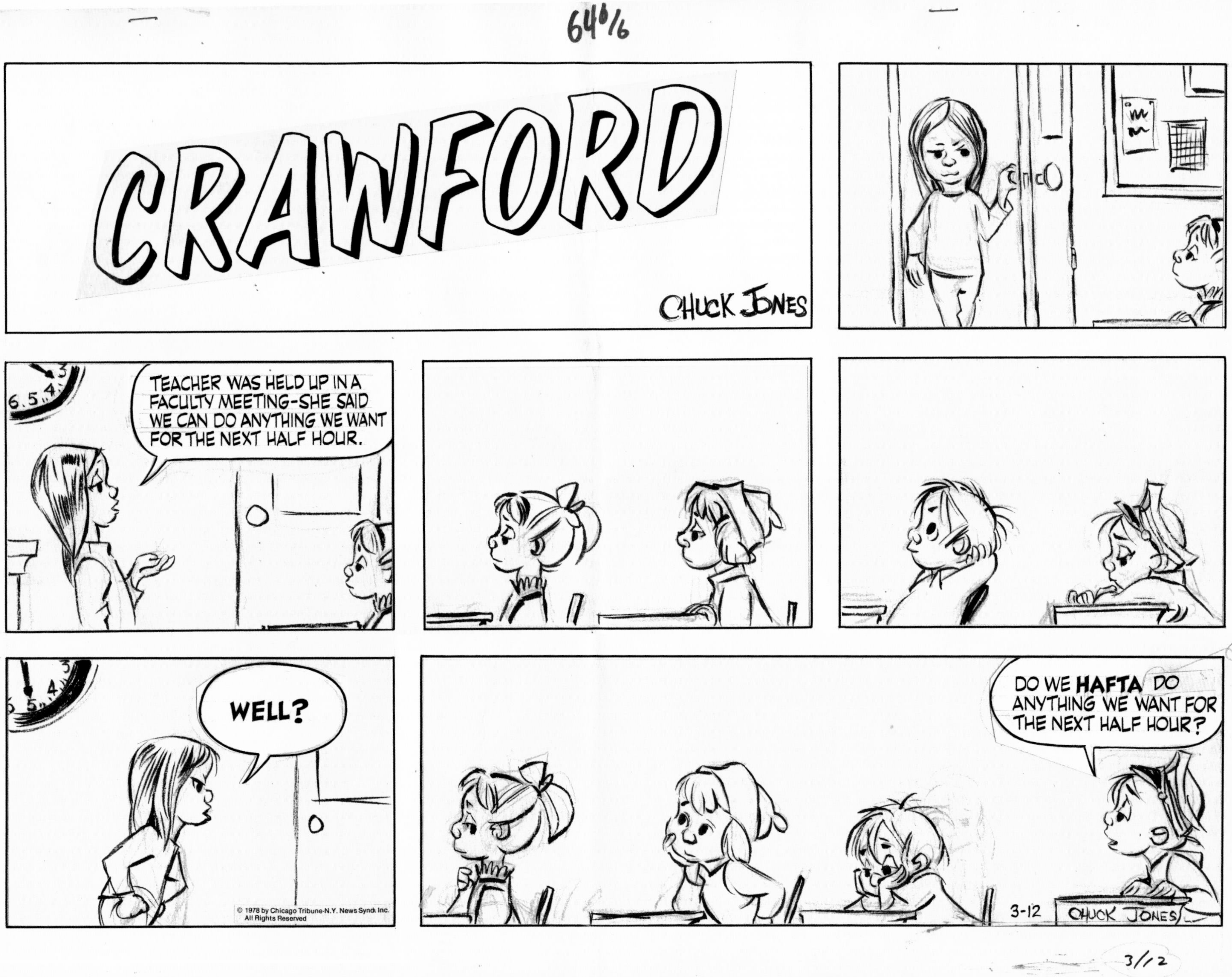
CRAWFORD
CHUCK JONES
TEACHER WAS HELD UP IN A FACULTY MEETING-SHE SAID WE CAN DO ANYTHING WE WANT FOR THE NEXT HALF HOUR.
WELL?
© 1978 by Chicago Tribune-N.Y. News Synd. Inc. All Rights Reserved
DO WE **HAFTA** DO ANYTHING WE WANT FOR THE NEXT HALF HOUR?
3-12
CHUCK JONES

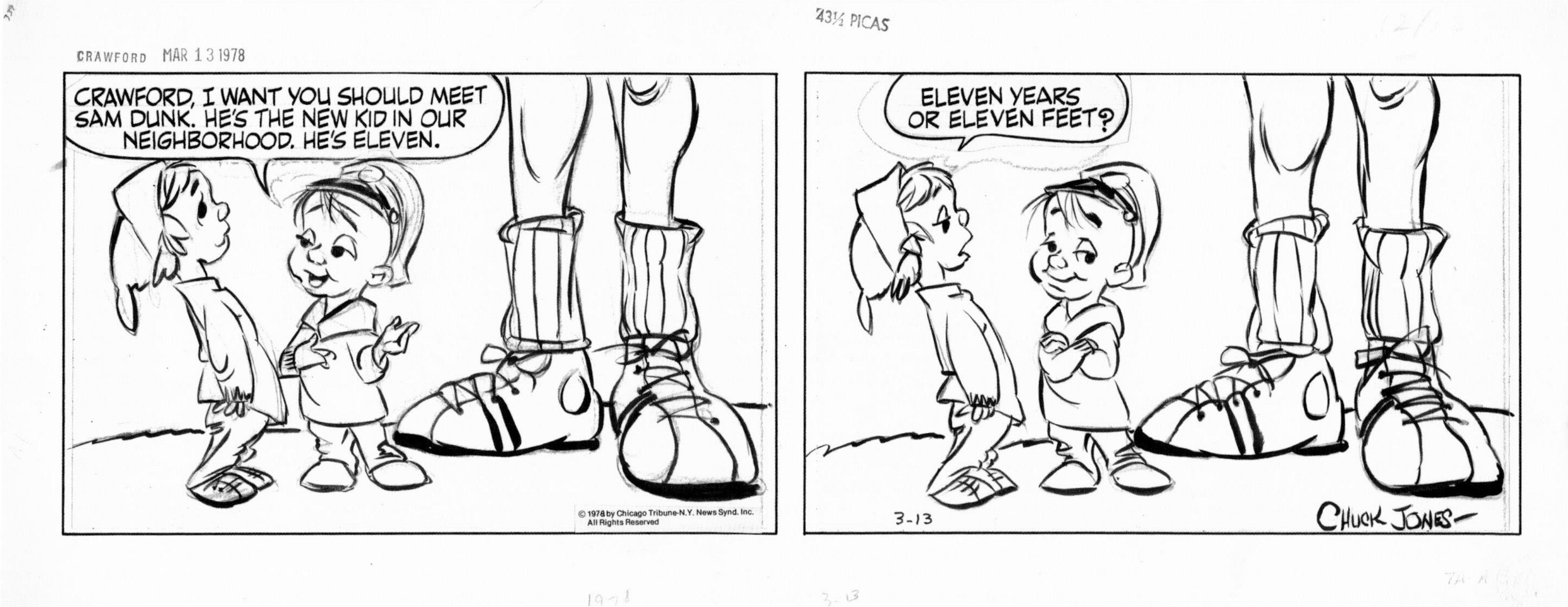
43½ PICAS
CRAWFORD MAR 13 1978
CRAWFORD, I WANT YOU SHOULD MEET SAM DUNK. HE'S THE NEW KID IN OUR NEIGHBORHOOD. HE'S ELEVEN.
ELEVEN YEARS OR ELEVEN FEET?
© 1978 by Chicago Tribune-N.Y. News Synd. Inc. All Rights Reserved
3-13
CHUCK JONES

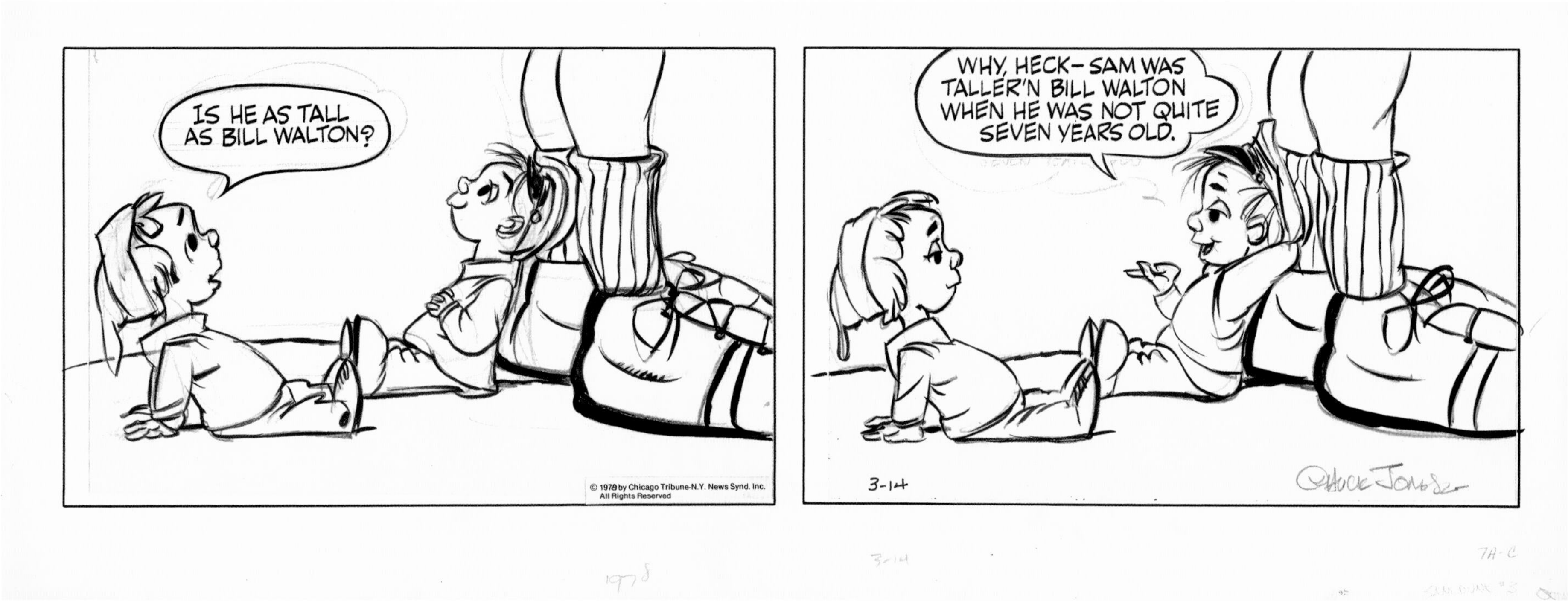
IS HE AS TALL AS BILL WALTON?
WHY, HECK—SAM WAS TALLER'N BILL WALTON WHEN HE WAS NOT QUITE SEVEN YEARS OLD.
© 1978 by Chicago Tribune-N.Y. News Synd. Inc. All Rights Reserved
3-14
CHUCK JONES

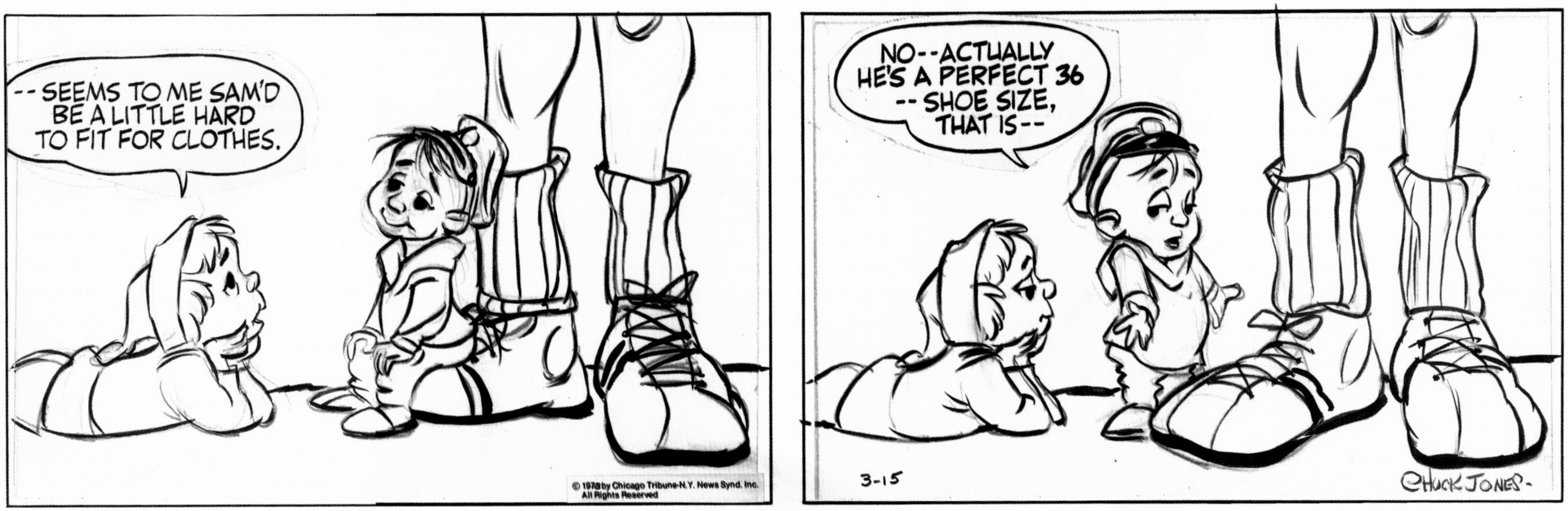
-- SEEMS TO ME SAM'D BE A LITTLE HARD TO FIT FOR CLOTHES.
NO--ACTUALLY HE'S A PERFECT 36 --SHOE SIZE, THAT IS--
© 1978 by Chicago Tribune-N.Y. News Synd. Inc. All Rights Reserved
3-15
CHUCK JONES

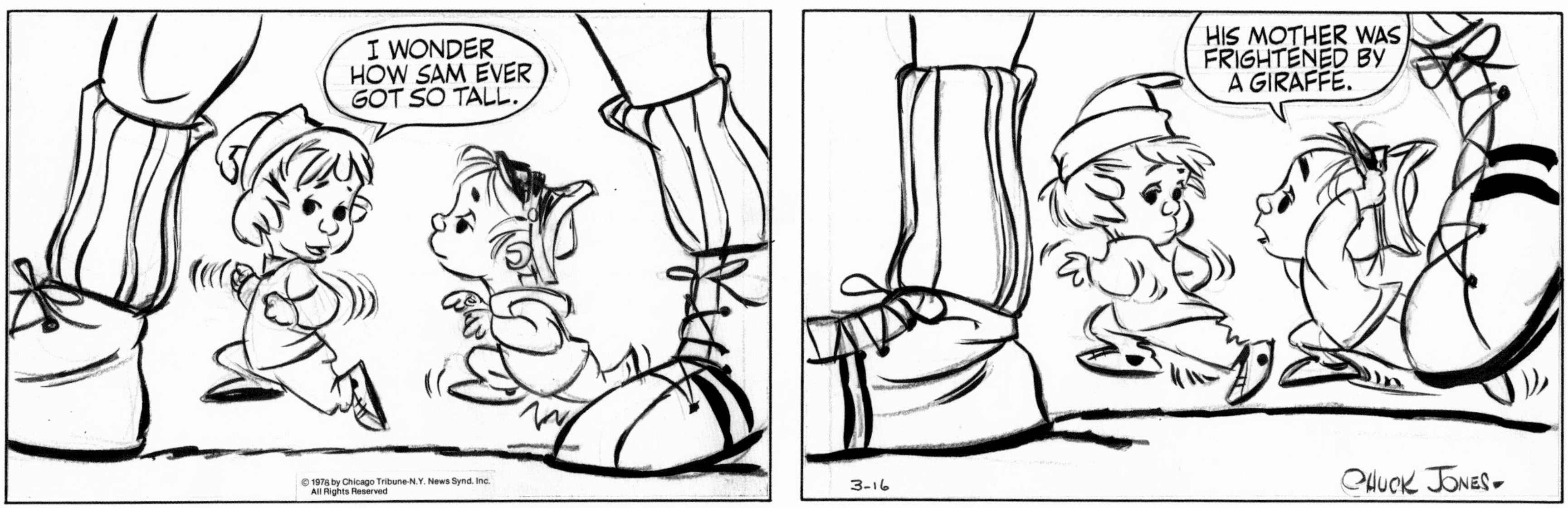
I WONDER HOW SAM EVER GOT SO TALL.
HIS MOTHER WAS FRIGHTENED BY A GIRAFFE.
© 1978 by Chicago Tribune-N.Y. News Synd. Inc. All Rights Reserved
3-16
CHUCK JONES

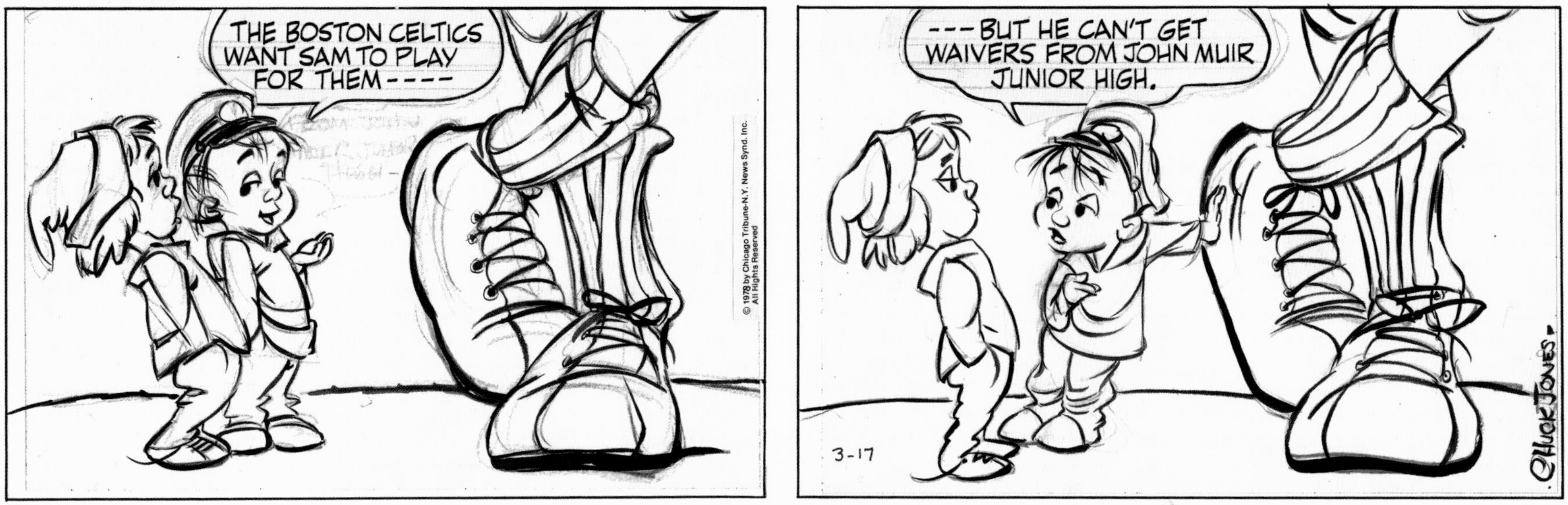
THE BOSTON CELTICS WANT SAM TO PLAY FOR THEM----
© 1978 by Chicago Tribune-N.Y. News Synd. Inc. All Rights Reserved
---BUT HE CAN'T GET WAIVERS FROM JOHN MUIR JUNIOR HIGH.
3-17
CHUCK JONES

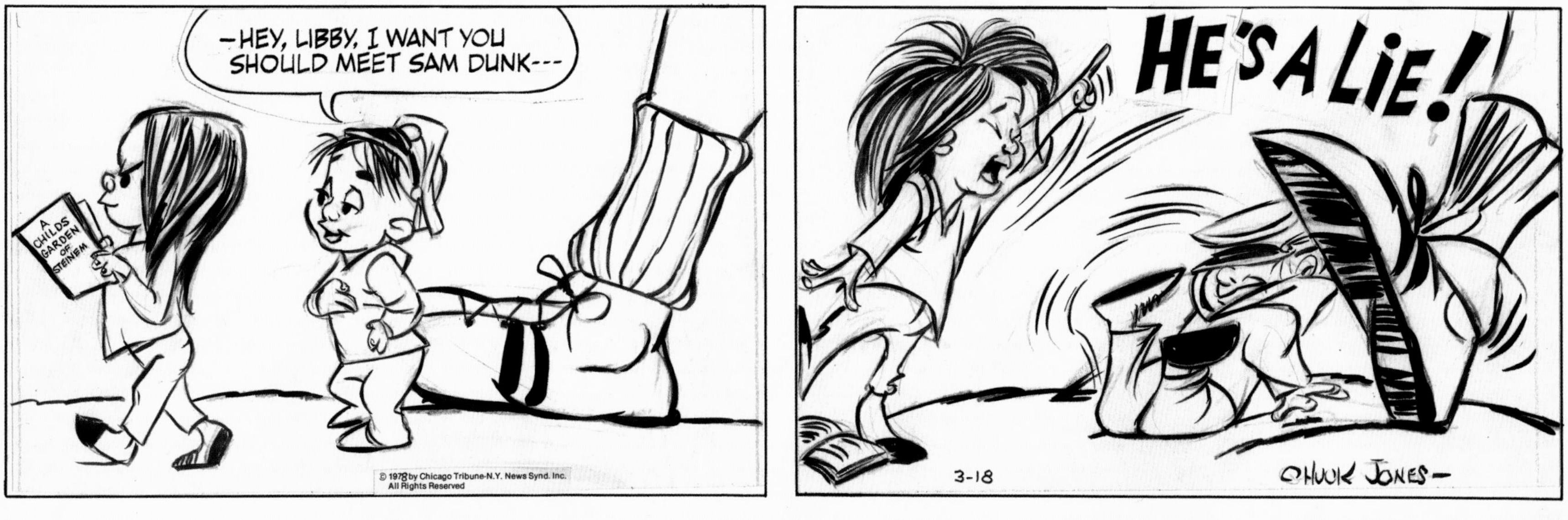
-HEY, LIBBY, I WANT YOU SHOULD MEET SAM DUNK---
A CHILDS GARDEN OF STEINEM
© 1978 by Chicago Tribune-N.Y. News Synd. Inc. All Rights Reserved
HE'S A LIE!
3-18
CHUCK JONES-

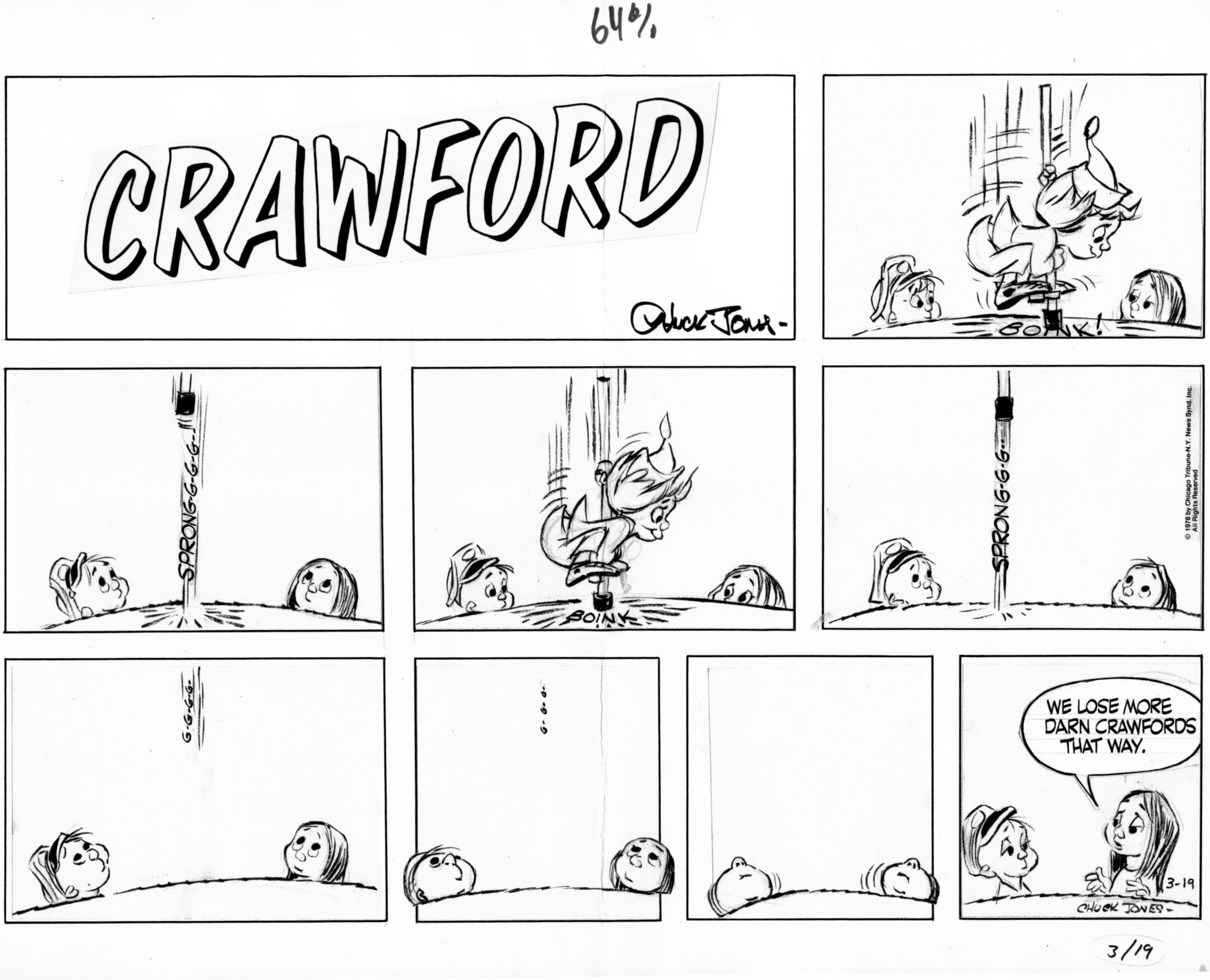
64%
CRAWFORD
CHUCK JONES
BOINK!
SPRONG-G-G-G-
BOINK
SPRONG-G-G-
© 1978 by Chicago Tribune-N.Y. News Synd. Inc. All Rights Reserved
G-G-G-G-
G-G-G-
WE LOSE MORE DARN CRAWFORDS THAT WAY.
3-19
CHUCK JONES
3/19

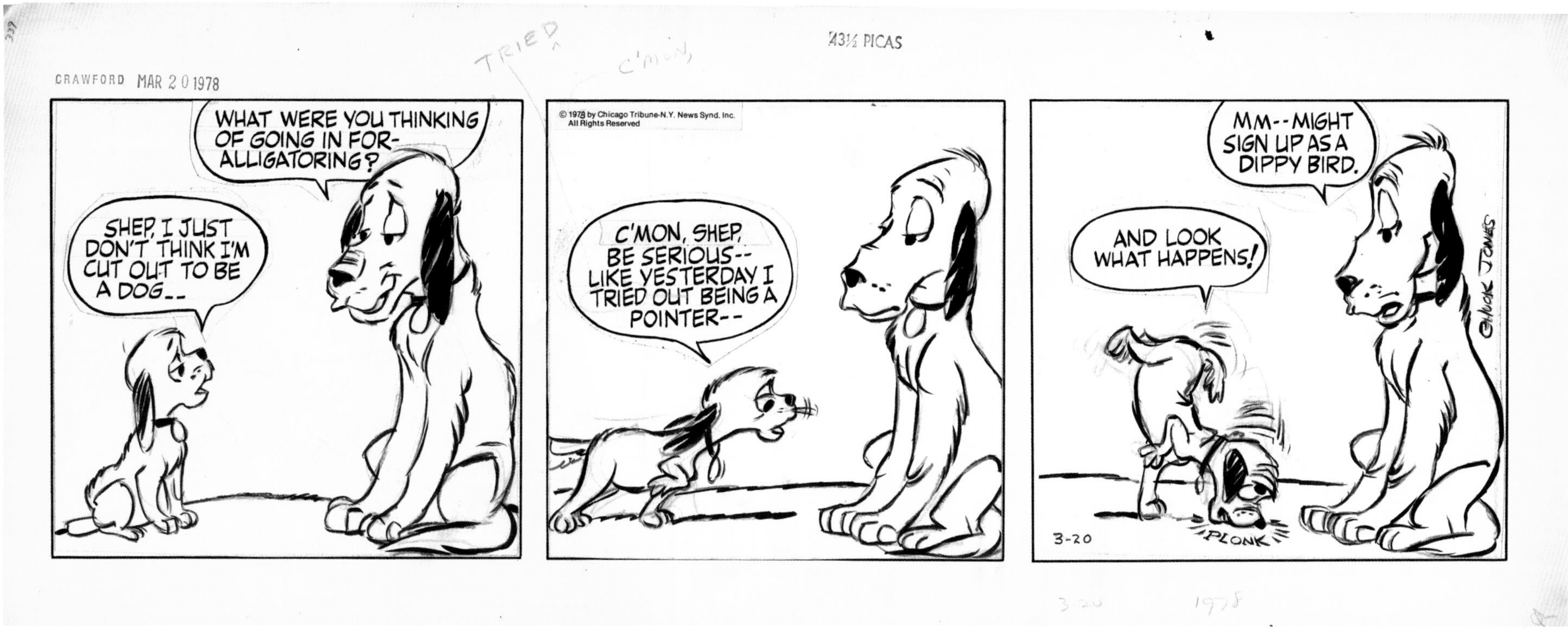
CRAWFORD MAR 2 0 1978
43½ PICAS
TRIED
C'MON,
WHAT WERE YOU THINKING OF GOING IN FOR- ALLIGATORING?
SHEP, I JUST DON'T THINK I'M CUT OUT TO BE A DOG--
© 1978 by Chicago Tribune-N.Y. News Synd. Inc. All Rights Reserved
C'MON, SHEP, BE SERIOUS-- LIKE YESTERDAY I TRIED OUT BEING A POINTER--
MM--MIGHT SIGN UP AS A DIPPY BIRD.
AND LOOK WHAT HAPPENS!
CHUCK JONES
PLONK
3-20

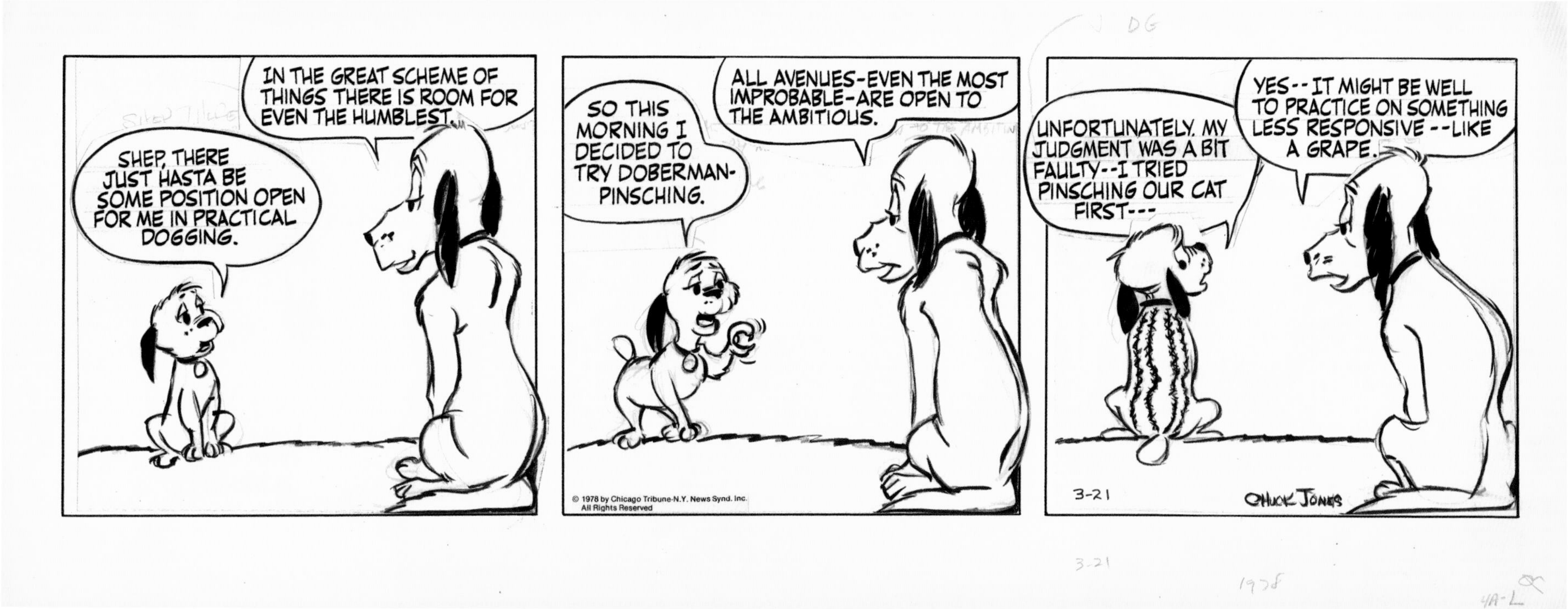
IN THE GREAT SCHEME OF THINGS THERE IS ROOM FOR EVEN THE HUMBLEST.
SHEP, THERE JUST HASTA BE SOME POSITION OPEN FOR ME IN PRACTICAL DOGGING.
ALL AVENUES-EVEN THE MOST IMPROBABLE-ARE OPEN TO THE AMBITIOUS.
SO THIS MORNING I DECIDED TO TRY DOBERMAN-PINSCHING.
© 1978 by Chicago Tribune-N.Y. News Synd. Inc. All Rights Reserved
YES--IT MIGHT BE WELL TO PRACTICE ON SOMETHING LESS RESPONSIVE--LIKE A GRAPE.
UNFORTUNATELY, MY JUDGMENT WAS A BIT FAULTY--I TRIED PINSCHING OUR CAT FIRST---
3-21
CHUCK JONES

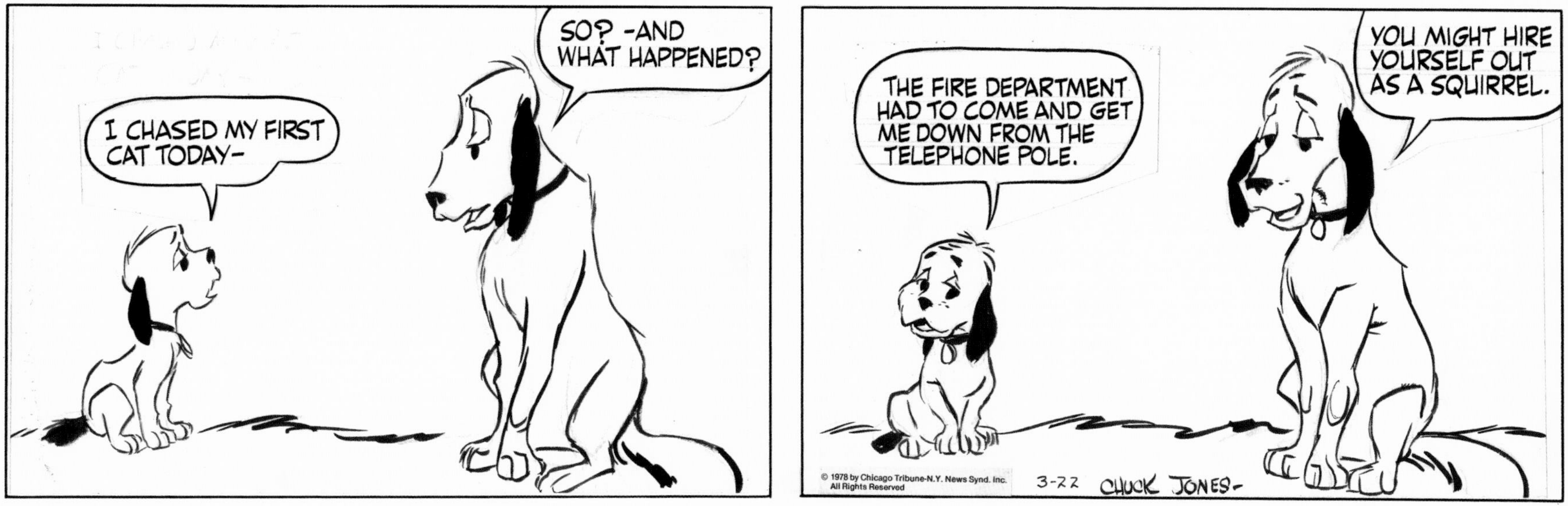
I CHASED MY FIRST CAT TODAY-
SO? -AND WHAT HAPPENED?
THE FIRE DEPARTMENT HAD TO COME AND GET ME DOWN FROM THE TELEPHONE POLE.
YOU MIGHT HIRE YOURSELF OUT AS A SQUIRREL.
© 1978 by Chicago Tribune-N.Y. News Synd. Inc. All Rights Reserved
3-22
CHUCK JONES-

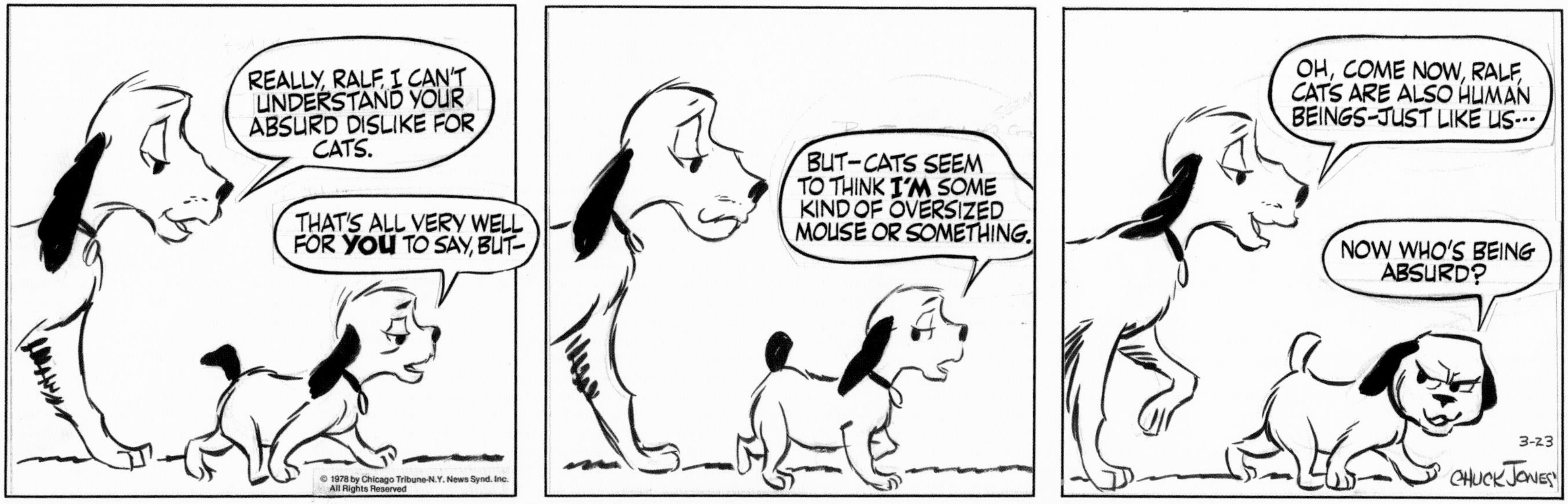
REALLY, RALF, I CAN'T UNDERSTAND YOUR ABSURD DISLIKE FOR CATS.
THAT'S ALL VERY WELL FOR YOU TO SAY, BUT-
© 1978 by Chicago Tribune-N.Y. News Synd. Inc. All Rights Reserved
BUT-CATS SEEM TO THINK I'M SOME KIND OF OVERSIZED MOUSE OR SOMETHING.
OH, COME NOW, RALF, CATS ARE ALSO HUMAN BEINGS-JUST LIKE US...
NOW WHO'S BEING ABSURD?
3-23
CHUCK JONES

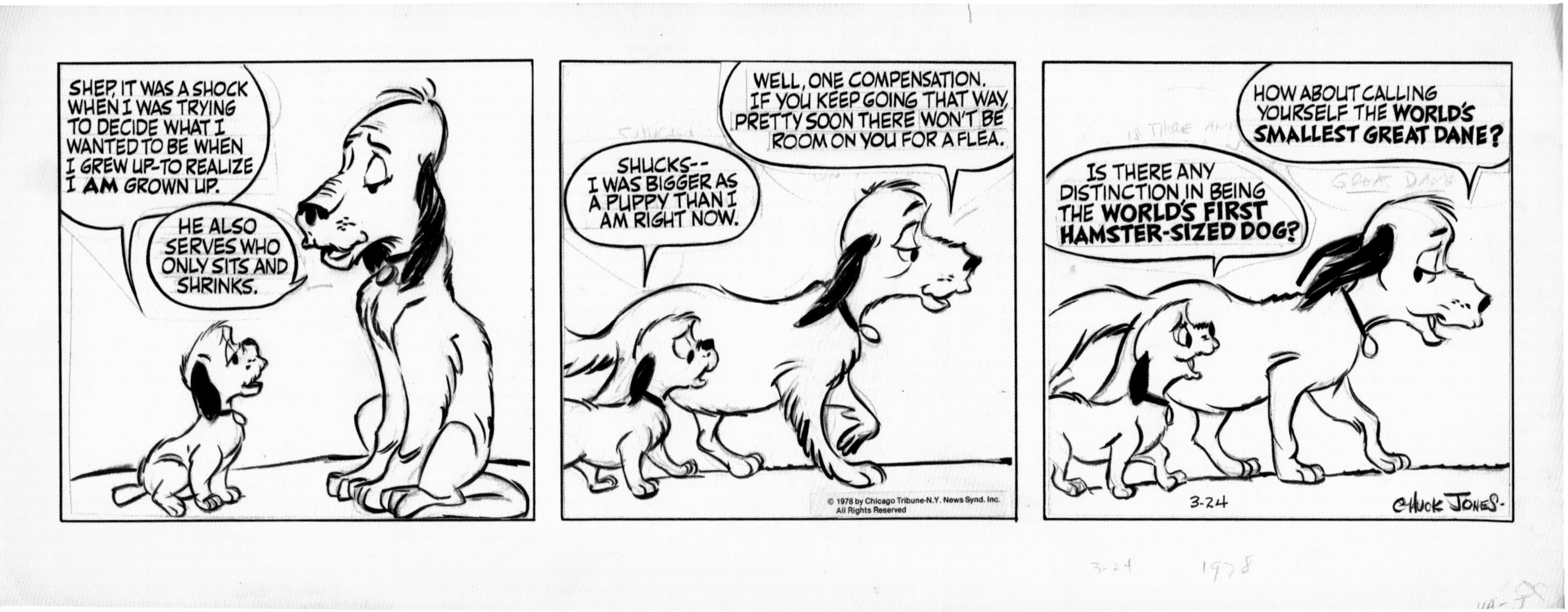
SHEP, IT WAS A SHOCK WHEN I WAS TRYING TO DECIDE WHAT I WANTED TO BE WHEN I GREW UP-TO REALIZE I **AM** GROWN UP.
HE ALSO SERVES WHO ONLY SITS AND SHRINKS.
SHUCKS-- I WAS BIGGER AS A PUPPY THAN I AM RIGHT NOW.
WELL, ONE COMPENSATION. IF YOU KEEP GOING THAT WAY, PRETTY SOON THERE WON'T BE ROOM ON YOU FOR A FLEA.
IS THERE ANY DISTINCTION IN BEING THE **WORLD'S FIRST HAMSTER-SIZED DOG?**
HOW ABOUT CALLING YOURSELF THE **WORLD'S SMALLEST GREAT DANE?**
© 1978 by Chicago Tribune-N.Y. News Synd. Inc. All Rights Reserved
3-24
CHUCK JONES

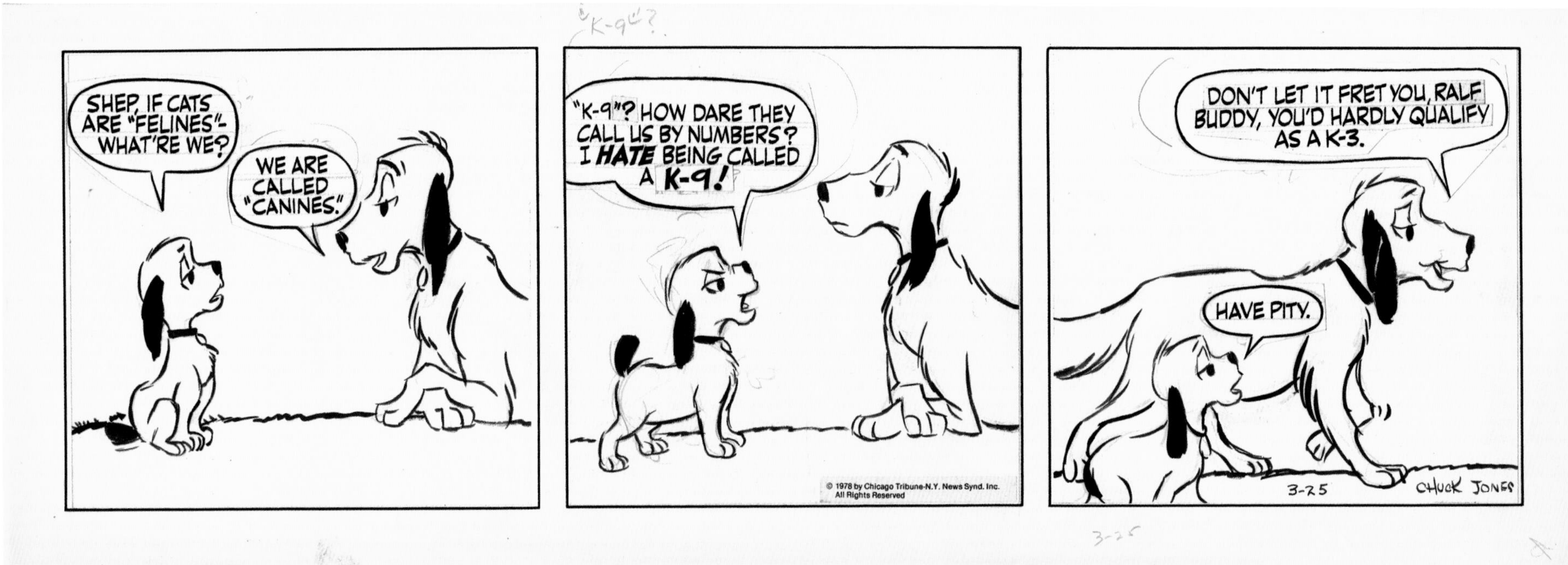
SHEP, IF CATS ARE "FELINES"- WHAT'RE WE?
WE ARE CALLED "CANINES."
"K-9"? HOW DARE THEY CALL US BY NUMBERS? I ***HATE*** BEING CALLED A **K-9!**
DON'T LET IT FRET YOU, RALF BUDDY, YOU'D HARDLY QUALIFY AS A K-3.
HAVE PITY.
© 1978 by Chicago Tribune-N.Y. News Synd. Inc. All Rights Reserved
3-25
CHUCK JONES

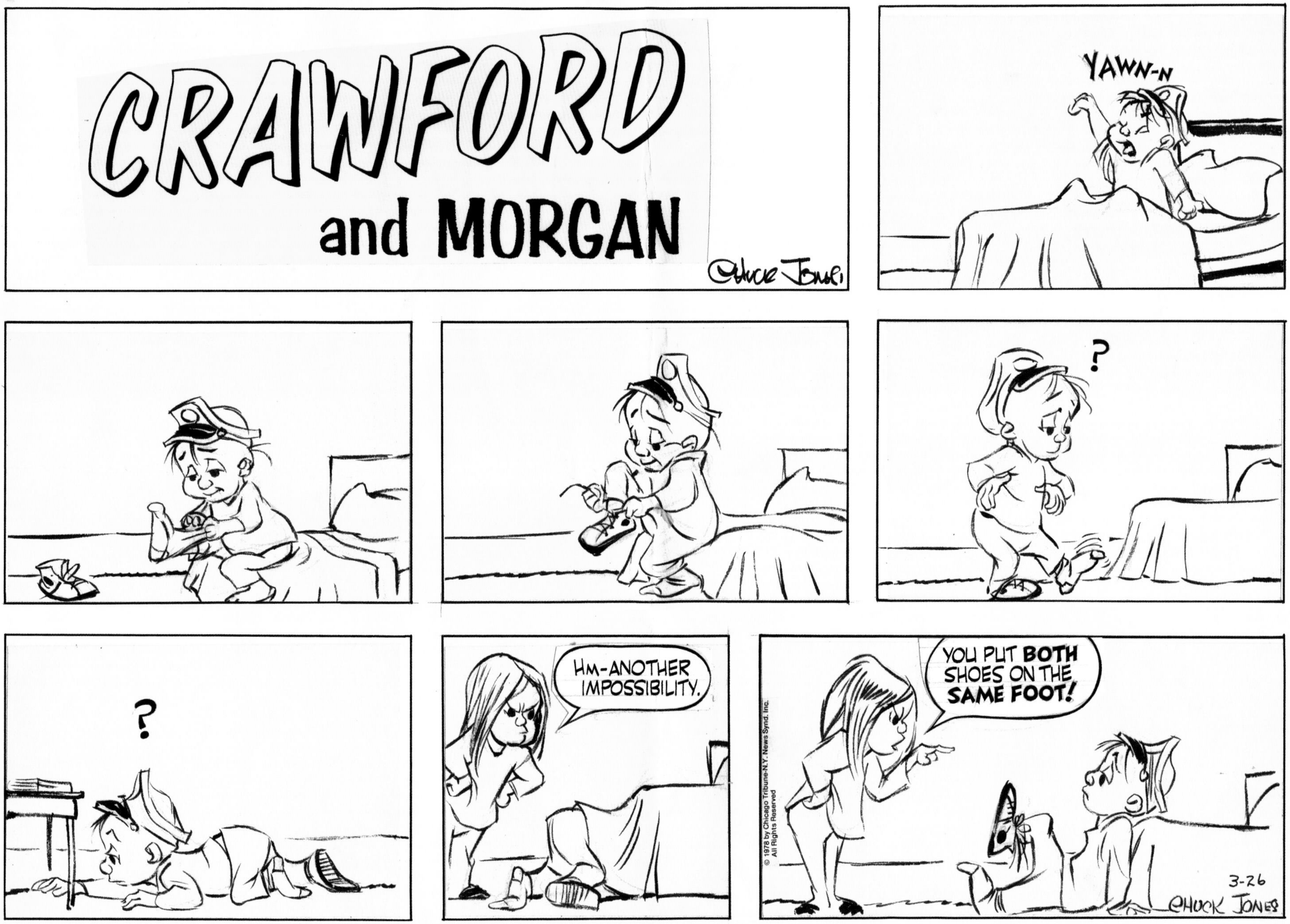

CRAWFORD
and MORGAN
CHUCK JONES
YAWN-N
?
?
HM-ANOTHER IMPOSSIBILITY.
© 1978 by Chicago Tribune-N.Y. News Synd. Inc. All Rights Reserved
YOU PUT **BOTH** SHOES ON THE **SAME FOOT!**
3-26
CHUCK JONES

3/26

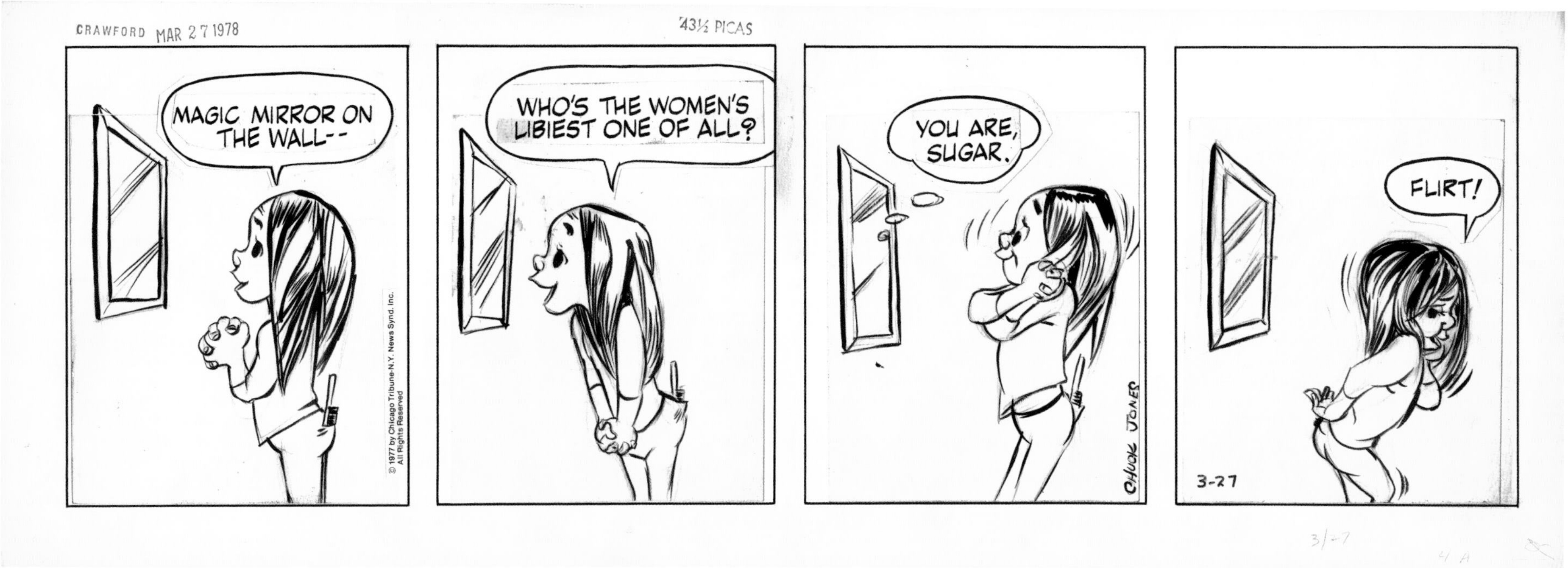
CRAWFORD MAR 27 1978
43½ PICAS
MAGIC MIRROR ON THE WALL--
WHO'S THE WOMEN'S LIBIEST ONE OF ALL?
© 1977 by Chicago Tribune-N.Y. News Synd. Inc. All Rights Reserved
YOU ARE, SUGAR.
CHUCK JONES
FLIRT!
3-27

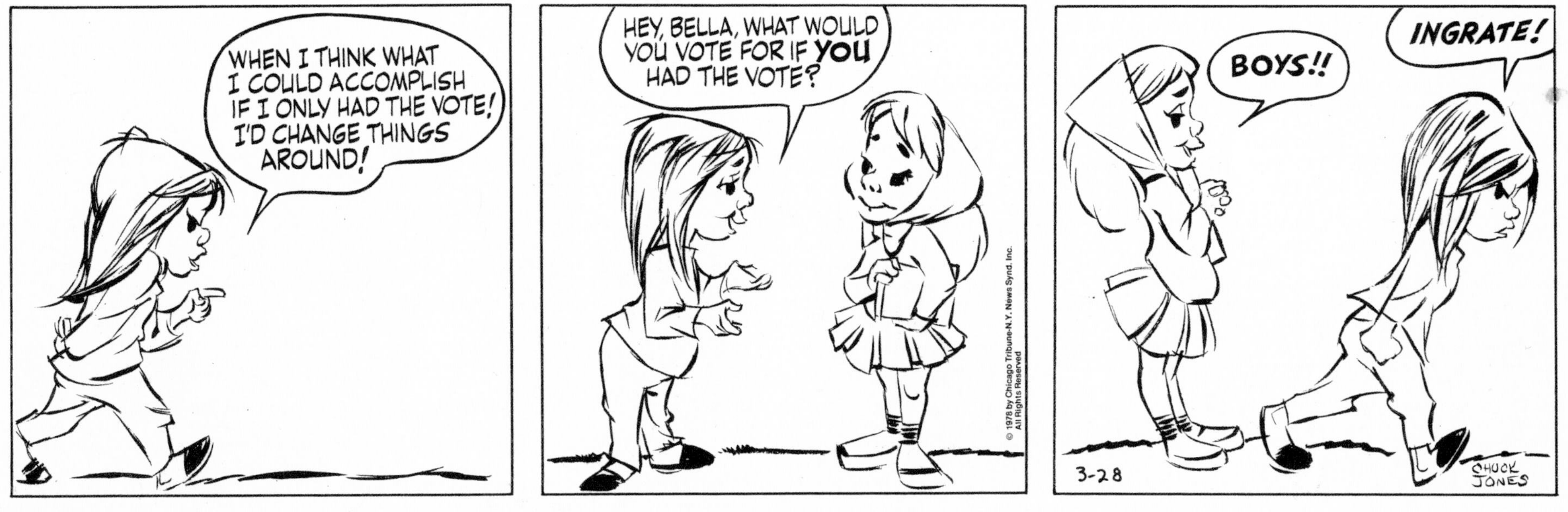
WHEN I THINK WHAT I COULD ACCOMPLISH IF I ONLY HAD THE VOTE! I'D CHANGE THINGS AROUND!
HEY, BELLA, WHAT WOULD YOU VOTE FOR IF YOU HAD THE VOTE?
© 1978 by Chicago Tribune-N.Y. News Synd. Inc. All Rights Reserved
BOYS!!
INGRATE!
3-28
CHUCK JONES

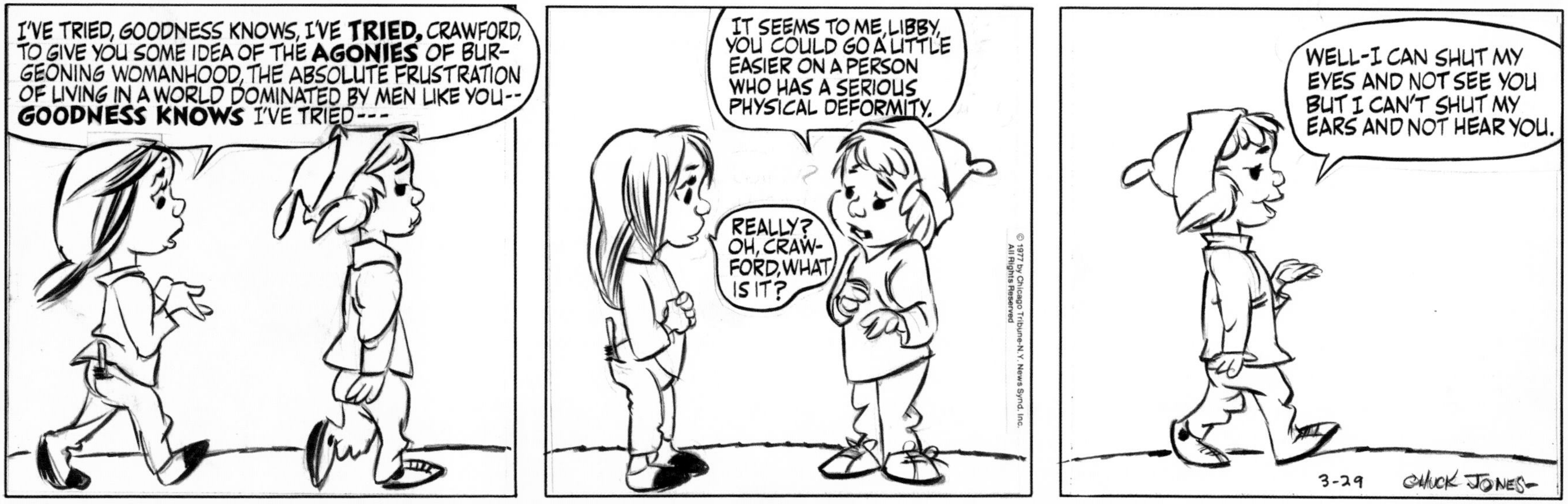
I'VE TRIED, GOODNESS KNOWS, I'VE **TRIED,** CRAWFORD, TO GIVE YOU SOME IDEA OF THE **AGONIES** OF BURGEONING WOMANHOOD, THE ABSOLUTE FRUSTRATION OF LIVING IN A WORLD DOMINATED BY MEN LIKE YOU-- **GOODNESS KNOWS** I'VE TRIED---
IT SEEMS TO ME, LIBBY, YOU COULD GO A LITTLE EASIER ON A PERSON WHO HAS A SERIOUS PHYSICAL DEFORMITY.
REALLY? OH, CRAWFORD, WHAT IS IT?
© 1977 by Chicago Tribune-N.Y. News Synd., Inc. All Rights Reserved
WELL-I CAN SHUT MY EYES AND NOT SEE YOU BUT I CAN'T SHUT MY EARS AND NOT HEAR YOU.
3-29 CHUCK JONES

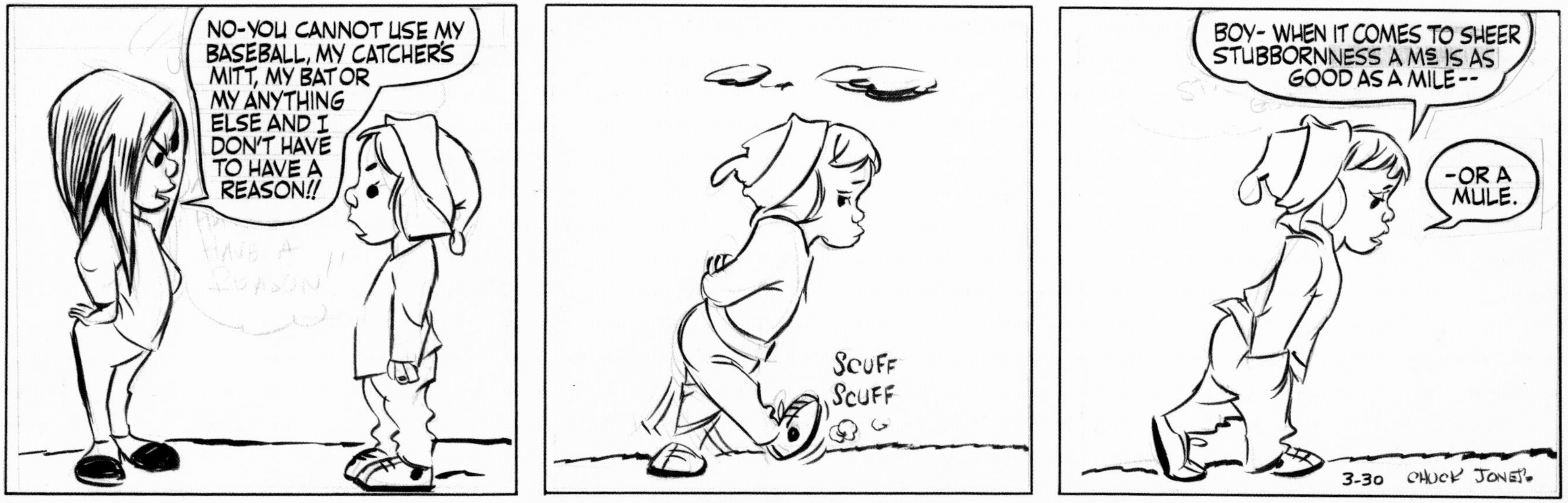
NO-YOU CANNOT USE MY BASEBALL, MY CATCHER'S MITT, MY BAT OR MY ANYTHING ELSE AND I DON'T HAVE TO HAVE A REASON!!
SCUFF SCUFF
BOY- WHEN IT COMES TO SHEER STUBBORNNESS A Ms IS AS GOOD AS A MILE--
-OR A MULE.
3-30 CHUCK JONES

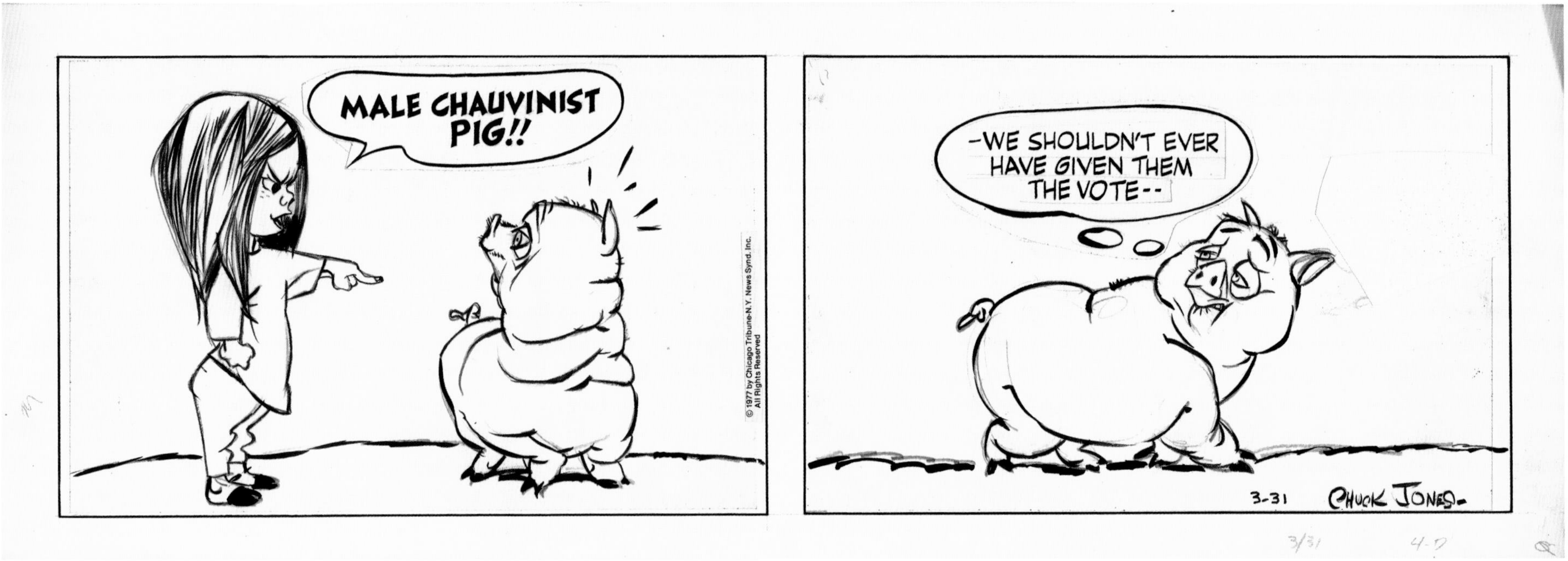
MALE CHAUVINIST PIG!!
© 1977 by Chicago Tribune-N.Y. News Synd. Inc. All Rights Reserved
-WE SHOULDN'T EVER HAVE GIVEN THEM THE VOTE--
3-31
CHUCK JONES

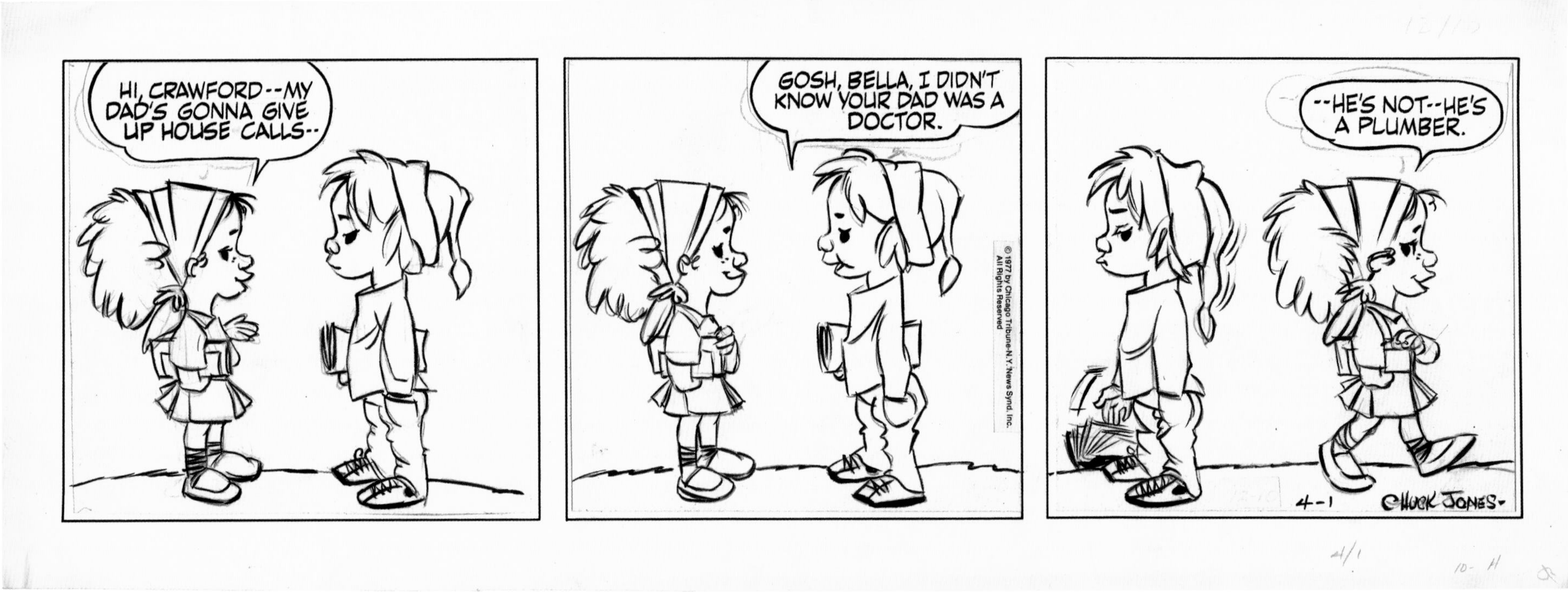
HI, CRAWFORD--MY DAD'S GONNA GIVE UP HOUSE CALLS--
GOSH, BELLA, I DIDN'T KNOW YOUR DAD WAS A DOCTOR.
© 1977 by Chicago Tribune-N.Y. News Synd. Inc. All Rights Reserved
--HE'S NOT--HE'S A PLUMBER.
4-1
CHUCK JONES

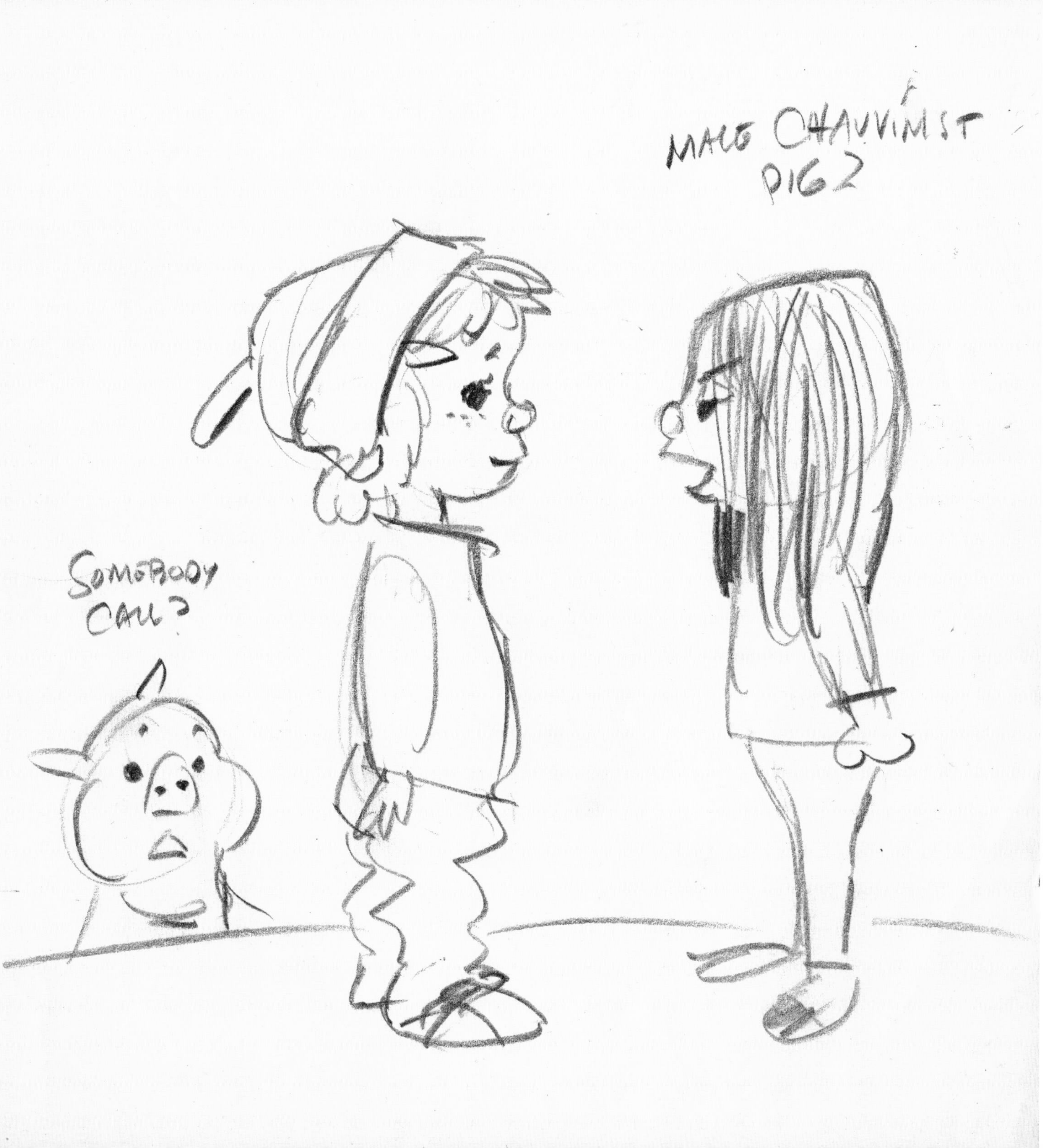
MALE CHAUVINIST PIG?
SOMEBODY CALL?

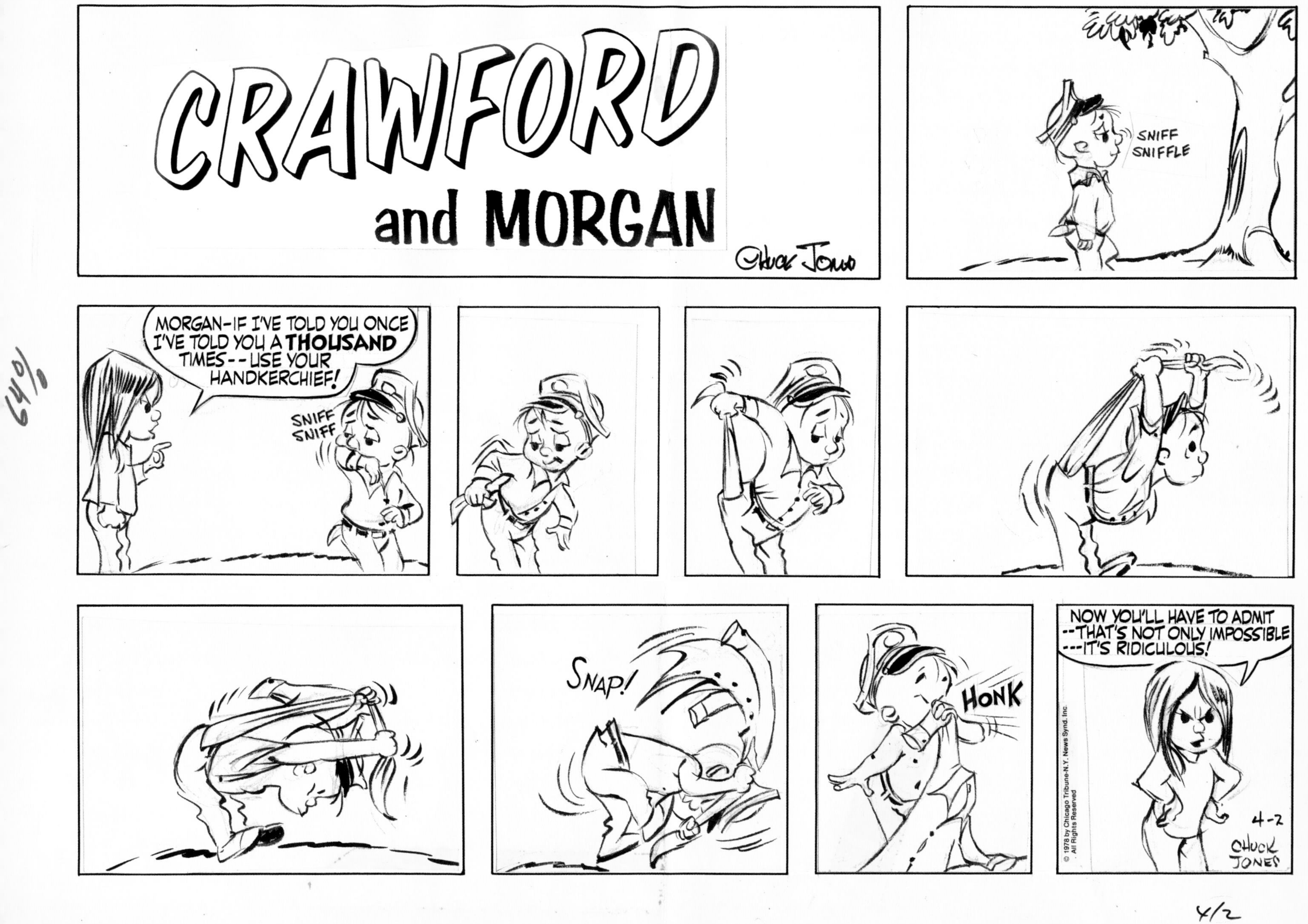
CRAWFORD
and MORGAN
©Chuck Jones
SNIFF
SNIFFLE
MORGAN-IF I'VE TOLD YOU ONCE I'VE TOLD YOU A **THOUSAND** TIMES--USE YOUR HANDKERCHIEF!
SNIFF
SNIFF
SNAP!
HONK
NOW YOU'LL HAVE TO ADMIT --THAT'S NOT ONLY IMPOSSIBLE ---IT'S RIDICULOUS!
© 1978 by Chicago Tribune-N.Y. News Synd. Inc. All Rights Reserved
4-2
CHUCK JONES
64%
4/2

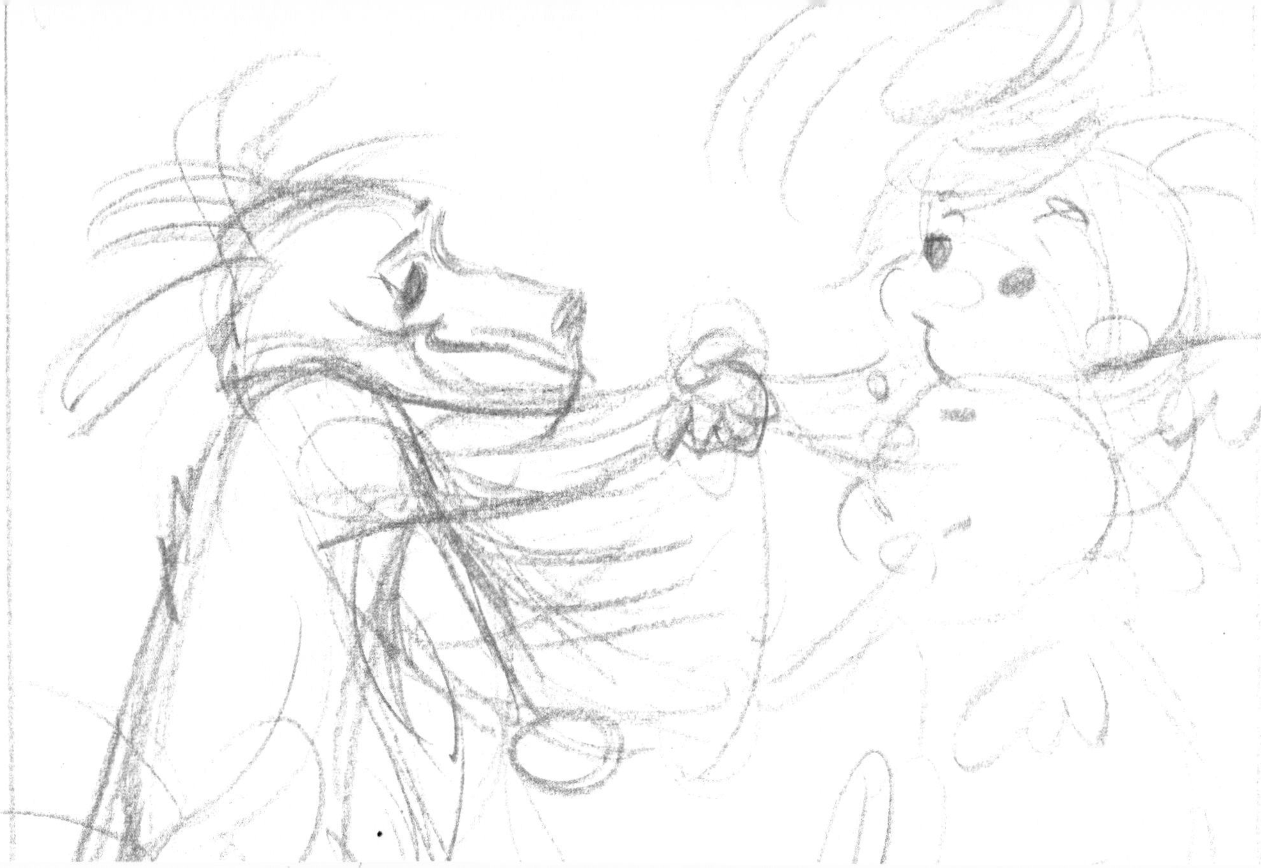

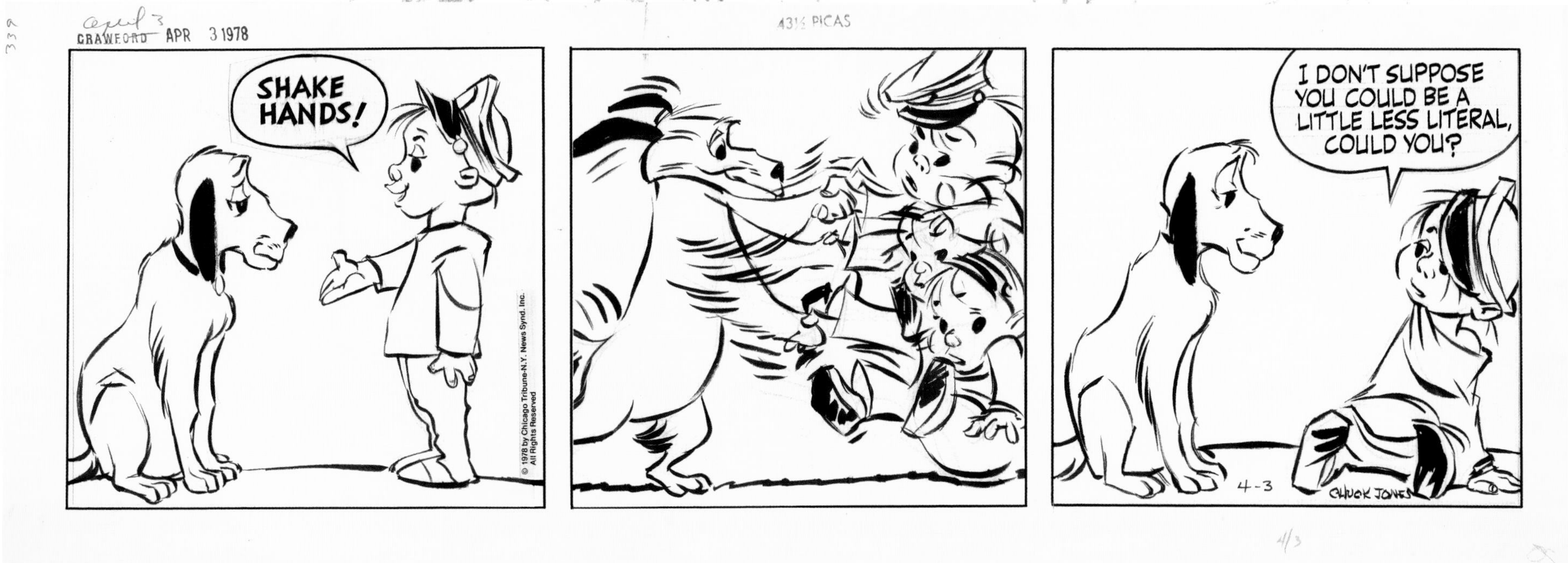
CRAWFORD APR 3 1978
43½ PICAS
SHAKE HANDS!
© 1978 by Chicago Tribune-N.Y. News Synd. Inc. All Rights Reserved
I DON'T SUPPOSE YOU COULD BE A LITTLE LESS LITERAL, COULD YOU?
4-3
CHUCK JONES

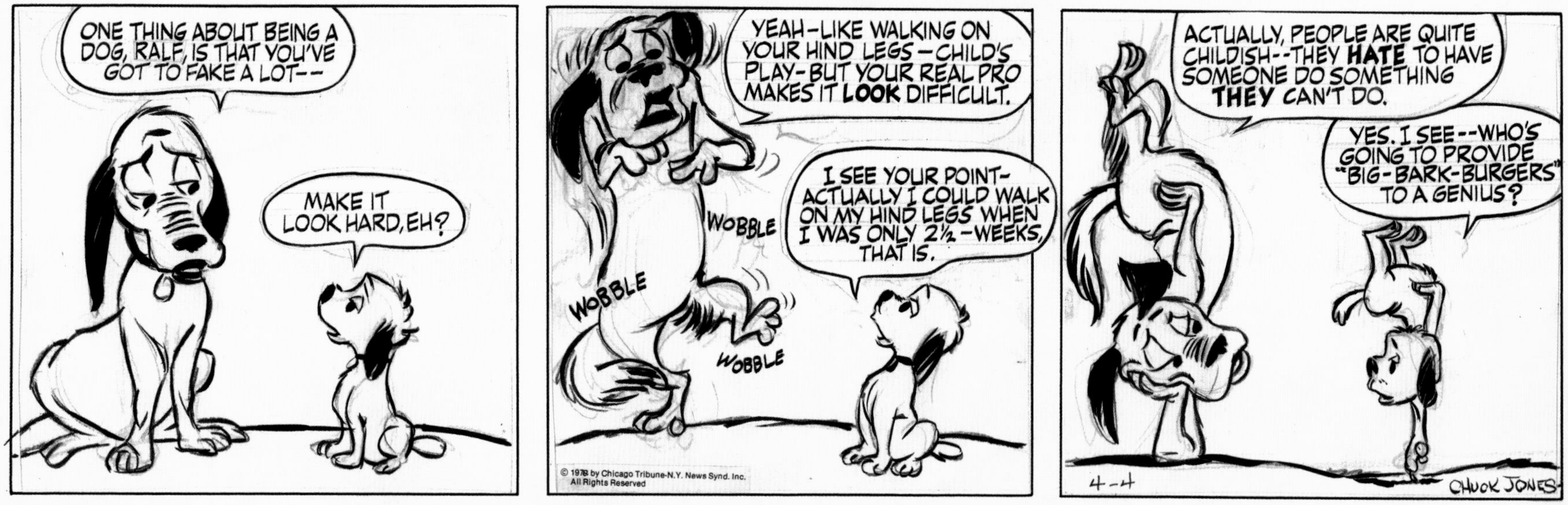
ONE THING ABOUT BEING A DOG, RALF, IS THAT YOU'VE GOT TO FAKE A LOT--
MAKE IT LOOK HARD, EH?
YEAH-LIKE WALKING ON YOUR HIND LEGS-CHILD'S PLAY-BUT YOUR REAL PRO MAKES IT **LOOK** DIFFICULT.
WOBBLE
WOBBLE
WOBBLE
I SEE YOUR POINT-ACTUALLY I COULD WALK ON MY HIND LEGS WHEN I WAS ONLY 2½-WEEKS, THAT IS.
© 1978 by Chicago Tribune-N.Y. News Synd. Inc. All Rights Reserved
ACTUALLY, PEOPLE ARE QUITE CHILDISH--THEY **HATE** TO HAVE SOMEONE DO SOMETHING **THEY** CAN'T DO.
YES. I SEE--WHO'S GOING TO PROVIDE "BIG-BARK-BURGERS" TO A GENIUS?
4-4
CHUCK JONES

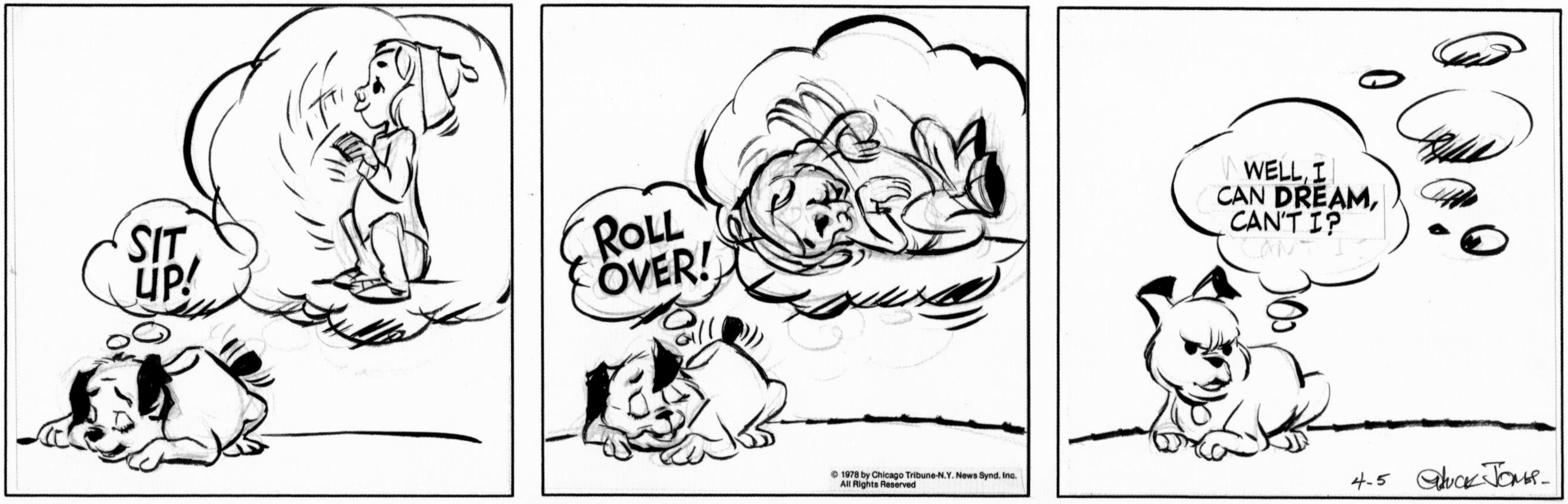
SIT UP!
ROLL OVER!
© 1978 by Chicago Tribune-N.Y. News Synd. Inc. All Rights Reserved
WELL, I CAN **DREAM**, CAN'T I?
4-5
CHUCK JONES

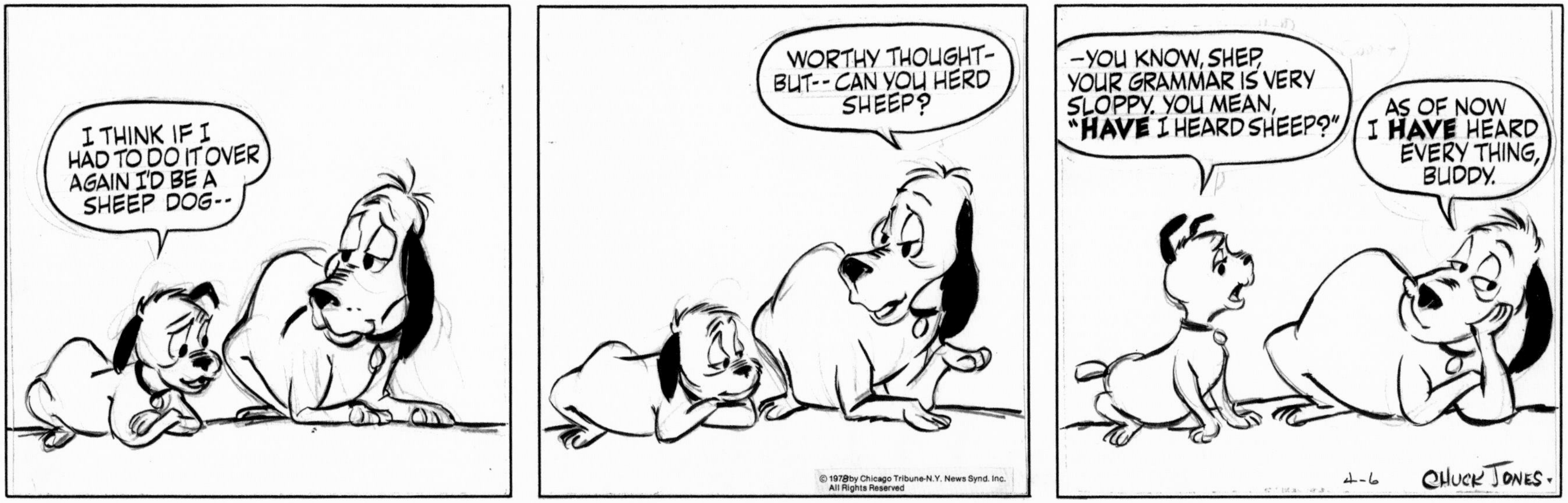
I THINK IF I HAD TO DO IT OVER AGAIN I'D BE A SHEEP DOG--
WORTHY THOUGHT-BUT--CAN YOU HERD SHEEP?
© 1978 by Chicago Tribune-N.Y. News Synd. Inc. All Rights Reserved
-YOU KNOW, SHEP, YOUR GRAMMAR IS VERY SLOPPY. YOU MEAN, "HAVE I HEARD SHEEP?"
AS OF NOW I HAVE HEARD EVERY THING, BUDDY.
4-6
CHUCK JONES

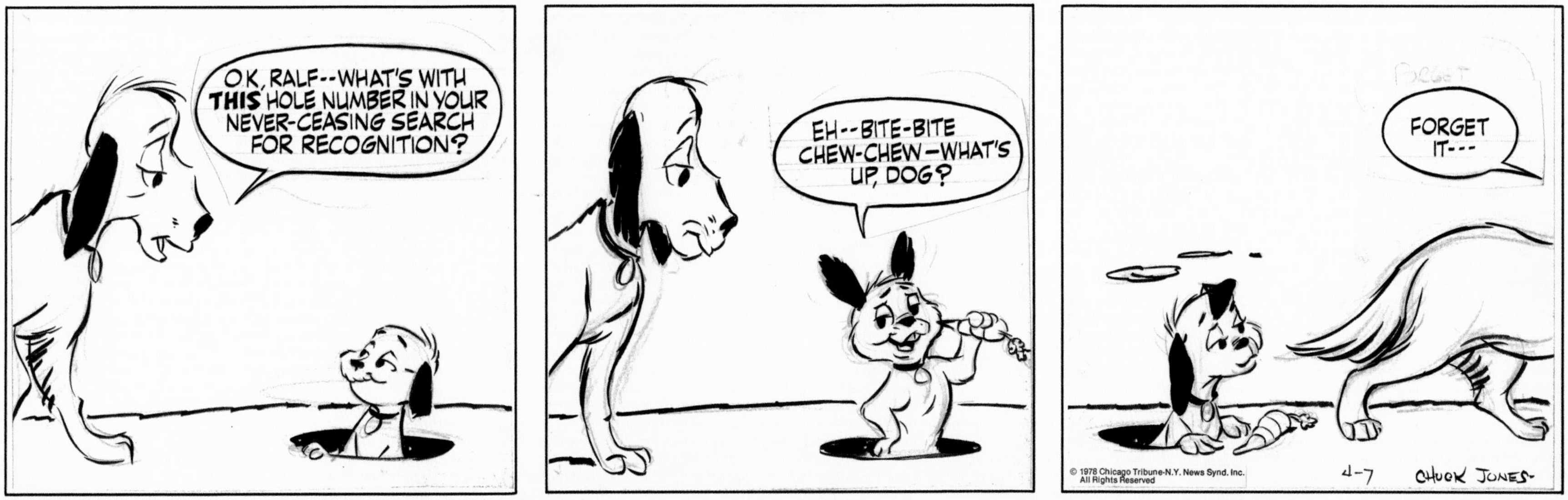
O.K. RALF--WHAT'S WITH THIS HOLE NUMBER IN YOUR NEVER-CEASING SEARCH FOR RECOGNITION?
EH--BITE-BITE CHEW-CHEW-WHAT'S UP, DOG?
FORGET IT---
© 1978 Chicago Tribune-N.Y. News Synd. Inc. All Rights Reserved
4-7
CHUCK JONES

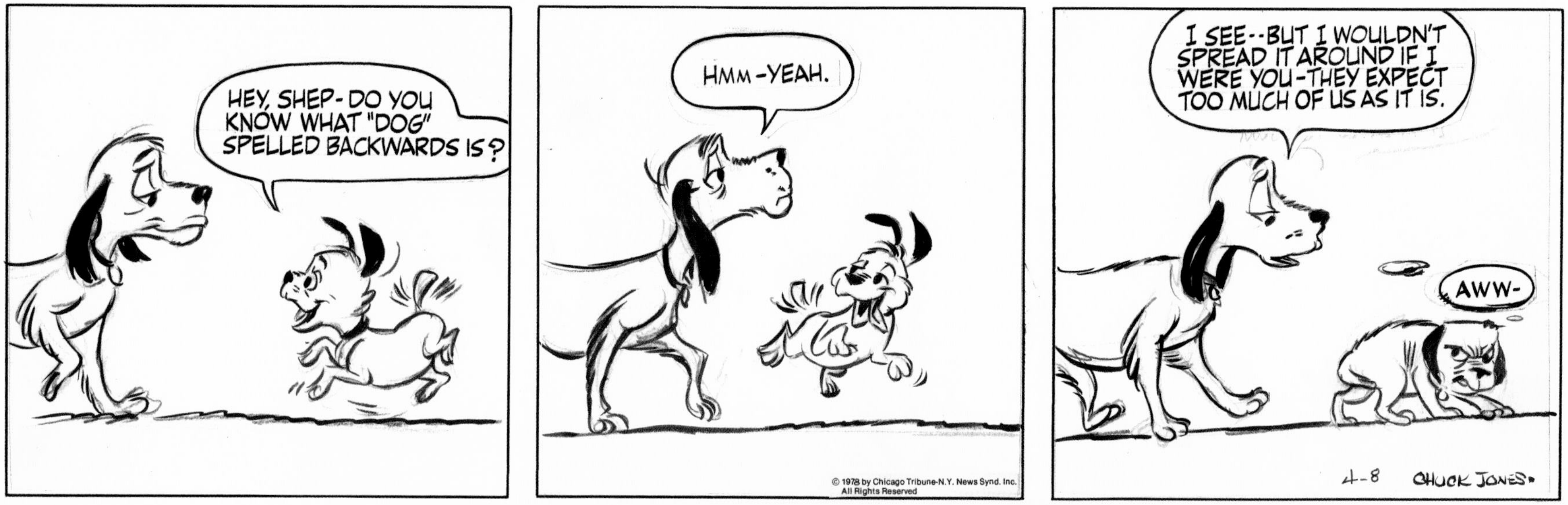
HEY, SHEP- DO YOU KNOW WHAT "DOG" SPELLED BACKWARDS IS?
HMM-YEAH.
© 1978 by Chicago Tribune-N.Y. News Synd. Inc. All Rights Reserved
I SEE--BUT I WOULDN'T SPREAD IT AROUND IF I WERE YOU-THEY EXPECT TOO MUCH OF US AS IT IS.
AWW-
4-8
CHUCK JONES

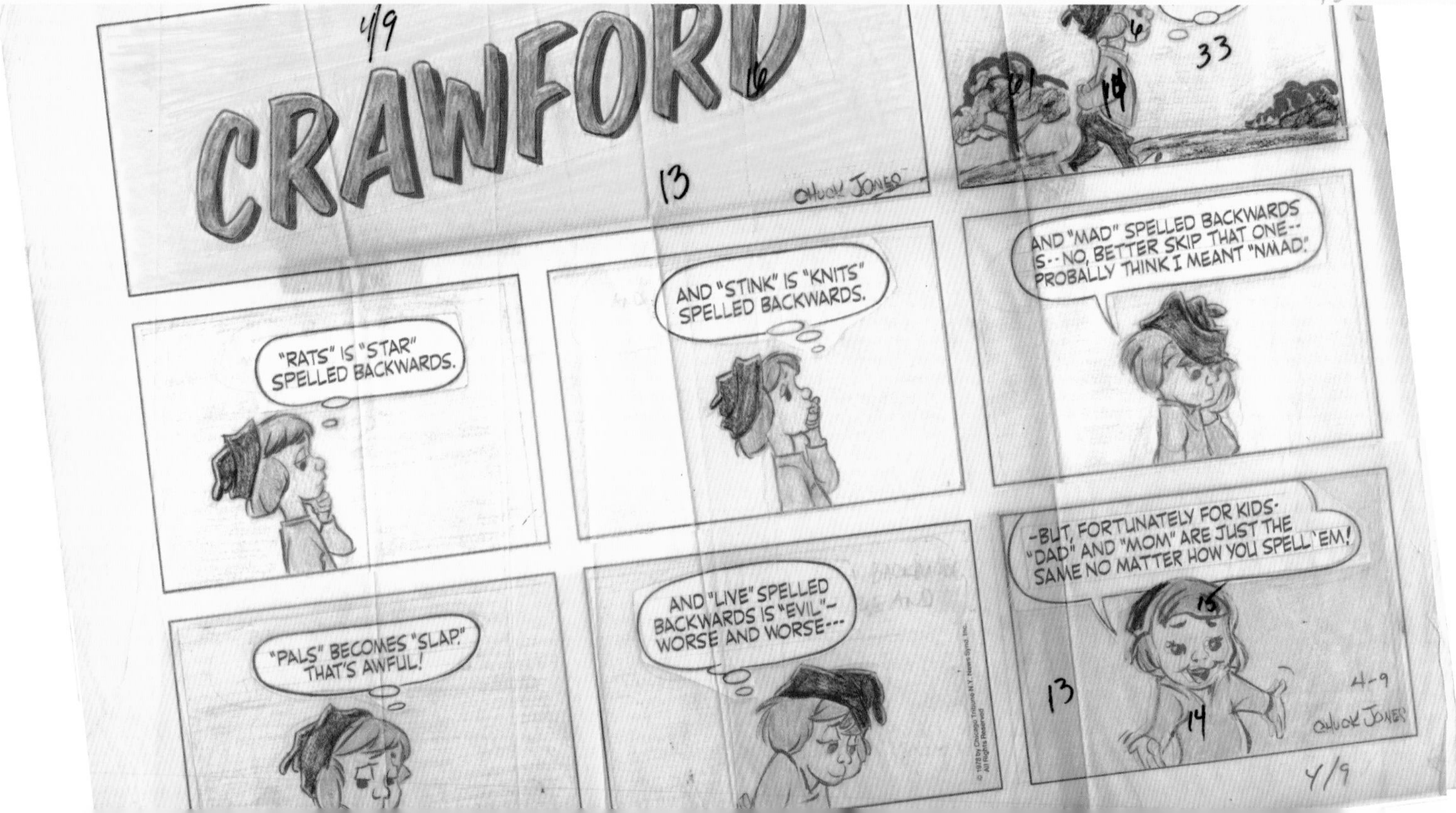
4/9
CRAWFORD
CHUCK JONES
"RATS" IS "STAR" SPELLED BACKWARDS.
AND "STINK" IS "KNITS" SPELLED BACKWARDS.
AND "MAD" SPELLED BACKWARDS IS--NO, BETTER SKIP THAT ONE--PROBABLY THINK I MEANT "NMAD."
"PALS" BECOMES "SLAP." THAT'S AWFUL!
AND "LIVE" SPELLED BACKWARDS IS "EVIL"-WORSE AND WORSE---
-BUT, FORTUNATELY FOR KIDS-"DAD" AND "MOM" ARE JUST THE SAME NO MATTER HOW YOU SPELL 'EM!
4-9
CHUCK JONES

Chuck Jones's color guide for the engravers.

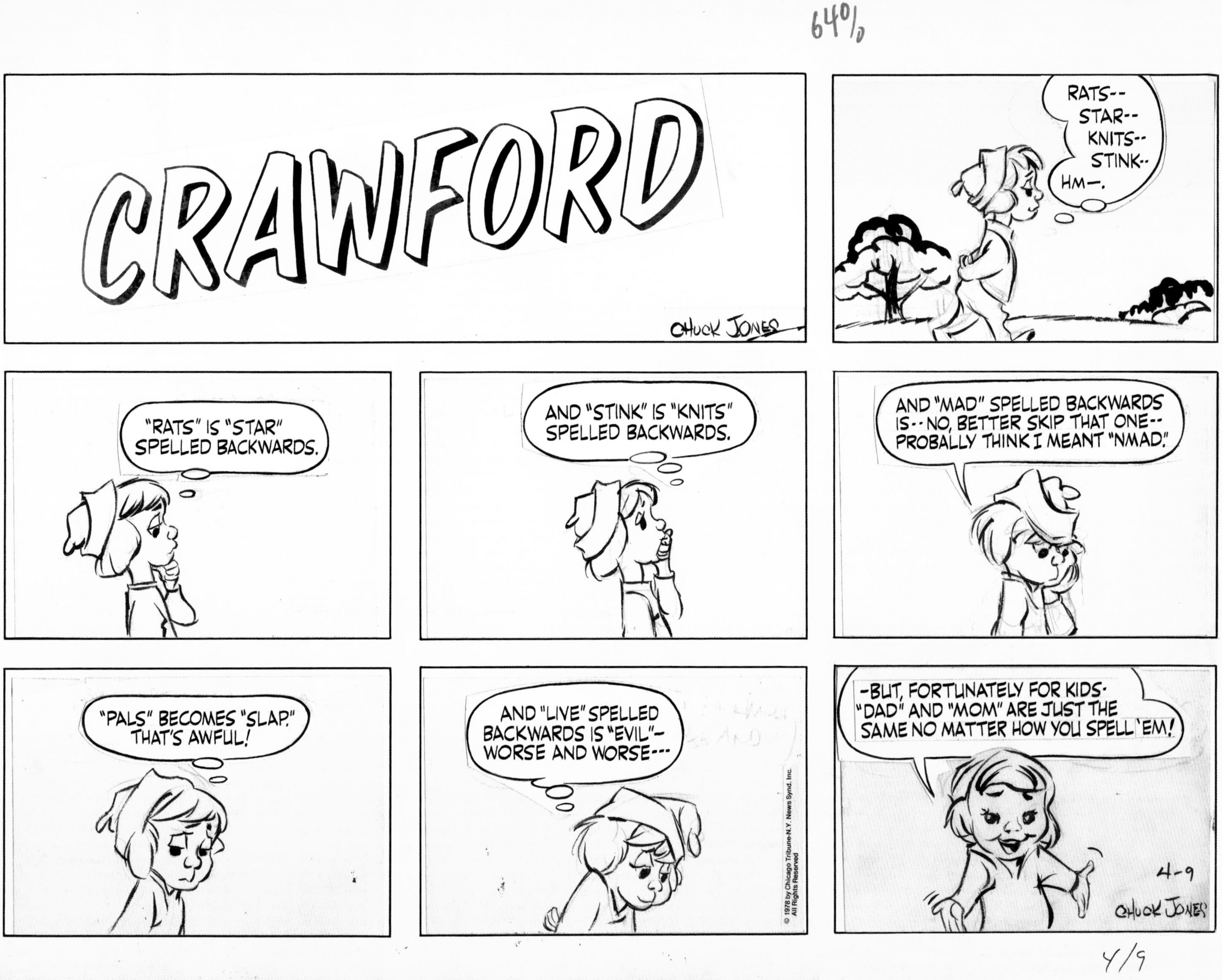
64%
CRAWFORD
CHUCK JONES
RATS-- STAR-- KNITS-- STINK-- HM—.
"RATS" IS "STAR" SPELLED BACKWARDS.
AND "STINK" IS "KNITS" SPELLED BACKWARDS.
AND "MAD" SPELLED BACKWARDS IS-- NO, BETTER SKIP THAT ONE-- PROBALLY THINK I MEANT "NMAD."
"PALS" BECOMES "SLAP." THAT'S AWFUL!
AND "LIVE" SPELLED BACKWARDS IS "EVIL"— WORSE AND WORSE---
© 1978 by Chicago Tribune-N.Y. News Synd. Inc. All Rights Reserved
-BUT, FORTUNATELY FOR KIDS- "DAD" AND "MOM" ARE JUST THE SAME NO MATTER HOW YOU SPELL 'EM!
4-9
CHUCK JONES
4/9

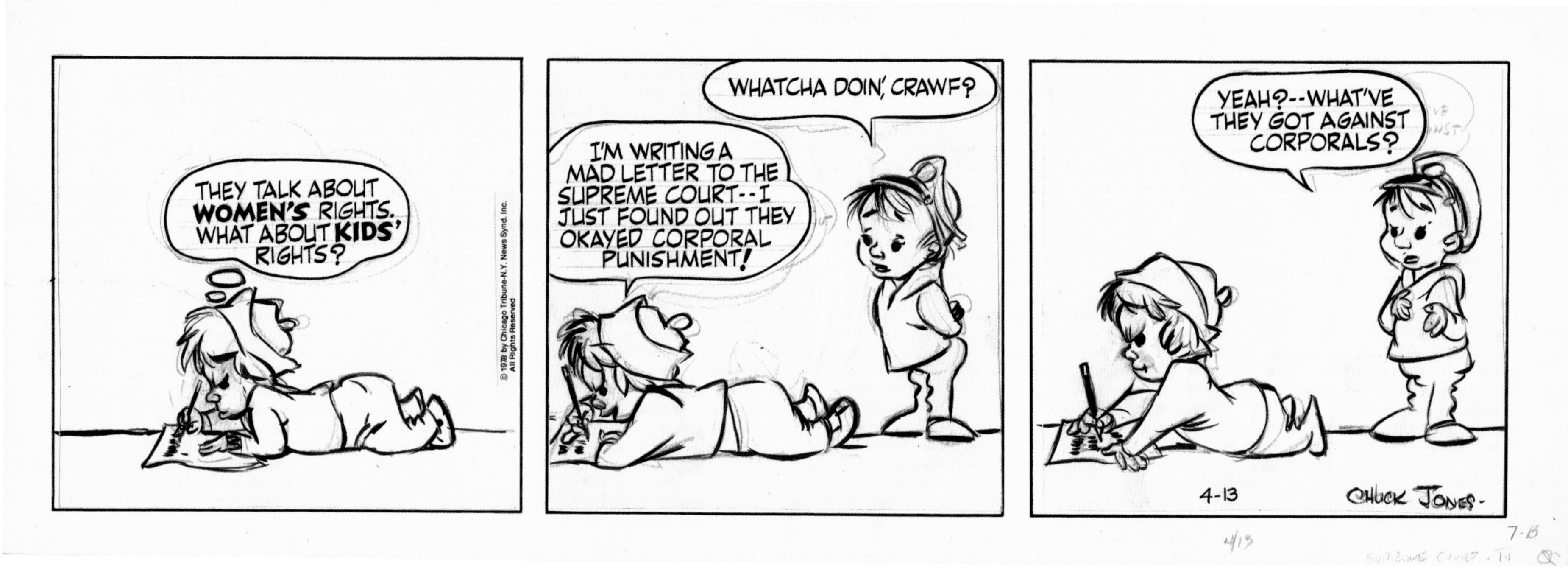
THEY TALK ABOUT **WOMEN'S** RIGHTS. WHAT ABOUT **KIDS'** RIGHTS?
© 1978 by Chicago Tribune-N.Y. News Synd. Inc. All Rights Reserved
WHATCHA DOIN', CRAWF?
I'M WRITING A MAD LETTER TO THE SUPREME COURT--I JUST FOUND OUT THEY OKAYED CORPORAL PUNISHMENT!
YEAH?--WHAT'VE THEY GOT AGAINST CORPORALS?
4-13
CHUCK JONES

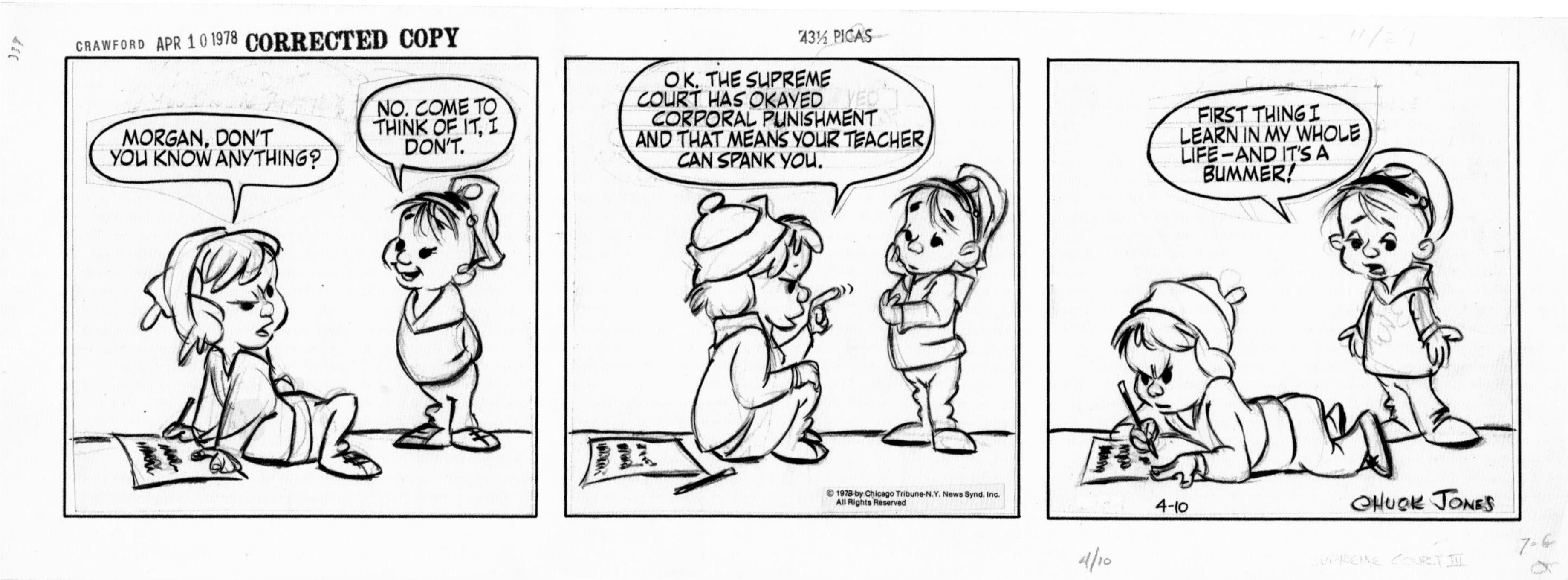
CRAWFORD APR 10 1978 CORRECTED COPY
43½ PICAS
MORGAN, DON'T YOU KNOW ANYTHING?
NO. COME TO THINK OF IT, I DON'T.
O.K. THE SUPREME COURT HAS OKAYED CORPORAL PUNISHMENT AND THAT MEANS YOUR TEACHER CAN SPANK YOU.
© 1978 by Chicago Tribune-N.Y. News Synd. Inc. All Rights Reserved
FIRST THING I LEARN IN MY WHOLE LIFE–AND IT'S A BUMMER!
4-10
CHUCK JONES

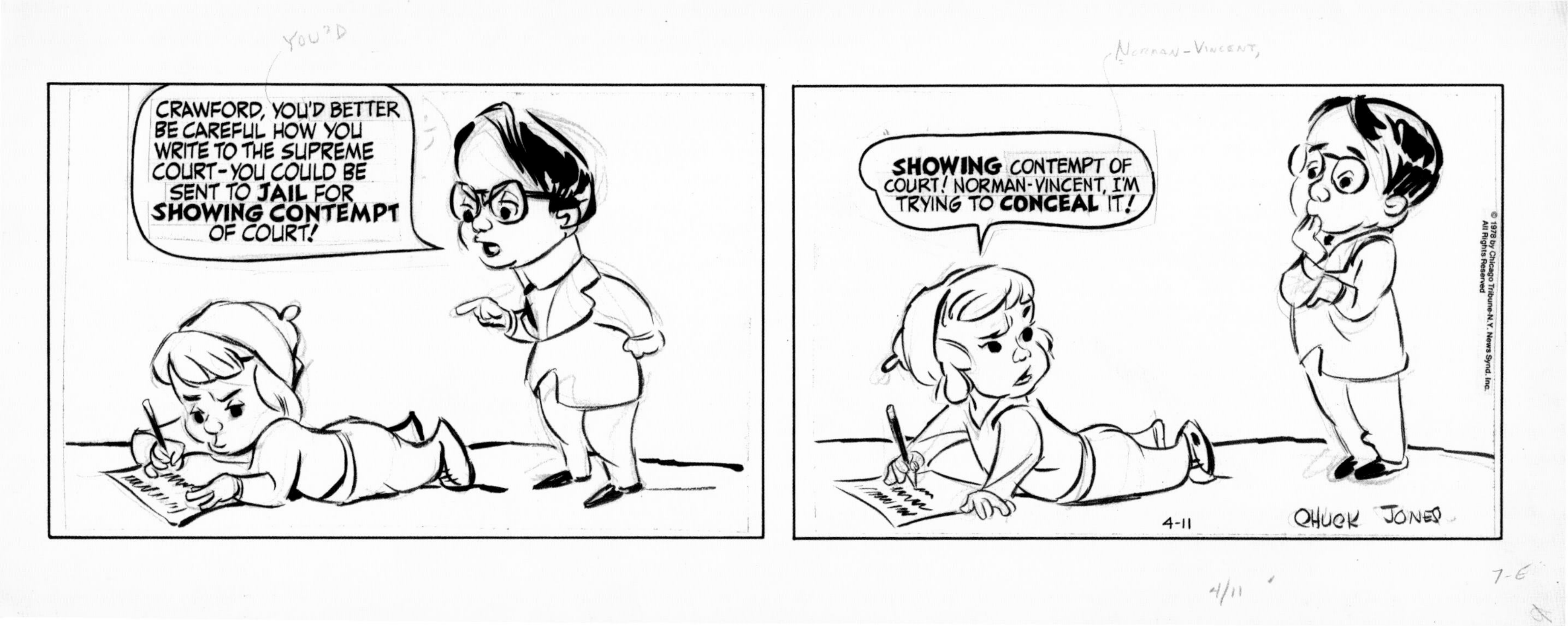
CRAWFORD, YOU'D BETTER BE CAREFUL HOW YOU WRITE TO THE SUPREME COURT-YOU COULD BE SENT TO JAIL FOR SHOWING CONTEMPT OF COURT!
SHOWING CONTEMPT OF COURT! NORMAN-VINCENT, I'M TRYING TO CONCEAL IT!
4-11
CHUCK JONES
© 1978 by Chicago Tribune-N.Y. News Synd. Inc. All Rights Reserved

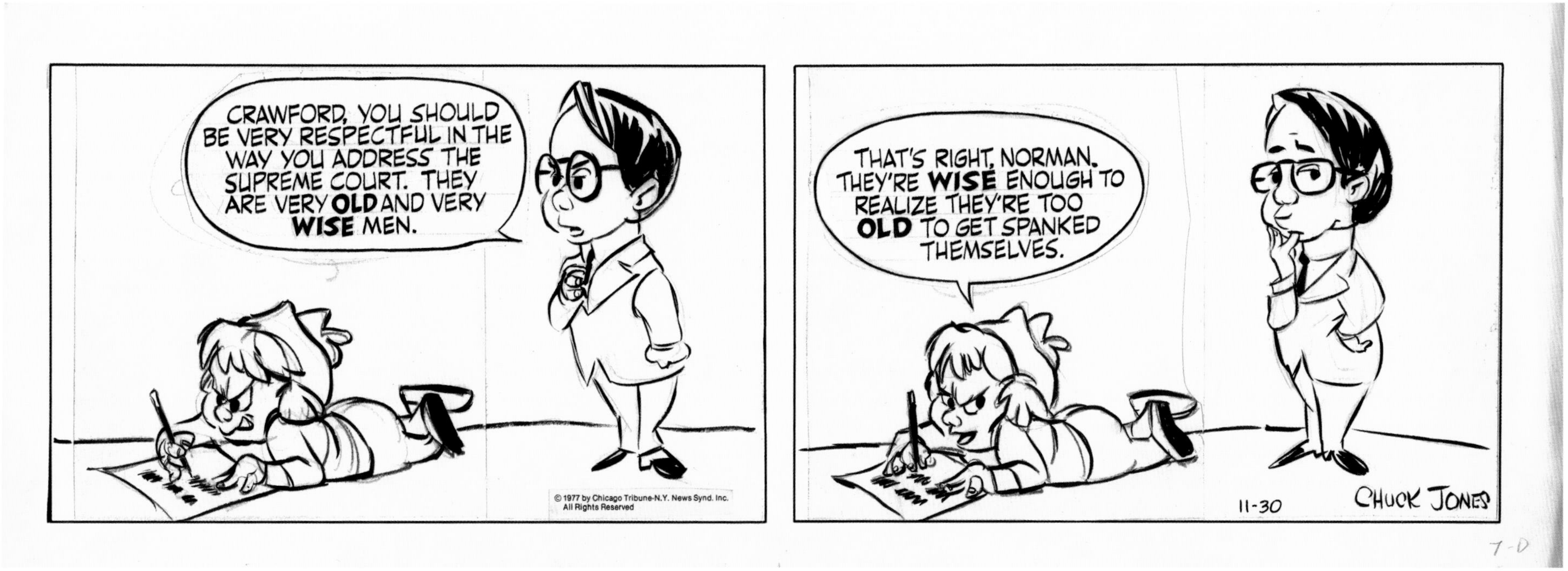
CRAWFORD, YOU SHOULD BE VERY RESPECTFUL IN THE WAY YOU ADDRESS THE SUPREME COURT. THEY ARE VERY OLD AND VERY WISE MEN.
THAT'S RIGHT, NORMAN. THEY'RE WISE ENOUGH TO REALIZE THEY'RE TOO OLD TO GET SPANKED THEMSELVES.
© 1977 by Chicago Tribune-N.Y. News Synd. Inc. All Rights Reserved
11-30
CHUCK JONES

Unpublished strip—an earlier, alternate version of the daily at top that was published on April 11.

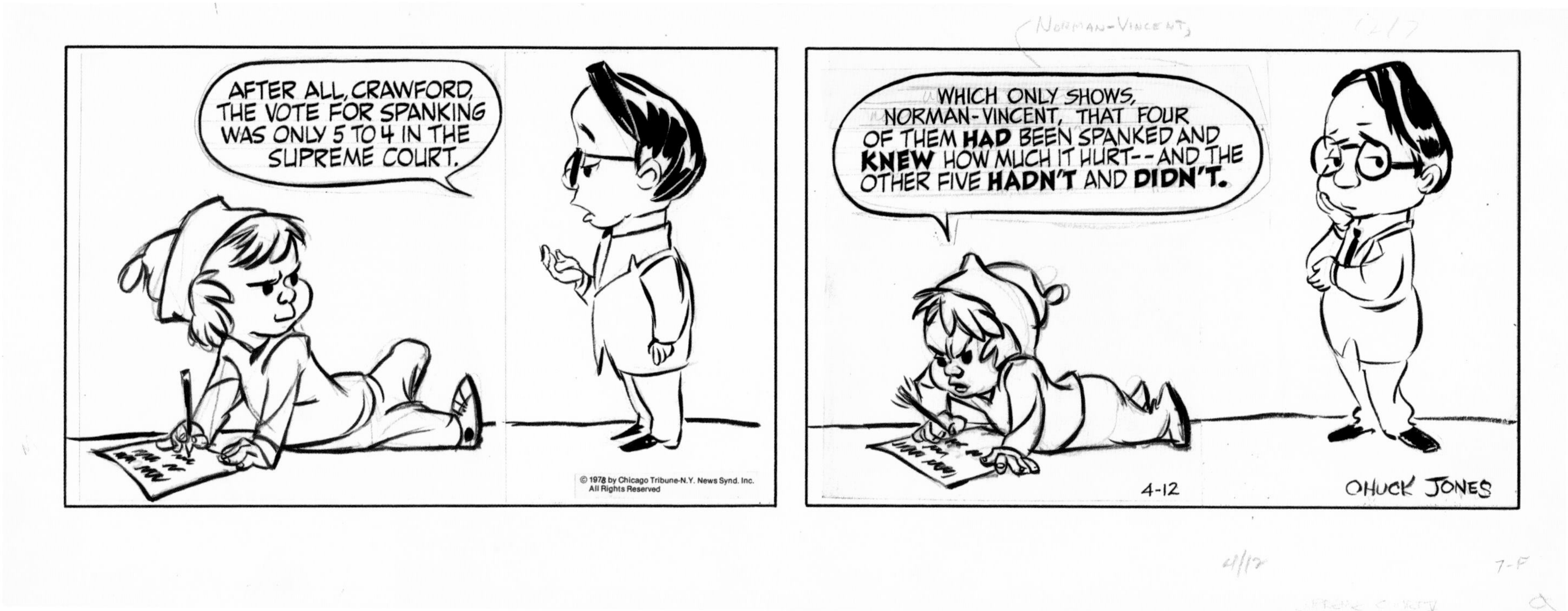
NORMAN-VINCENT
AFTER ALL, CRAWFORD, THE VOTE FOR SPANKING WAS ONLY 5 TO 4 IN THE SUPREME COURT.
© 1978 by Chicago Tribune-N.Y. News Synd. Inc. All Rights Reserved
WHICH ONLY SHOWS, NORMAN-VINCENT, THAT FOUR OF THEM **HAD** BEEN SPANKED AND **KNEW** HOW MUCH IT HURT--AND THE OTHER FIVE **HADN'T** AND **DIDN'T.**
4-12
CHUCK JONES

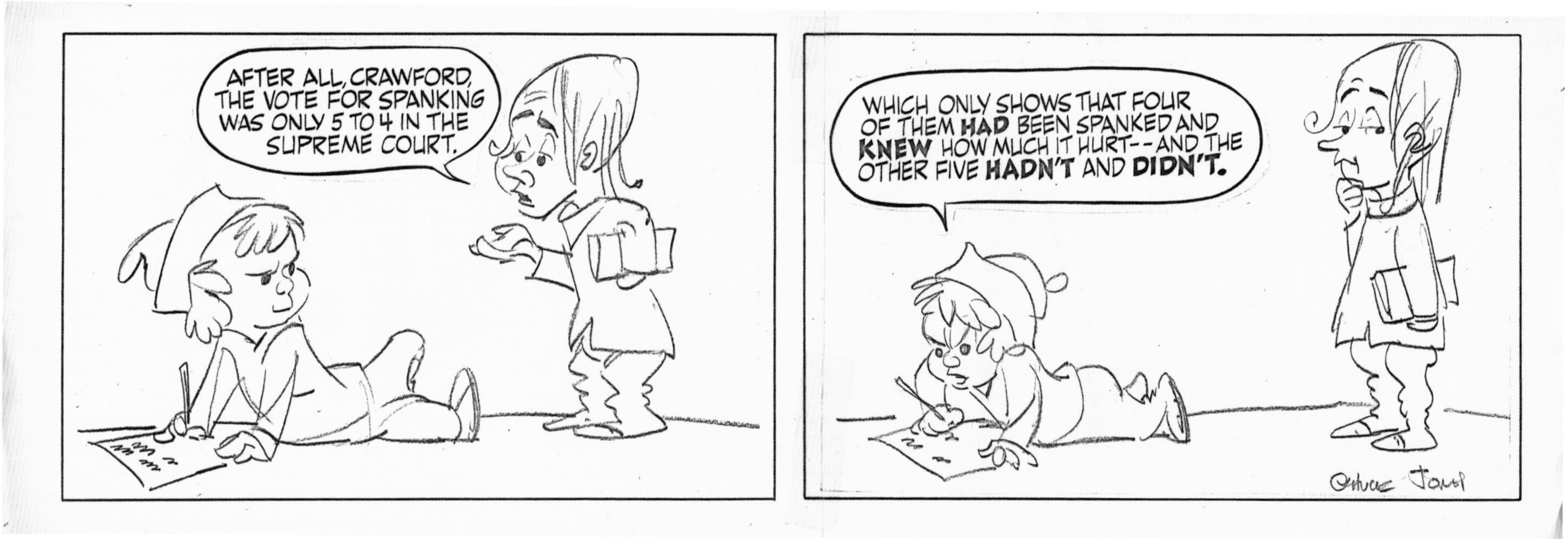
AFTER ALL, CRAWFORD, THE VOTE FOR SPANKING WAS ONLY 5 TO 4 IN THE SUPREME COURT.
WHICH ONLY SHOWS THAT FOUR OF THEM **HAD** BEEN SPANKED AND **KNEW** HOW MUCH IT HURT--AND THE OTHER FIVE **HADN'T** AND **DIDN'T.**

Earlier rendition of Norman-Vincent.

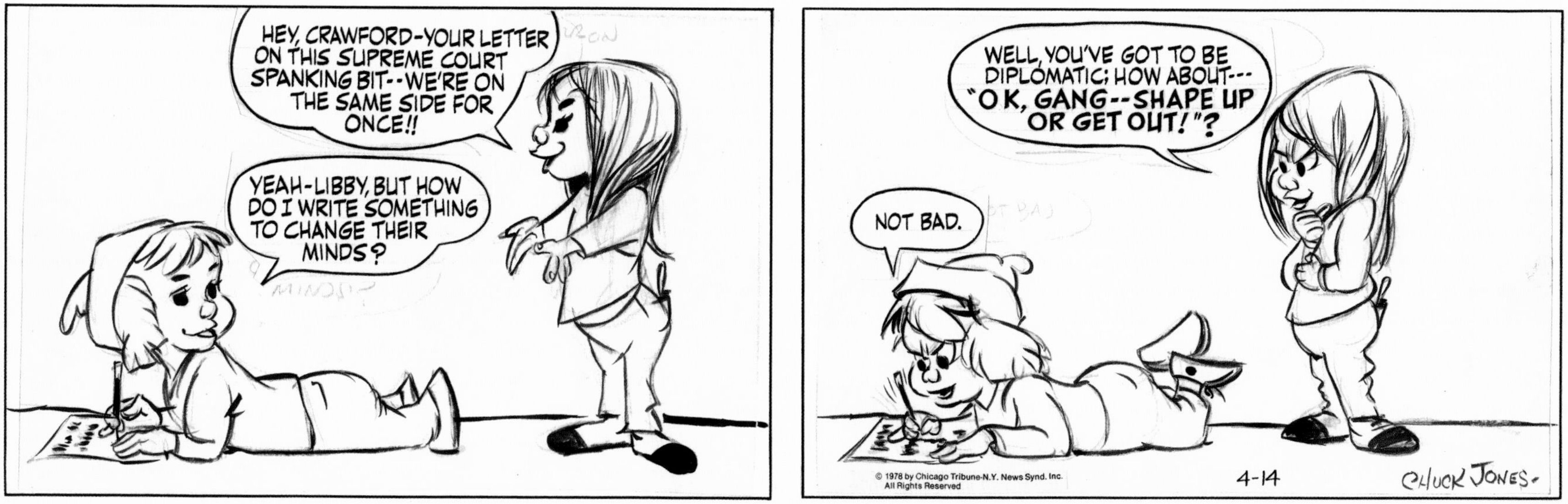
HEY, CRAWFORD-YOUR LETTER ON THIS SUPREME COURT SPANKING BIT--WE'RE ON THE SAME SIDE FOR ONCE!!
YEAH-LIBBY, BUT HOW DO I WRITE SOMETHING TO CHANGE THEIR MINDS?
WELL, YOU'VE GOT TO BE DIPLOMATIC; HOW ABOUT--- "O K, GANG--SHAPE UP OR GET OUT!"?
NOT BAD.
© 1978 by Chicago Tribune-N.Y. News Synd. Inc. All Rights Reserved
4-14
CHUCK JONES

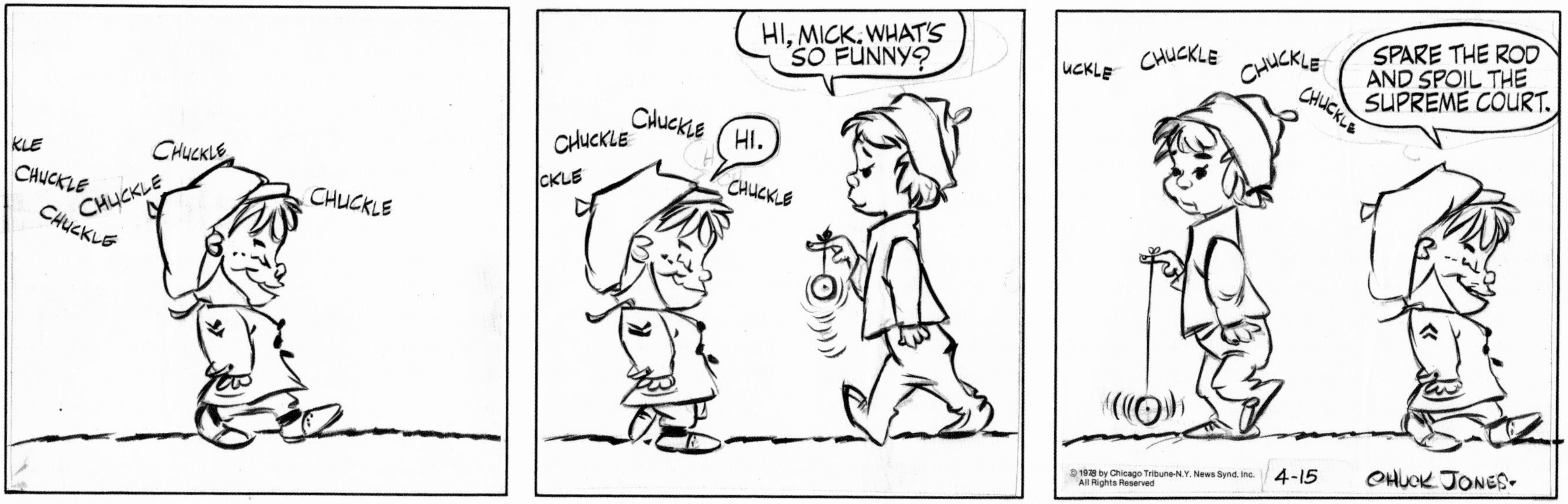
KLE
CHUCKLE
CHUCKLE
CHUCKLE
CHUCKLE
CHUCKLE
CHUCKLE CHUCKLE
CKLE
HI.
CHUCKLE
HI, MICK. WHAT'S SO FUNNY?
UCKLE CHUCKLE CHUCKLE CHUCKLE
SPARE THE ROD AND SPOIL THE SUPREME COURT.
© 1978 by Chicago Tribune-N.Y. News Synd. Inc. All Rights Reserved
4-15
CHUCK JONES

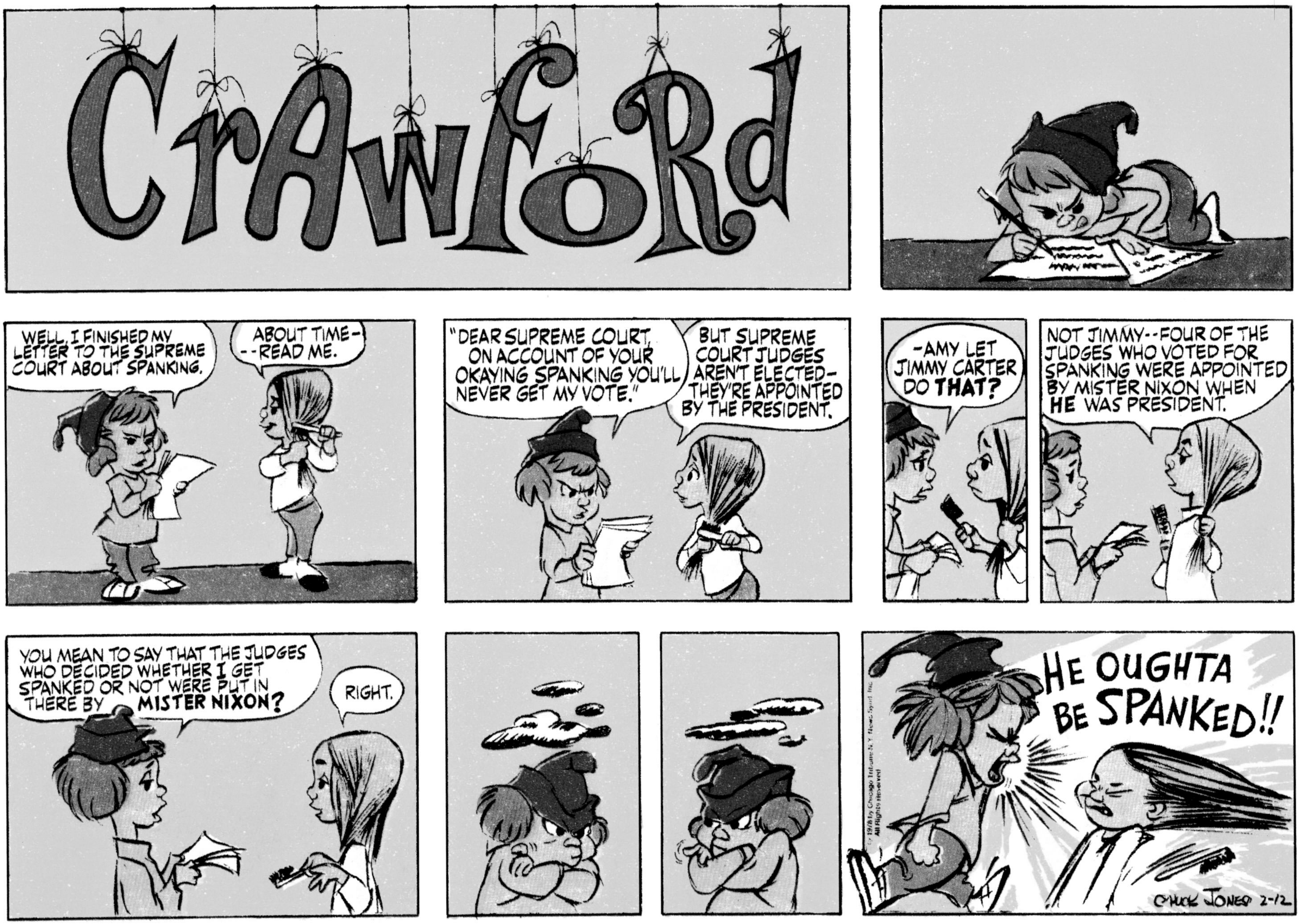
CRAWFORD
WELL, I FINISHED MY LETTER TO THE SUPREME COURT ABOUT SPANKING.
ABOUT TIME- -READ ME.
"DEAR SUPREME COURT, ON ACCOUNT OF YOUR OKAYING SPANKING YOU'LL NEVER GET MY VOTE."
BUT SUPREME COURT JUDGES AREN'T ELECTED- THEY'RE APPOINTED BY THE PRESIDENT.
-AMY LET JIMMY CARTER DO **THAT?**
NOT JIMMY--FOUR OF THE JUDGES WHO VOTED FOR SPANKING WERE APPOINTED BY MISTER NIXON WHEN **HE** WAS PRESIDENT.
YOU MEAN TO SAY THAT THE JUDGES WHO DECIDED WHETHER **I** GET SPANKED OR NOT WERE PUT IN THERE BY **MISTER NIXON?**
RIGHT.
HE OUGHTA BE SPANKED!!
CHUCK JONES 2-12

The February 12, 1978 Sunday page inserted in its proper order following April 15 per Chuck Jones's notes.

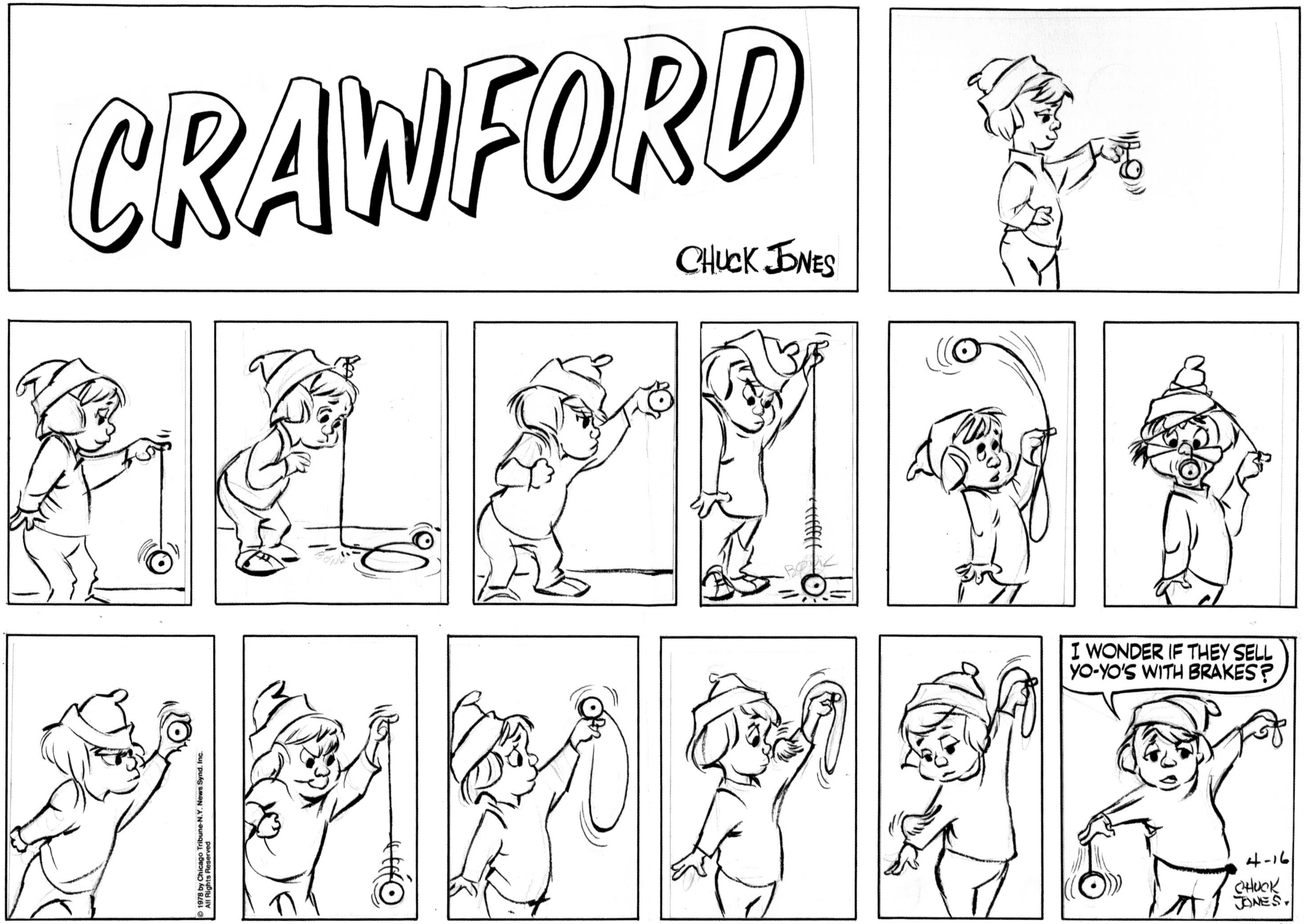
CRAWFORD
CHUCK JONES
© 1978 by Chicago Tribune-N.Y. News Synd. Inc.
All Rights Reserved
I WONDER IF THEY SELL YO-YO'S WITH BRAKES?
4-16
CHUCK JONES.

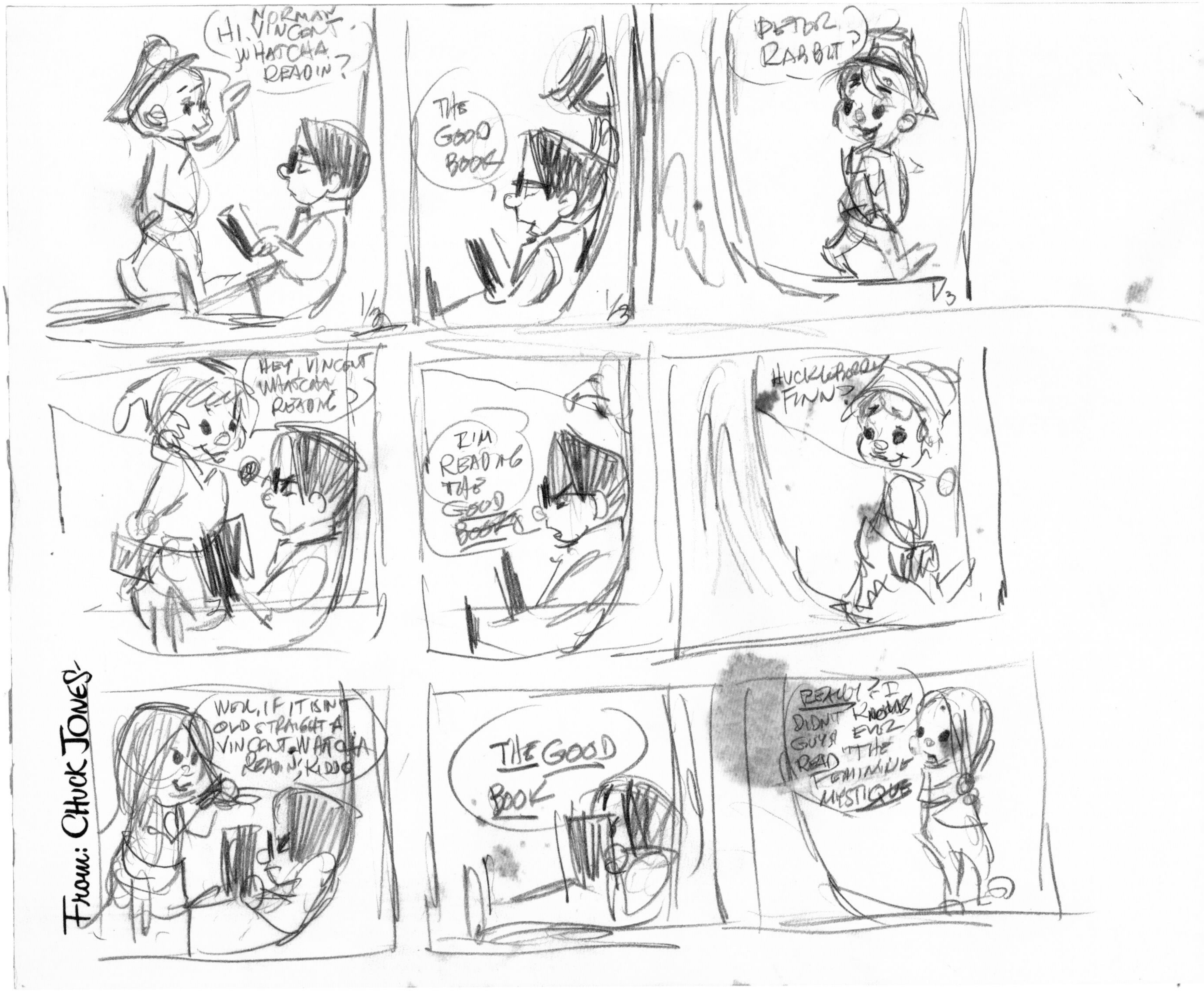
HI, NORMAN VINCENT. WHATCHA READIN?
THE GOOD BOOK
PETER RABBIT?
HEY, VINCENT WHATCHA READIN'
I'M READING THE GOOD BOOK
HUCKLEBERRY FINN?
WELL, IF IT ISN'T OLD STRAIGHT A VINCENT. WATCHA READIN', KIDDO
THE GOOD BOOK
REALLY? I DIDN'T KNOW GUYS EVER READ "THE FEMININE MYSTIQUE"
From: CHUCK JONES

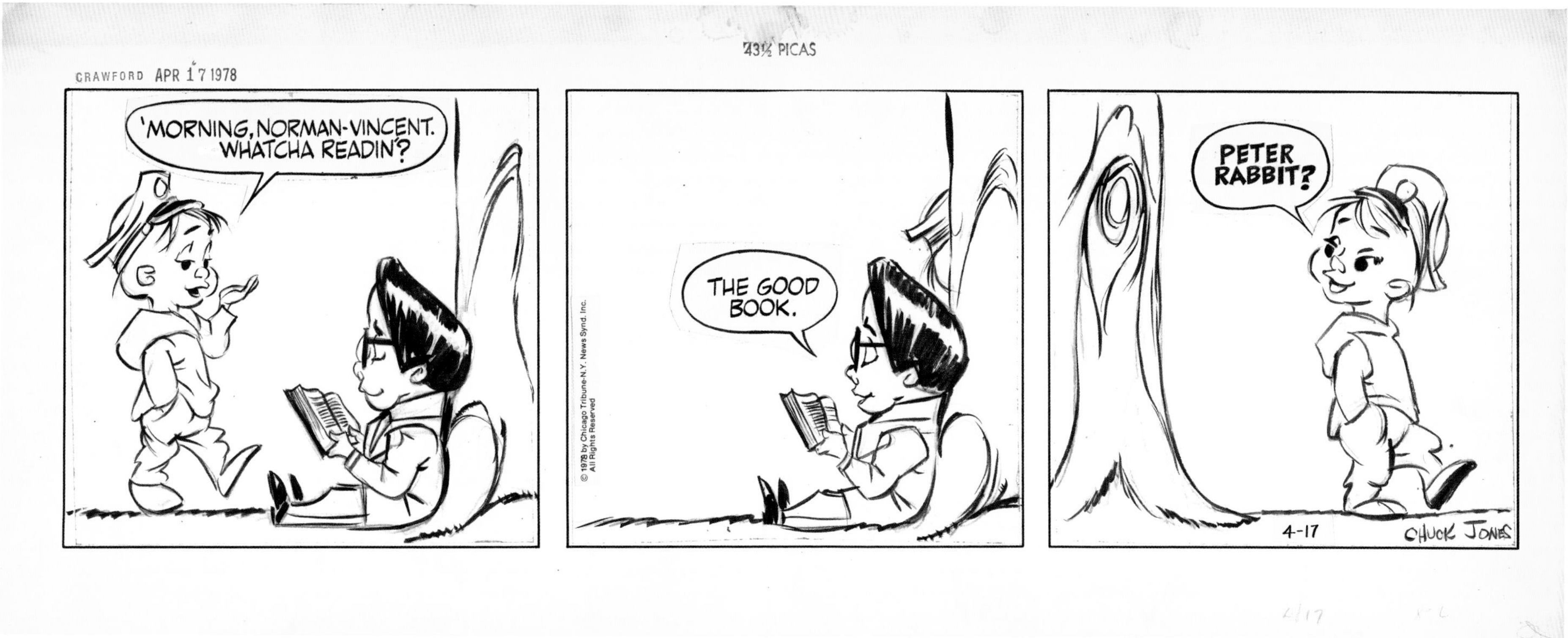
CRAWFORD APR 17 1978
43½ PICAS
'MORNING, NORMAN-VINCENT. WHATCHA READIN'?
THE GOOD BOOK.
© 1978 by Chicago Tribune-N.Y. News Synd. Inc. All Rights Reserved
PETER RABBIT?
4-17
CHUCK JONES

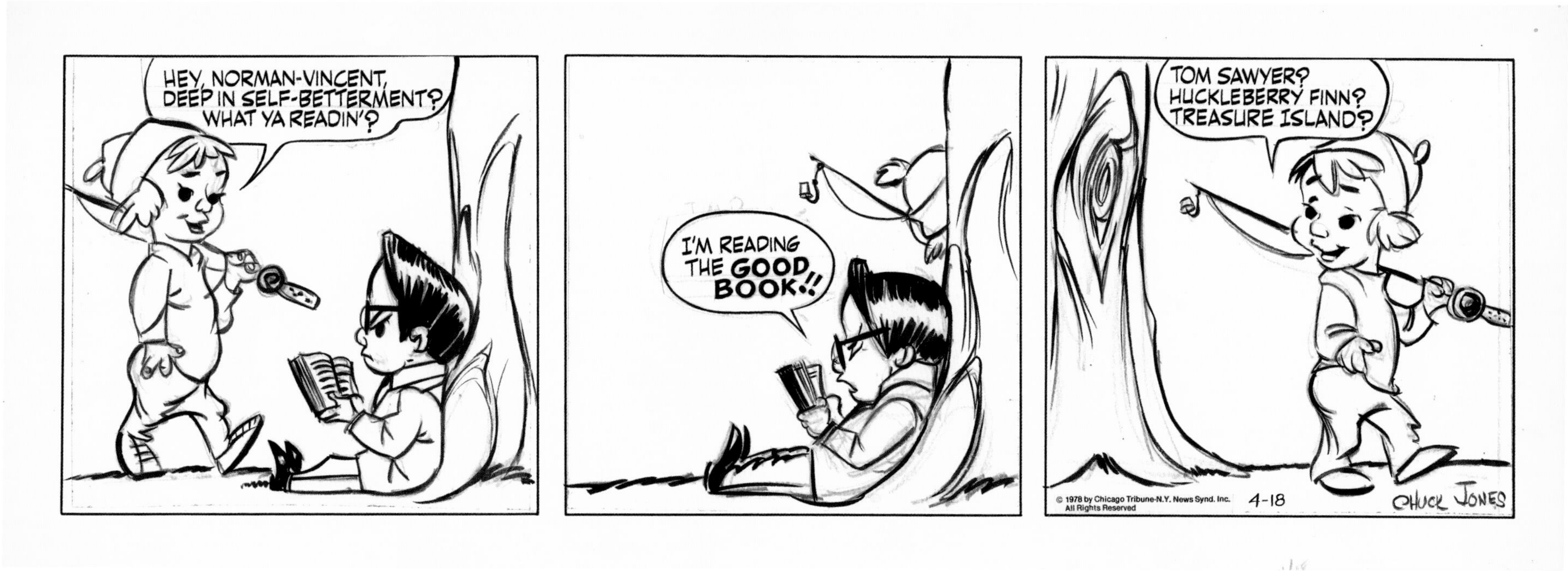
HEY, NORMAN-VINCENT, DEEP IN SELF-BETTERMENT? WHAT YA READIN'?
I'M READING THE GOOD BOOK.!!
TOM SAWYER? HUCKLEBERRY FINN? TREASURE ISLAND?
© 1978 by Chicago Tribune-N.Y. News Synd. Inc. All Rights Reserved
4-18
CHUCK JONES

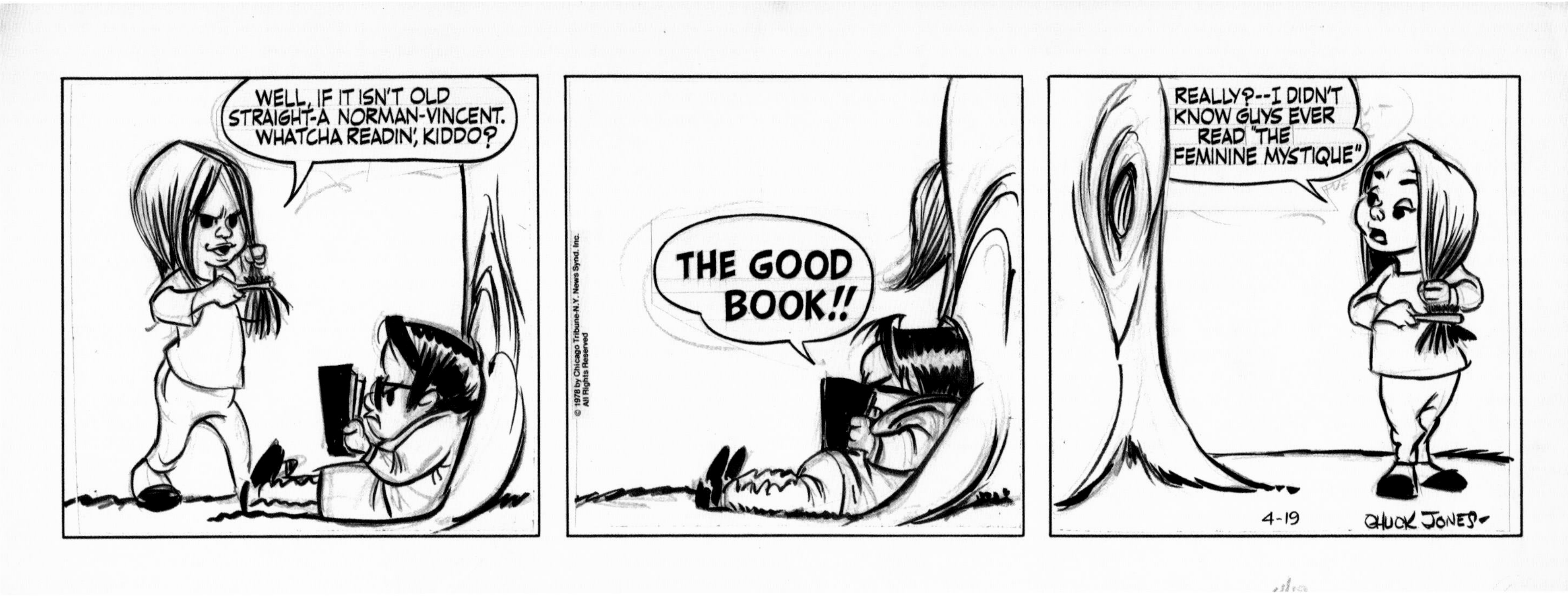
WELL, IF IT ISN'T OLD STRAIGHT-A NORMAN-VINCENT. WHATCHA READIN', KIDDO?
© 1978 by Chicago Tribune-N.Y. News Synd. Inc. All Rights Reserved
THE GOOD BOOK!!
REALLY?--I DIDN'T KNOW GUYS EVER READ "THE FEMININE MYSTIQUE"
4-19
CHUCK JONES

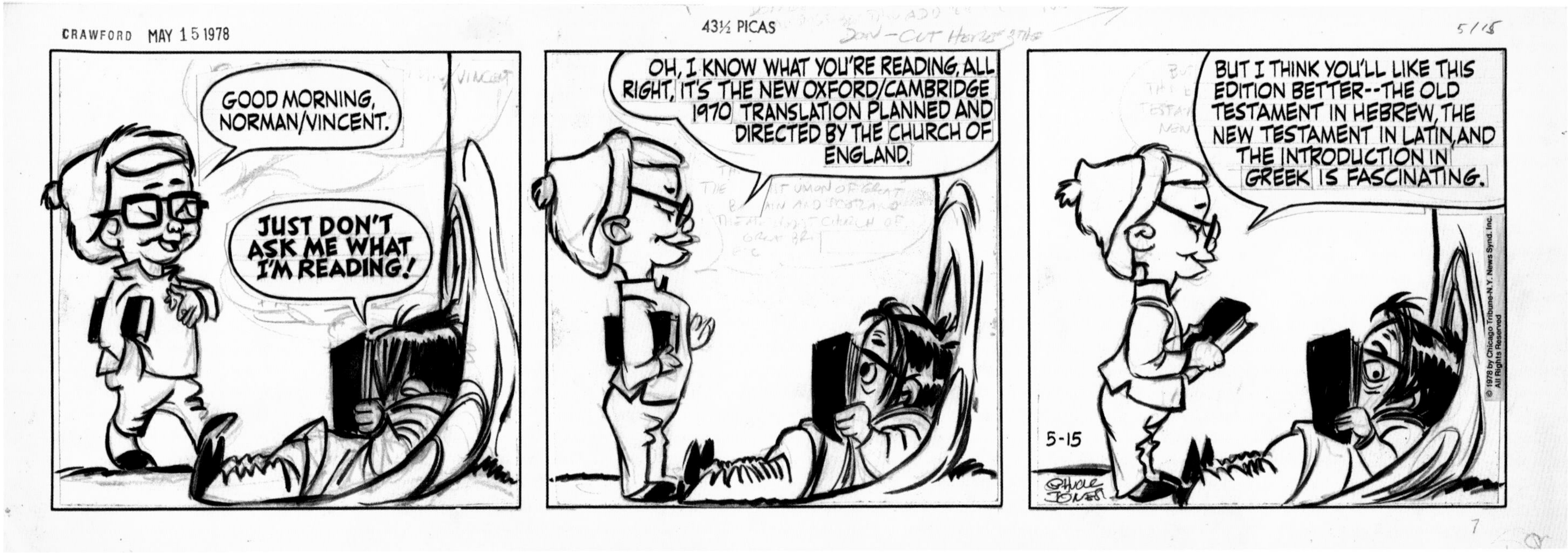
CRAWFORD MAY 15 1978
43½ PICAS
5/15
GOOD MORNING, NORMAN/VINCENT.
JUST DON'T ASK ME WHAT I'M READING!
OH, I KNOW WHAT YOU'RE READING, ALL RIGHT, IT'S THE NEW OXFORD/CAMBRIDGE 1970 TRANSLATION PLANNED AND DIRECTED BY THE CHURCH OF ENGLAND.
BUT I THINK YOU'LL LIKE THIS EDITION BETTER--THE OLD TESTAMENT IN HEBREW, THE NEW TESTAMENT IN LATIN, AND THE INTRODUCTION IN GREEK IS FASCINATING.
© 1978 by Chicago Tribune-N.Y. News Synd. Inc. All Rights Reserved
5-15
CHUCK JONES

The May 15-17, 1978 dailies inserted in their proper order following April 19 per Chuck Jones's notes.

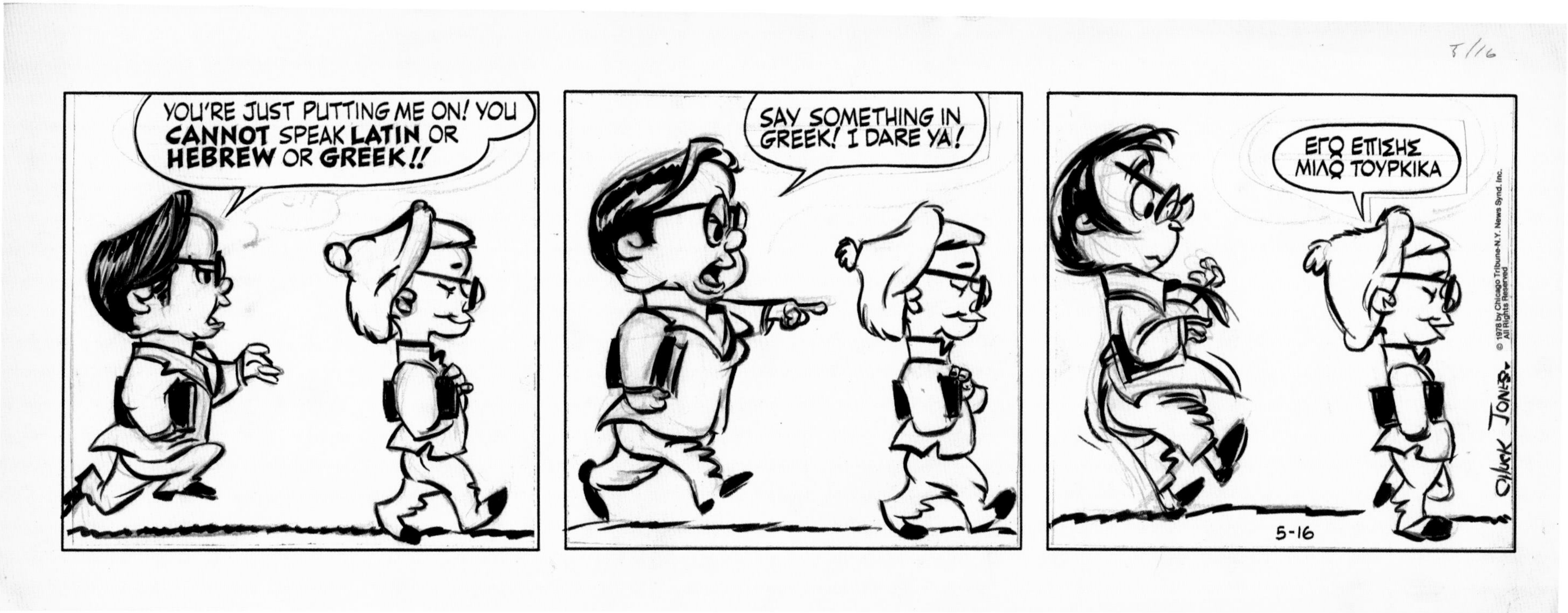
5/16
YOU'RE JUST PUTTING ME ON! YOU **CANNOT** SPEAK **LATIN** OR **HEBREW** OR **GREEK**!!
SAY SOMETHING IN GREEK! I DARE YA!
ΕΓΩ ΕΠΙΣΗΣ ΜΙΛΩ ΤΟΥΡΚΙΚΑ
© 1978 by Chicago Tribune-N.Y. News Synd. Inc. All Rights Reserved
CHUCK JONES
5-16

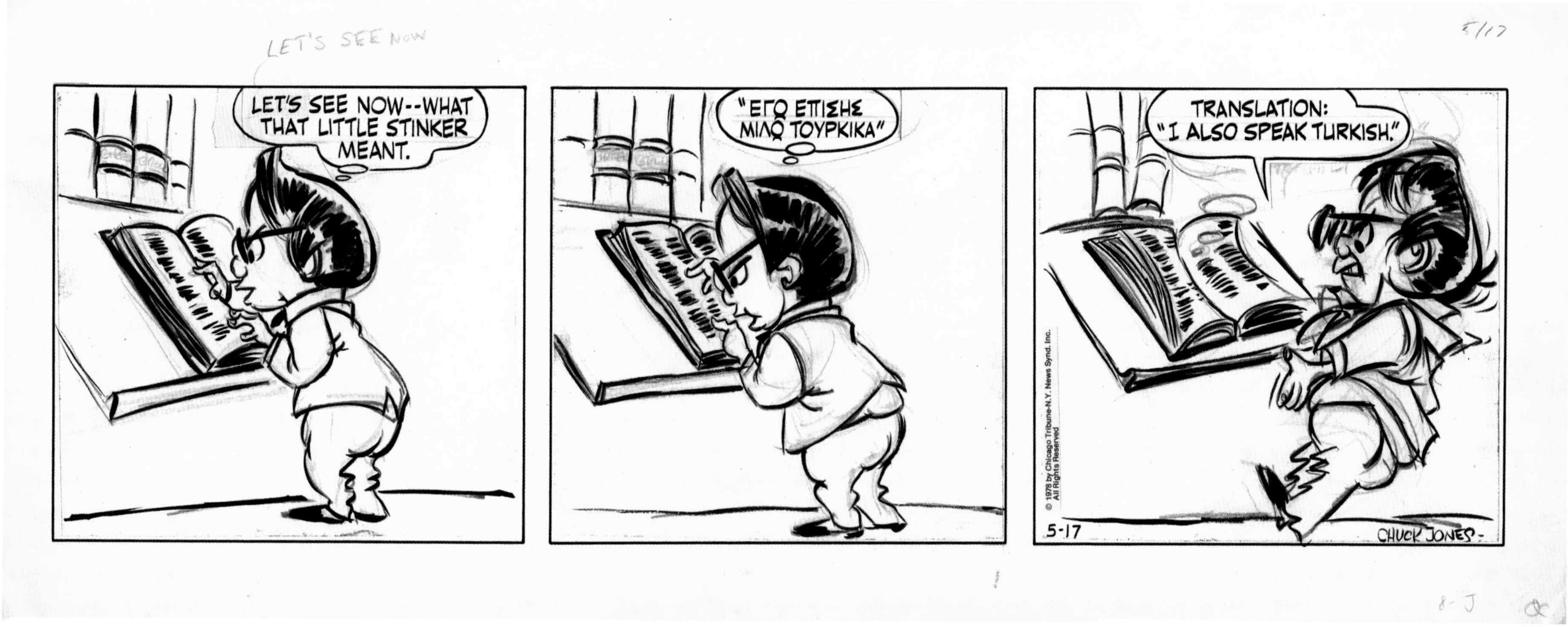
LET'S SEE NOW
5/17
LET'S SEE NOW--WHAT THAT LITTLE STINKER MEANT.
"ΕΓΩ ΕΠΙΣΗΣ ΜΙΛΩ ΤΟΥΡΚΙΚΑ"
TRANSLATION: "I ALSO SPEAK TURKISH."
© 1978 by Chicago Tribune-N.Y. News Synd. Inc. All Rights Reserved
5-17
CHUCK JONES
8-J

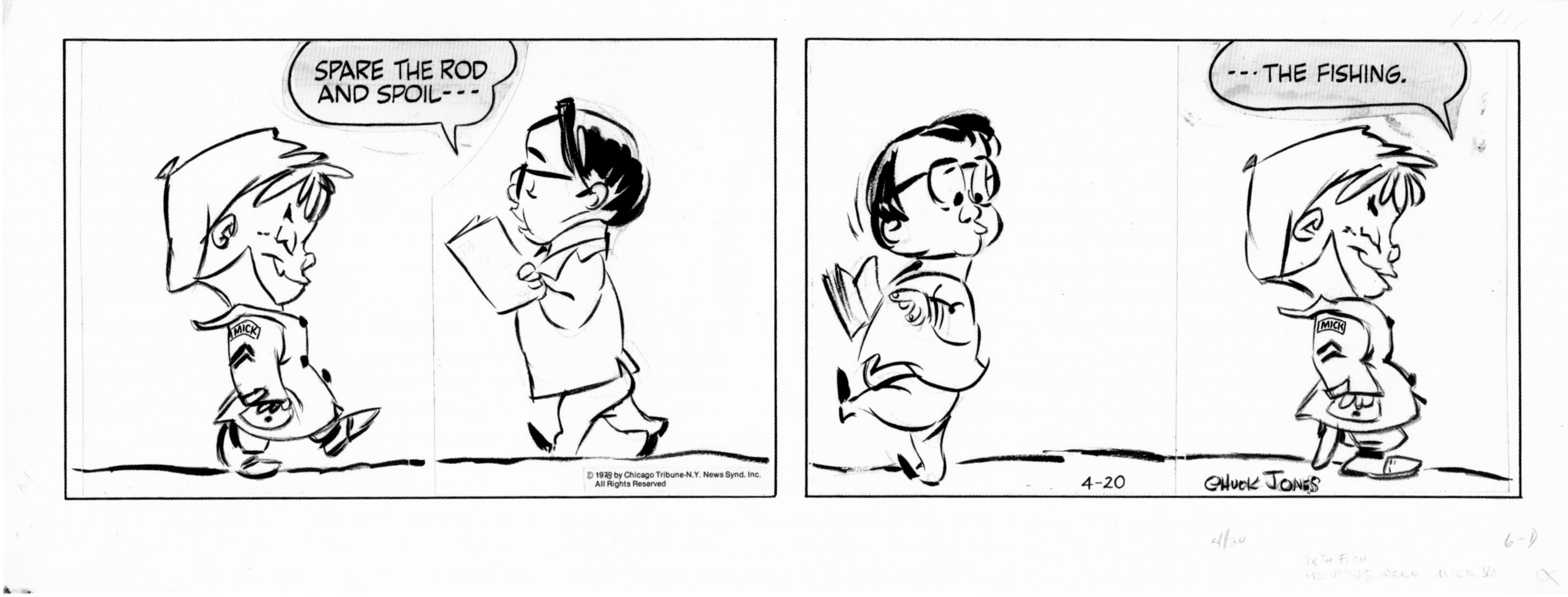
SPARE THE ROD AND SPOIL---
MICK
© 1978 by Chicago Tribune-N.Y. News Synd. Inc.
All Rights Reserved
---THE FISHING.
MICK
4-20
CHUCK JONES

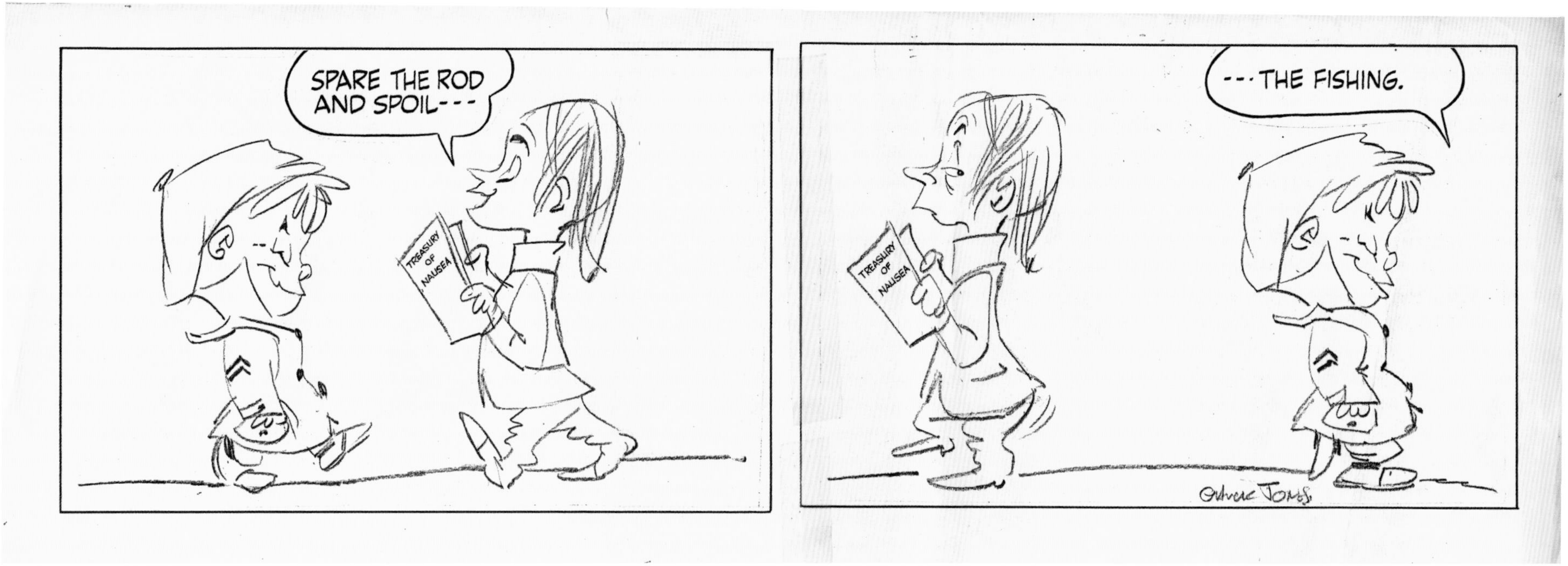
SPARE THE ROD AND SPOIL---
TREASURY OF NAUSEA
TREASURY OF NAUSEA
---THE FISHING.
CHUCK JONES

Earlier rendition of Norman-Vincent.

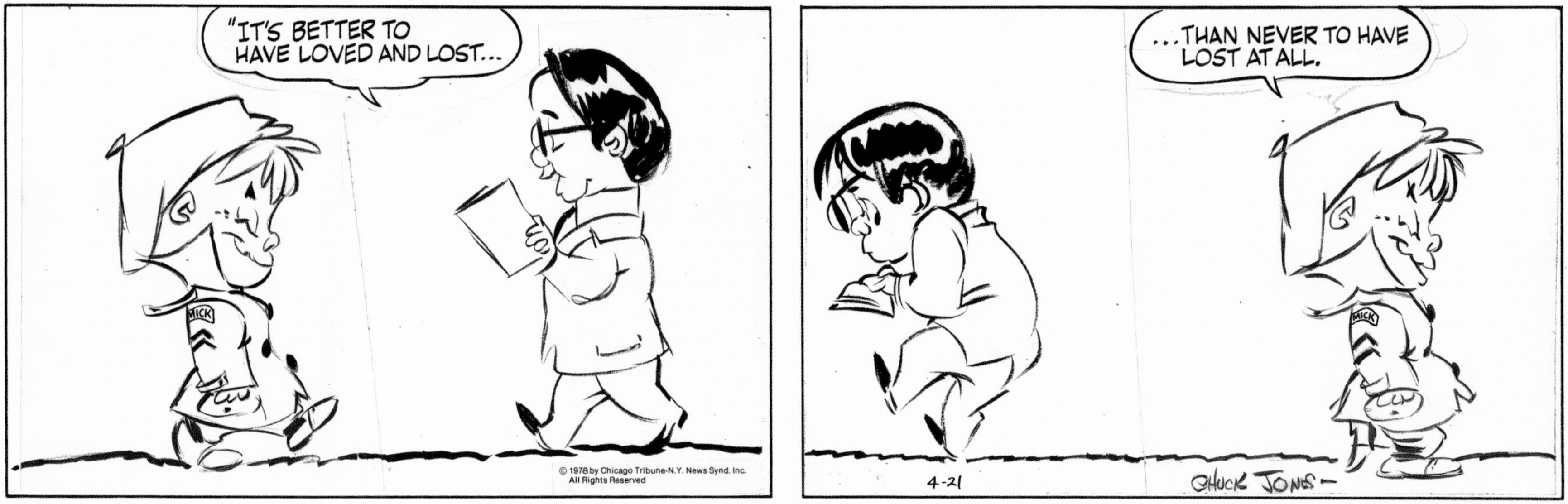
"IT'S BETTER TO HAVE LOVED AND LOST...
© 1978 by Chicago Tribune-N.Y. News Synd. Inc. All Rights Reserved
...THAN NEVER TO HAVE LOST AT ALL.
4-21
CHUCK JONES

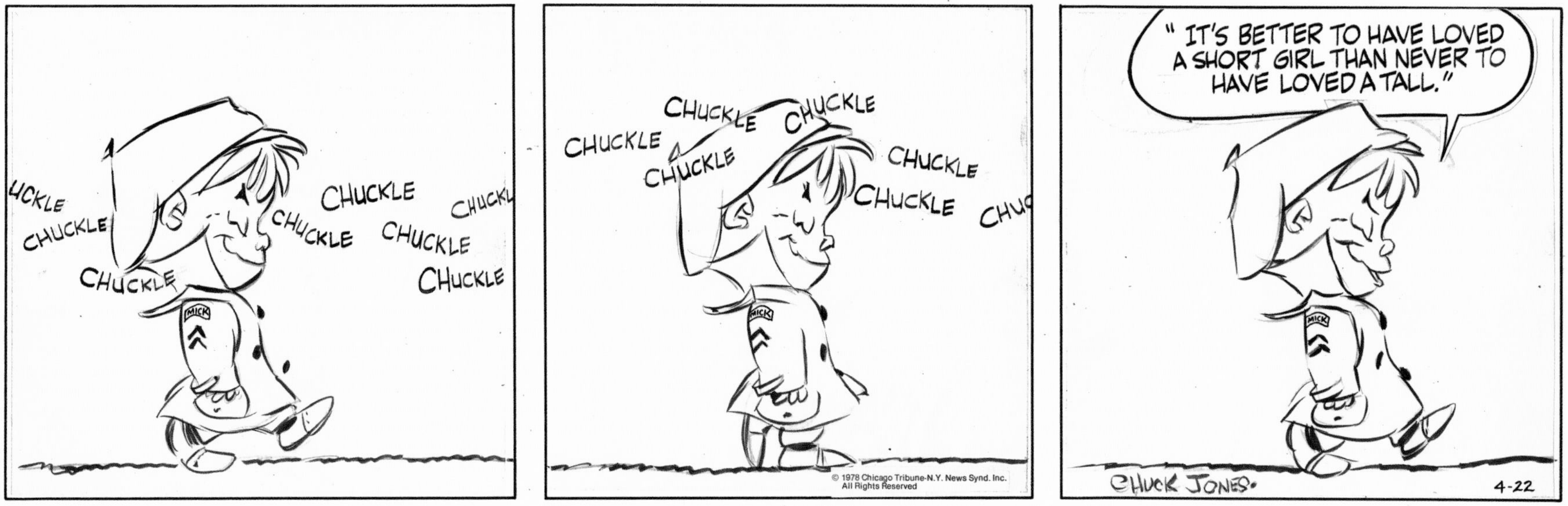
CHUCKLE CHUCKLE CHUCKLE CHUCKLE CHUCKLE CHUCKLE CHUCKLE
CHUCKLE CHUCKLE CHUCKLE CHUCKLE CHUCKLE CHUCKLE
© 1978 Chicago Tribune-N.Y. News Synd. Inc. All Rights Reserved
" IT'S BETTER TO HAVE LOVED A SHORT GIRL THAN NEVER TO HAVE LOVED A TALL."
CHUCK JONES
4-22

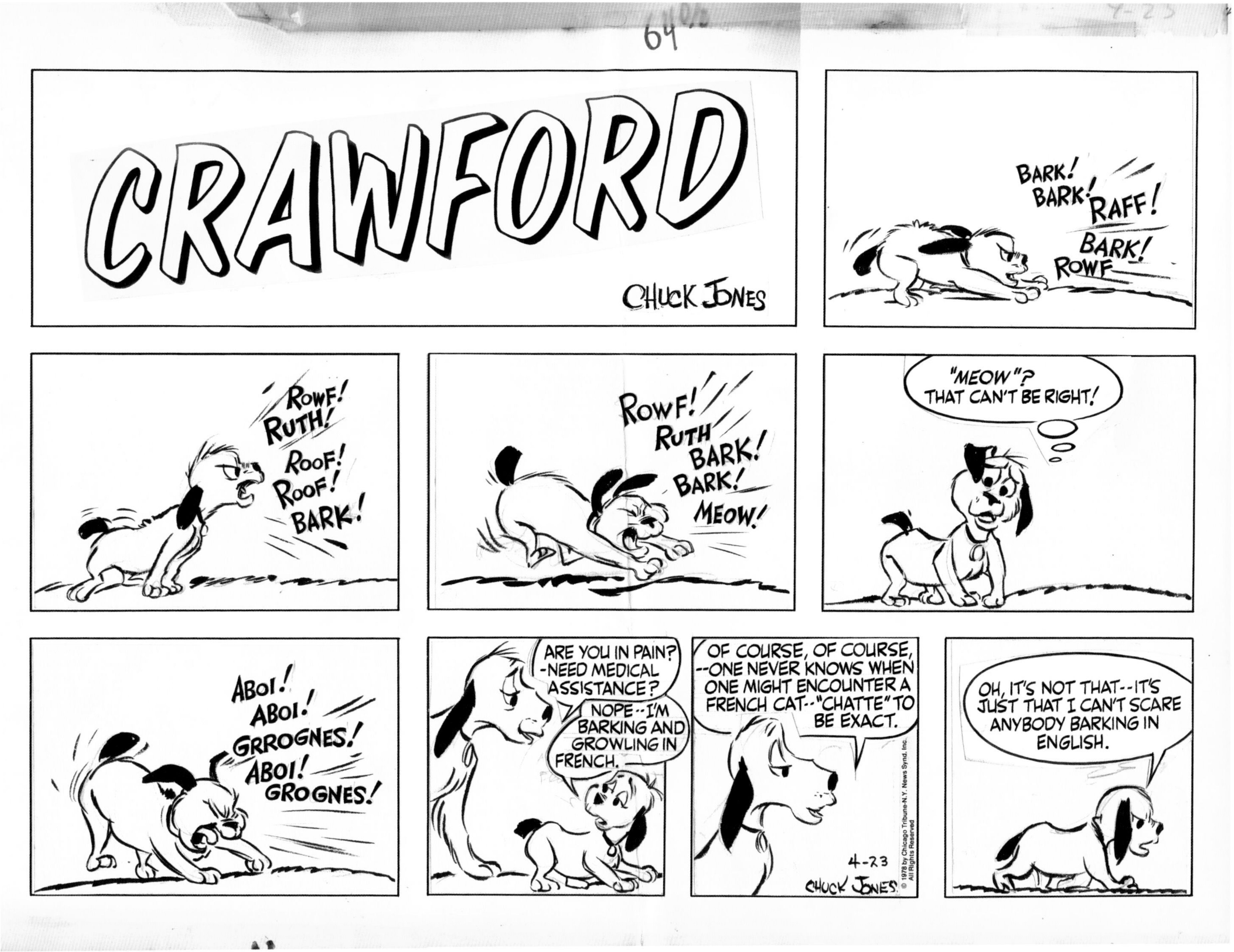
CRAWFORD
CHUCK JONES
BARK! BARK! RAFF! BARK! ROWF
ROWF! RUTH! ROOF! ROOF! BARK!
ROWF! RUTH BARK! BARK! MEOW!
"MEOW"? THAT CAN'T BE RIGHT!
ABOI! ABOI! GRROGNES! ABOI! GROGNES!
ARE YOU IN PAIN? -NEED MEDICAL ASSISTANCE?
NOPE--I'M BARKING AND GROWLING IN FRENCH.
OF COURSE, OF COURSE, --ONE NEVER KNOWS WHEN ONE MIGHT ENCOUNTER A FRENCH CAT--"CHATTE" TO BE EXACT.
4-23
CHUCK JONES
© 1978 by Chicago Tribune-N.Y. News Synd. Inc. All Rights Reserved
OH, IT'S NOT THAT--IT'S JUST THAT I CAN'T SCARE ANYBODY BARKING IN ENGLISH.

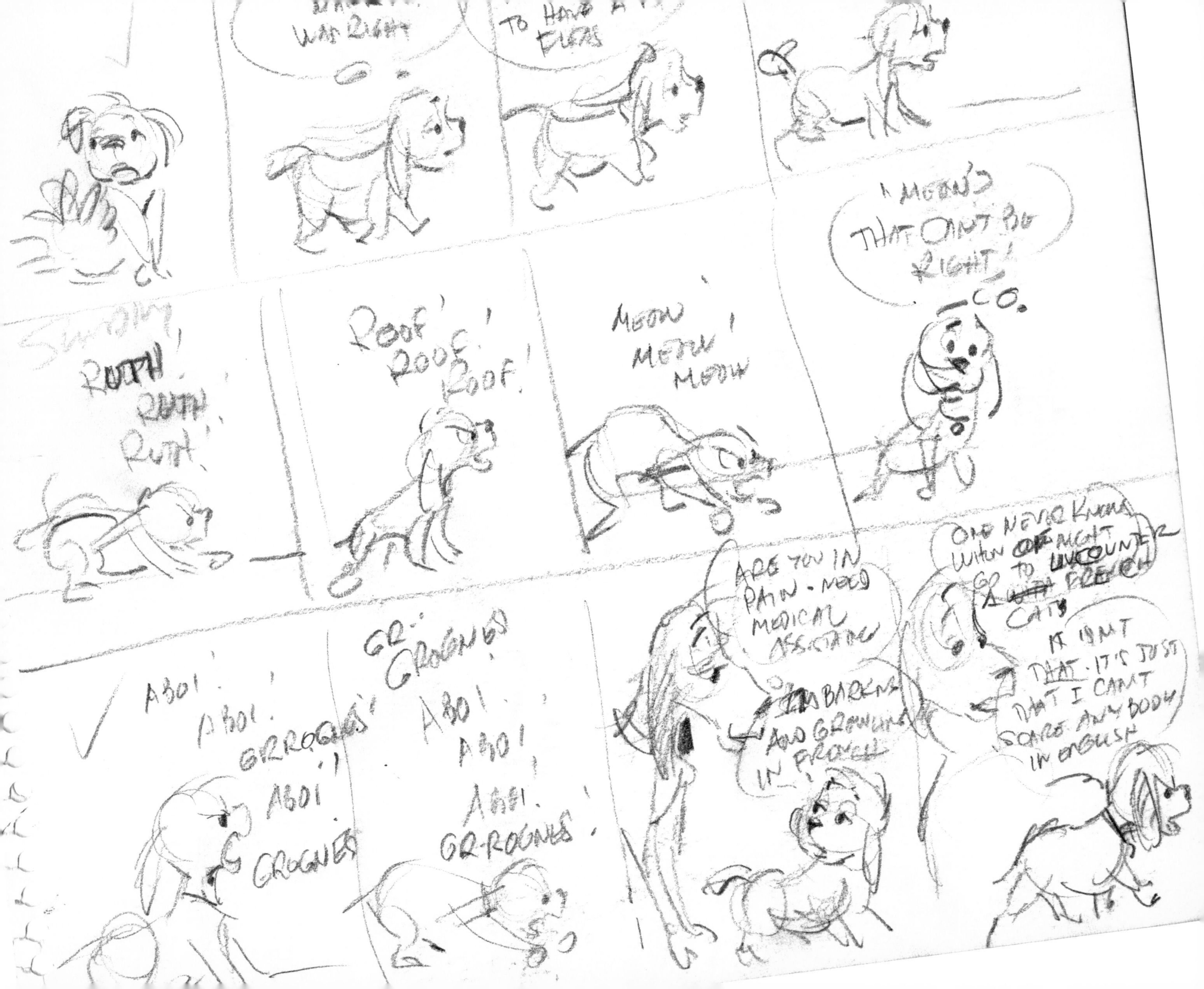
WAS RIGHT
TO HAVE A FLEAS
MEOW? THAT CAN'T BE RIGHT!
RUTH! RUTH! RUTH!
ROOF! ROOF! ROOF!
MEOW MEOW MEOW
ABOI! ABOI! GRROGNES! ABOI GROGNES
GR- GROGNES! ABOI! ABOI! ABOI! GR-ROGNES!
ARE YOU IN PAIN - NEED MEDICAL ASSISTANCE
I'M BARKING AND GROWLING IN FRENCH
ONE NEVER KNOWS WHEN ONE MIGHT GO TO ENCOUNTER A FRENCH CAT
IT ISN'T THAT. IT'S JUST THAT I CAN'T SCARE ANYBODY IN ENGLISH

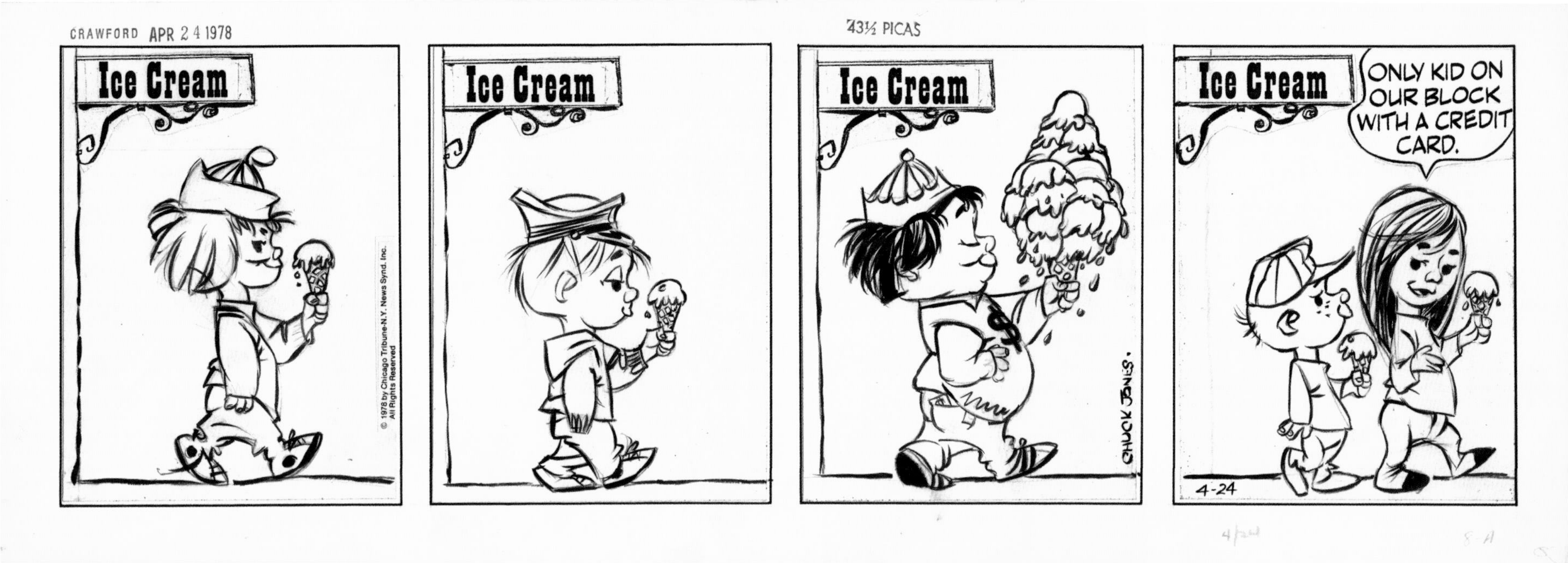
CRAWFORD APR 24 1978
43½ PICAS
Ice Cream
© 1978 by Chicago Tribune-N.Y. News Synd. Inc. All Rights Reserved
Ice Cream
Ice Cream
CHUCK JONES
Ice Cream
ONLY KID ON OUR BLOCK WITH A CREDIT CARD.
4-24
4/24
8-A

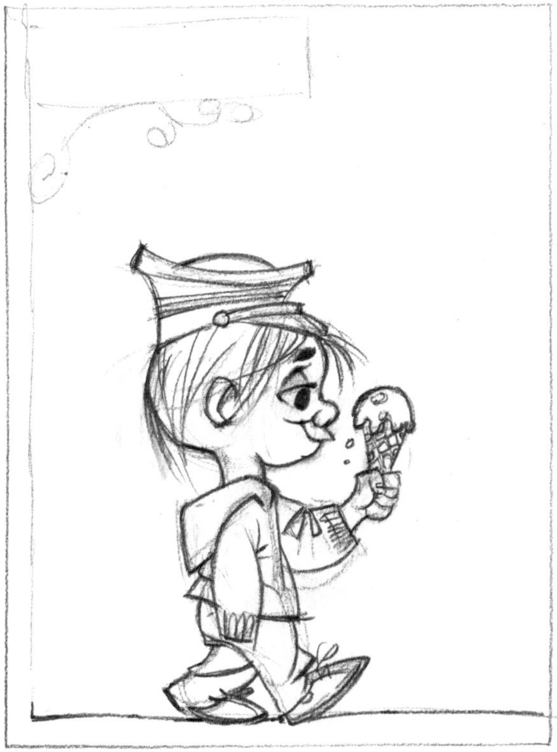

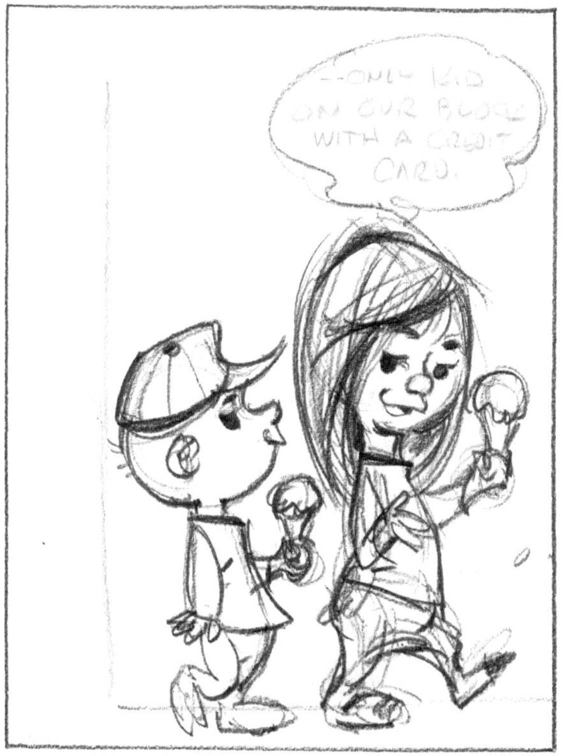
ONLY KID ON OUR BLOCK WITH A CREDIT CARD.

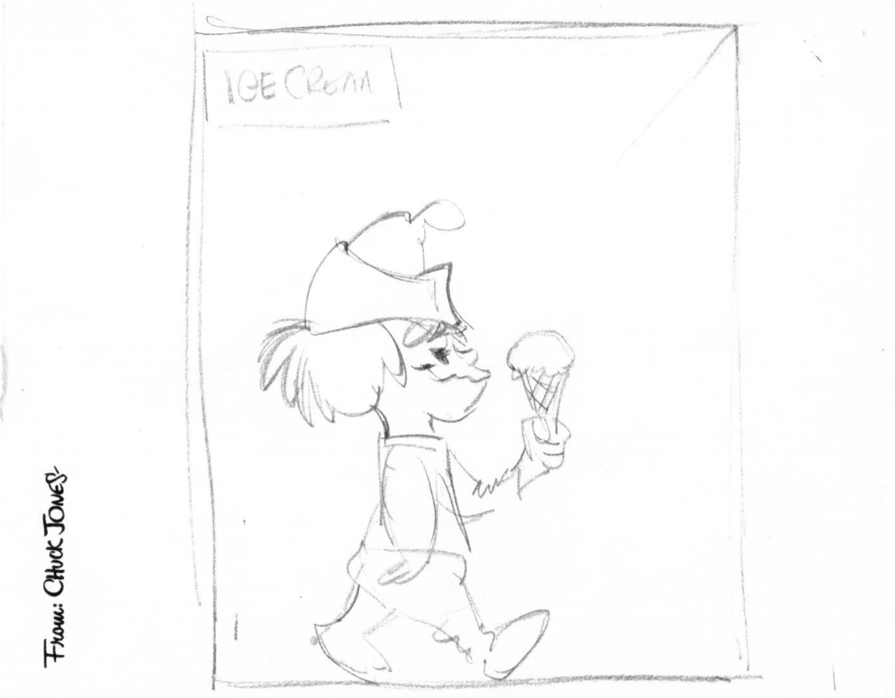
ICE CREAM
From: Chuck Jones

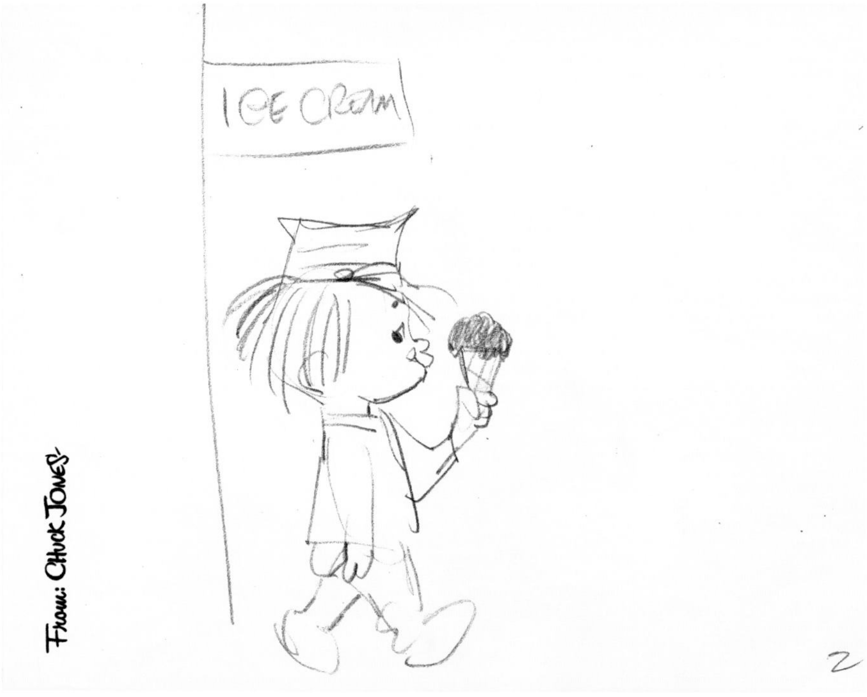
ICE CREAM
From: Chuck Jones
2

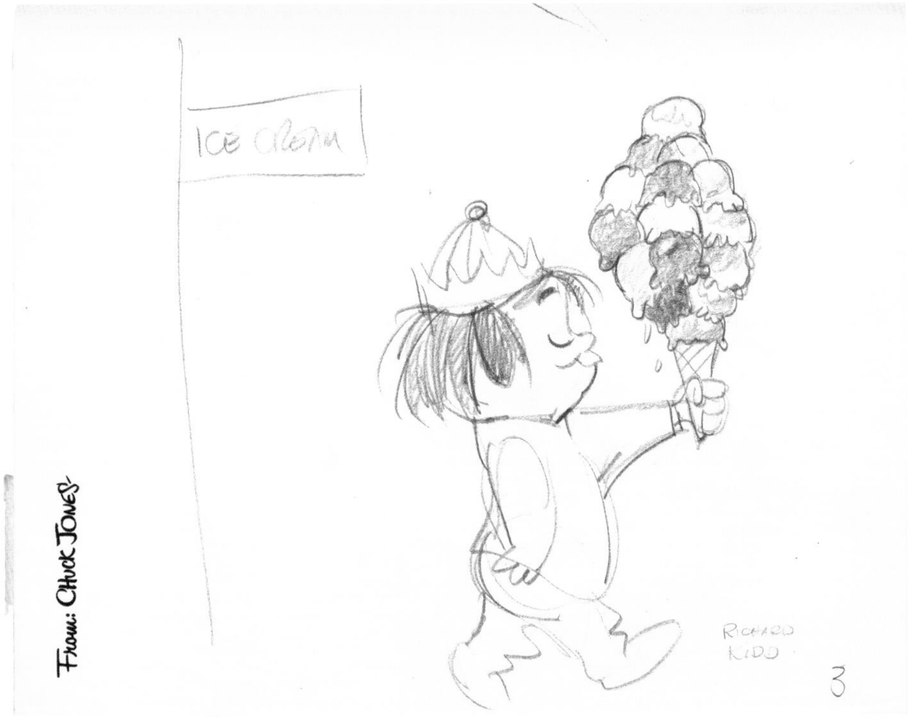
ICE CREAM
From: Chuck Jones
RICHARD KIDD
3

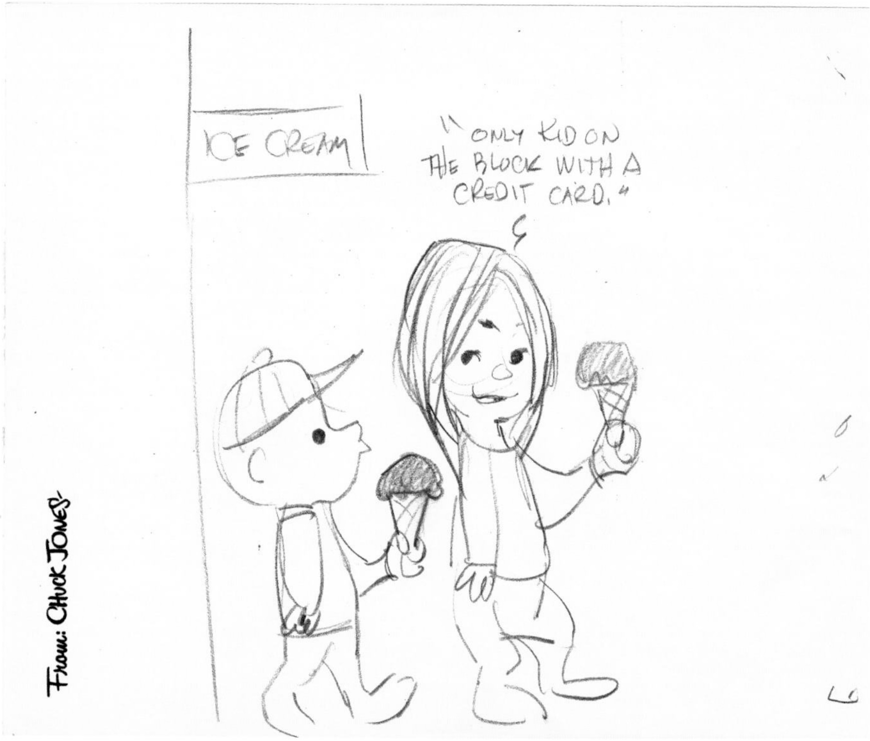
ICE CREAM
"ONLY KID ON THE BLOCK WITH A CREDIT CARD."
From: Chuck Jones

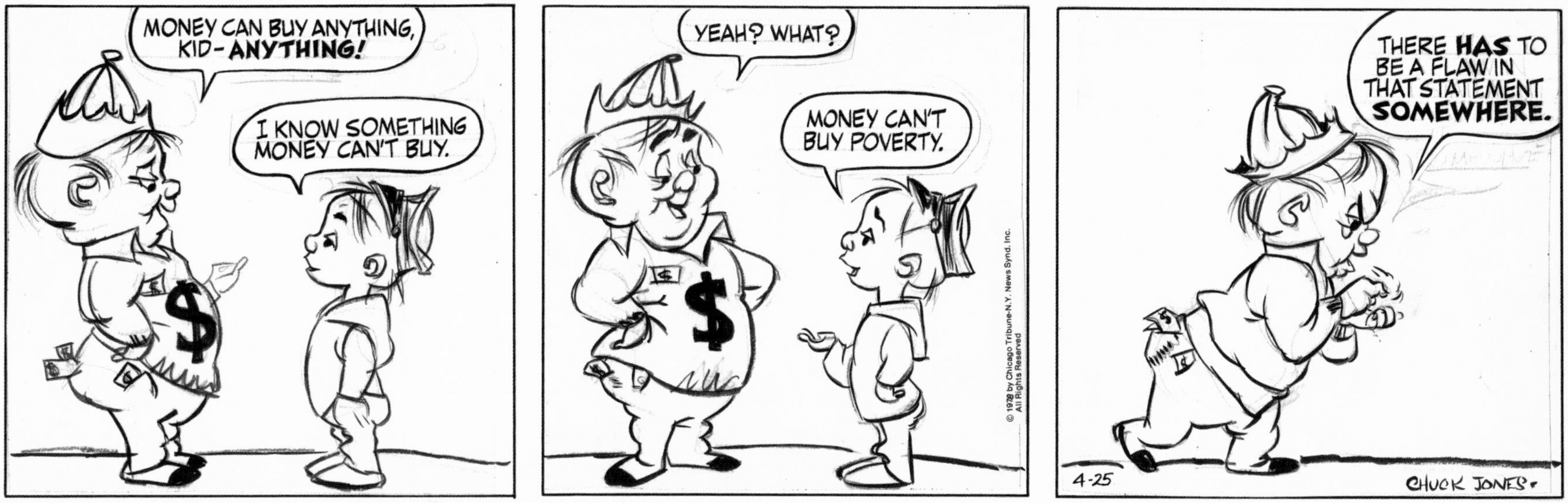
MONEY CAN BUY ANYTHING, KID-**ANYTHING!**
I KNOW SOMETHING MONEY CAN'T BUY.
YEAH? WHAT?
MONEY CAN'T BUY POVERTY.
© 1978 by Chicago Tribune-N.Y. News Synd. Inc. All Rights Reserved
THERE **HAS** TO BE A FLAW IN THAT STATEMENT **SOMEWHERE.**
4-25
CHUCK JONES

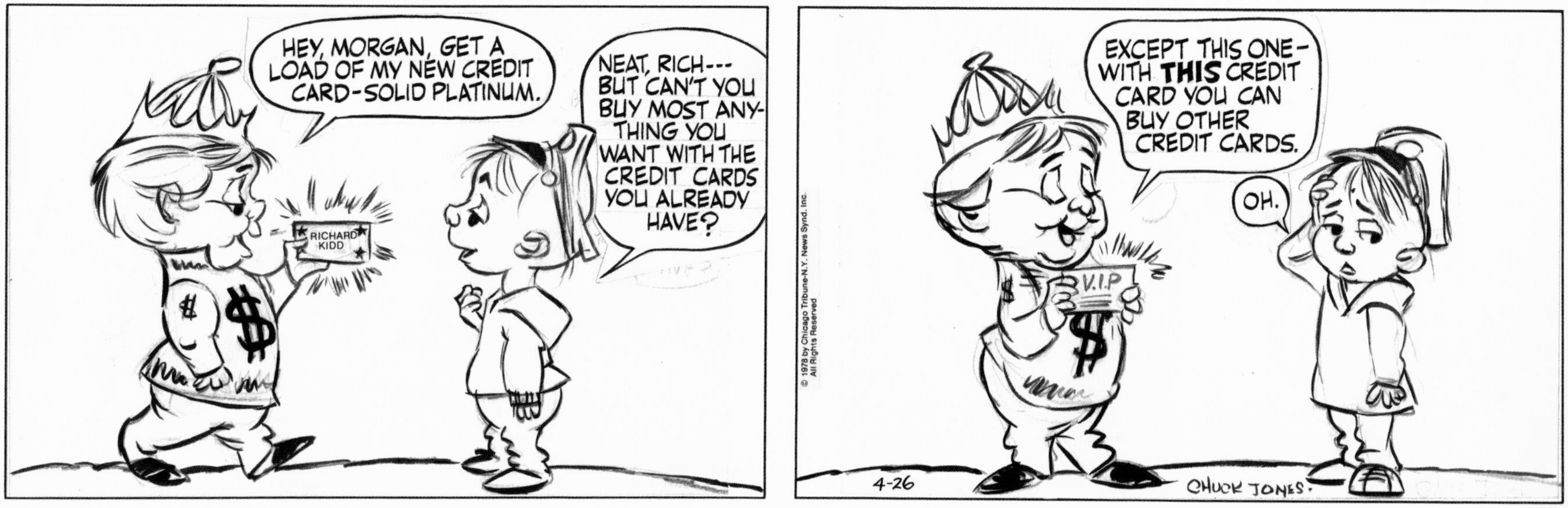
HEY, MORGAN, GET A LOAD OF MY NEW CREDIT CARD-SOLID PLATINUM.
RICHARD KIDD
NEAT, RICH--- BUT CAN'T YOU BUY MOST ANY-THING YOU WANT WITH THE CREDIT CARDS YOU ALREADY HAVE?
© 1978 by Chicago Tribune-N.Y. News Synd. Inc. All Rights Reserved
EXCEPT THIS ONE- WITH **THIS** CREDIT CARD YOU CAN BUY OTHER CREDIT CARDS.
V.I.P
OH.
4-26
CHUCK JONES

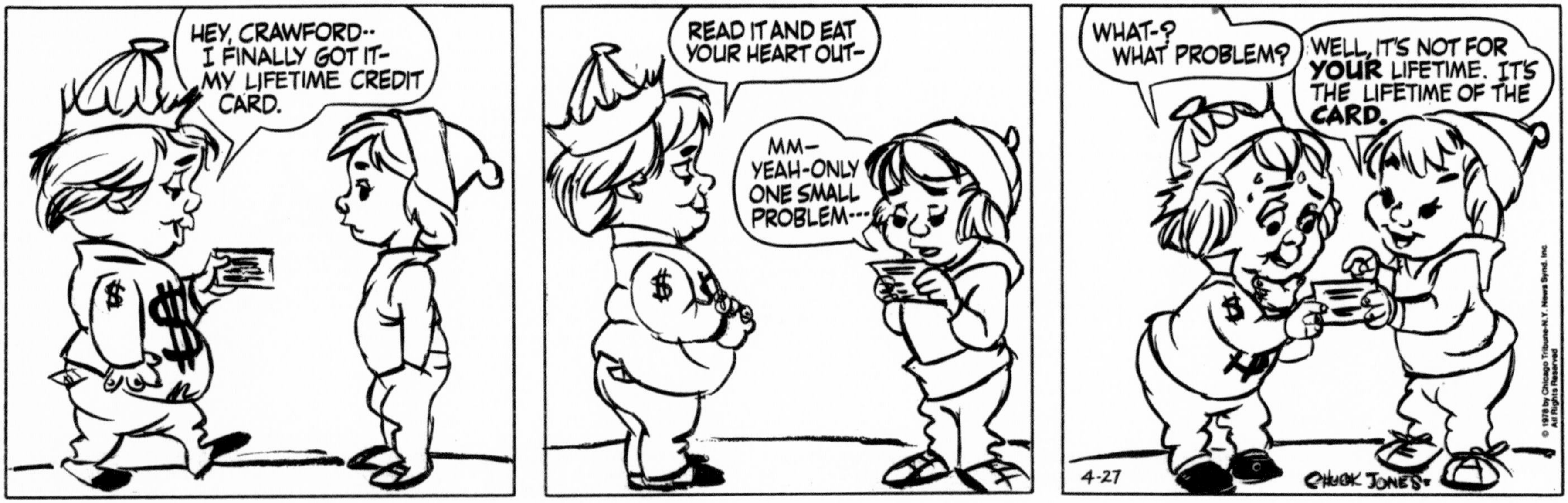
HEY, CRAWFORD-- I FINALLY GOT IT- MY LIFETIME CREDIT CARD.
READ IT AND EAT YOUR HEART OUT-
MM- YEAH-ONLY ONE SMALL PROBLEM---
WHAT-? WHAT PROBLEM?
WELL, IT'S NOT FOR **YOUR** LIFETIME. IT'S THE LIFETIME OF THE **CARD.**
4-27
CHUCK JONES
© 1978 by Chicago Tribune-N.Y. News Synd. Inc. All Rights Reserved

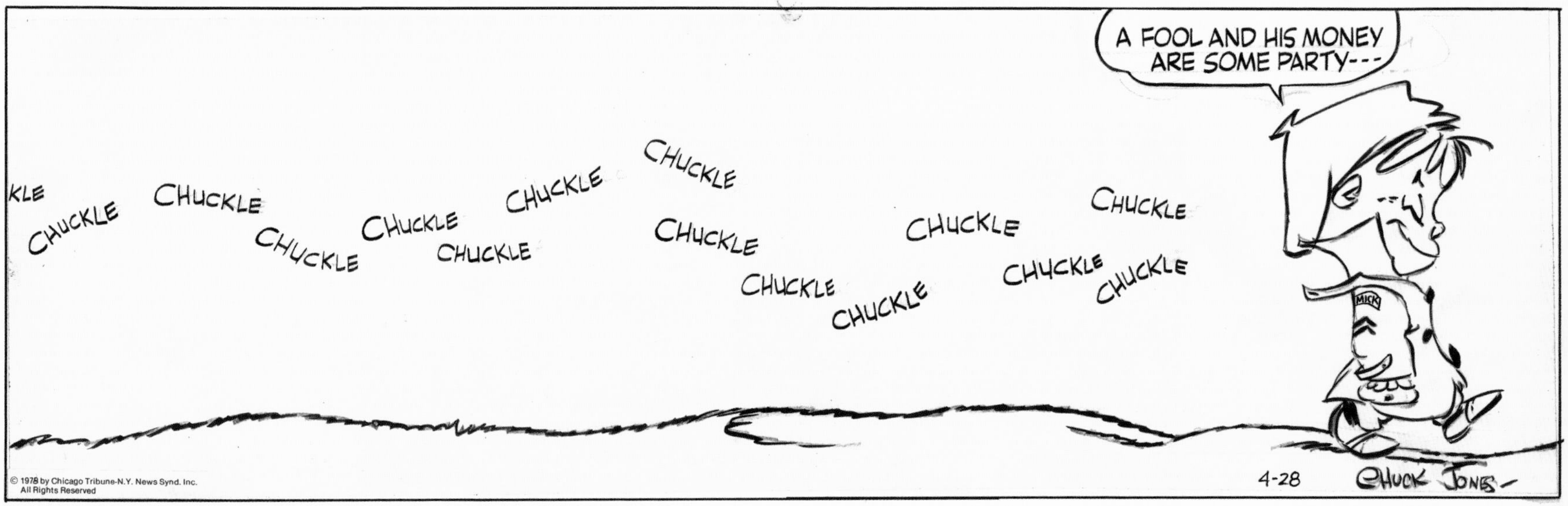
A FOOL AND HIS MONEY ARE SOME PARTY---
KLE
CHUCKLE
CHUCKLE
CHUCKLE
CHUCKLE
CHUCKLE
CHUCKLE
CHUCKLE
CHUCKLE
CHUCKLE
CHUCKLE
CHUCKLE
CHUCKLE
CHUCKLE
CHUCKLE
CHUCKLE
© 1978 by Chicago Tribune-N.Y. News Synd. Inc. All Rights Reserved
4-28
CHUCK JONES
4/28

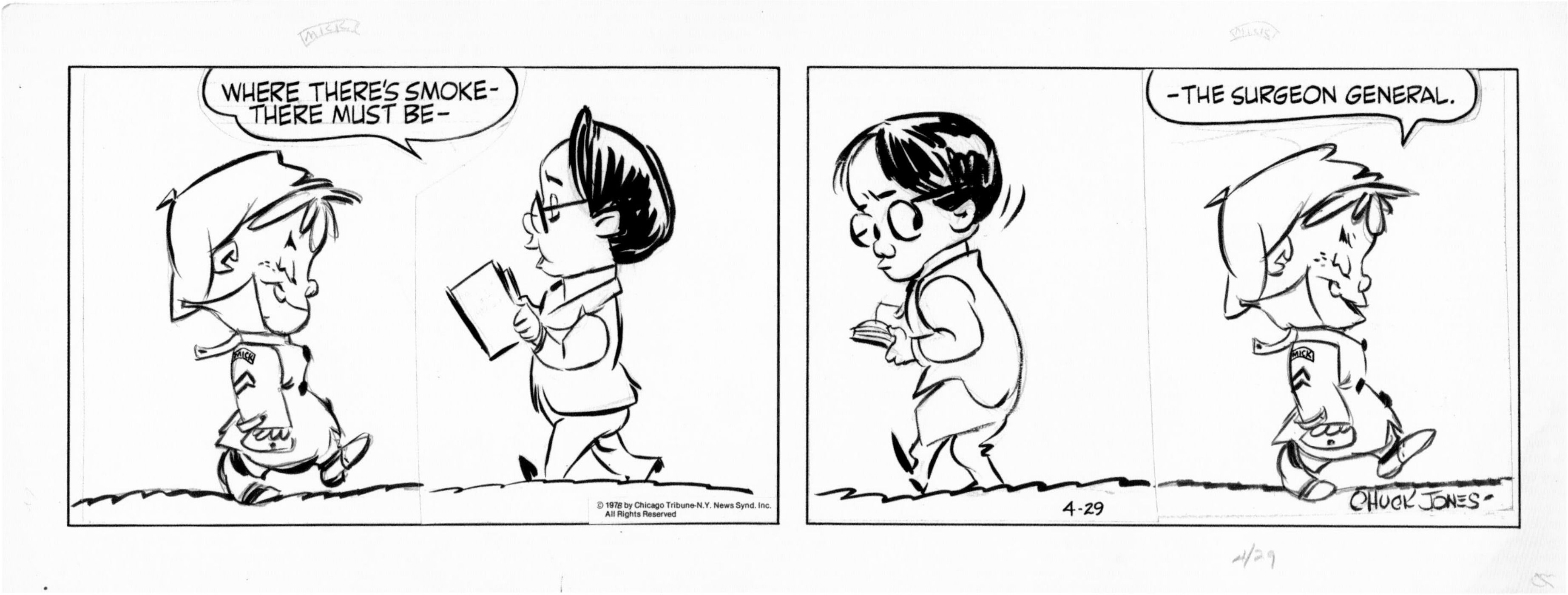
WHERE THERE'S SMOKE-
THERE MUST BE-
© 1978 by Chicago Tribune-N.Y. News Synd. Inc.
All Rights Reserved
-THE SURGEON GENERAL.
4-29
CHUCK JONES

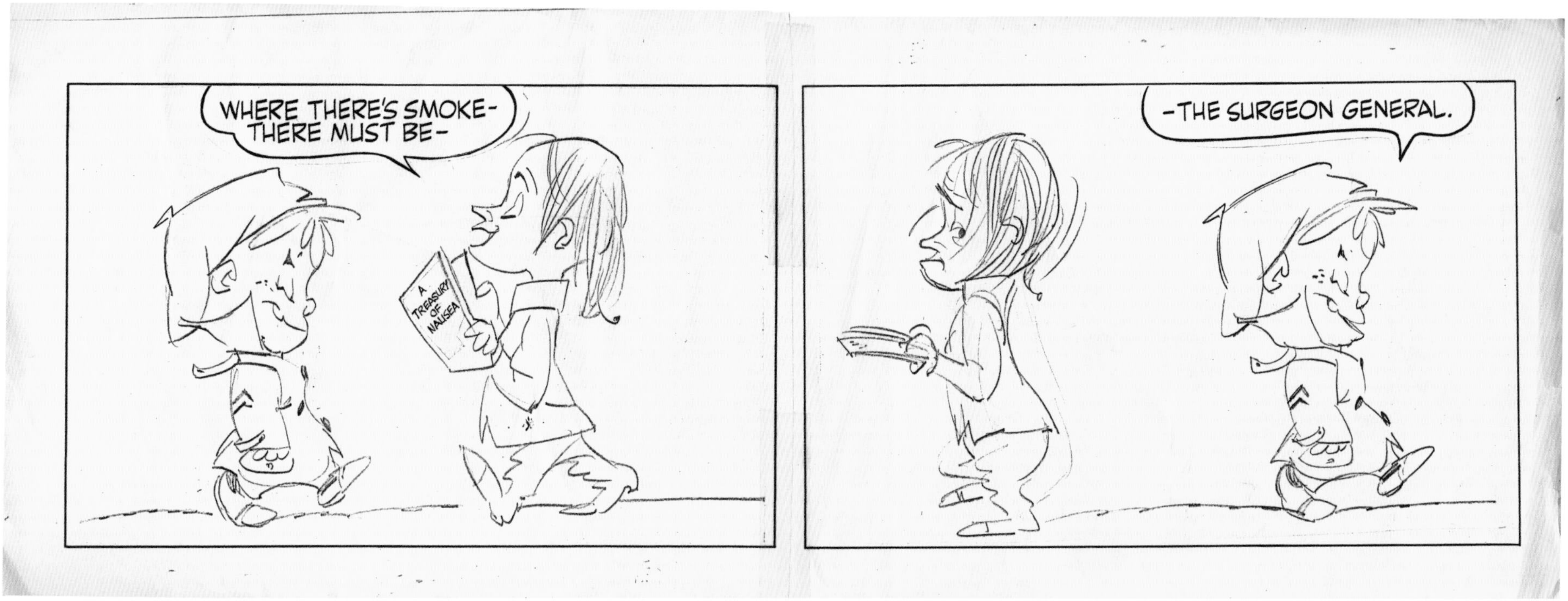
WHERE THERE'S SMOKE-
THERE MUST BE-
A TREASURY OF NAUSEA
-THE SURGEON GENERAL.

Earlier rendition of Norman-Vincent.

64%

4-30

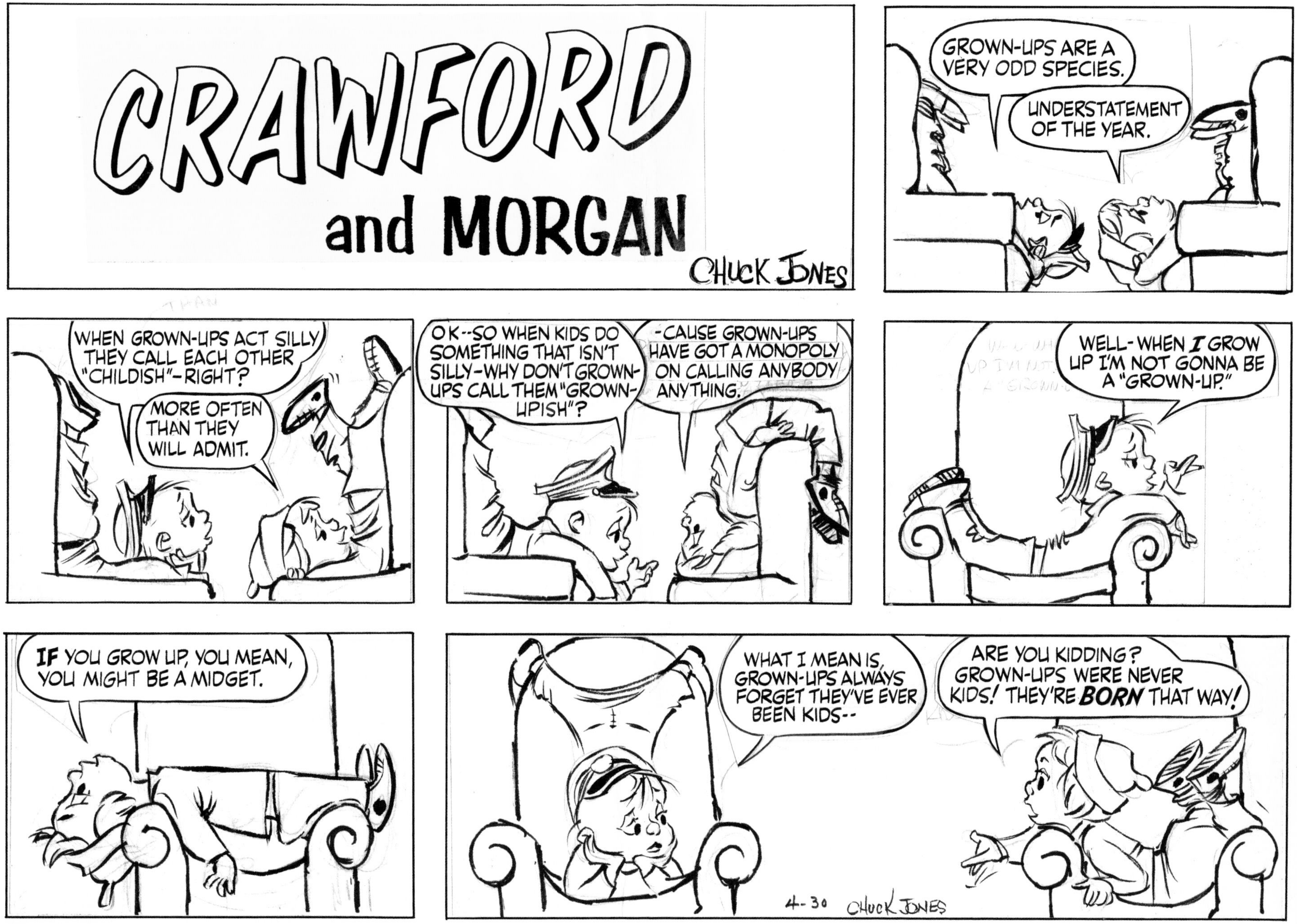
CRAWFORD
and MORGAN
CHUCK JONES
GROWN-UPS ARE A VERY ODD SPECIES.
UNDERSTATEMENT OF THE YEAR.
WHEN GROWN-UPS ACT SILLY THEY CALL EACH OTHER "CHILDISH"-RIGHT?
MORE OFTEN THAN THEY WILL ADMIT.
OK--SO WHEN KIDS DO SOMETHING THAT ISN'T SILLY-WHY DON'T GROWN-UPS CALL THEM "GROWN-UPISH"?
-CAUSE GROWN-UPS HAVE GOT A MONOPOLY ON CALLING ANYBODY ANYTHING.
WELL-WHEN I GROW UP I'M NOT GONNA BE A "GROWN-UP."
IF YOU GROW UP, YOU MEAN, YOU MIGHT BE A MIDGET.
WHAT I MEAN IS, GROWN-UPS ALWAYS FORGET THEY'VE EVER BEEN KIDS--
ARE YOU KIDDING? GROWN-UPS WERE NEVER KIDS! THEY'RE BORN THAT WAY!
4-30 CHUCK JONES

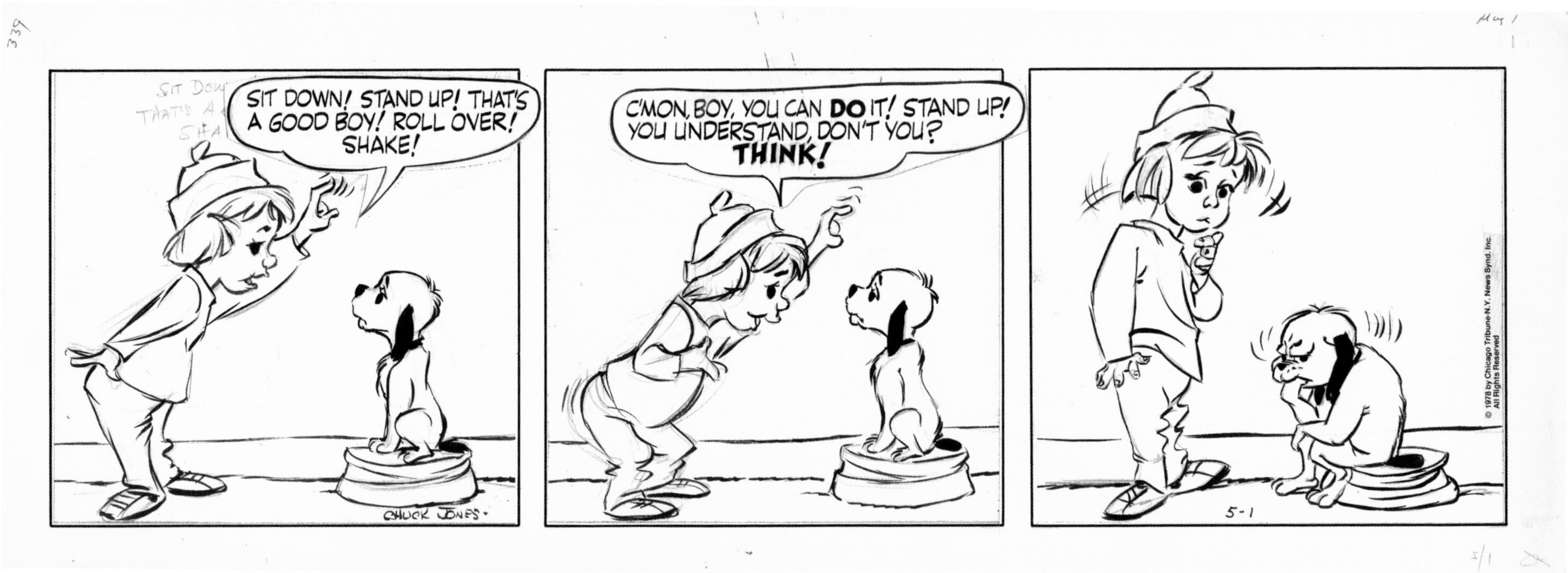
SIT DOWN! STAND UP! THAT'S A GOOD BOY! ROLL OVER! SHAKE!
CHUCK JONES
C'MON, BOY, YOU CAN DO IT! STAND UP! YOU UNDERSTAND, DON'T YOU? THINK!
5-1
© 1978 by Chicago Tribune-N.Y. News Synd. Inc. All Rights Reserved

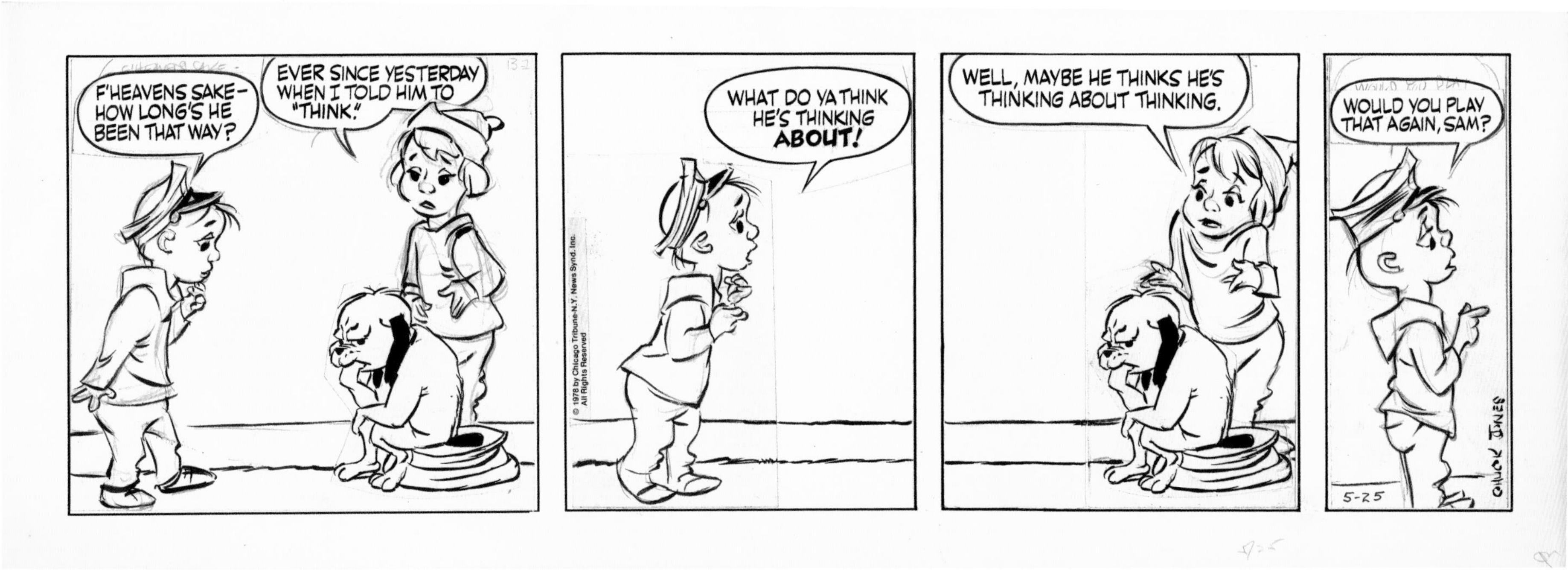
F'HEAVENS SAKE– HOW LONG'S HE BEEN THAT WAY?
EVER SINCE YESTERDAY WHEN I TOLD HIM TO "THINK."
© 1978 by Chicago Tribune-N.Y. News Synd. Inc. All Rights Reserved
WHAT DO YA THINK HE'S THINKING ABOUT!
WELL, MAYBE HE THINKS HE'S THINKING ABOUT THINKING.
WOULD YOU PLAY THAT AGAIN, SAM?
CHUCK JONES
5-25

The May 25, 1978 daily moved to its correct position.

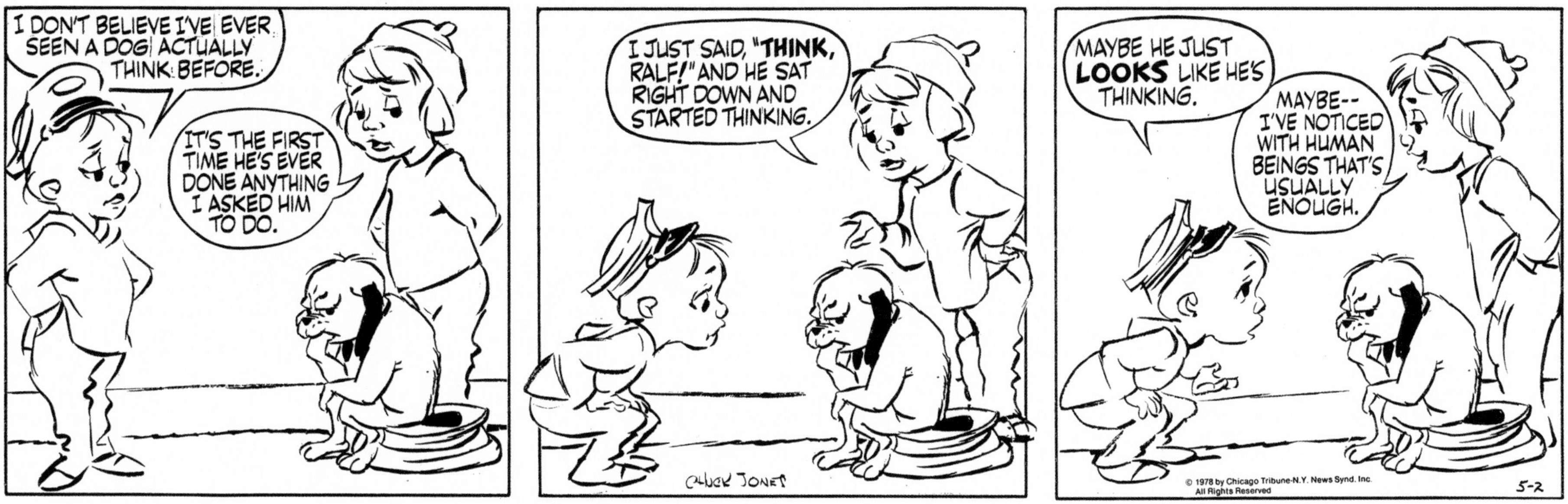
I DON'T BELIEVE I'VE EVER SEEN A DOG ACTUALLY THINK BEFORE.
IT'S THE FIRST TIME HE'S EVER DONE ANYTHING I ASKED HIM TO DO.
I JUST SAID, "THINK, RALF!" AND HE SAT RIGHT DOWN AND STARTED THINKING.
MAYBE HE JUST LOOKS LIKE HE'S THINKING.
MAYBE-- I'VE NOTICED WITH HUMAN BEINGS THAT'S USUALLY ENOUGH.
CHUCK JONES
© 1978 by Chicago Tribune-N.Y. News Synd. Inc. All Rights Reserved
5-2

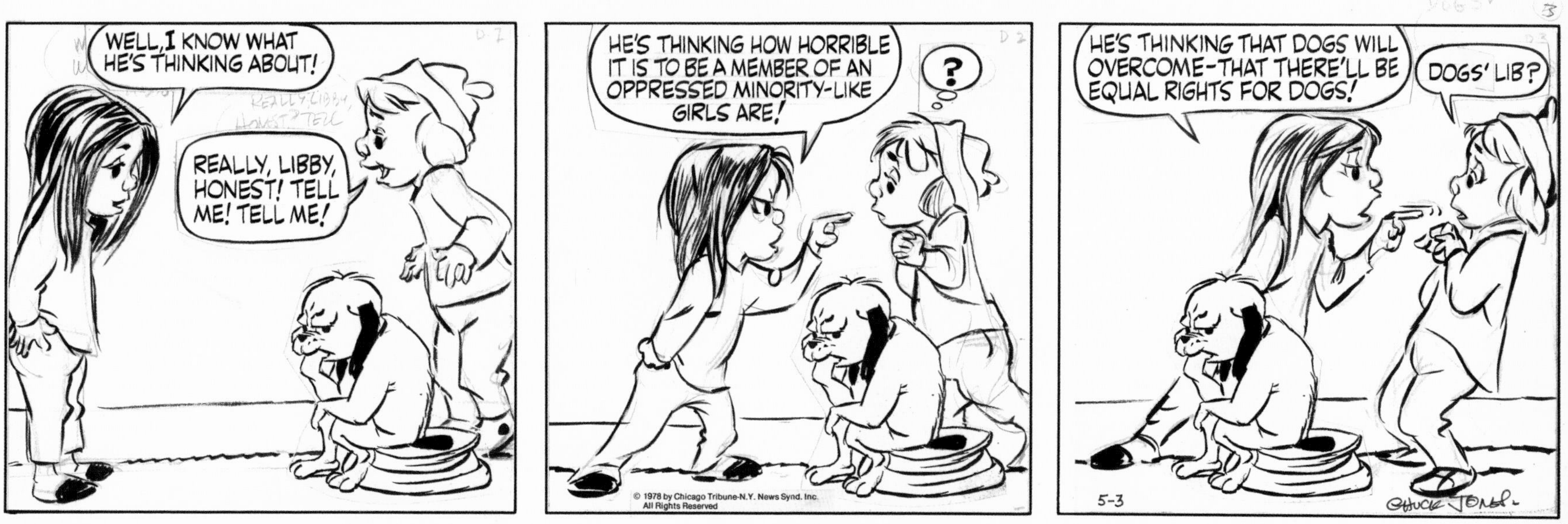
WELL, I KNOW WHAT HE'S THINKING ABOUT!
REALLY, LIBBY, HONEST! TELL ME! TELL ME!
HE'S THINKING HOW HORRIBLE IT IS TO BE A MEMBER OF AN OPPRESSED MINORITY-LIKE GIRLS ARE!
?
© 1978 by Chicago Tribune-N.Y. News Synd. Inc. All Rights Reserved
HE'S THINKING THAT DOGS WILL OVERCOME-THAT THERE'LL BE EQUAL RIGHTS FOR DOGS!
DOGS' LIB?
5-3
CHUCK JONES

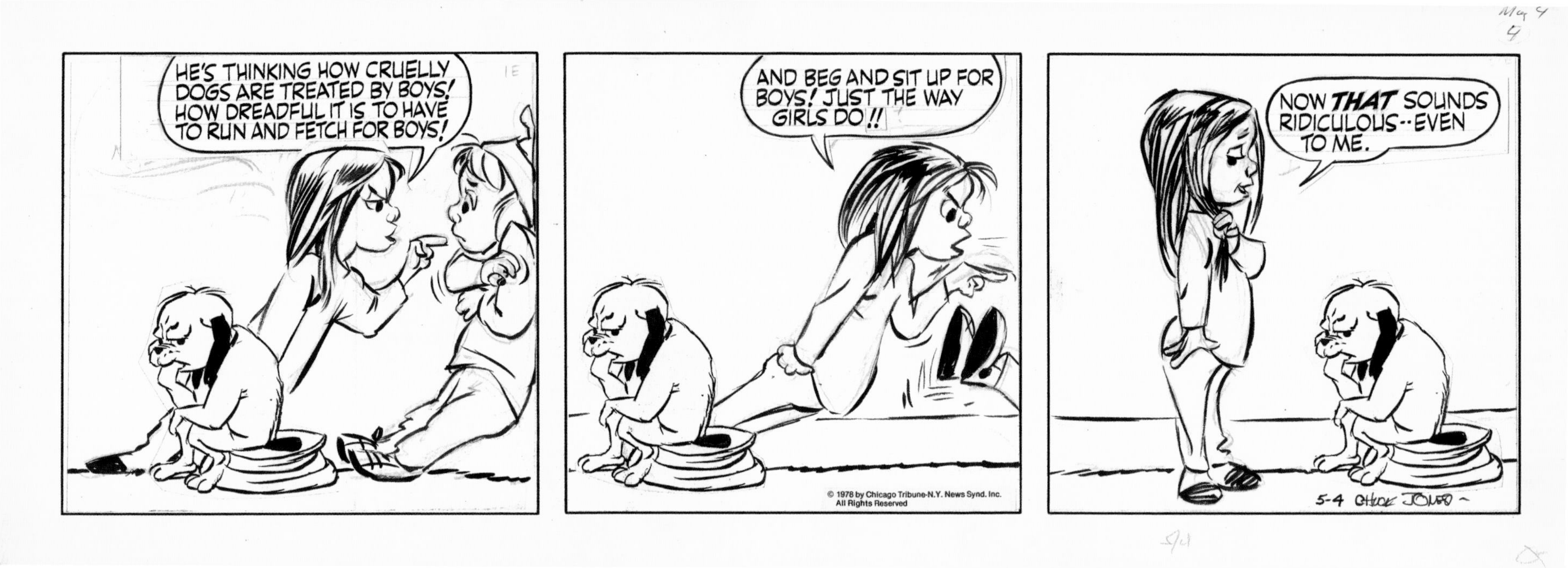
HE'S THINKING HOW CRUELLY DOGS ARE TREATED BY BOYS! HOW DREADFUL IT IS TO HAVE TO RUN AND FETCH FOR BOYS!
AND BEG AND SIT UP FOR BOYS! JUST THE WAY GIRLS DO!!
© 1978 by Chicago Tribune-N.Y. News Synd. Inc. All Rights Reserved
NOW **THAT** SOUNDS RIDICULOUS--EVEN TO ME.
5-4 CHUCK JONES

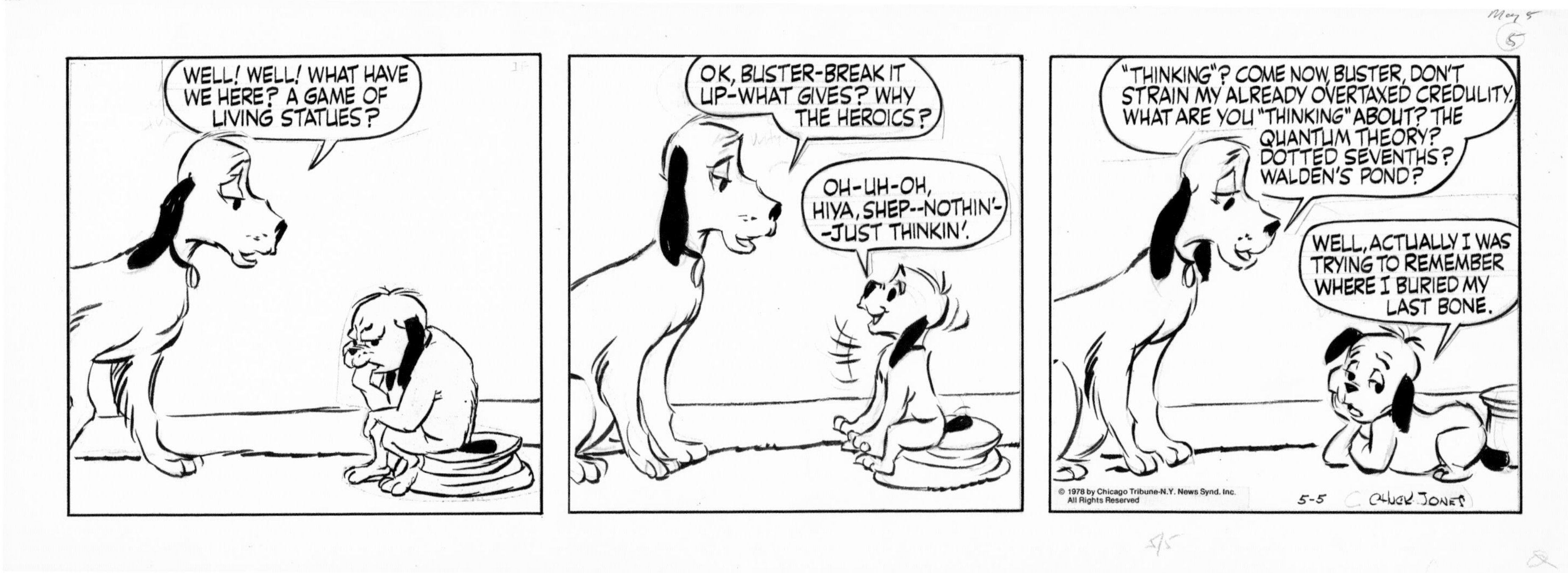
WELL! WELL! WHAT HAVE WE HERE? A GAME OF LIVING STATUES?
OK, BUSTER-BREAK IT UP-WHAT GIVES? WHY THE HEROICS?
OH-UH-OH, HIYA, SHEP--NOTHIN'--JUST THINKIN'.
"THINKING"? COME NOW, BUSTER, DON'T STRAIN MY ALREADY OVERTAXED CREDULITY. WHAT ARE YOU "THINKING" ABOUT? THE QUANTUM THEORY? DOTTED SEVENTHS? WALDEN'S POND?
WELL, ACTUALLY I WAS TRYING TO REMEMBER WHERE I BURIED MY LAST BONE.
© 1978 by Chicago Tribune-N.Y. News Synd. Inc. All Rights Reserved
5-5 CHUCK JONES

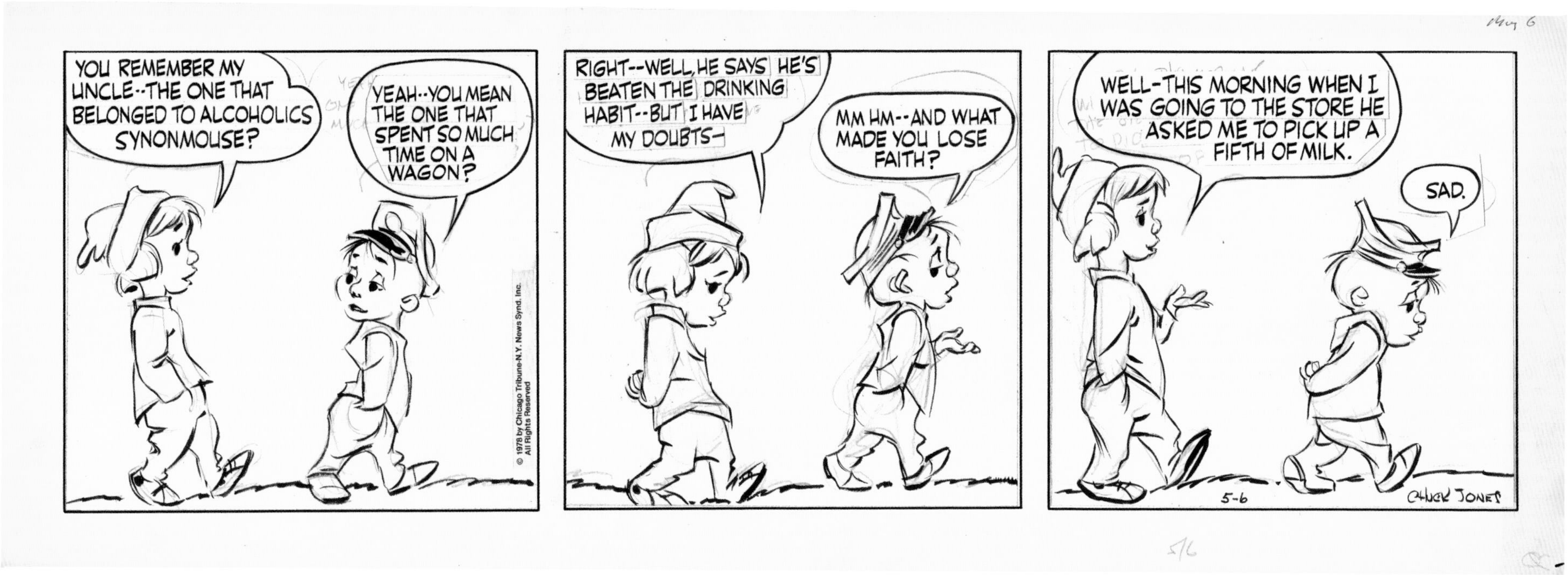
YOU REMEMBER MY UNCLE--THE ONE THAT BELONGED TO ALCOHOLICS SYNONMOUSE?
YEAH--YOU MEAN THE ONE THAT SPENT SO MUCH TIME ON A WAGON?
© 1978 by Chicago Tribune-N.Y. News Synd. Inc. All Rights Reserved
RIGHT--WELL, HE SAYS HE'S BEATEN THE DRINKING HABIT--BUT I HAVE MY DOUBTS—
MM HM--AND WHAT MADE YOU LOSE FAITH?
WELL-THIS MORNING WHEN I WAS GOING TO THE STORE HE ASKED ME TO PICK UP A FIFTH OF MILK.
SAD.
5-6
CHUCK JONES

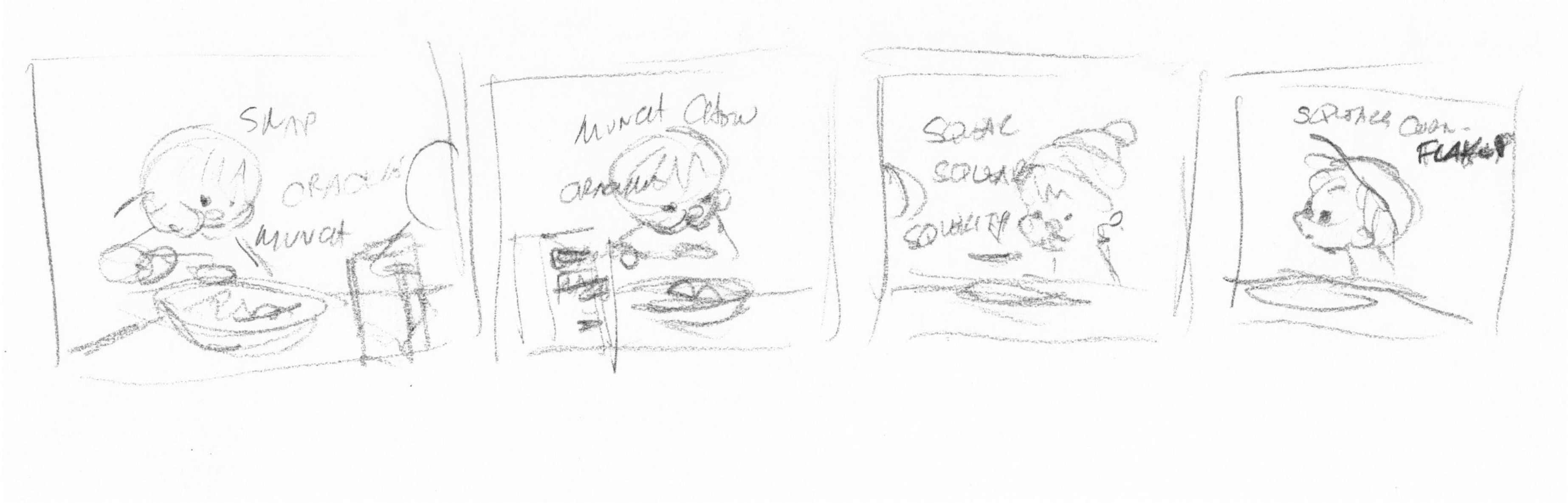

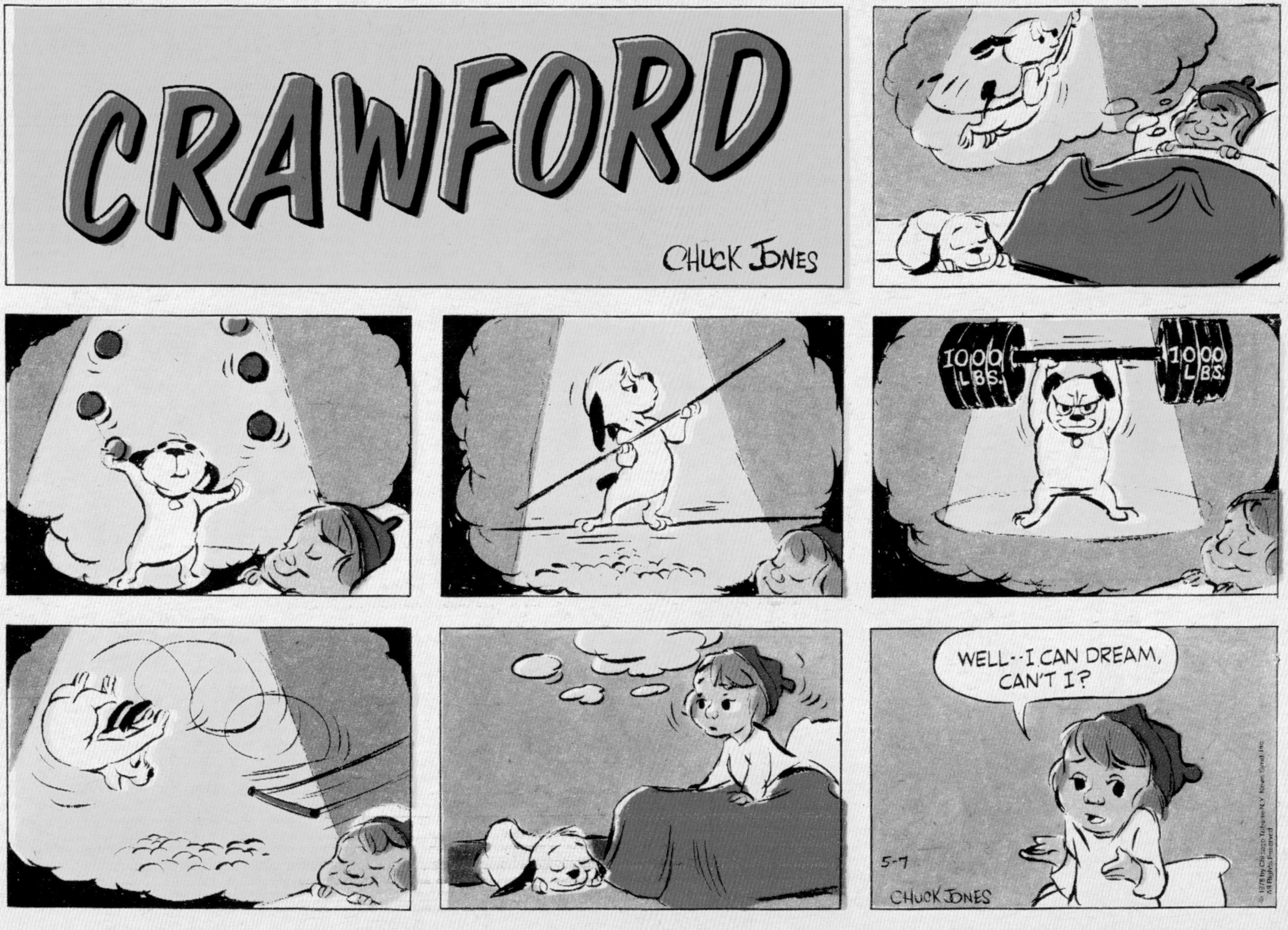
CRAWFORD
CHUCK JONES
1000 LBS.
1000 LBS.
WELL--I CAN DREAM, CAN'T I?
5-7
CHUCK JONES

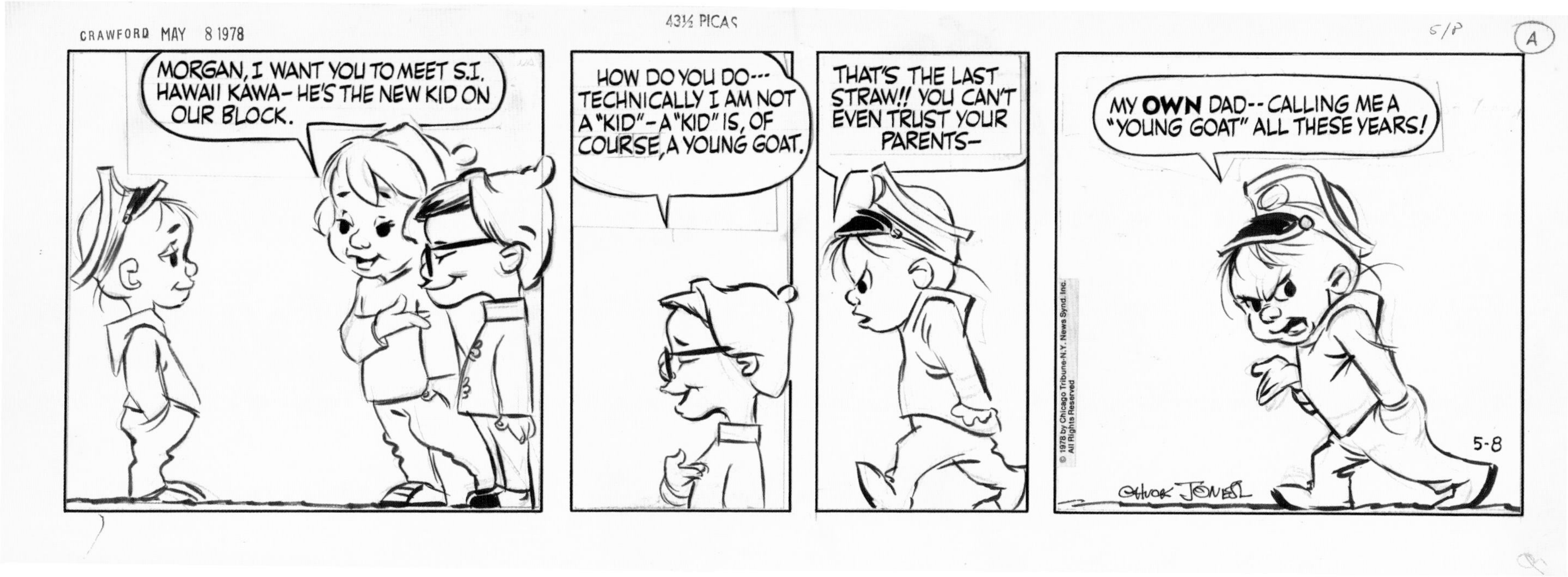
CRAWFORD MAY 8 1978
43½ PICAS
5/8
A
MORGAN, I WANT YOU TO MEET S.I. HAWAII KAWA– HE'S THE NEW KID ON OUR BLOCK.
HOW DO YOU DO--- TECHNICALLY I AM NOT A "KID"–A "KID" IS, OF COURSE, A YOUNG GOAT.
THAT'S THE LAST STRAW!! YOU CAN'T EVEN TRUST YOUR PARENTS–
MY **OWN** DAD--CALLING ME A "YOUNG GOAT" ALL THESE YEARS!
© 1978 by Chicago Tribune-N.Y. News Synd. Inc. All Rights Reserved
5-8
CHUCK JONES

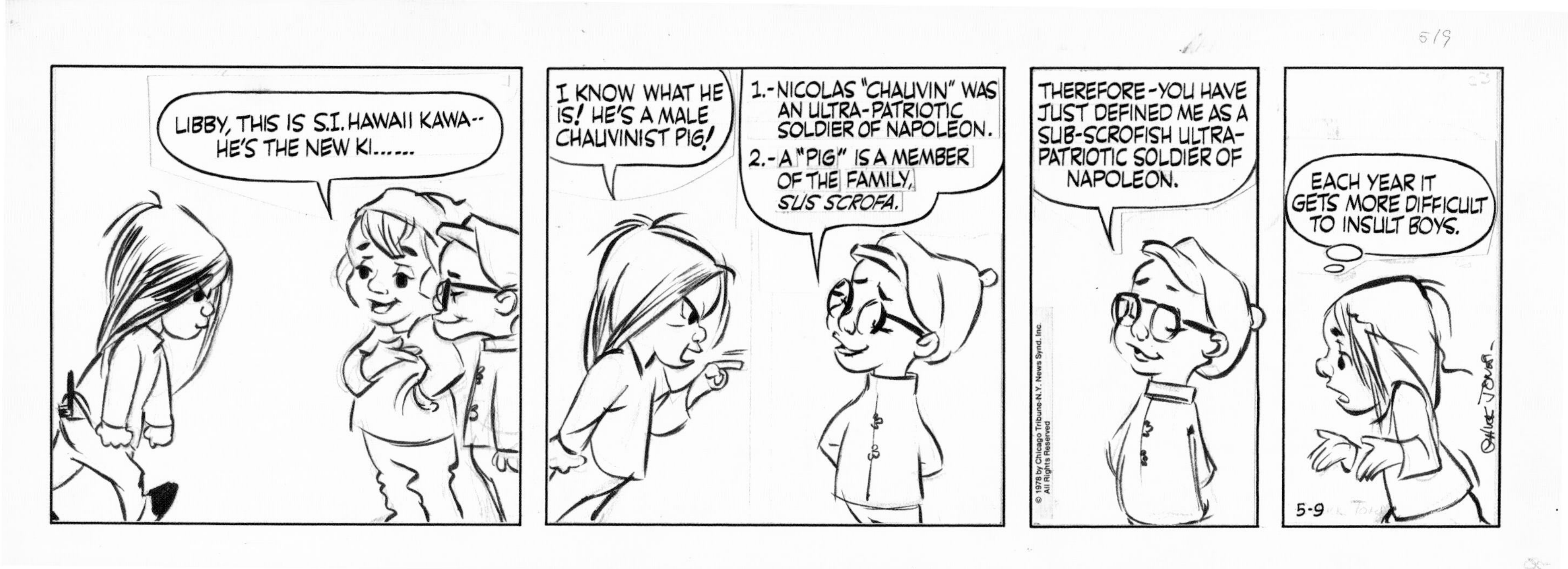
5/9
LIBBY, THIS IS S.I. HAWAII KAWA-- HE'S THE NEW KI......
I KNOW WHAT HE IS! HE'S A MALE CHAUVINIST PIG!
1.-NICOLAS "CHAUVIN" WAS AN ULTRA-PATRIOTIC SOLDIER OF NAPOLEON.
2.-A "PIG" IS A MEMBER OF THE FAMILY, *SUS SCROFA.*
THEREFORE-YOU HAVE JUST DEFINED ME AS A SUB-SCROFISH ULTRA-PATRIOTIC SOLDIER OF NAPOLEON.
© 1978 by Chicago Tribune-N.Y. News Synd. Inc. All Rights Reserved
EACH YEAR IT GETS MORE DIFFICULT TO INSULT BOYS.
CHUCK JONES
5-9

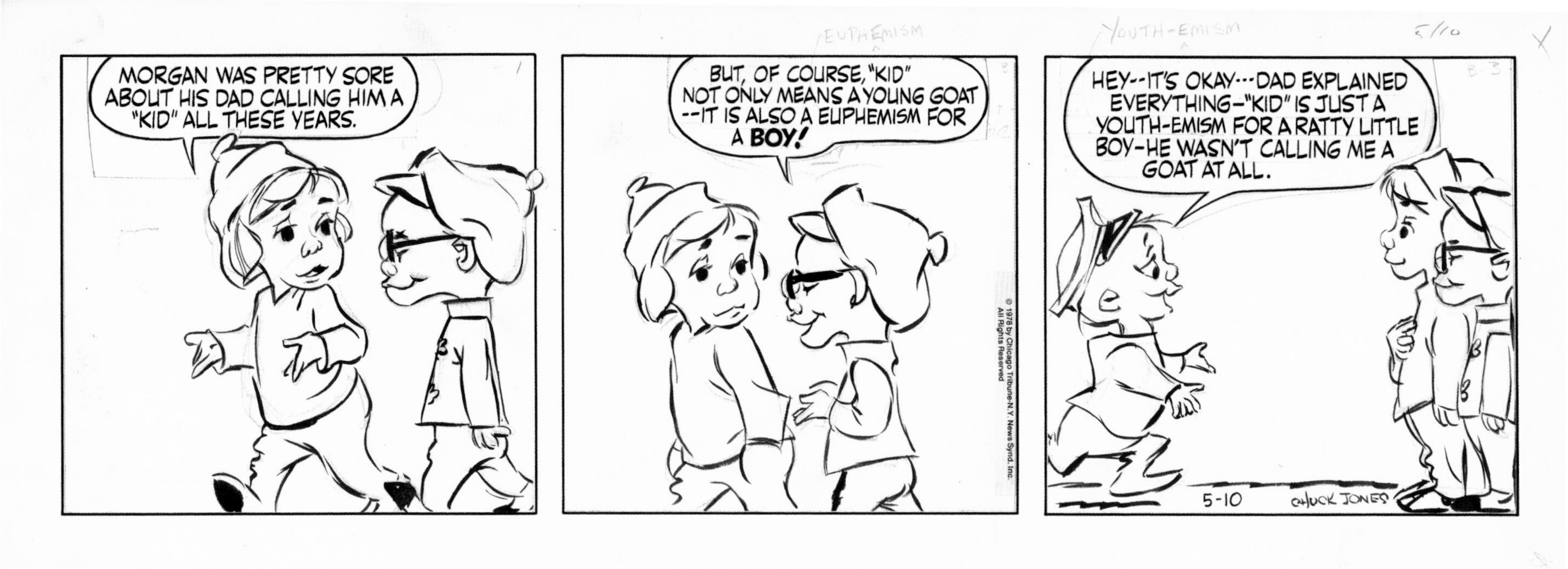
MORGAN WAS PRETTY SORE ABOUT HIS DAD CALLING HIM A "KID" ALL THESE YEARS.
BUT, OF COURSE, "KID" NOT ONLY MEANS A YOUNG GOAT --IT IS ALSO A EUPHEMISM FOR A **BOY!**
HEY--IT'S OKAY---DAD EXPLAINED EVERYTHING--"KID" IS JUST A YOUTH-EMISM FOR A RATTY LITTLE BOY-HE WASN'T CALLING ME A GOAT AT ALL.
© 1978 by Chicago Tribune-N.Y. News Synd. Inc. All Rights Reserved
5-10
CHUCK JONES

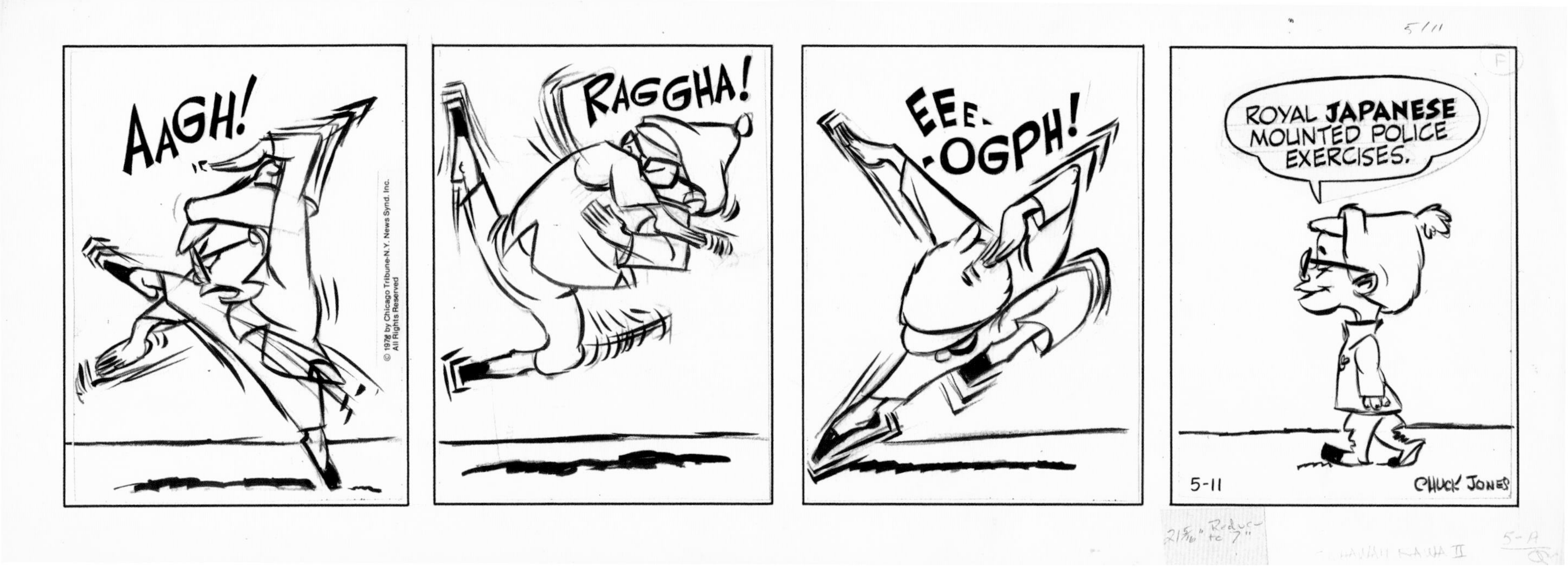
AAGH!
RAGGHA!
EEE-OGPH!
ROYAL **JAPANESE** MOUNTED POLICE EXERCISES.
© 1978 by Chicago Tribune-N.Y. News Synd. Inc. All Rights Reserved
5-11
CHUCK JONES

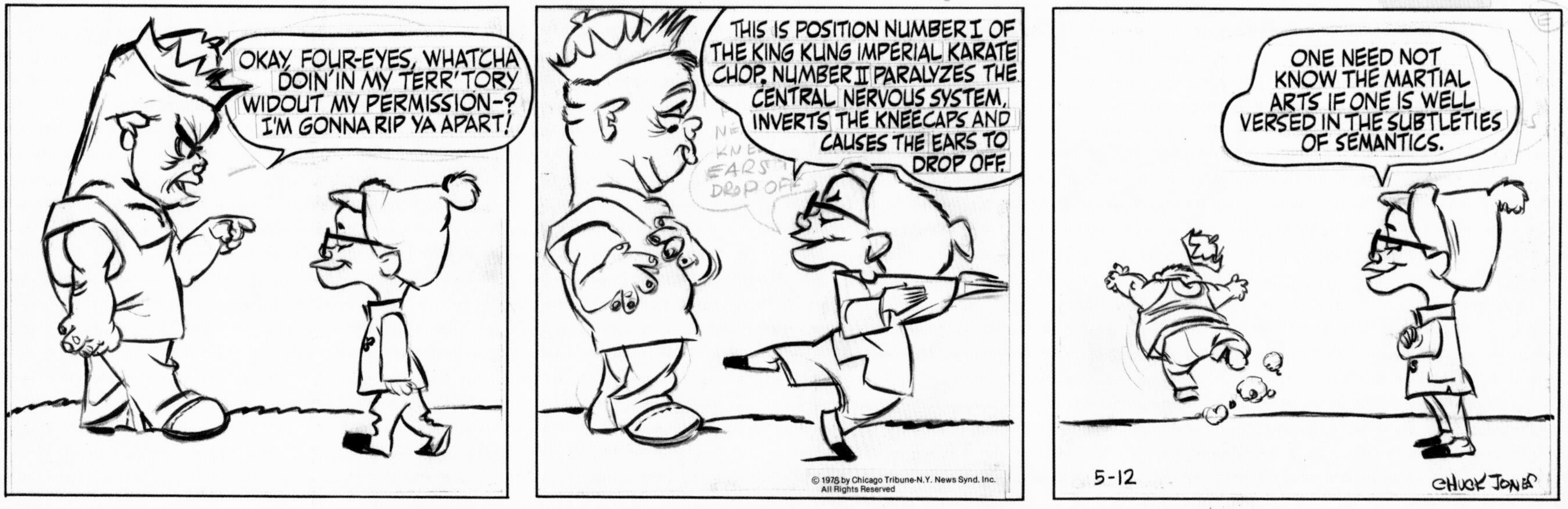
OKAY, FOUR-EYES, WHATCHA DOIN' IN MY TERR'TORY WIDOUT MY PERMISSION-? I'M GONNA RIP YA APART!
THIS IS POSITION NUMBER I OF THE KING KUNG IMPERIAL KARATE CHOP. NUMBER II PARALYZES THE CENTRAL NERVOUS SYSTEM, INVERTS THE KNEECAPS AND CAUSES THE EARS TO DROP OFF.
ONE NEED NOT KNOW THE MARTIAL ARTS IF ONE IS WELL VERSED IN THE SUBTLETIES OF SEMANTICS.
© 1978 by Chicago Tribune-N.Y. News Synd. Inc. All Rights Reserved
5-12
CHUCK JONES

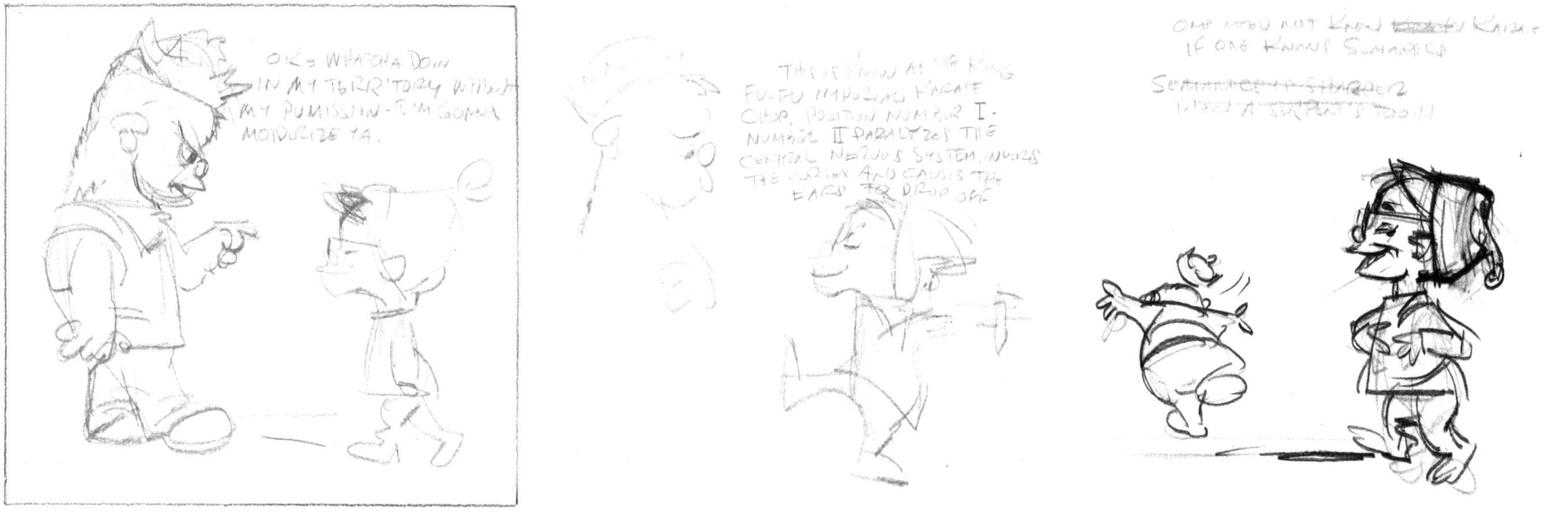

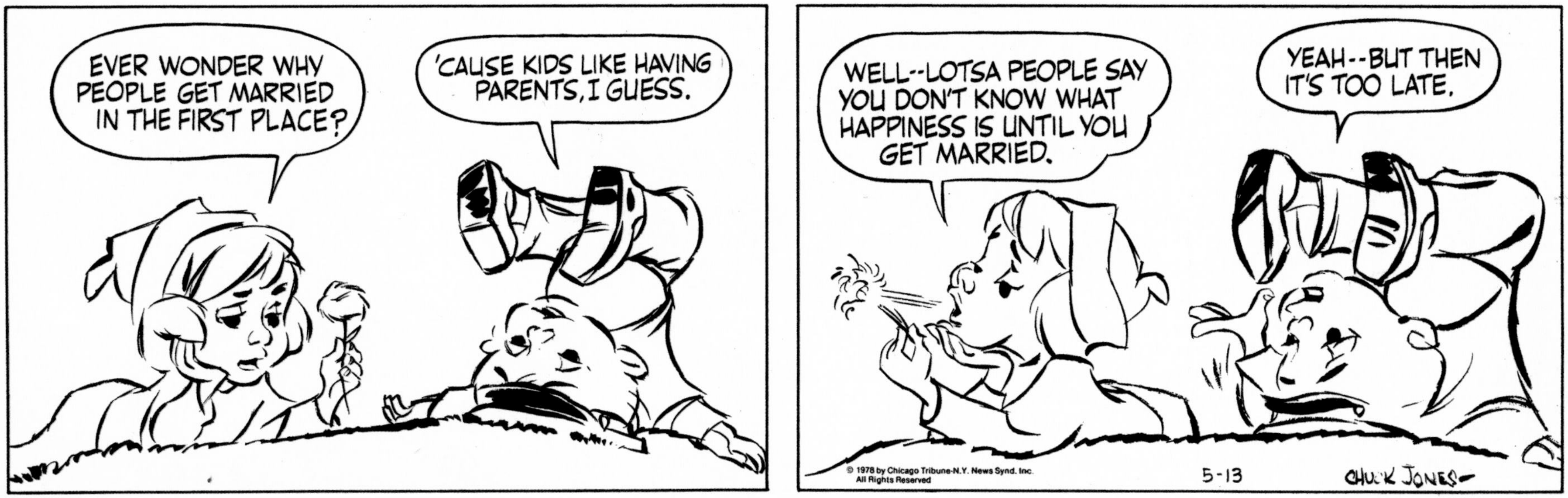

EVER WONDER WHY PEOPLE GET MARRIED IN THE FIRST PLACE?
'CAUSE KIDS LIKE HAVING PARENTS, I GUESS.
WELL--LOTSA PEOPLE SAY YOU DON'T KNOW WHAT HAPPINESS IS UNTIL YOU GET MARRIED.
YEAH--BUT THEN IT'S TOO LATE.
© 1978 by Chicago Tribune-N.Y. News Synd. Inc. All Rights Reserved
5-13
CHUCK JONES

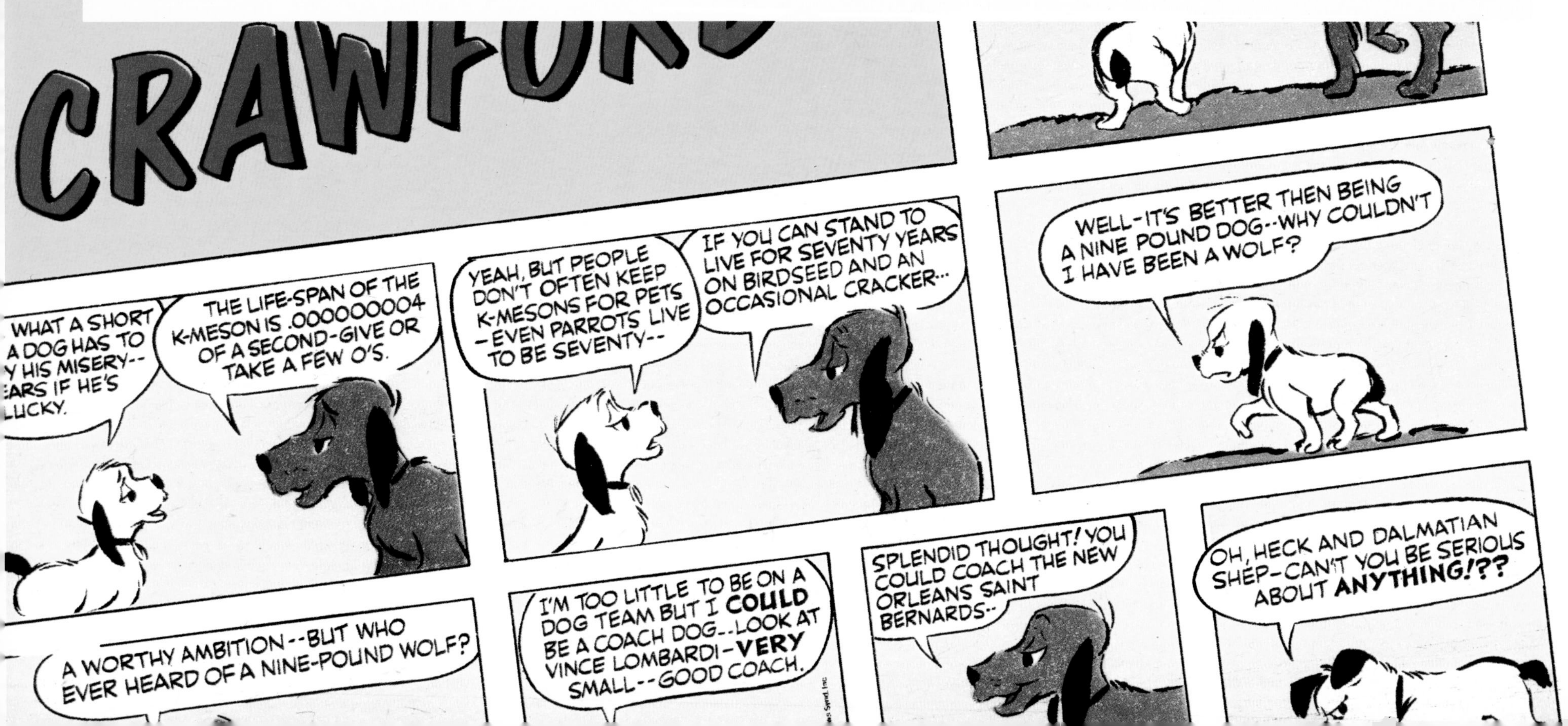

CRAWFOR
WHAT A SHORT
A DOG HAS TO
Y HIS MISERY--
EARS IF HE'S
LUCKY.
THE LIFE-SPAN OF THE K-MESON IS .000000004 OF A SECOND-GIVE OR TAKE A FEW O'S.
YEAH, BUT PEOPLE DON'T OFTEN KEEP K-MESONS FOR PETS -EVEN PARROTS LIVE TO BE SEVENTY--
IF YOU CAN STAND TO LIVE FOR SEVENTY YEARS ON BIRDSEED AND AN OCCASIONAL CRACKER...
WELL-IT'S BETTER THEN BEING A NINE POUND DOG--WHY COULDN'T I HAVE BEEN A WOLF?
A WORTHY AMBITION--BUT WHO EVER HEARD OF A NINE-POUND WOLF?
I'M TOO LITTLE TO BE ON A DOG TEAM BUT I COULD BE A COACH DOG--LOOK AT VINCE LOMBARDI-VERY SMALL--GOOD COACH.
SPLENDID THOUGHT! YOU COULD COACH THE NEW ORLEANS SAINT BERNARDS--
OH, HECK AND DALMATIAN SHEP-CAN'T YOU BE SERIOUS ABOUT ANYTHING!??

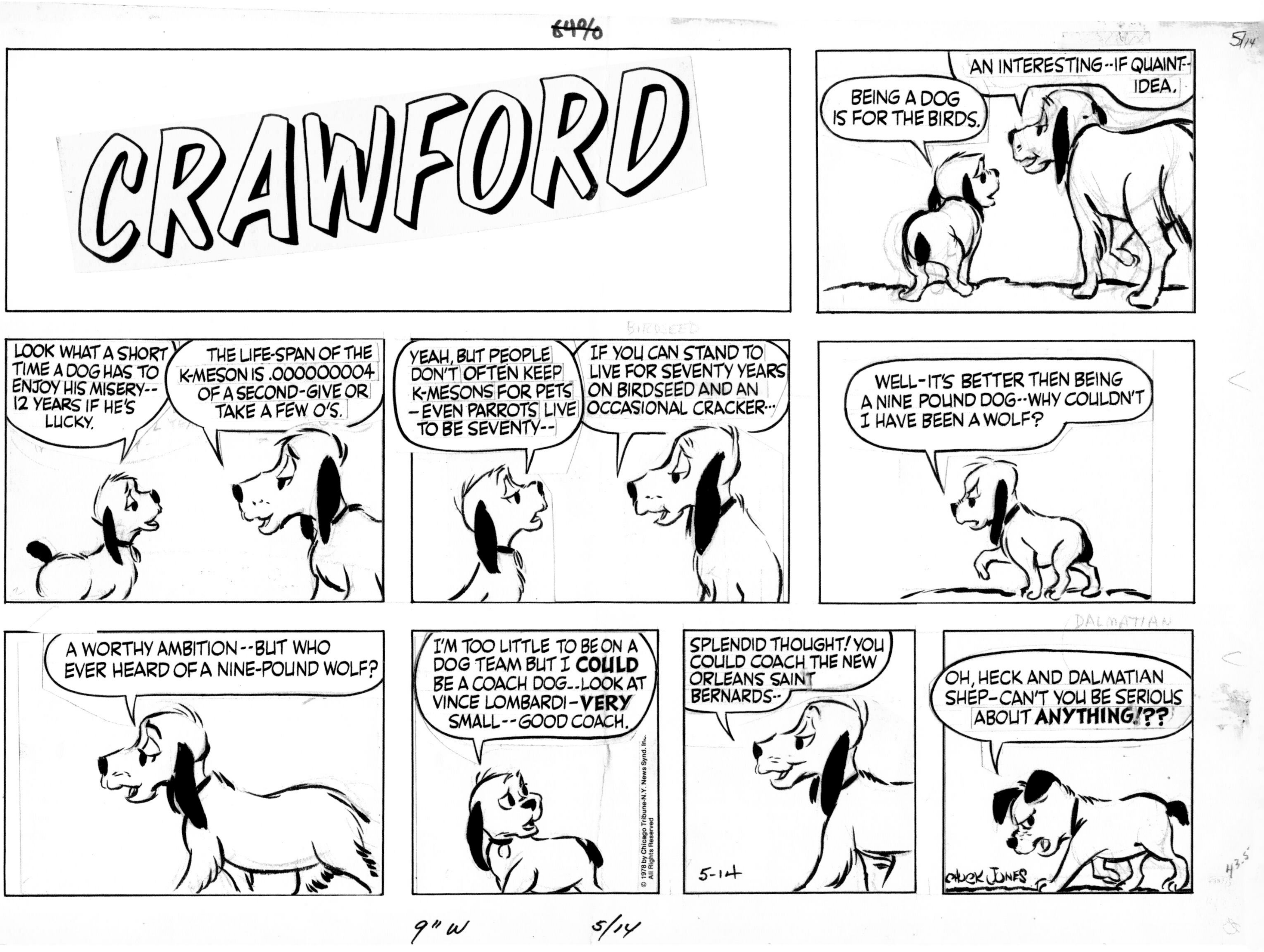
CRAWFORD
BEING A DOG IS FOR THE BIRDS.
AN INTERESTING--IF QUAINT--IDEA.
LOOK WHAT A SHORT TIME A DOG HAS TO ENJOY HIS MISERY--12 YEARS IF HE'S LUCKY.
THE LIFE-SPAN OF THE K-MESON IS .000000004 OF A SECOND-GIVE OR TAKE A FEW O'S.
YEAH, BUT PEOPLE DON'T OFTEN KEEP K-MESONS FOR PETS -EVEN PARROTS LIVE TO BE SEVENTY--
IF YOU CAN STAND TO LIVE FOR SEVENTY YEARS ON BIRDSEED AND AN OCCASIONAL CRACKER...
WELL-IT'S BETTER THEN BEING A NINE POUND DOG--WHY COULDN'T I HAVE BEEN A WOLF?
A WORTHY AMBITION--BUT WHO EVER HEARD OF A NINE-POUND WOLF?
I'M TOO LITTLE TO BE ON A DOG TEAM BUT I **COULD** BE A COACH DOG--LOOK AT VINCE LOMBARDI-**VERY** SMALL--GOOD COACH.
© 1978 by Chicago Tribune-N.Y. News Synd. Inc. All Rights Reserved
SPLENDID THOUGHT! YOU COULD COACH THE NEW ORLEANS SAINT BERNARDS--
5-14
OH, HECK AND DALMATIAN SHEP-CAN'T YOU BE SERIOUS ABOUT **ANYTHING!??**
CHUCK JONES

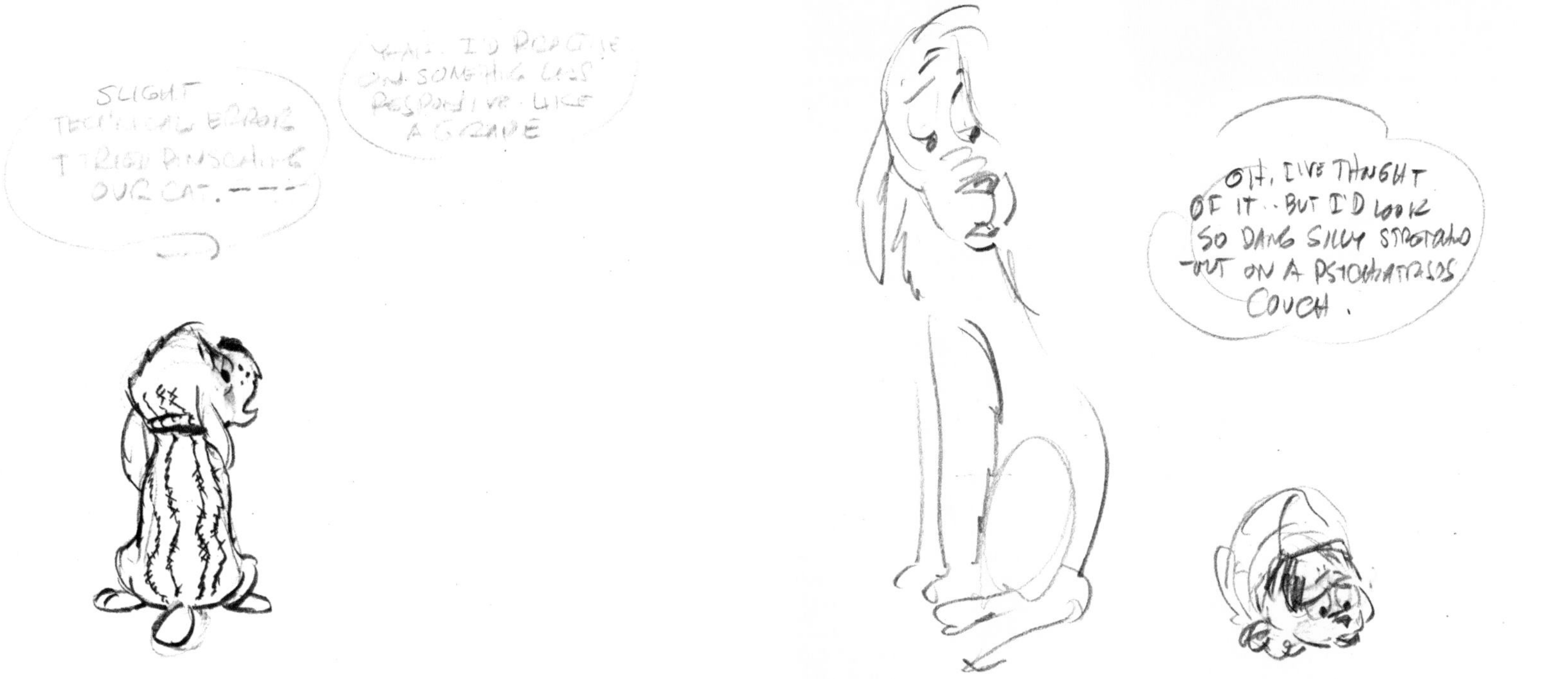

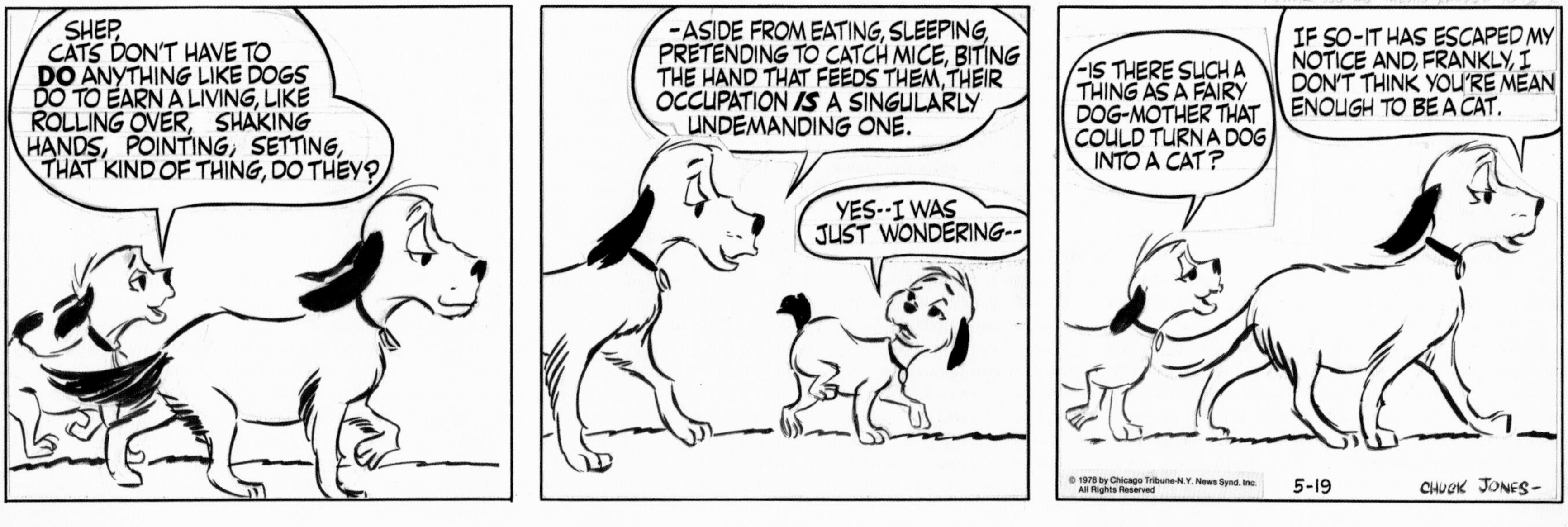

SHEP, CATS DON'T HAVE TO **DO** ANYTHING LIKE DOGS DO TO EARN A LIVING, LIKE ROLLING OVER, SHAKING HANDS, POINTING, SETTING, THAT KIND OF THING, DO THEY?
-ASIDE FROM EATING, SLEEPING, PRETENDING TO CATCH MICE, BITING THE HAND THAT FEEDS THEM, THEIR OCCUPATION ***IS*** A SINGULARLY UNDEMANDING ONE.
YES--I WAS JUST WONDERING--
-IS THERE SUCH A THING AS A FAIRY DOG-MOTHER THAT COULD TURN A DOG INTO A CAT?
IF SO-IT HAS ESCAPED MY NOTICE AND, FRANKLY, I DON'T THINK YOU'RE MEAN ENOUGH TO BE A CAT.
© 1978 by Chicago Tribune-N.Y. News Synd. Inc. All Rights Reserved
5-19
CHUCK JONES-

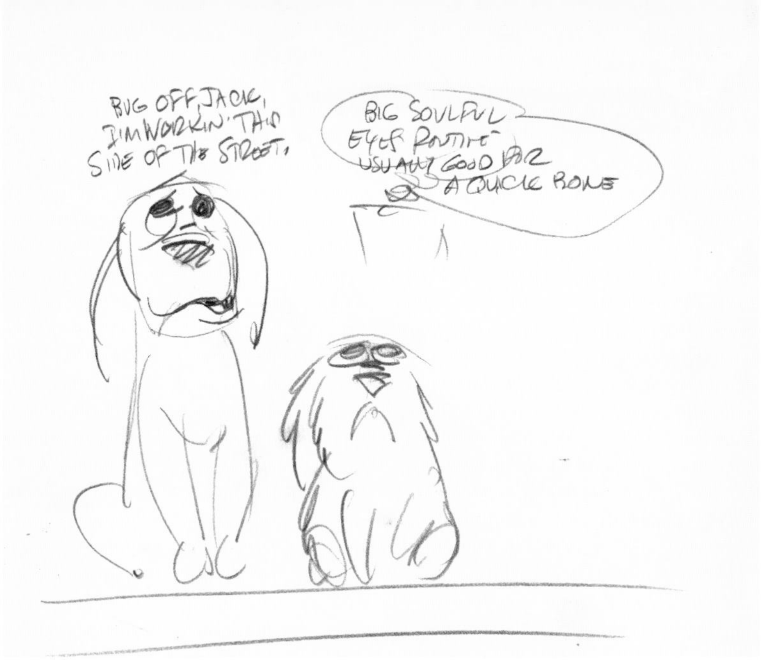
BUG OFF, JACK, I'M WORKIN' THIS SIDE OF THE STREET.
BIG SOULFUL EYES ROUTINE USUALLY GOOD FOR A QUICK BONE

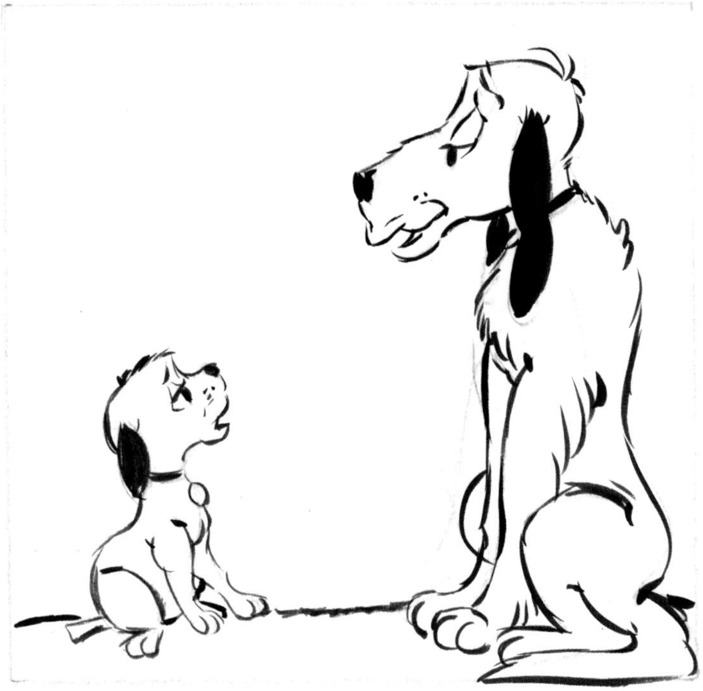

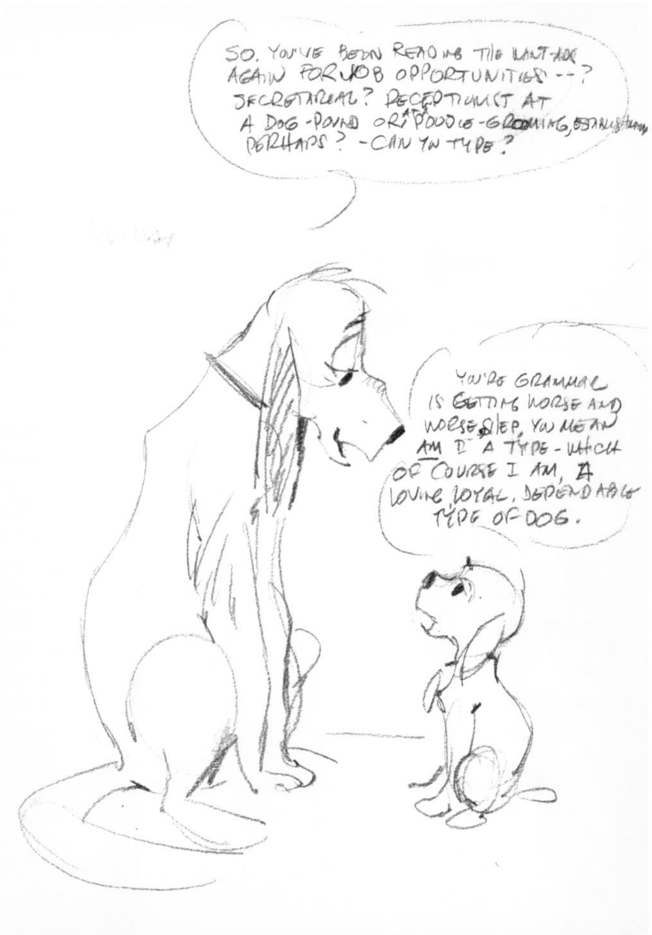
SO, YOU'VE BEEN READING THE WANT-ADS AGAIN FOR JOB OPPORTUNITIES --? SECRETARIAL? RECEPTIONIST AT A DOG-POUND OR AT A POODLE-GROOMING ESTABLISHMENT PERHAPS? -CAN YOU TYPE?
YOU'RE GRAMMAR IS GETTING WORSE AND WORSE, SKEP. YOU MEAN AM I A TYPE - WHICH OF COURSE I AM, A LOVING LOYAL, DEPENDABLE TYPE OF DOG.

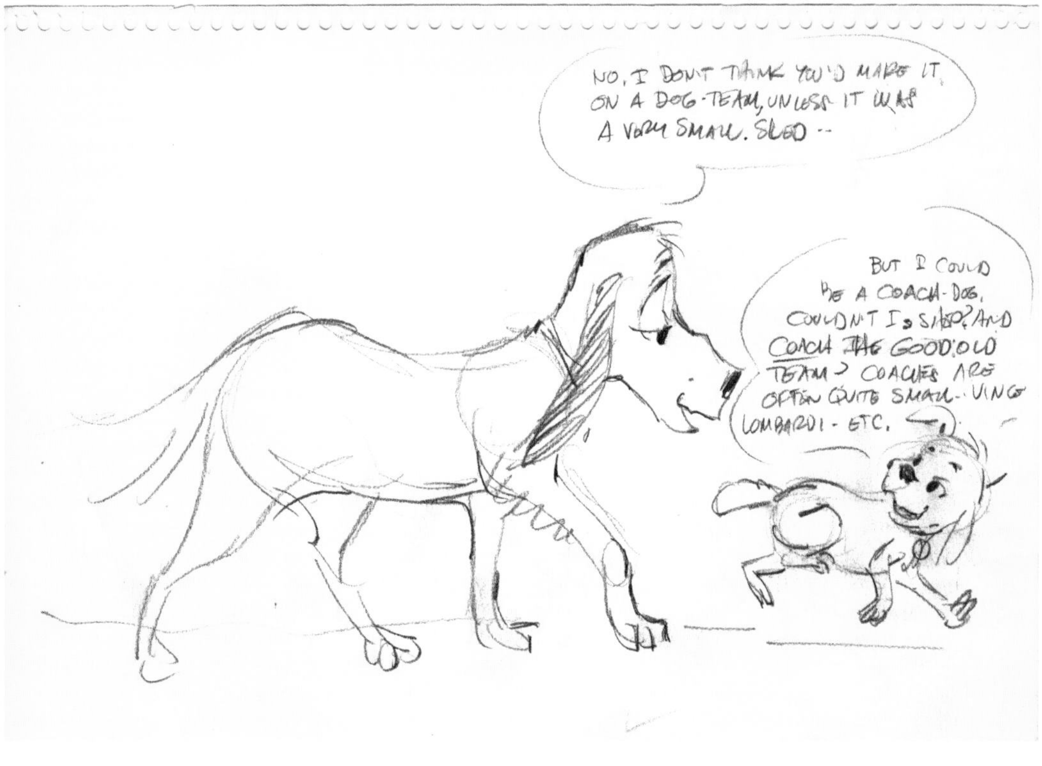
NO, I DON'T THINK YOU'D MAKE IT ON A DOG-TEAM, UNLESS IT WAS A VERY SMALL SLED --
BUT I COULD BE A COACH-DOG, COULDN'T I, SKEP? AND COACH THE GOOD OLD TEAM? COACHES ARE OFTEN QUITE SMALL - VINCE LOMBARDI - ETC.

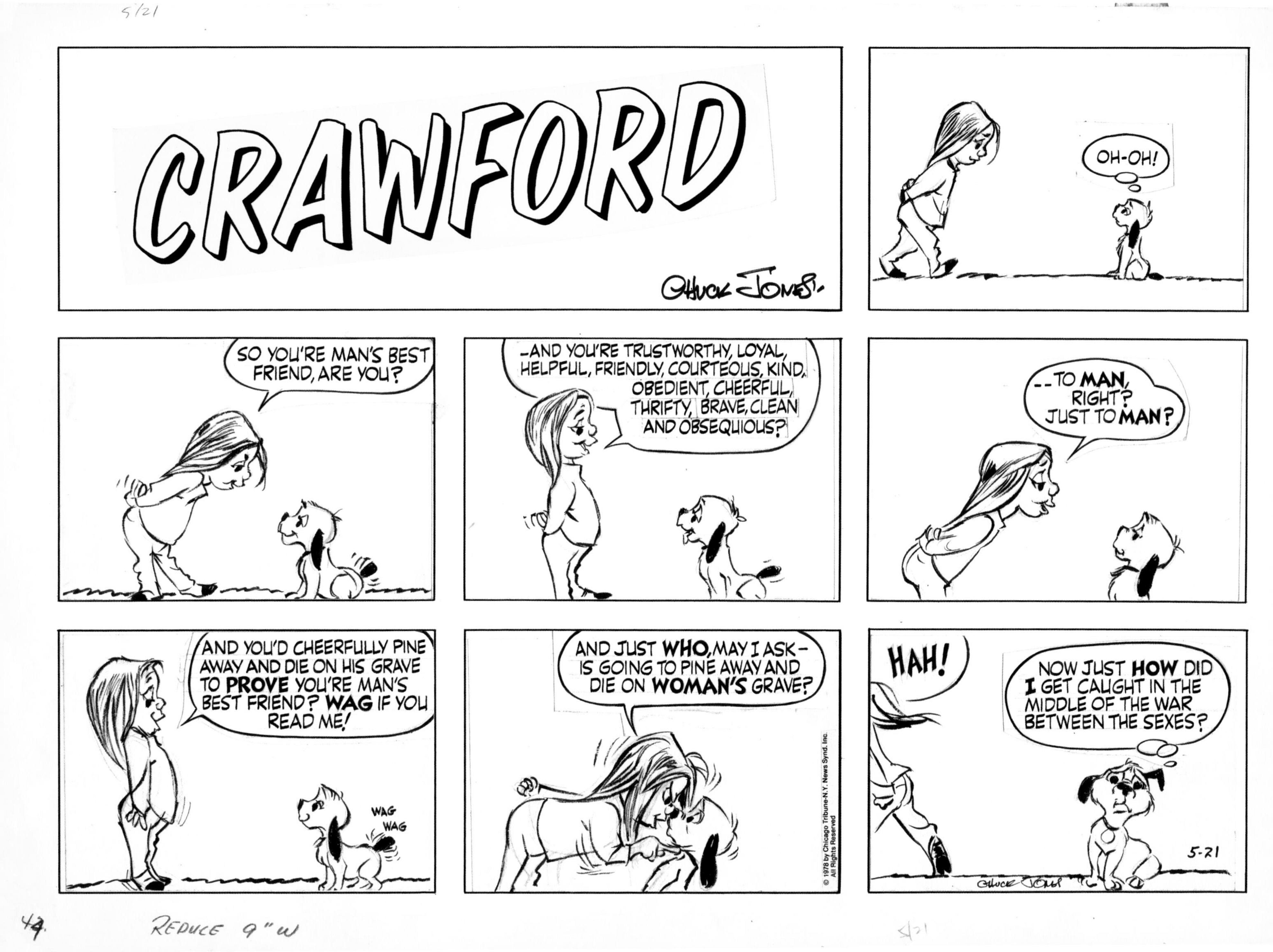
5/21
CRAWFORD
CHUCK JONES
OH-OH!
SO YOU'RE MAN'S BEST FRIEND, ARE YOU?
–AND YOU'RE TRUSTWORTHY, LOYAL, HELPFUL, FRIENDLY, COURTEOUS, KIND, OBEDIENT, CHEERFUL, THRIFTY, BRAVE, CLEAN AND OBSEQUIOUS?
--TO MAN, RIGHT? JUST TO MAN?
AND YOU'D CHEERFULLY PINE AWAY AND DIE ON HIS GRAVE TO PROVE YOU'RE MAN'S BEST FRIEND? WAG IF YOU READ ME!
WAG WAG
AND JUST WHO, MAY I ASK– IS GOING TO PINE AWAY AND DIE ON WOMAN'S GRAVE?
© 1978 by Chicago Tribune-N.Y. News Synd. Inc. All Rights Reserved
HAH!
NOW JUST HOW DID I GET CAUGHT IN THE MIDDLE OF THE WAR BETWEEN THE SEXES?
5-21
CHUCK JONES
44
REDUCE 9" W
5/21

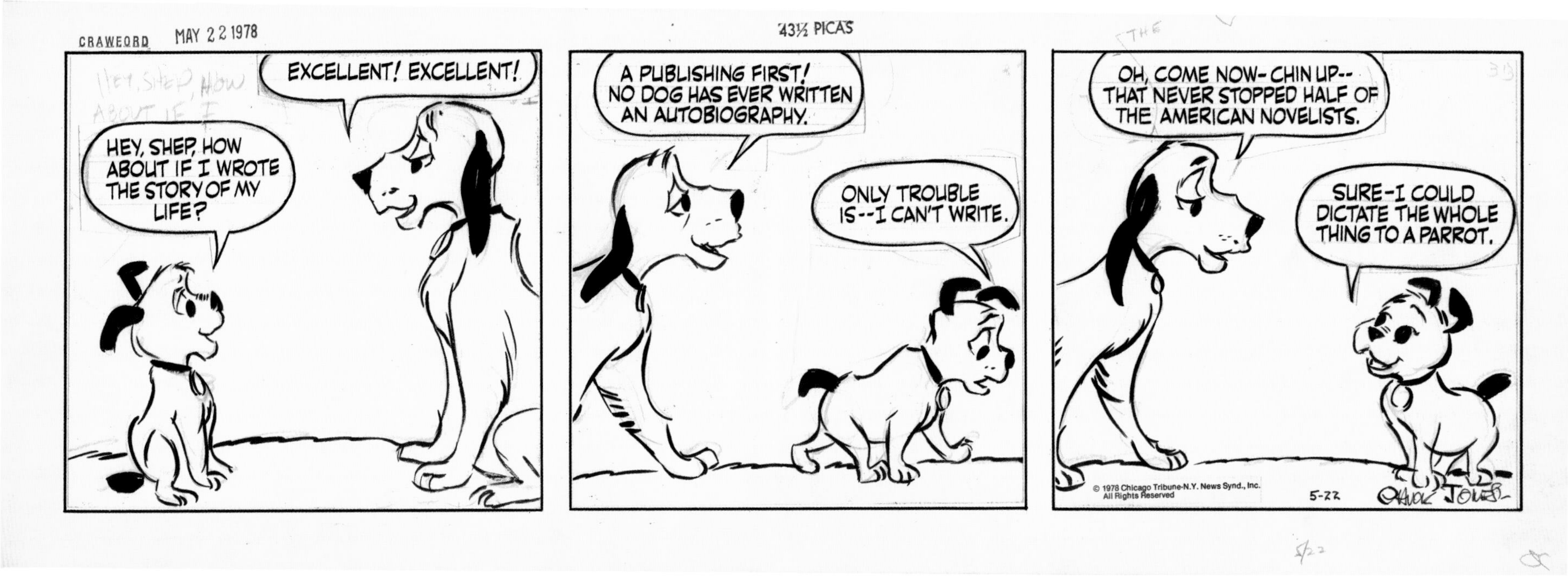
CRAWFORD MAY 22 1978
43½ PICAS
HEY, SHEP, HOW ABOUT IF I WROTE THE STORY OF MY LIFE?
EXCELLENT! EXCELLENT!
A PUBLISHING FIRST! NO DOG HAS EVER WRITTEN AN AUTOBIOGRAPHY.
ONLY TROUBLE IS--I CAN'T WRITE.
OH, COME NOW- CHIN UP-- THAT NEVER STOPPED HALF OF THE AMERICAN NOVELISTS.
SURE-I COULD DICTATE THE WHOLE THING TO A PARROT.
© 1978 Chicago Tribune-N.Y. News Synd., Inc. All Rights Reserved
5-22
CHUCK JONES

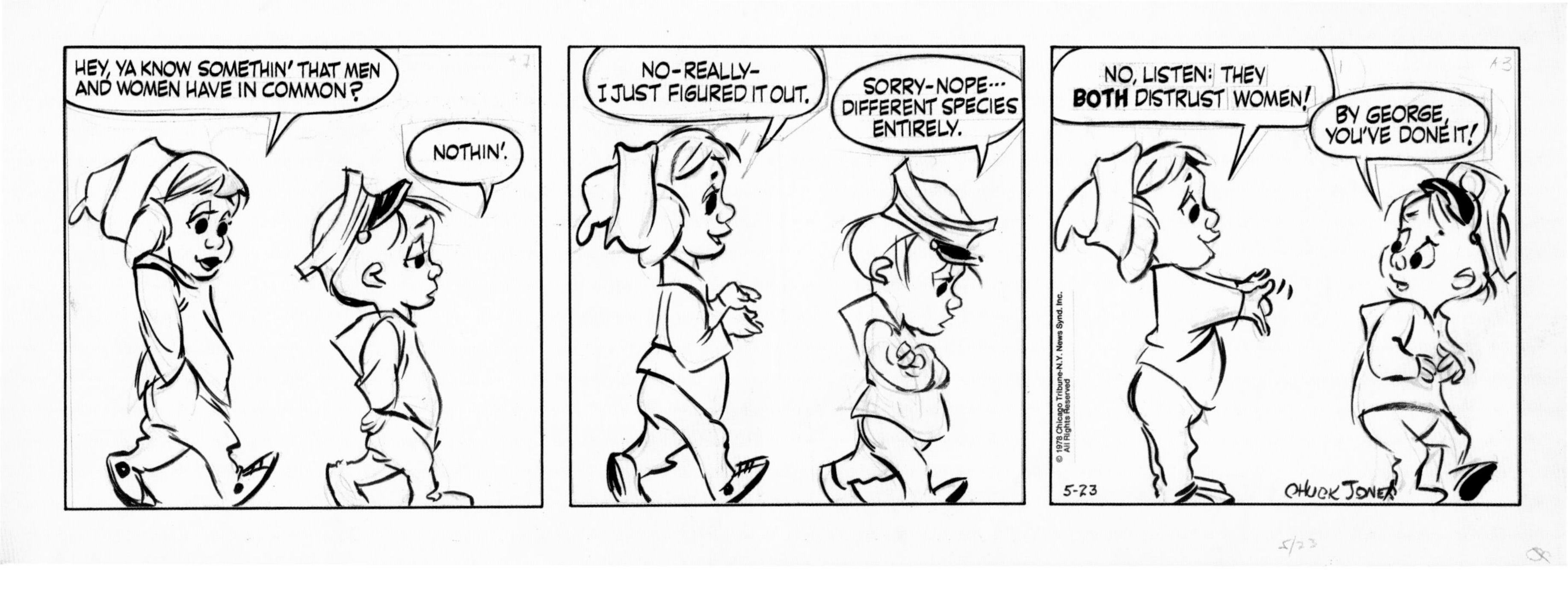
HEY, YA KNOW SOMETHIN' THAT MEN AND WOMEN HAVE IN COMMON?
NOTHIN'.
NO-REALLY- I JUST FIGURED IT OUT.
SORRY-NOPE... DIFFERENT SPECIES ENTIRELY.
NO, LISTEN: THEY **BOTH** DISTRUST WOMEN!
BY GEORGE, YOU'VE DONE IT!
© 1978 Chicago Tribune-N.Y. News Synd. Inc. All Rights Reserved
5-23
CHUCK JONES

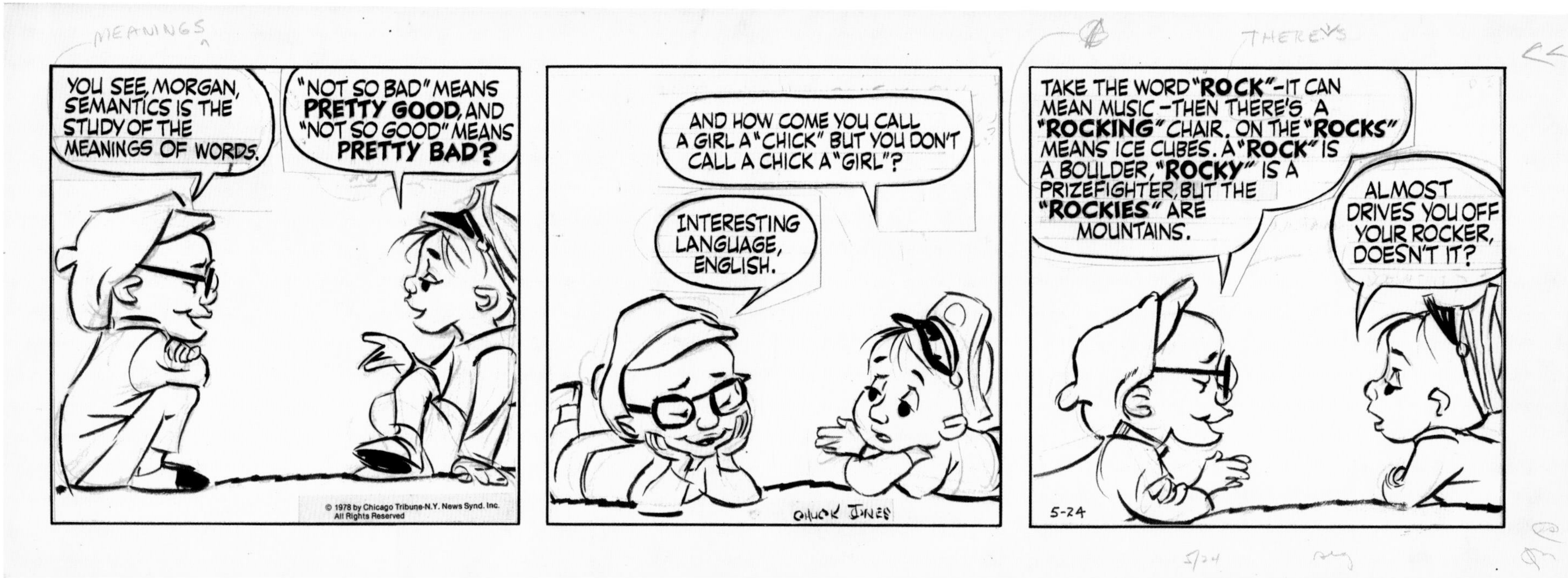
YOU SEE, MORGAN, SEMANTICS IS THE STUDY OF THE MEANINGS OF WORDS.
"NOT SO BAD" MEANS **PRETTY GOOD**, AND "NOT SO GOOD" MEANS **PRETTY BAD?**
AND HOW COME YOU CALL A GIRL A "CHICK" BUT YOU DON'T CALL A CHICK A "GIRL"?
INTERESTING LANGUAGE, ENGLISH.
TAKE THE WORD "**ROCK**"–IT CAN MEAN MUSIC–THEN THERE'S A "**ROCKING**" CHAIR. ON THE "**ROCKS**" MEANS ICE CUBES. A "**ROCK**" IS A BOULDER, "**ROCKY**" IS A PRIZEFIGHTER, BUT THE "**ROCKIES**" ARE MOUNTAINS.
ALMOST DRIVES YOU OFF YOUR ROCKER, DOESN'T IT?
© 1978 by Chicago Tribune-N.Y. News Synd. Inc. All Rights Reserved
CHUCK JONES
5-24

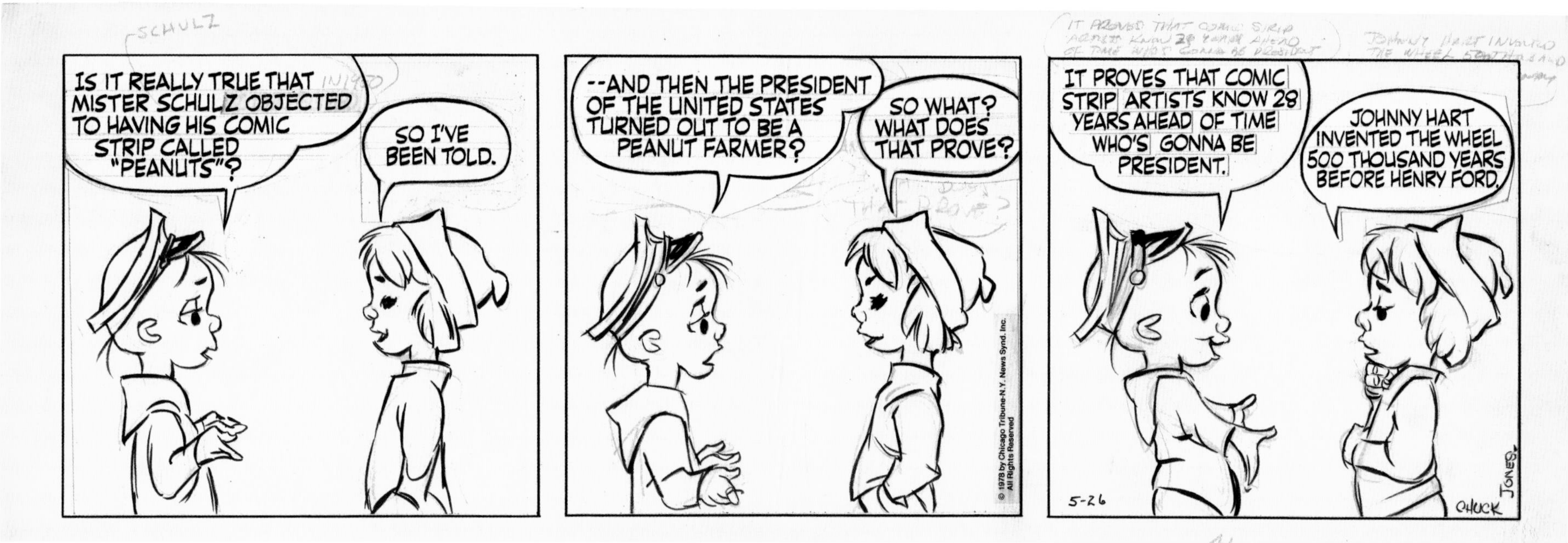
IS IT REALLY TRUE THAT MISTER SCHULZ OBJECTED TO HAVING HIS COMIC STRIP CALLED "PEANUTS"?
SO I'VE BEEN TOLD.
--AND THEN THE PRESIDENT OF THE UNITED STATES TURNED OUT TO BE A PEANUT FARMER?
SO WHAT? WHAT DOES THAT PROVE?
© 1978 by Chicago Tribune-N.Y. News Synd. Inc. All Rights Reserved
IT PROVES THAT COMIC STRIP ARTISTS KNOW 28 YEARS AHEAD OF TIME WHO'S GONNA BE PRESIDENT.
JOHNNY HART INVENTED THE WHEEL 500 THOUSAND YEARS BEFORE HENRY FORD.
5-26
CHUCK JONES

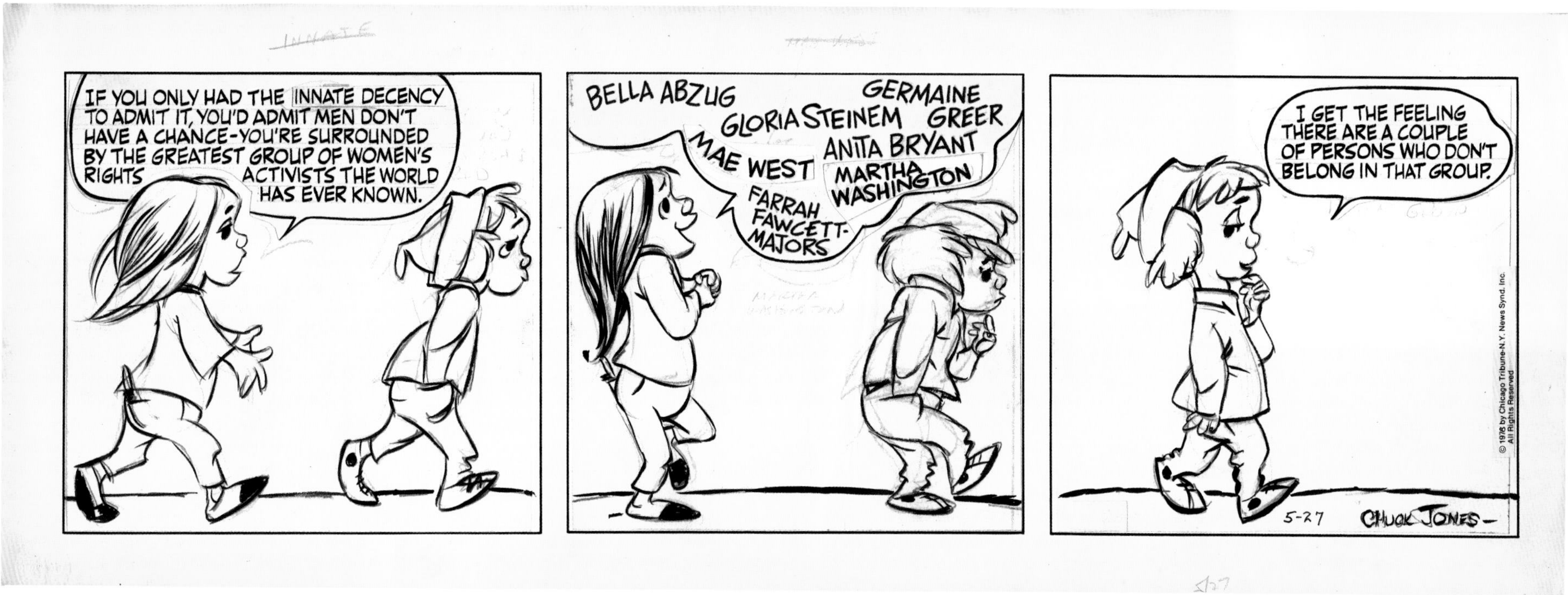
IF YOU ONLY HAD THE INNATE DECENCY TO ADMIT IT, YOU'D ADMIT MEN DON'T HAVE A CHANCE-YOU'RE SURROUNDED BY THE GREATEST GROUP OF WOMEN'S RIGHTS ACTIVISTS THE WORLD HAS EVER KNOWN.
BELLA ABZUG
GLORIA STEINEM
GERMAINE GREER
MAE WEST
ANITA BRYANT
MARTHA WASHINGTON
FARRAH FAWCETT-MAJORS
I GET THE FEELING THERE ARE A COUPLE OF PERSONS WHO DON'T BELONG IN THAT GROUP.
© 1976 by Chicago Tribune-N.Y. News Synd. Inc. All Rights Reserved
5-27
CHUCK JONES

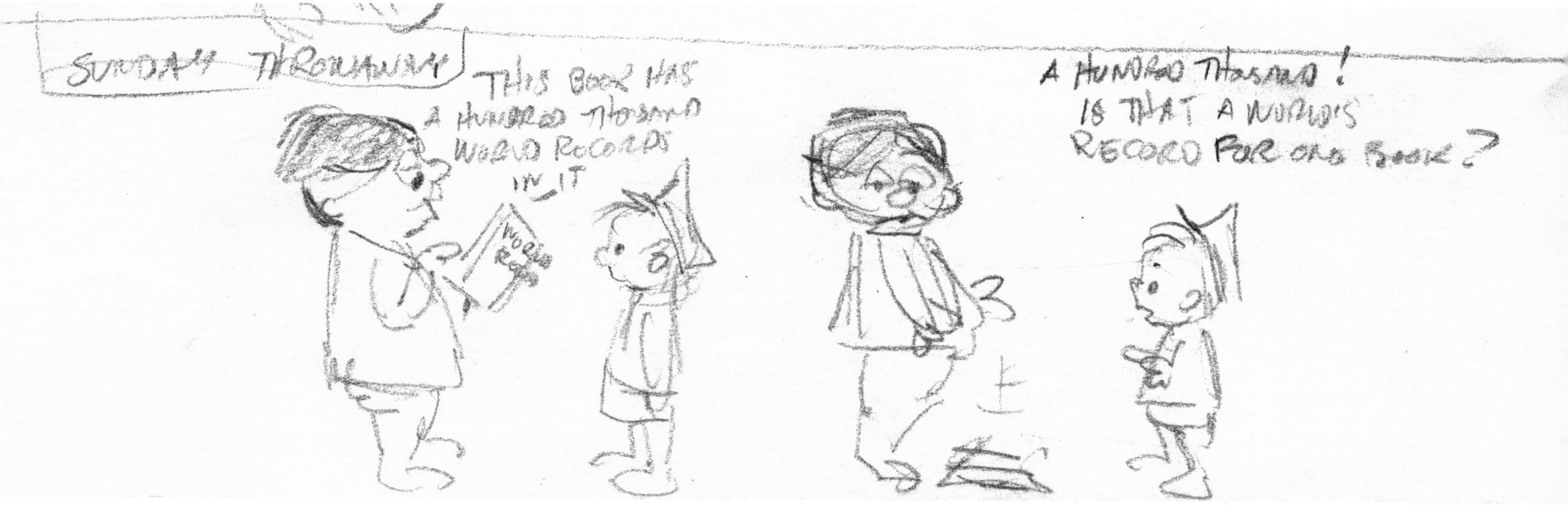
SUNDAY THROWAWAY
THIS BOOK HAS A HUNDRED THOUSAND WORLD RECORDS IN IT
A HUNDRED THOUSAND! IS THAT A WORLD'S RECORD FOR ONE BOOK?

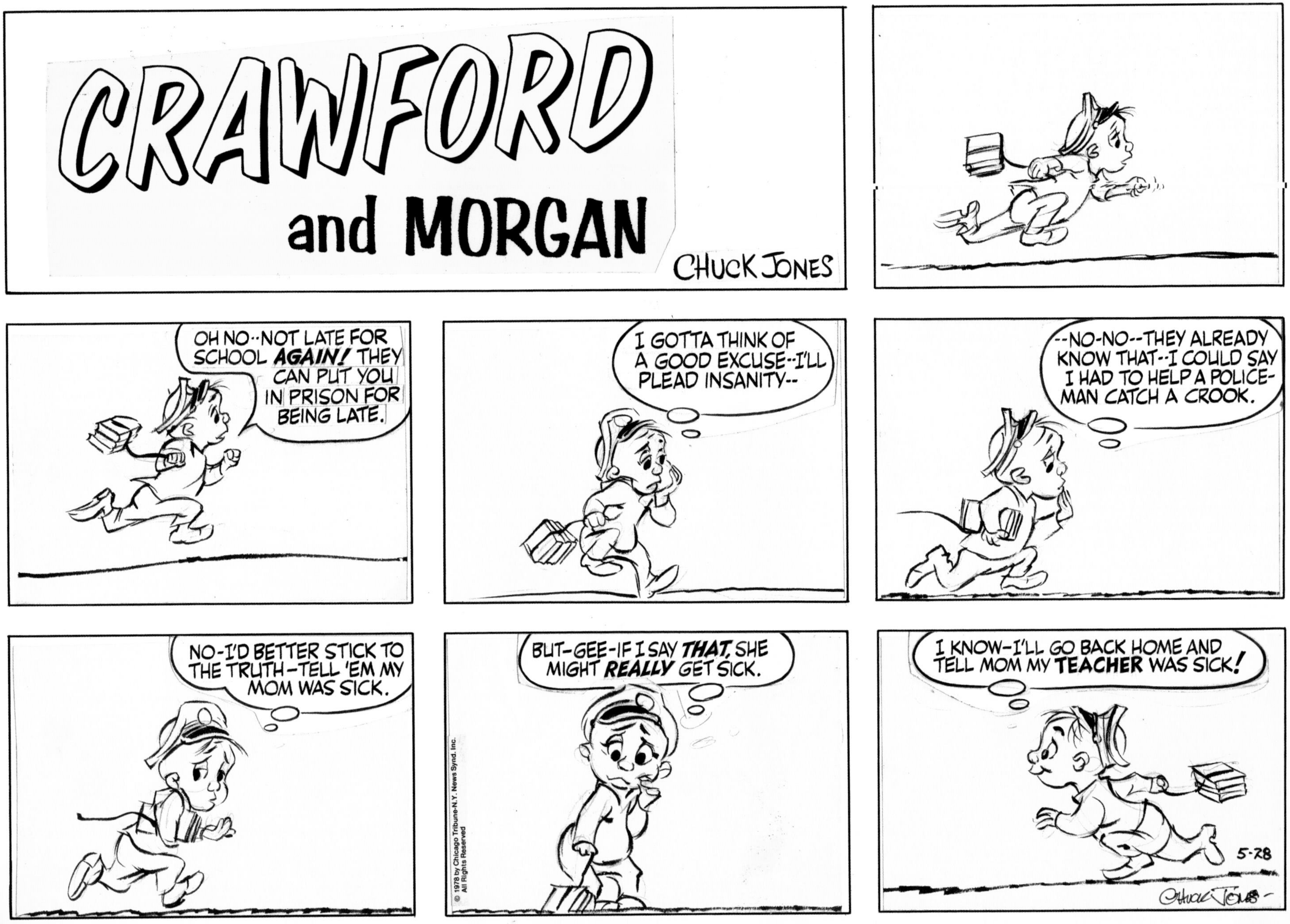
CRAWFORD and MORGAN
CHUCK JONES
OH NO--NOT LATE FOR SCHOOL AGAIN! THEY CAN PUT YOU IN PRISON FOR BEING LATE.
I GOTTA THINK OF A GOOD EXCUSE--I'LL PLEAD INSANITY--
--NO-NO--THEY ALREADY KNOW THAT--I COULD SAY I HAD TO HELP A POLICE-MAN CATCH A CROOK.
NO-I'D BETTER STICK TO THE TRUTH-TELL 'EM MY MOM WAS SICK.
© 1978 by Chicago Tribune-N.Y. News Synd. Inc. All Rights Reserved
BUT-GEE-IF I SAY THAT, SHE MIGHT REALLY GET SICK.
I KNOW-I'LL GO BACK HOME AND TELL MOM MY TEACHER WAS SICK!
5-28
CHUCK JONES

REDUCE 9" W 4A

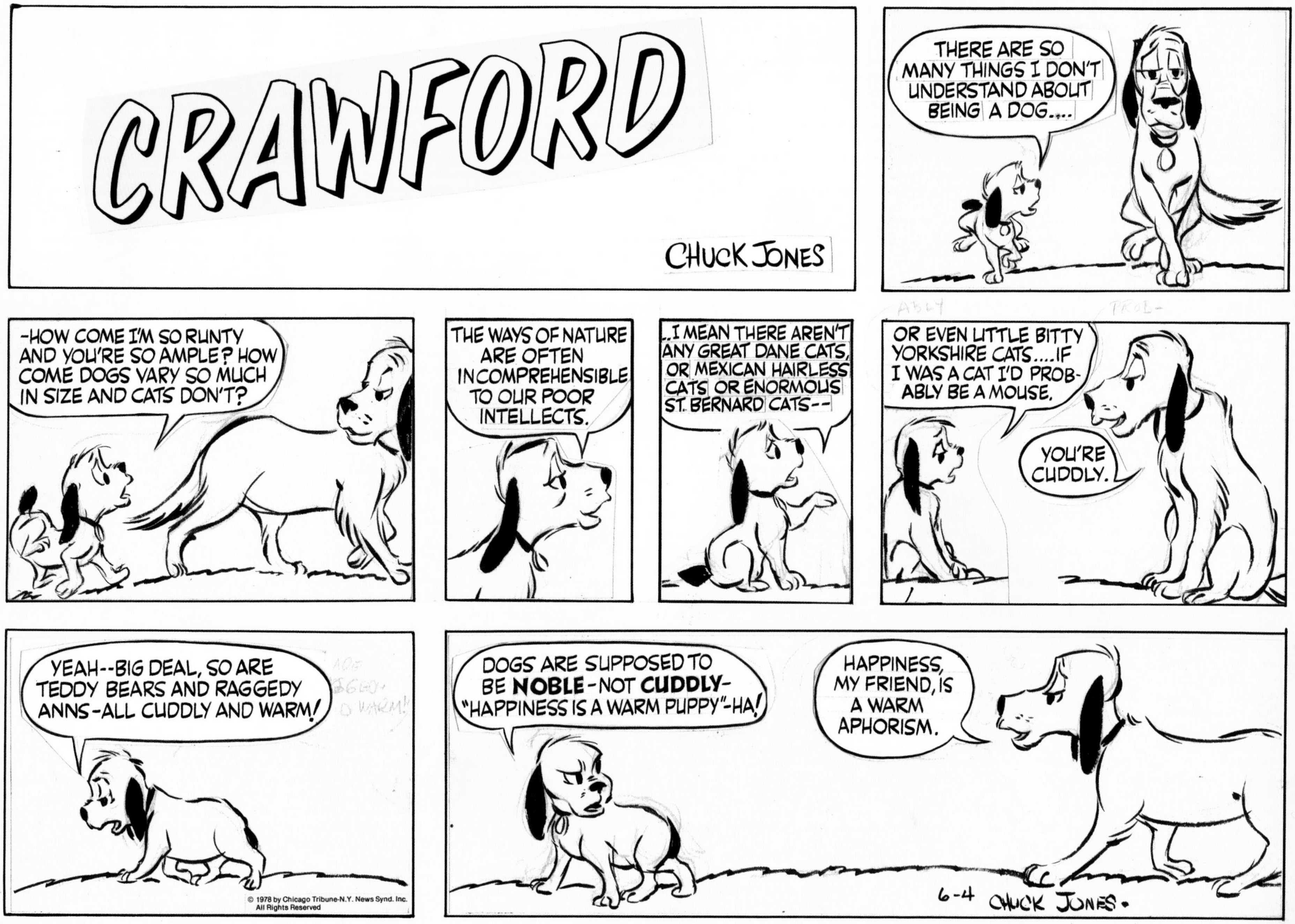
CRAWFORD
CHUCK JONES
THERE ARE SO MANY THINGS I DON'T UNDERSTAND ABOUT BEING A DOG....
-HOW COME I'M SO RUNTY AND YOU'RE SO AMPLE? HOW COME DOGS VARY SO MUCH IN SIZE AND CATS DON'T?
THE WAYS OF NATURE ARE OFTEN INCOMPREHENSIBLE TO OUR POOR INTELLECTS.
..I MEAN THERE AREN'T ANY GREAT DANE CATS, OR MEXICAN HAIRLESS CATS OR ENORMOUS ST. BERNARD CATS--
OR EVEN LITTLE BITTY YORKSHIRE CATS....IF I WAS A CAT I'D PROBABLY BE A MOUSE.
YOU'RE CUDDLY.
YEAH--BIG DEAL, SO ARE TEDDY BEARS AND RAGGEDY ANNS-ALL CUDDLY AND WARM!
DOGS ARE SUPPOSED TO BE **NOBLE**-NOT **CUDDLY**-"HAPPINESS IS A WARM PUPPY"-HA!
HAPPINESS, MY FRIEND, IS A WARM APHORISM.
© 1978 by Chicago Tribune-N.Y. News Synd. Inc. All Rights Reserved
6-4 CHUCK JONES

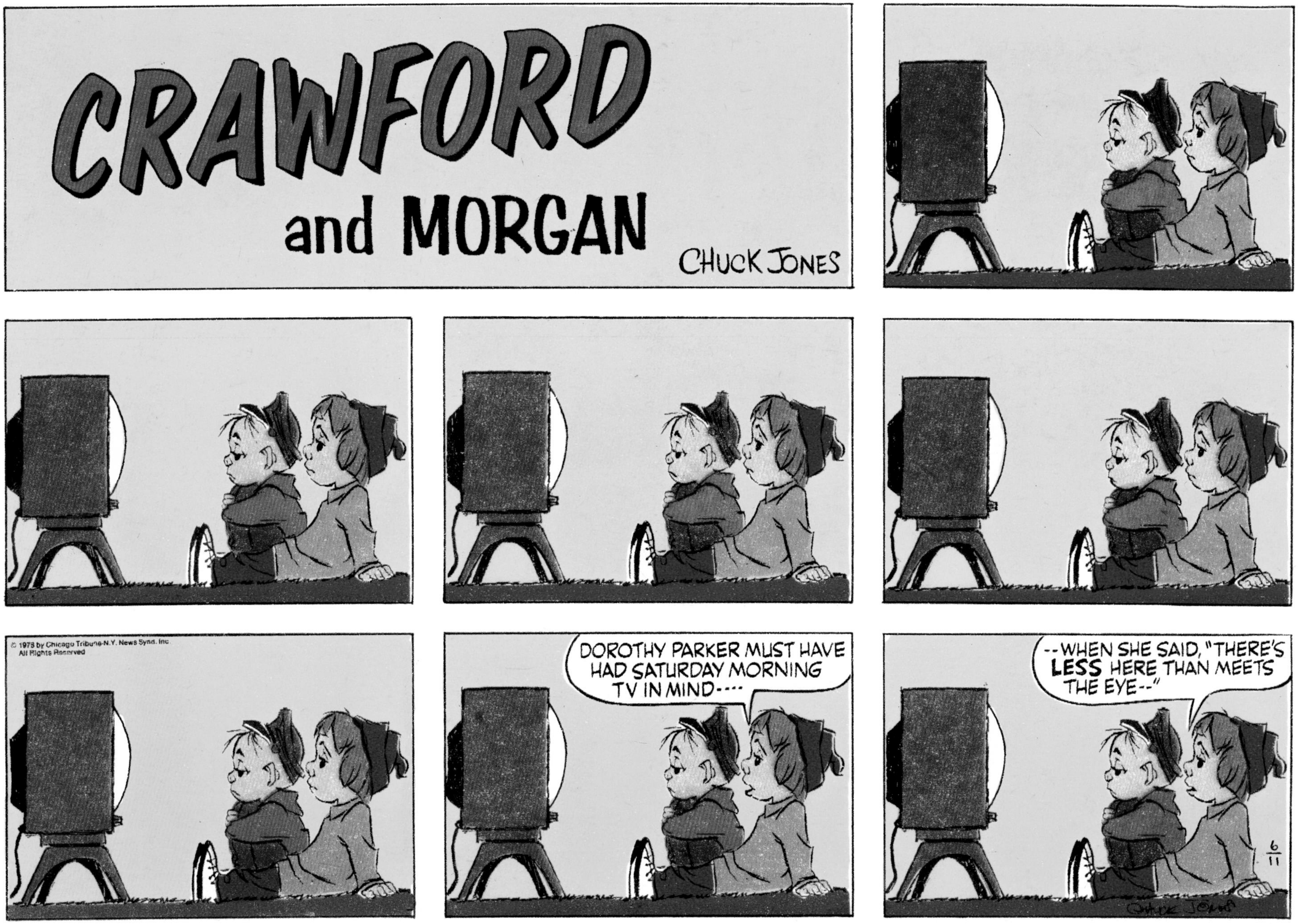
CRAWFORD
and MORGAN
CHUCK JONES
© 1978 by Chicago Tribune-N.Y. News Synd. Inc.
All Rights Reserved
DOROTHY PARKER MUST HAVE HAD SATURDAY MORNING TV IN MIND----
--WHEN SHE SAID, "THERE'S **LESS** HERE THAN MEETS THE EYE--"
6/11

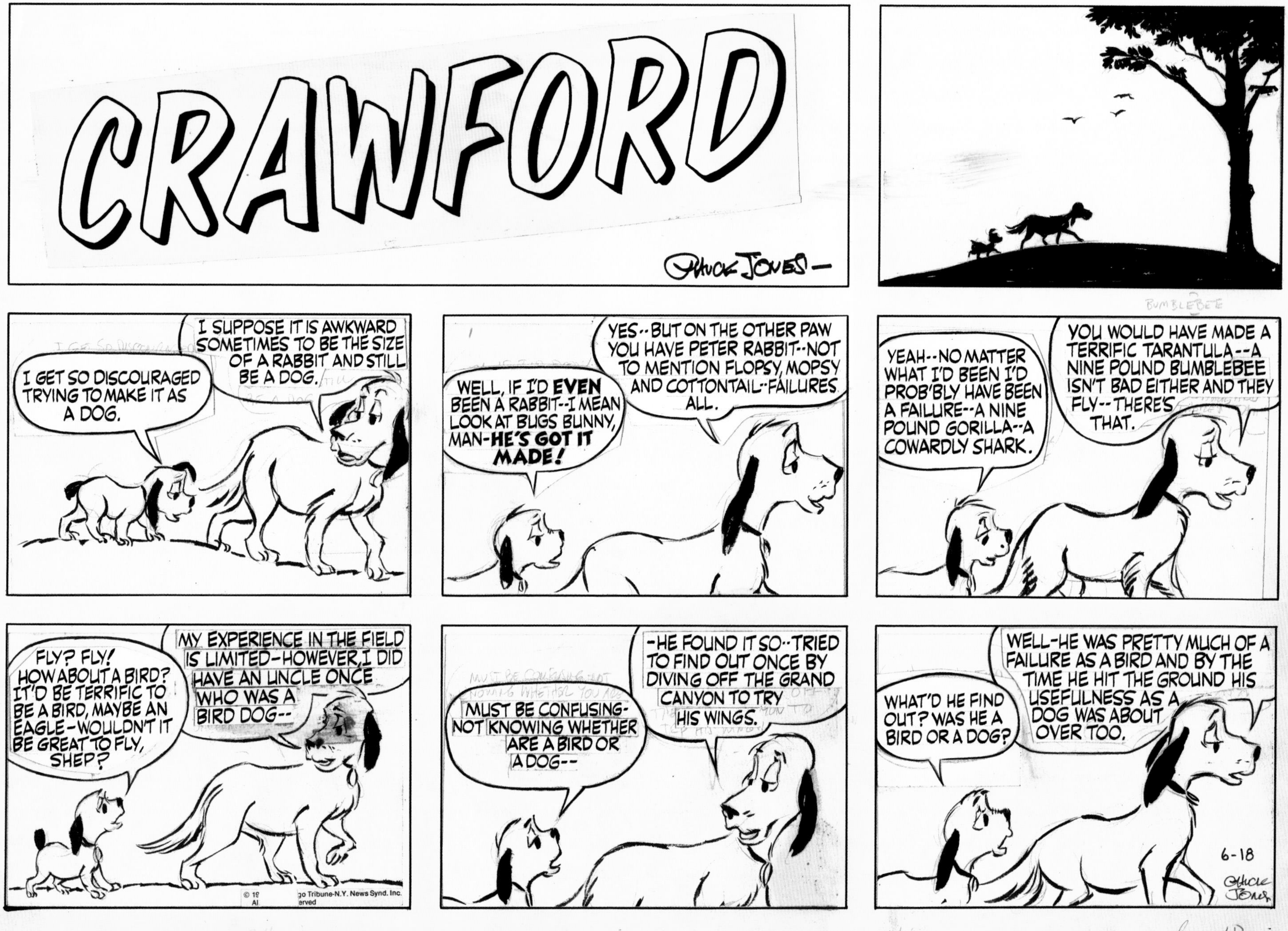
CRAWFORD
CHUCK JONES
I GET SO DISCOURAGED TRYING TO MAKE IT AS A DOG.
I SUPPOSE IT IS AWKWARD SOMETIMES TO BE THE SIZE OF A RABBIT AND STILL BE A DOG.
WELL, IF I'D **EVEN** BEEN A RABBIT--I MEAN LOOK AT BUGS BUNNY, MAN-**HE'S GOT IT MADE!**
YES--BUT ON THE OTHER PAW YOU HAVE PETER RABBIT--NOT TO MENTION FLOPSY, MOPSY AND COTTONTAIL--FAILURES ALL.
YEAH--NO MATTER WHAT I'D BEEN I'D PROB'BLY HAVE BEEN A FAILURE--A NINE POUND GORILLA--A COWARDLY SHARK.
YOU WOULD HAVE MADE A TERRIFIC TARANTULA--A NINE POUND BUMBLEBEE ISN'T BAD EITHER AND THEY FLY--THERE'S THAT.
FLY? FLY! HOW ABOUT A BIRD? IT'D BE TERRIFIC TO BE A BIRD, MAYBE AN EAGLE-WOULDN'T IT BE GREAT TO FLY, SHEP?
MY EXPERIENCE IN THE FIELD IS LIMITED-HOWEVER, I DID HAVE AN UNCLE ONCE WHO WAS A BIRD DOG--
MUST BE CONFUSING-NOT KNOWING WHETHER ARE A BIRD OR A DOG--
-HE FOUND IT SO--TRIED TO FIND OUT ONCE BY DIVING OFF THE GRAND CANYON TO TRY HIS WINGS.
WHAT'D HE FIND OUT? WAS HE A BIRD OR A DOG?
WELL-HE WAS PRETTY MUCH OF A FAILURE AS A BIRD AND BY THE TIME HE HIT THE GROUND HIS USEFULNESS AS A DOG WAS ABOUT OVER TOO.
6-18
CHUCK JONES
© 19 go Tribune-N.Y. News Synd. Inc.

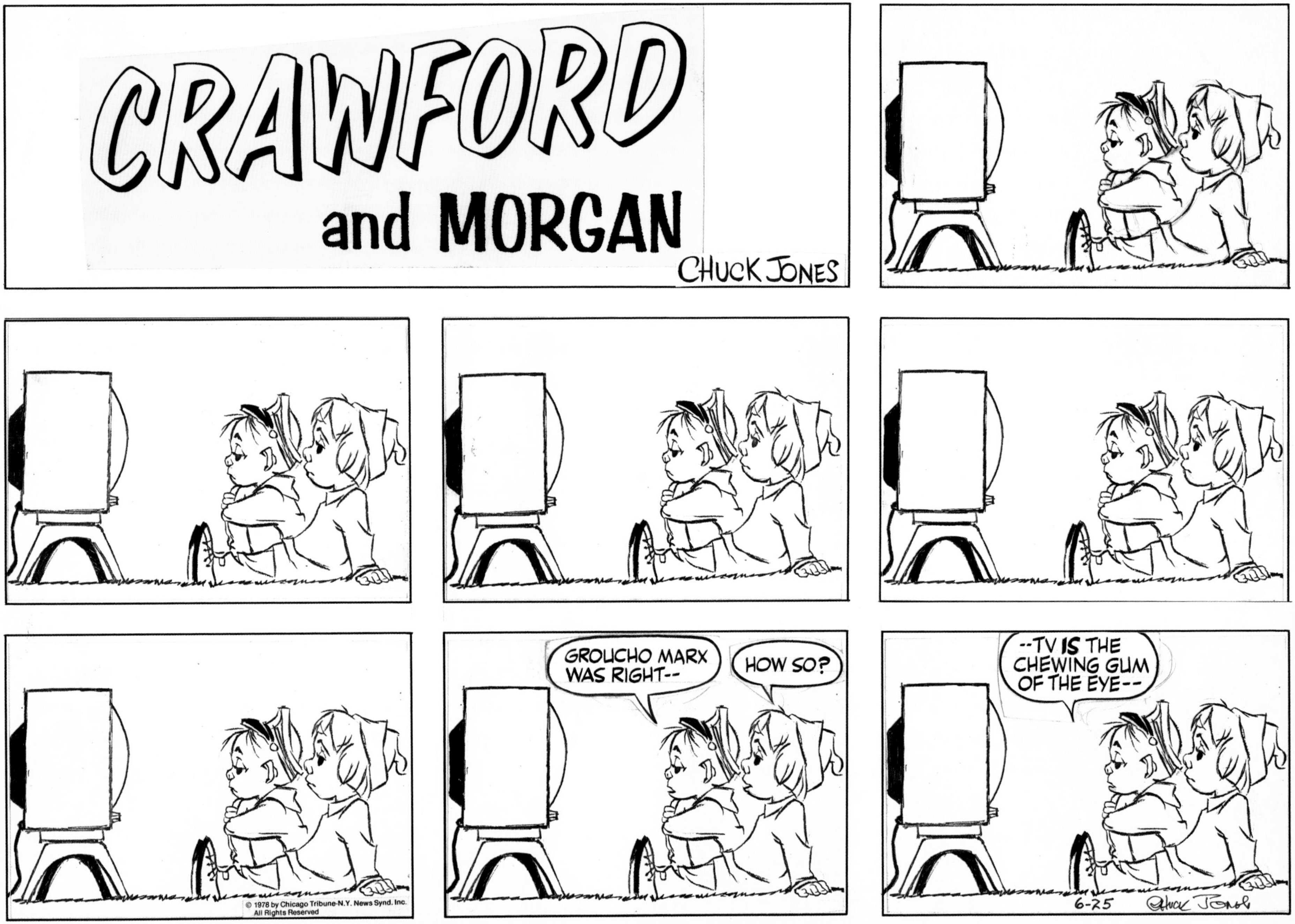
CRAWFORD and MORGAN
CHUCK JONES
GROUCHO MARX WAS RIGHT--
HOW SO?
--TV IS THE CHEWING GUM OF THE EYE--
6-25
Chuck Jones
© 1978 by Chicago Tribune-N.Y. News Synd. Inc. All Rights Reserved

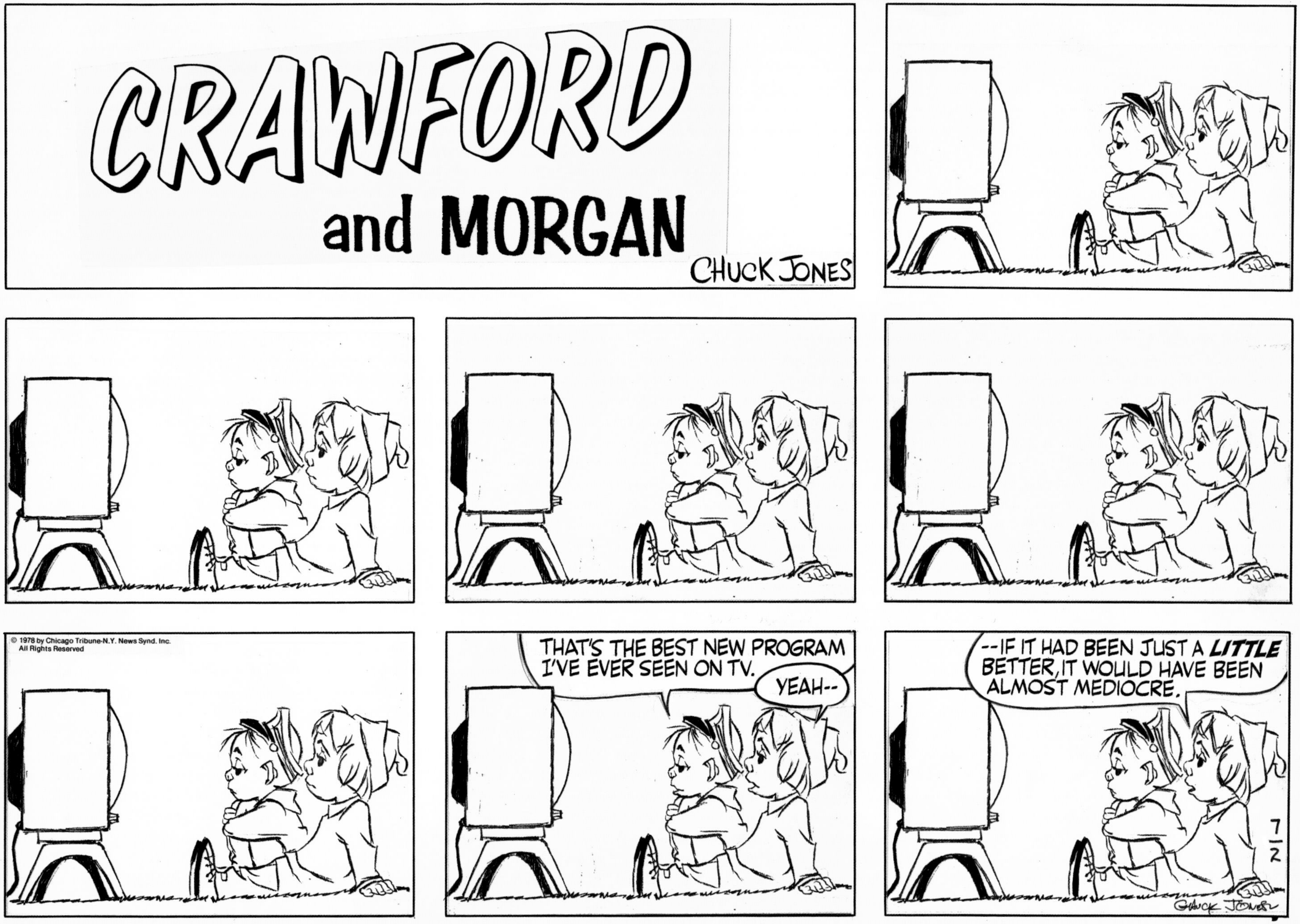
CRAWFORD
and MORGAN
CHUCK JONES
© 1978 by Chicago Tribune-N.Y. News Synd. Inc.
All Rights Reserved
THAT'S THE BEST NEW PROGRAM I'VE EVER SEEN ON TV.
YEAH--
--IF IT HAD BEEN JUST A LITTLE BETTER, IT WOULD HAVE BEEN ALMOST MEDIOCRE.
7/2
CHUCK JONES

Unpublished strips and unused gags

A series of unpublished strips and unused gags. Some strips—such as those for Thanksgiving and Christmas 1977—were shelved when the launch date of the series was pushed back to January 1978.

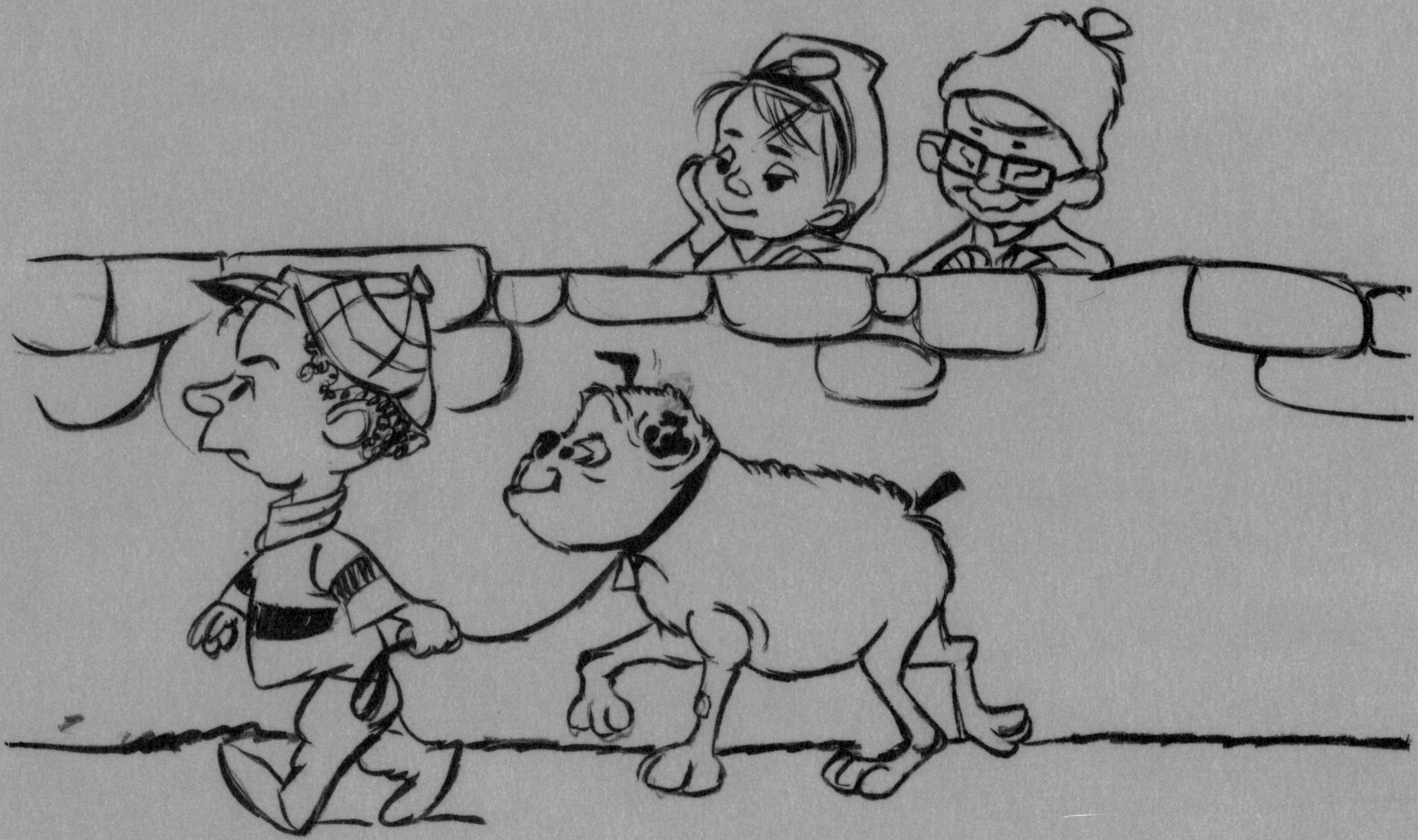

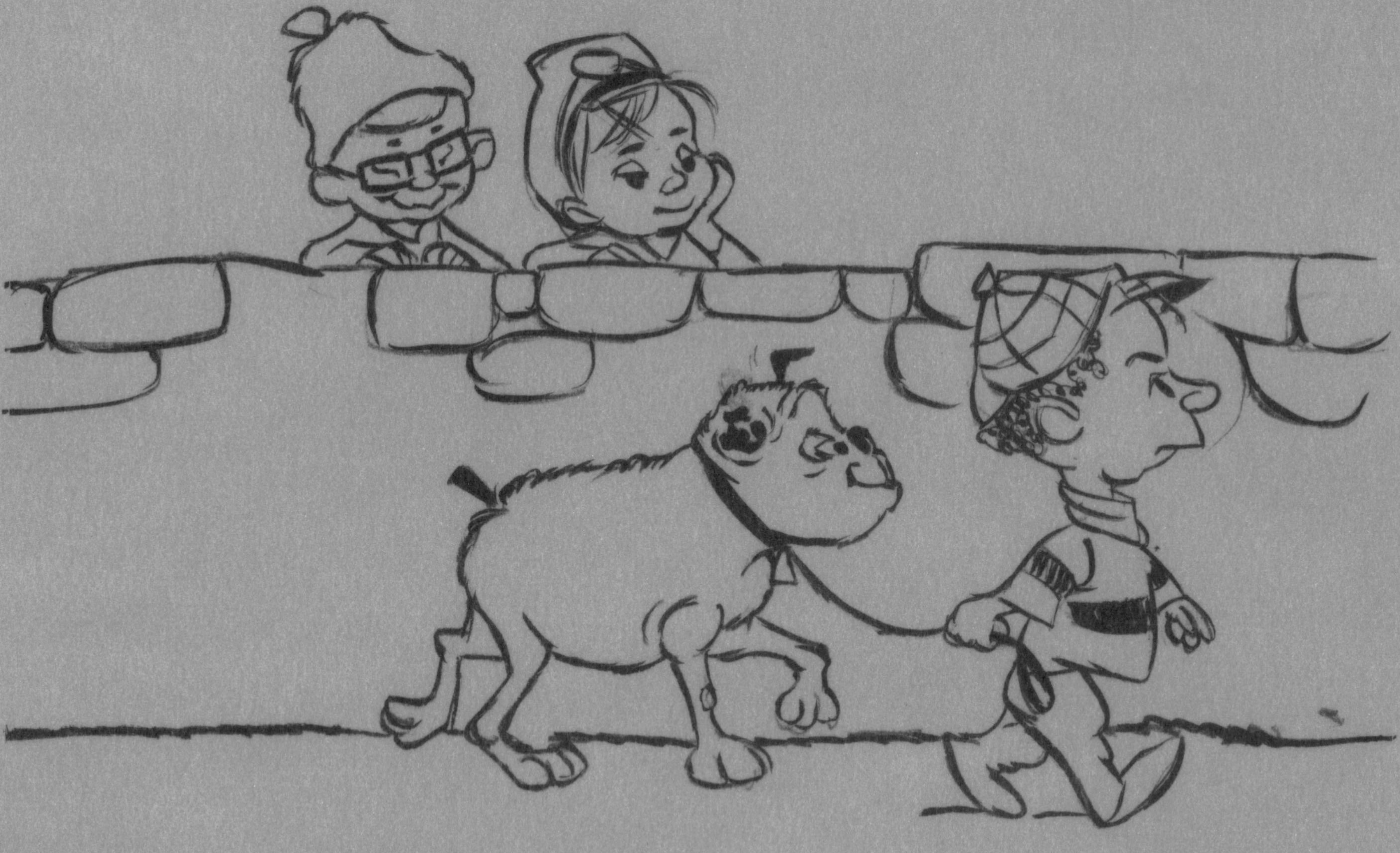

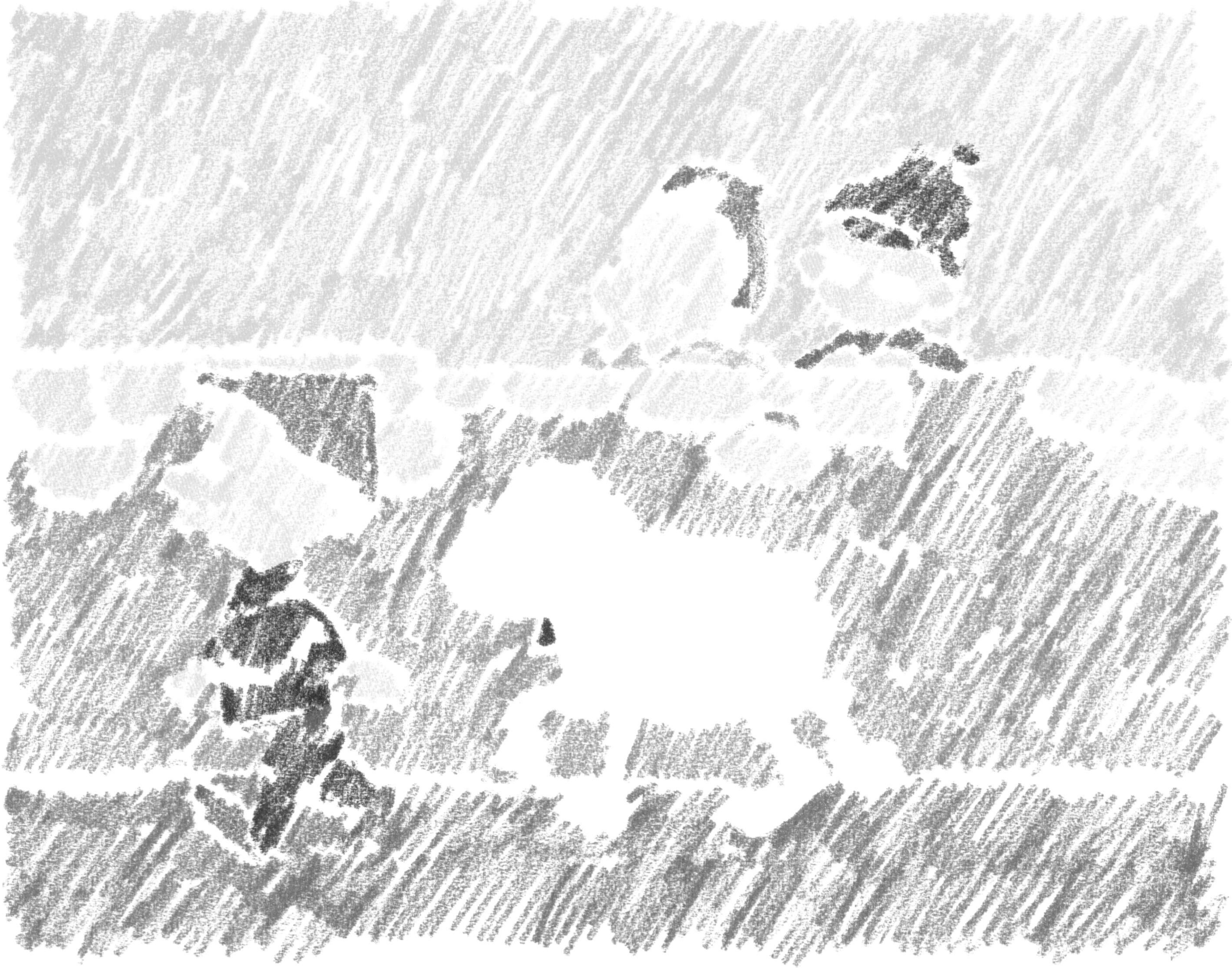

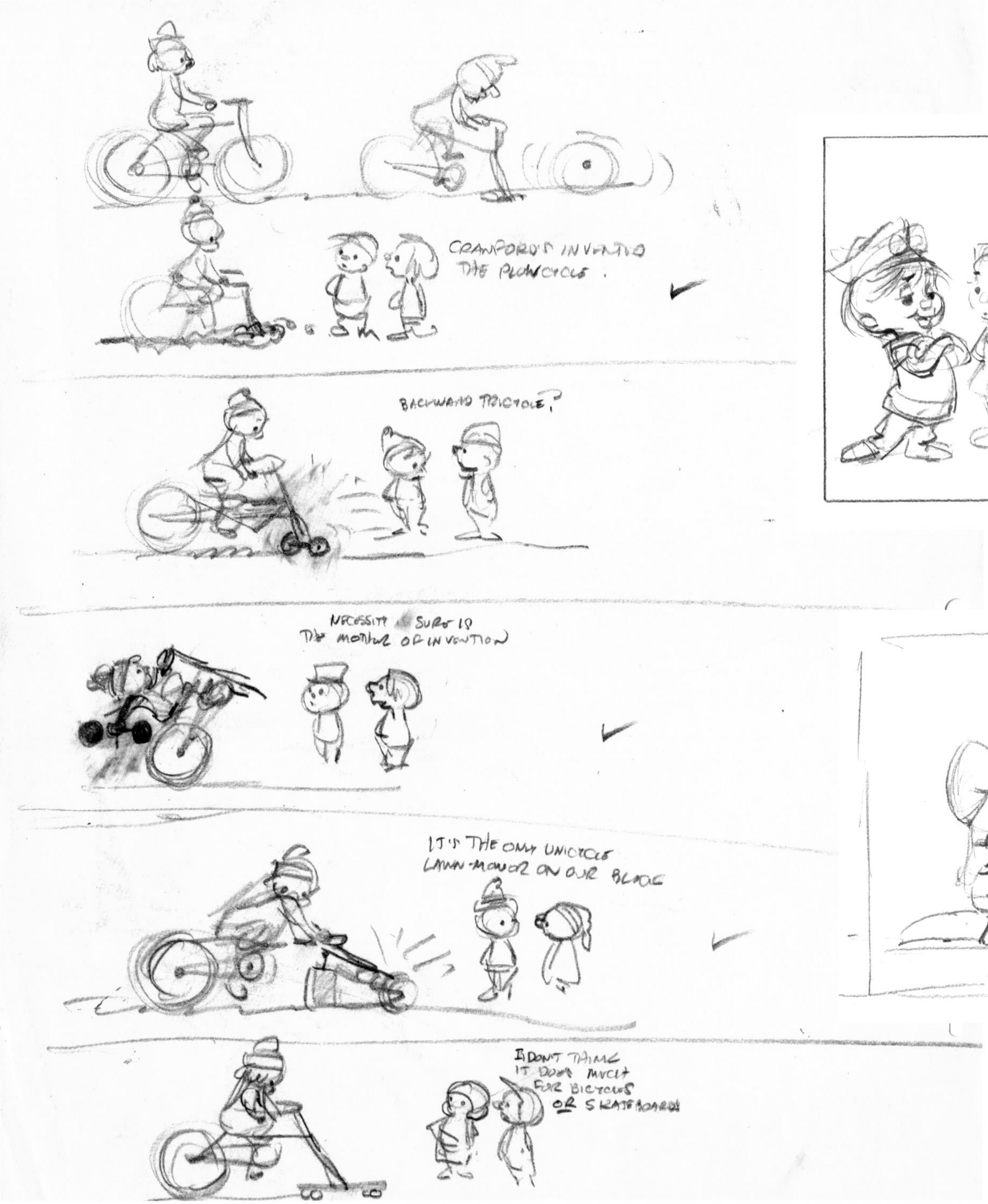
CRANFORD'S INVENTED THE PLOWCYCLE.
BACKWARD TRICYCLE?
NECESSITY SURE IS THE MOTHER OF INVENTION
IT'S THE ONLY UNICYCLE LAWN-MOWER ON OUR BLOCK
I DON'T THINK IT DOES MUCH FOR BICYCLES OR SKATEBOARDS

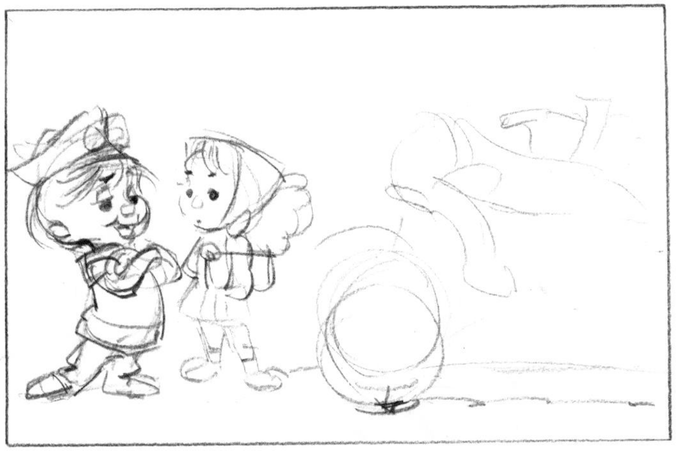

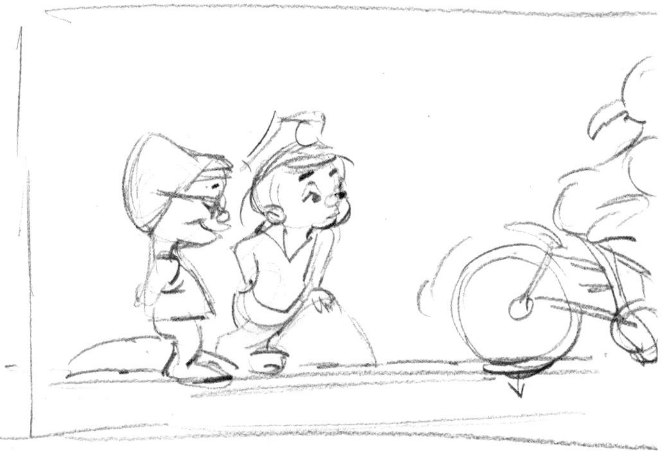

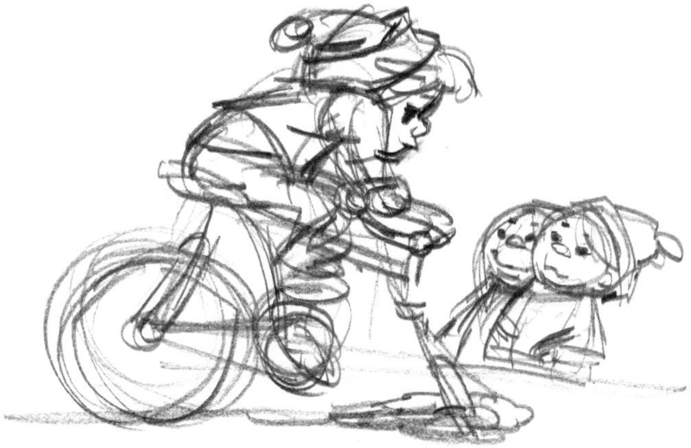

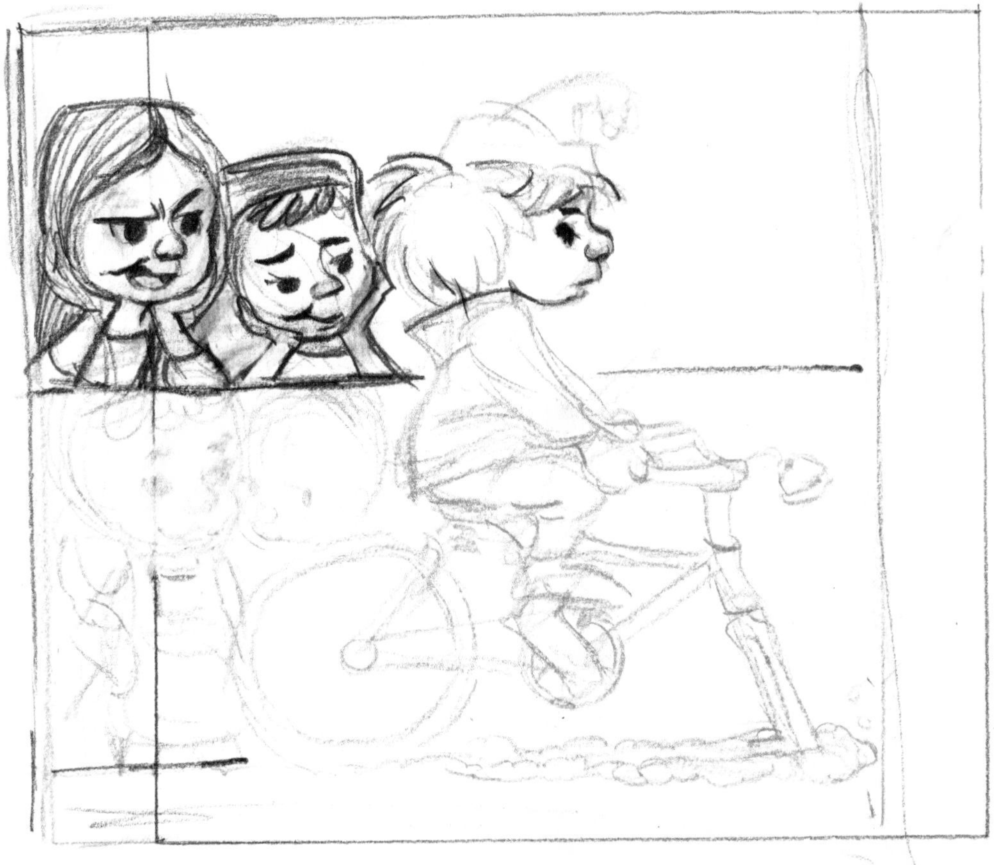

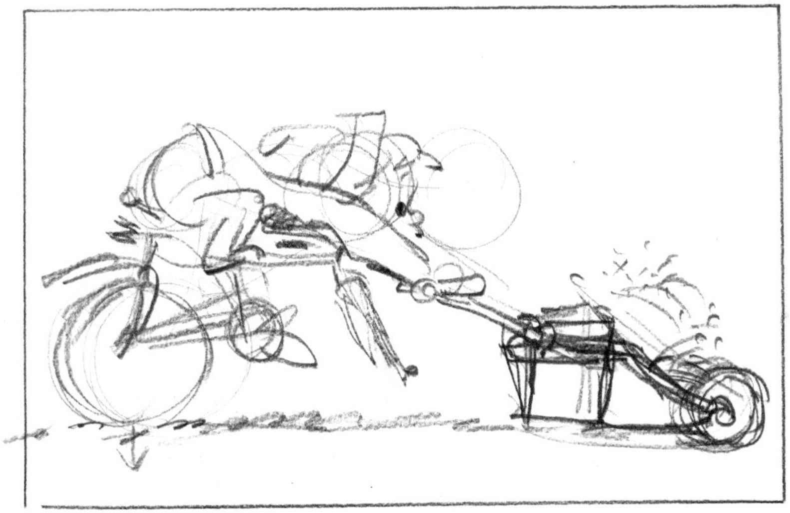

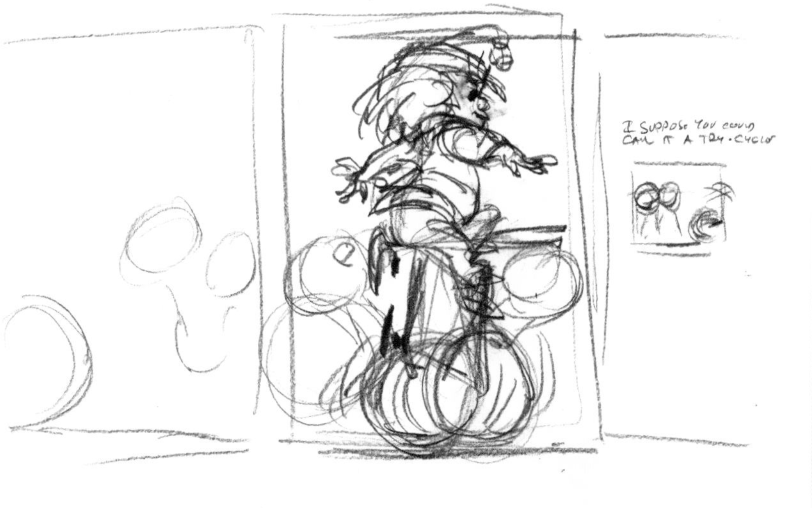
I SUPPOSE YOU COULD CALL IT A TRY-CYCLE

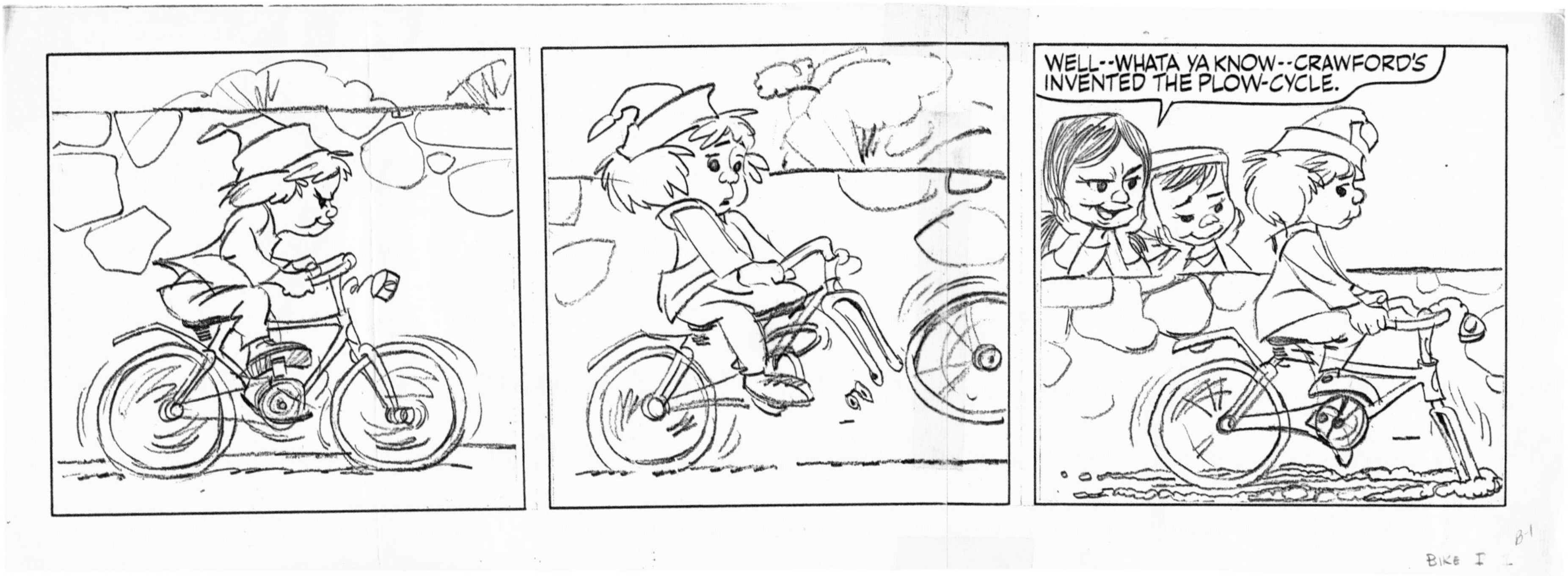
WELL--WHATA YA KNOW--CRAWFORD'S INVENTED THE PLOW-CYCLE.
BIKE I

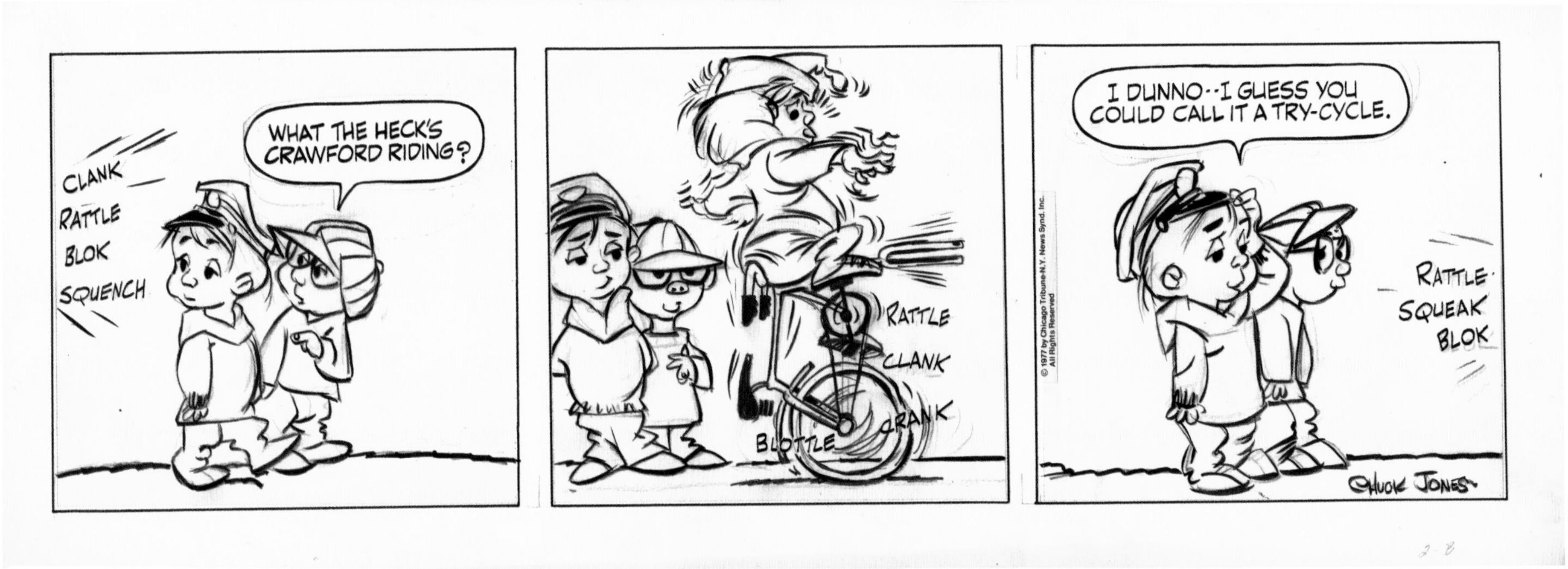
CLANK
RATTLE
BLOK
SQUENCH
WHAT THE HECK'S CRAWFORD RIDING?
RATTLE
CLANK
CRANK
BLOTTLE
© 1977 by Chicago Tribune-N.Y. News Synd. Inc. All Rights Reserved
I DUNNO--I GUESS YOU COULD CALL IT A TRY-CYCLE.
RATTLE
SQUEAK
BLOK
CHUCK JONES

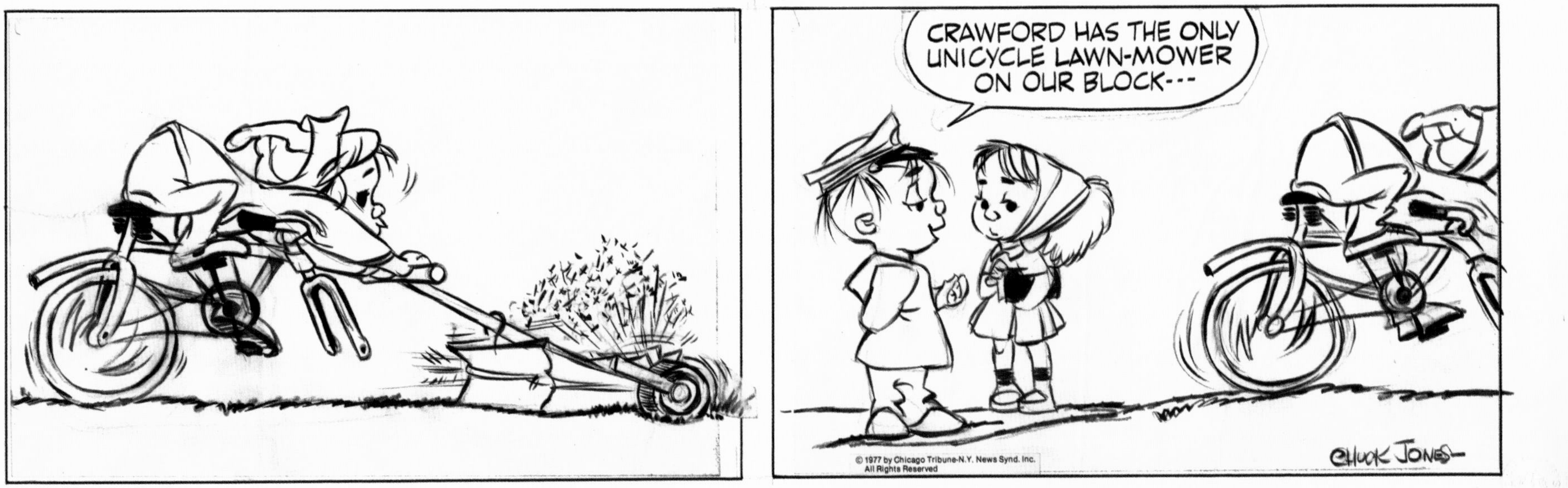
CRAWFORD HAS THE ONLY UNICYCLE LAWN-MOWER ON OUR BLOCK---
© 1977 by Chicago Tribune-N.Y. News Synd. Inc. All Rights Reserved
CHUCK JONES

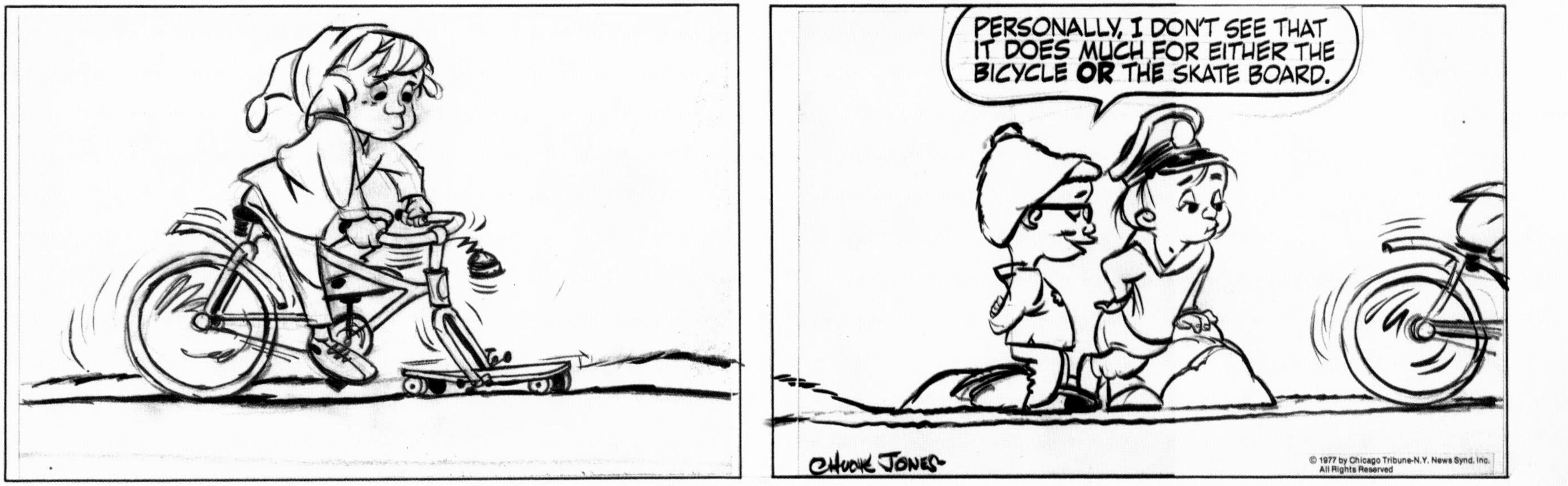
PERSONALLY, I DON'T SEE THAT IT DOES MUCH FOR EITHER THE BICYCLE **OR** THE SKATE BOARD.
CHUCK JONES
© 1977 by Chicago Tribune-N.Y. News Synd. Inc. All Rights Reserved

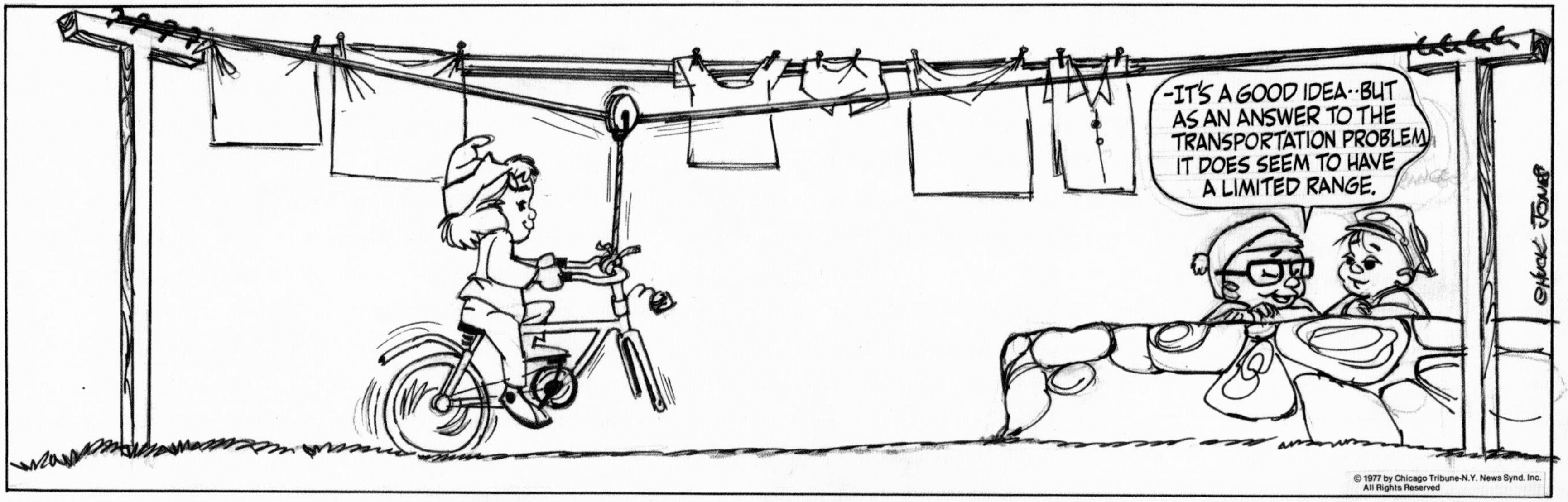
-IT'S A GOOD IDEA··BUT AS AN ANSWER TO THE TRANSPORTATION PROBLEM IT DOES SEEM TO HAVE A LIMITED RANGE.
CHUCK JONES
© 1977 by Chicago Tribune-N.Y. News Synd. Inc. All Rights Reserved

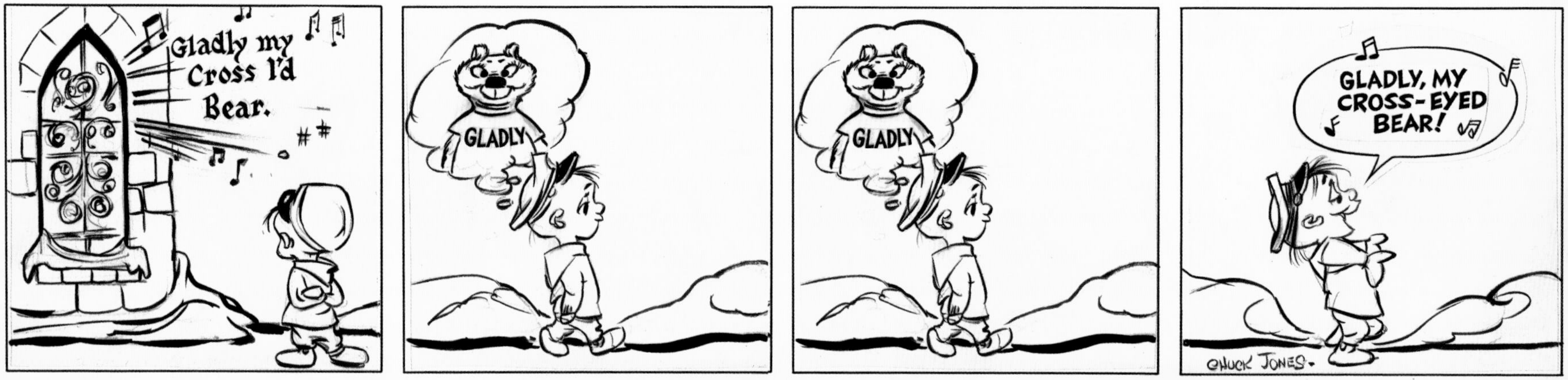
Gladly my Cross I'd Bear.
GLADLY
GLADLY
GLADLY, MY CROSS-EYED BEAR!
CHUCK JONES

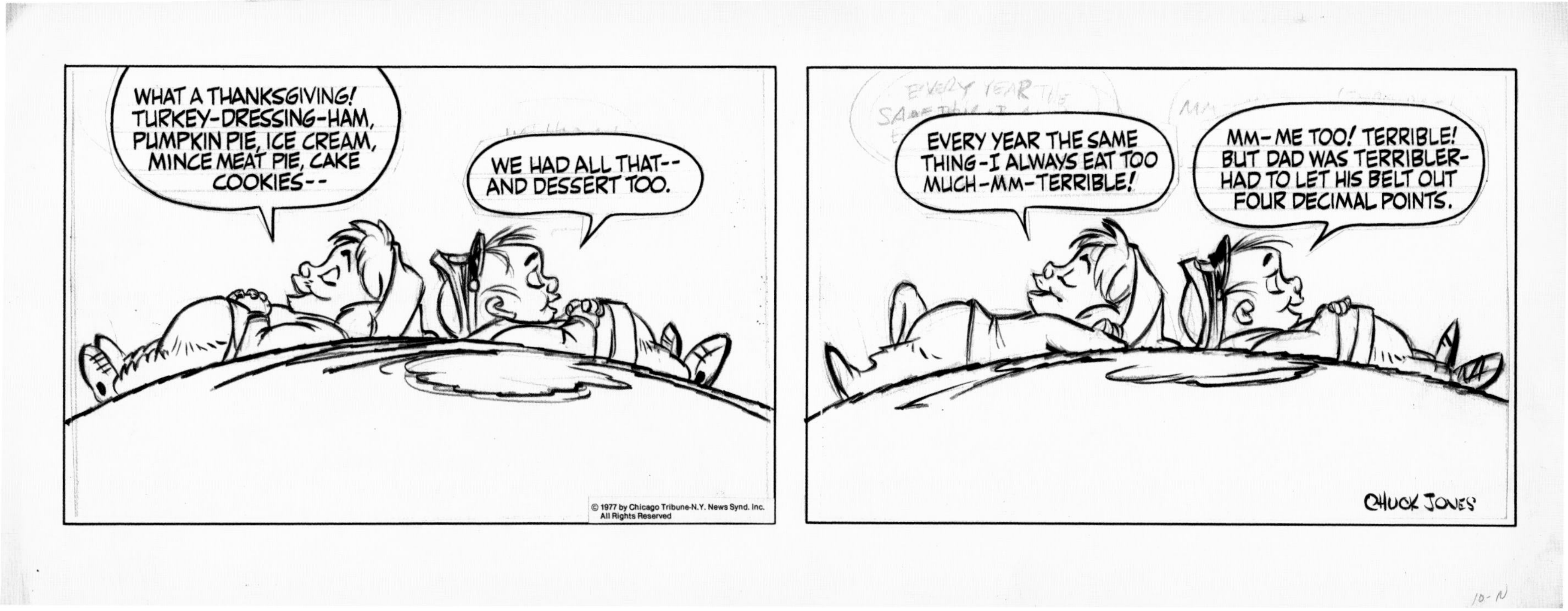
WHAT A THANKSGIVING! TURKEY-DRESSING-HAM, PUMPKIN PIE, ICE CREAM, MINCE MEAT PIE, CAKE COOKIES--
WE HAD ALL THAT--AND DESSERT TOO.
EVERY YEAR THE SAME THING-I ALWAYS EAT TOO MUCH-MM-TERRIBLE!
MM-ME TOO! TERRIBLE! BUT DAD WAS TERRIBLER-HAD TO LET HIS BELT OUT FOUR DECIMAL POINTS.
© 1977 by Chicago Tribune-N.Y. News Synd. Inc. All Rights Reserved
CHUCK JONES

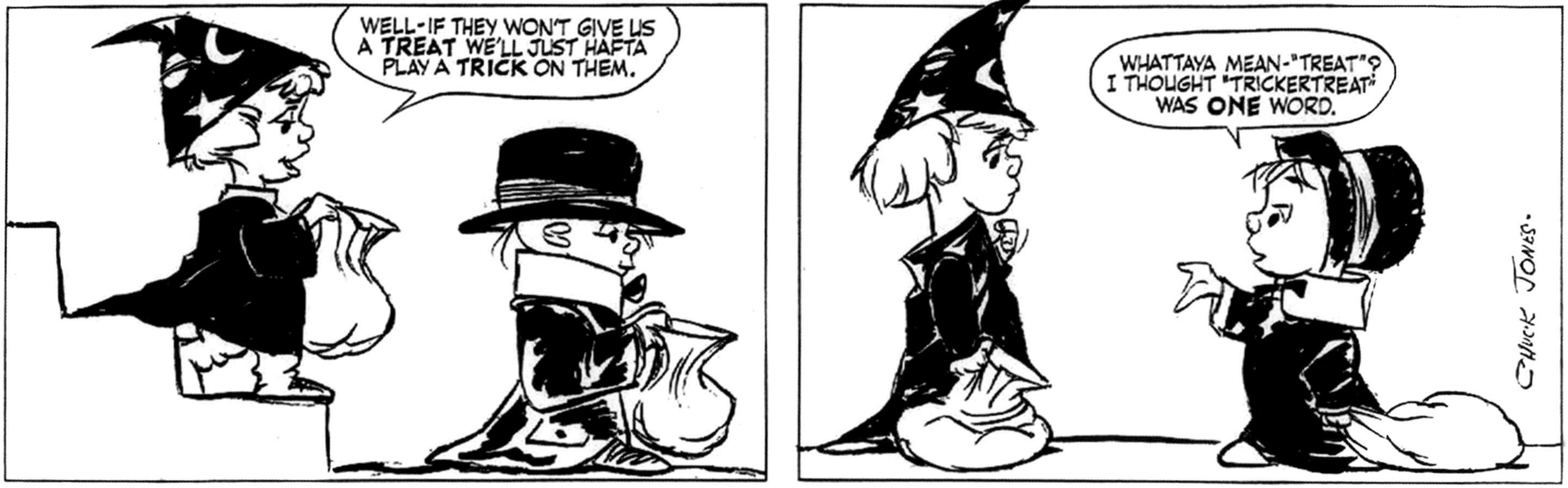
WELL-IF THEY WON'T GIVE US A **TREAT** WE'LL JUST HAFTA PLAY A **TRICK** ON THEM.
WHATTAYA MEAN-"TREAT"? I THOUGHT "TRICKERTREAT" WAS **ONE** WORD.
CHUCK JONES.

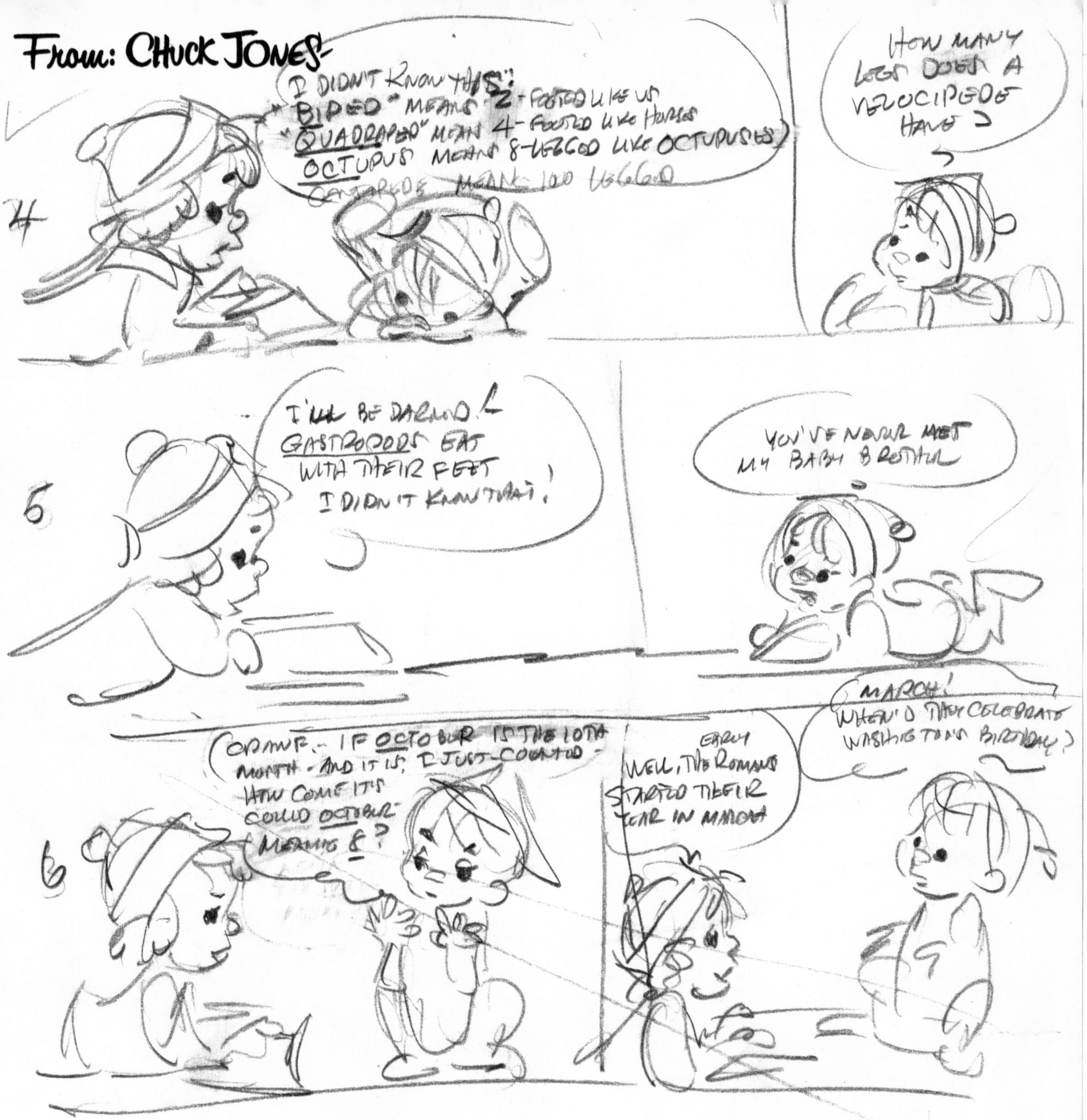
From: CHUCK JONES
I DIDN'T KNOW THIS! "BIPED" MEANS 2-FOOTED LIKE US "QUADRAPED" MEAN 4-FOOTED LIKE HORSES OCTUPUS MEANS 8-LEGGED LIKE OCTUPUSES CENTIPEDE MEANS 100 LEGGED
HOW MANY LEGS DOES A VELOCIPEDE HAVE?
I'LL BE DARNED! GASTROPODS EAT WITH THEIR FEET I DIDN'T KNOW THAT!
YOU'VE NEVER MET MY BABY BROTHER
IF OCTOBER IS THE 10TH MONTH — AND IT IS, I JUST COUNTED — HOW COME IT'S CALLED OCTOBER MEANING 8?
WELL, THE EARLY ROMANS STARTED THEIR YEAR IN MARCH
MARCH! WHEN'D THEY CELEBRATE WASHINGTON'S BIRTHDAY?

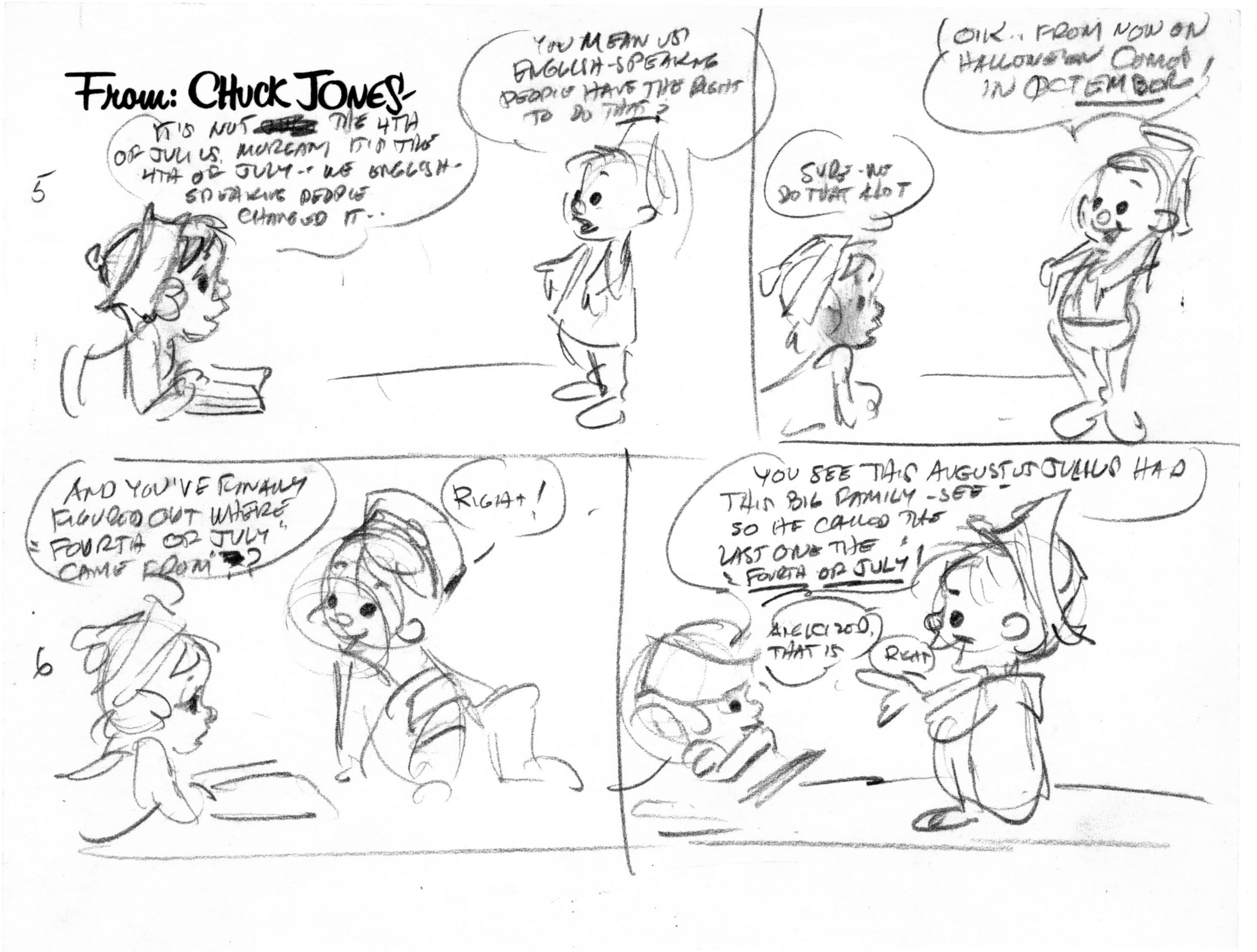
From: Chuck Jones
5
IT'S NOT THE 4TH OF JULIUS MORGAN IT'S THE 4TH OF JULY -- WE ENGLISH-SPEAKING PEOPLE CHANGED IT..
YOU MEAN US ENGLISH-SPEAKING PEOPLE HAVE THE RIGHT TO DO THAT?
SURE -- WE DO THAT ALOT
OK.. FROM NOW ON HALLOWEEN COMES IN OCTEMBER!
6
AND YOU'VE FINALLY FIGURED OUT WHERE "FOURTH OF JULY" CAME FROM?
RIGHT!
YOU SEE THIS AUGUSTUS JULIUS HAD THIS BIG FAMILY -- SEE -- SO HE CALLED THE LAST ONE THE "FOURTH OF JULY"!
THAT IS
RIGHT

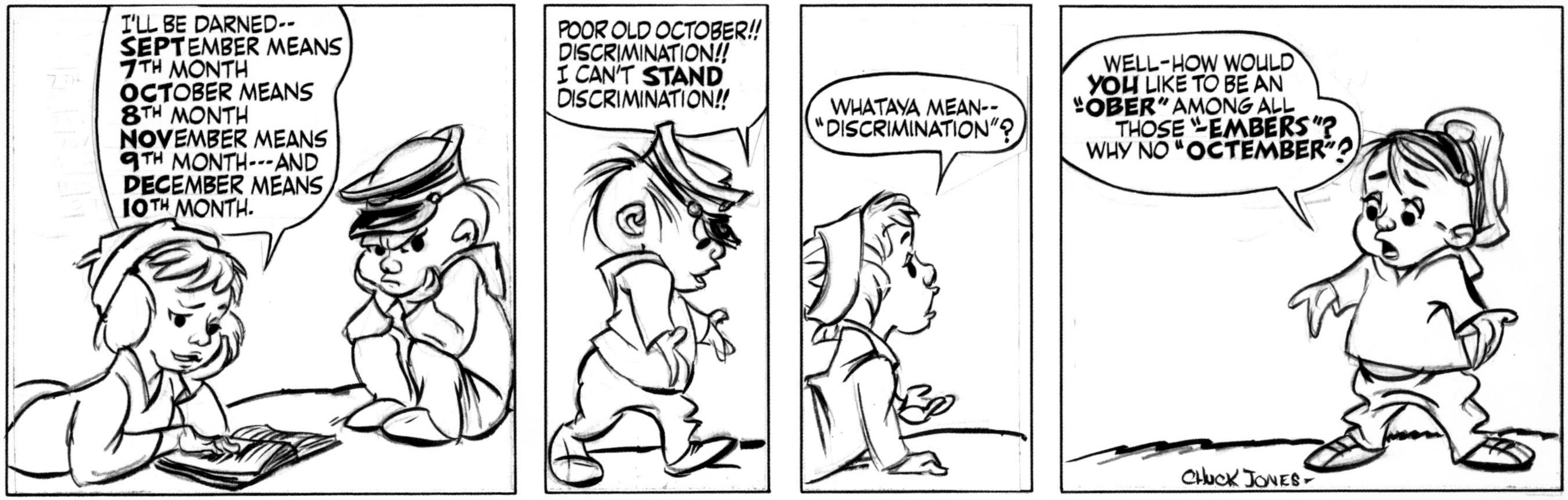
I'LL BE DARNED-- SEPTEMBER MEANS 7TH MONTH OCTOBER MEANS 8TH MONTH NOVEMBER MEANS 9TH MONTH---AND DECEMBER MEANS 10TH MONTH.
POOR OLD OCTOBER!! DISCRIMINATION!! I CAN'T STAND DISCRIMINATION!!
WHATAYA MEAN-- "DISCRIMINATION"?
WELL-HOW WOULD YOU LIKE TO BE AN "OBER" AMONG ALL THOSE "-EMBERS"? WHY NO "OCTEMBER"?
CHUCK JONES-

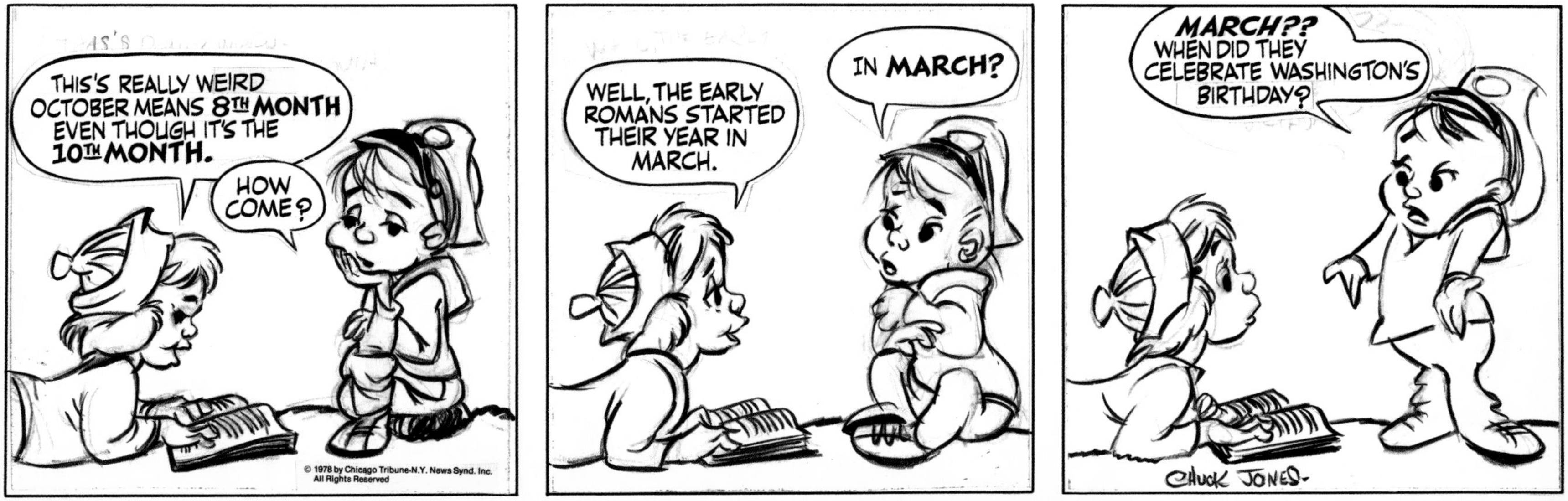
THIS'S REALLY WEIRD OCTOBER MEANS 8TH MONTH EVEN THOUGH IT'S THE 10TH MONTH.
HOW COME?
© 1978 by Chicago Tribune-N.Y. News Synd. Inc. All Rights Reserved
WELL, THE EARLY ROMANS STARTED THEIR YEAR IN MARCH.
IN MARCH?
MARCH?? WHEN DID THEY CELEBRATE WASHINGTON'S BIRTHDAY?
CHUCK JONES-

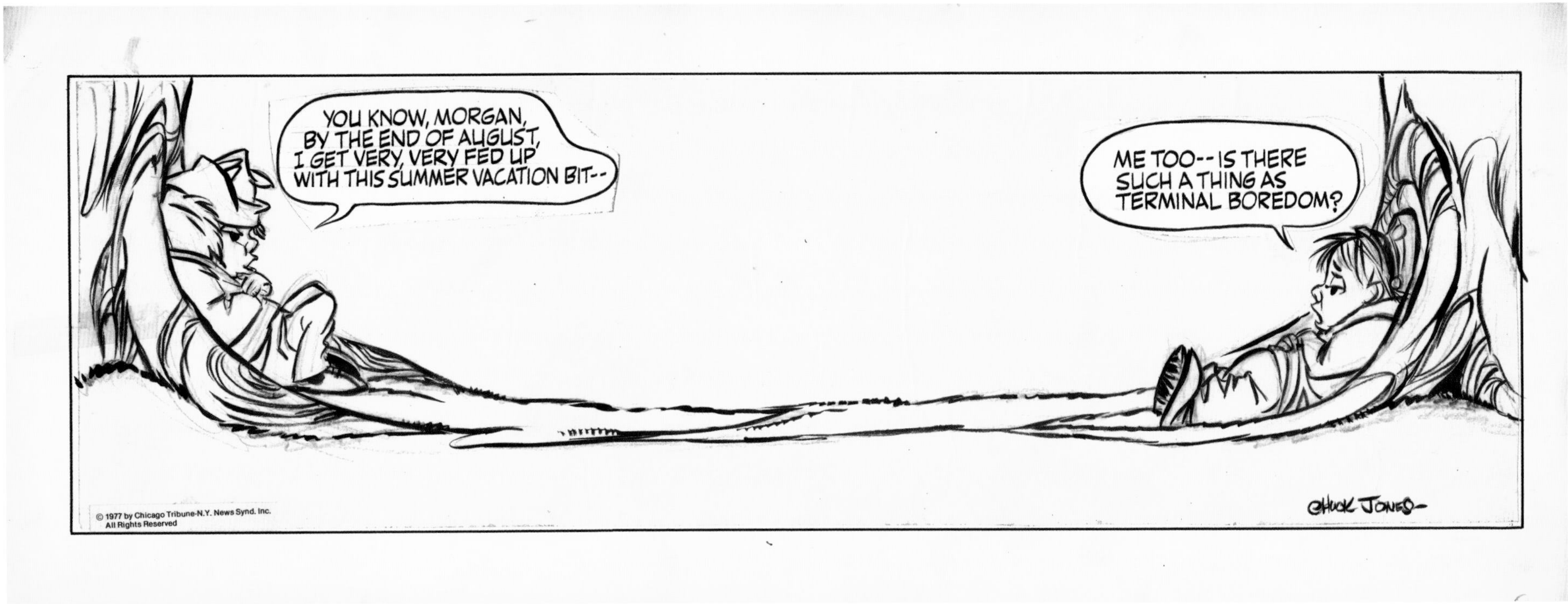
YOU KNOW, MORGAN, BY THE END OF AUGUST, I GET VERY, VERY FED UP WITH THIS SUMMER VACATION BIT--
ME TOO--IS THERE SUCH A THING AS TERMINAL BOREDOM?
© 1977 by Chicago Tribune-N.Y. News Synd. Inc. All Rights Reserved
CHUCK JONES

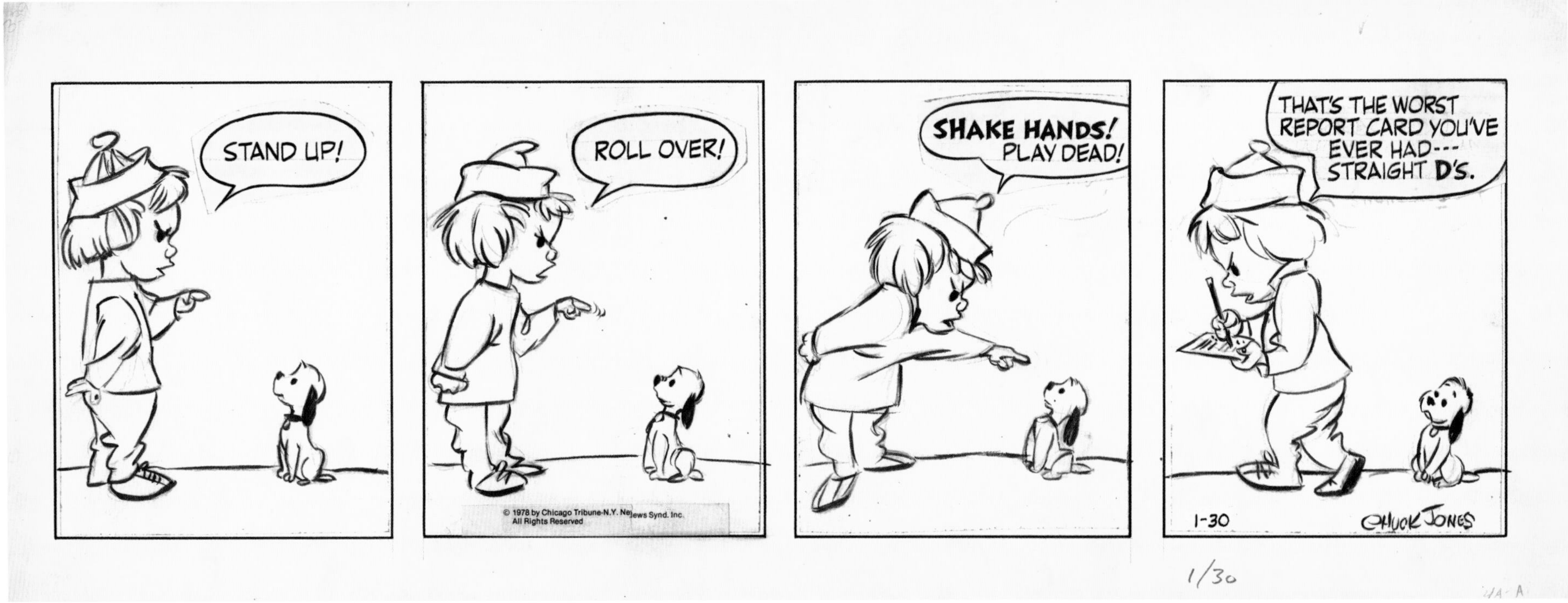
STAND UP!
ROLL OVER!
SHAKE HANDS! PLAY DEAD!
THAT'S THE WORST REPORT CARD YOU'VE EVER HAD--- STRAIGHT D'S.
© 1978 by Chicago Tribune-N.Y. News Synd. Inc. All Rights Reserved
1-30
CHUCK JONES
1/30

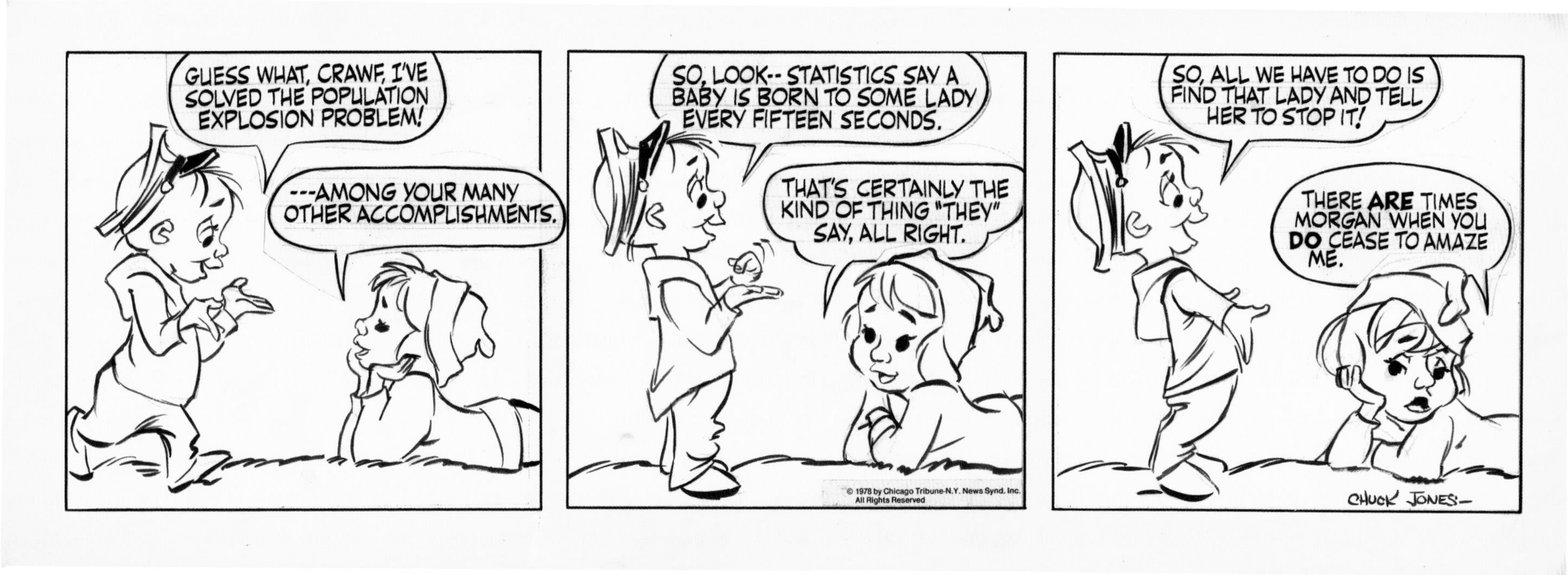
GUESS WHAT, CRAWF, I'VE SOLVED THE POPULATION EXPLOSION PROBLEM!
---AMONG YOUR MANY OTHER ACCOMPLISHMENTS.
SO, LOOK-- STATISTICS SAY A BABY IS BORN TO SOME LADY EVERY FIFTEEN SECONDS.
THAT'S CERTAINLY THE KIND OF THING "THEY" SAY, ALL RIGHT.
© 1978 by Chicago Tribune-N.Y. News Synd. Inc. All Rights Reserved
SO, ALL WE HAVE TO DO IS FIND THAT LADY AND TELL HER TO STOP IT!
THERE **ARE** TIMES MORGAN WHEN YOU **DO** CEASE TO AMAZE ME.
CHUCK JONES

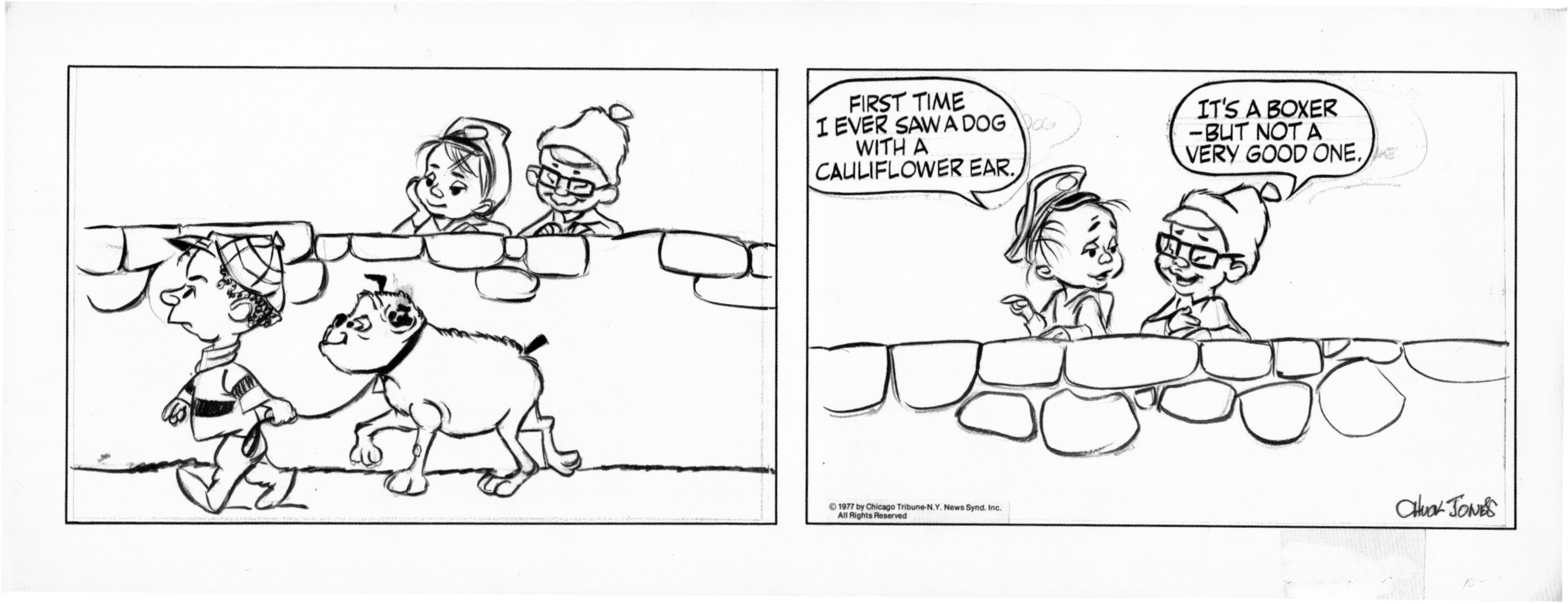
FIRST TIME I EVER SAW A DOG WITH A CAULIFLOWER EAR.
IT'S A BOXER –BUT NOT A VERY GOOD ONE.
© 1977 by Chicago Tribune-N.Y. News Synd. Inc. All Rights Reserved
CHUCK JONES

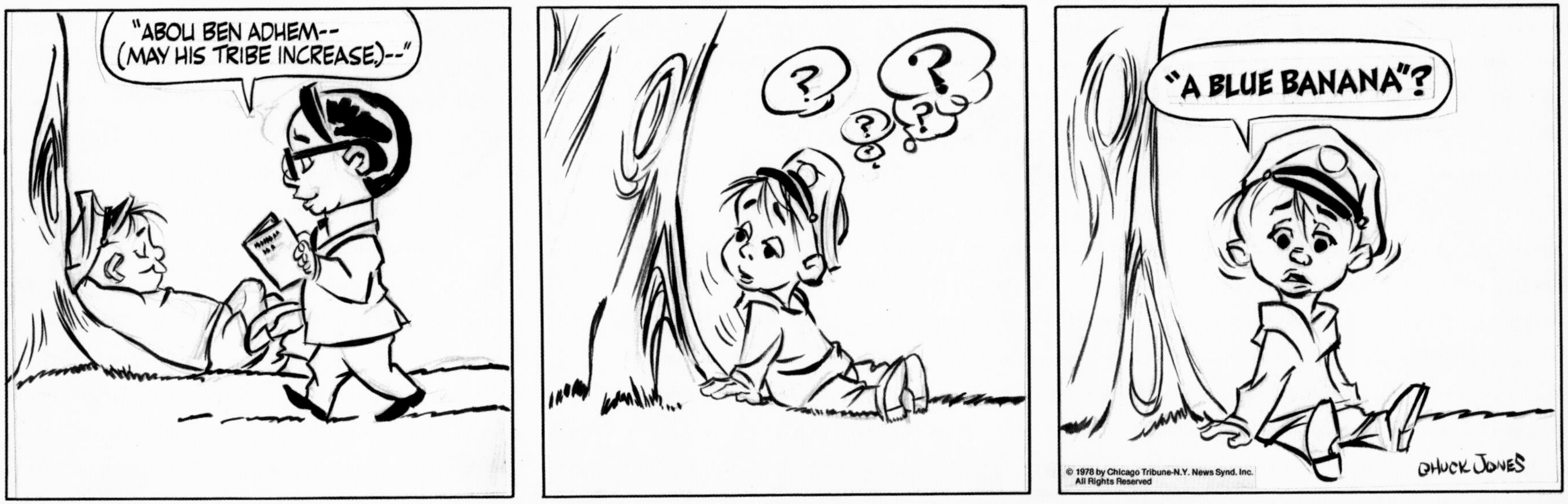
"ABOU BEN ADHEM--
(MAY HIS TRIBE INCREASE.)--"
?
?
?
?
"A BLUE BANANA"?
© 1978 by Chicago Tribune-N.Y. News Synd. Inc.
All Rights Reserved
CHUCK JONES

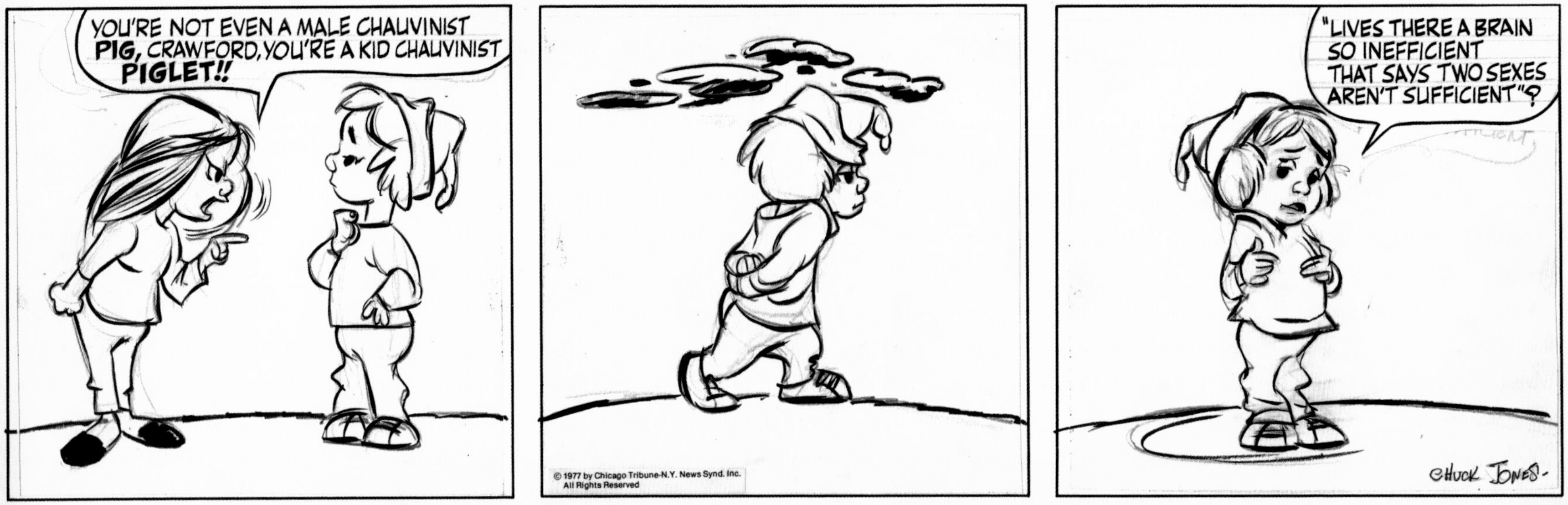
YOU'RE NOT EVEN A MALE CHAUVINIST **PIG,** CRAWFORD, YOU'RE A KID CHAUVINIST **PIGLET!!**
© 1977 by Chicago Tribune-N.Y. News Synd. Inc.
All Rights Reserved
"LIVES THERE A BRAIN SO INEFFICIENT THAT SAYS TWO SEXES AREN'T SUFFICIENT"?
CHUCK JONES-

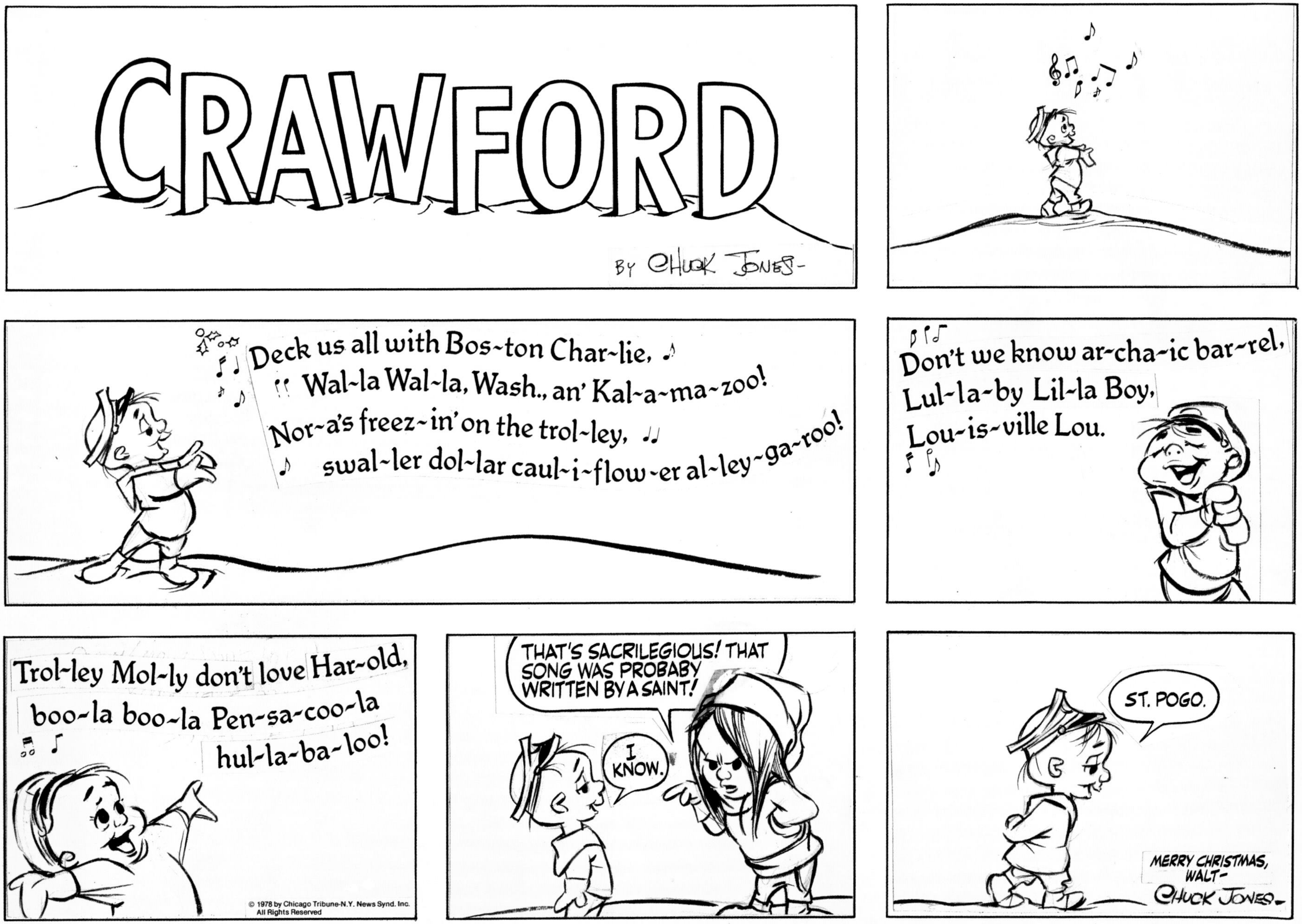
CRAWFORD
BY CHUCK JONES
Deck us all with Bos~ton Char~lie,
Wal~la Wal~la, Wash., an' Kal~a~ma~zoo!
Nor~a's freez~in' on the trol~ley,
swal~ler dol~lar caul~i~flow~er al~ley~ga~roo!
Don't we know ar~cha~ic bar~rel,
Lul~la~by Lil~la Boy,
Lou~is~ville Lou.
Trol~ley Mol~ly don't love Har~old,
boo~la boo~la Pen~sa~coo~la
hul~la~ba~loo!
© 1978 by Chicago Tribune-N.Y. News Synd. Inc. All Rights Reserved
THAT'S SACRILEGIOUS! THAT SONG WAS PROBABY WRITTEN BY A SAINT!
I KNOW.
ST. POGO.
MERRY CHRISTMAS, WALT—
CHUCK JONES—

Morgan is singing the first stanza of the Christmas carol sung annually by the citizens of Okefenokee Swamp in Walt Kelly's *Pogo*. Coincidentally, Kelly's middle name was Crawford.

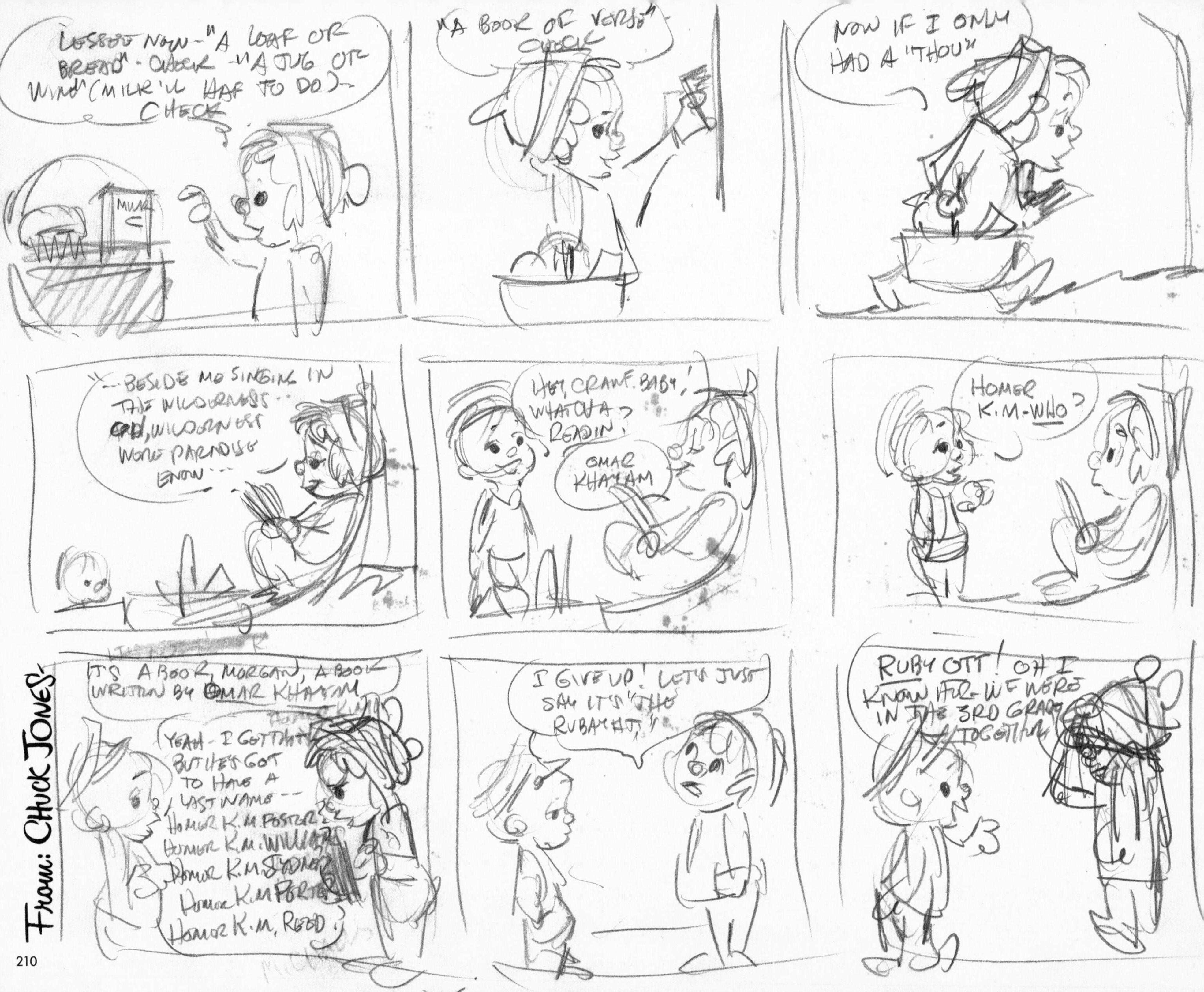
LESSEE NOW—"A LOAF OF BREAD"—CHECK—"A JUG OF WINE" (MILK'LL HAF TO DO)—CHECK
"A BOOK OF VERSE"—CHECK
NOW IF I ONLY HAD A "THOU"
"...BESIDE ME SINGING IN THE WILDERNESS—OH, WILDERNESS WERE PARADISE ENOW..."
HEY, CRANE BABY, WHATCHA READIN'?
OMAR KHAYAM
HOMER K.M.-WHO?
IT'S A BOOK, MORGAN, A BOOK WRITTEN BY OMAR KHAYAM
YEAH—I GOT THAT BUT HE'S GOT TO HAVE A LAST NAME—HOMER K.M. FOSTER? HOMER K.M. PORTER? HOMER K.M. REED?
I GIVE UP! LET'S JUST SAY IT'S "THE RUBAYAT"!
RUBY OTT! OH I KNOW HER—WE WERE IN THE 3RD GRADE TOGETHER

From: Chuck Jones

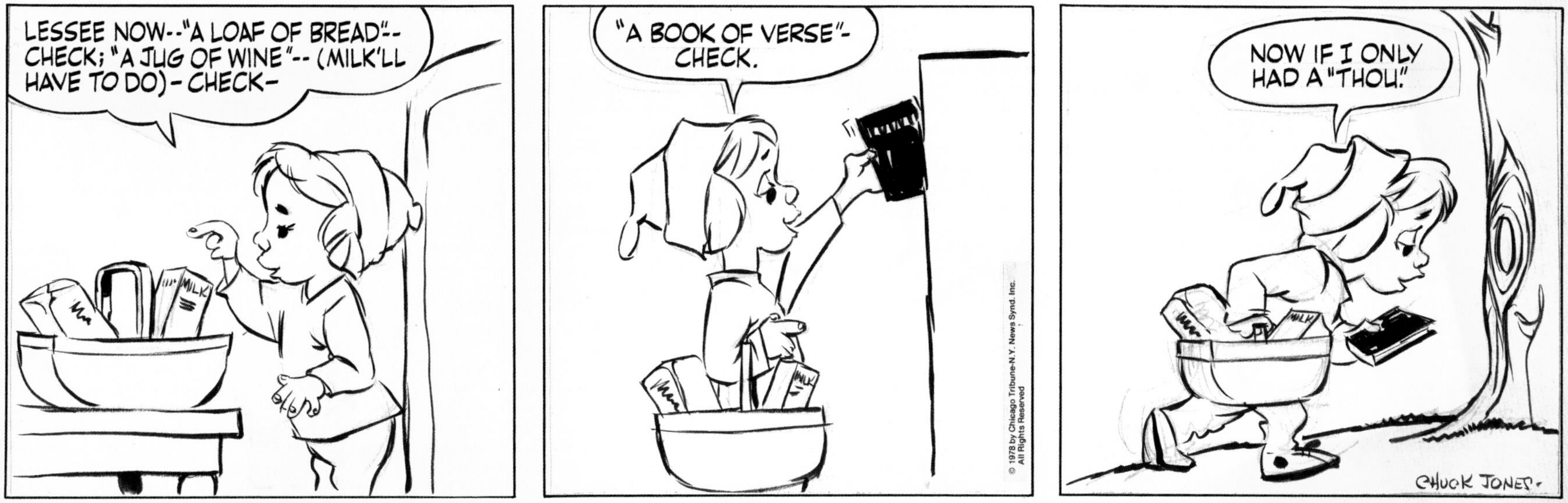
LESSEE NOW--"A LOAF OF BREAD"-CHECK; "A JUG OF WINE"-- (MILK'LL HAVE TO DO)-CHECK-
"A BOOK OF VERSE"-CHECK.
© 1978 by Chicago Tribune-N.Y. News Synd. Inc. All Rights Reserved
NOW IF I ONLY HAD A "THOU."
CHUCK JONES

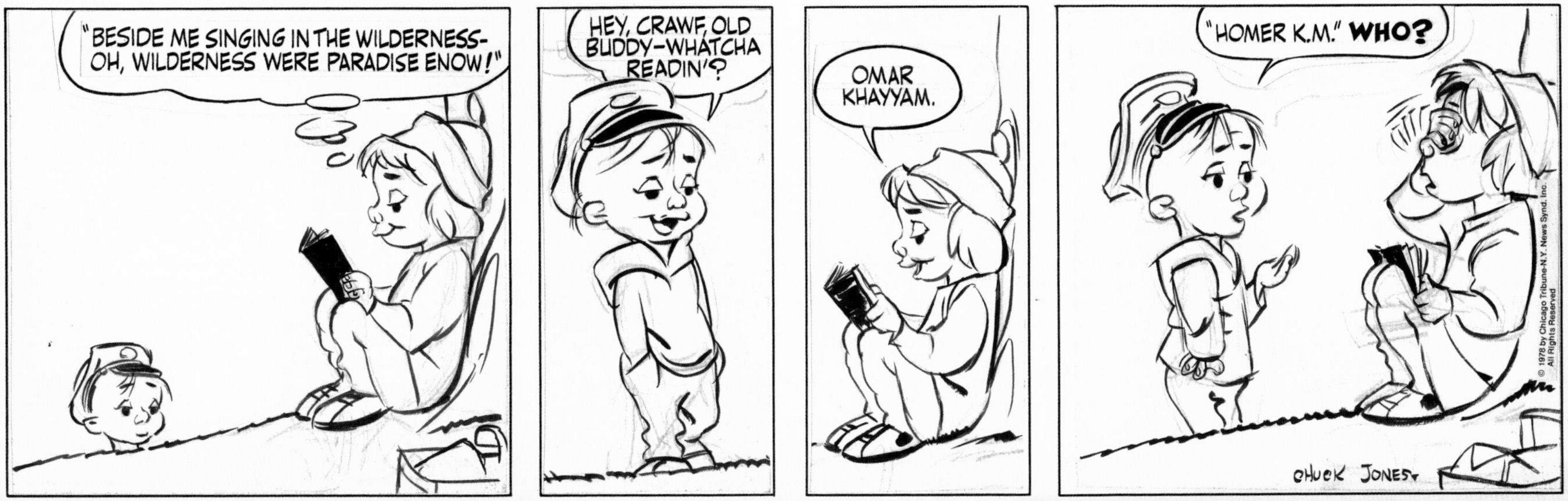
"BESIDE ME SINGING IN THE WILDERNESS-OH, WILDERNESS WERE PARADISE ENOW!"
HEY, CRAWF, OLD BUDDY-WHATCHA READIN'?
OMAR KHAYYAM.
"HOMER K.M." WHO?
© 1978 by Chicago Tribune-N.Y. News Synd. Inc. All Rights Reserved
CHUCK JONES

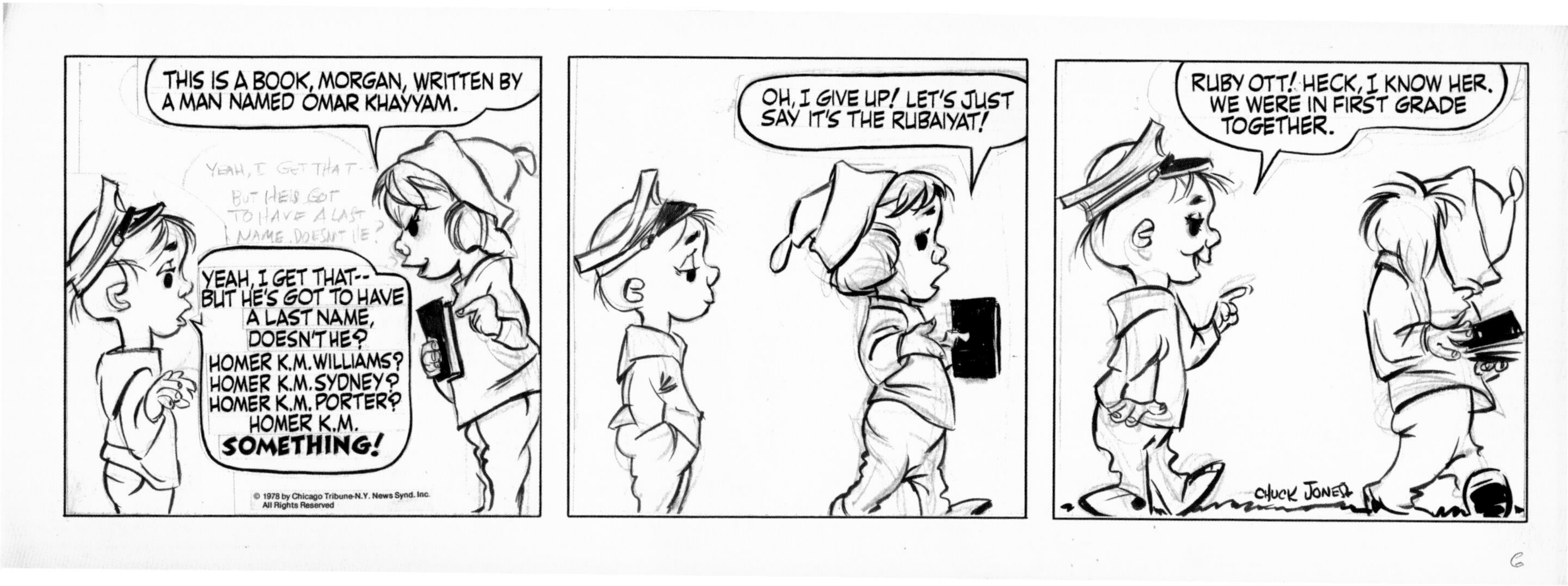
THIS IS A BOOK, MORGAN, WRITTEN BY A MAN NAMED OMAR KHAYYAM.
YEAH, I GET THAT-- BUT HE'S GOT TO HAVE A LAST NAME, DOESN'T HE? HOMER K.M. WILLIAMS? HOMER K.M. SYDNEY? HOMER K.M. PORTER? HOMER K.M. SOMETHING!
© 1978 by Chicago Tribune-N.Y. News Synd. Inc. All Rights Reserved
OH, I GIVE UP! LET'S JUST SAY IT'S THE RUBAIYAT!
RUBY OTT! HECK, I KNOW HER. WE WERE IN FIRST GRADE TOGETHER.
CHUCK JONES

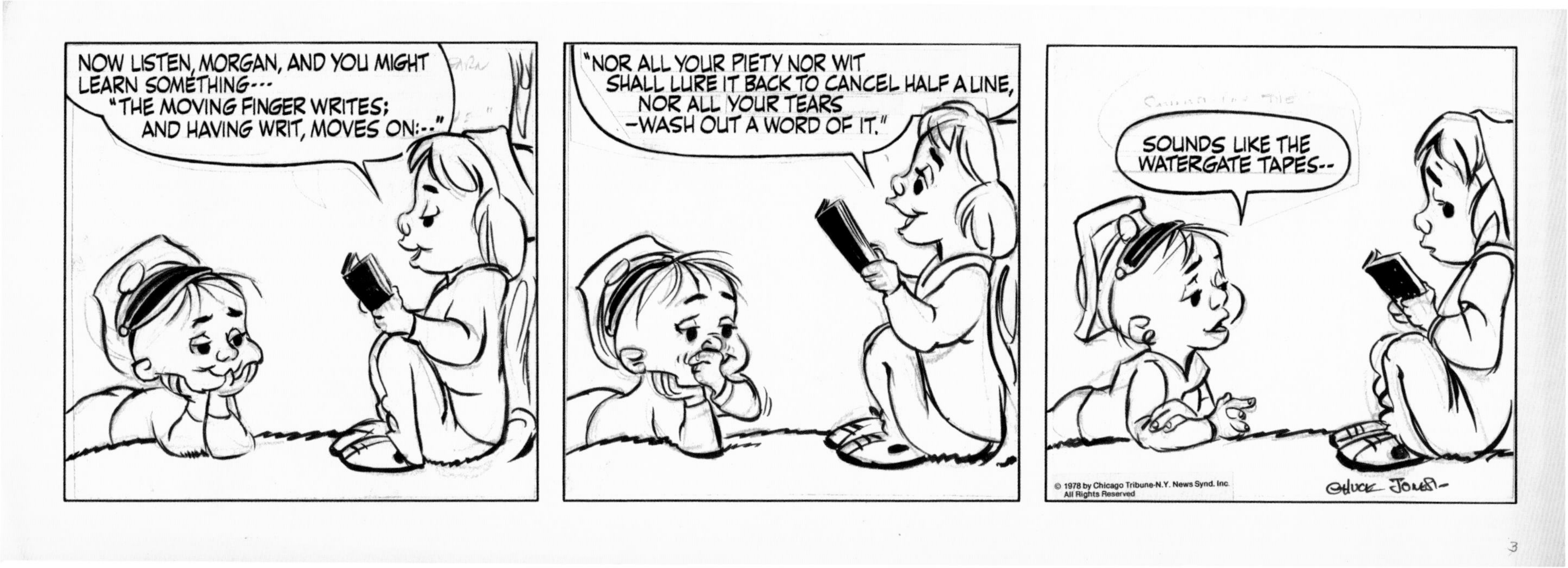
NOW LISTEN, MORGAN, AND YOU MIGHT LEARN SOMETHING--- "THE MOVING FINGER WRITES; AND HAVING WRIT, MOVES ON:--"
"NOR ALL YOUR PIETY NOR WIT SHALL LURE IT BACK TO CANCEL HALF A LINE, NOR ALL YOUR TEARS -WASH OUT A WORD OF IT."
SOUNDS LIKE THE WATERGATE TAPES--
© 1978 by Chicago Tribune-N.Y. News Synd. Inc. All Rights Reserved
CHUCK JONES

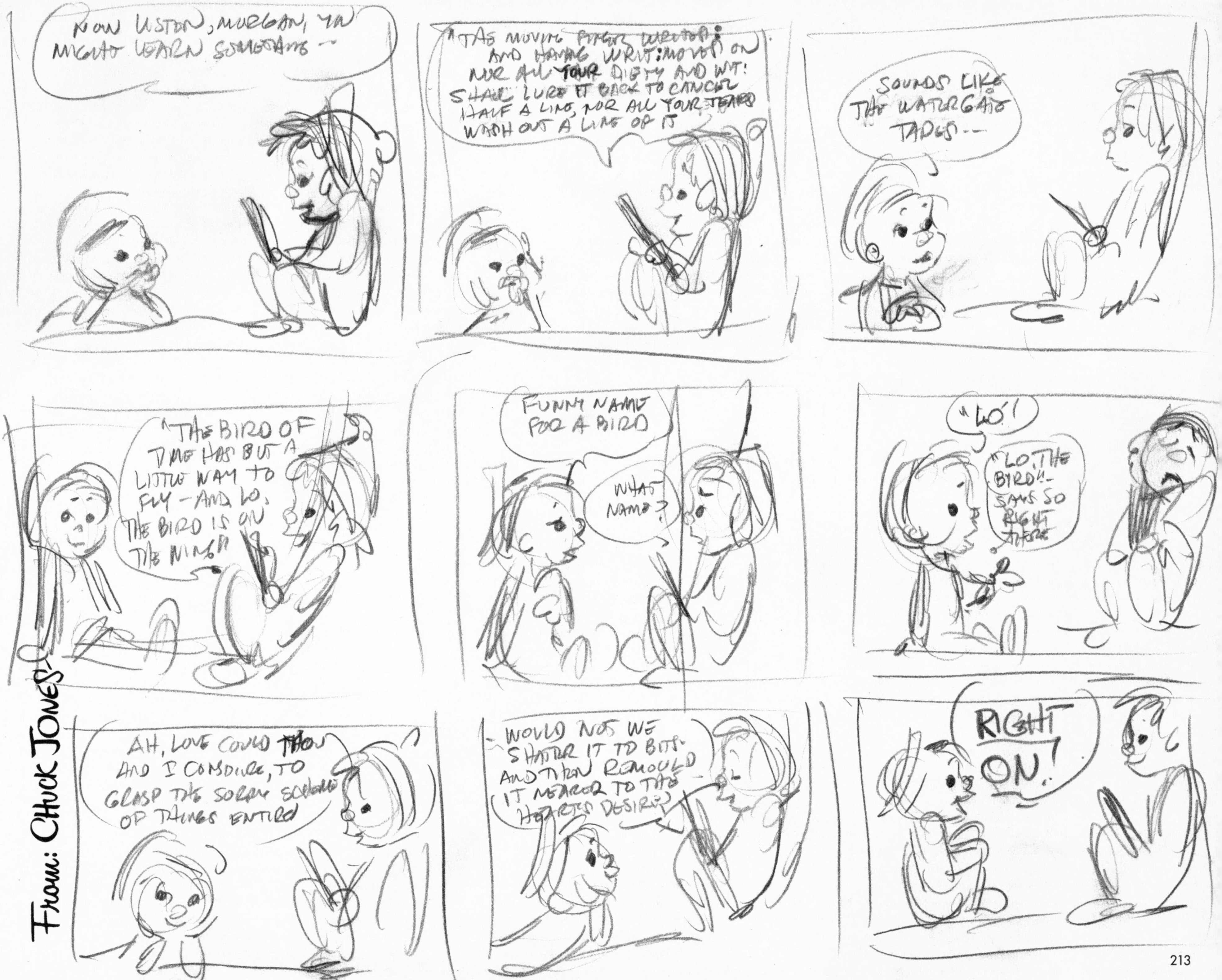
NOW LISTEN, MORGAN, YOU MIGHT LEARN SOMETHING --
"THE MOVING FINGER WRITES; AND HAVING WRIT, MOVES ON NOR ALL YOUR PIETY AND WIT SHALL LURE IT BACK TO CANCEL HALF A LINE, NOR ALL YOUR TEARS WASH OUT A LINE OF IT
SOUNDS LIKE THE WATERGATE TAPES...
"THE BIRD OF TIME HAS BUT A LITTLE WAY TO FLY – AND LO, THE BIRD IS ON THE WING!"
FUNNY NAME FOR A BIRD
WHAT NAME?
"LO"!
"LO, THE BIRD"! SAYS SO RIGHT THERE
AH, LOVE COULD THOU AND I CONSPIRE, TO GRASP THE SORRY SCHEME OF THINGS ENTIRE
WOULD NOT WE SHATTER IT TO BITS AND THEN REMOULD IT NEARER TO THE HEART'S DESIRE?
RIGHT ON!
From: CHUCK JONES

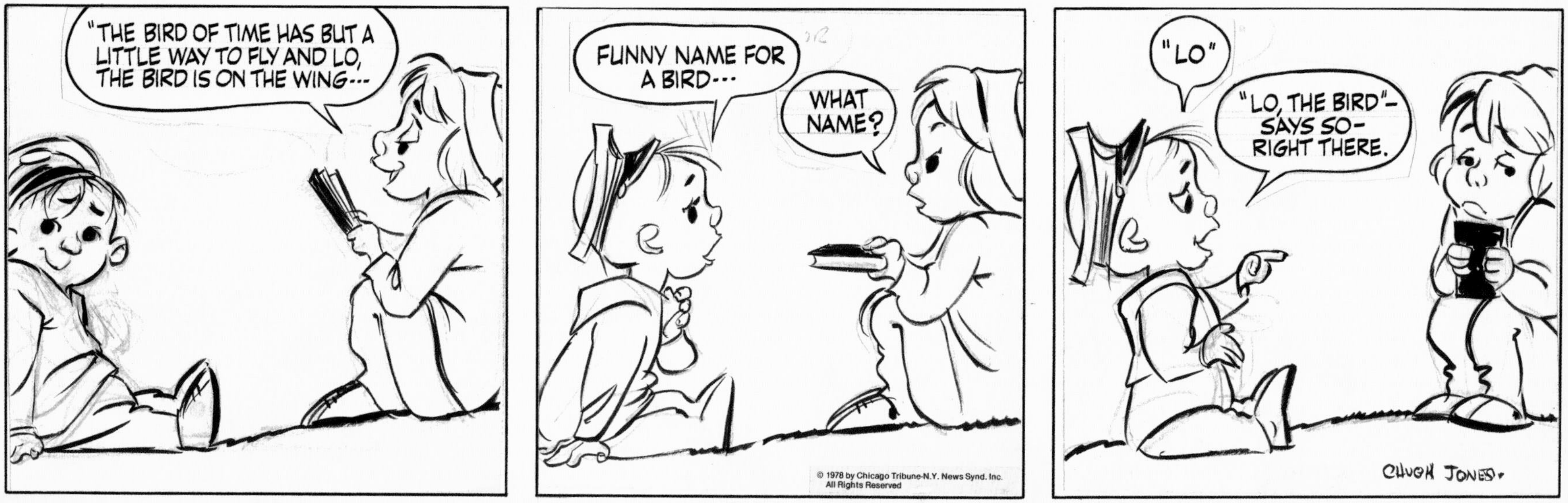
"THE BIRD OF TIME HAS BUT A LITTLE WAY TO FLY AND LO, THE BIRD IS ON THE WING---
FUNNY NAME FOR A BIRD---
WHAT NAME?
© 1978 by Chicago Tribune-N.Y. News Synd. Inc. All Rights Reserved
"LO"
"LO, THE BIRD"– SAYS SO– RIGHT THERE.
CHUCK JONES

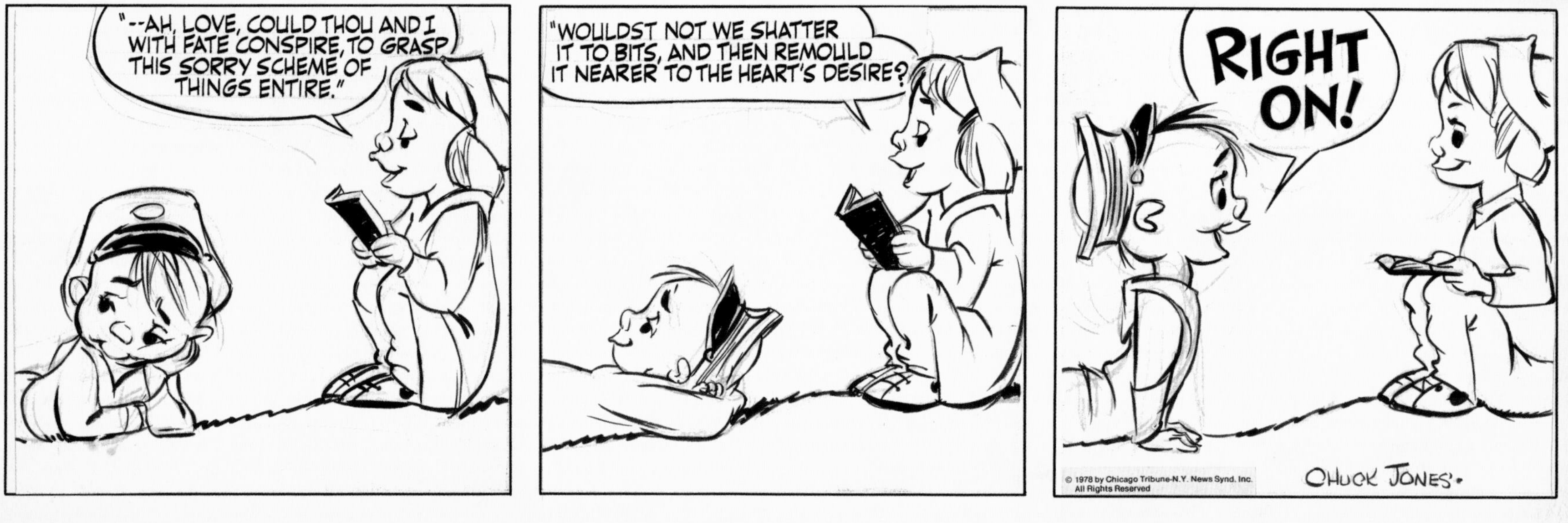
"--AH, LOVE, COULD THOU AND I WITH FATE CONSPIRE, TO GRASP THIS SORRY SCHEME OF THINGS ENTIRE."
"WOULDST NOT WE SHATTER IT TO BITS, AND THEN REMOULD IT NEARER TO THE HEART'S DESIRE?"
RIGHT ON!
© 1978 by Chicago Tribune-N.Y. News Synd. Inc. All Rights Reserved
CHUCK JONES

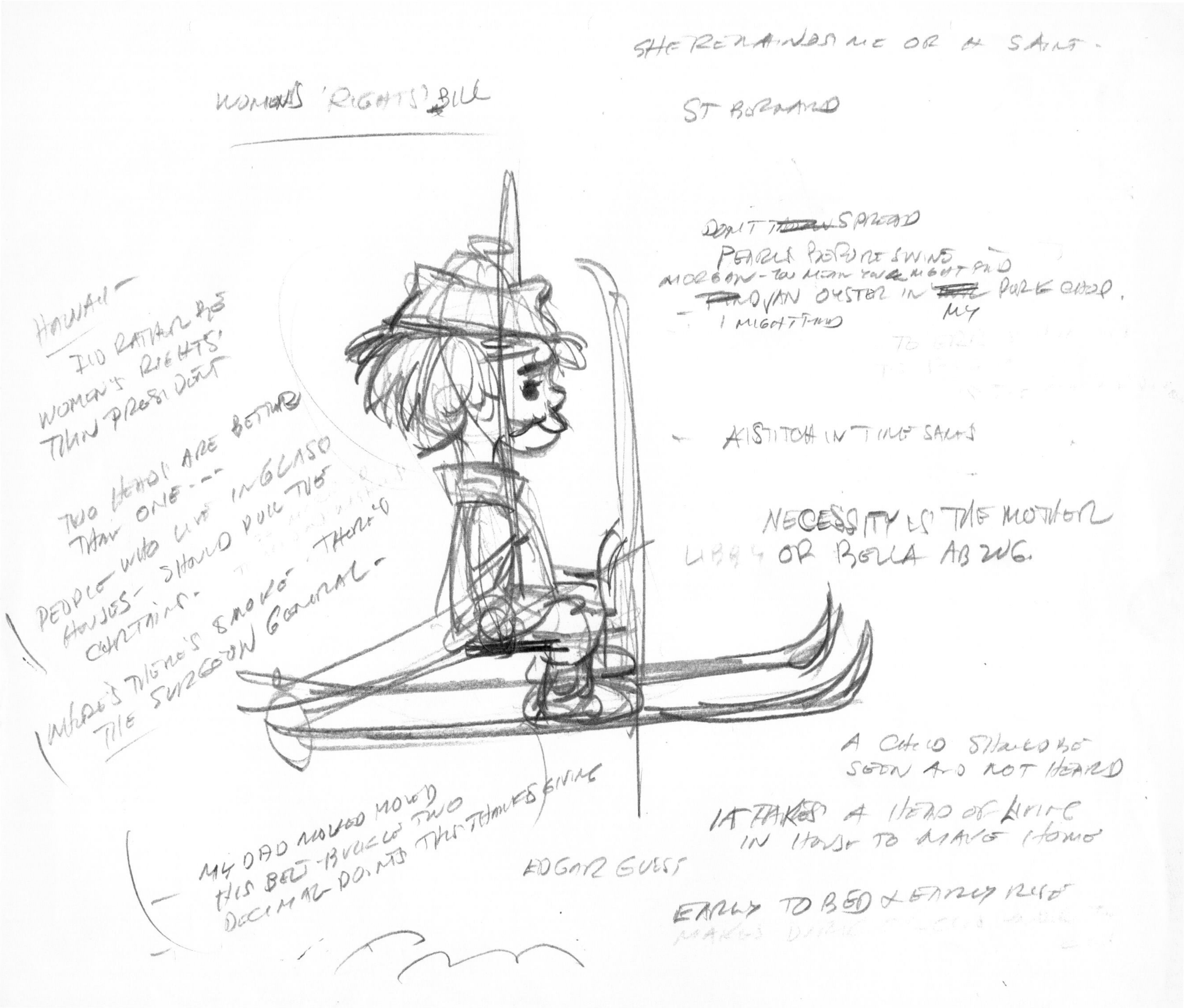
WOMENS 'RIGHTS' BILL
ST BERNARD
DON'T SPREAD PEARLS BEFORE SWINE
A STITCH IN TIME SAVES
NECESSITY IS THE MOTHER
OR BELLA ABZUG.
A CHILD SHOULD BE SEEN AND NOT HEARD
IT TAKES A HEAP OF LIVING IN HOUSE TO MAKE HOME
EDGAR GUEST
EARLY TO BED & EARLY RISE
I'D RATHER BE WOMEN'S RIGHTS THAN PRESIDENT
TWO HEADS ARE BETTER THAN ONE ---
PEOPLE WHO LIVE IN GLASS HOUSES - SHOULD PULL THE CURTAINS.
WHERE'S THERE'S SMOKE THERE'S THE SURGEON GENERAL -
MY DAD MOVED HIS BELT BUCKLE TWO DECIMAL POINTS THIS THANKSGIVING

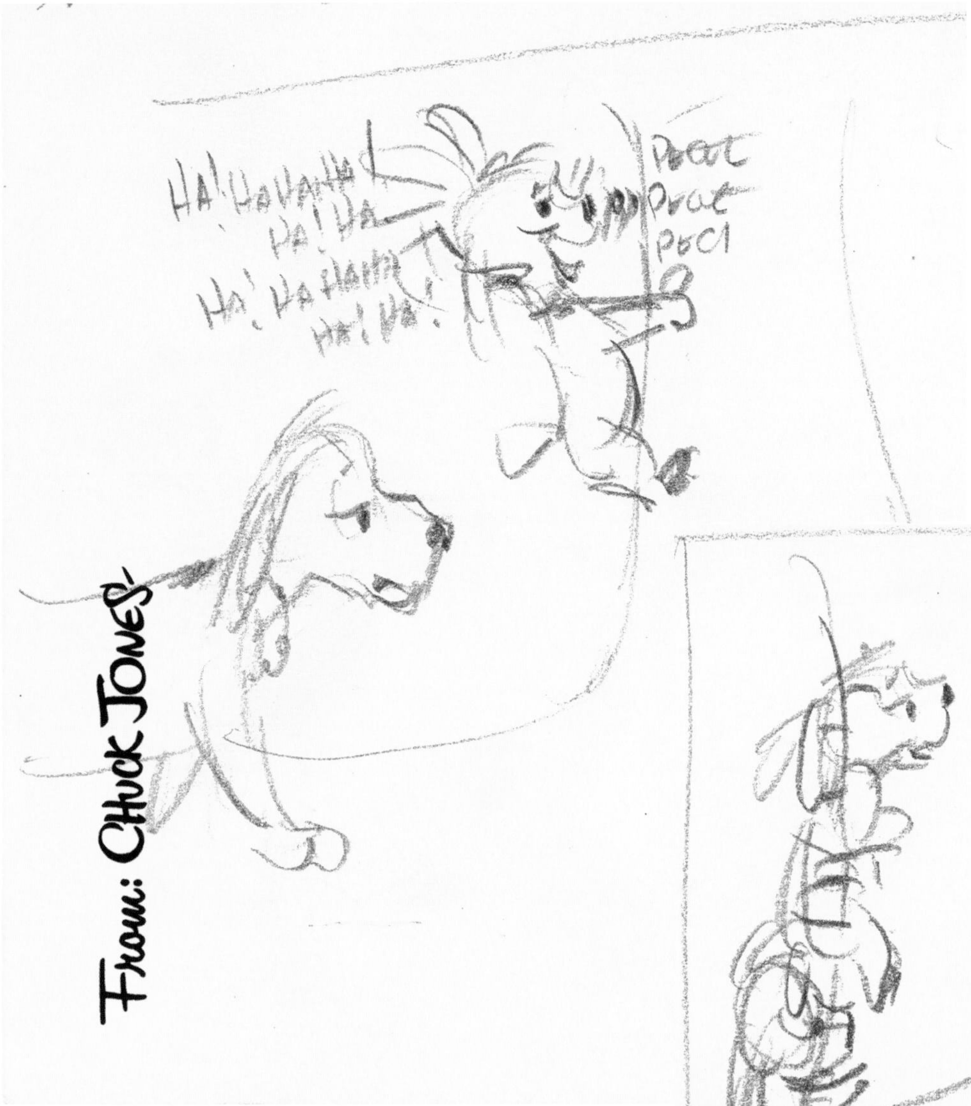
HA! HA HA HA! HA! HA!
HA! HA HA HA! HA! HA!
PECK
PECK
PECK
From: CHUCK JONES

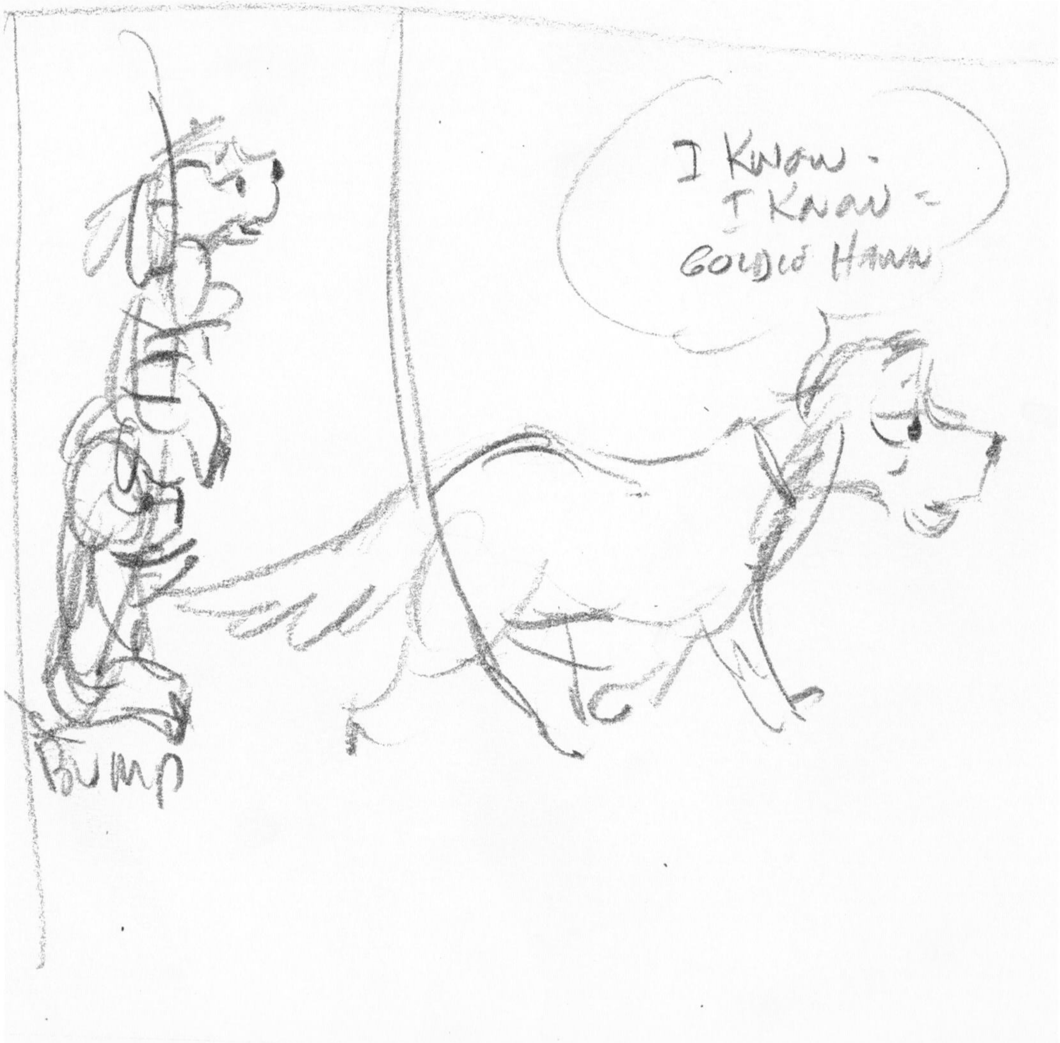
I KNOW -
I KNOW -
GOLDIE HAWN
BUMP

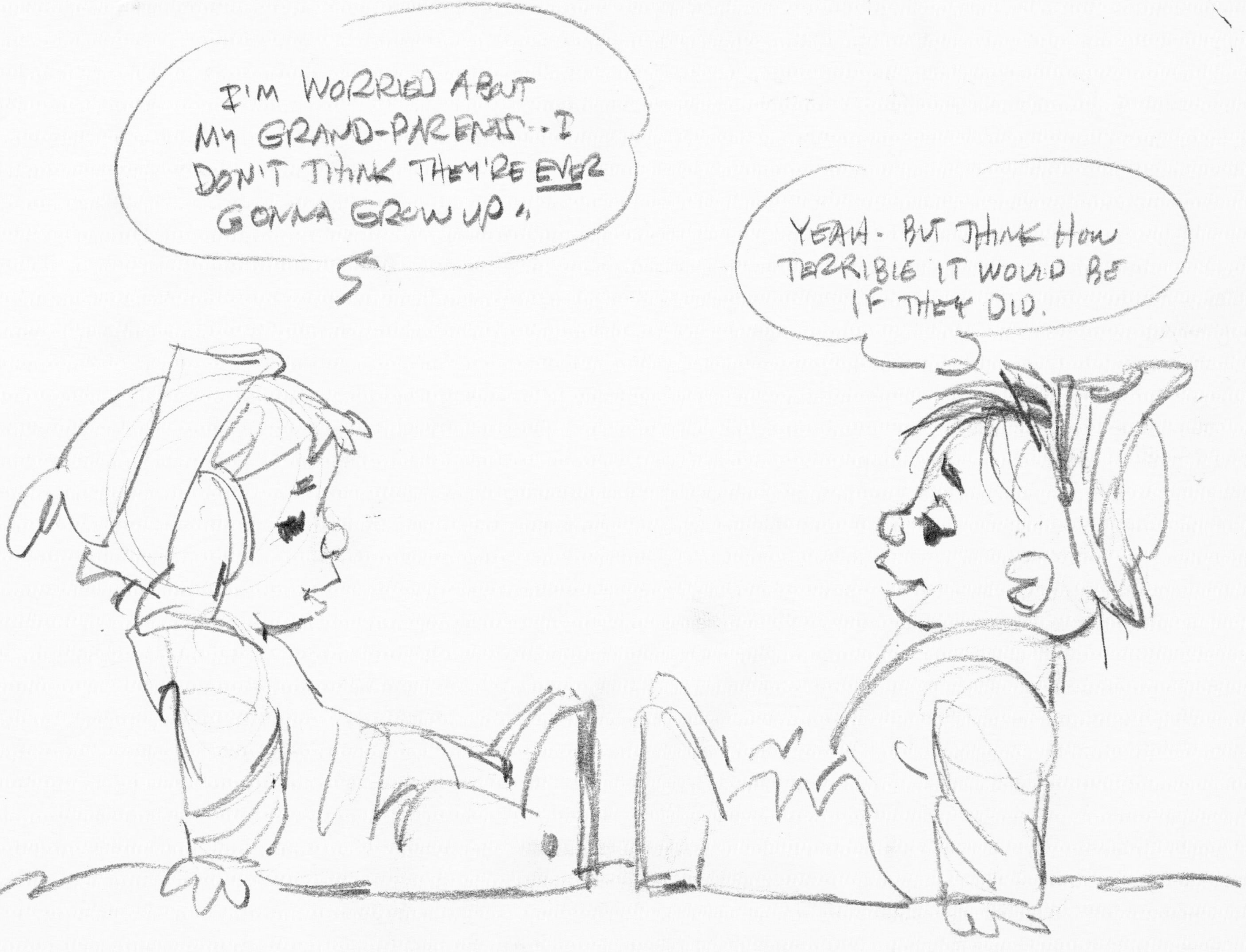
I'M WORRIED ABOUT MY GRAND-PARENTS.. I DON'T THINK THEY'RE EVER GONNA GROW UP.
YEAH. BUT THINK HOW TERRIBLE IT WOULD BE IF THEY DID.

10 - 1977

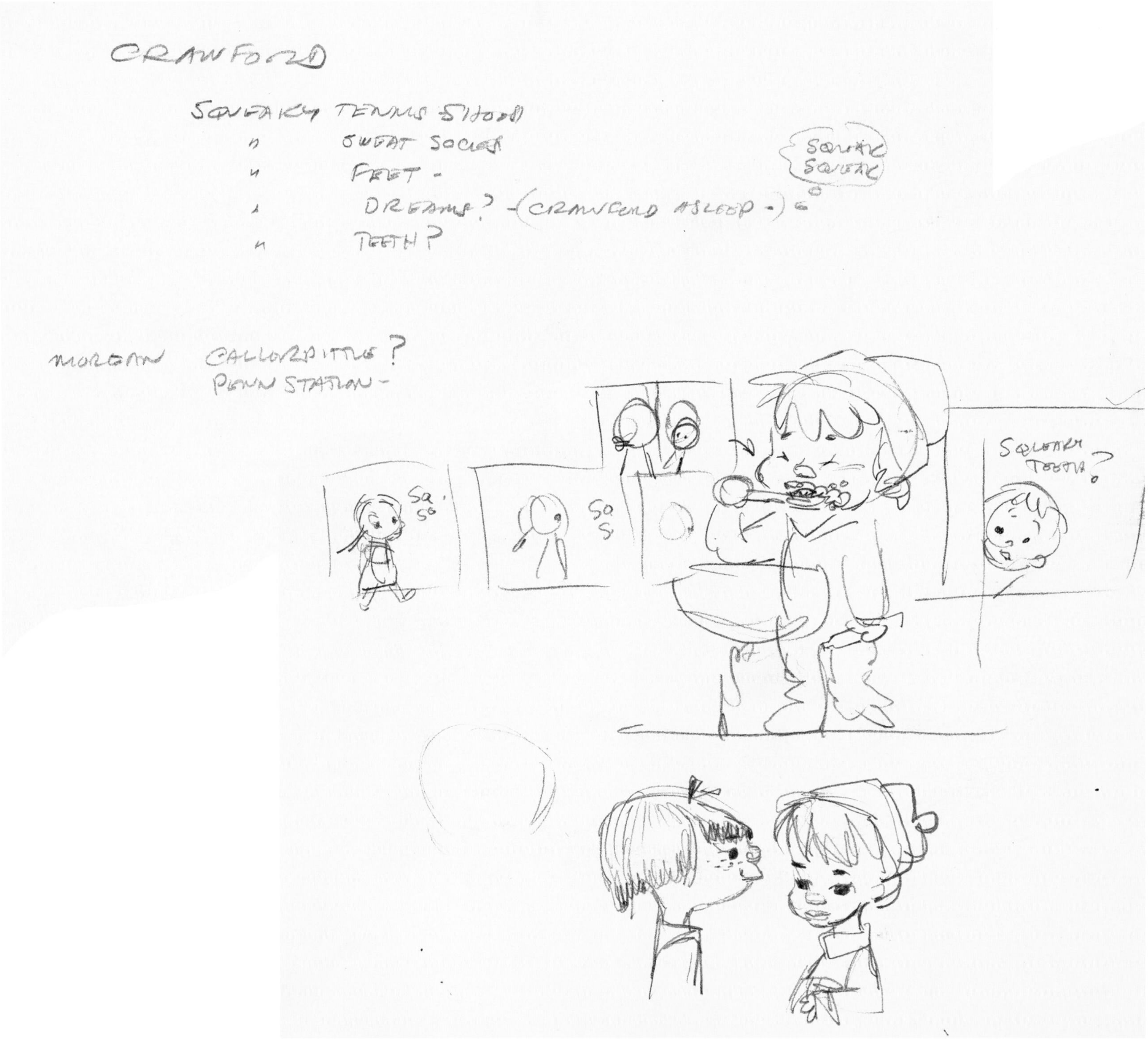
CRAWFORD
SQUEAKY TENNIS SHOES
" SWEAT SOCKS
" FEET -
" DREAMS? -(CRAWFORD ASLEEP -)
" TEETH?
SQUEAK SQUEAK
PENN STATION -
SQUEAKY TEETH?

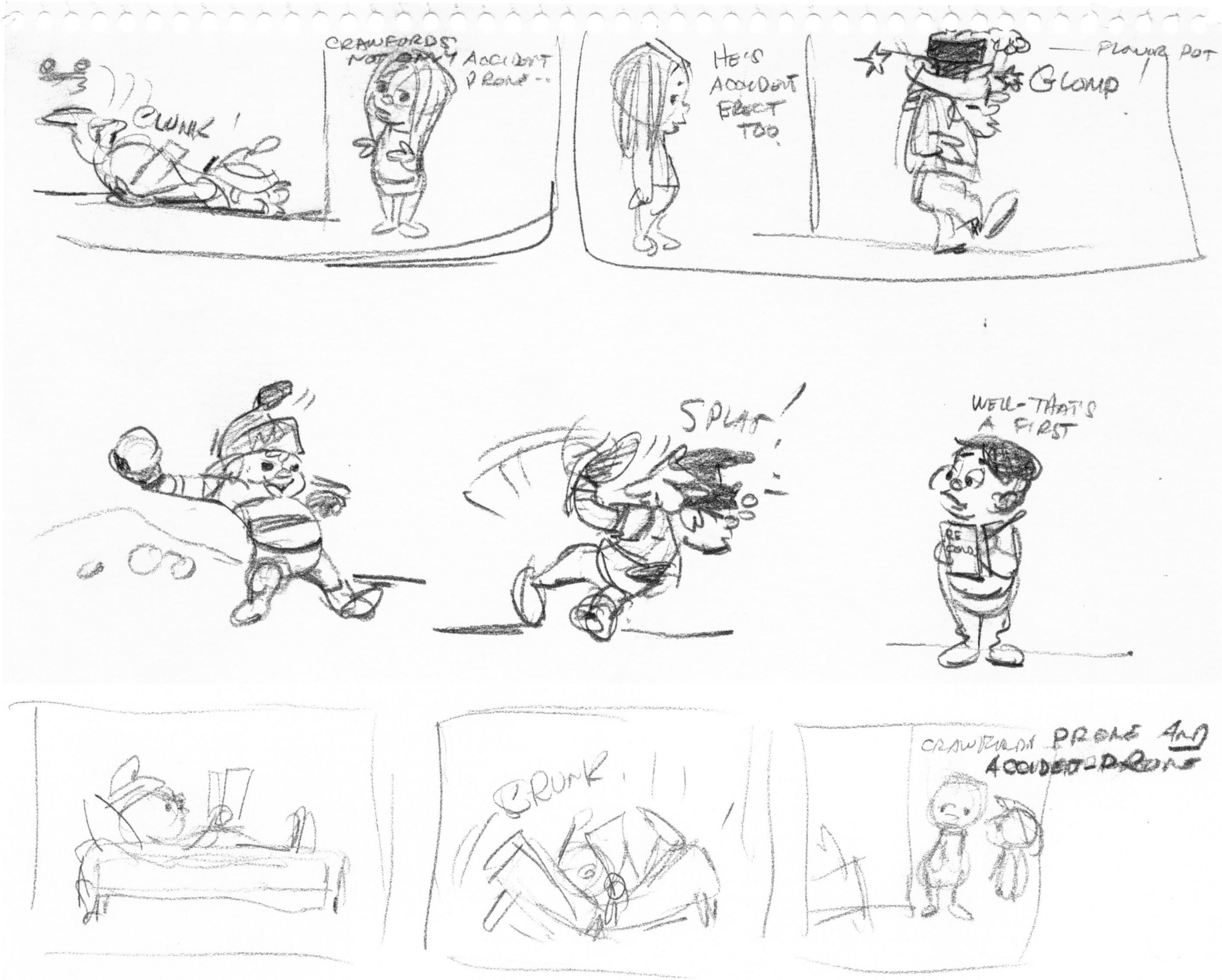
CLUNK!
CRAWFORDS NOT ONLY ACCIDENT PRONE...
HE'S ACCIDENT ERECT TOO.
FLOWER POT
GLOMP
SPLAT!
WELL-THAT'S A FIRST
CRUNK
PRONE AND
ACCIDENT-PRONE

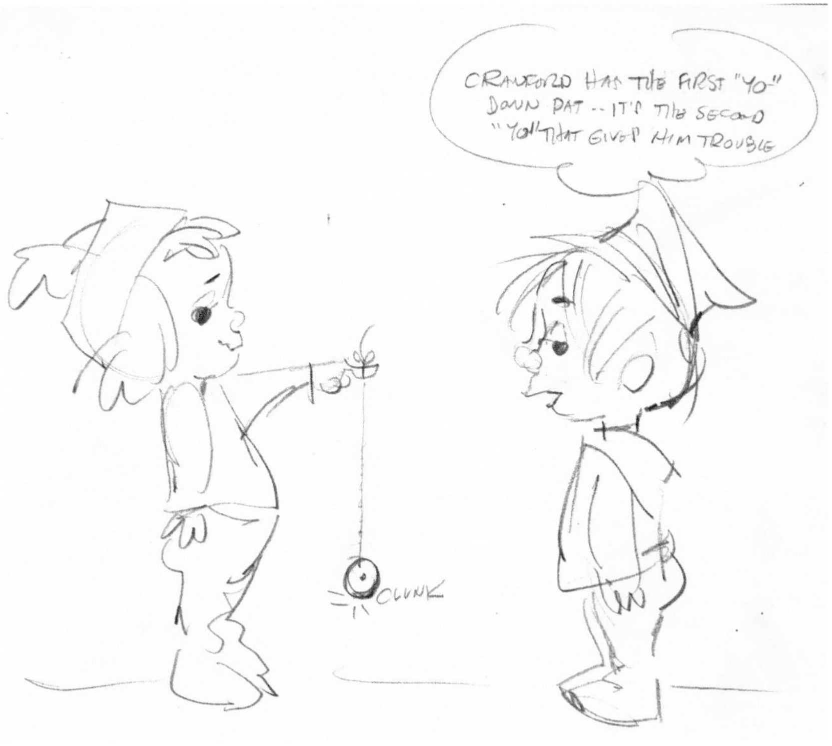
CRAWFORD HAS THE FIRST "YO" DOWN PAT -- IT'S THE SECOND "YO" THAT GIVES HIM TROUBLE
CLUNK

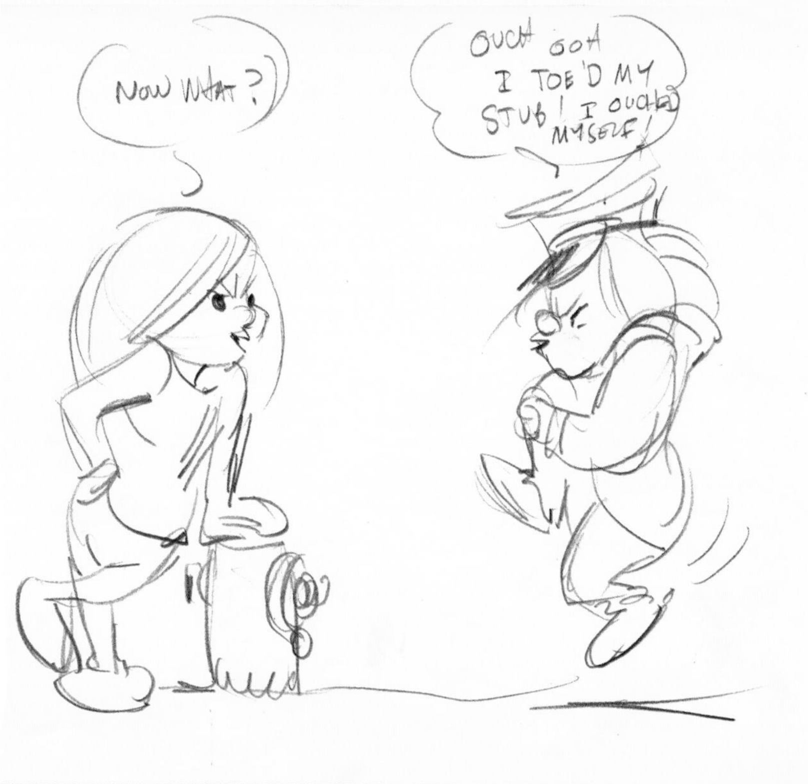
NOW WHAT?
OUCH GOSH I TOE'D MY STUB! I OUCHED MYSELF!

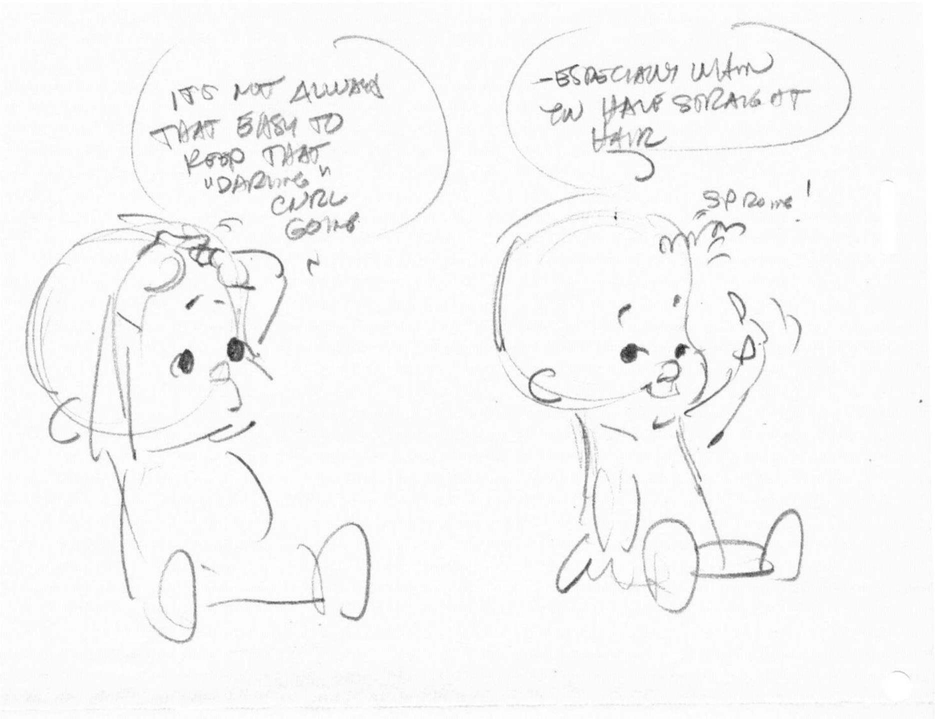
IT'S NOT ALWAYS THAT EASY TO KEEP THAT "DARLING" CURL GOING
—ESPECIALLY WHEN YOU HAVE STRAIGHT HAIR
SPROING!

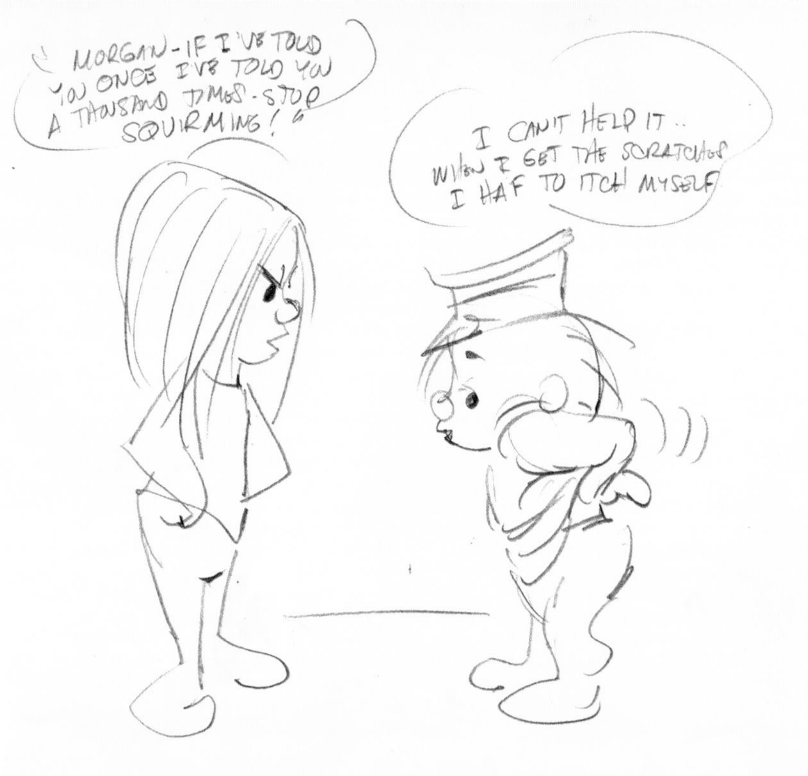
MORGAN - IF I'VE TOLD YOU ONCE I'VE TOLD YOU A THOUSAND TIMES - STOP SQUIRMING!
I CAN'T HELP IT.. WHEN I GET THE SCRATCHES I HAF TO ITCH MYSELF

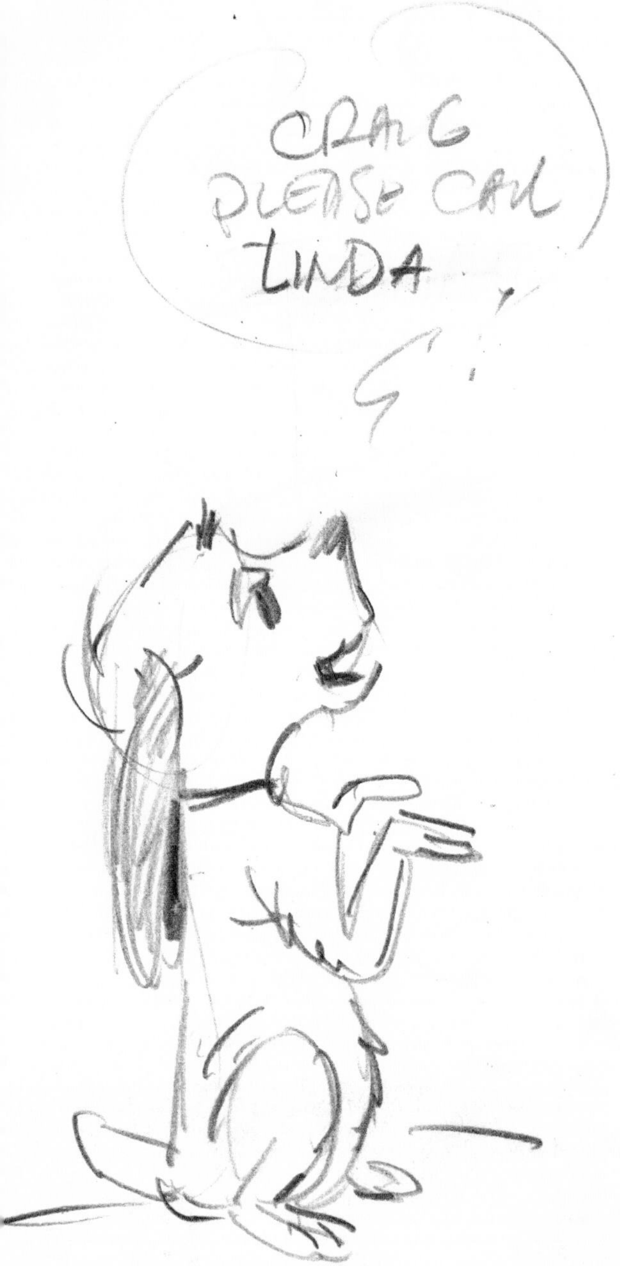
CRAIG
PLEASE CALL
LINDA

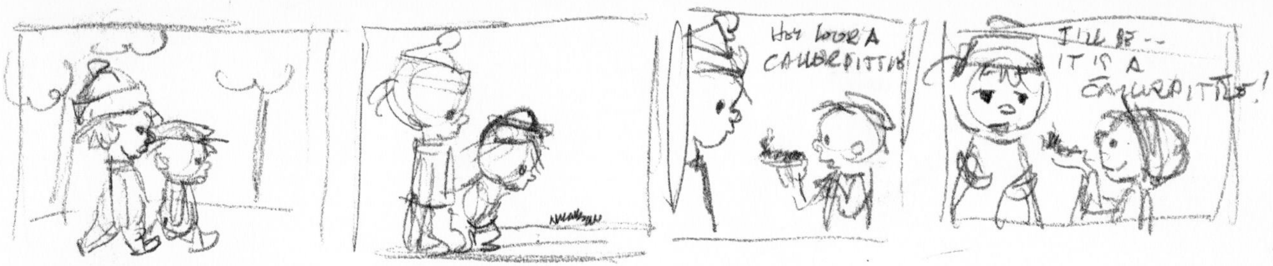
I'LL BE --
IT IS A

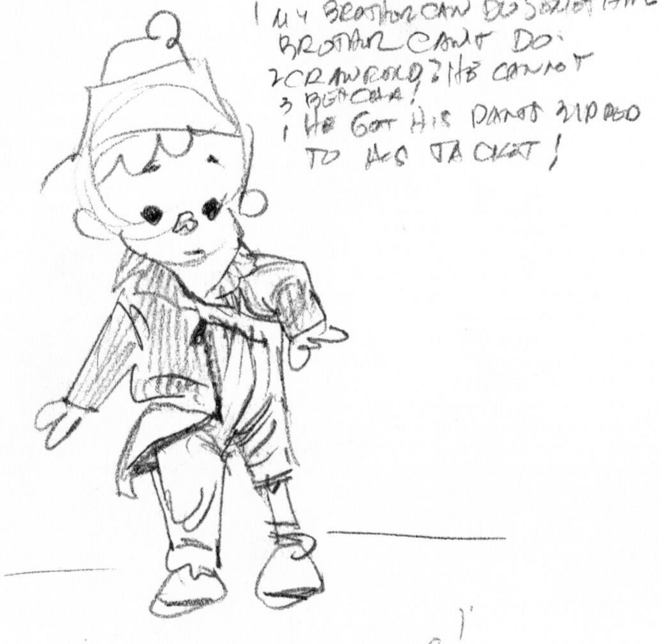
1 MY BROTHER CAN DO SOMETHING YOUR
BROTHER CAN'T DO:
2 CRAWFORD? HE CANNOT
3 BETCHA!
1 HE GOT HIS PANTS ZIPPED
TO HIS JACKET!

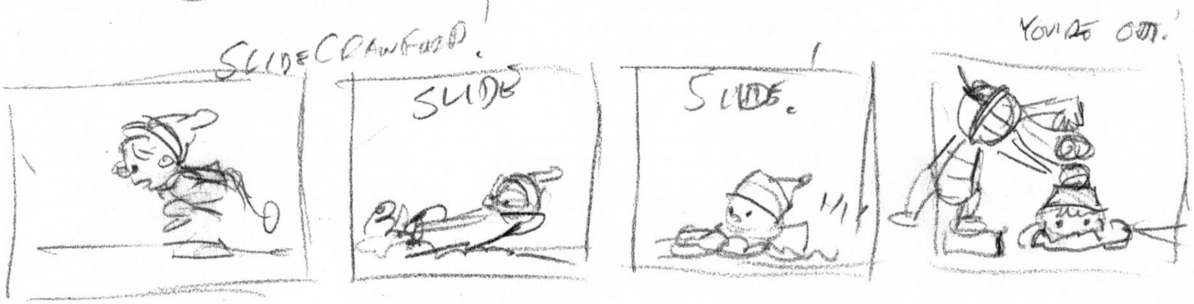
SLIDE CRAWFORD!
SLIDE
SLIDE.
YOU'RE OUT!

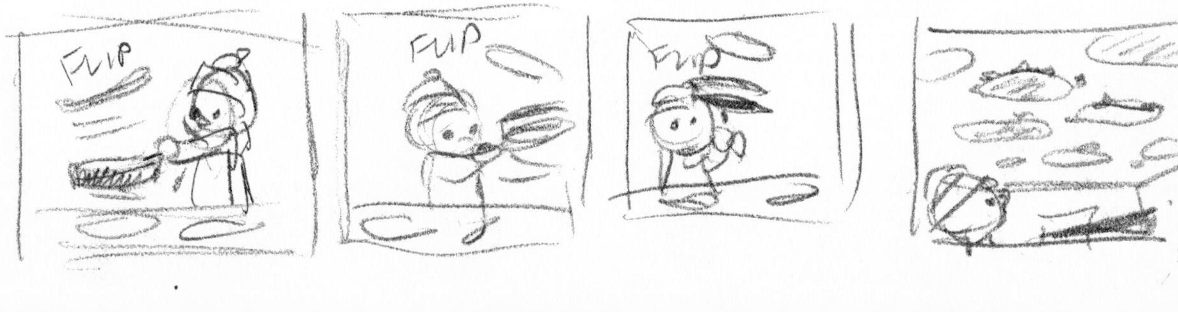
FLIP
FLIP
FLIP

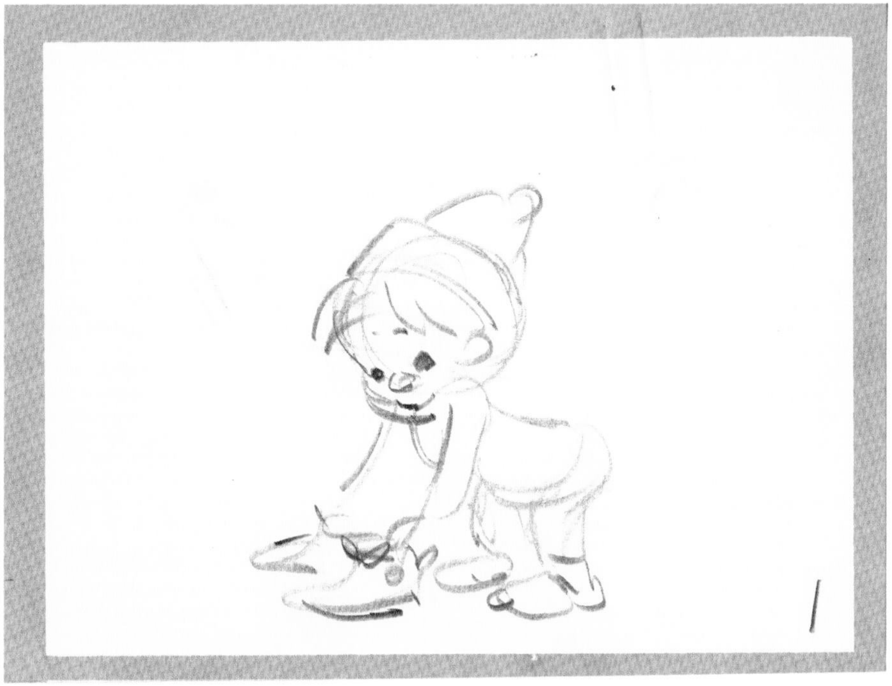
1

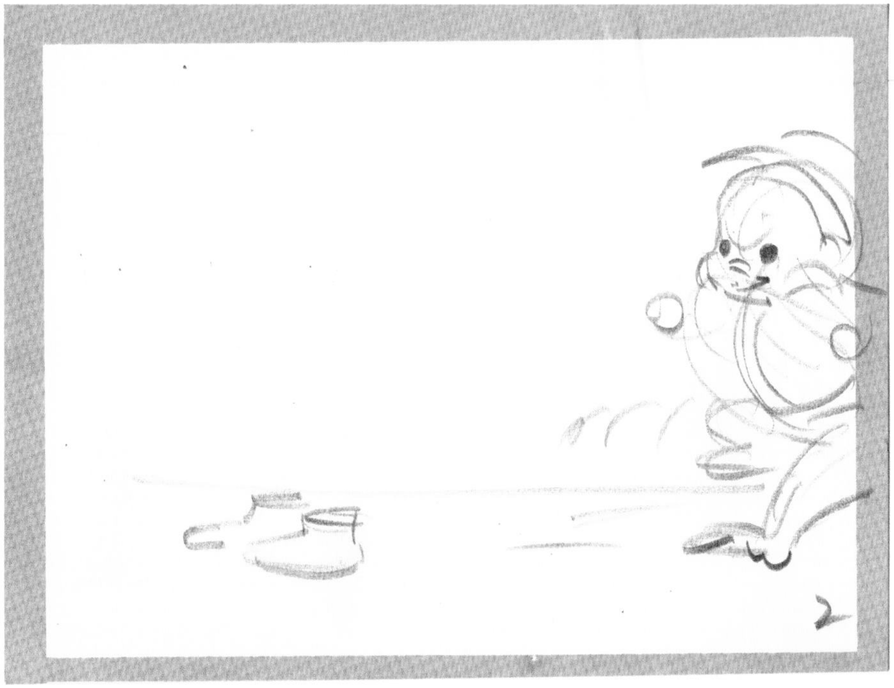
2

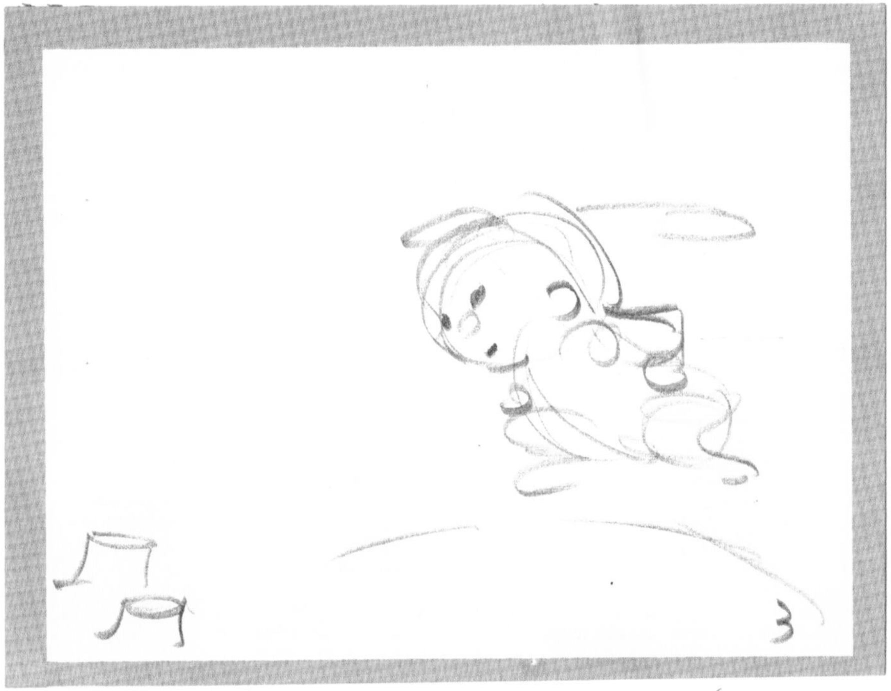
3

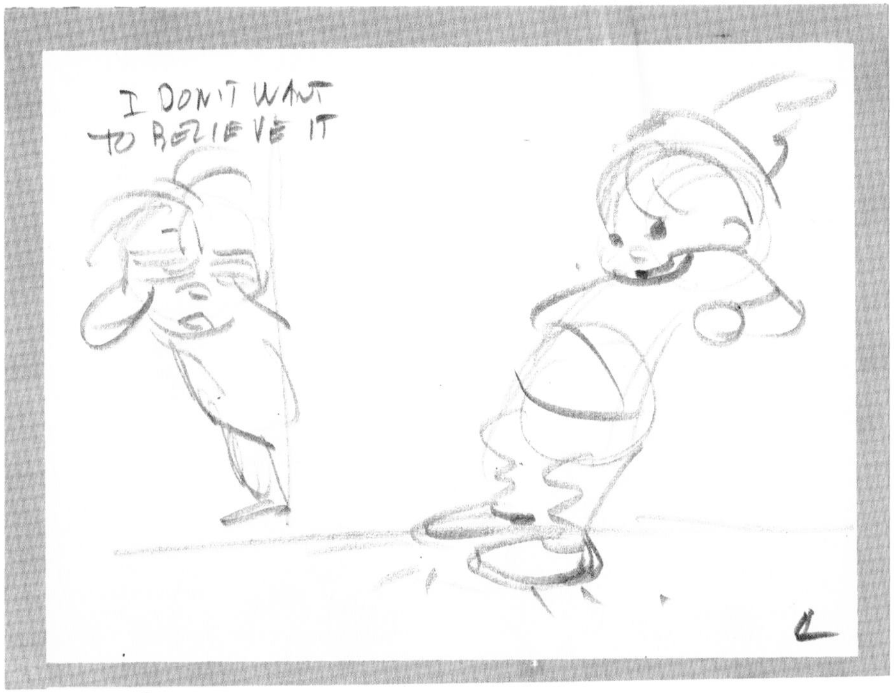
I DONT WANT
TO BELIEVE IT
4

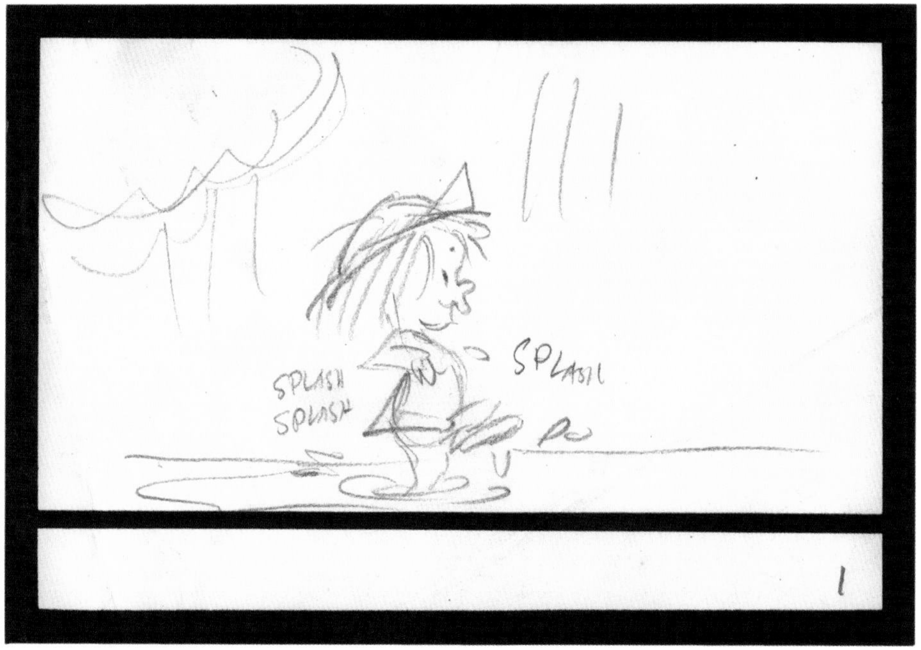
SPLASH
SPLASH
SPLASH
1

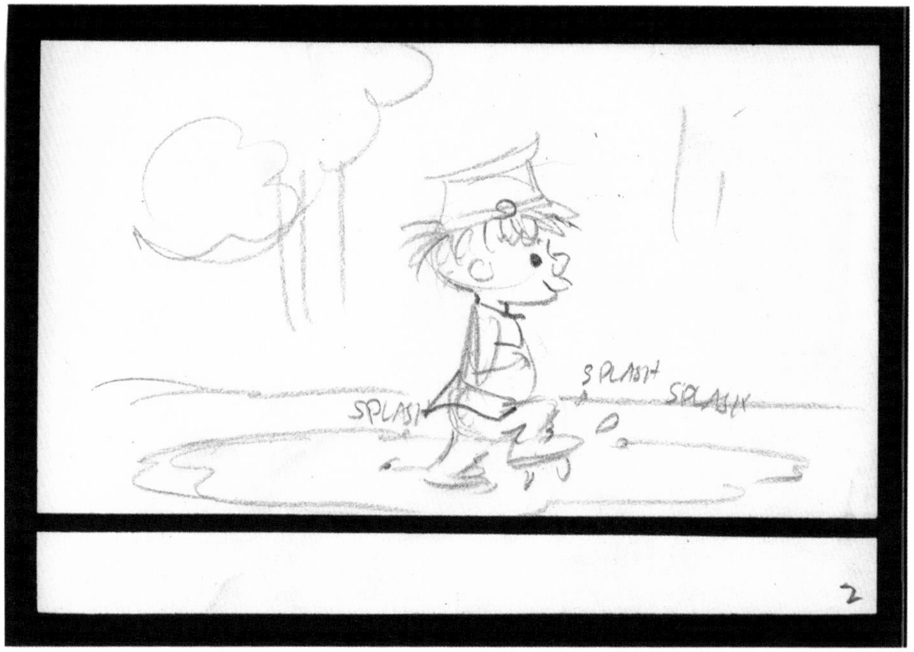
SPLASH
SPLASH
SPLASH
2

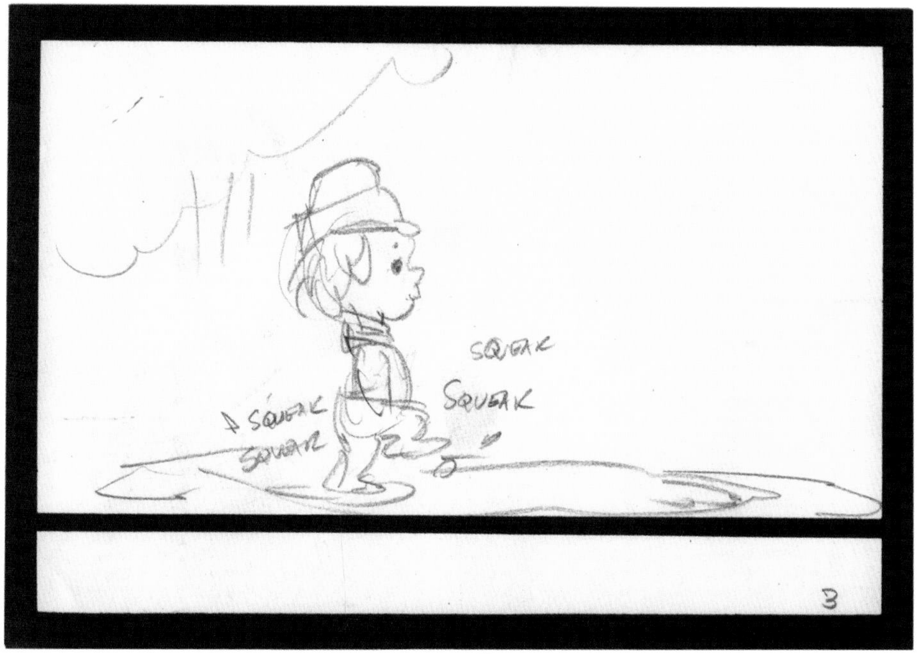
SQUEAK
SQUEAK
SQUEAK
SQUEAK
3

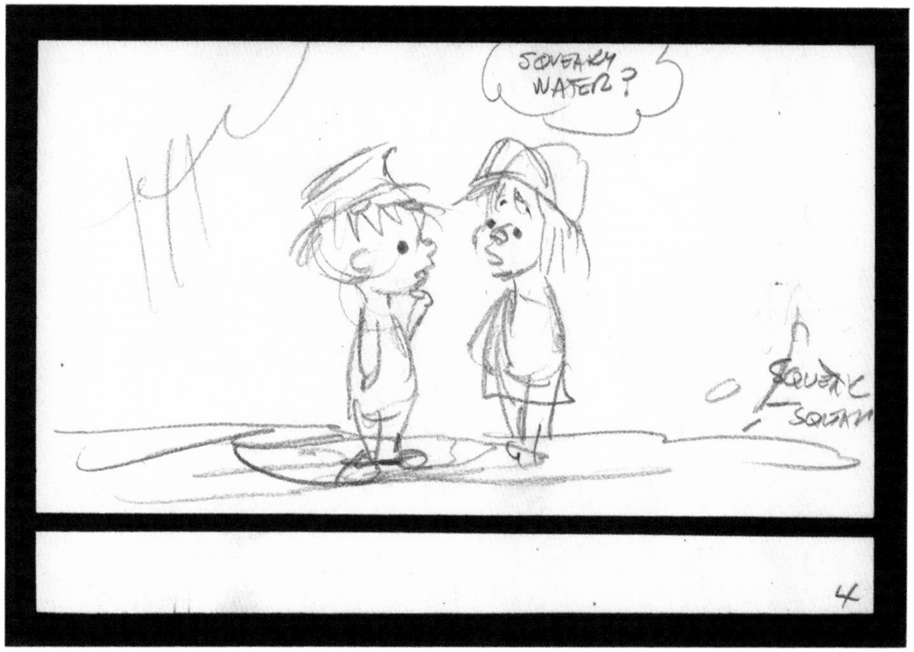
SQUEAKY WATER?
SQUEAK
SQUEAK
4

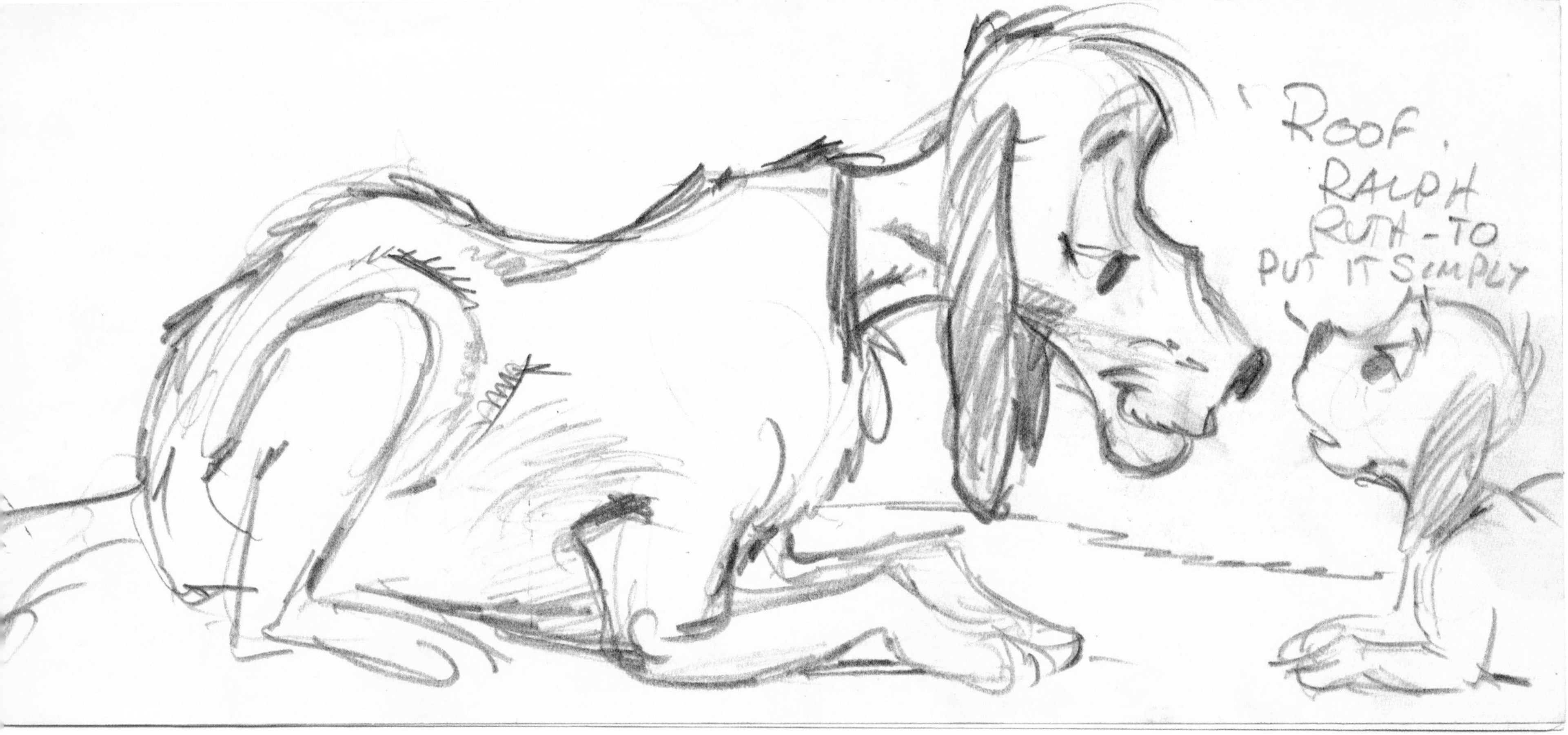
ROOF. RALPH RUTH - TO PUT IT SIMPLY

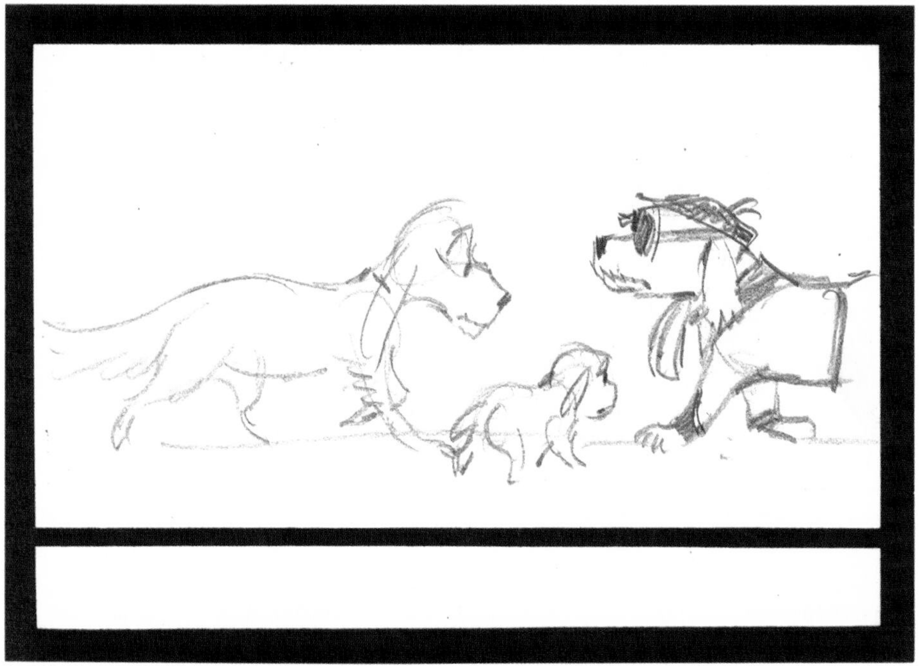

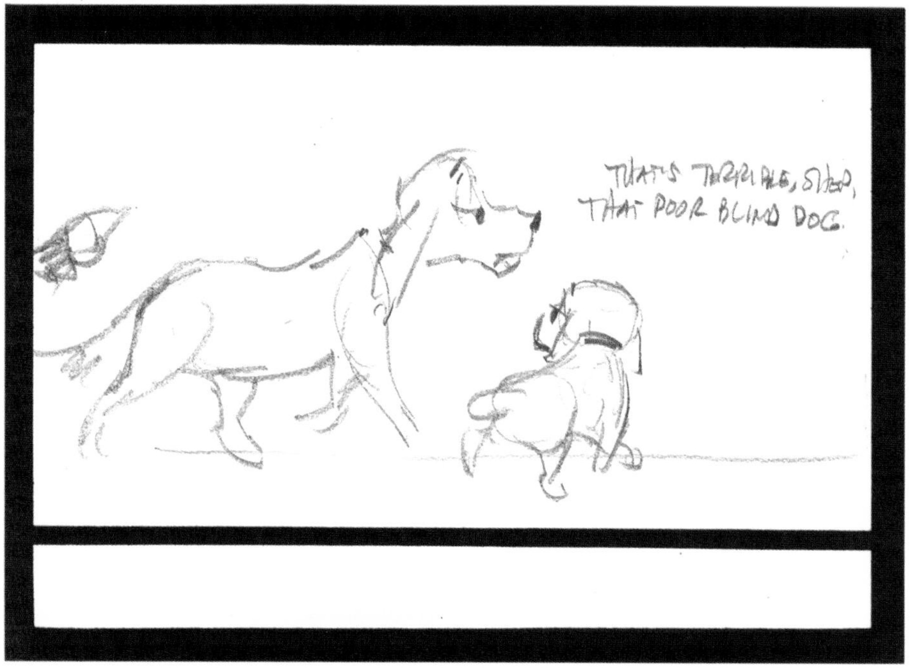
THAT'S TERRIBLE, SISTER,
THAT POOR BLIND DOG.

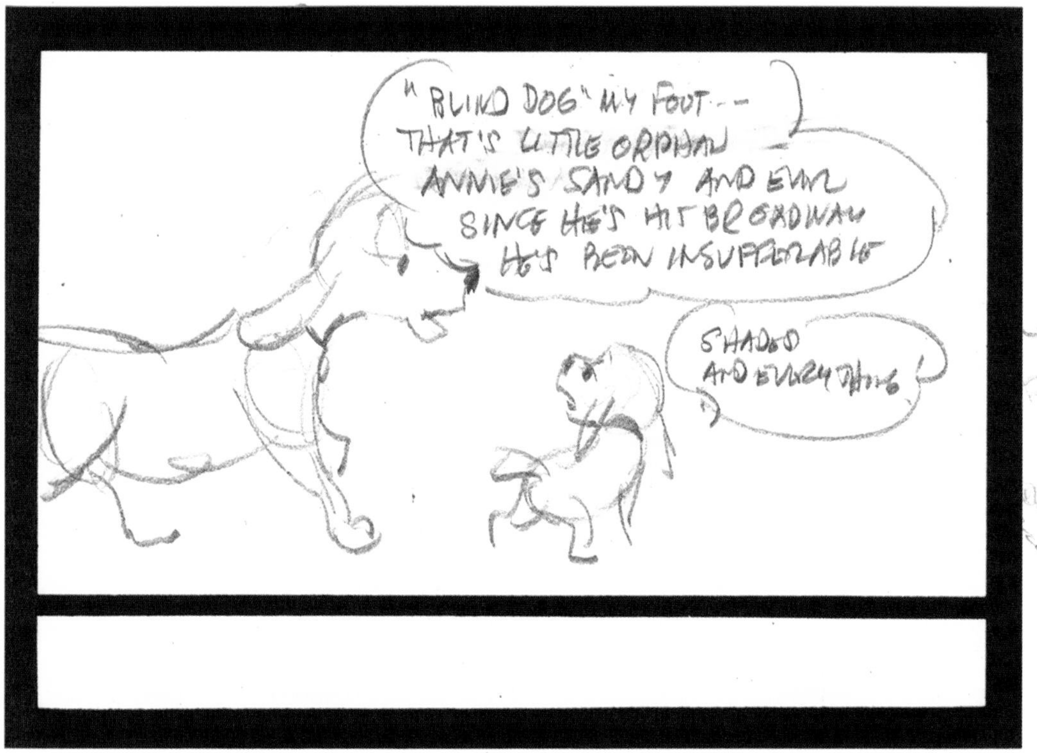
"BLIND DOG" MY FOOT-- THAT'S LITTLE ORPHAN ANNIE'S SANDY AND EVER SINCE HE'S HIT BROADWAY HE'S BEEN INSUFFERABLE
SHADES AND EVERYTHING

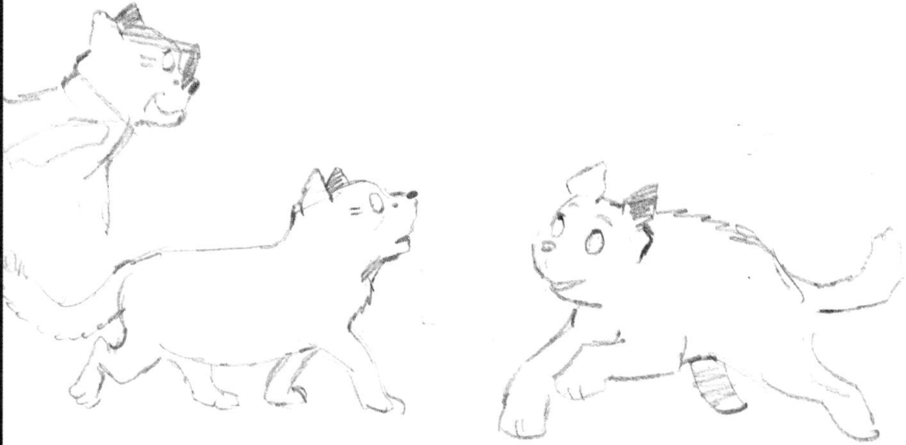

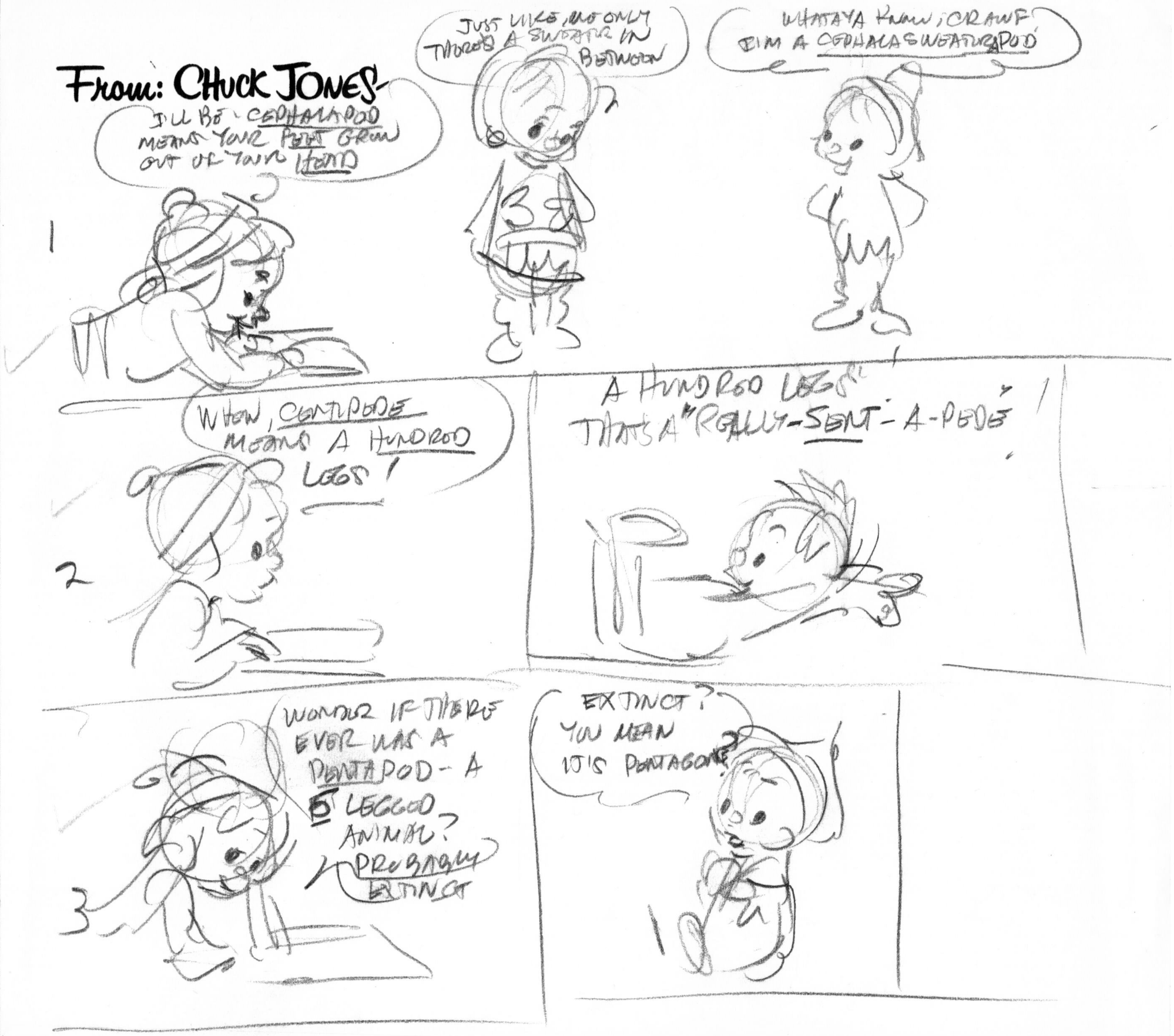
From: CHUCK JONES
I'LL BE · CEPHALAPOD MEANS YOUR FEET GROW OUT OF YOUR HEAD
JUST LIKE ME ONLY THERE'S A SWEATER IN BETWEEN
WHATAYA KNOW, CRAWF! I'M A CEPHALASWEATERPOD
1
WHEW, CENTIPEDE MEANS A HUNDRED LEGS!
2
A HUNDRED LEGS! THAT'S A "REALLY-SENT-A-PEDE"
WONDER IF THERE EVER WAS A PENTAPOD - A 5 LEGGED ANIMAL? PROBABLY EXTINCT
3
EXTINCT? YOU MEAN IT'S PENTAGONE?

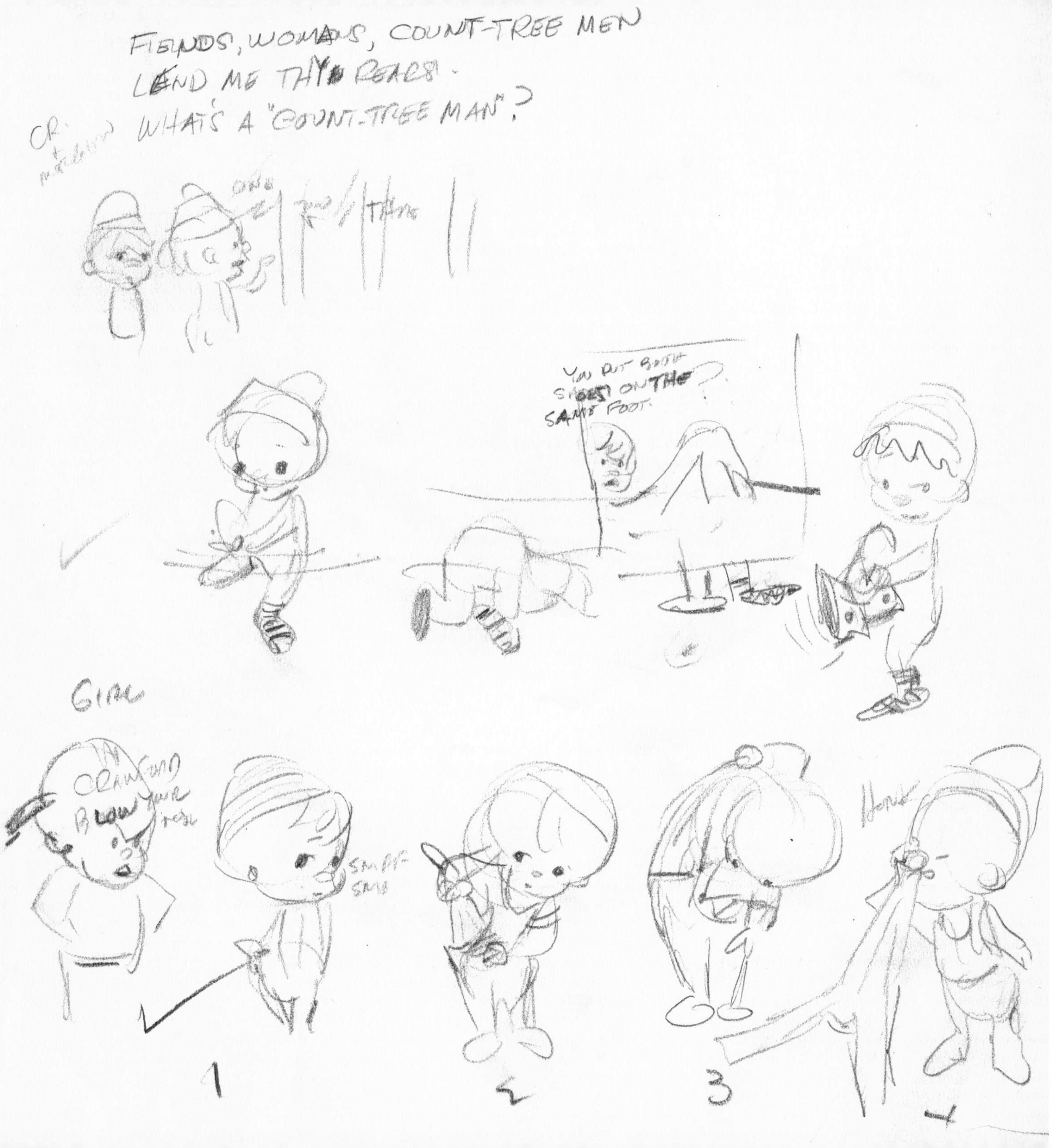
FIENDS, WOMANS, COUNT-TREE MEN
LEND ME THY REARS.
WHAT'S A "COUNT-TREE MAN"?
YOU PUT BOTH SHOES ON THE SAME FOOT.
GIRL
1
2
3
4

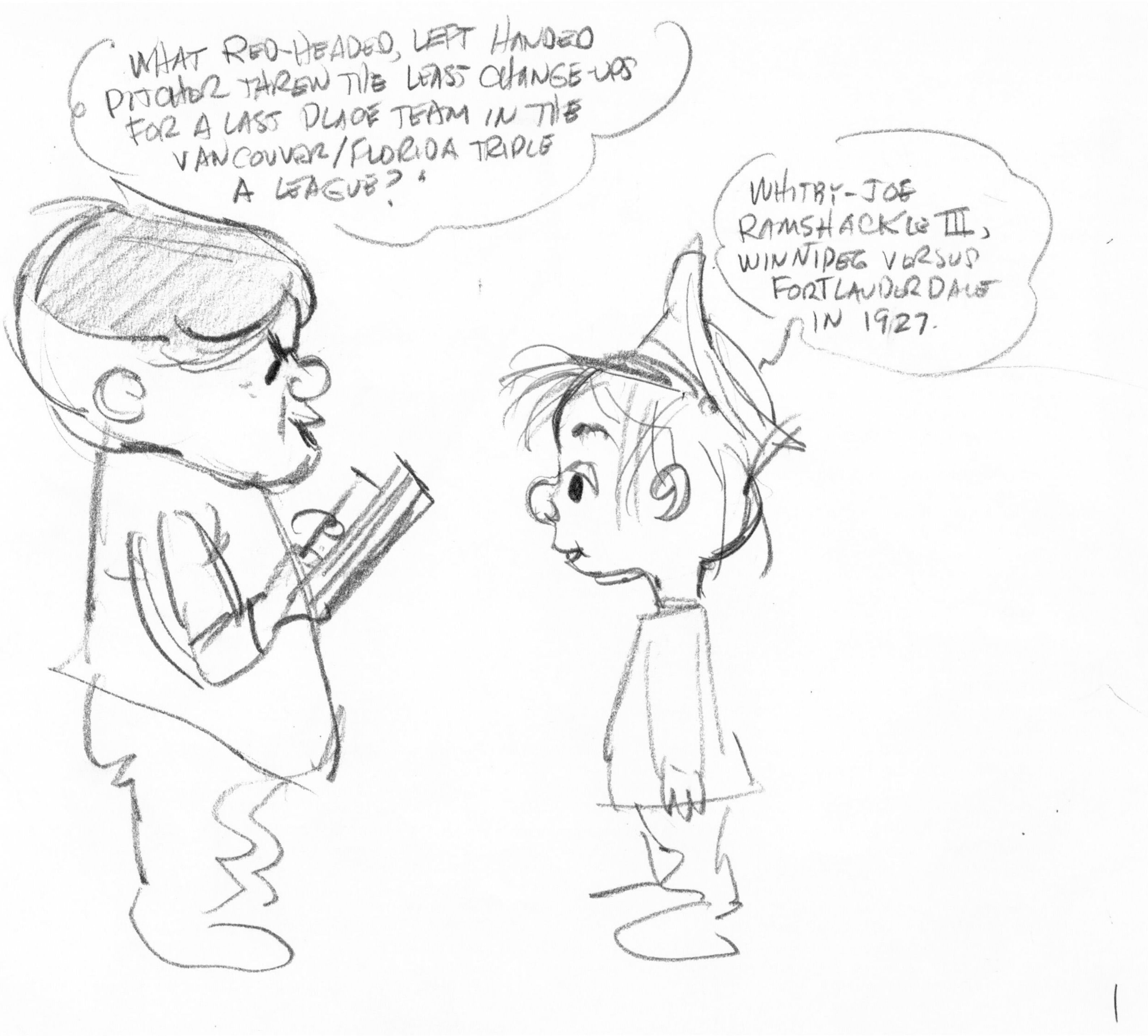
WHAT RED-HEADED, LEFT HANDED PITCHER THREW THE LEAST CHANGE-UPS FOR A LAST PLACE TEAM IN THE VANCOUVER/FLORIDA TRIPLE A LEAGUE?
WHITBY-JOE RAMSHACKLE III, WINNIPEG VERSUS FORTLAUDERDALE IN 1927.

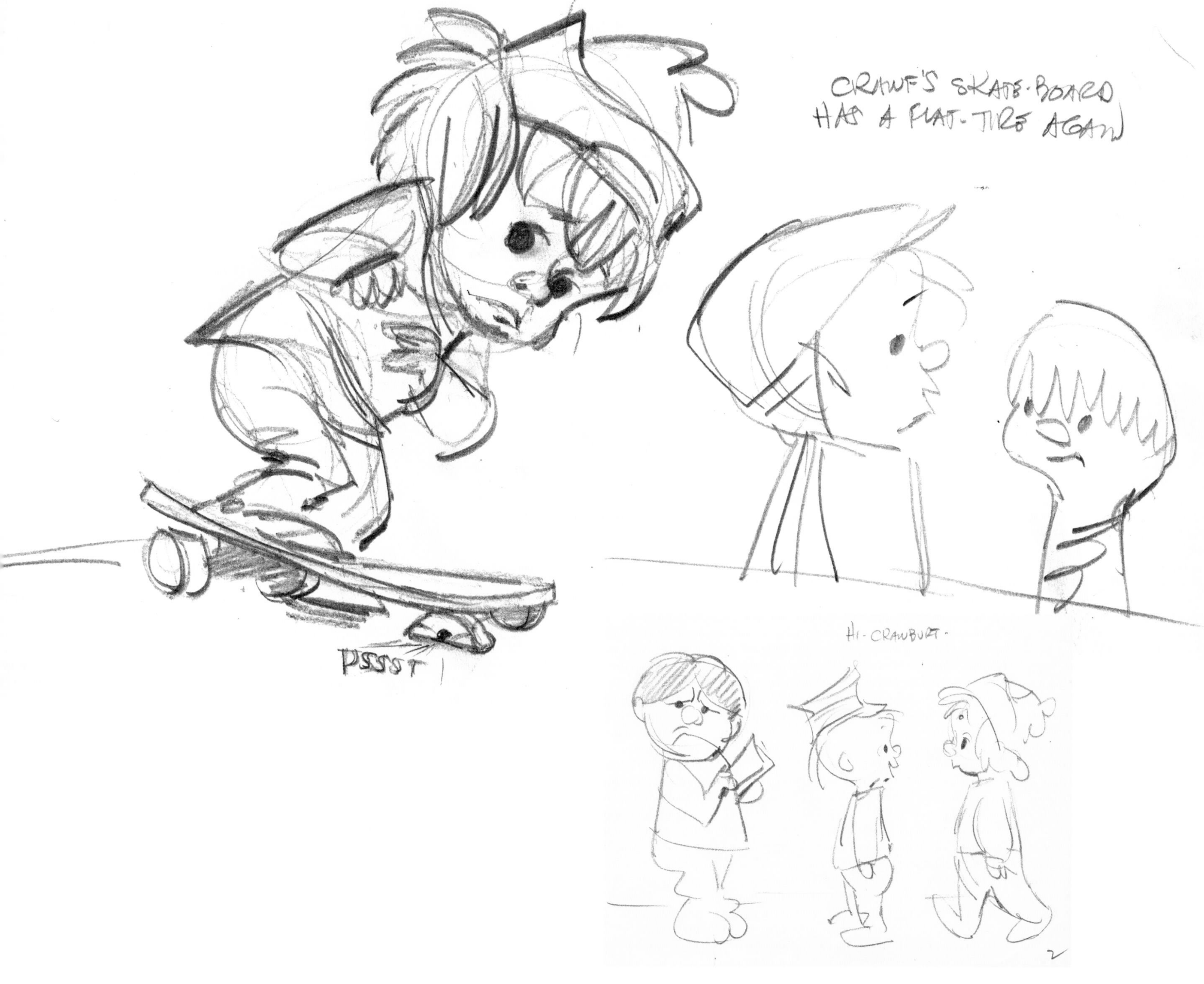
CRAWF'S SKATE-BOARD
HAS A FLAT-TIRE AGAIN
PSSST
HI-CRAWBURT-

DRIBBLE DRIBBLE
DRIBBLE

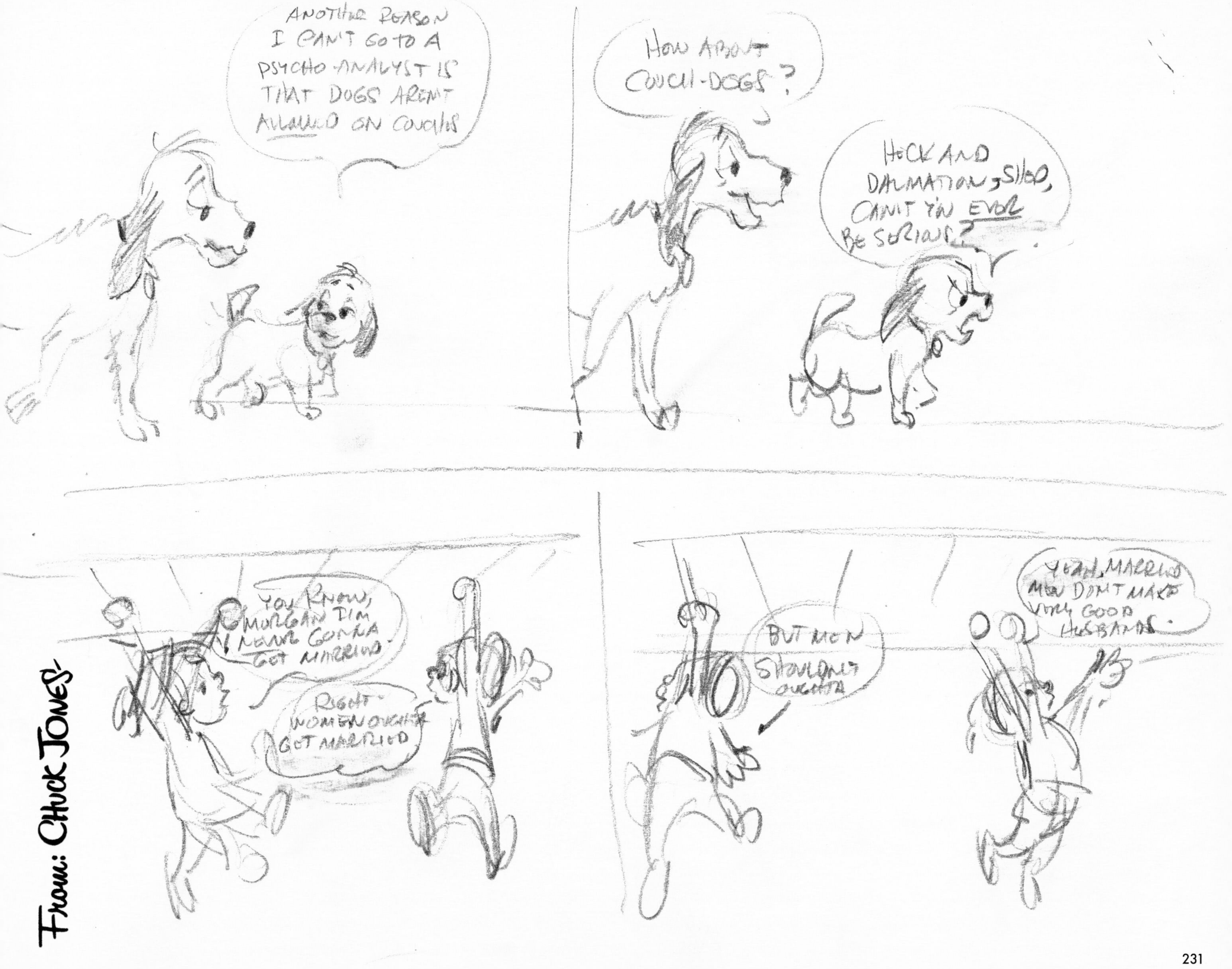

ANOTHER REASON I CAN'T GO TO A PSYCHO-ANALYST IS THAT DOGS AREN'T ALLOWED ON COUCHES
HOW ABOUT COUCH-DOGS?
HECK AND DALMATION, SHOO, CAN'T YOU EVER BE SERIOUS?
YOU KNOW, MORGAN I'M NEVER GONNA GET MARRIED
RIGHT. WOMEN OUGHTA GET MARRIED
BUT MEN SHOULDN'T OUGHTA
YEAH, MARRIED MEN DON'T MAKE VERY GOOD HUSBANDS.
From: Chuck Jones

From: CHUCK JONES

MICK TWAIN (WITH AN OCCASIONAL HAND (FROM) A MARK*)
HE IS CONSUMED BY A DEEP INNER AMUSEMENT
WITH THE HUMAN CONDITION, WITH THE LANGUAGE
AND WITH ALL ABSURDITIES. HE IS LIKE A
SMALL IDLING FERRARI - WITH SMALL SPURTS
OF SPEECH · ·

CHUCKLE
CHUCKLE
CHUCKLE
CHUCKLE
CHUCKLE
CHUCKLE
CHUCKLE
CHUCKLE

"LOOSEN" AND "UNLOOSEN" MEAN THE SAME THING

"IT'S BETTER TO HAVE LOVED A SHORT GIRL THAN NEVER TO HAVE LOVED A TALL"

"IT'S BETTER TO HAVE LOVED AND LOST THAN NEVER TO HAVE LOST AT ALL

"LOVE IS A MANY SPLINTERED THING"

"LOVE IS A MANY SPLINTED THING."

("A CHICKEN IS AN EGG'S WAY OF GETTING ANOTHER EGG.

WORKING BACKWARDS ON LAST ED. AND ON REVERSE SAMPLES > "LIVE" IS "EVIL SPELLED BACKWARDS!

"KNITS" IS "STINK SPELLED BACKWARDS"

MY DAD SAYS HE'S NEVER MET A MAN HE DIDN'T LIKE - EXCEPT WILL ROGERS"

"ONE THING ADAM 'N EVE HAD GOING FOR THEM - THEY ESCAPED TEETHIN'"

232

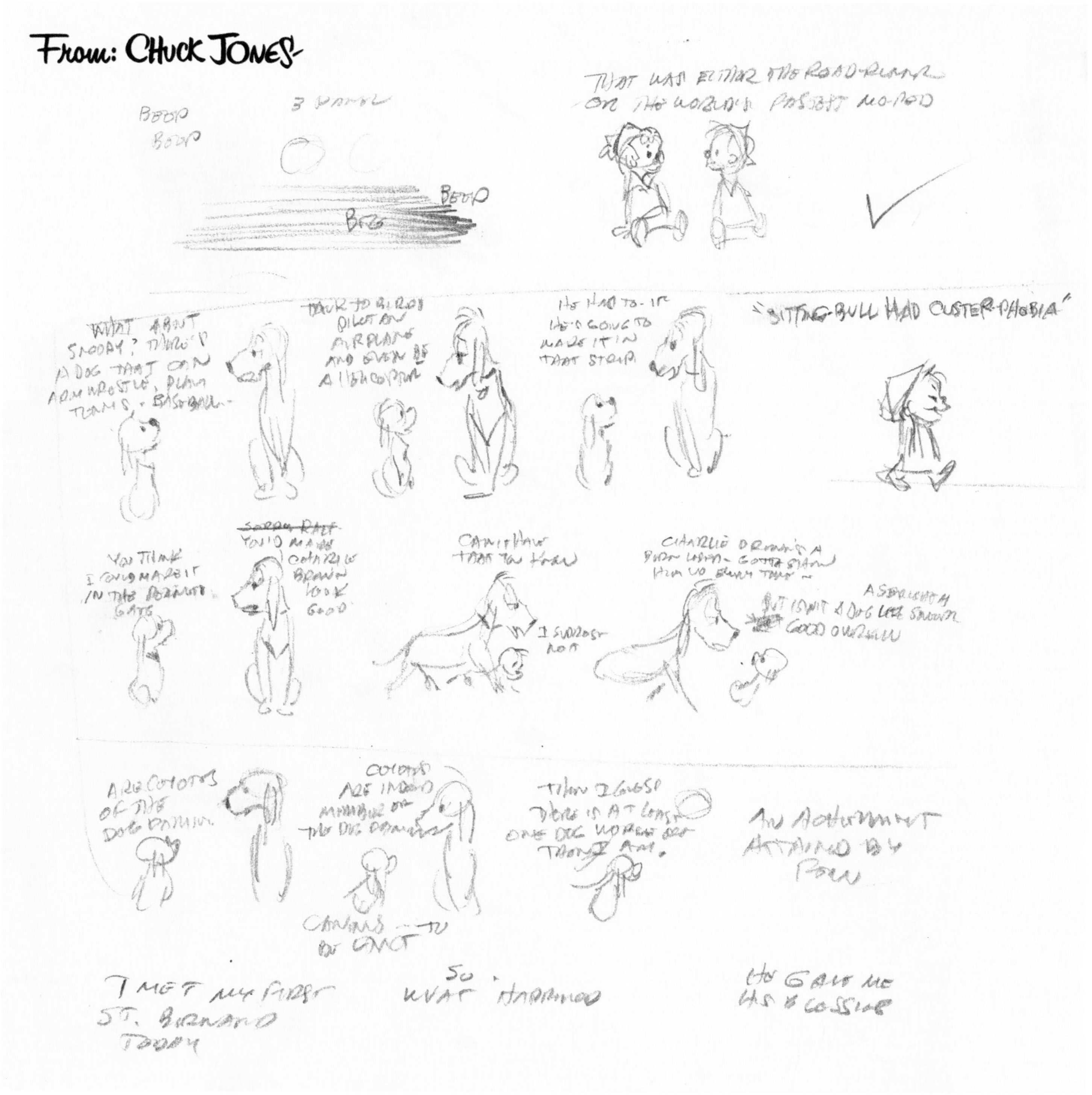
From: CHUCK JONES
BEEP
BEEP
BEEP
THAT WAS EITHER THE ROAD-RUNNER OR THE WORLD'S FASTEST MO-PED
HE HAD TO - IF HE'S GOING TO MAKE IT IN THAT STRIP
"SITTING-BULL HAD CUSTER-PHOBIA"
YOU'D MAKE CHARLIE BROWN LOOK GOOD
I SUPPOSE NOT
ARE COYOTES OF THE DOG FAMILY
THEN I GUESS THERE IS AT LEAST ONE DOG WORSE OFF THAN I AM.
I MET MY FIRST ST. BERNARD TODAY
SO WHAT HAPPENED

The storyboards

Newly discovered in Chuck Jones's files: this near-complete set of storyboards for a proposed 1969 *Crawford* TV series.

--here comes CRAWFORD

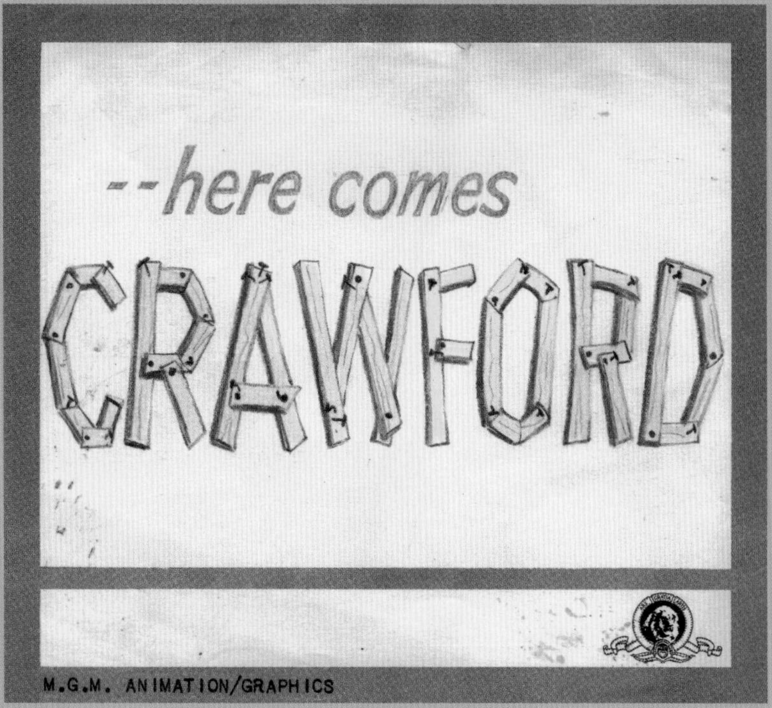
--here comes
CRAWFORD
M.G.M. ANIMATION/GRAPHICS

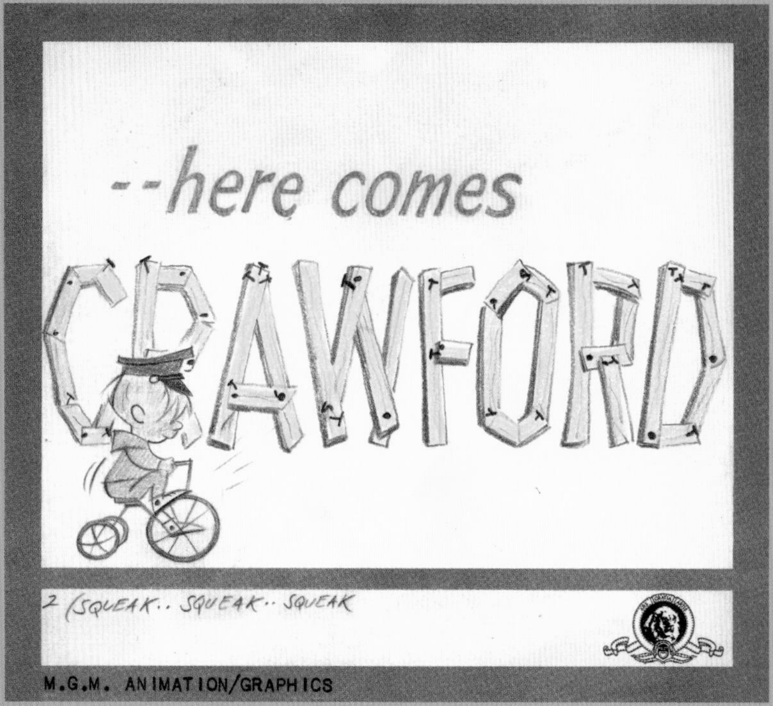
--here comes
CRAWFORD
2 (SQUEAK.. SQUEAK.. SQUEAK
M.G.M. ANIMATION/GRAPHICS

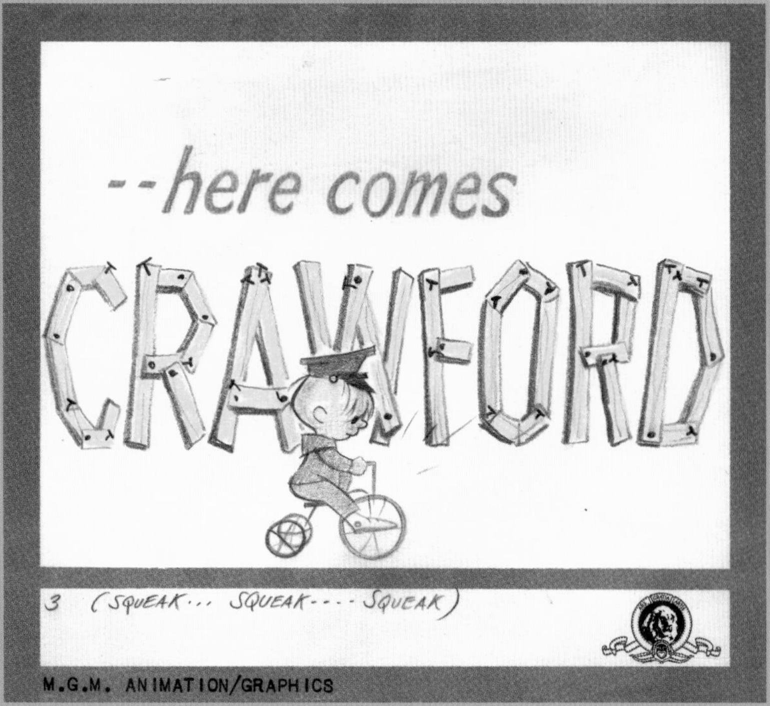
--here comes
CRAWFORD
3 (SQUEAK... SQUEAK---- SQUEAK)
M.G.M. ANIMATION/GRAPHICS

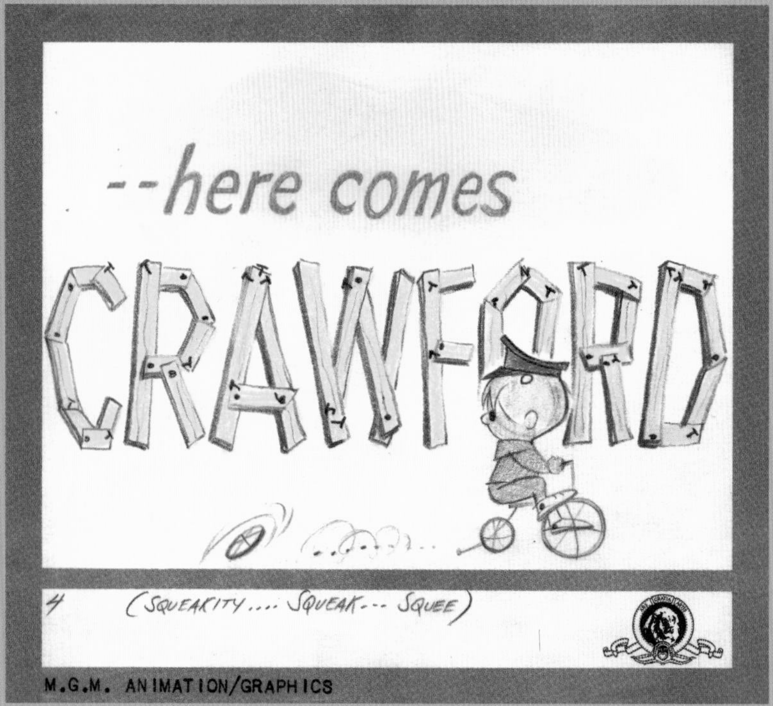
--here comes
CRAWFORD
4 (SQUEAKITY.... SQUEAK--- SQUEE)
M.G.M. ANIMATION/GRAPHICS

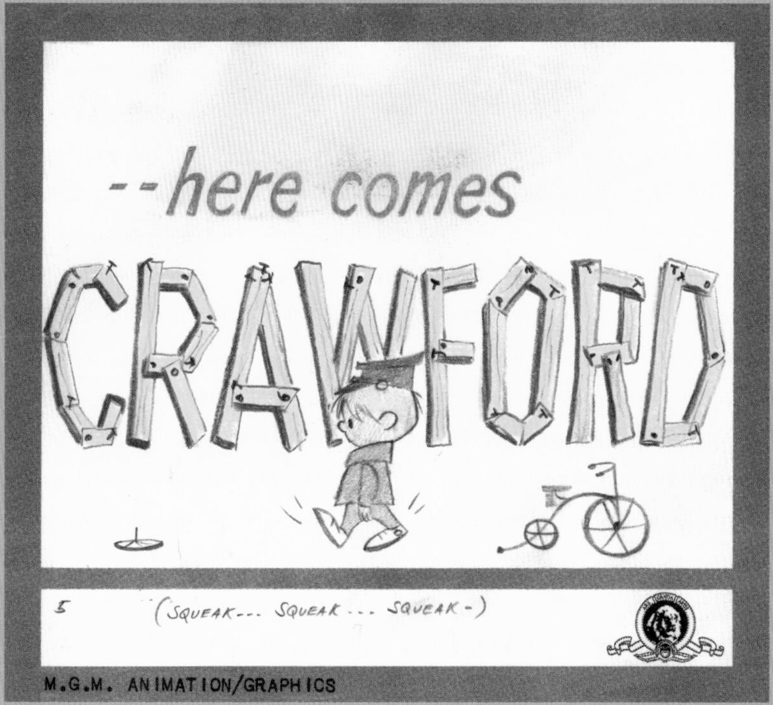
--here comes
CRAWFORD
5
(SQUEAK--- SQUEAK --- SQUEAK-)
M.G.M. ANIMATION/GRAPHICS

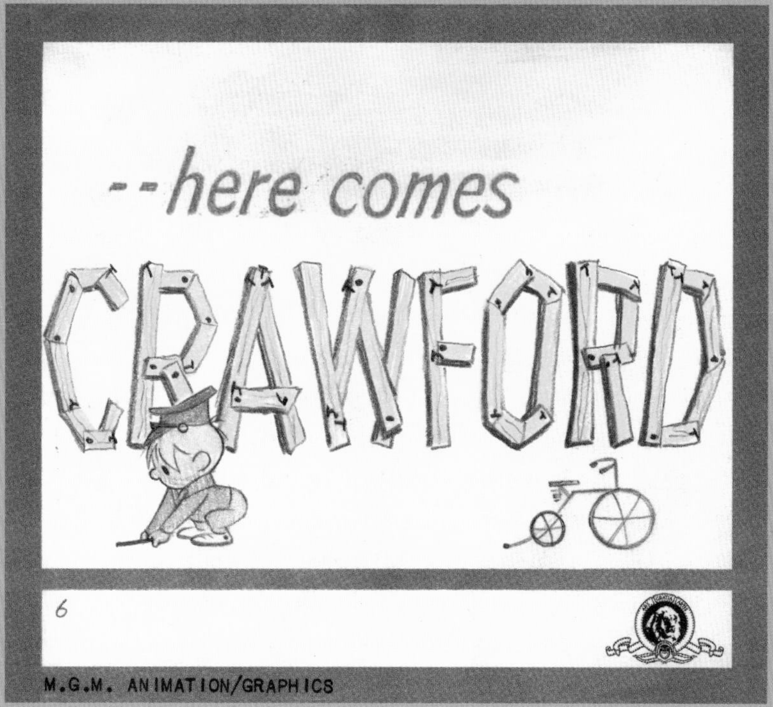
--here comes
CRAWFORD
6
M.G.M. ANIMATION/GRAPHICS

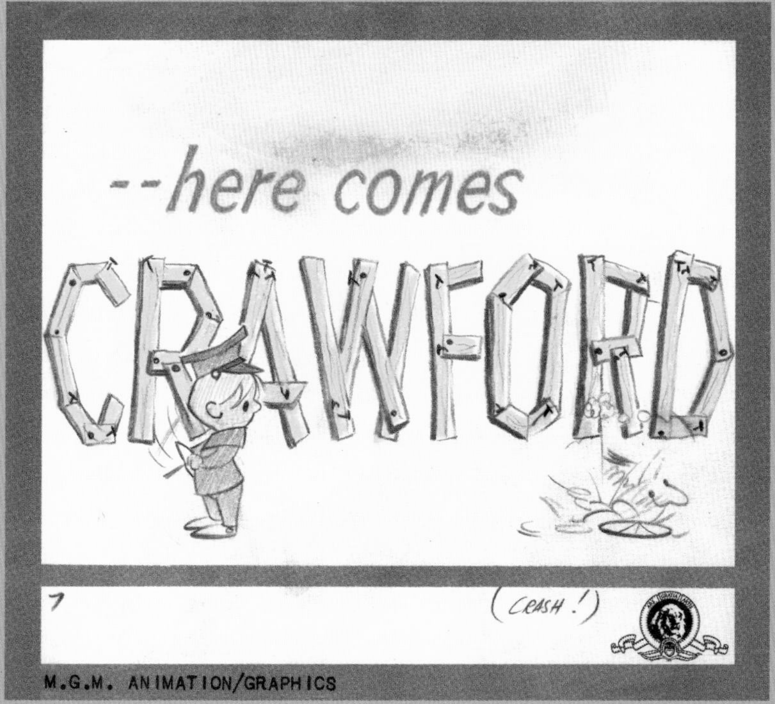
--here comes
CRAWFORD
7
(CRASH!)
M.G.M. ANIMATION/GRAPHICS

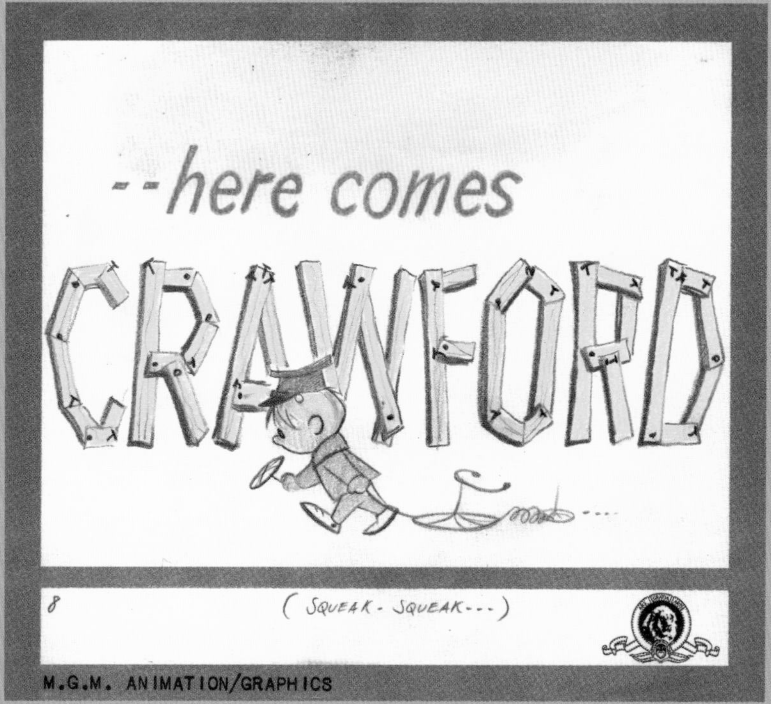
--here comes
CRAWFORD
8
(SQUEAK- SQUEAK---)
M.G.M. ANIMATION/GRAPHICS

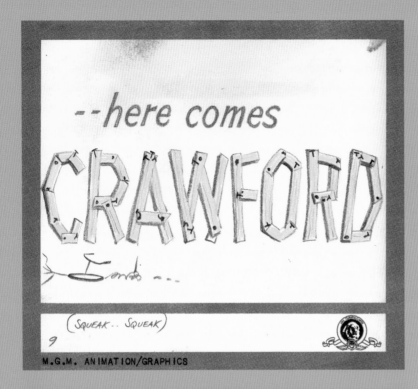

--here comes
CRAWFORD

(SQUEAK.. SQUEAK)
9

M.G.M. ANIMATION/GRAPHICS

--here comes
CRAWFORD

10
(CRR - - - R·R·RACK -)

M.G.M. ANIMATION/GRAPHICS

--here comes

11

M.G.M. ANIMATION/GRAPHICS

12   SILENCE

M.G.M. ANIMATION/GRAPHICS

238

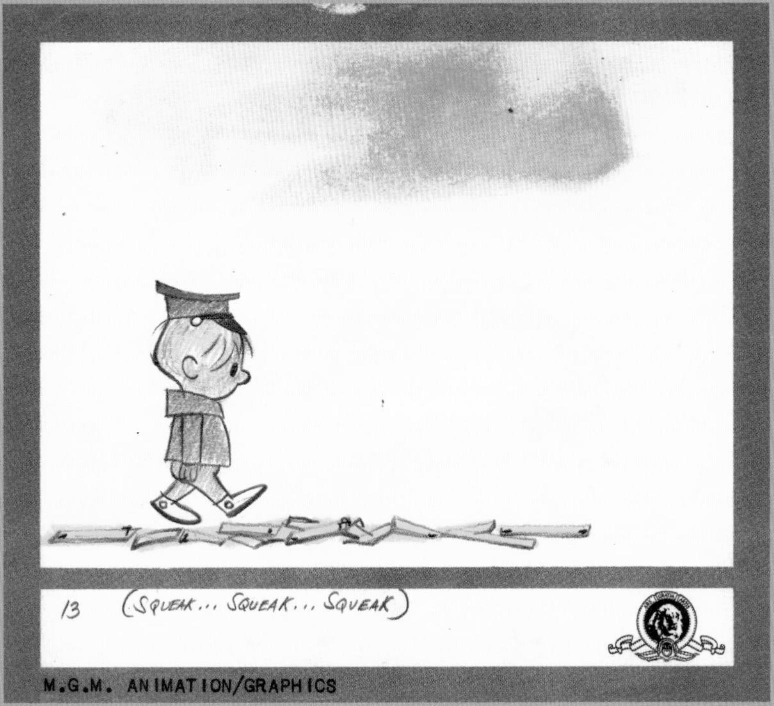
13
(SQUEAK... SQUEAK... SQUEAK)
M.G.M. ANIMATION/GRAPHICS

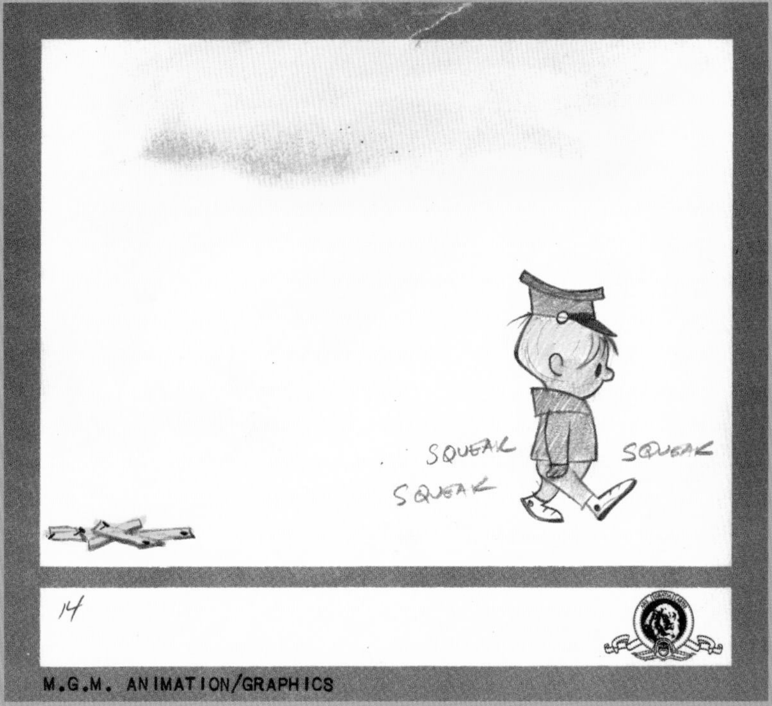
SQUEAK
SQUEAK
SQUEAK
14
M.G.M. ANIMATION/GRAPHICS

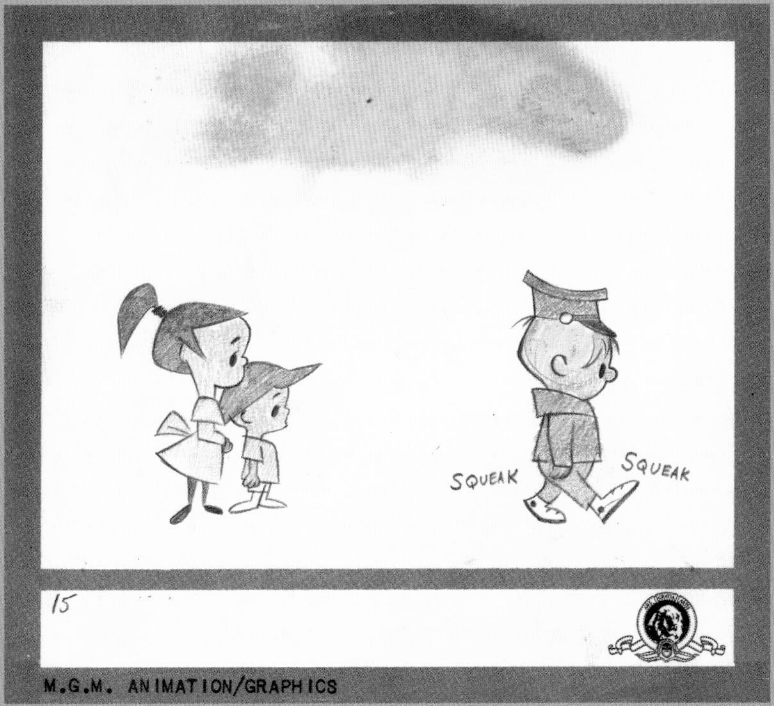
SQUEAK
SQUEAK
15
M.G.M. ANIMATION/GRAPHICS

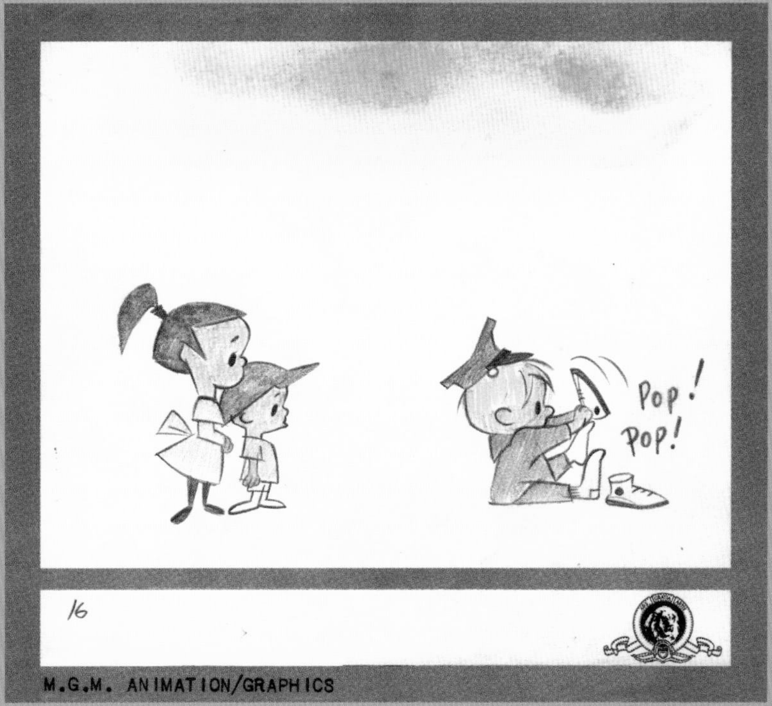
Pop!
Pop!
16
M.G.M. ANIMATION/GRAPHICS

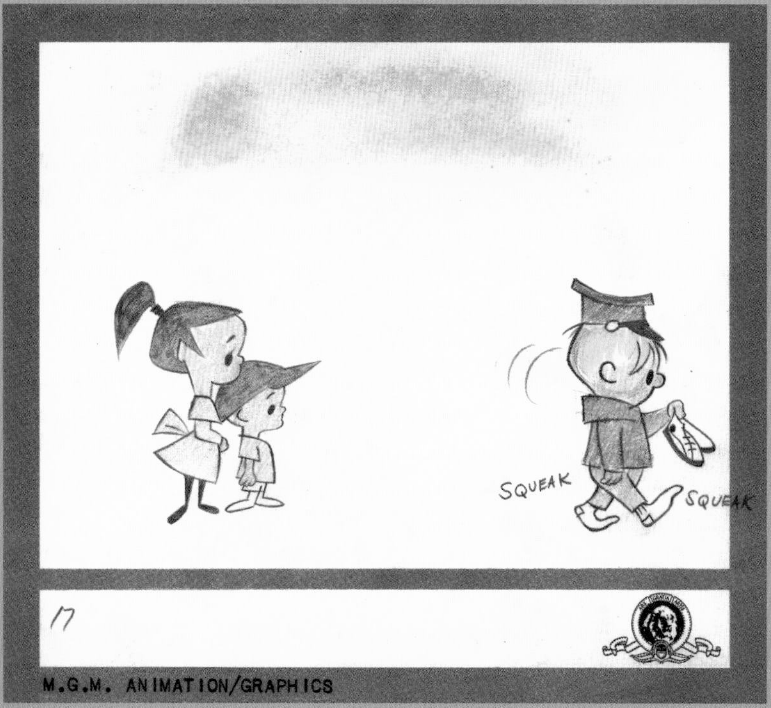
SQUEAK
SQUEAK
17
M.G.M. ANIMATION/GRAPHICS

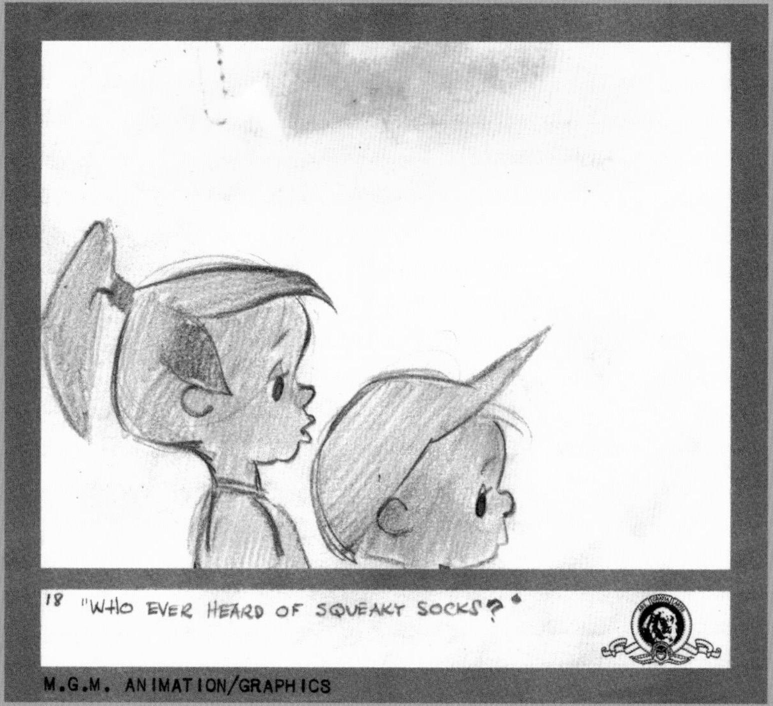
18 "WHO EVER HEARD OF SQUEAKY SOCKS?"
M.G.M. ANIMATION/GRAPHICS

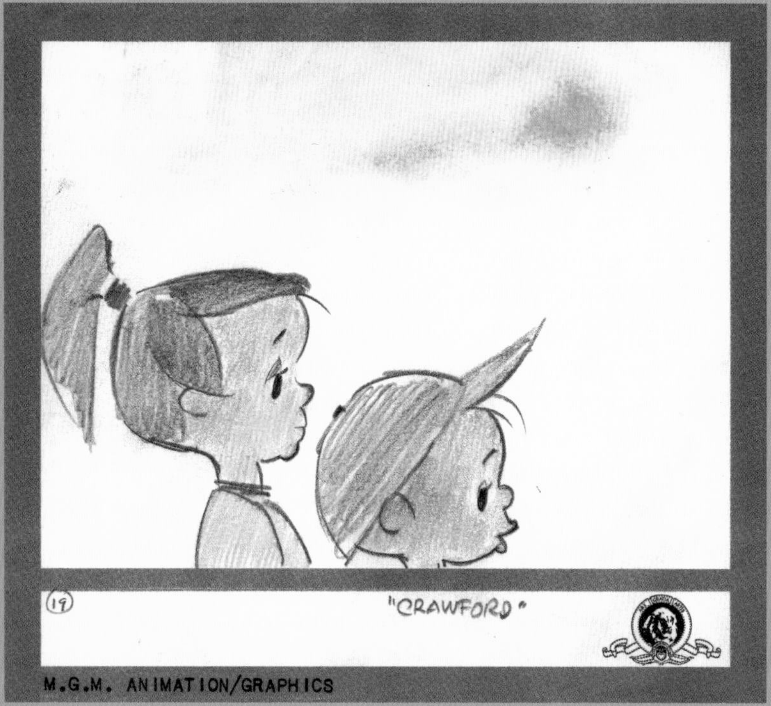
19
"CRAWFORD"
M.G.M. ANIMATION/GRAPHICS

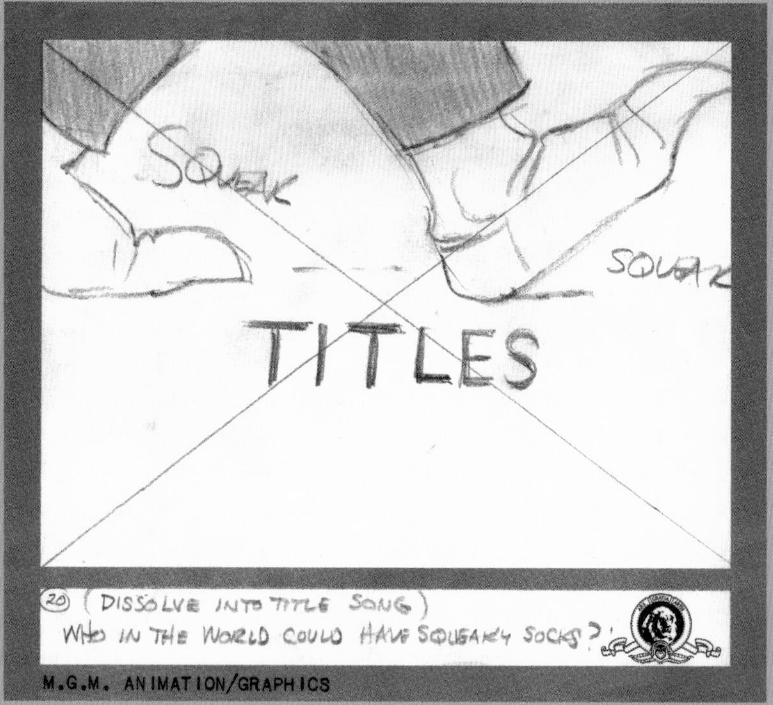
SQUEAK
SQUEAK
TITLES
20 (DISSOLVE INTO TITLE SONG)
WHO IN THE WORLD COULD HAVE SQUEAKY SOCKS?
M.G.M. ANIMATION/GRAPHICS

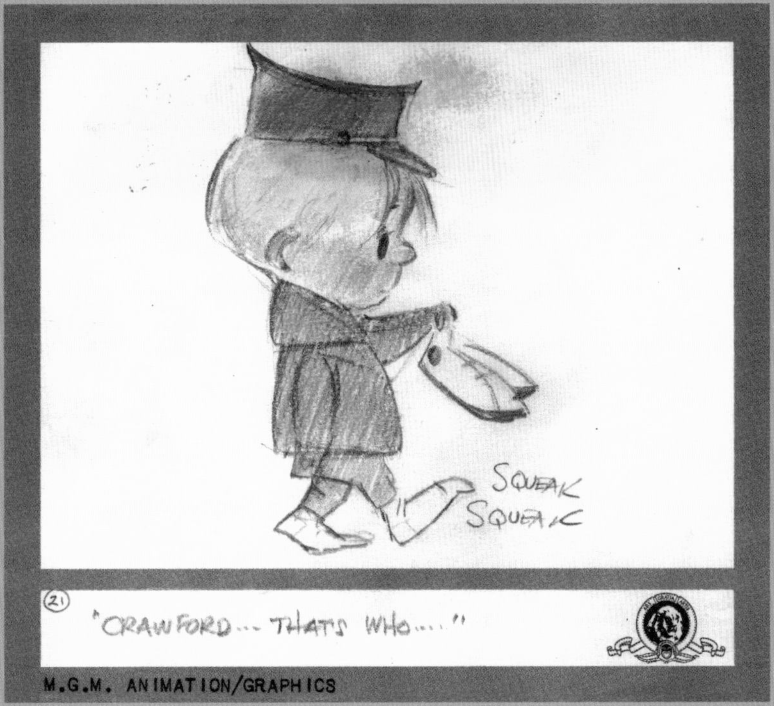
SQUEAK
SQUEAK
21 "CRAWFORD... THAT'S WHO...."
M.G.M. ANIMATION/GRAPHICS

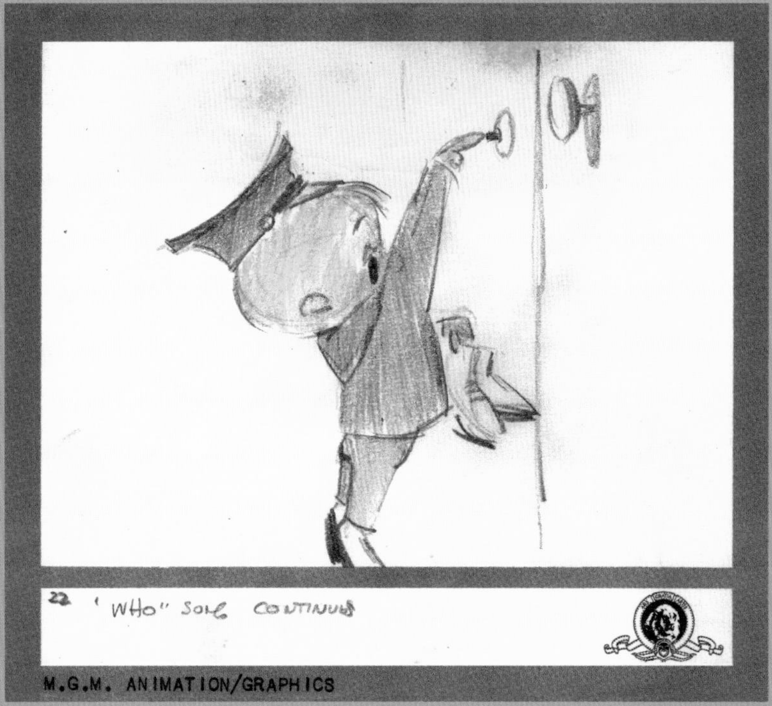
22 'WHO" SONG CONTINUES
M.G.M. ANIMATION/GRAPHICS

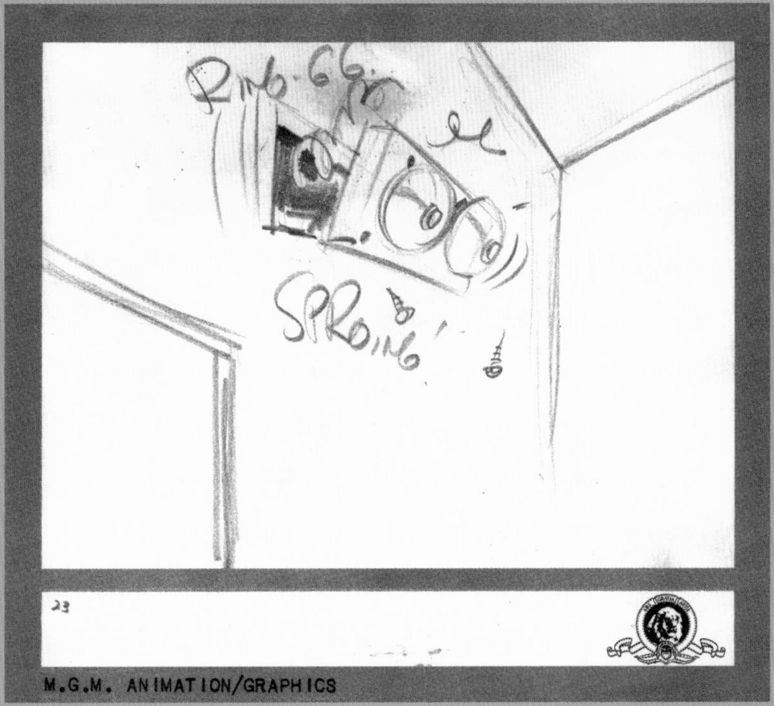
SPROING!
23
M.G.M. ANIMATION/GRAPHICS

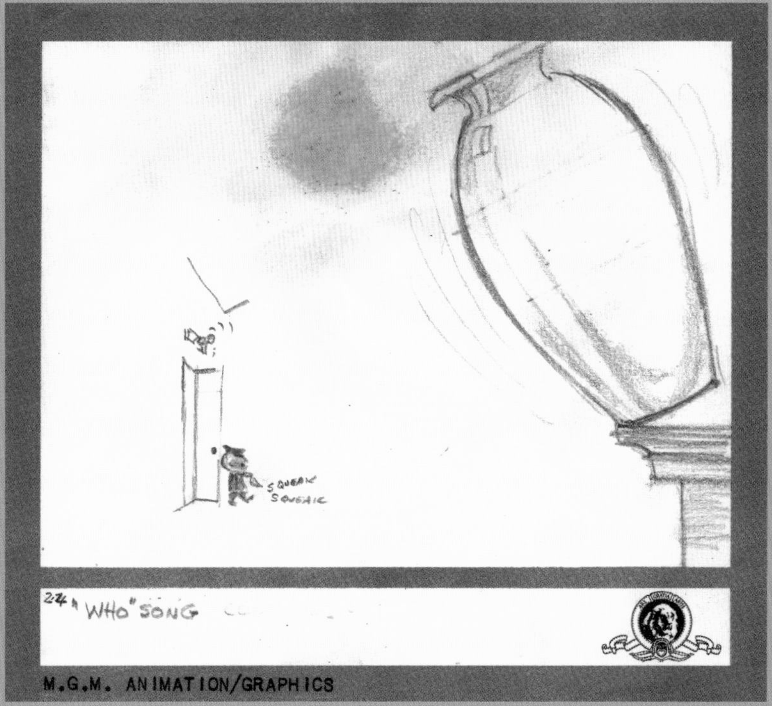
SQUEAK
SQUEAK
24 "WHO" SONG
M.G.M. ANIMATION/GRAPHICS

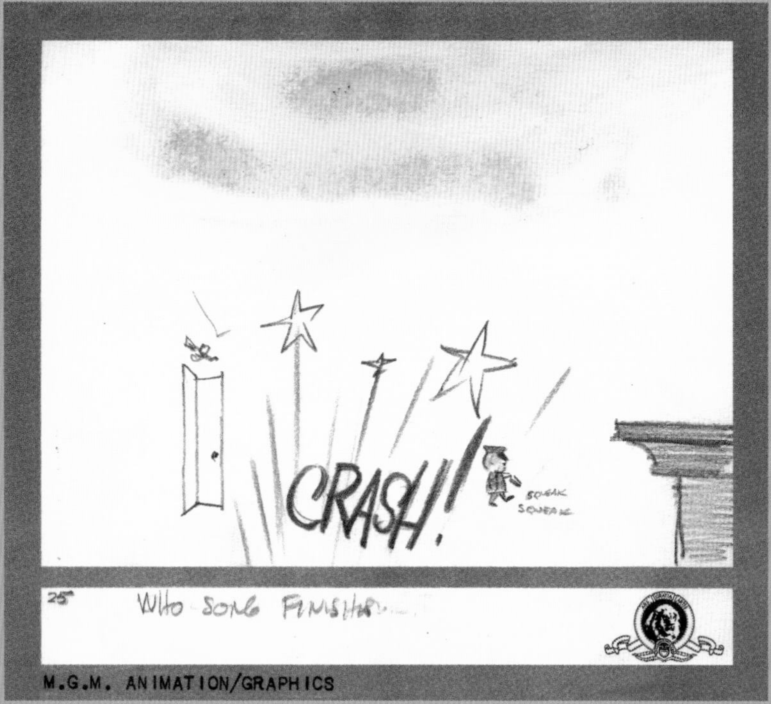
CRASH!
SQUEAK
SQUEAK
25
WHO SONG FINISHES...
M.G.M. ANIMATION/GRAPHICS

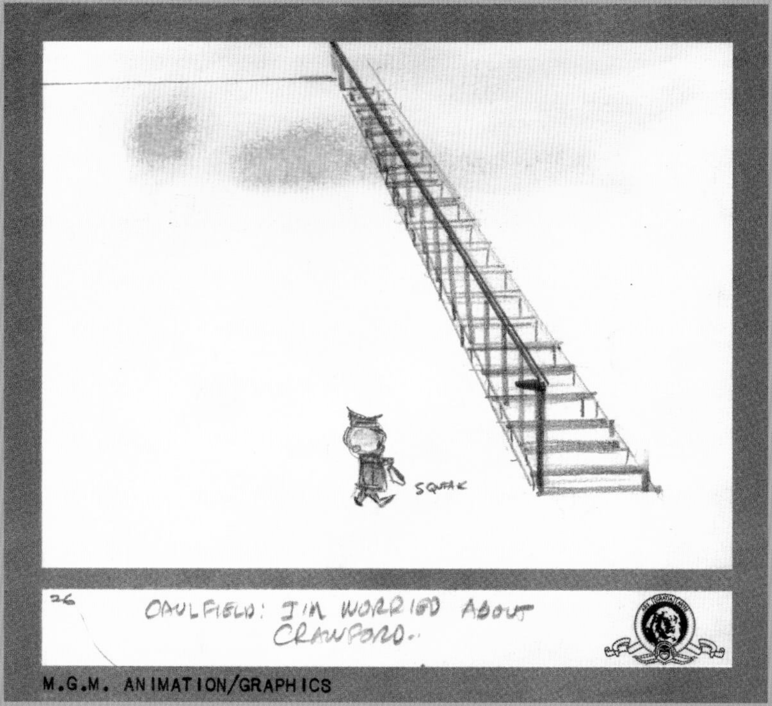
SQUEAK
26
CAULFIELD: I'M WORRIED ABOUT CRAWFORD..
M.G.M. ANIMATION/GRAPHICS

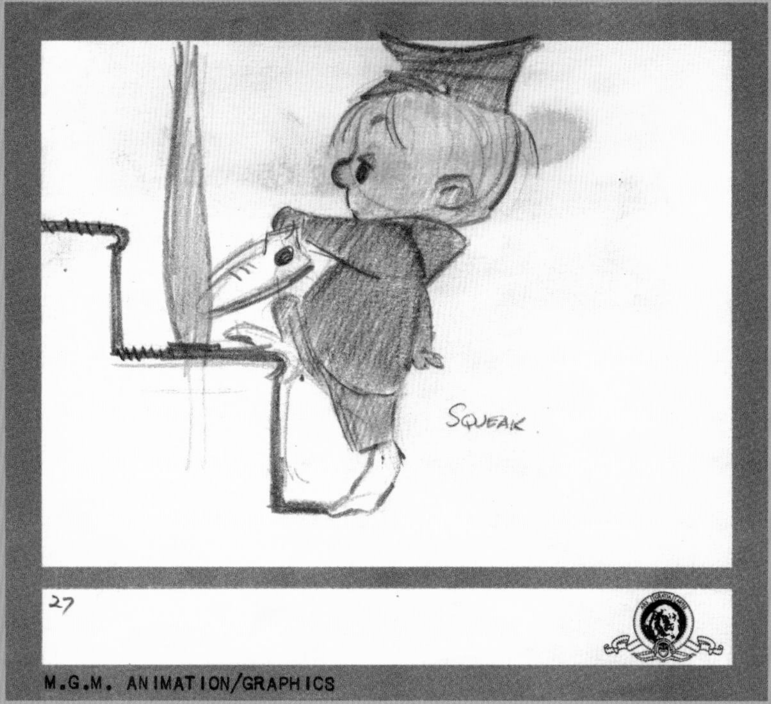
SQUEAK
27
M.G.M. ANIMATION/GRAPHICS

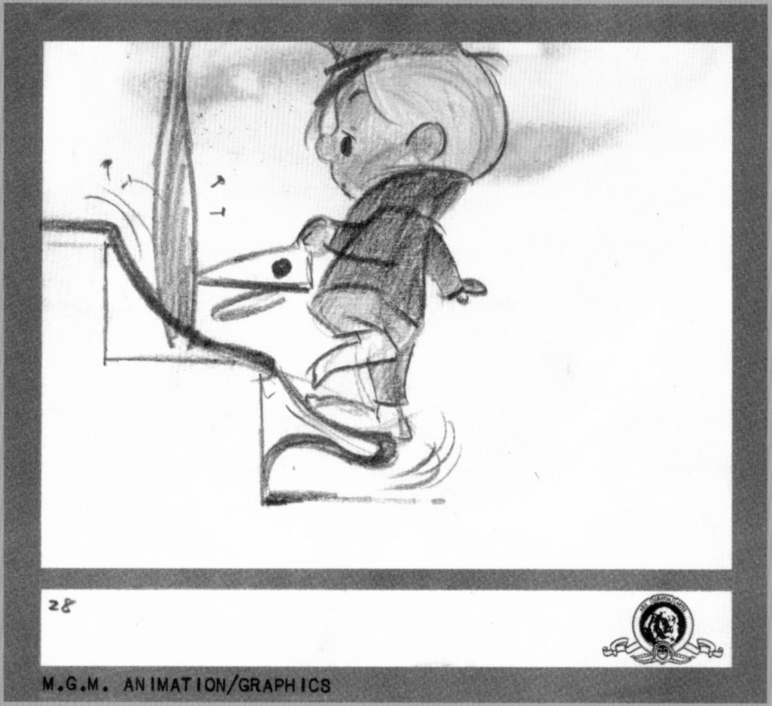
28
M.G.M. ANIMATION/GRAPHICS

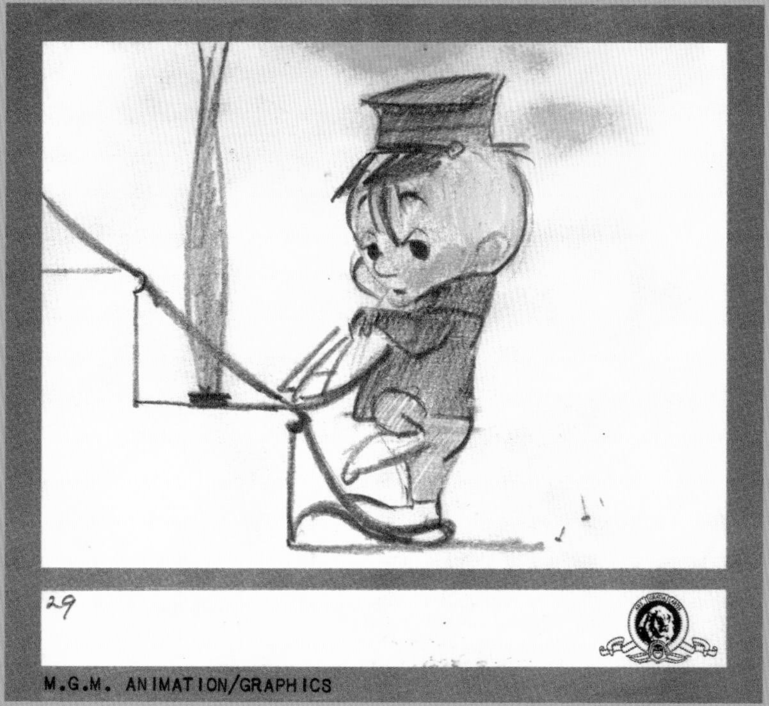
29
M.G.M. ANIMATION/GRAPHICS

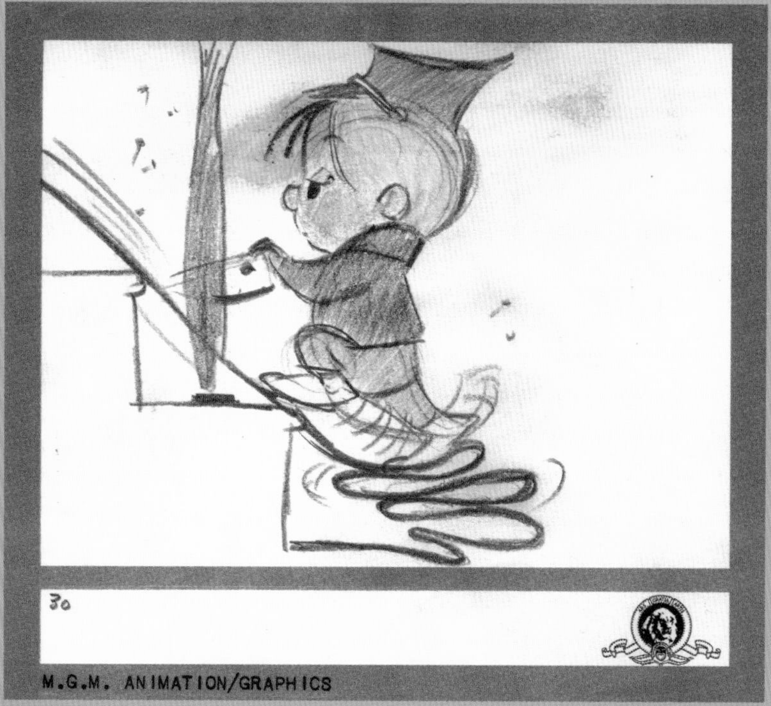
30
M.G.M. ANIMATION/GRAPHICS

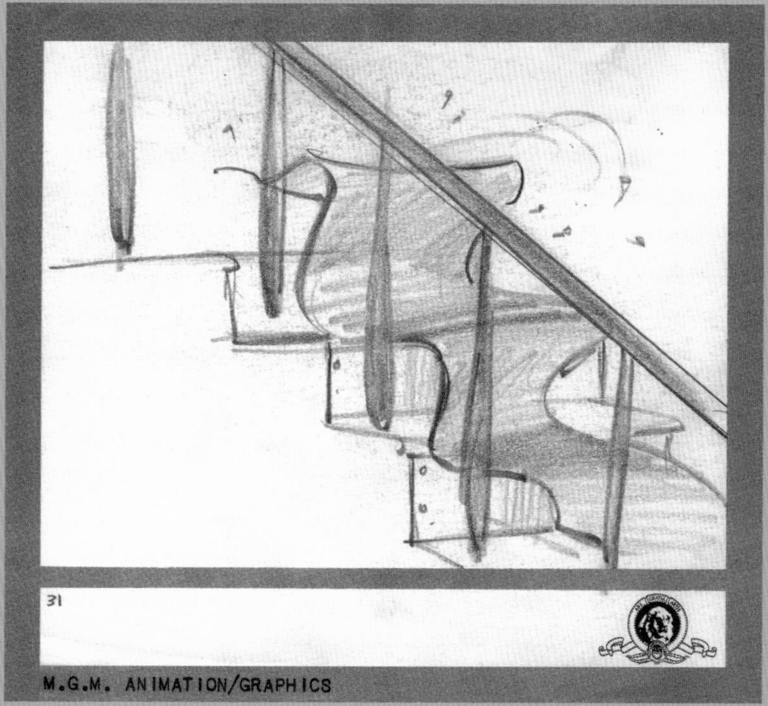
31
M.G.M. ANIMATION/GRAPHICS

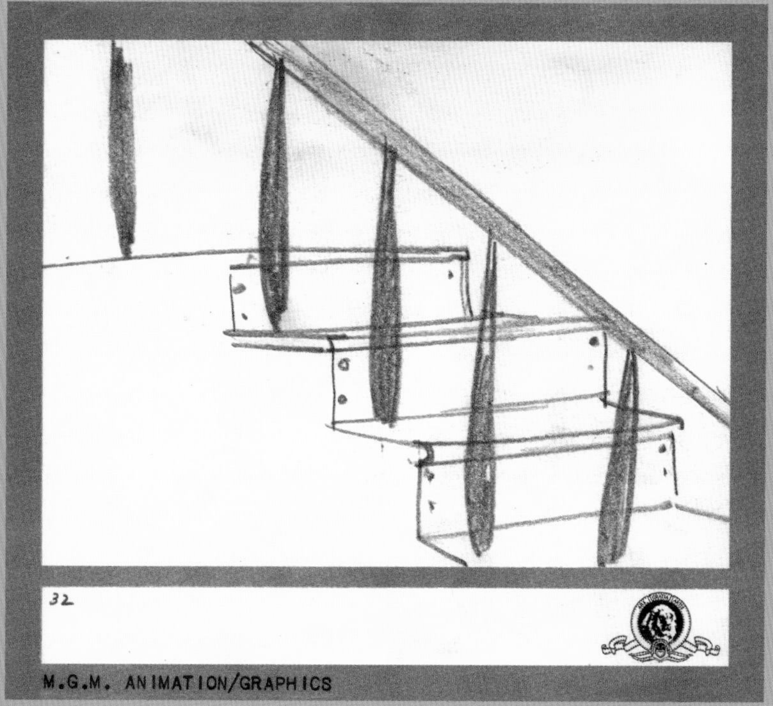
32
M.G.M. ANIMATION/GRAPHICS

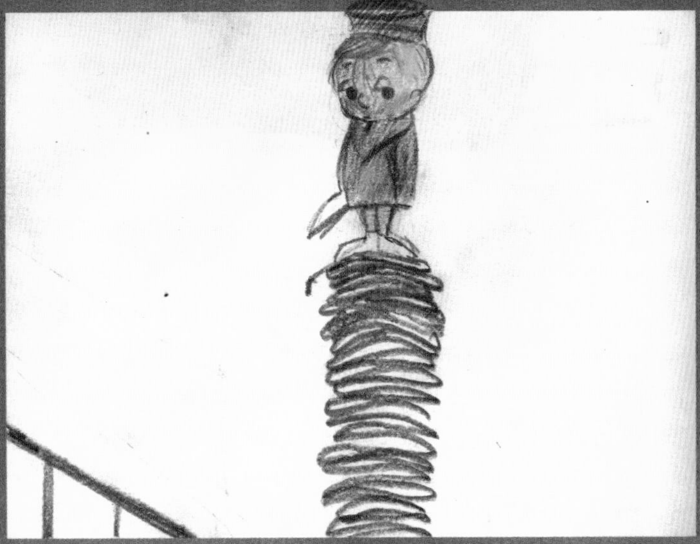

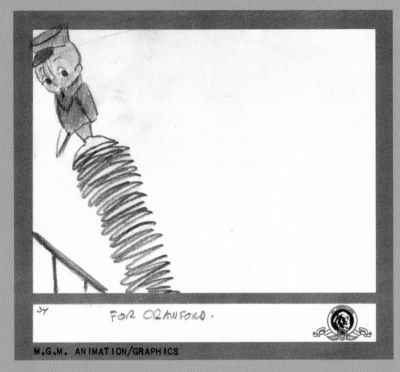

33 CAULFIELD - NO, NOT THAT. THAT'S NORMAL

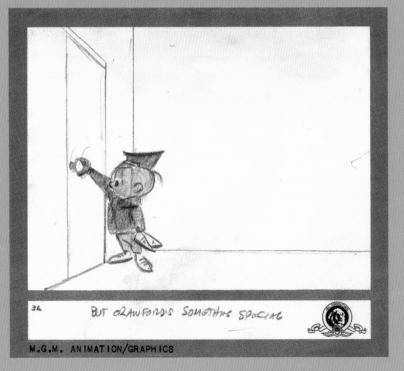

M.G.M. ANIMATION/GRAPHICS

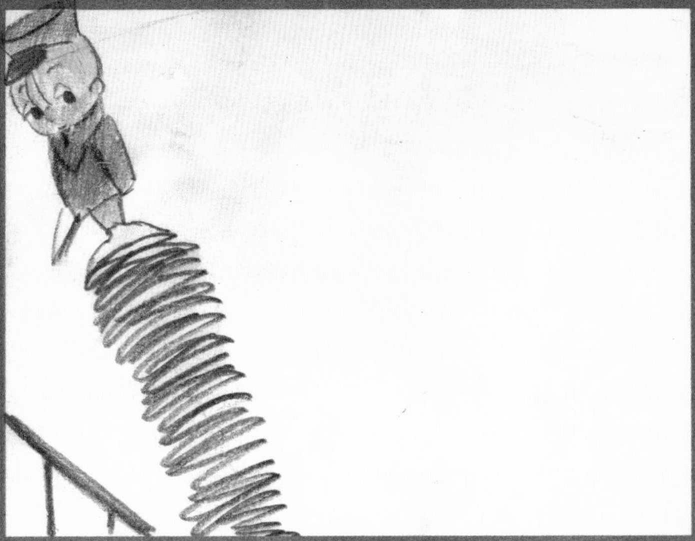

34 FOR CRAWFORD.

M.G.M. ANIMATION/GRAPHICS

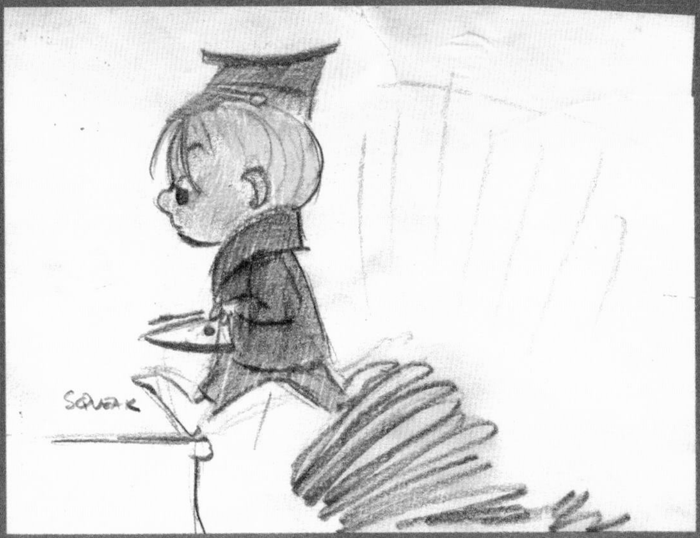
SQUEAK

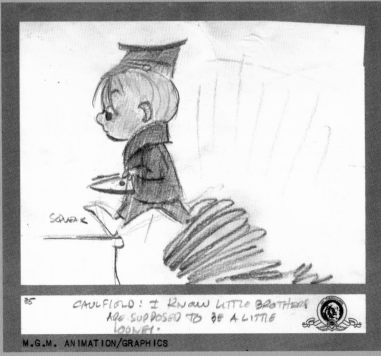

35 CAULFIELD: I KNOW LITTLE BROTHERS ARE SUPPOSED TO BE A LITTLE LOONEY.

M.G.M. ANIMATION/GRAPHICS

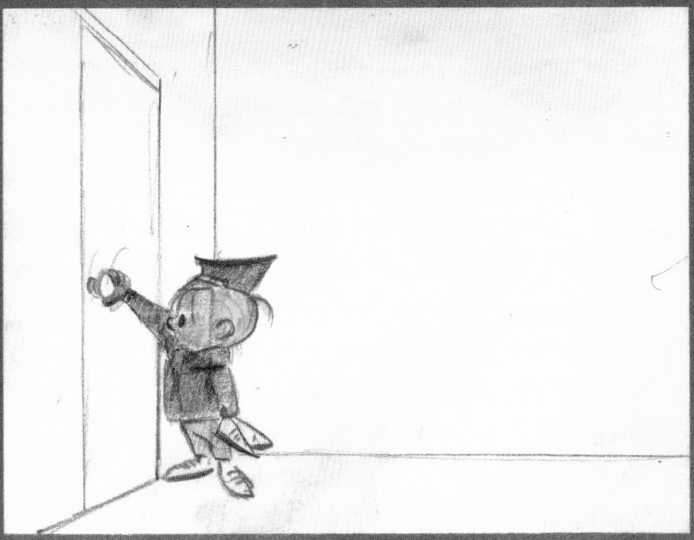

36 BUT CRAWFORD'S SOMETHING SPECIAL

M.G.M. ANIMATION/GRAPHICS

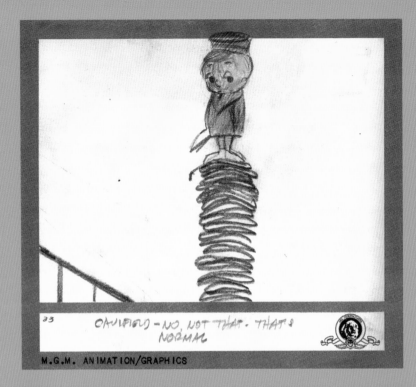

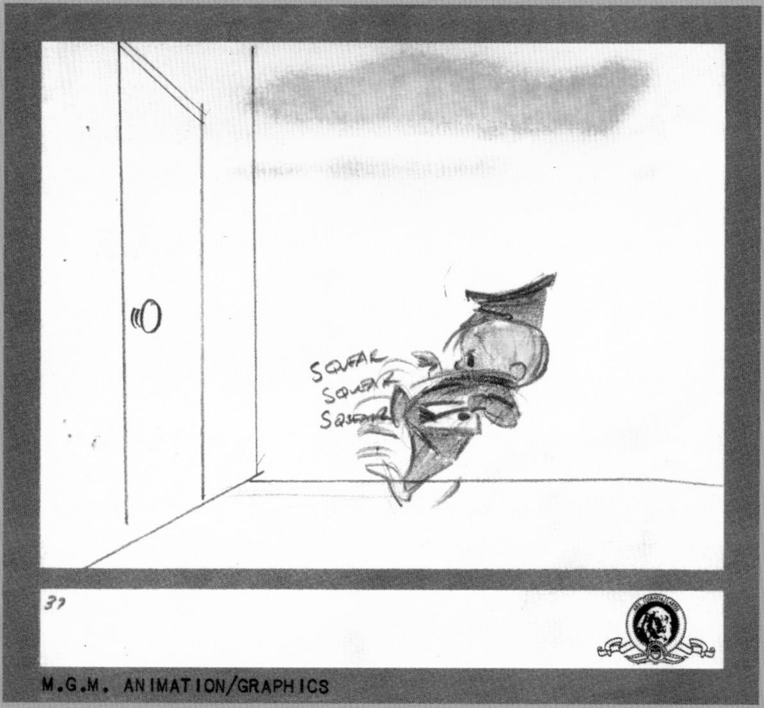
SQUEAK
SQUEAK
SQUEAK
37
M.G.M. ANIMATION/GRAPHICS

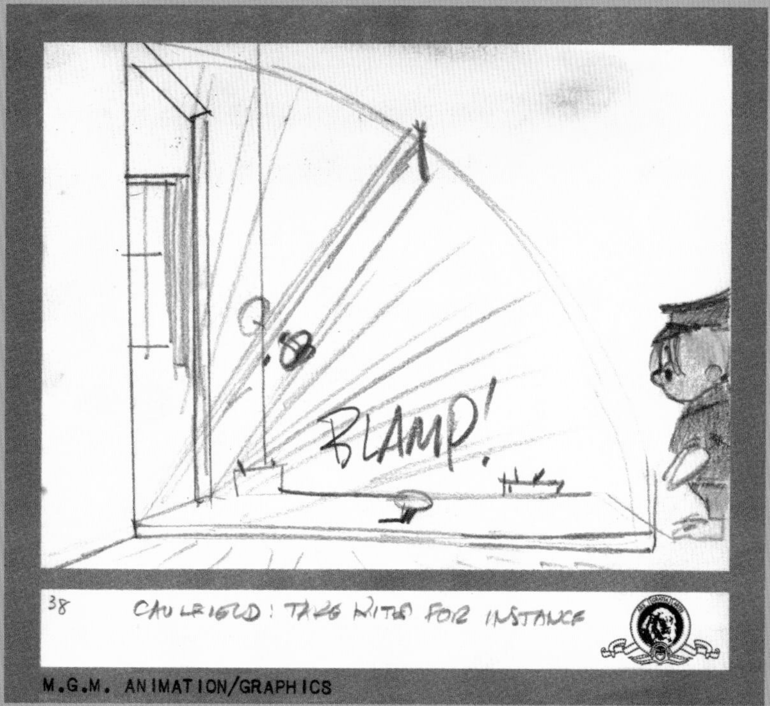
BLAMP!
38 CAULFIELD: TAKE KITES FOR INSTANCE
M.G.M. ANIMATION/GRAPHICS

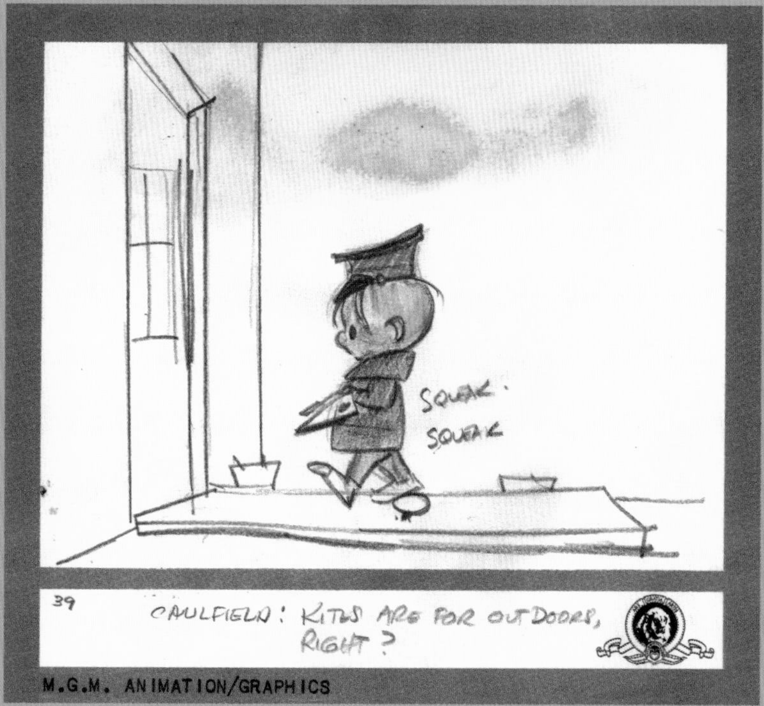
SQUEAK
SQUEAK
39 CAULFIELD: KITES ARE FOR OUTDOORS, RIGHT?
M.G.M. ANIMATION/GRAPHICS

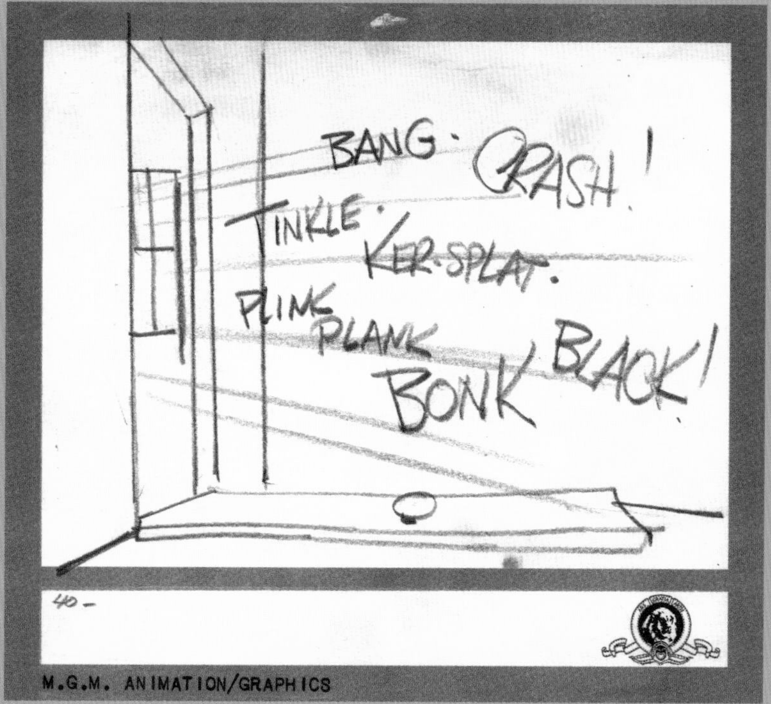
BANG. CRASH!
TINKLE. KER-SPLAT.
PLINK PLANK
BONK
BLACK!
40-
M.G.M. ANIMATION/GRAPHICS

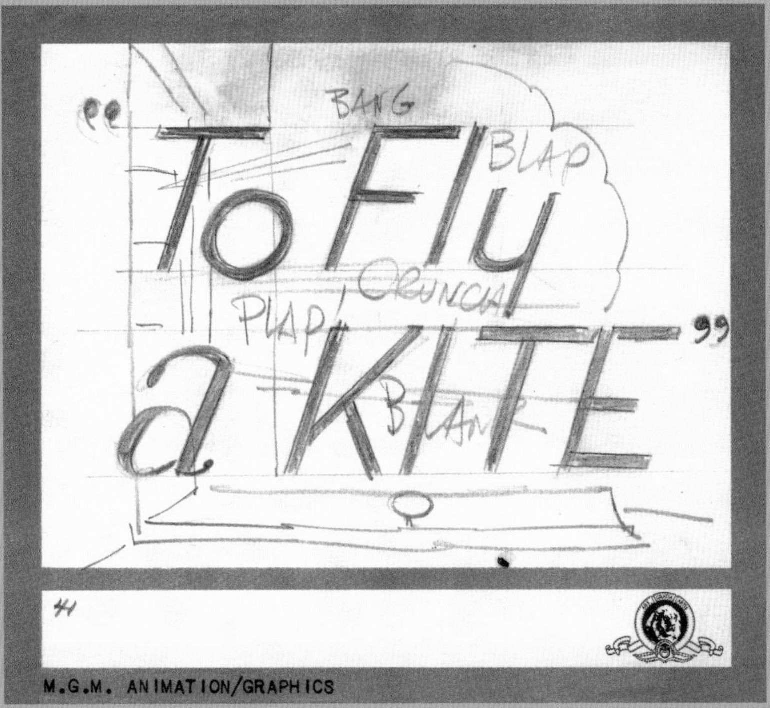

BANG
BLAP
"To Fly a KITE"
PLAP
41
M.G.M. ANIMATION/GRAPHICS

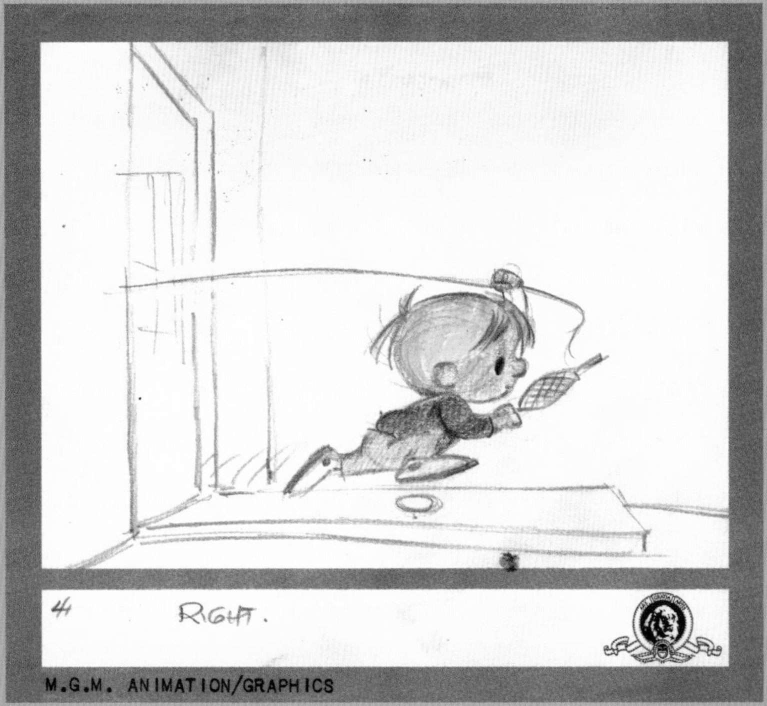

41
RIGHT.
M.G.M. ANIMATION/GRAPHICS

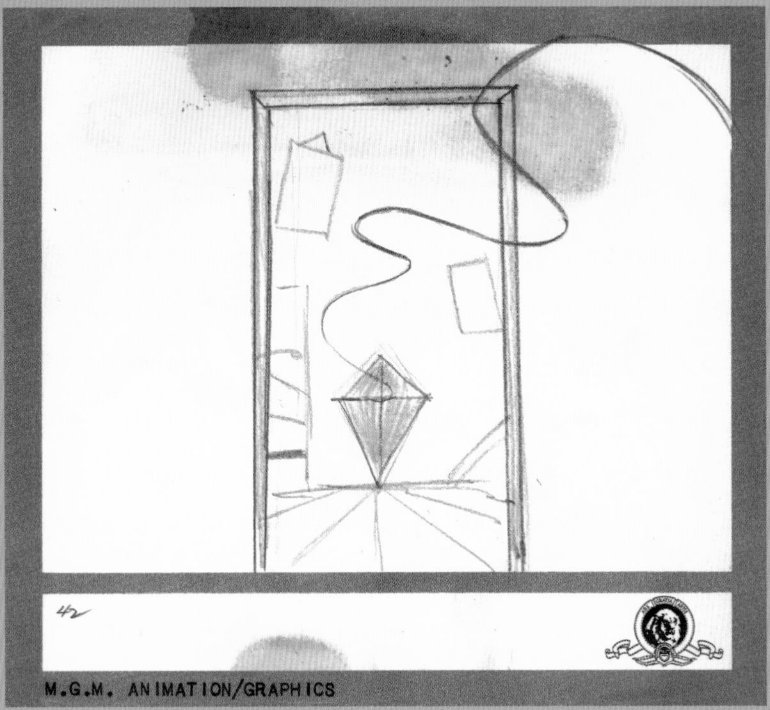

42
M.G.M. ANIMATION/GRAPHICS

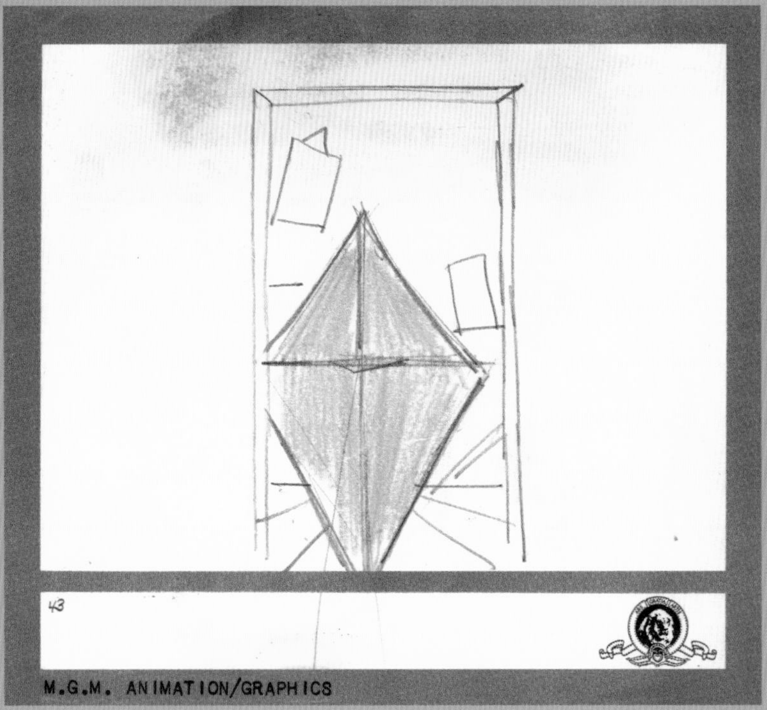

43
M.G.M. ANIMATION/GRAPHICS

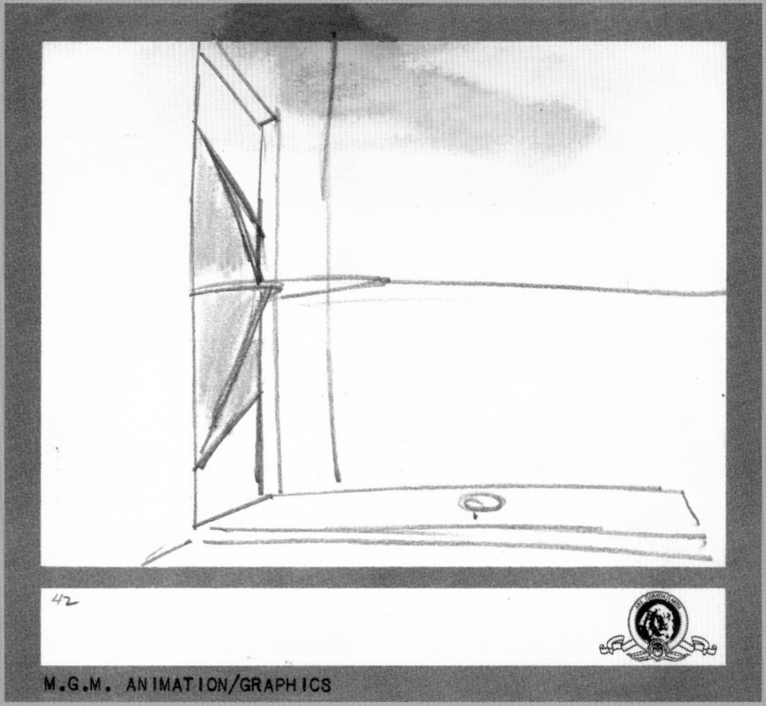
42
M.G.M. ANIMATION/GRAPHICS

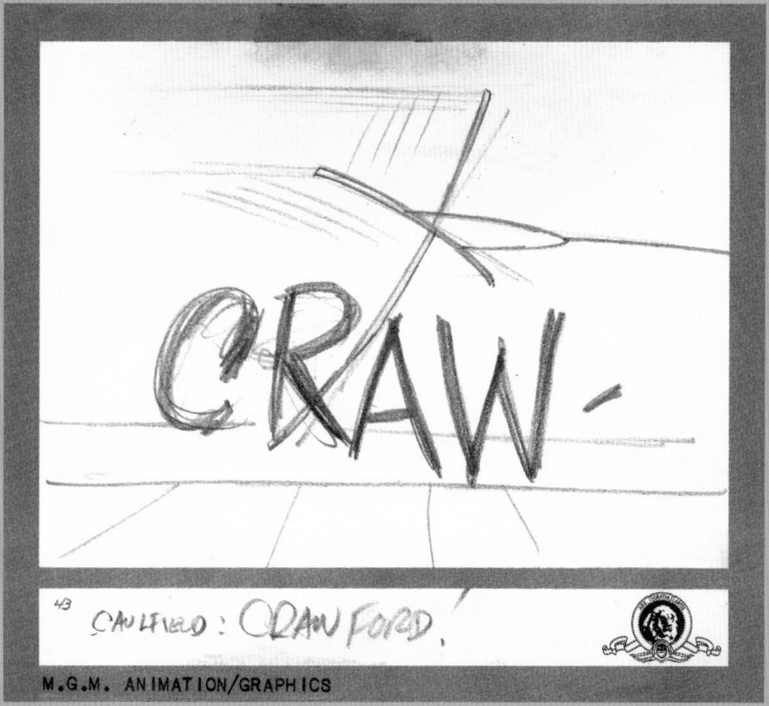
CRAW-
43
CAULFIELD: CRAWFORD!
M.G.M. ANIMATION/GRAPHICS

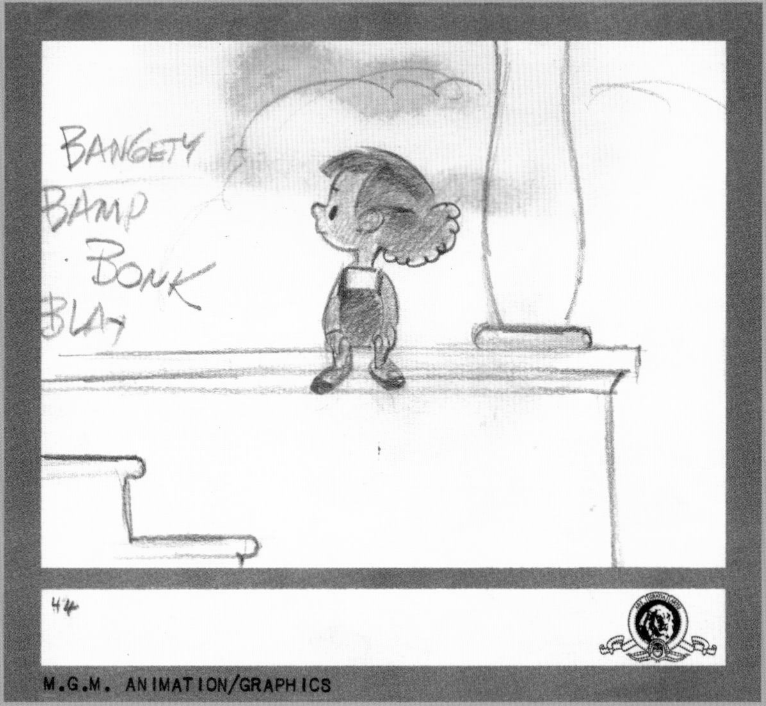
BANGETY
BAMP
BONK
44
M.G.M. ANIMATION/GRAPHICS

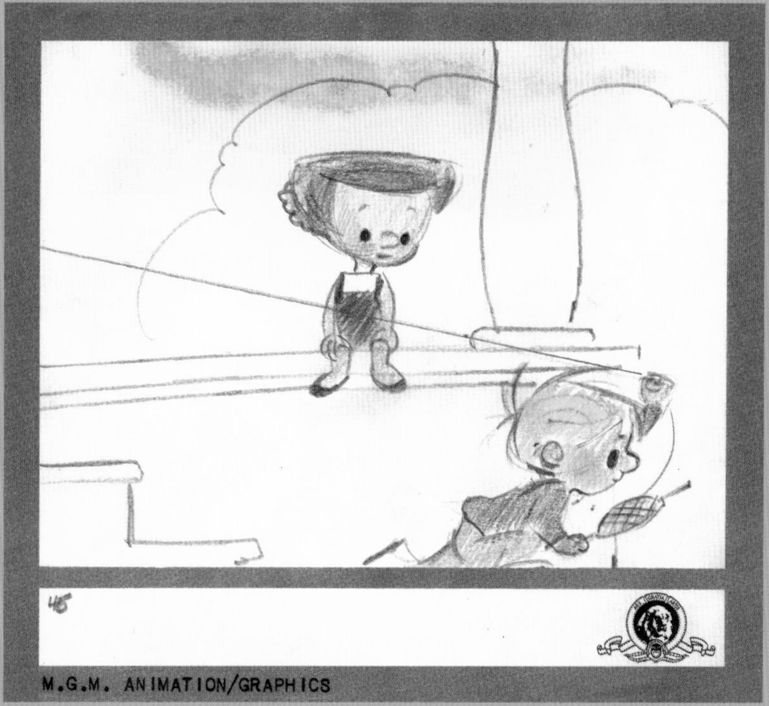
45
M.G.M. ANIMATION/GRAPHICS

WTSH

46

M.G.M. ANIMATION/GRAPHICS

47

M.G.M. ANIMATION/GRAPHICS

CRAW

48

M.G.M. ANIMATION/GRAPHICS

FORD!

49 (BRAKE SQUEAL)

M.G.M. ANIMATION/GRAPHICS

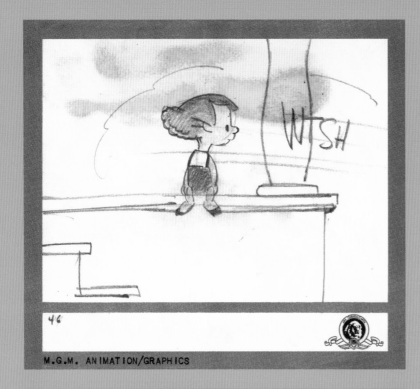

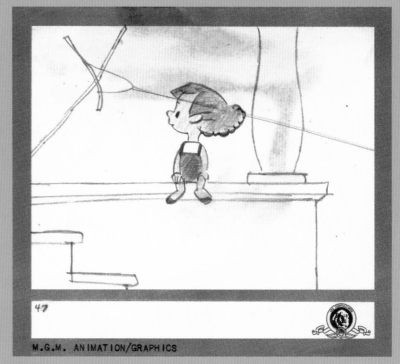

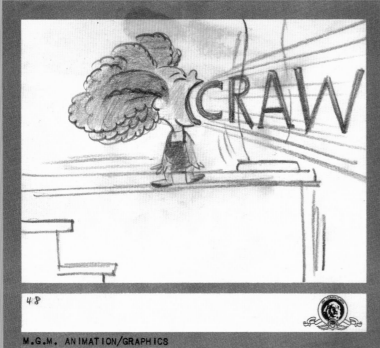

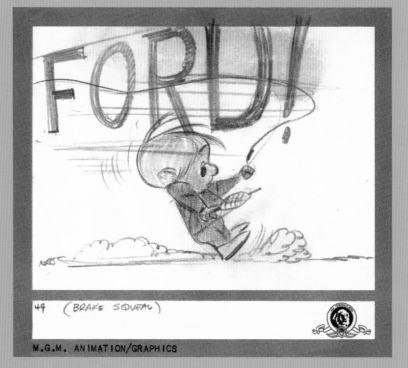

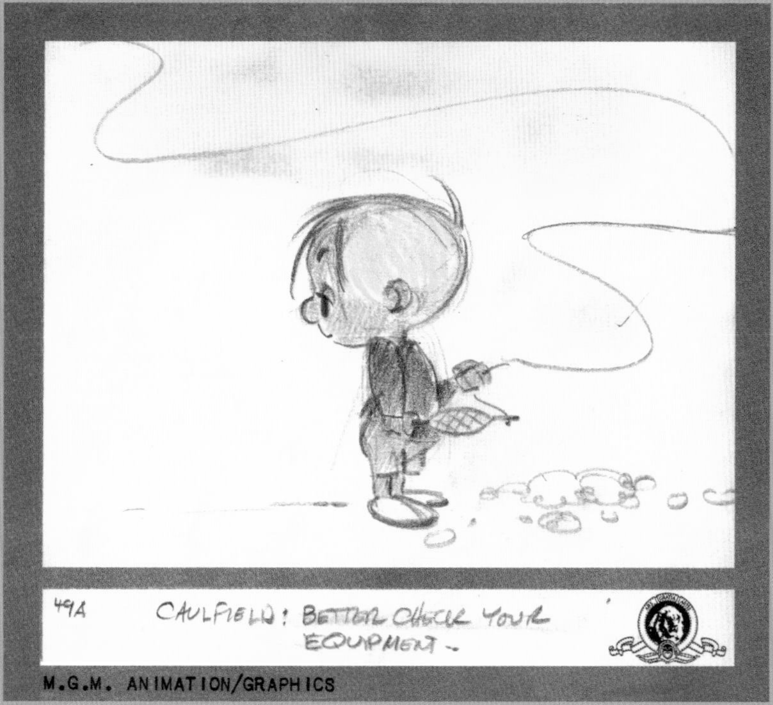
49A CAULFIELD: BETTER CHECK YOUR EQUIPMENT..
M.G.M. ANIMATION/GRAPHICS

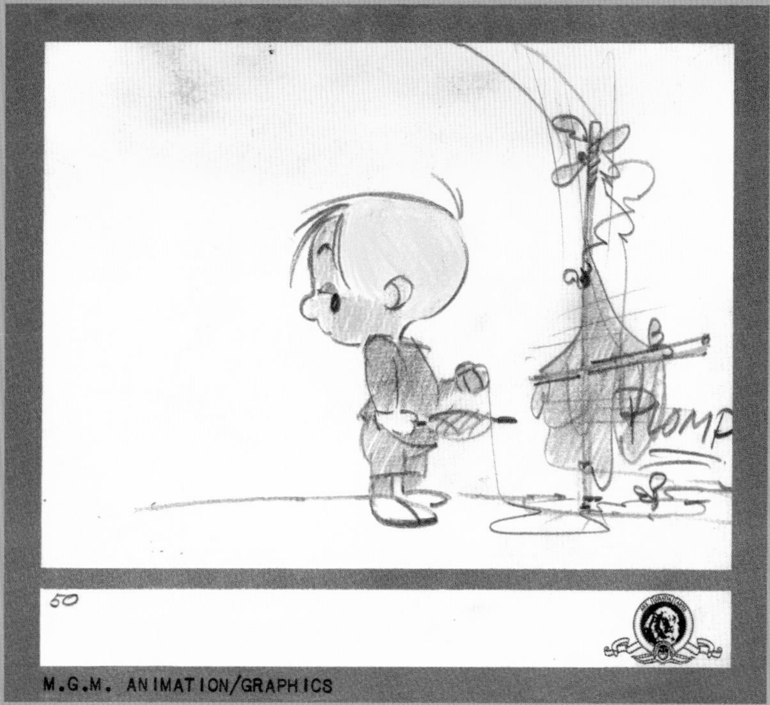
PLOMP
50
M.G.M. ANIMATION/GRAPHICS

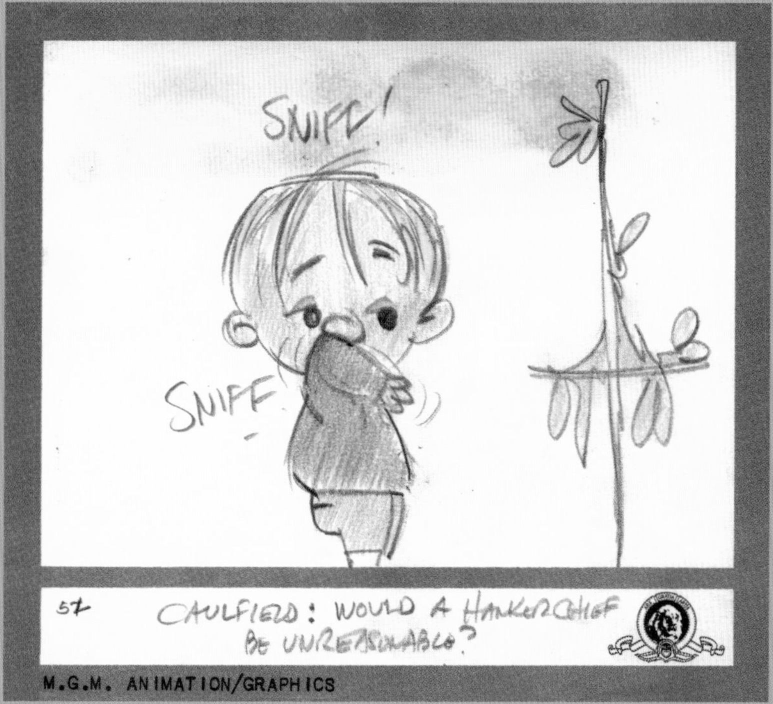
SNIFF!
SNIFF
57 CAULFIELD: WOULD A HANKERCHIEF BE UNREASONABLE?
M.G.M. ANIMATION/GRAPHICS

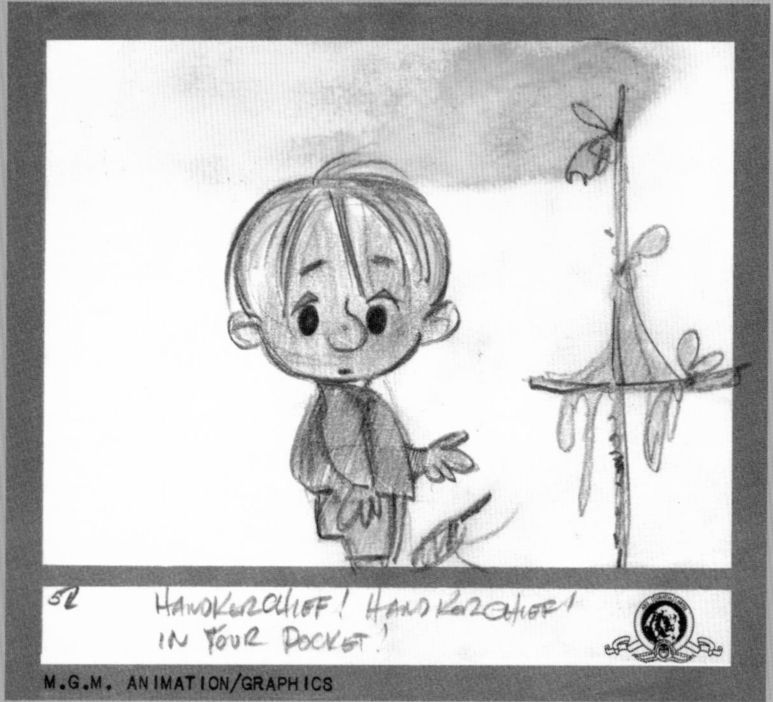
58 HANDKERCHIEF! HANDKERCHIEF! IN YOUR POCKET!
M.G.M. ANIMATION/GRAPHICS

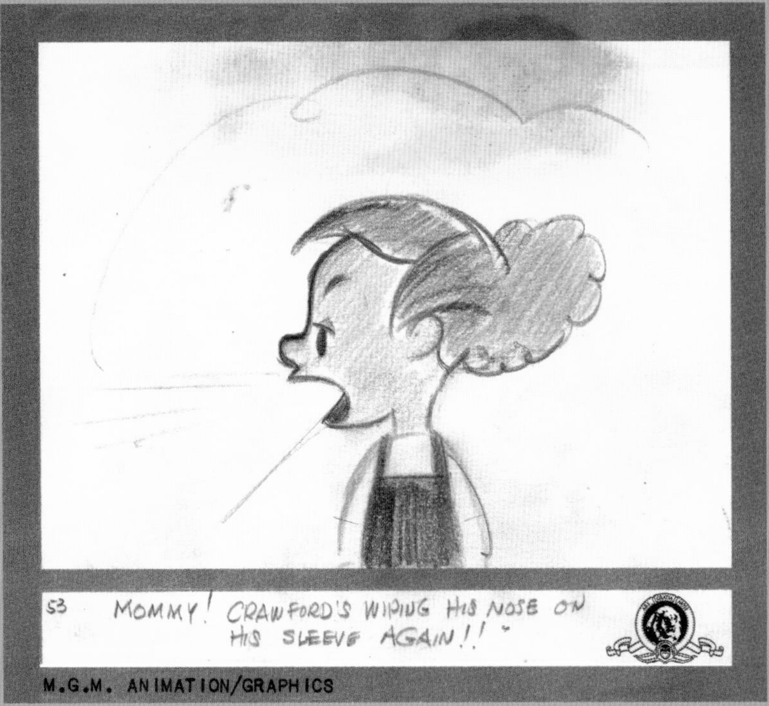
53 MOMMY! CRAWFORD'S WIPING HIS NOSE ON HIS SLEEVE AGAIN!!"
M.G.M. ANIMATION/GRAPHICS

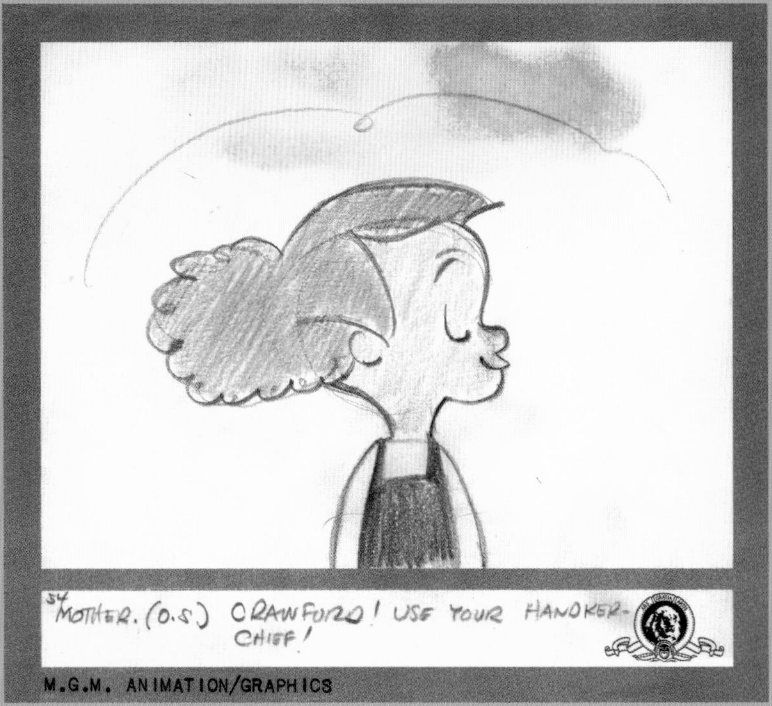
54 MOTHER. (O.S.) CRAWFORD! USE YOUR HANDKER-CHIEF!
M.G.M. ANIMATION/GRAPHICS

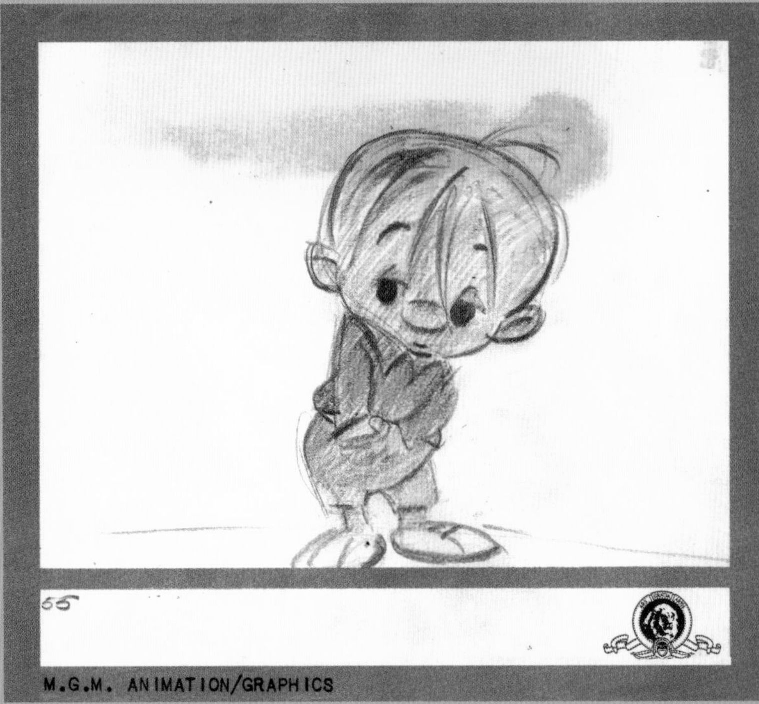
55
M.G.M. ANIMATION/GRAPHICS

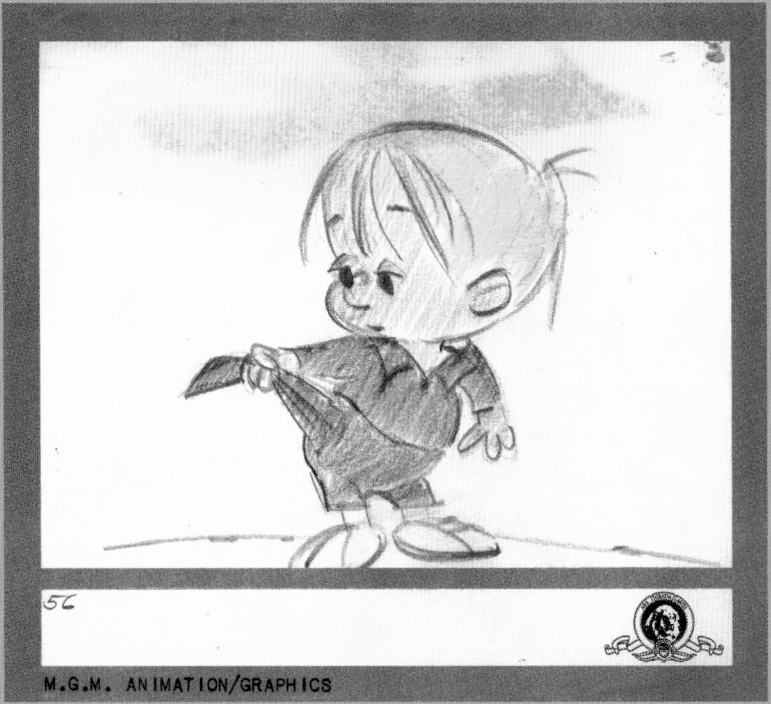
56
M.G.M. ANIMATION/GRAPHICS

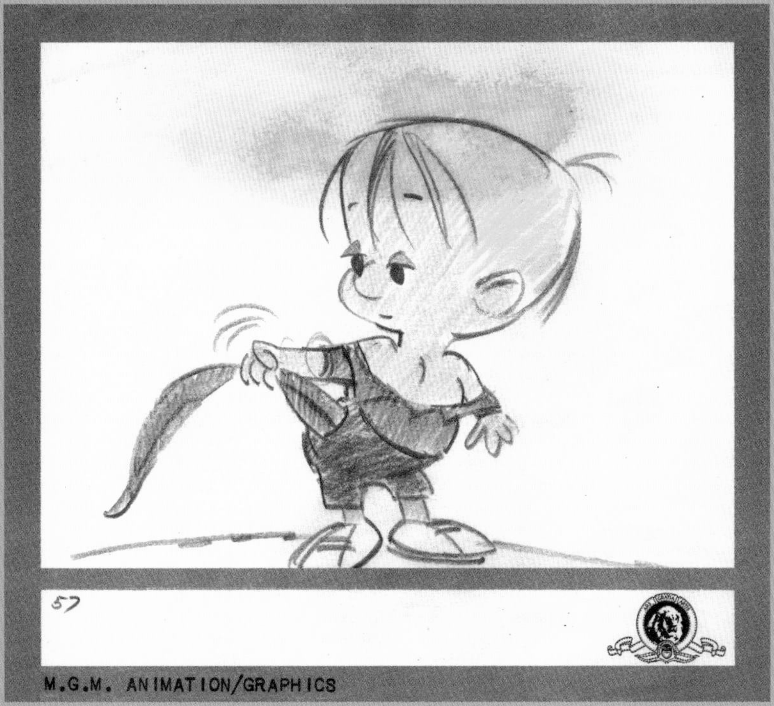
57
M.G.M. ANIMATION/GRAPHICS

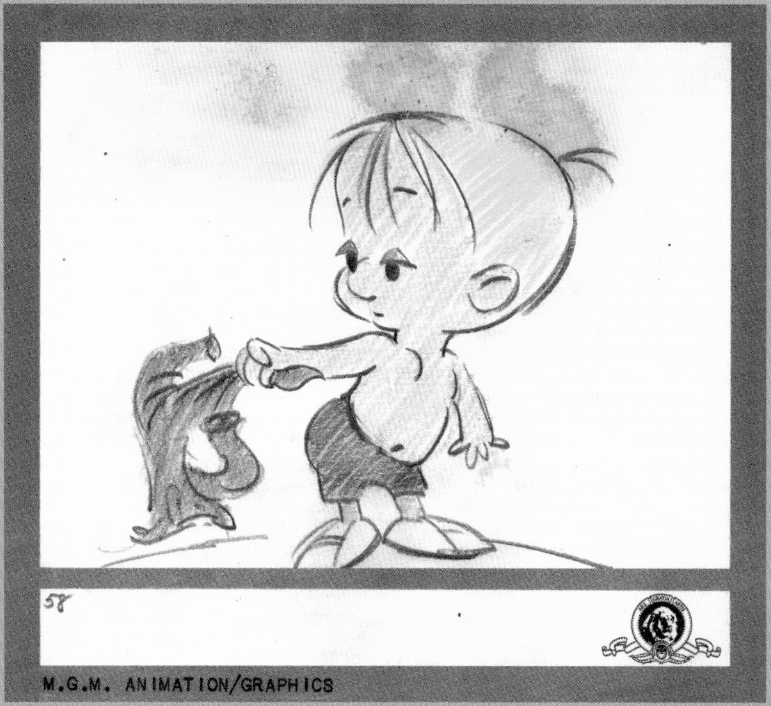
58
M.G.M. ANIMATION/GRAPHICS

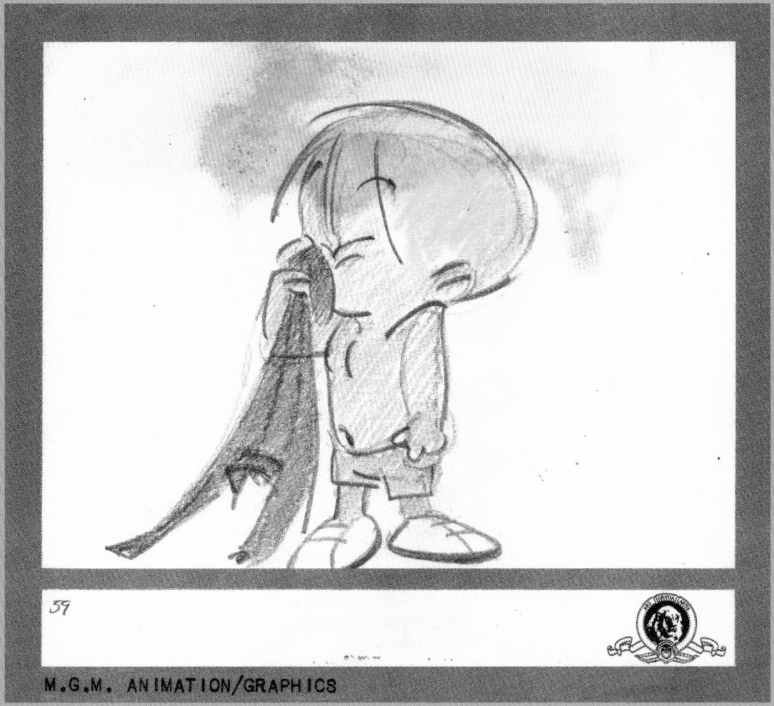
59
M.G.M. ANIMATION/GRAPHICS

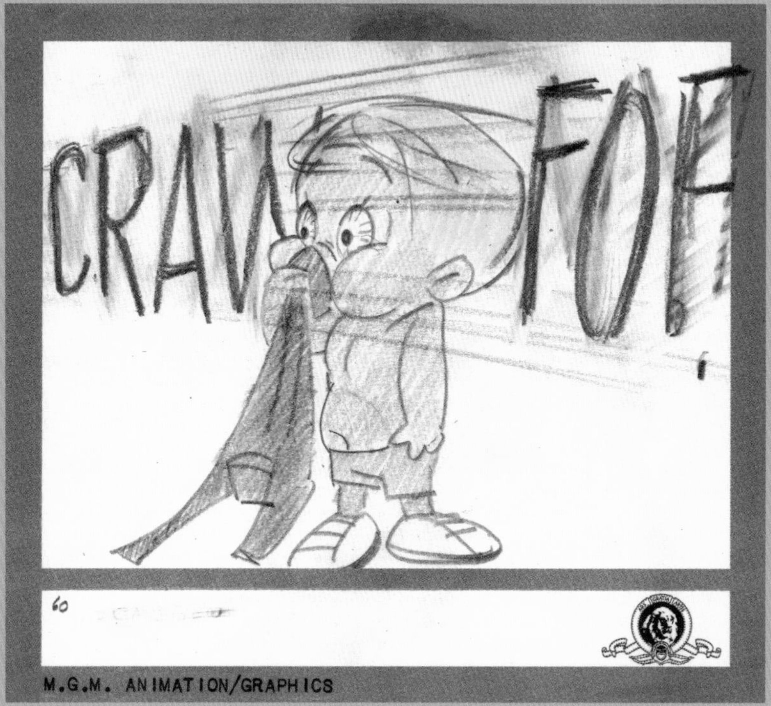
CRAW
60
M.G.M. ANIMATION/GRAPHICS

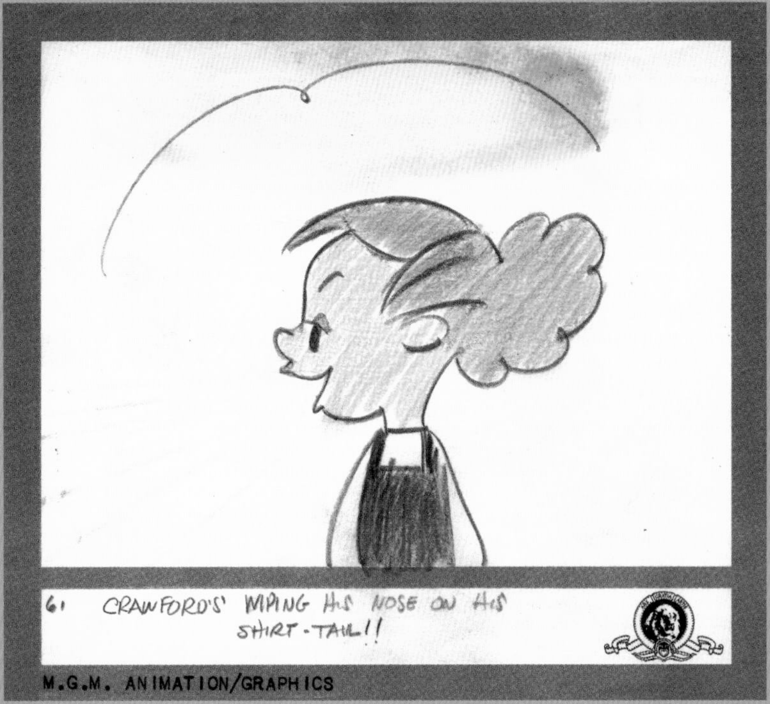
61 CRAWFORD'S' WIPING HIS NOSE ON HIS SHIRT-TAIL!!
M.G.M. ANIMATION/GRAPHICS

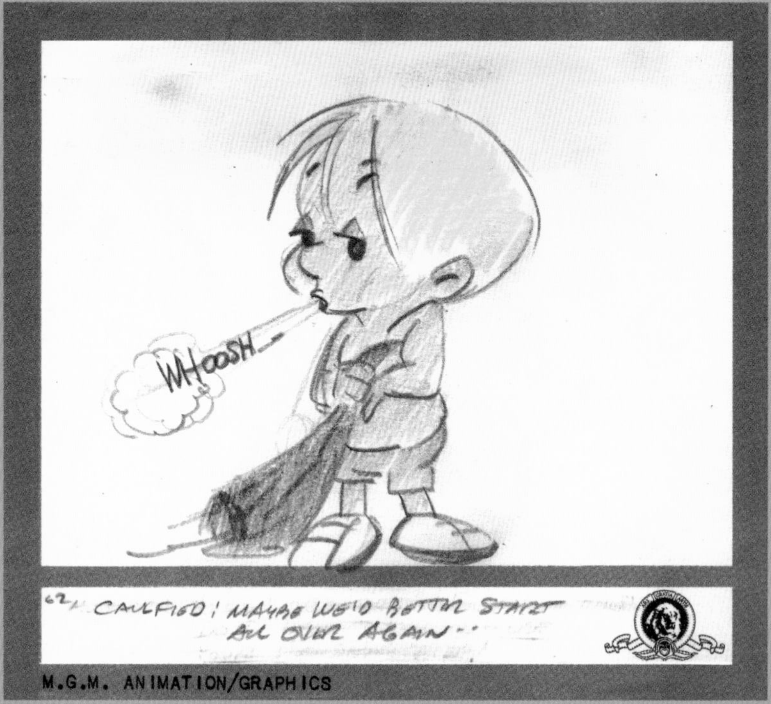
WHOOSH
62 CAULFIELD: MAYBE WE'D BETTER START ALL OVER AGAIN..
M.G.M. ANIMATION/GRAPHICS

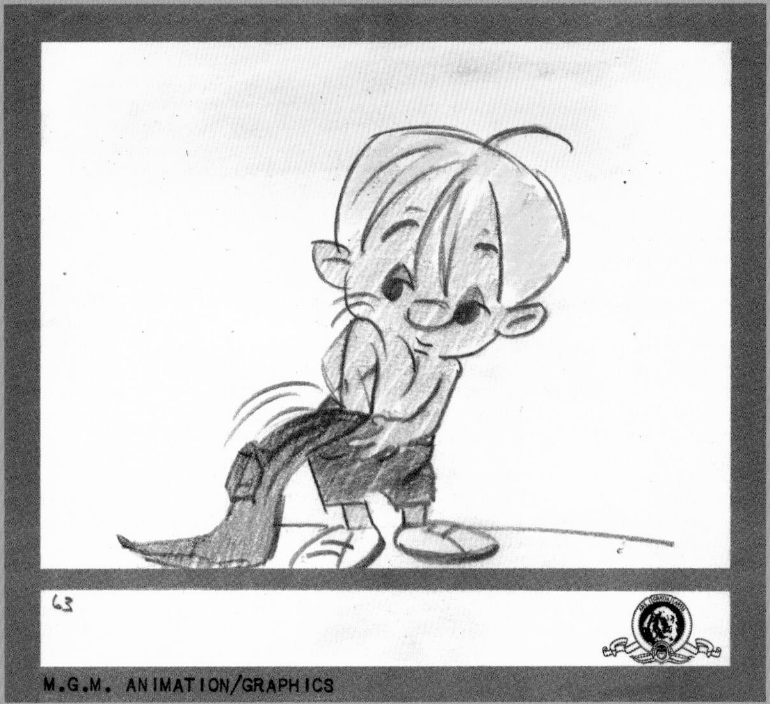
63
M.G.M. ANIMATION/GRAPHICS

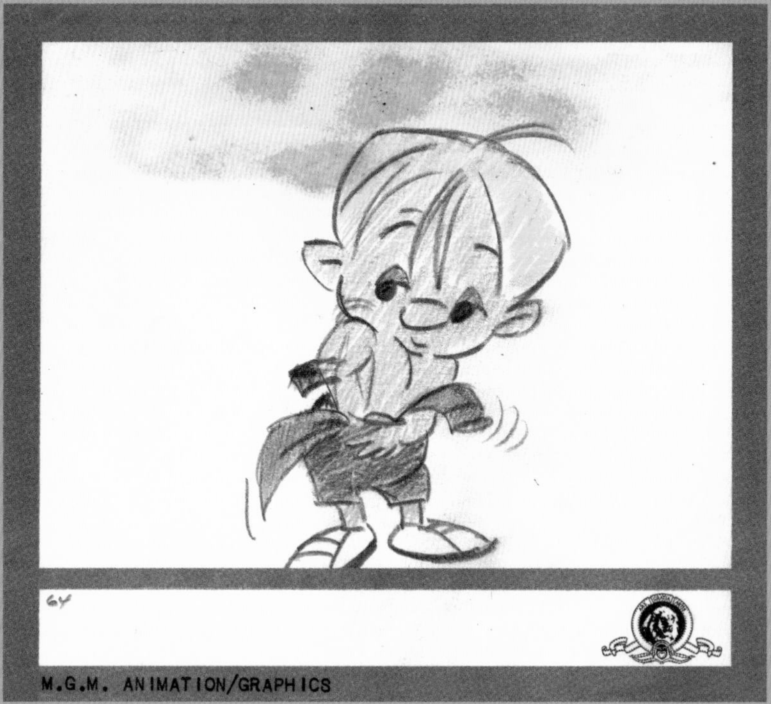
64
M.G.M. ANIMATION/GRAPHICS

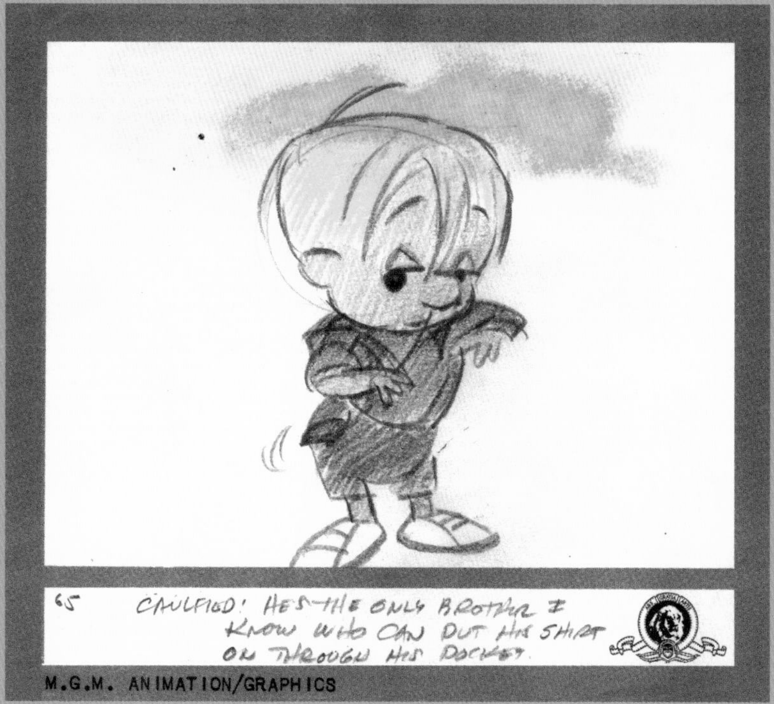
65 CAULFIED: HE'S THE ONLY BROTHER I KNOW WHO CAN PUT HIS SHIRT ON THROUGH HIS POCKET.
M.G.M. ANIMATION/GRAPHICS

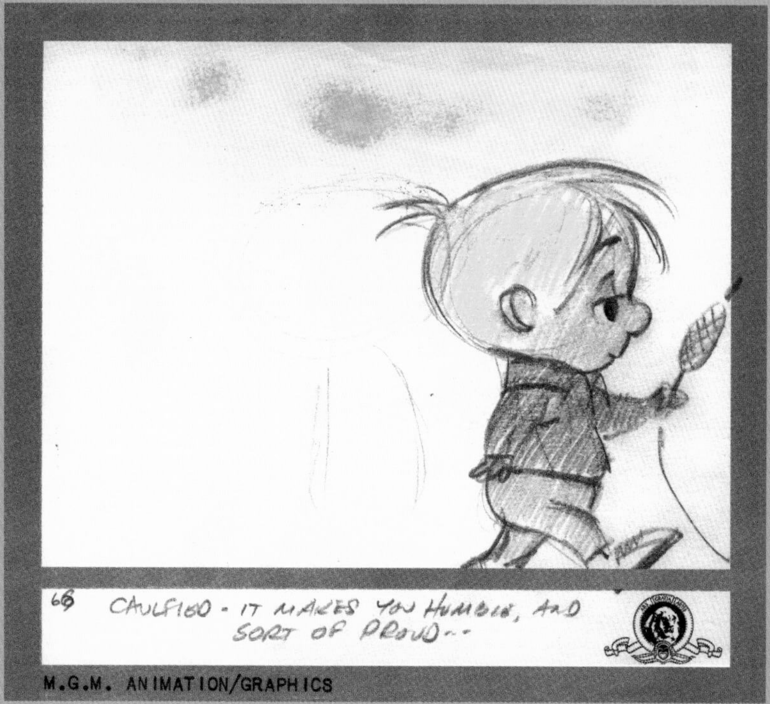
66 CAULFIED - IT MAKES YOU HUMBLE, AND SORT OF PROUD--
M.G.M. ANIMATION/GRAPHICS

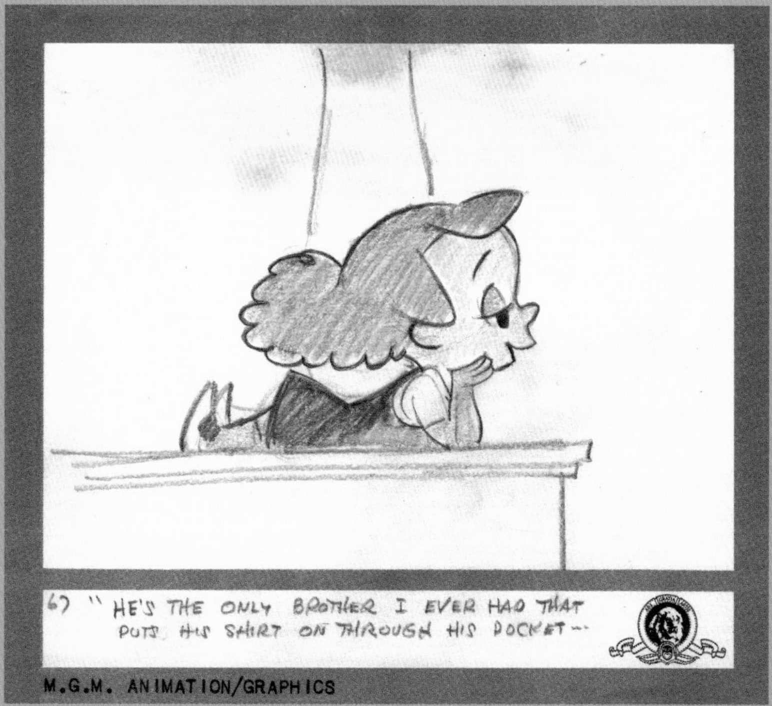
67 "HE'S THE ONLY BROTHER I EVER HAD THAT PUTS HIS SHIRT ON THROUGH HIS POCKET--
M.G.M. ANIMATION/GRAPHICS

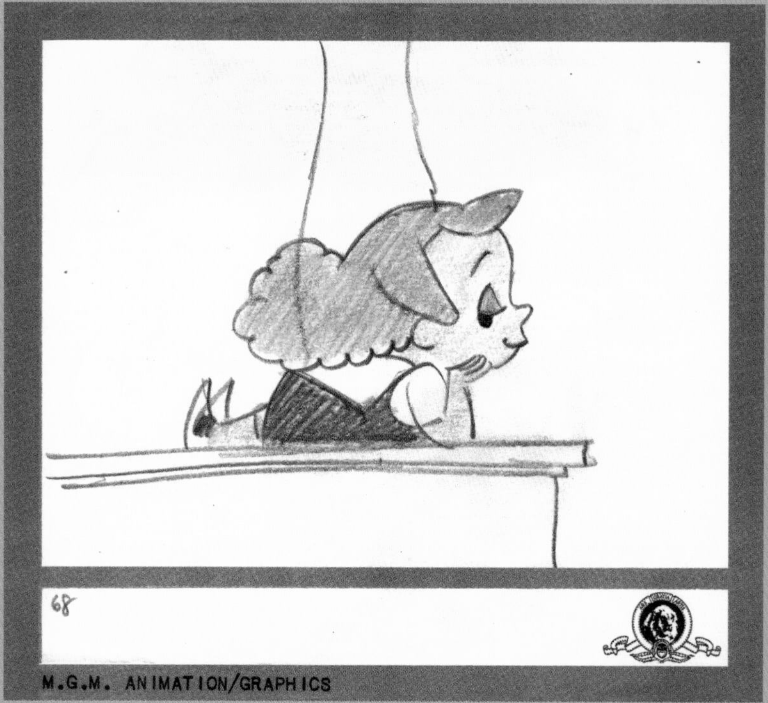
68
M.G.M. ANIMATION/GRAPHICS

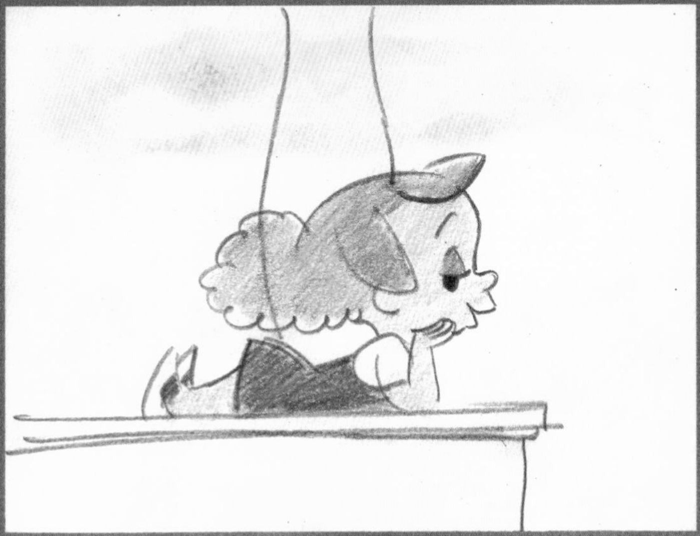

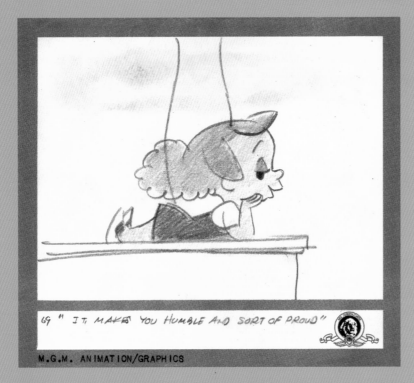

69 "IT MAKES YOU HUMBLE AND SORT OF PROUD"

M.G.M. ANIMATION/GRAPHICS

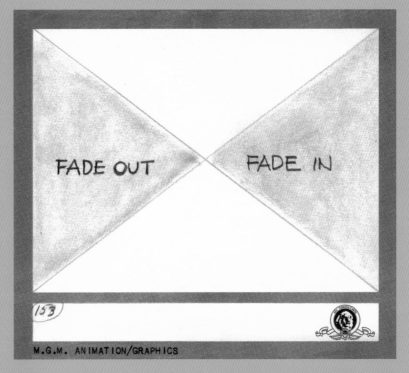

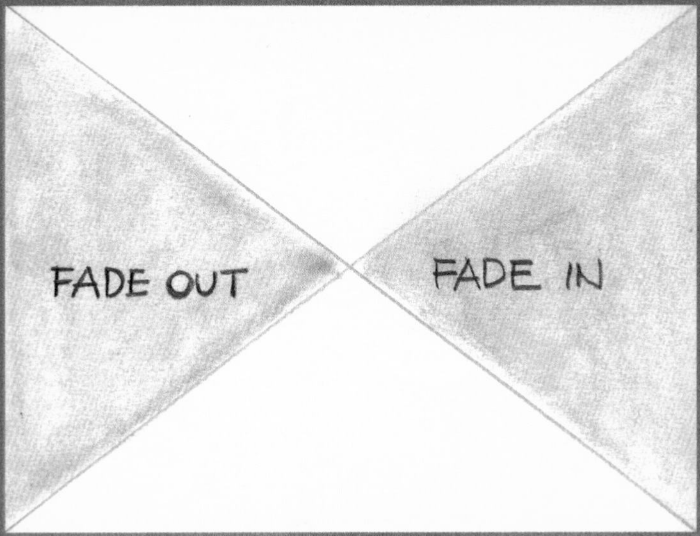
FADE OUT
FADE IN

153

M.G.M. ANIMATION/GRAPHICS

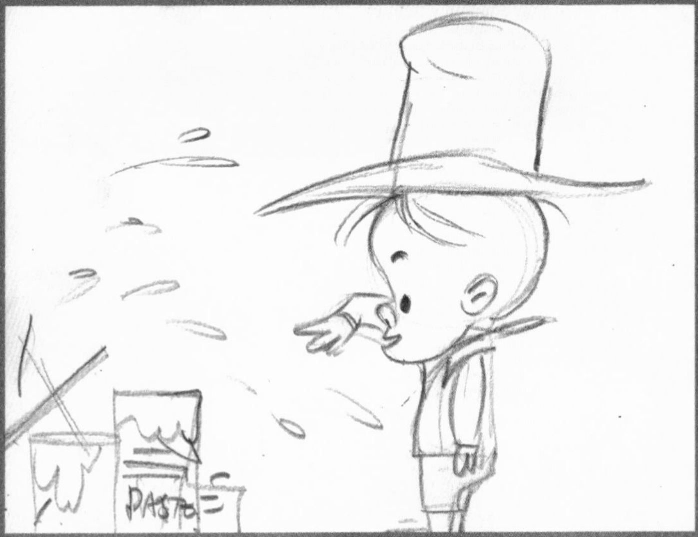
PASTE

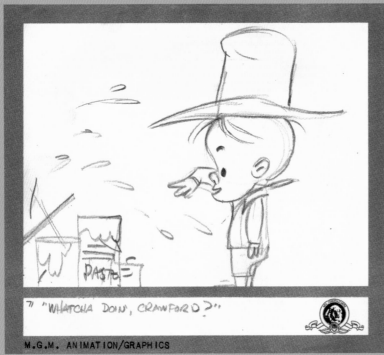

71 "WHATCHA DOIN', CRAWFORD?"

M.G.M. ANIMATION/GRAPHICS

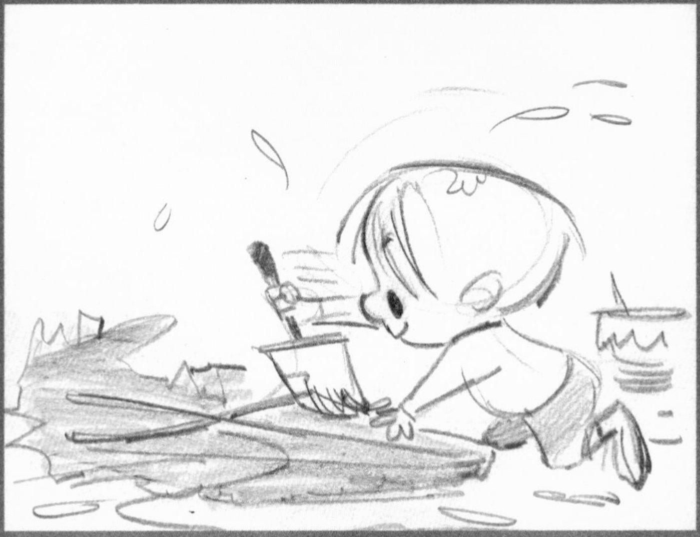

72

M.G.M. ANIMATION/GRAPHICS

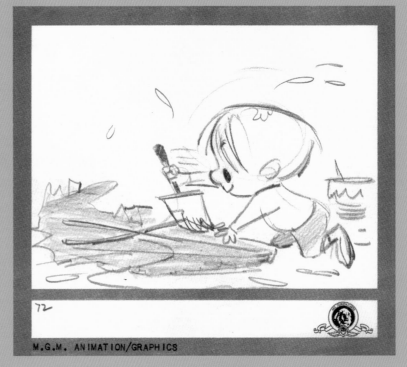

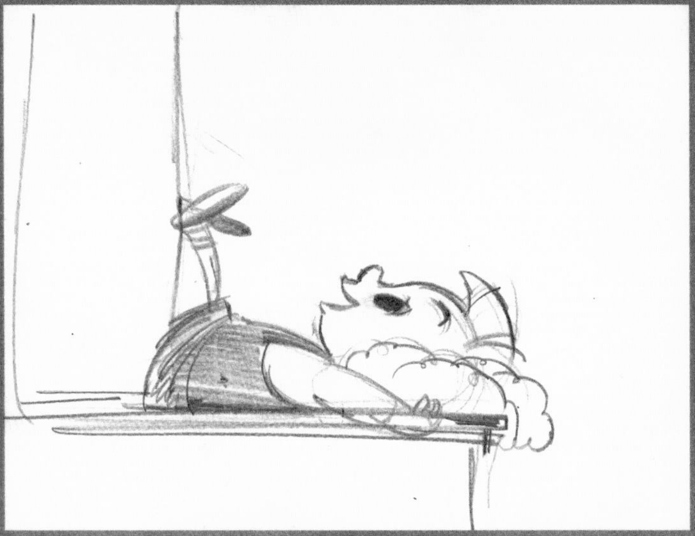

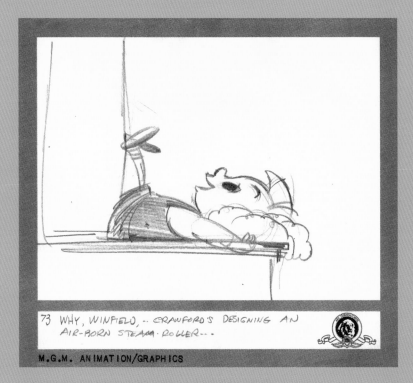

73 WHY, WINFIELD,-- CRAWFORD'S DESIGNING AN AIR-BORN STEAM-ROLLER---

M.G.M. ANIMATION/GRAPHICS

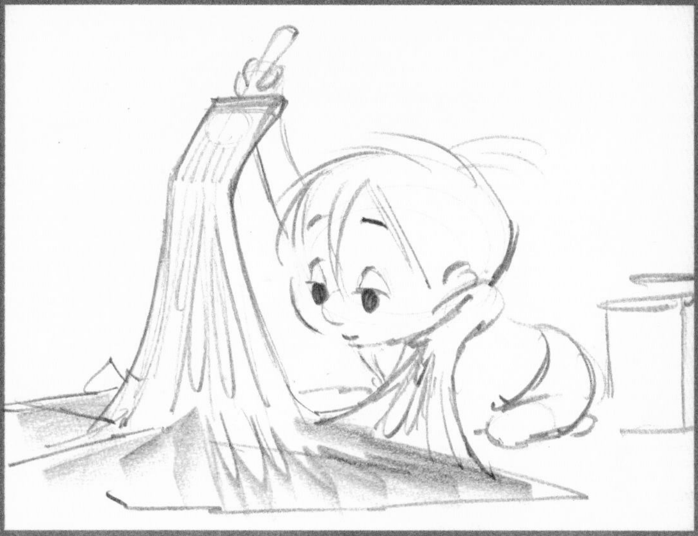

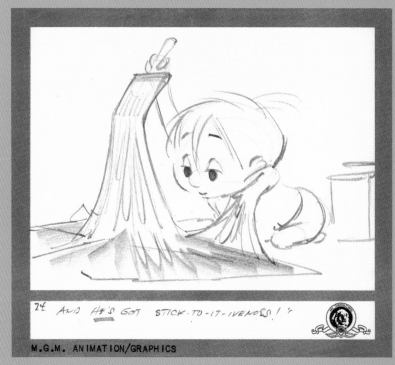

74 AND HE'S GOT STICK-TO-IT-IVENESS!

M.G.M. ANIMATION/GRAPHICS

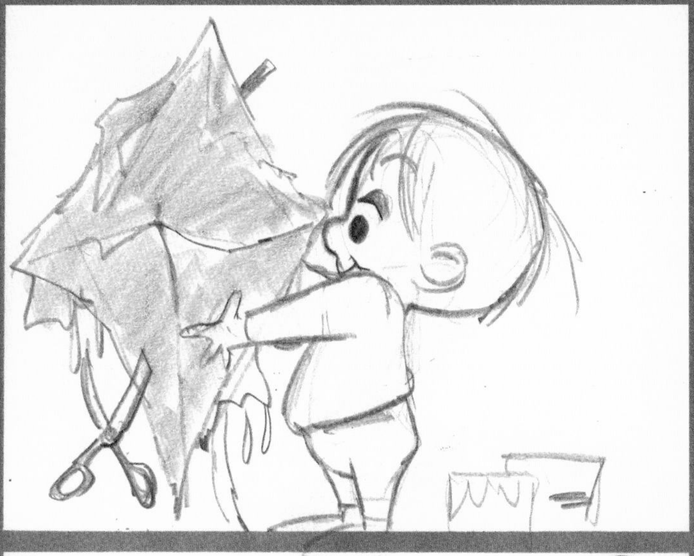

75

M.G.M. ANIMATION/GRAPHICS

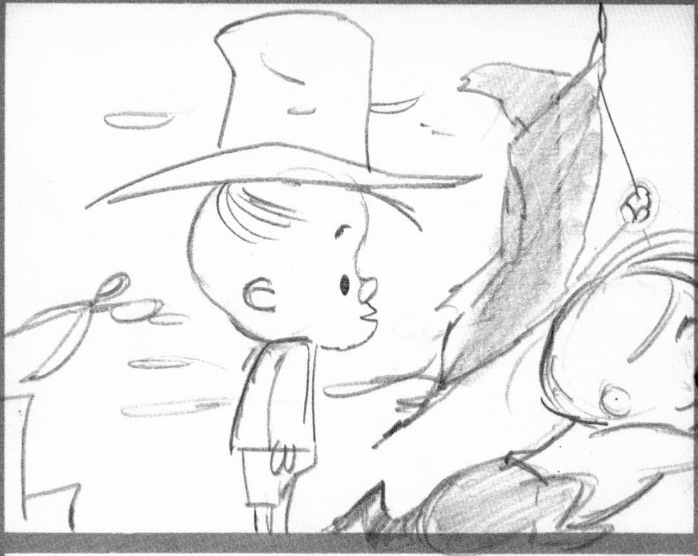

76 I'D STILL BE INTERESTED TO KNOW WHAT IT IS---

M.G.M. ANIMATION/GRAPHICS

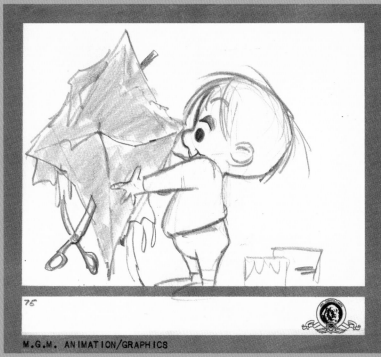

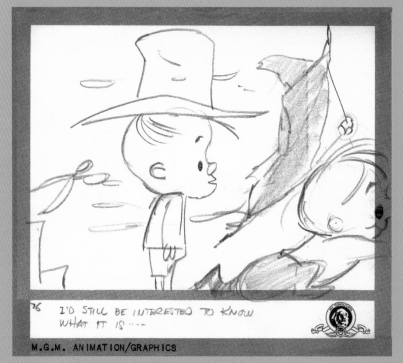

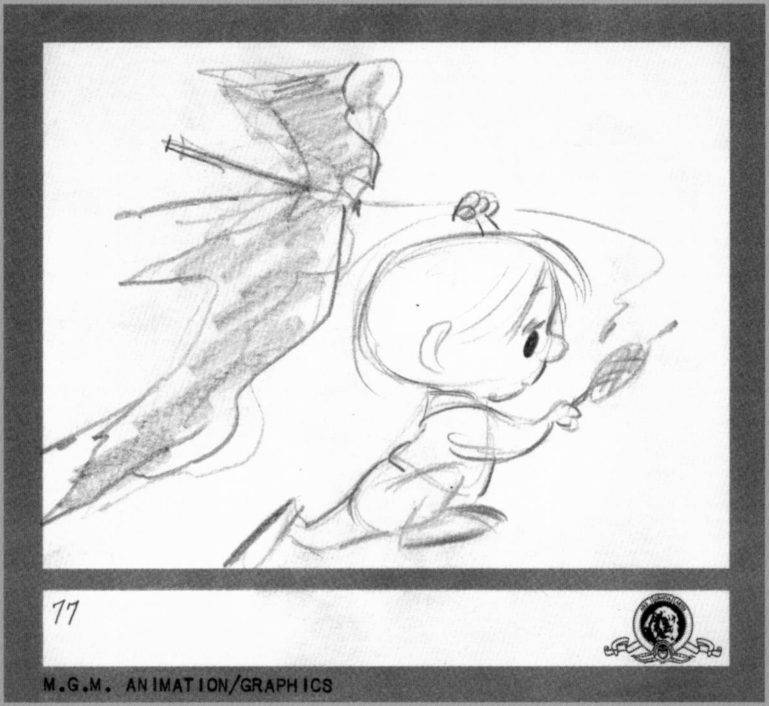
77
M.G.M. ANIMATION/GRAPHICS

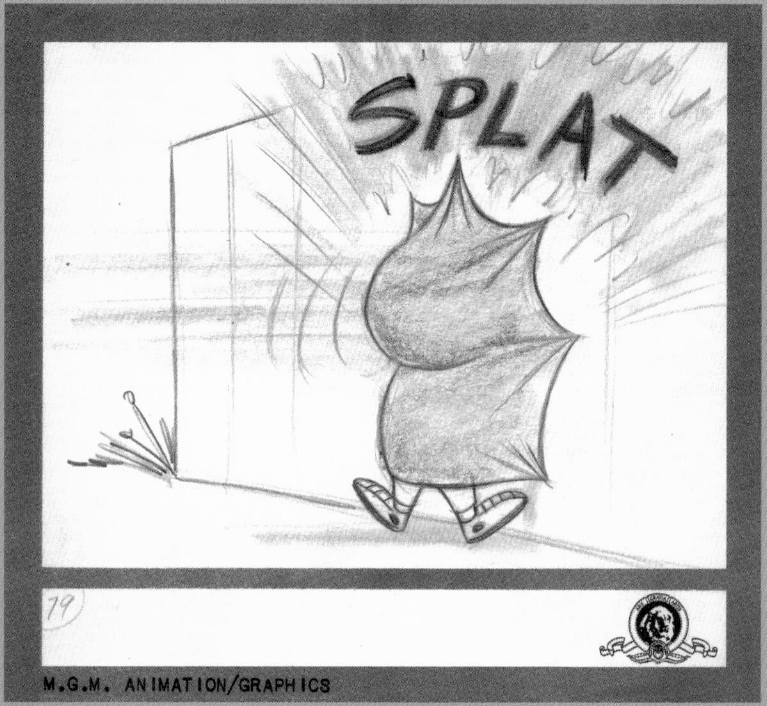
SPLAT
79
M.G.M. ANIMATION/GRAPHICS

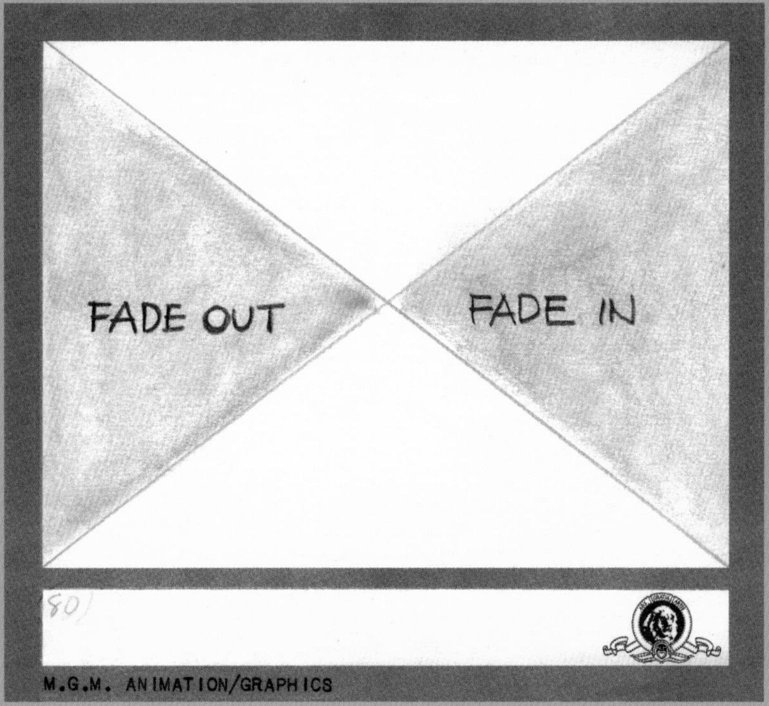
FADE OUT
FADE IN
80
M.G.M. ANIMATION/GRAPHICS

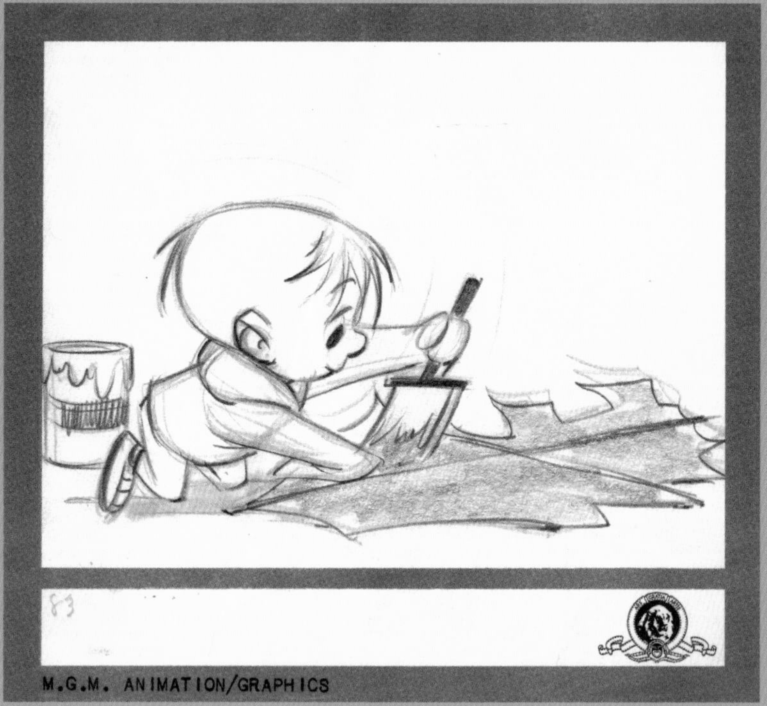
83
M.G.M. ANIMATION/GRAPHICS

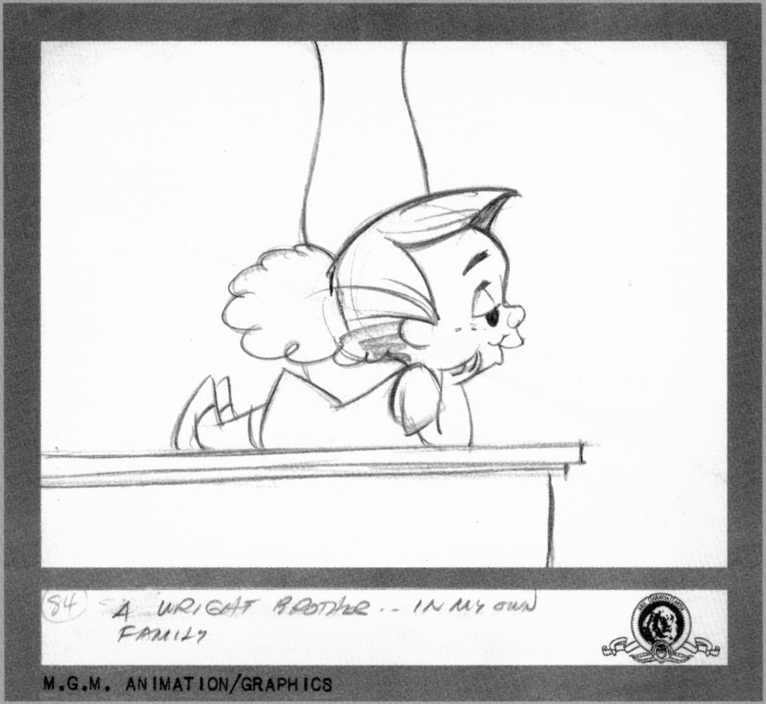
84
A WRIGHT BROTHER .. IN MY OWN FAMILY
M.G.M. ANIMATION/GRAPHICS

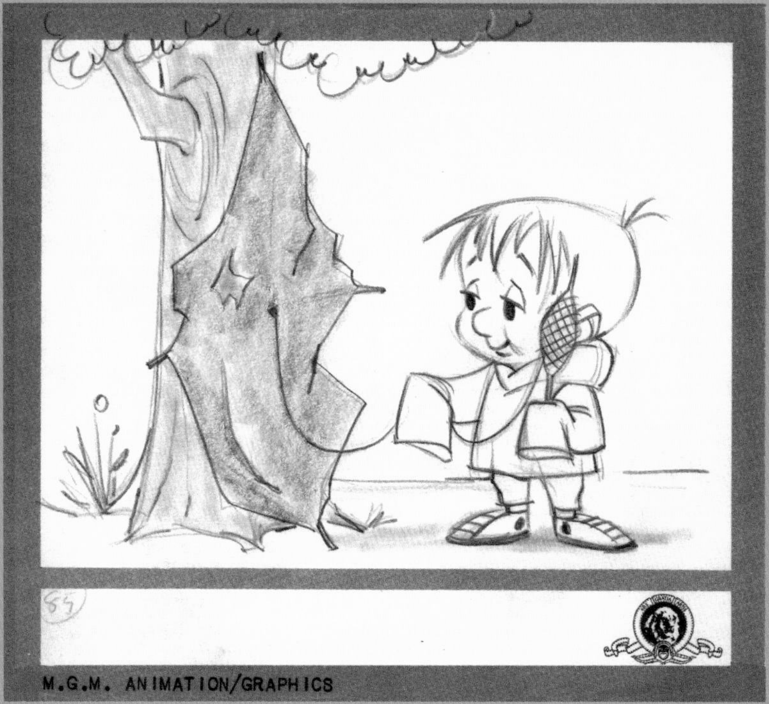
85
M.G.M. ANIMATION/GRAPHICS

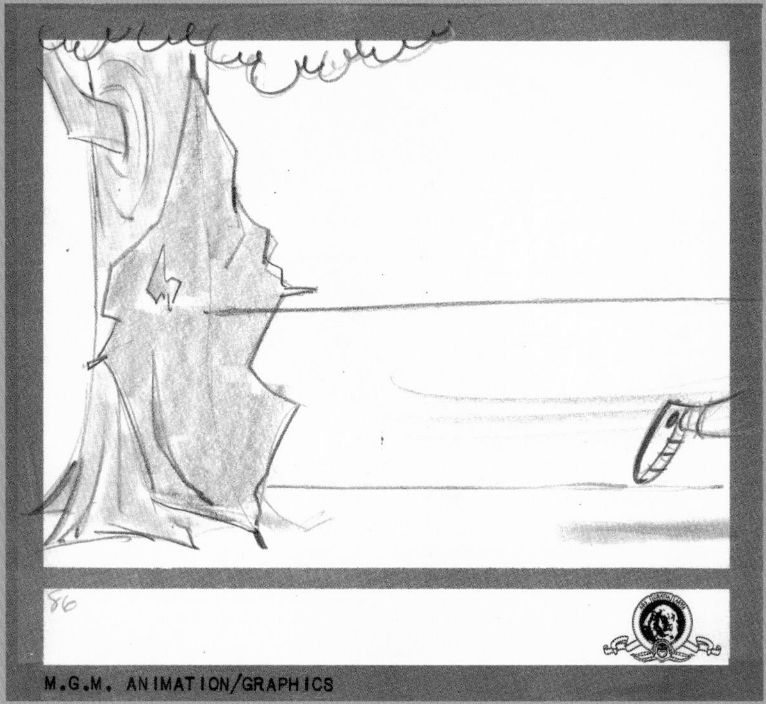
86
M.G.M. ANIMATION/GRAPHICS

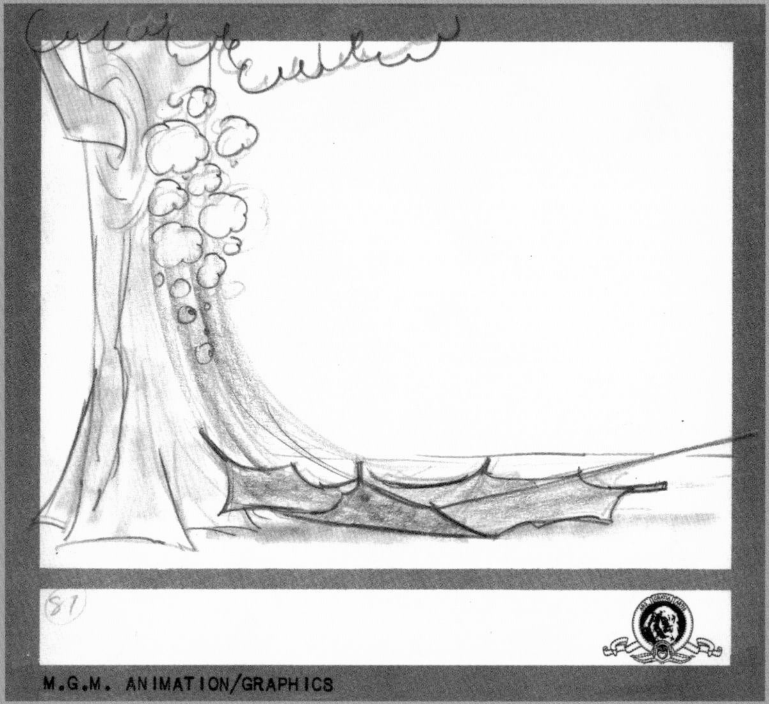
87
M.G.M. ANIMATION/GRAPHICS

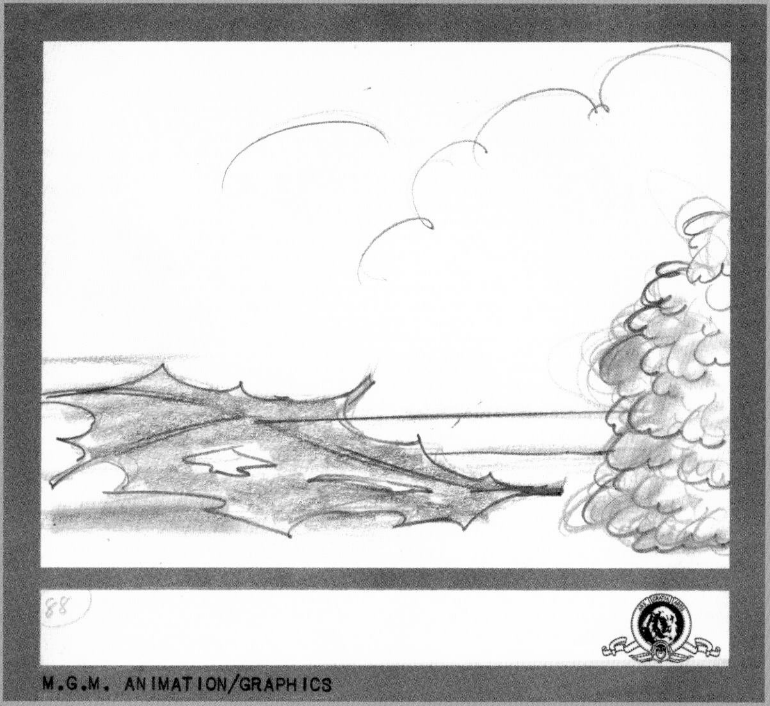
88
M.G.M. ANIMATION/GRAPHICS

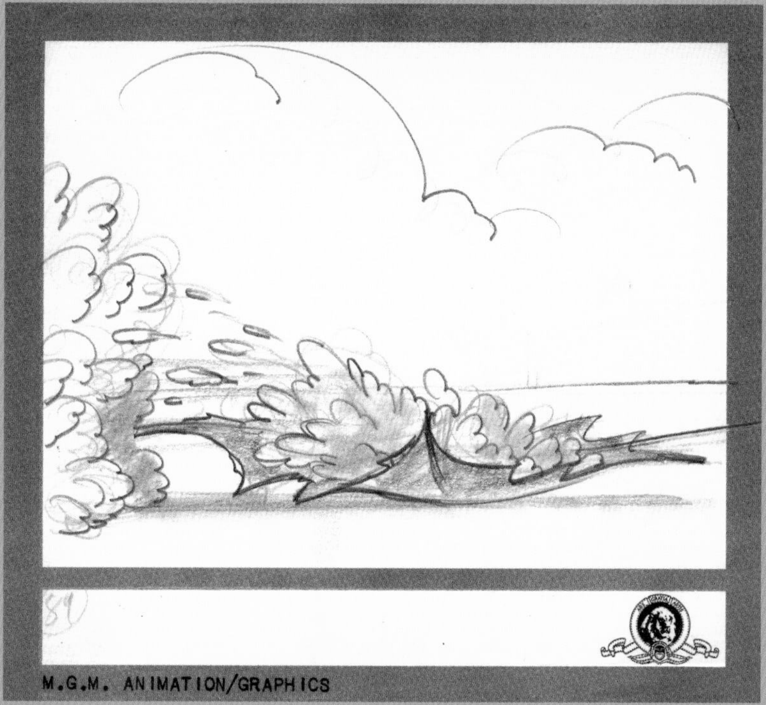
89
M.G.M. ANIMATION/GRAPHICS

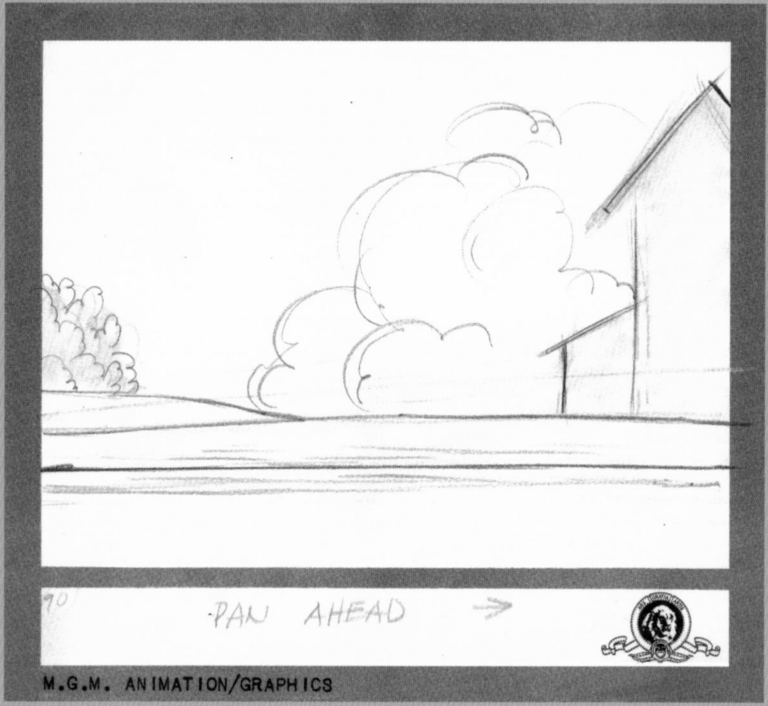
90
PAN AHEAD →
M.G.M. ANIMATION/GRAPHICS

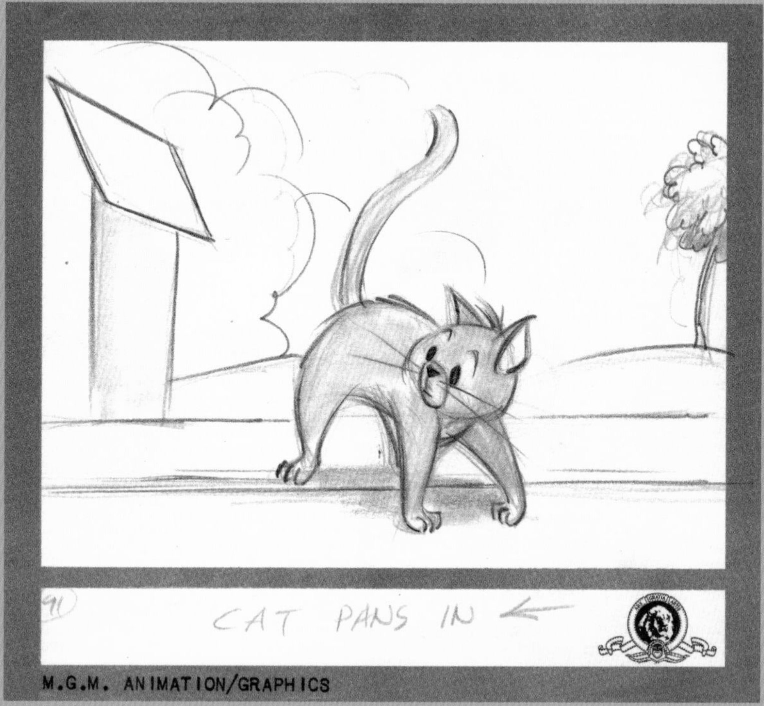
91
CAT PANS IN ←
M.G.M. ANIMATION/GRAPHICS

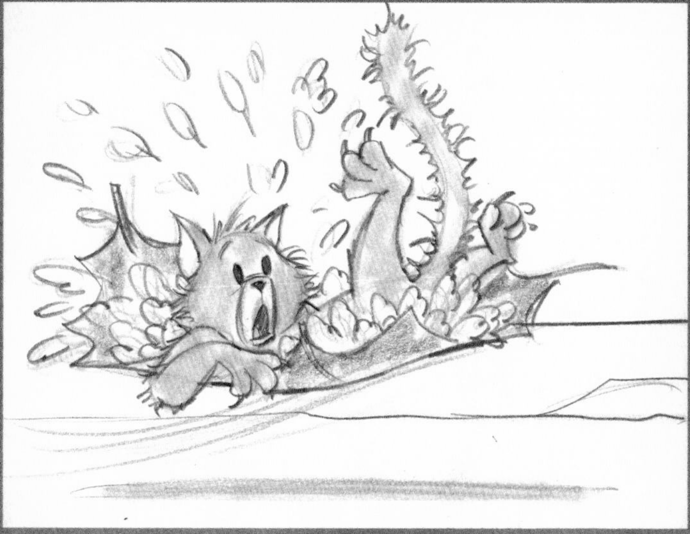

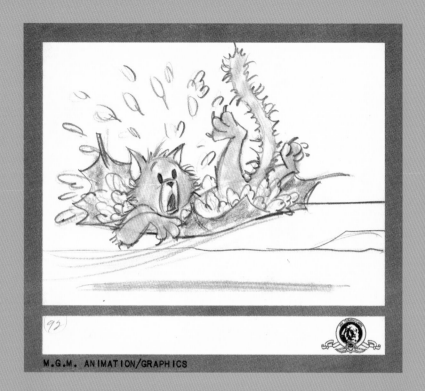

92

M.G.M. ANIMATION/GRAPHICS

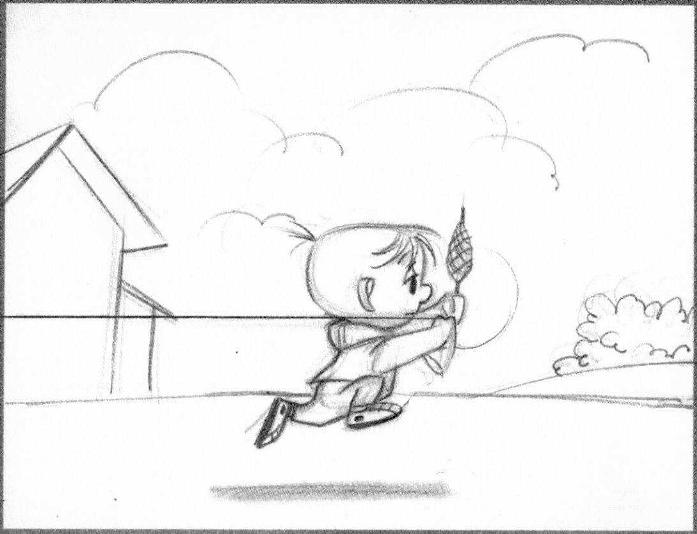

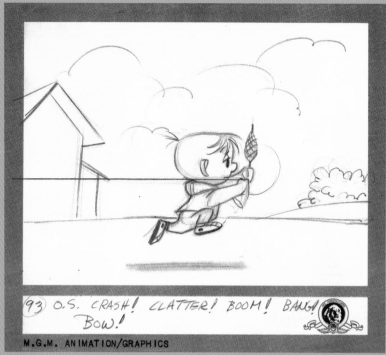

93 O.S. CRASH! CLATTER! BOOM! BANG! BOW!

M.G.M. ANIMATION/GRAPHICS

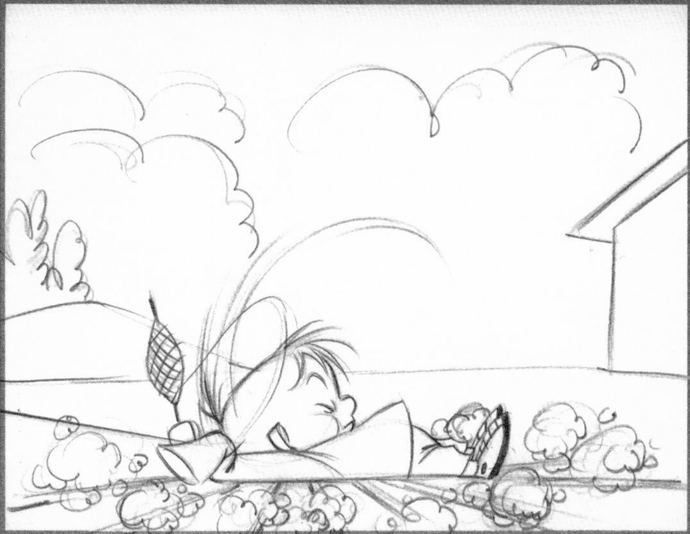

94 HE IS JERKED BACKWARDS
SPLAT!

M.G.M. ANIMATION/GRAPHICS

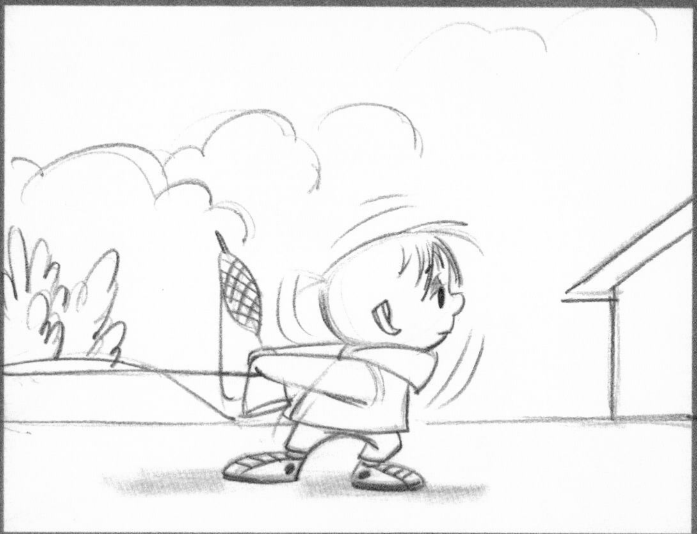

95

M.G.M. ANIMATION/GRAPHICS

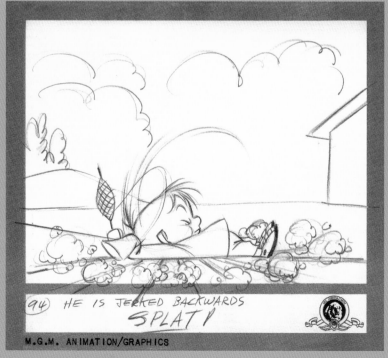

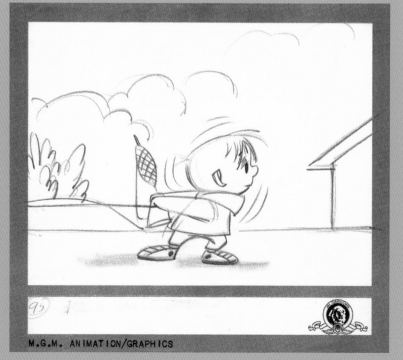

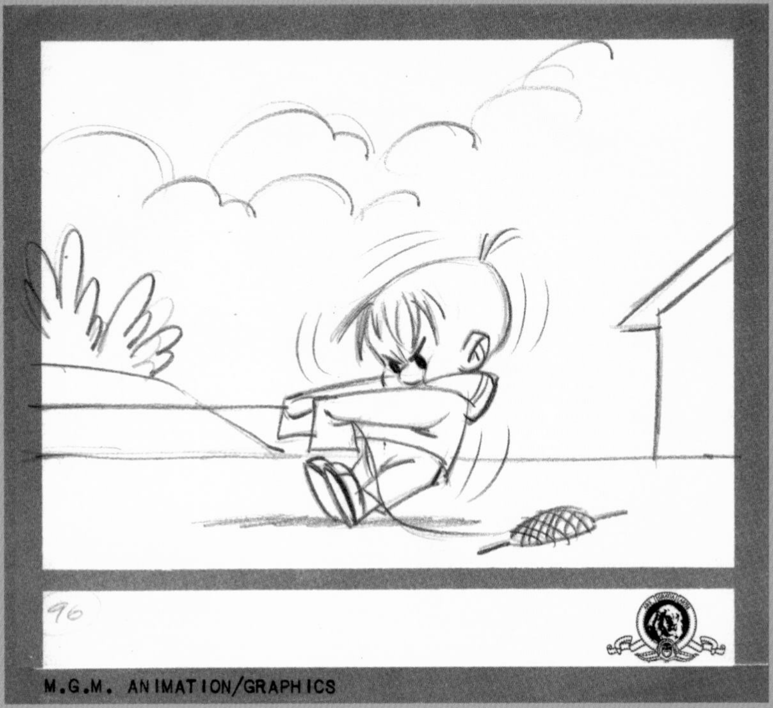
96
M.G.M. ANIMATION/GRAPHICS

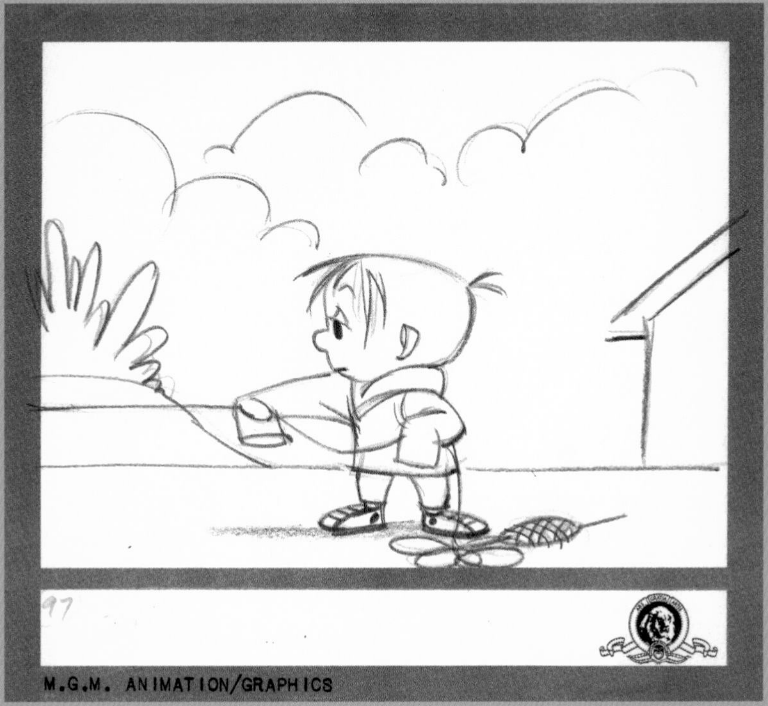
97
M.G.M. ANIMATION/GRAPHICS

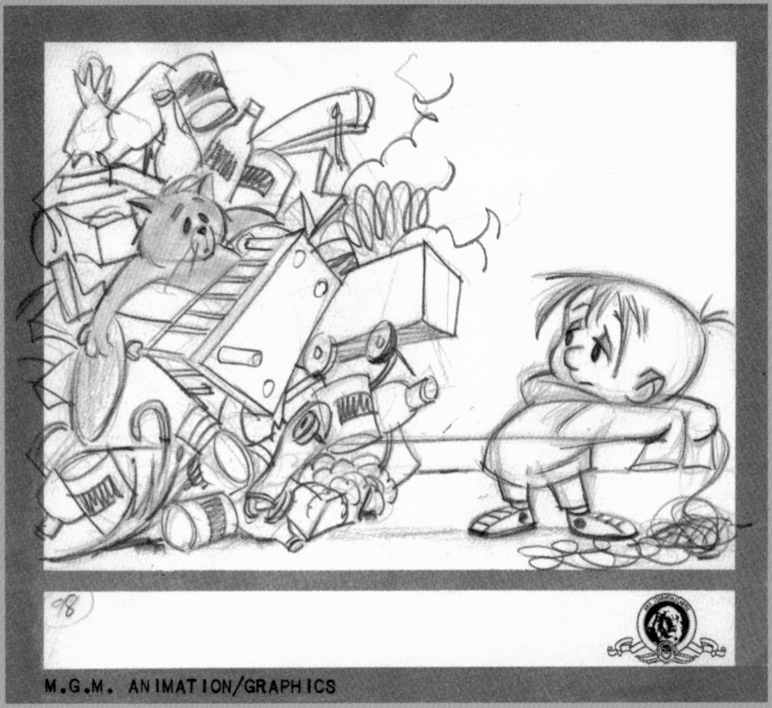
98
M.G.M. ANIMATION/GRAPHICS

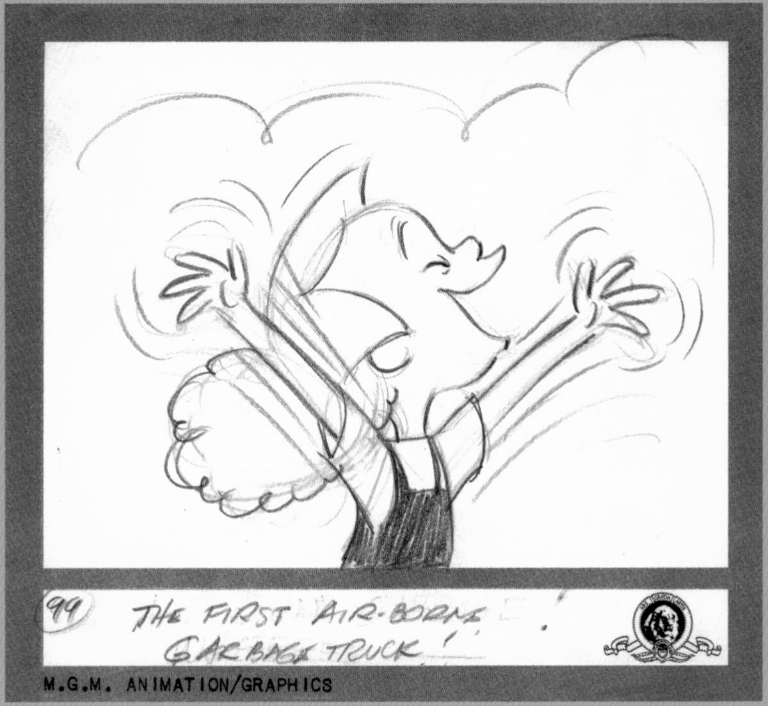
99
THE FIRST AIR-BORNE
GARBAGE TRUCK!
M.G.M. ANIMATION/GRAPHICS

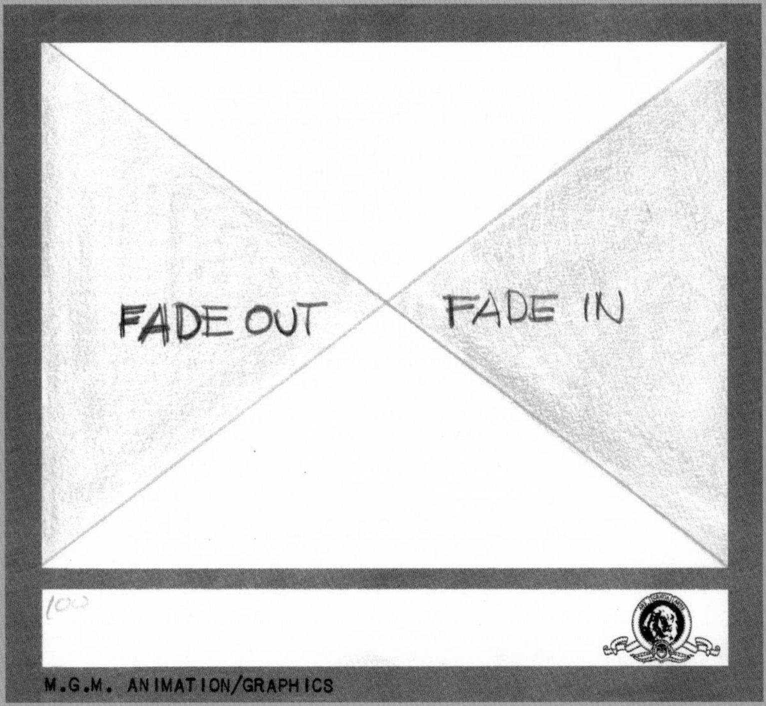
FADE OUT
FADE IN
100
M.G.M. ANIMATION/GRAPHICS

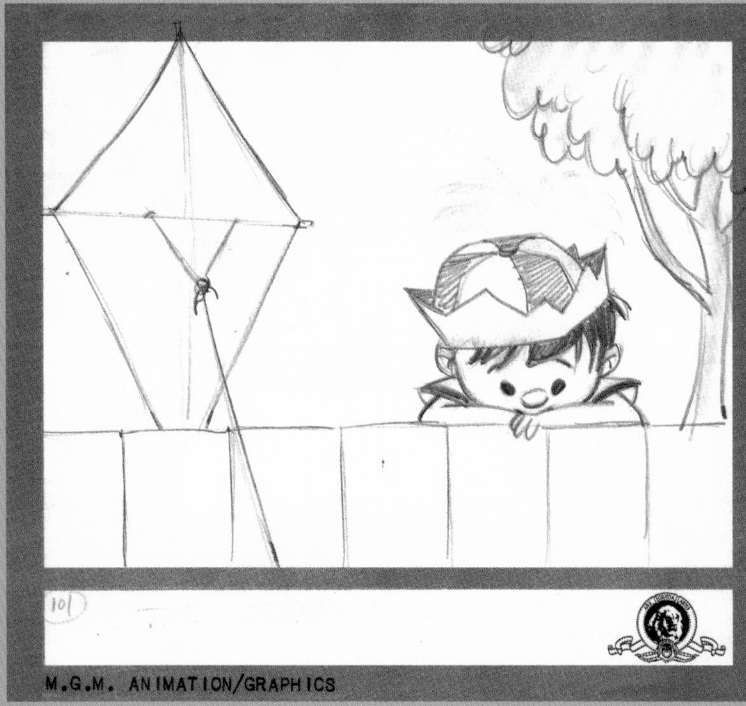
101
M.G.M. ANIMATION/GRAPHICS

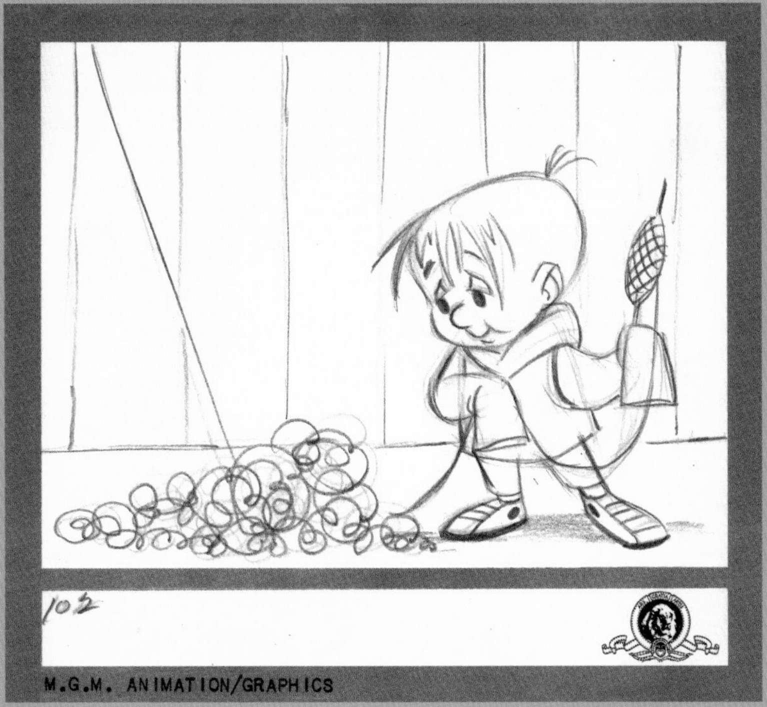
102
M.G.M. ANIMATION/GRAPHICS

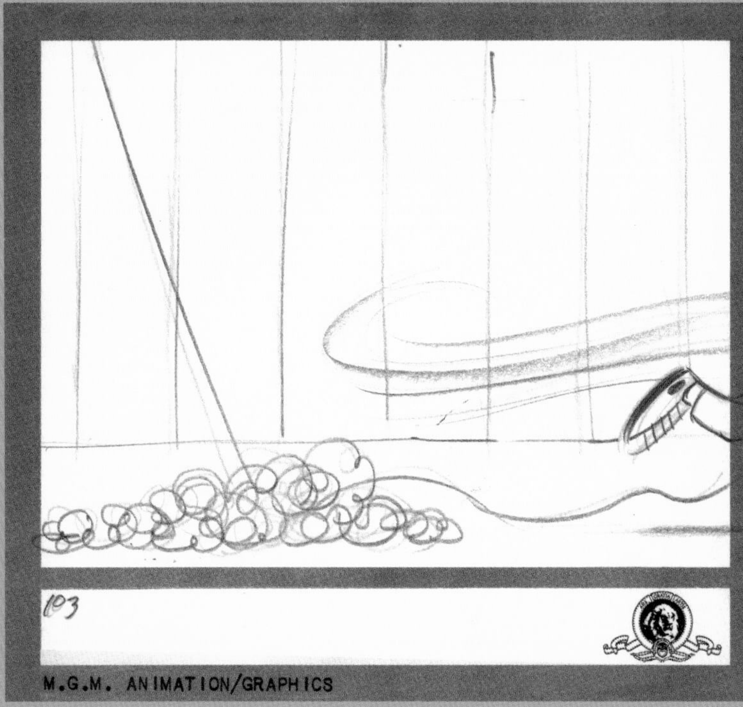
103
M.G.M. ANIMATION/GRAPHICS

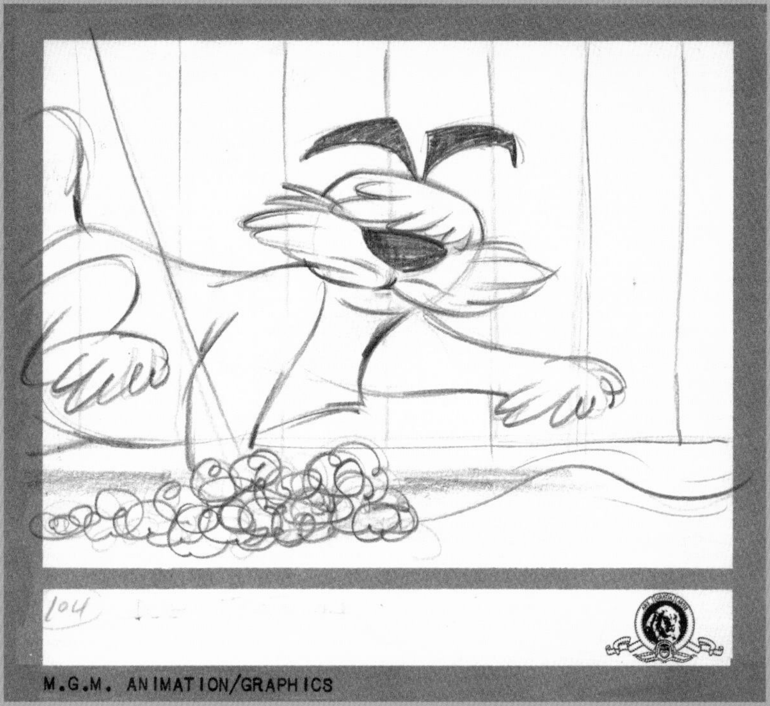
104
M.G.M. ANIMATION/GRAPHICS

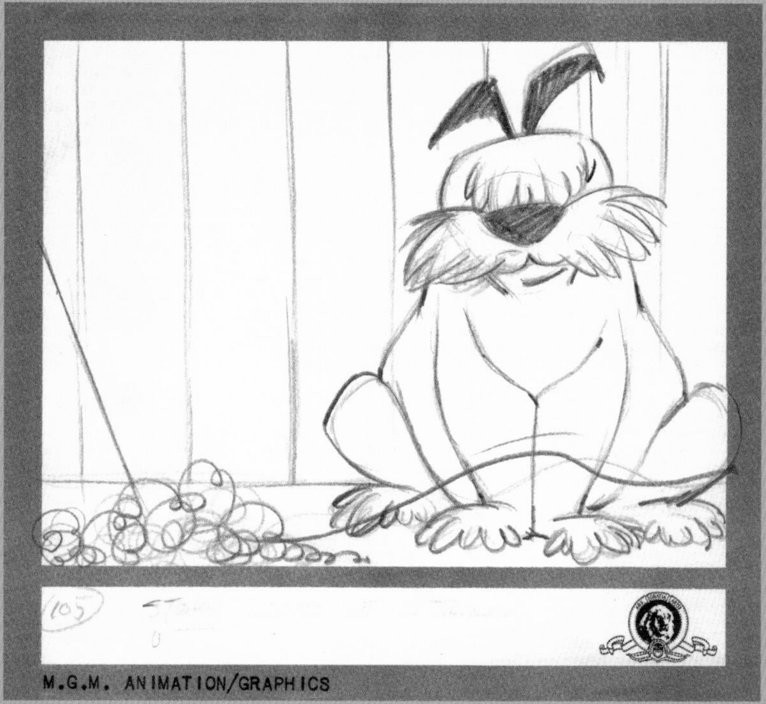
105
M.G.M. ANIMATION/GRAPHICS

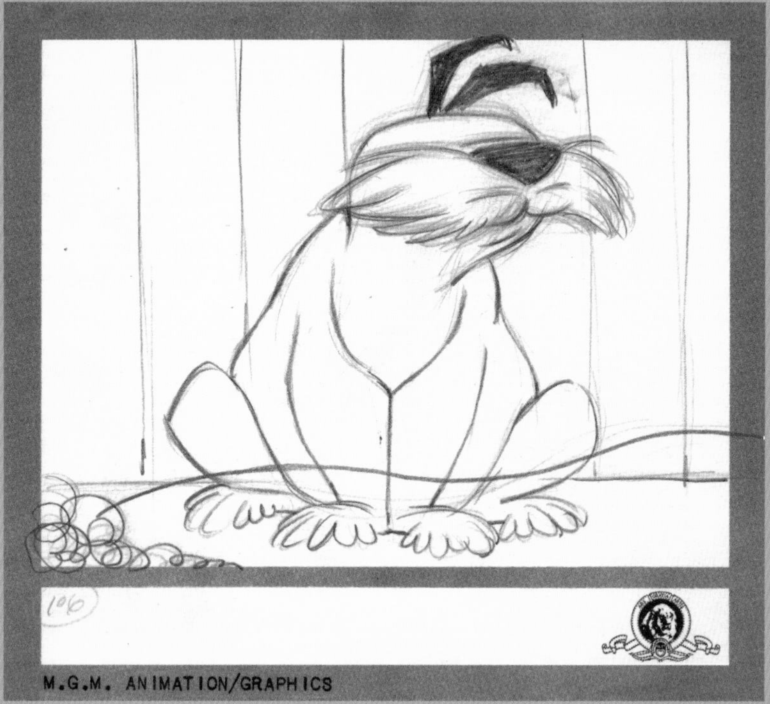
106
M.G.M. ANIMATION/GRAPHICS

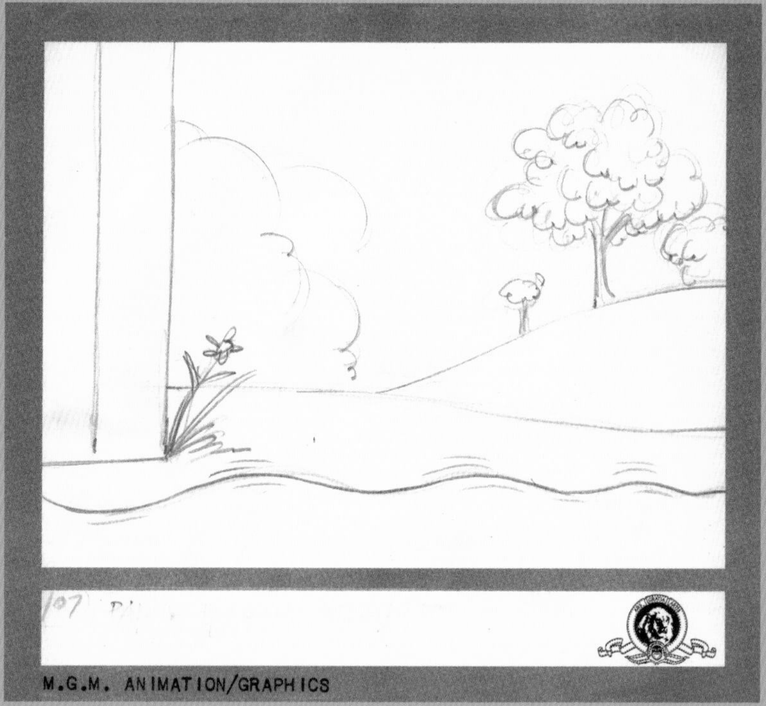
107
M.G.M. ANIMATION/GRAPHICS

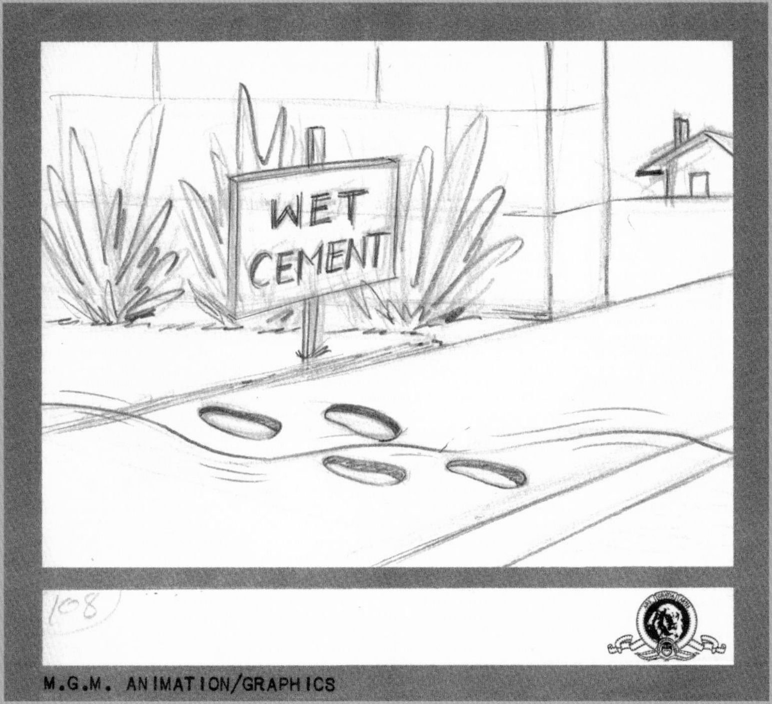
WET
CEMENT
108
M.G.M. ANIMATION/GRAPHICS

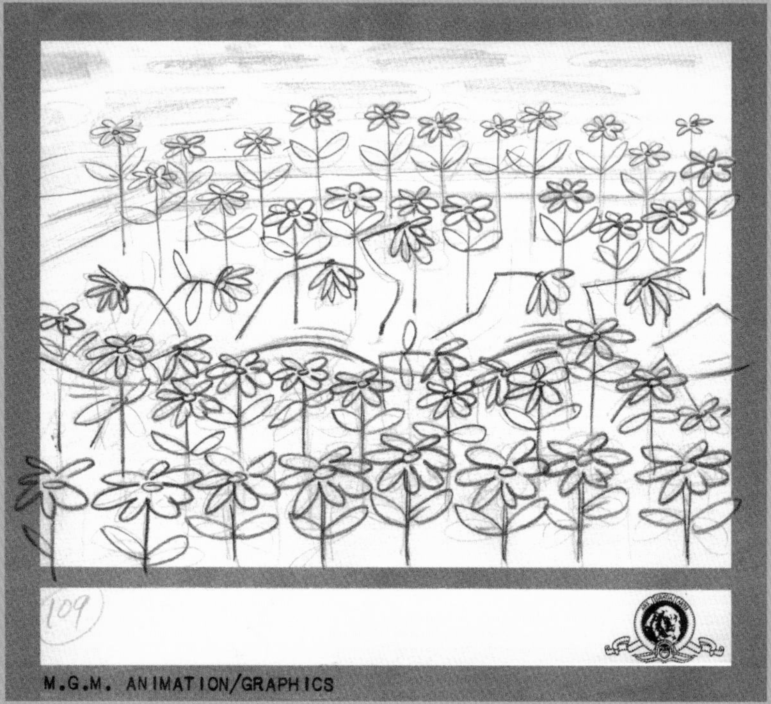
109
M.G.M. ANIMATION/GRAPHICS

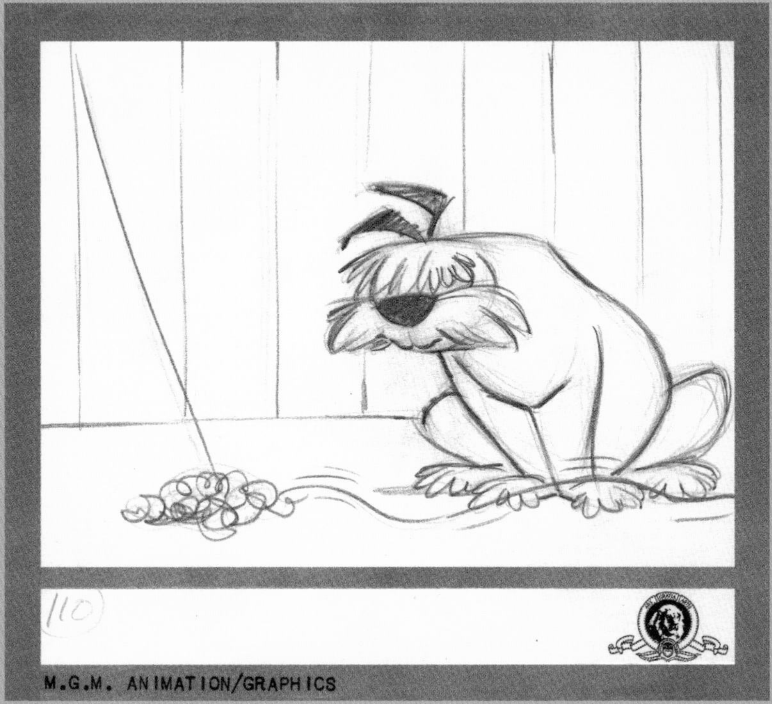
110
M.G.M. ANIMATION/GRAPHICS

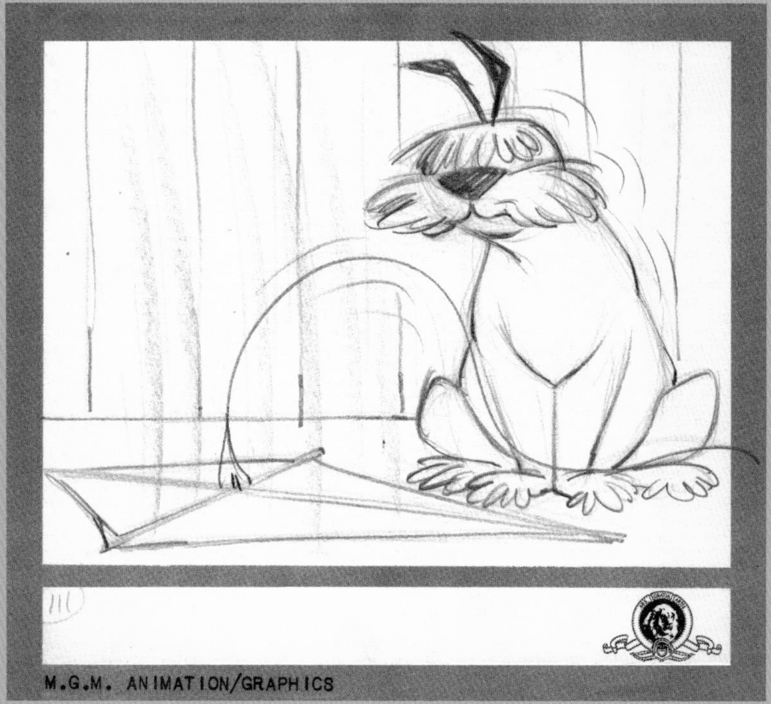
111
M.G.M. ANIMATION/GRAPHICS

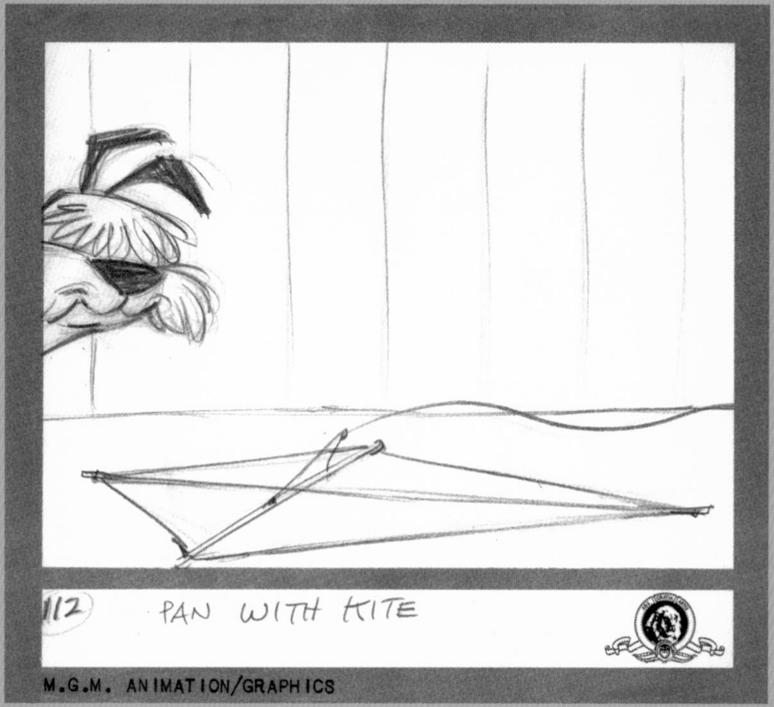
112
PAN WITH KITE
M.G.M. ANIMATION/GRAPHICS

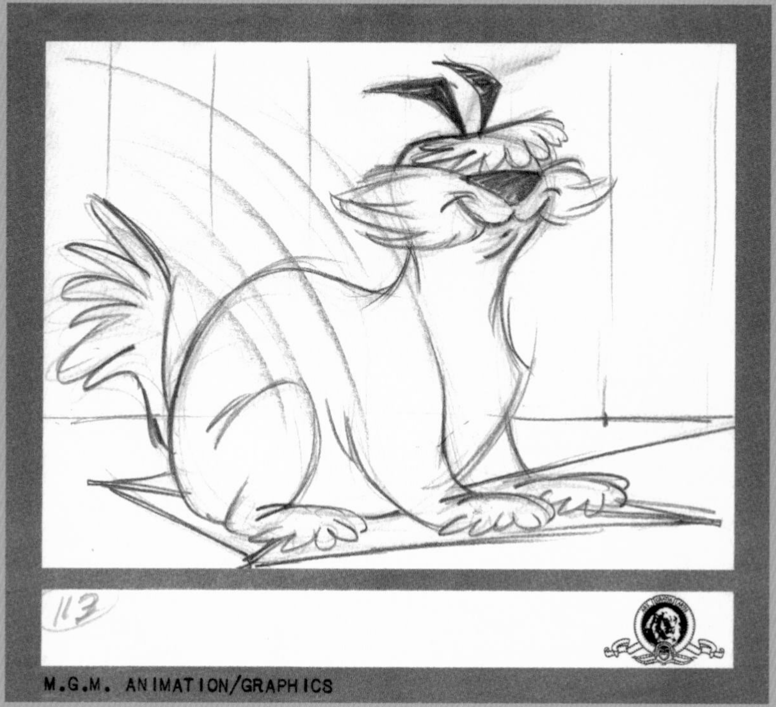
113
M.G.M. ANIMATION/GRAPHICS

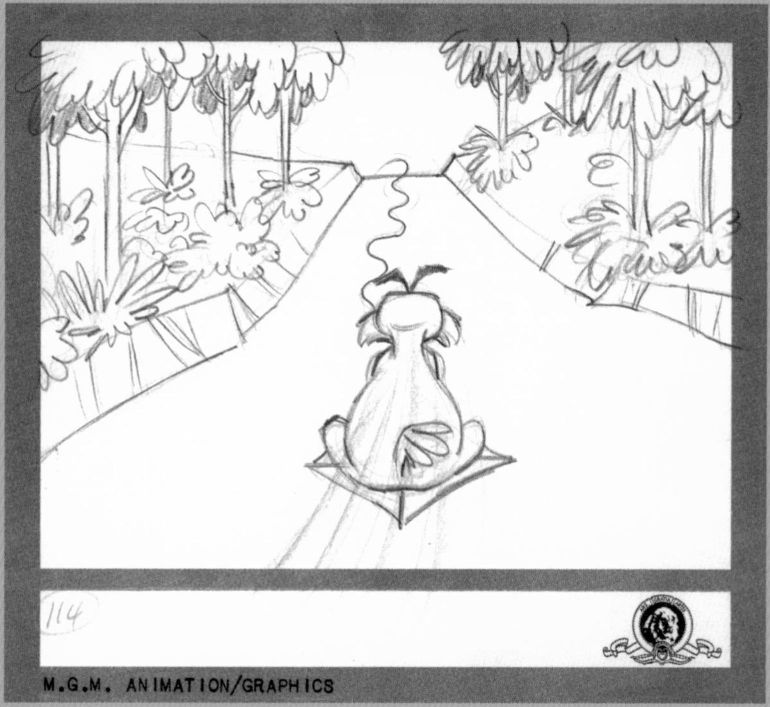
114
M.G.M. ANIMATION/GRAPHICS

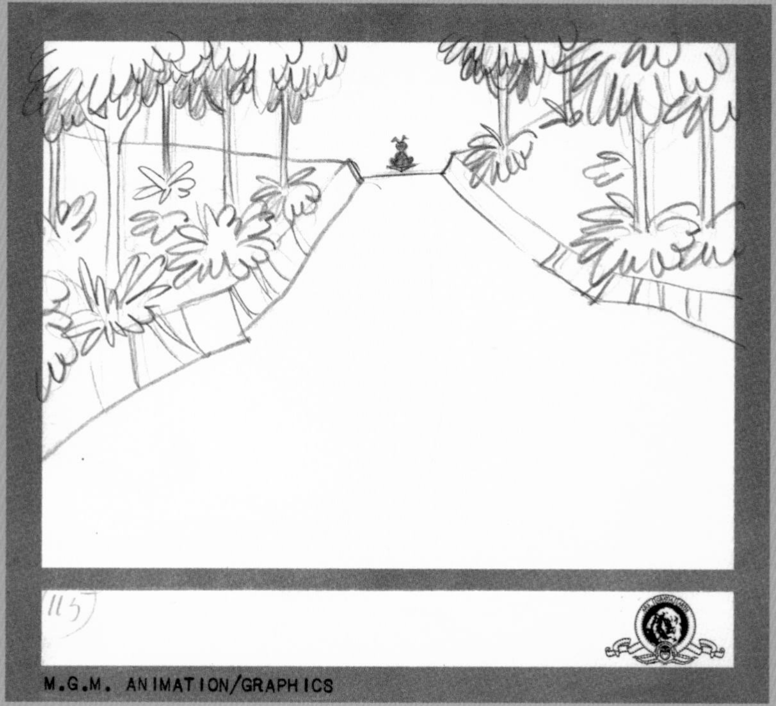
115
M.G.M. ANIMATION/GRAPHICS

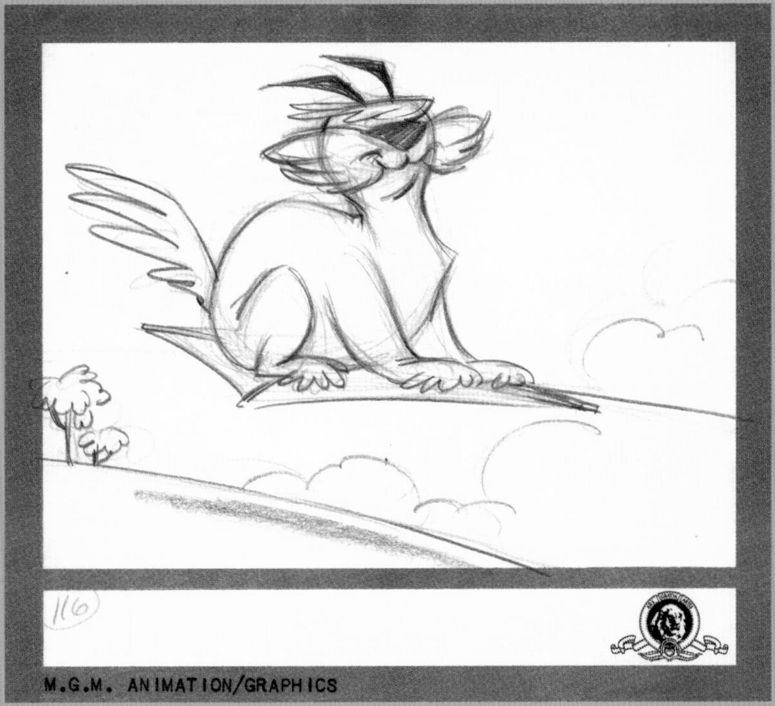
116
M.G.M. ANIMATION/GRAPHICS

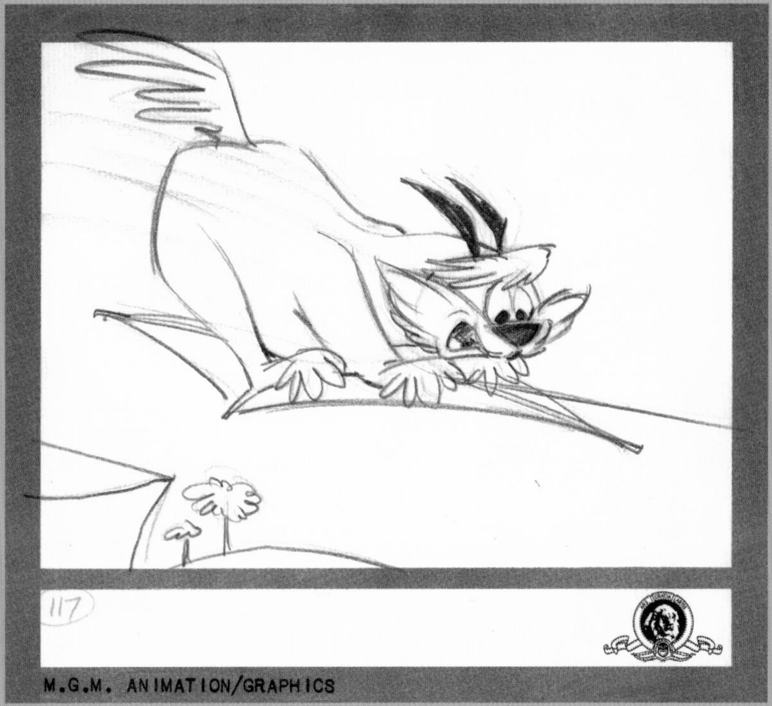
117
M.G.M. ANIMATION/GRAPHICS

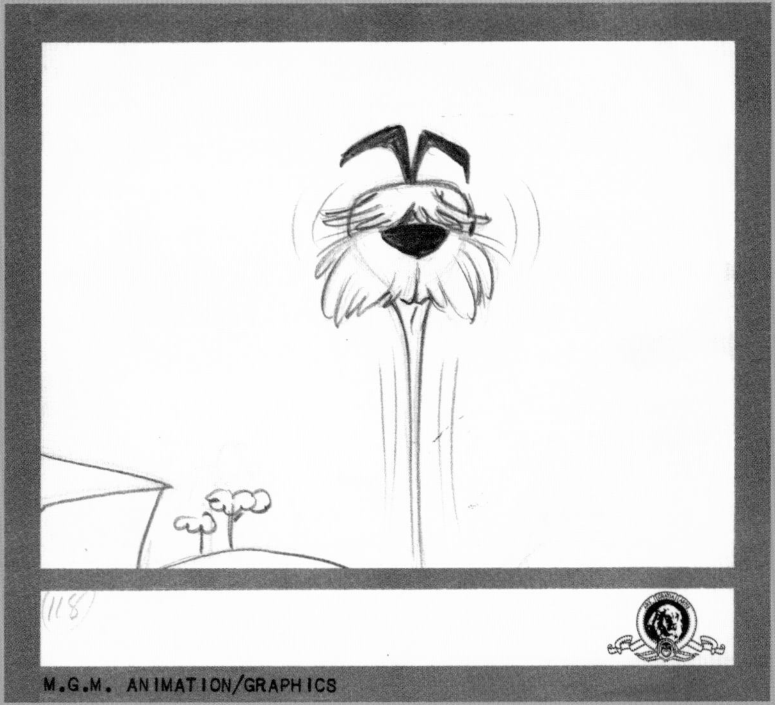
118
M.G.M. ANIMATION/GRAPHICS

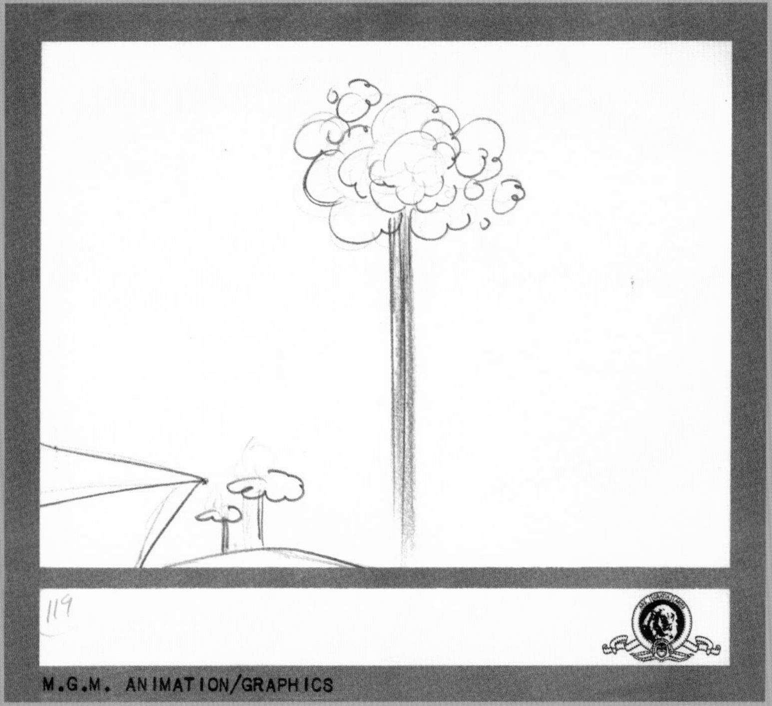
119
M.G.M. ANIMATION/GRAPHICS

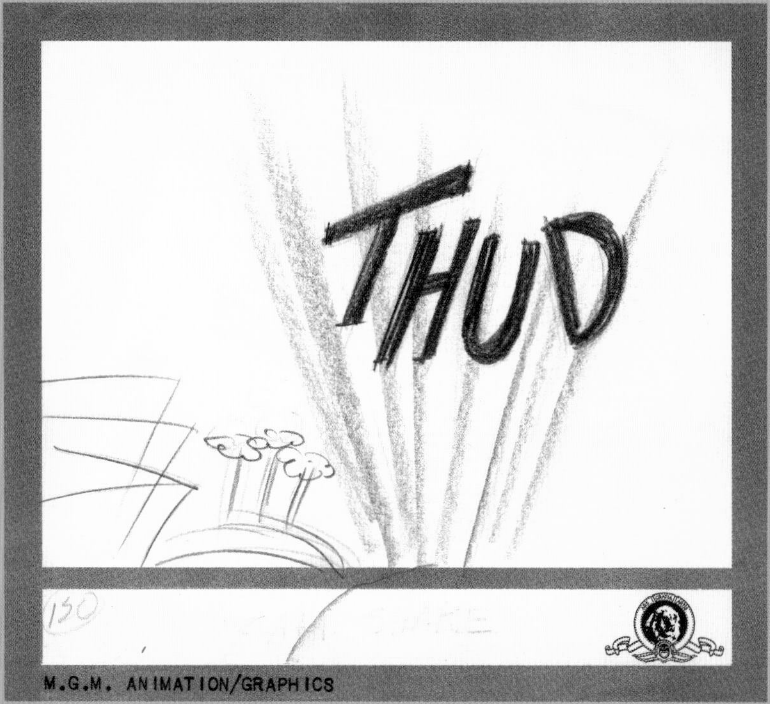
THUD
120
M.G.M. ANIMATION/GRAPHICS

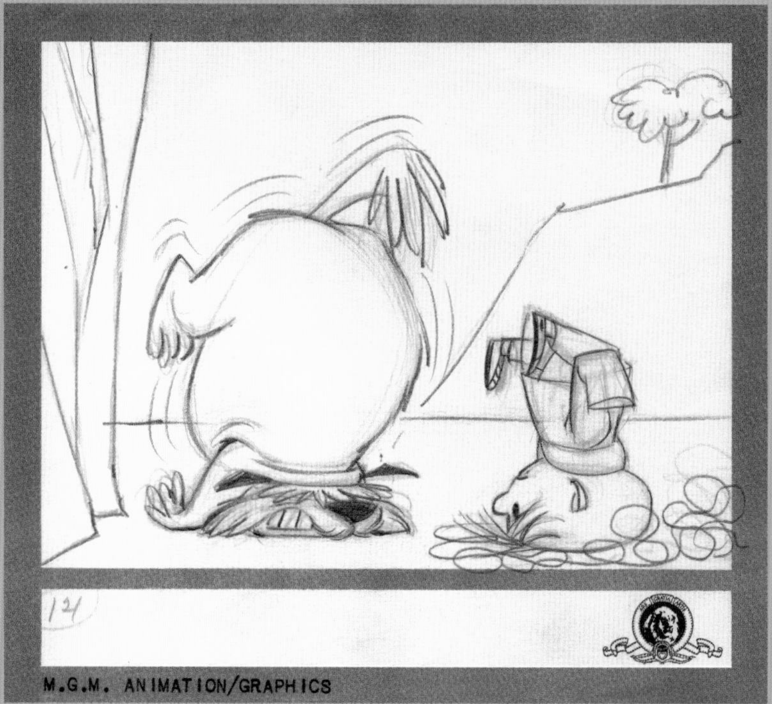
121
M.G.M. ANIMATION/GRAPHICS

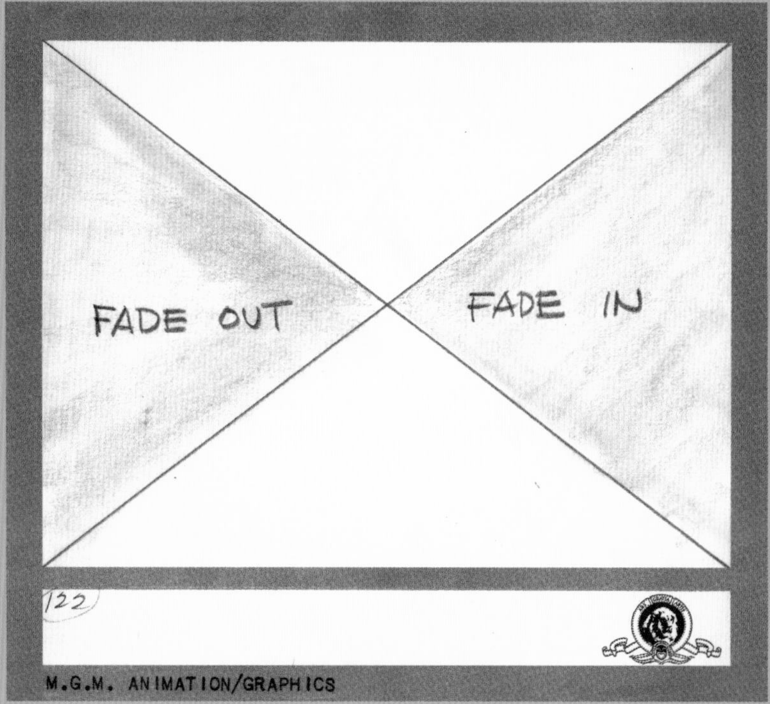
FADE OUT
FADE IN
122
M.G.M. ANIMATION/GRAPHICS

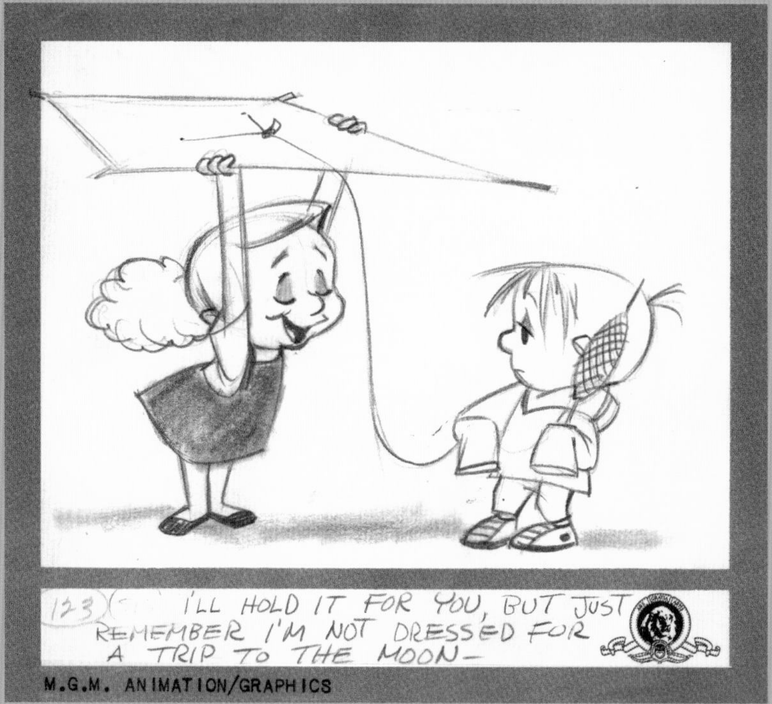
123
I'LL HOLD IT FOR YOU, BUT JUST REMEMBER I'M NOT DRESSED FOR A TRIP TO THE MOON—
M.G.M. ANIMATION/GRAPHICS

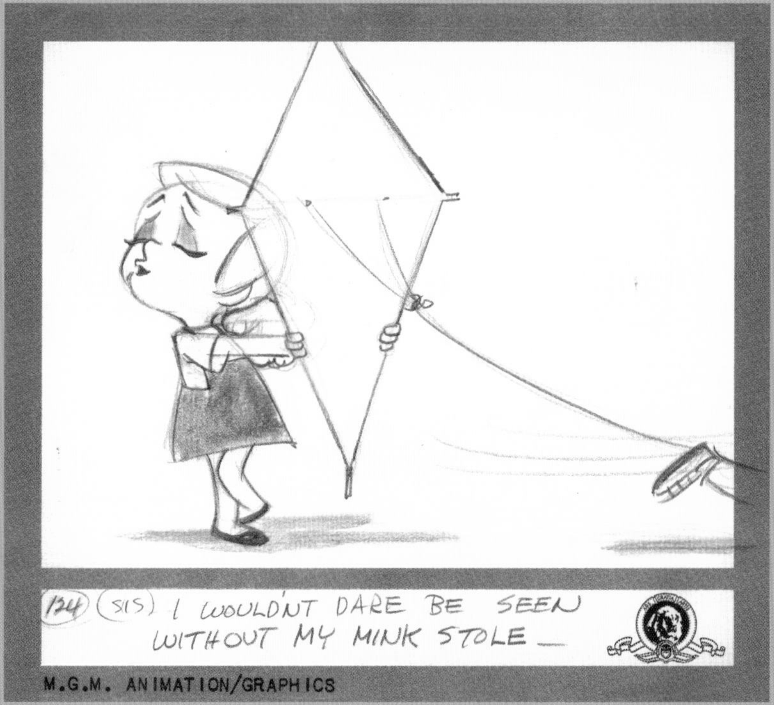
124 (SIS) I WOULD'NT DARE BE SEEN WITHOUT MY MINK STOLE _
M.G.M. ANIMATION/GRAPHICS

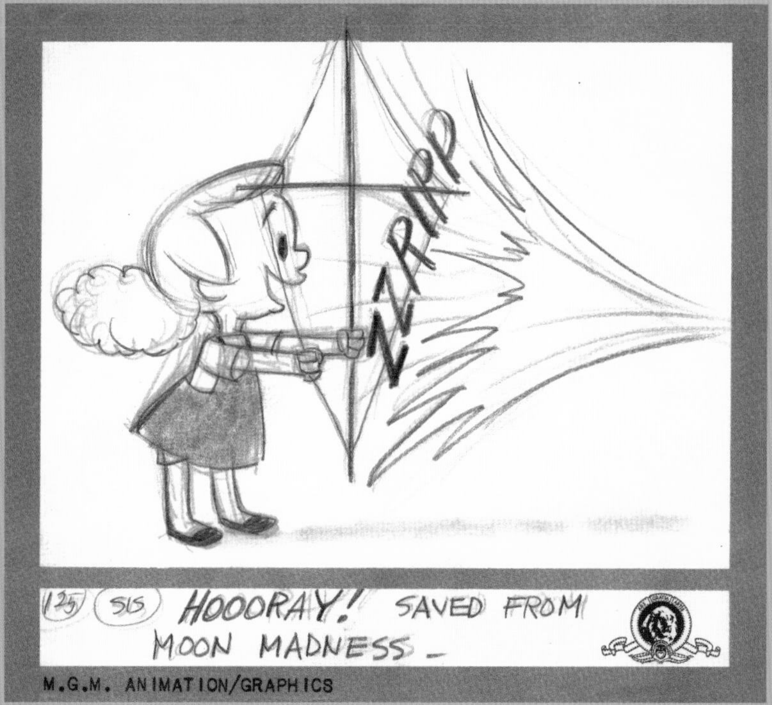
ZZRIPP
125 (SIS) HOOORAY! SAVED FROM MOON MADNESS _
M.G.M. ANIMATION/GRAPHICS

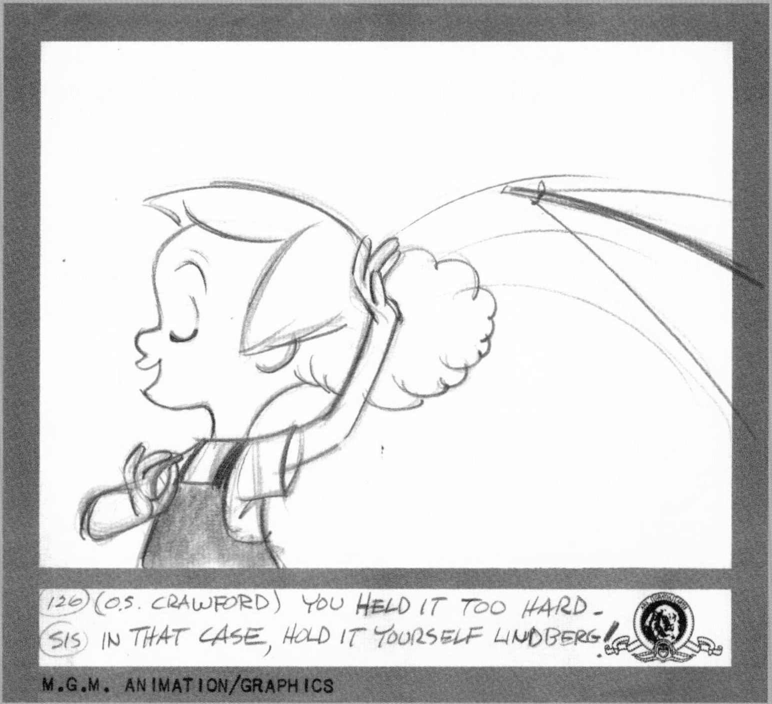
126 (O.S. CRAWFORD) YOU HELD IT TOO HARD -
(SIS) IN THAT CASE, HOLD IT YOURSELF LINDBERG!
M.G.M. ANIMATION/GRAPHICS

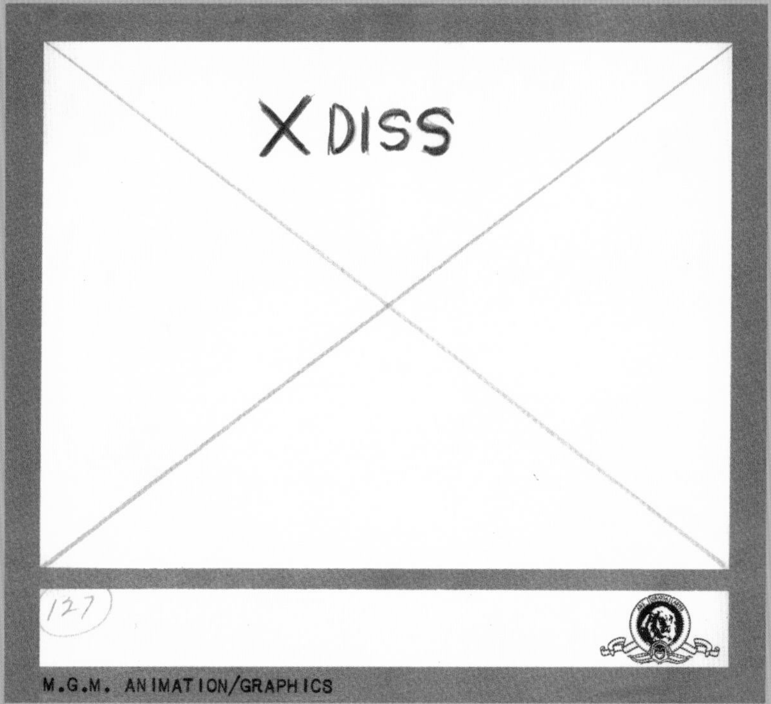
X DISS
127
M.G.M. ANIMATION/GRAPHICS

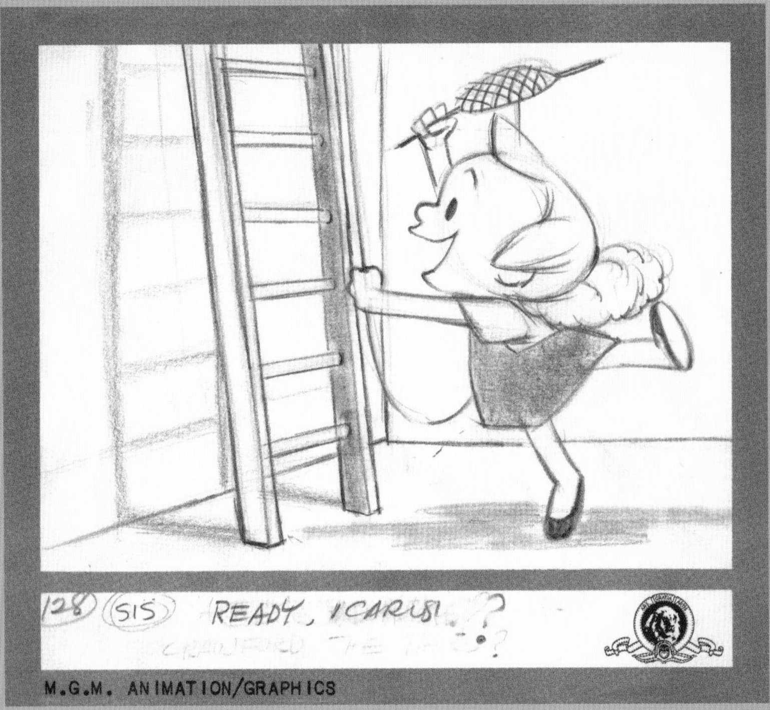
128 (515) READY, ICARUS!
M.G.M. ANIMATION/GRAPHICS

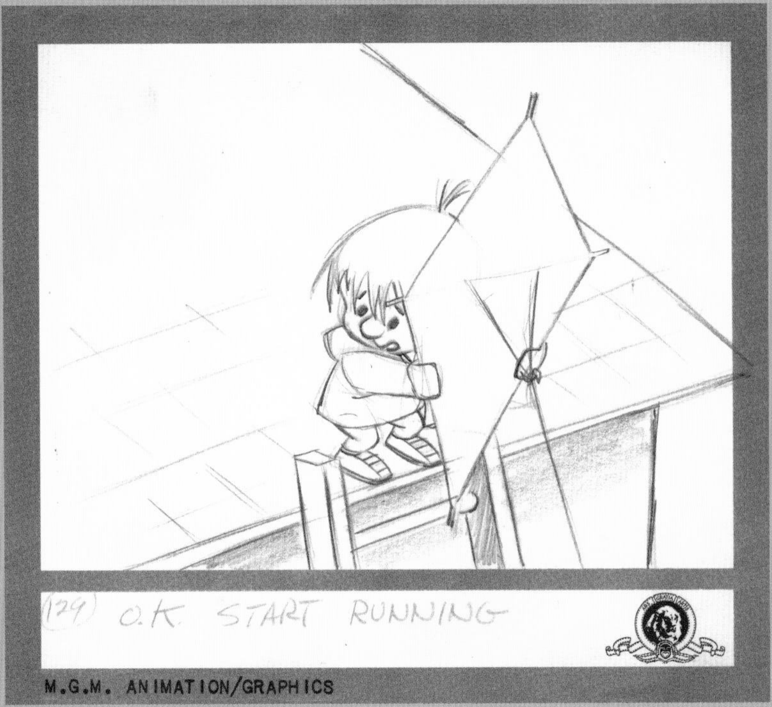
129 O.K. START RUNNING
M.G.M. ANIMATION/GRAPHICS

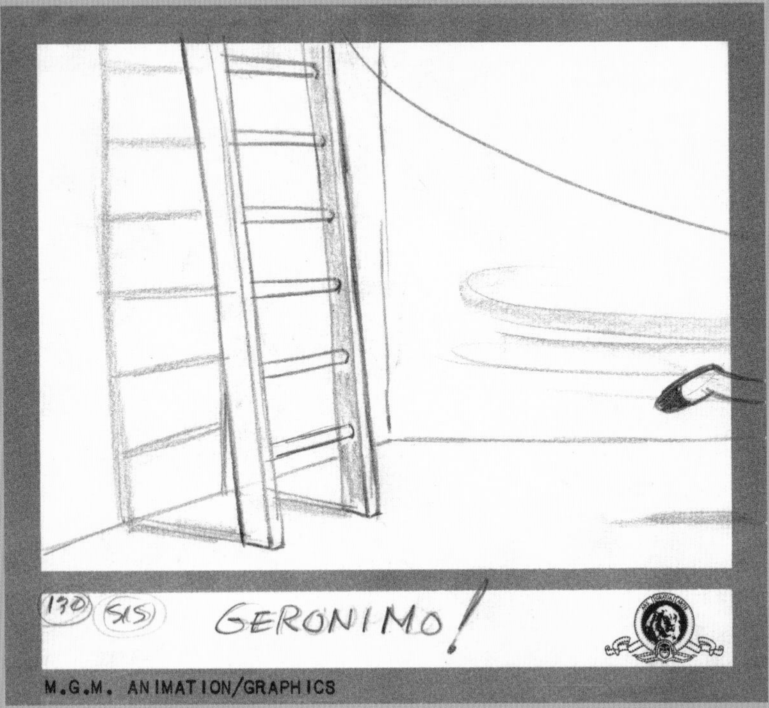
130 (515) GERONIMO!
M.G.M. ANIMATION/GRAPHICS

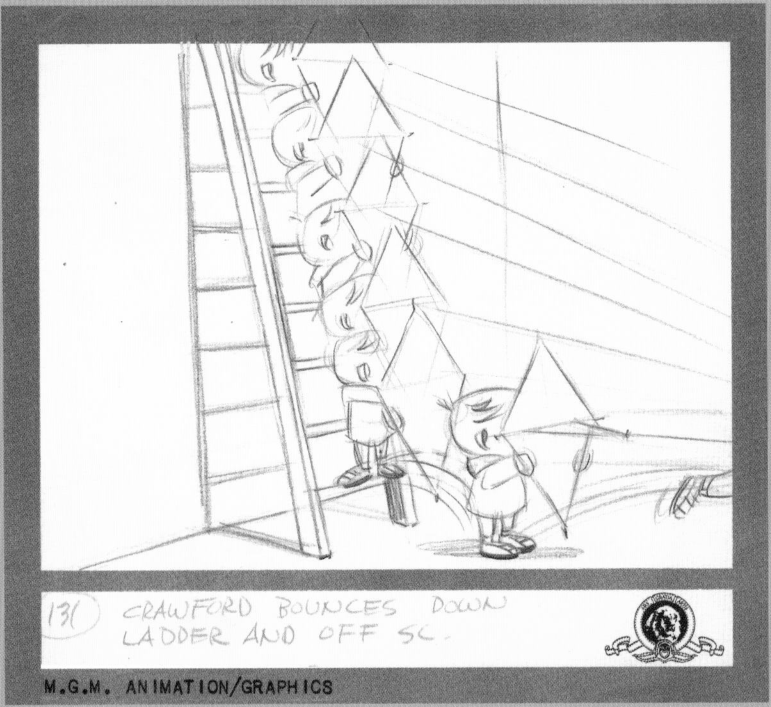
131 CRAWFORD BOUNCES DOWN
LADDER AND OFF SC.
M.G.M. ANIMATION/GRAPHICS

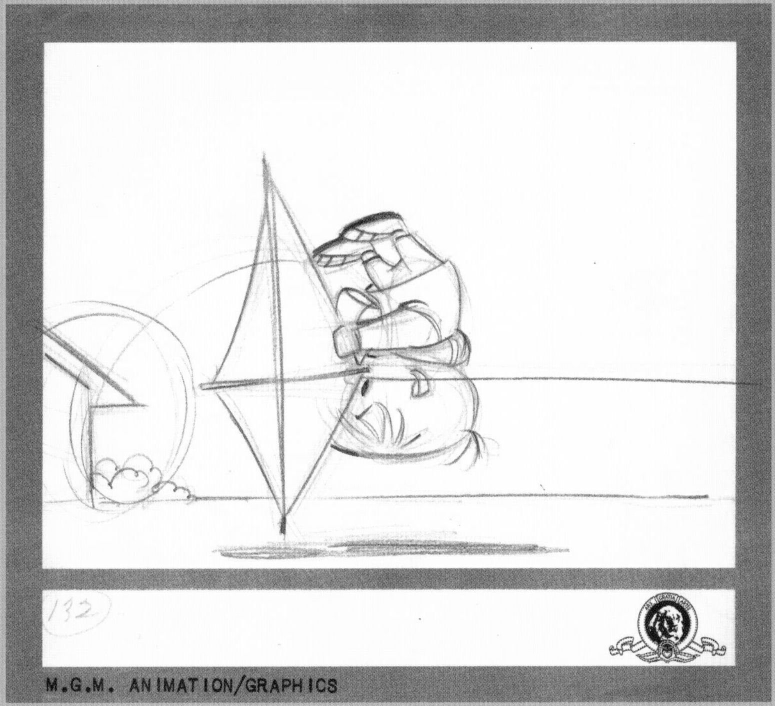
132
M.G.M. ANIMATION/GRAPHICS

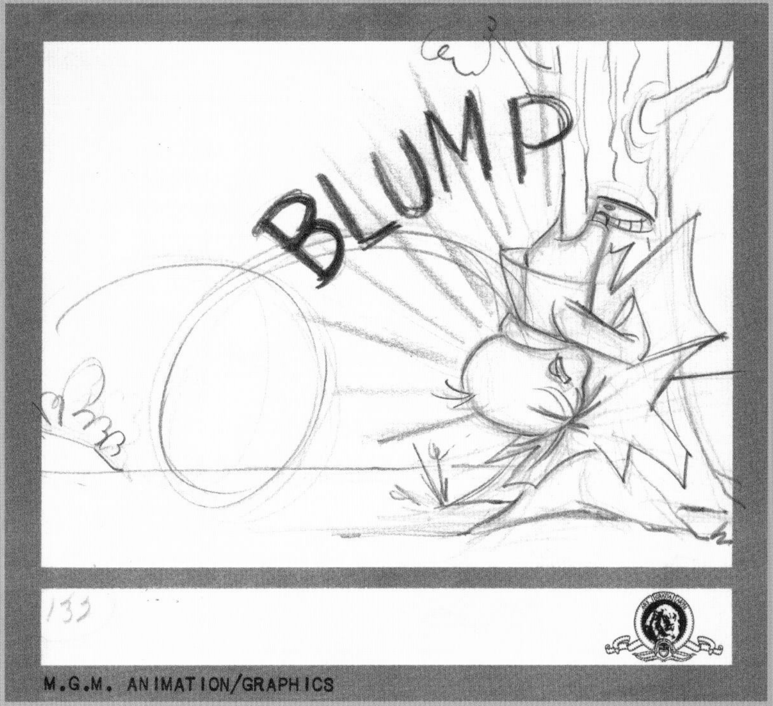
BLUMP
M.G.M. ANIMATION/GRAPHICS

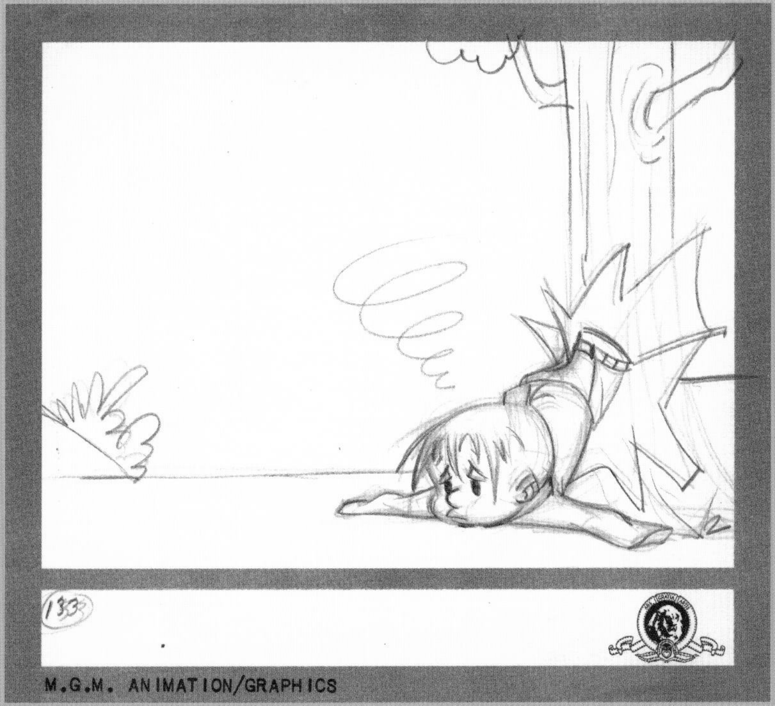
M.G.M. ANIMATION/GRAPHICS

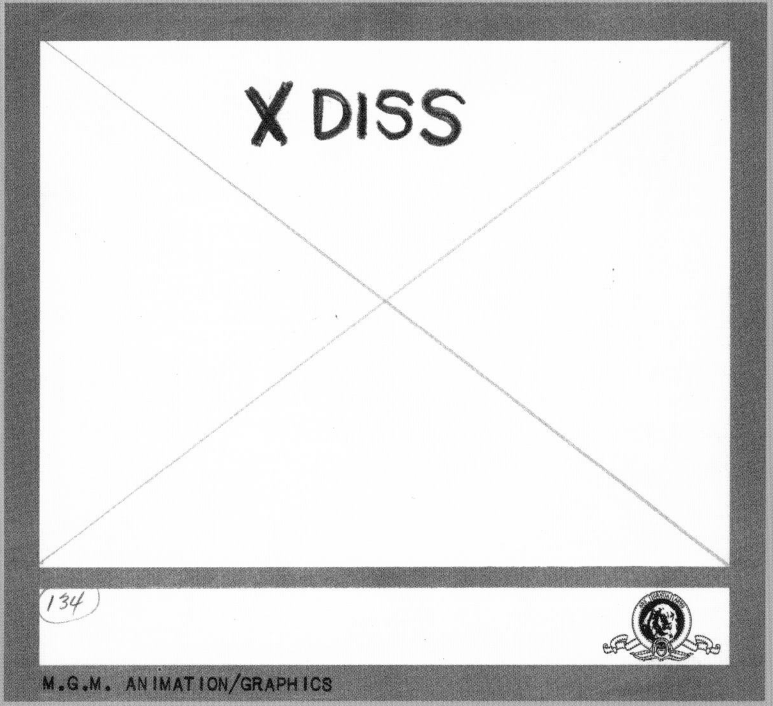
X DISS
134
M.G.M. ANIMATION/GRAPHICS

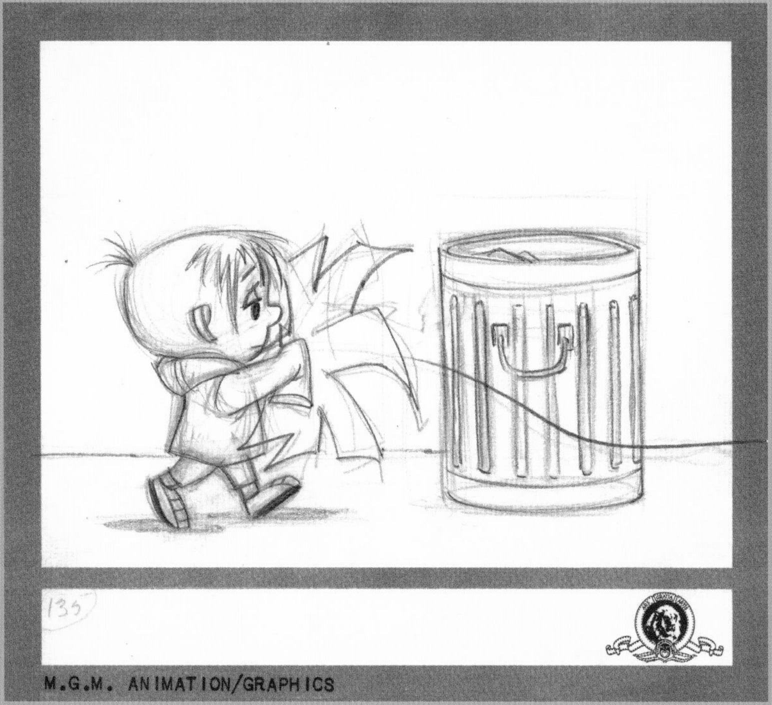
135
M.G.M. ANIMATION/GRAPHICS

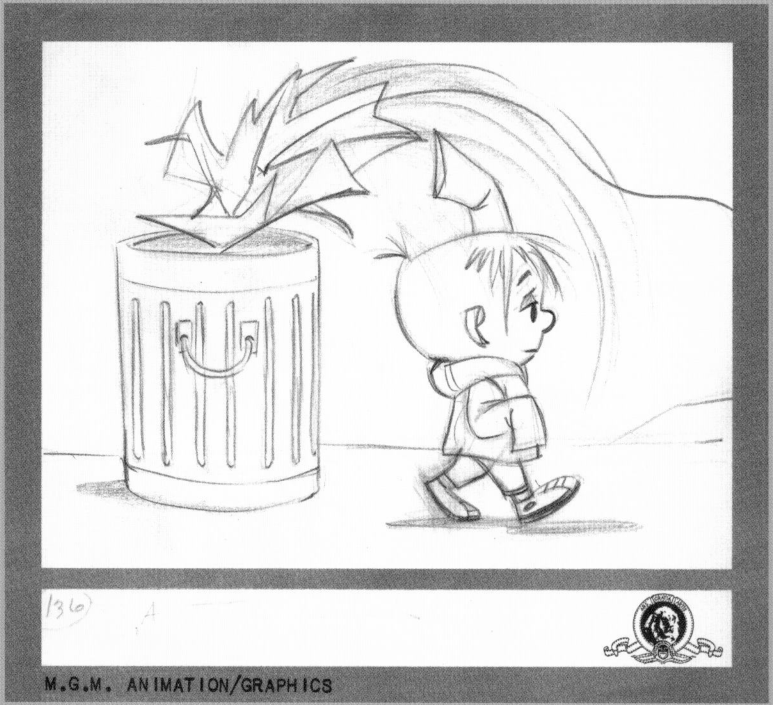
136
M.G.M. ANIMATION/GRAPHICS

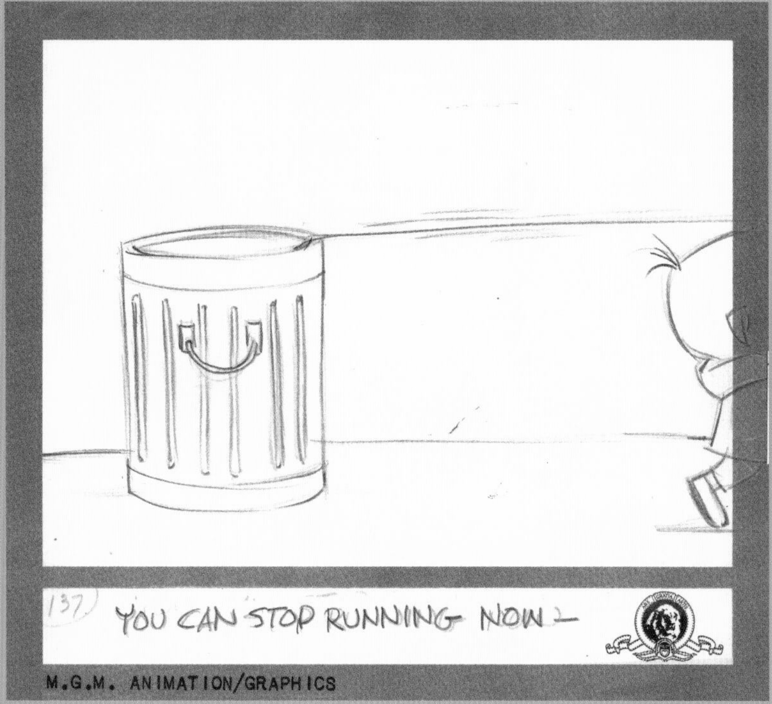
137
YOU CAN STOP RUNNING NOW –
M.G.M. ANIMATION/GRAPHICS

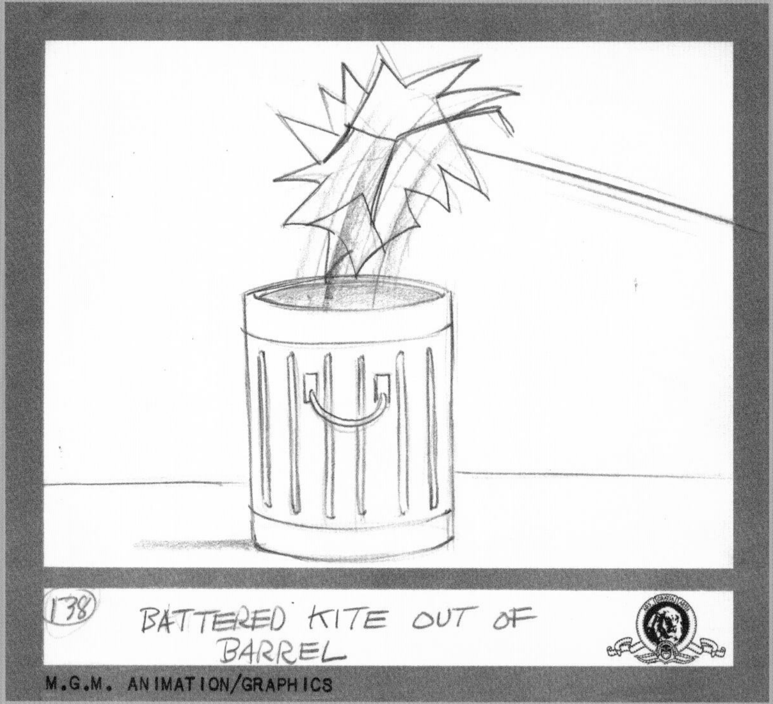
138
BATTERED KITE OUT OF BARREL
M.G.M. ANIMATION/GRAPHICS

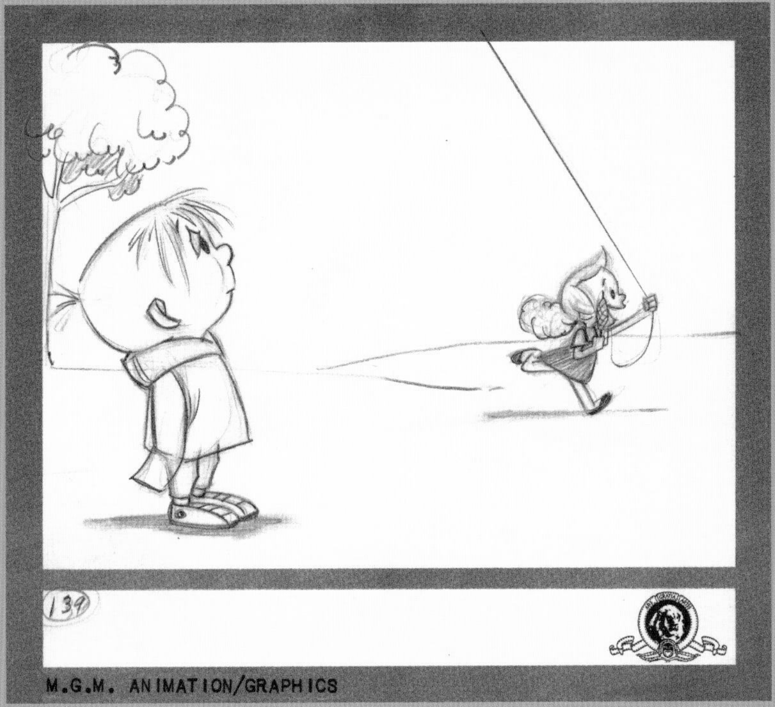

139
M.G.M. ANIMATION/GRAPHICS

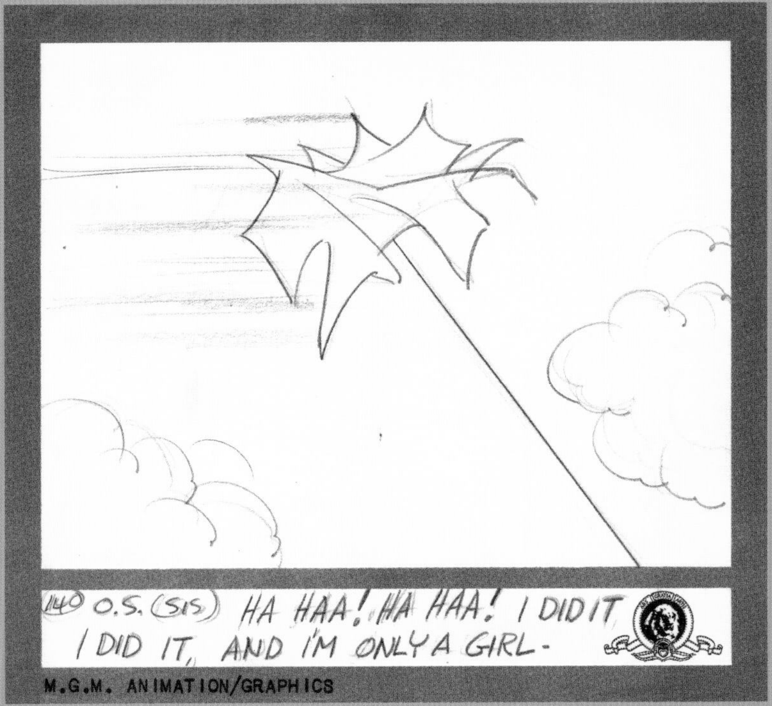

140 O.S. (SIS) HA HAA! HA HAA! I DID IT
I DID IT, AND I'M ONLY A GIRL-
M.G.M. ANIMATION/GRAPHICS

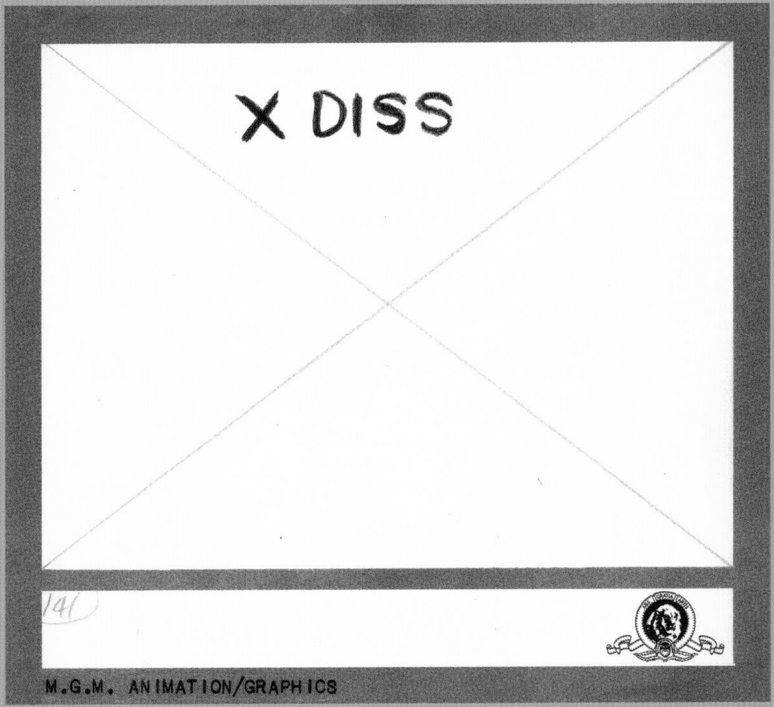

X DISS
141
M.G.M. ANIMATION/GRAPHICS

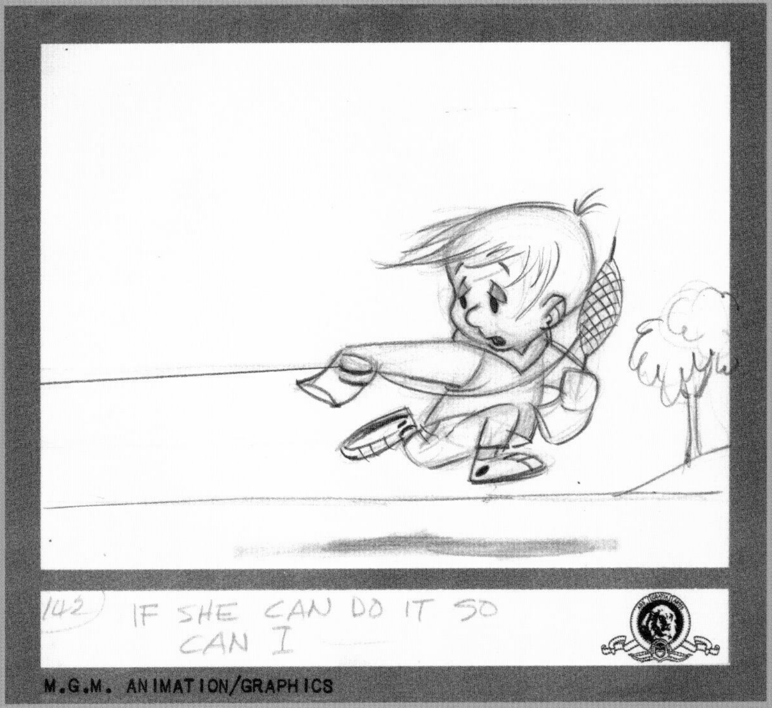

142 IF SHE CAN DO IT SO
CAN I
M.G.M. ANIMATION/GRAPHICS

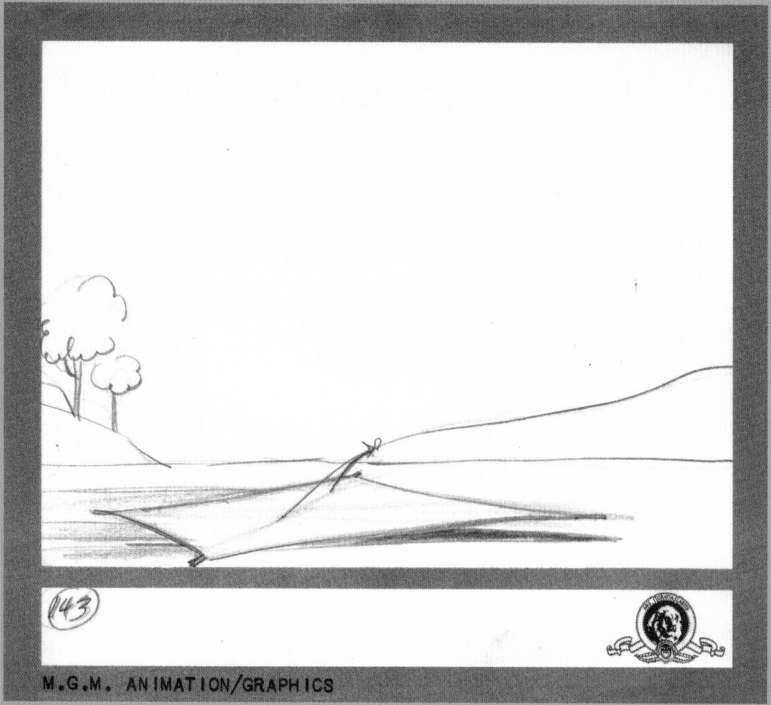
143
M.G.M. ANIMATION/GRAPHICS

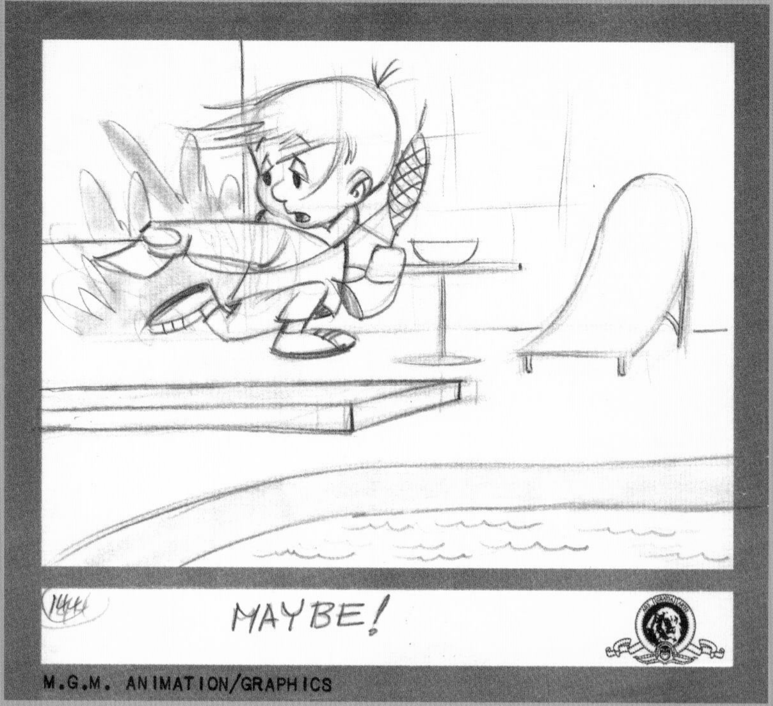
144
MAYBE!
M.G.M. ANIMATION/GRAPHICS

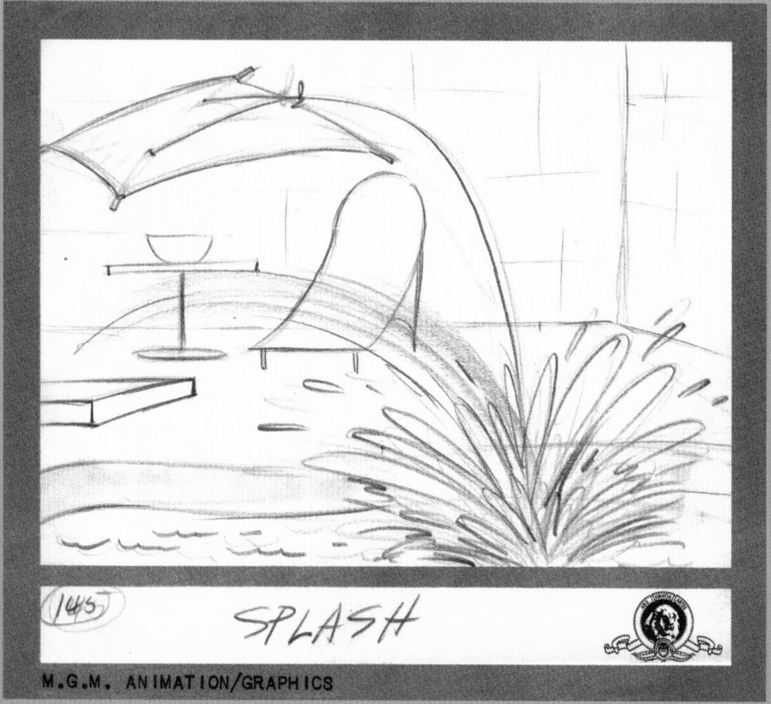
145
SPLASH
M.G.M. ANIMATION/GRAPHICS

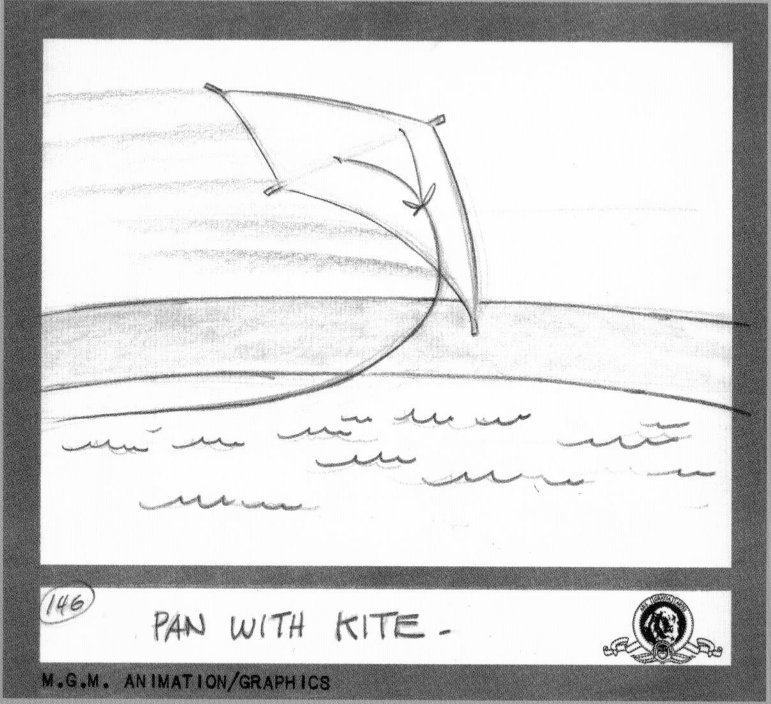
146
PAN WITH KITE -
M.G.M. ANIMATION/GRAPHICS

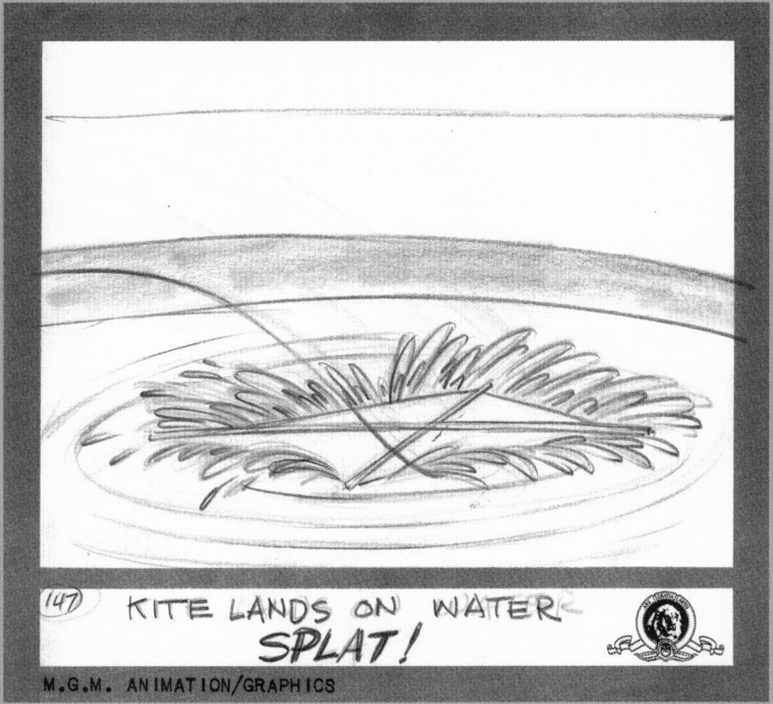
147 KITE LANDS ON WATER
SPLAT!
M.G.M. ANIMATION/GRAPHICS

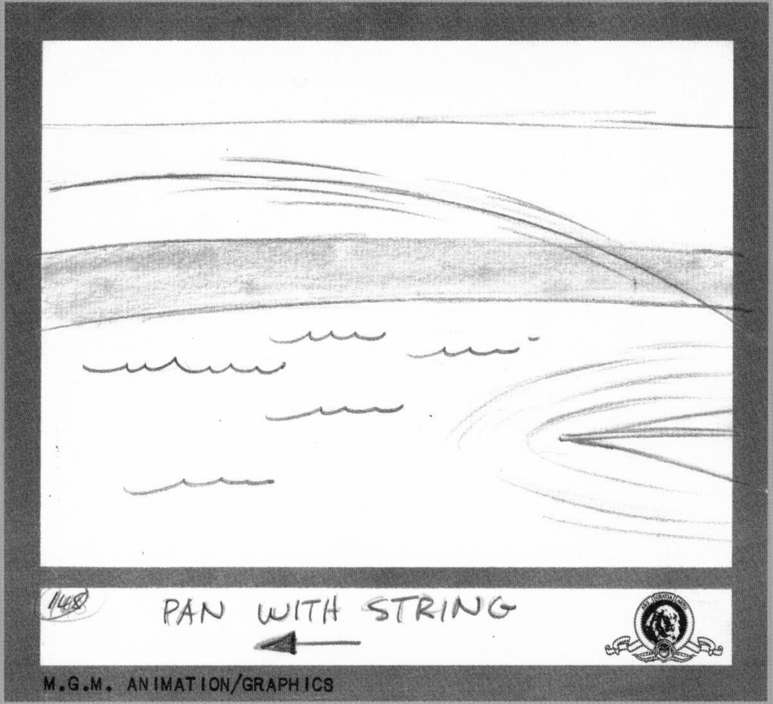
148 PAN WITH STRING
M.G.M. ANIMATION/GRAPHICS

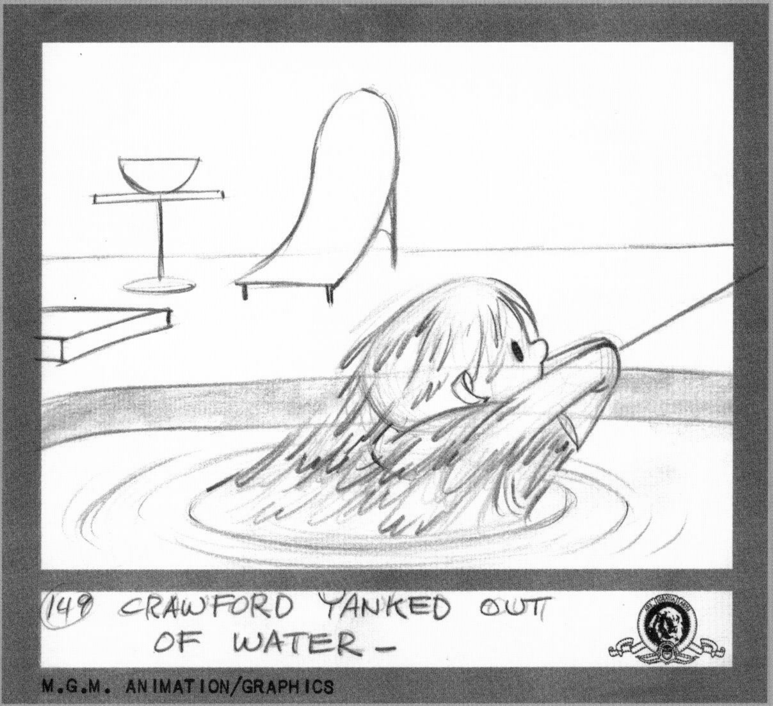
149 CRAWFORD YANKED OUT
OF WATER –
M.G.M. ANIMATION/GRAPHICS

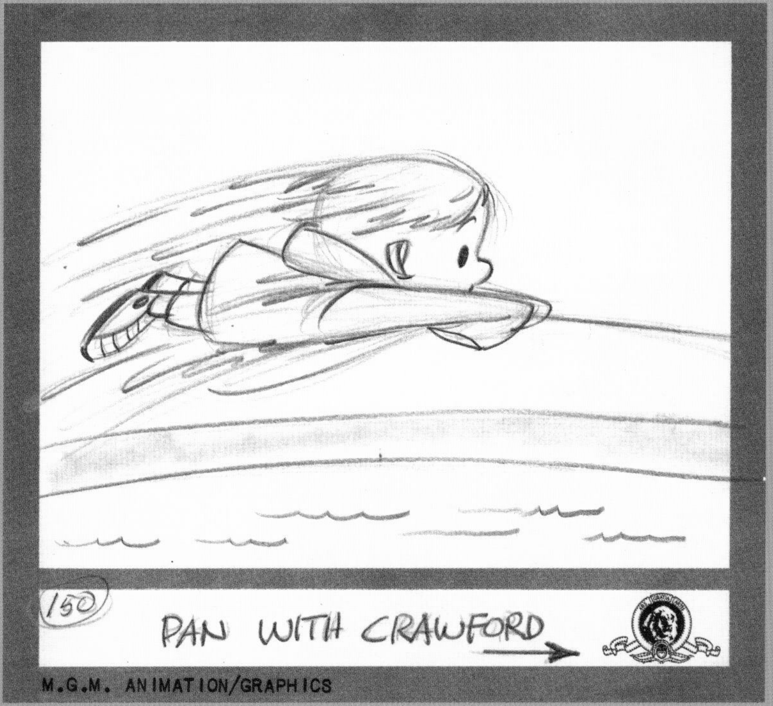
150 PAN WITH CRAWFORD
M.G.M. ANIMATION/GRAPHICS

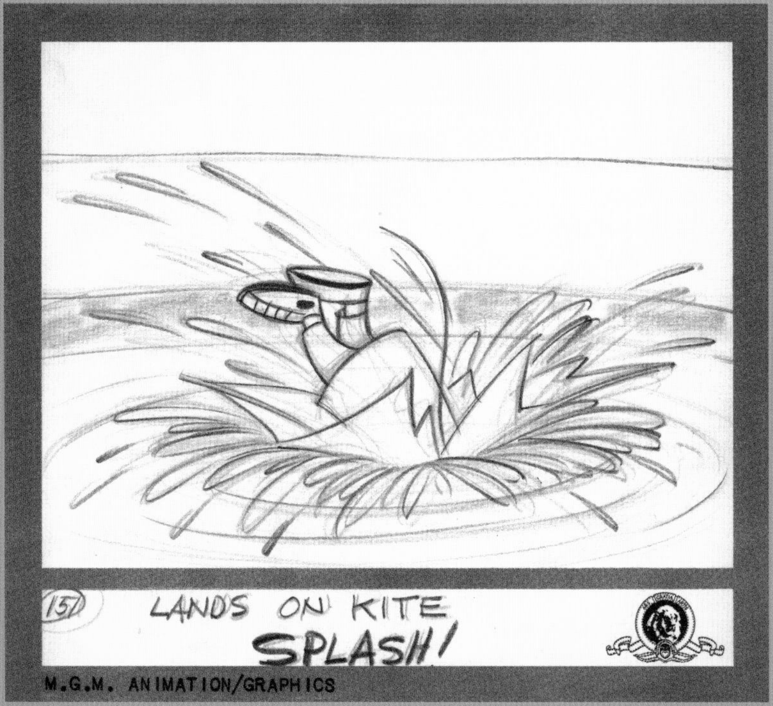
151 LANDS ON KITE
SPLASH!
M.G.M. ANIMATION/GRAPHICS

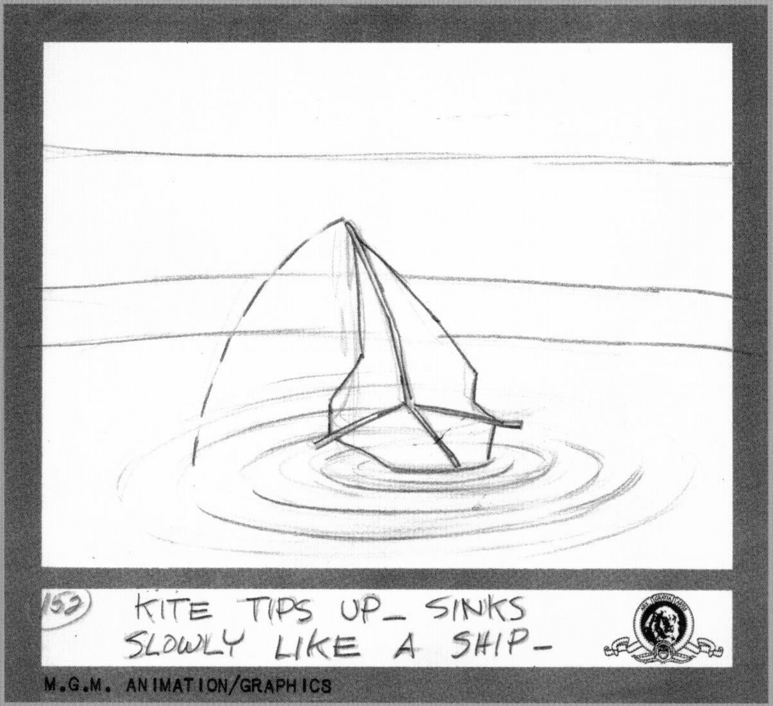
152 KITE TIPS UP_ SINKS SLOWLY LIKE A SHIP_
M.G.M. ANIMATION/GRAPHICS

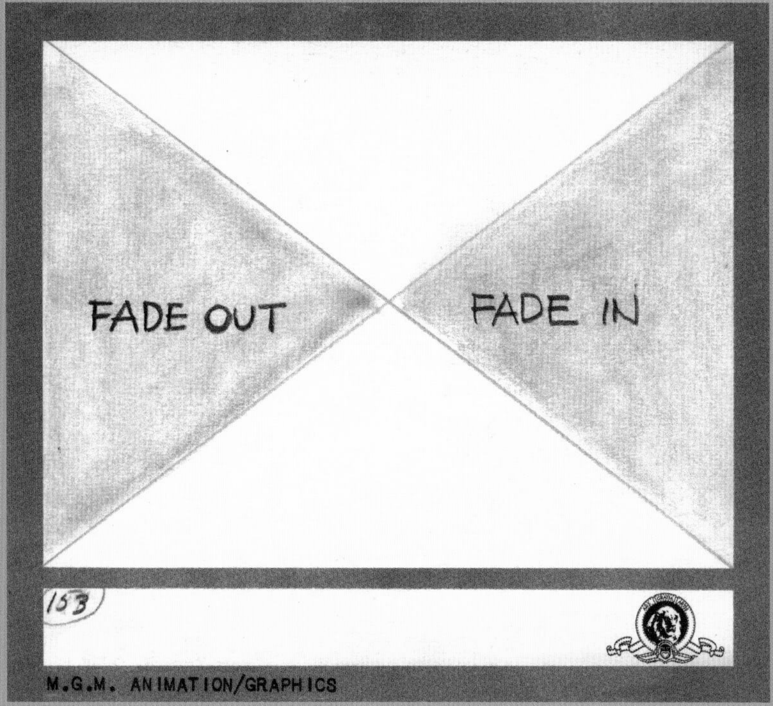
FADE OUT
FADE IN
153
M.G.M. ANIMATION/GRAPHICS

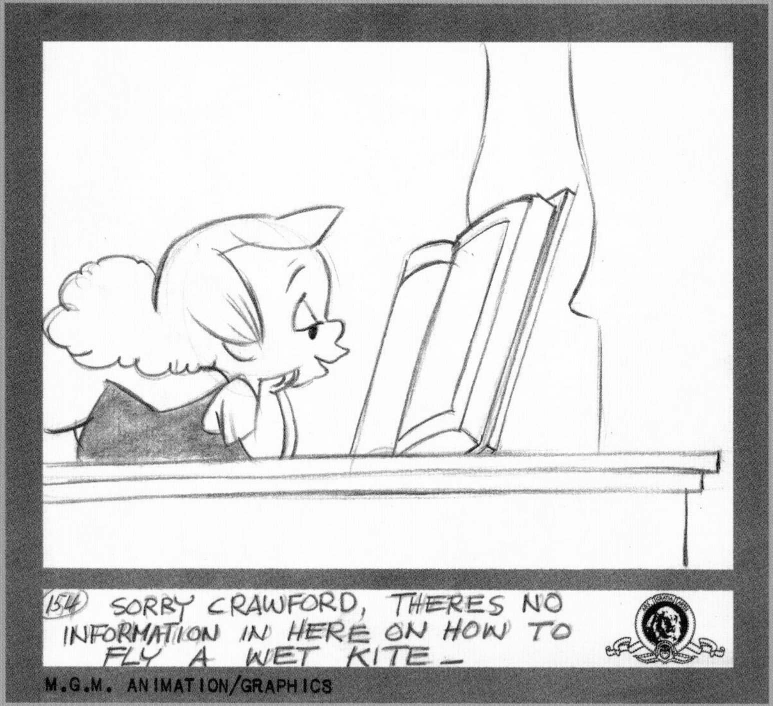
154 SORRY CRAWFORD, THERES NO INFORMATION IN HERE ON HOW TO FLY A WET KITE_
M.G.M. ANIMATION/GRAPHICS

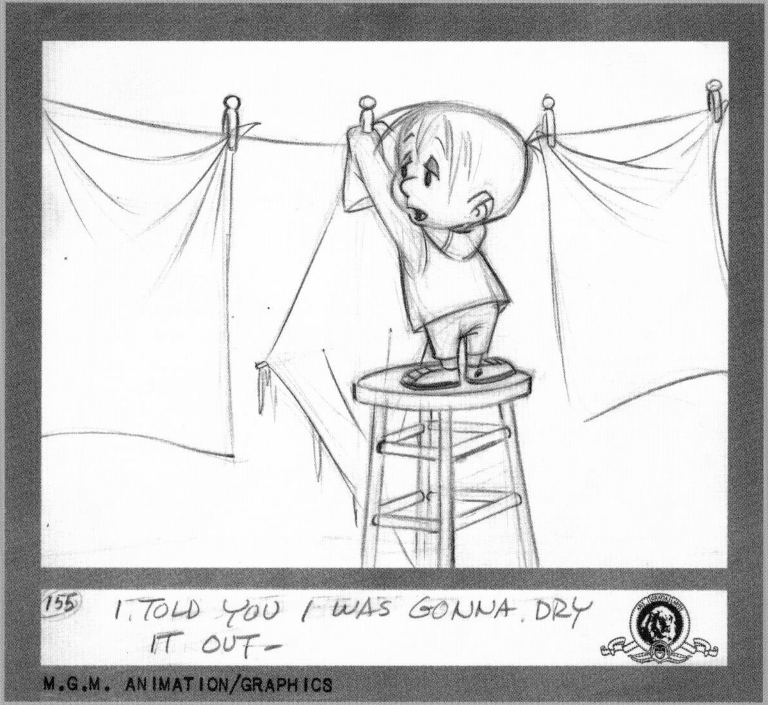
155
I TOLD YOU I WAS GONNA DRY IT OUT –
M.G.M. ANIMATION/GRAPHICS

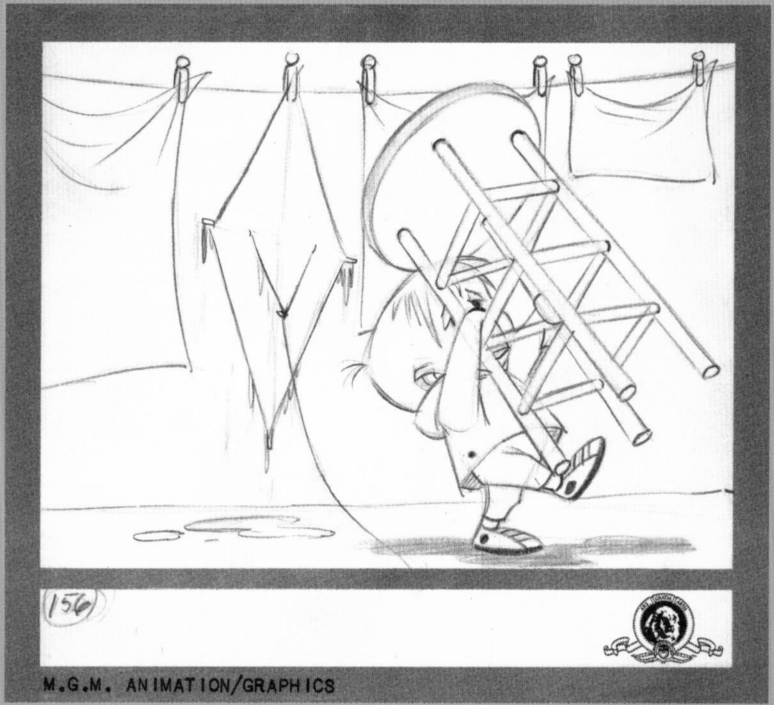
156
M.G.M. ANIMATION/GRAPHICS

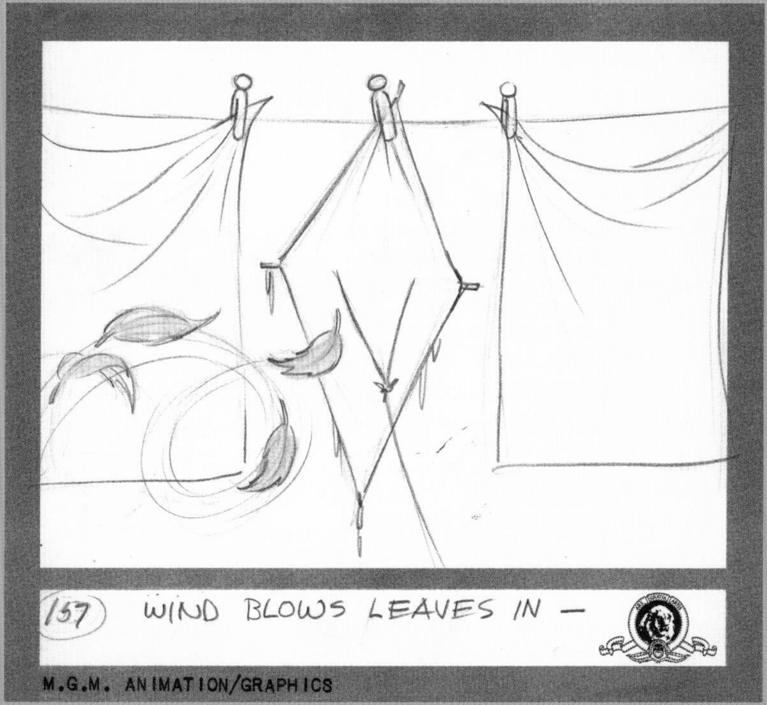
157
WIND BLOWS LEAVES IN –
M.G.M. ANIMATION/GRAPHICS

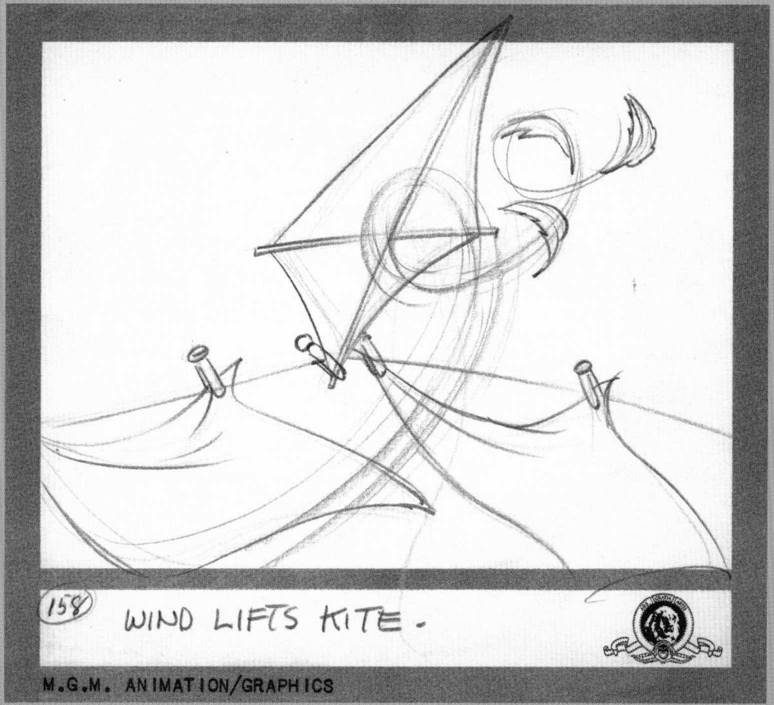
158
WIND LIFTS KITE –
M.G.M. ANIMATION/GRAPHICS

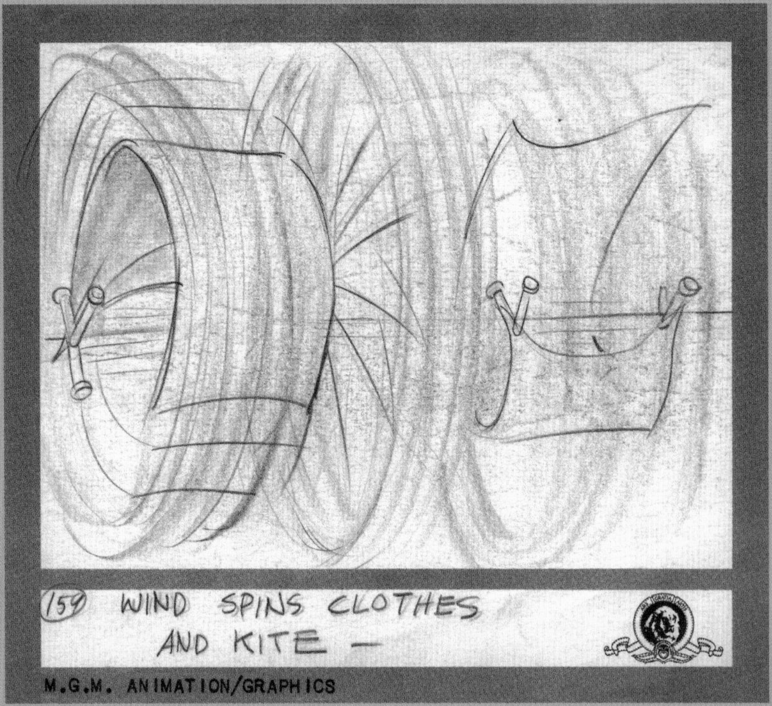
159 WIND SPINS CLOTHES
AND KITE —
M.G.M. ANIMATION/GRAPHICS

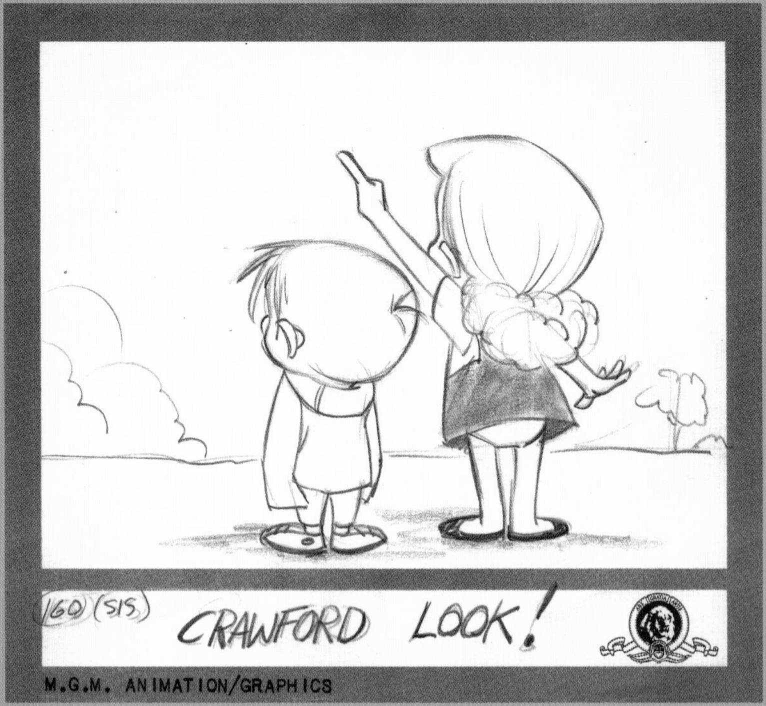
160 (SIS)
CRAWFORD LOOK!
M.G.M. ANIMATION/GRAPHICS

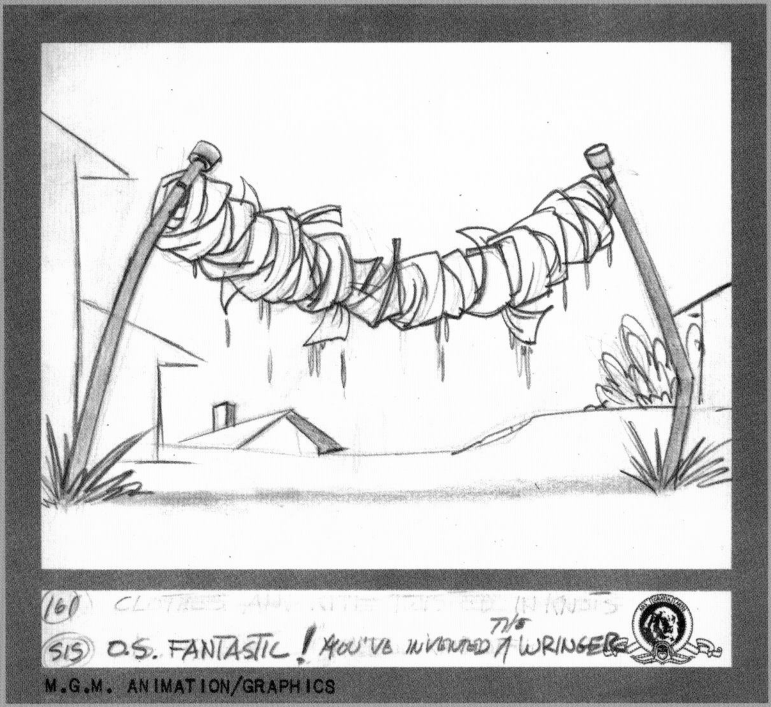
161
SIS O.S. FANTASTIC! YOU'VE INVENTED A WRINGER
M.G.M. ANIMATION/GRAPHICS

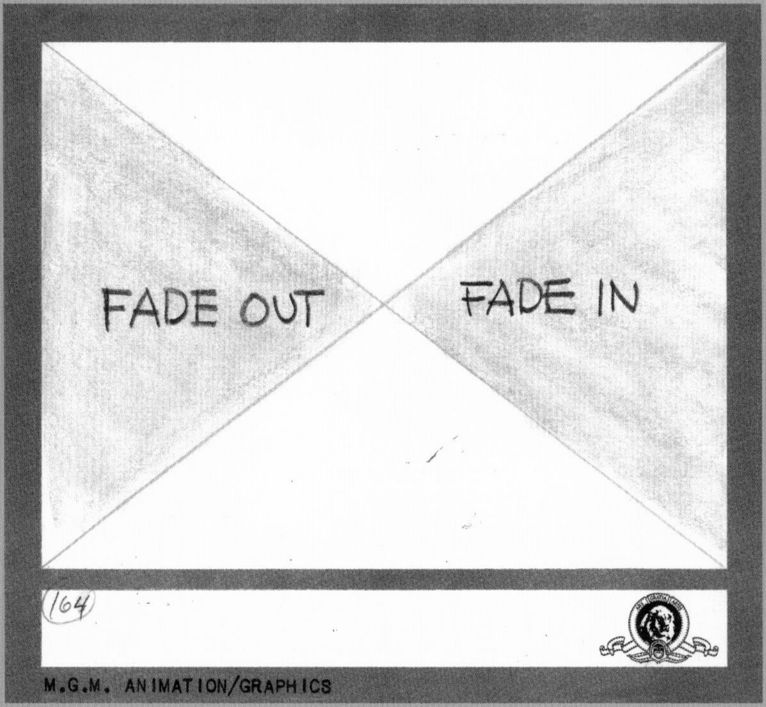
FADE OUT
FADE IN
164
M.G.M. ANIMATION/GRAPHICS

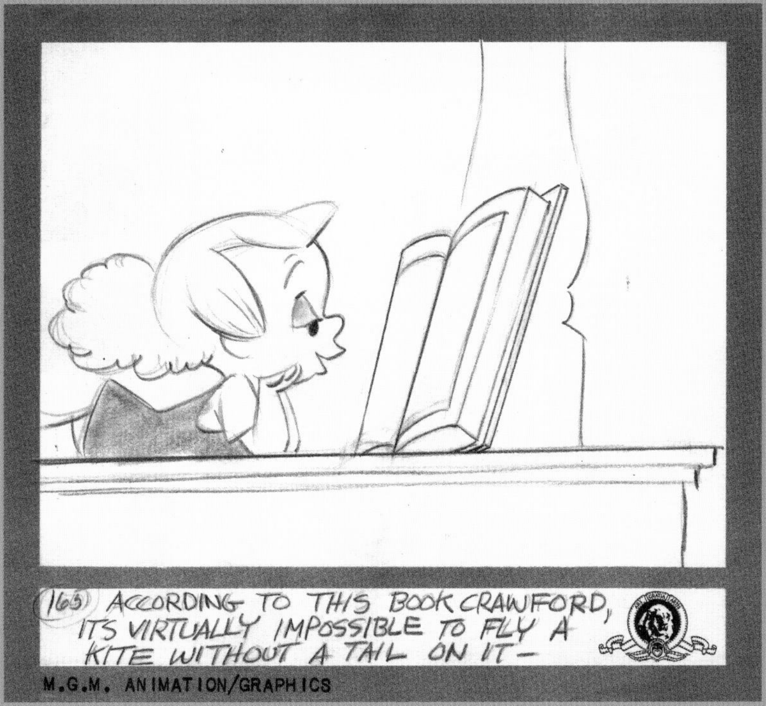
165 ACCORDING TO THIS BOOK CRAWFORD, ITS VIRTUALLY IMPOSSIBLE TO FLY A KITE WITHOUT A TAIL ON IT—
M.G.M. ANIMATION/GRAPHICS

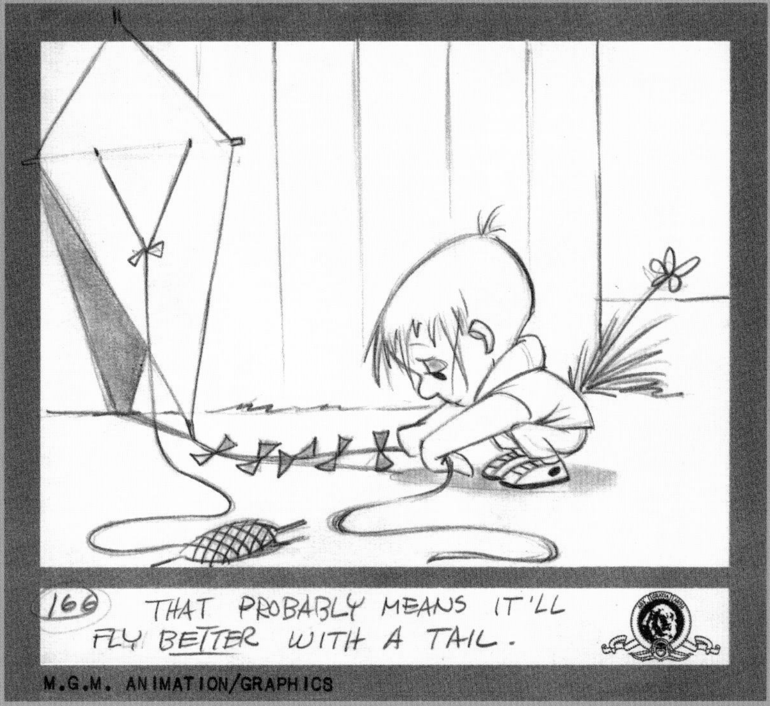
166 THAT PROBABLY MEANS IT'LL FLY BETTER WITH A TAIL.
M.G.M. ANIMATION/GRAPHICS

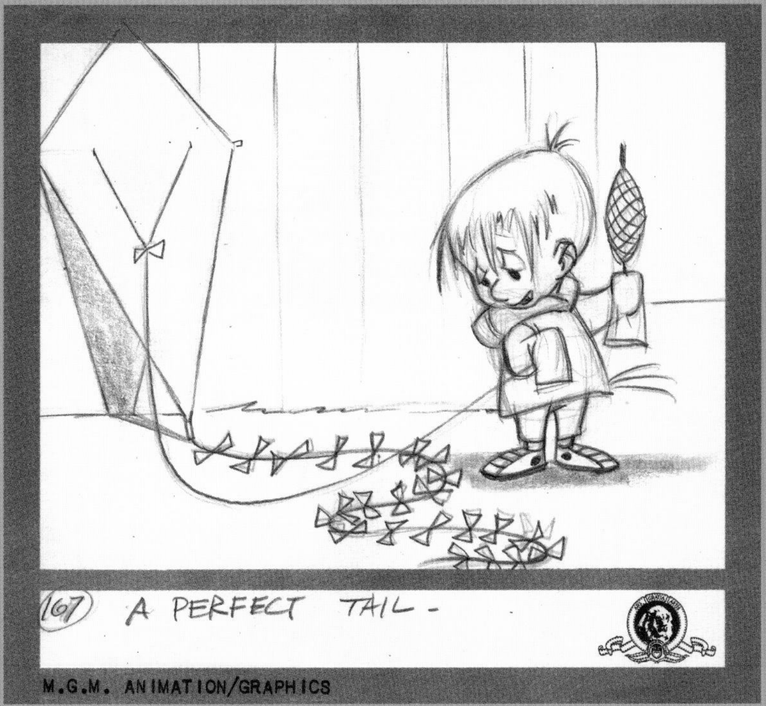
167 A PERFECT TAIL.
M.G.M. ANIMATION/GRAPHICS

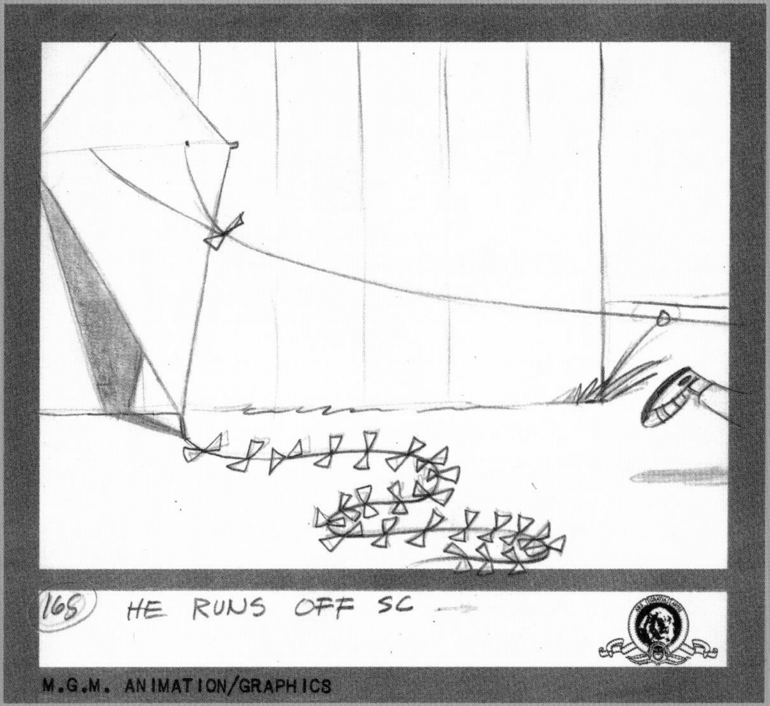
168 HE RUNS OFF SC —
M.G.M. ANIMATION/GRAPHICS

169 PAN WITH KITE →

M.G.M. ANIMATION/GRAPHICS

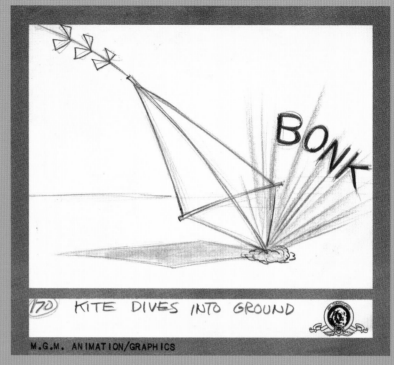

170 KITE DIVES INTO GROUND

BONK

M.G.M. ANIMATION/GRAPHICS

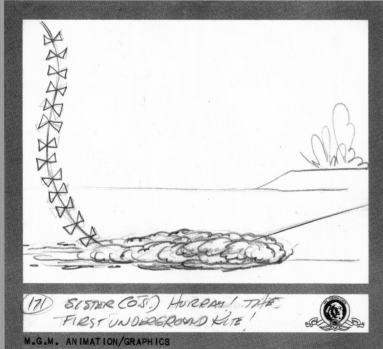

171 SISTER (O.S.) HURRAY! THE FIRST UNDERGROUND KITE!

M.G.M. ANIMATION/GRAPHICS

173 CRAWFORD LOOKS BACK —

M.G.M. ANIMATION/GRAPHICS

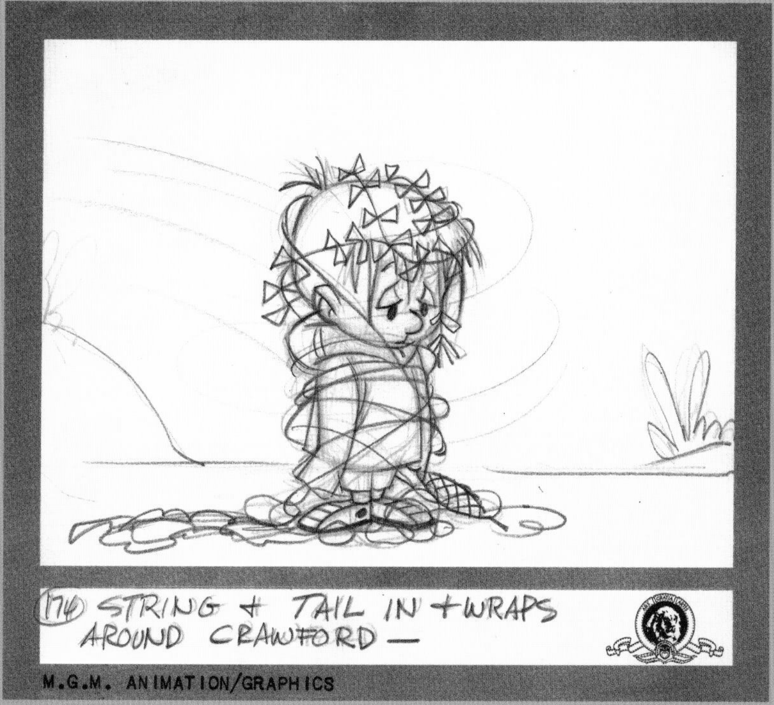
(174) STRING + TAIL IN + WRAPS AROUND CRAWFORD—
M.G.M. ANIMATION/GRAPHICS

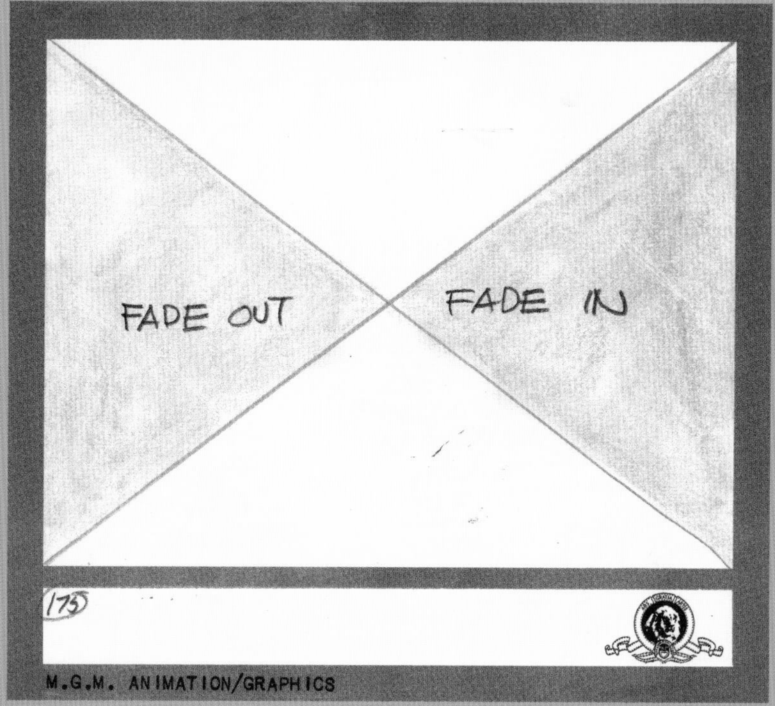
FADE OUT
FADE IN
(175)
M.G.M. ANIMATION/GRAPHICS

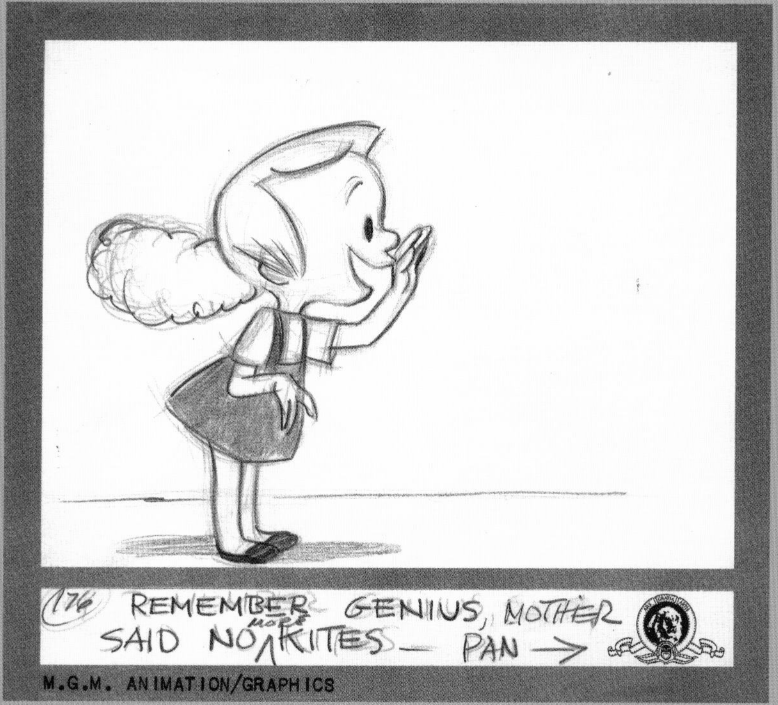
(176) REMEMBER GENIUS, MOTHER SAID NO MORE KITES— PAN →
M.G.M. ANIMATION/GRAPHICS

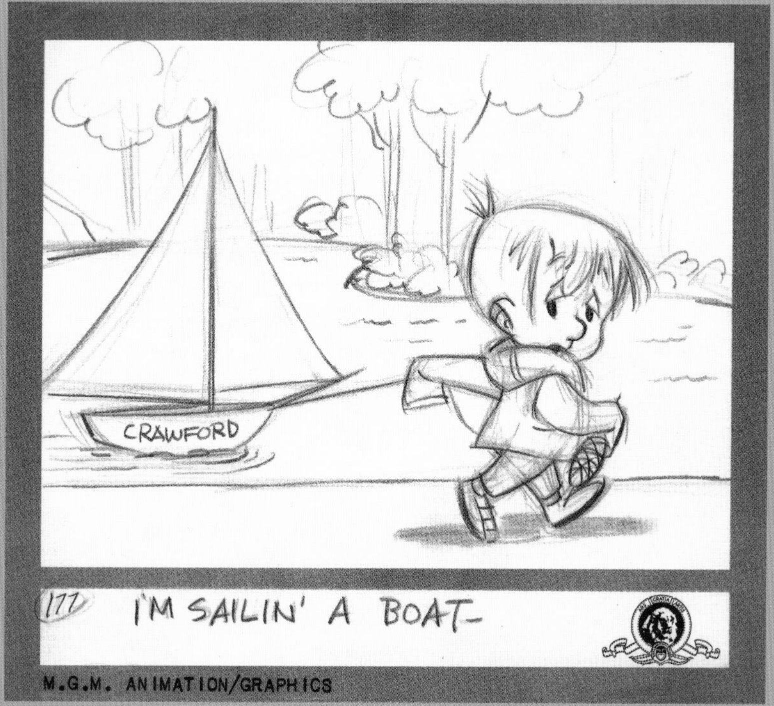
CRAWFORD
(177) I'M SAILIN' A BOAT—
M.G.M. ANIMATION/GRAPHICS

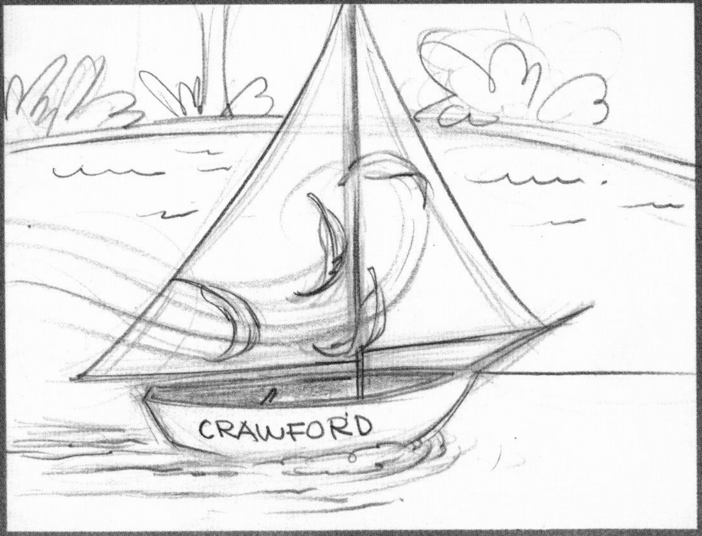
CRAWFORD

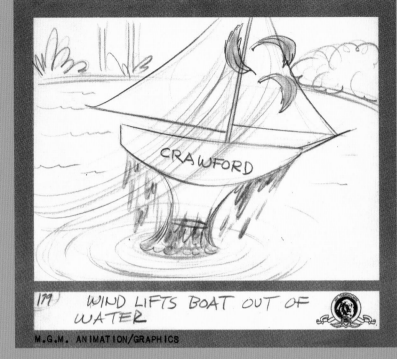

(178) (SIS) O.S. WELL AT LEAST YOU CAN'T SET FIRE TO THE WATER

M.G.M. ANIMATION/GRAPHICS

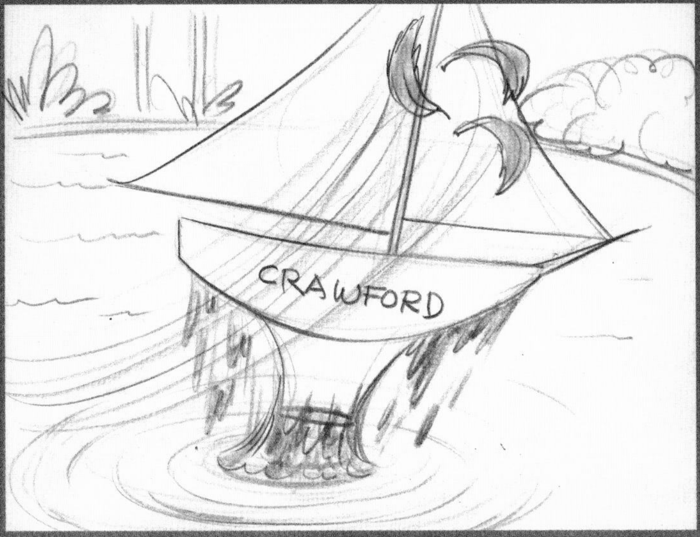
CRAWFORD

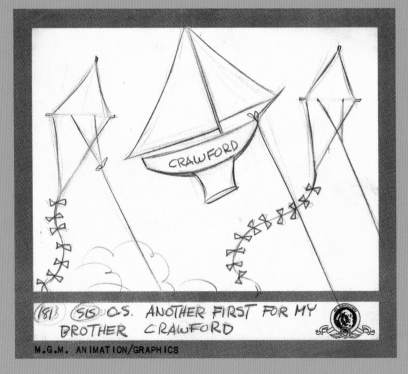

(179) WIND LIFTS BOAT OUT OF WATER

M.G.M. ANIMATION/GRAPHICS

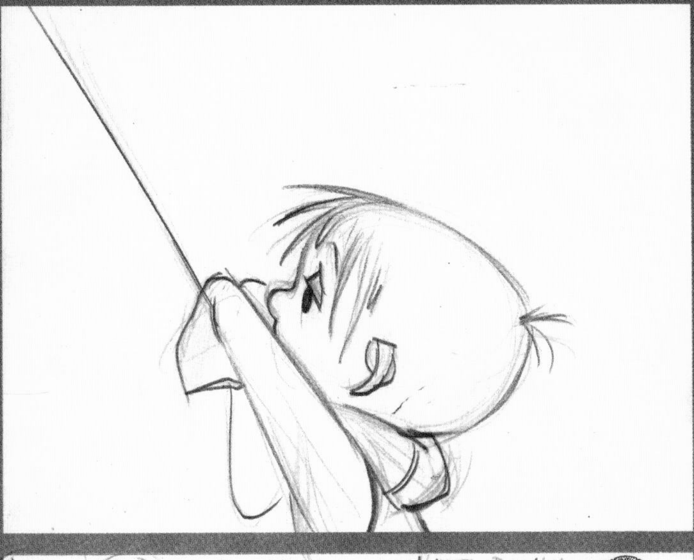

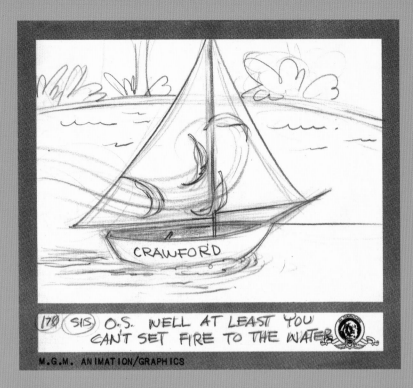

(180) (SIS) O.S. WELL WHAT DO YOU KNOW-

M.G.M. ANIMATION/GRAPHICS

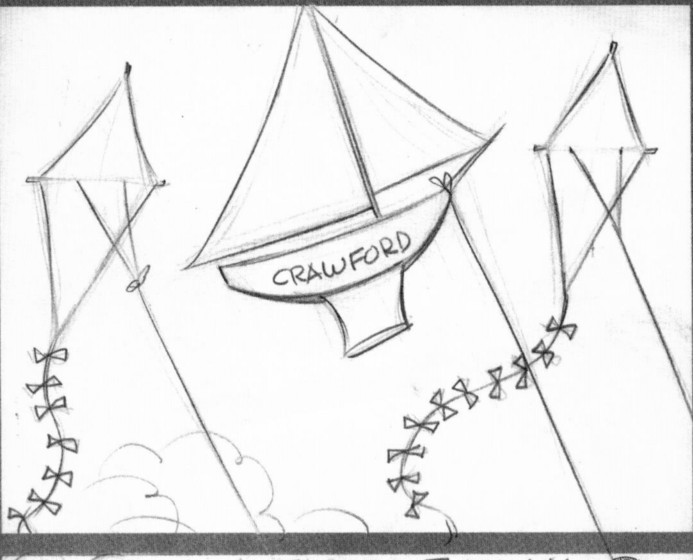
CRAWFORD

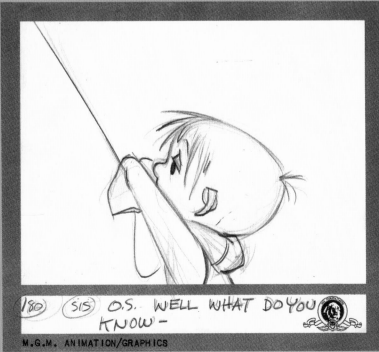

(181) (SIS) O.S. ANOTHER FIRST FOR MY BROTHER CRAWFORD

M.G.M. ANIMATION/GRAPHICS

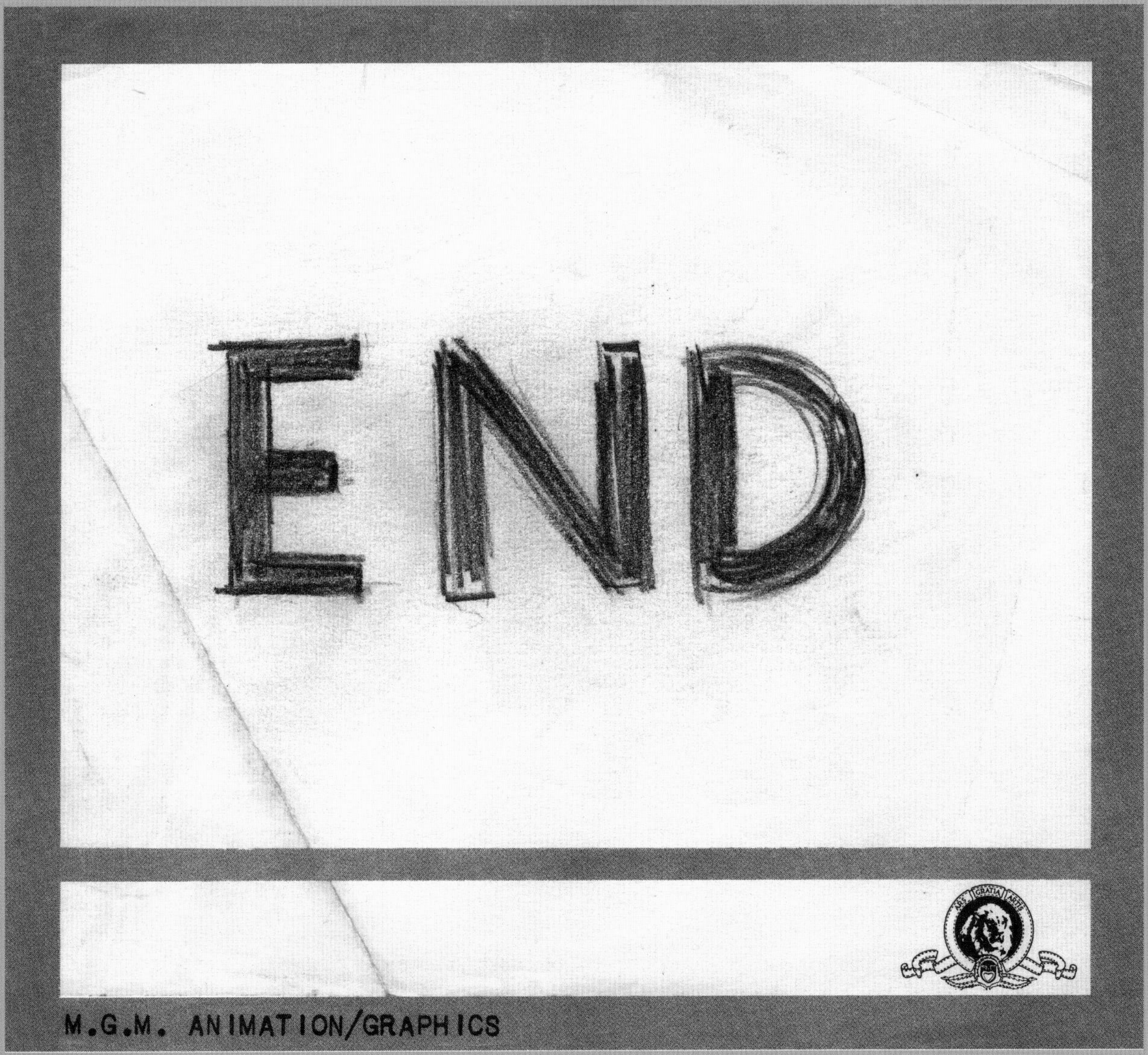
END
M.G.M. ANIMATION/GRAPHICS

SOURCES

BOOKS:

Beck, Jerry. *The Animated Movie Guide*. Chicago: Chicago Review Press, 2005.

Beck, Jerry (ed.). *Animation Art*. New York: Harper Design International, 2004.

Beck, Jerry and Will Freidwald. *Looney Tunes and Merrie Melodies: A Complete Illustrated Guide to the Warner Bros. Cartoons*. New York: Holt, 1989.

Beck, Jerry and Will Freidwald. *Warner Bros. Animation Art*. n.p.: Universe, 1997.

Crouch, Bill Jr. (ed.). *Phi Beta Pogo*. New York: Simon & Shuster, 1989.

Furness, Maureen (ed.). *Chuck Jones Conversations*. Jackson: University Press of Mississippi, 2005.

Garcia, Roger (ed.). *Frank Tashlin*. n.p.: British Film Institute, 1994.

Grant, John. *Masters of Animation*. London, BT Batford, 2001.

Iwerks, Leslie and Kenworthy, John D. *The Hand Behind the Mouse*. New York: Disney Editions, 2001

Jones, Chuck. *Chuck Amuck: The Life and Times of an Animated Cartoonist*. New York: Farrar, Straus & Giraux, New York, 1989.

Jones, Chuck. *Chuck Reducks: Drawing from the Fun Side of Life*. New York: Warner, 1996.

Kelly, Selby Daily and Steve Thompson. *Pogo Files for Pogophiles*. Richfield, MS: Spring Hollow Books, 1992.

Kenner, Hugh. *Chuck Jones: A Flurry of Drawings*. Berkley: University of California Press, 1994.

Lenburg, Jeff. *The Encyclopedia of Animated Cartoons (2nd ed.)*. New York: Checkmark, 1999.

McKinnon, Robert J. *Stepping Into the Picture: Cartoon Designer Maurice Noble*. Jackson: University Press of Mississippi, 2008.

Maltin, Leonard. *Of Mice and Magic (revised ed.)*. New York: Plume, 1987.

Mazurkewich, Karen. *Cartoon Capers: The History of Canadian Animators*. Toronto: McArthur, 1999.

Morgan, Judith and Neil. *Dr. Seuss and Mr. Geisel: A Biography*. New York: Random, 1995.

Van Citters, Darrell. *Mister Magoo's Christmas Carol: The Making of the First Animated Christmas Special*. Los Angeles: Oxberry, 2008.

Willliams, Richard. *Animator's Survival Kit*. London: Faber & Faber, 2001.

ARTICLES:

Crawford, Tom. "Crawdad's Crossroads." Bemidji *Pioneer*, 15 Dec. 1977: 4

Du Brow, Rick. "ABC-TV Offering 'Curiosity Shop.'" Redland *Daily Facts*, 3 Sep, 1971: 10

Gabriel, Joyce. "New Shows Are For, Not About, Children." Pulaski *Times*, 16 Aug. 1971: 8

Mills, Cynthia. "High Court Allows Spanking in School."

Shay, Mary. "Forecast of TV Fans." Tucson *Daily Citizen*, 28 Aug. 1971: 22

Smith, Cecil. "No is a No-No for ABC'S Chuck Jones." Portsmouth *Times*, 5 Jan. 1971: 8.

Smith, Cecil. "Views on Television: Curious Mr. Jones and His Curiosity Shop." Victoria *Advocate*, 29 Aug, 1971: 8

Warren, Ina. "Cartoonist known as Story-boarder." Lethbridge *Herald*, 5 Aug. 1977: 20

"Animated Special Conveys History." Jefferson City *Post-Tribune*, 6 Jun. 1976: 4

"Children's Series to Make Debut." Florence *Morning News Saturday*, 27 Mar. 1971: 3

"Commercial-Free TV Hours Asked." Des Moines *Register*, 13 Feb. 1970: 7

"NEA Approves CBS Show." Des Moines *Sunday Register*, 8 Feb. 1971: 5-TV

"Pogo Birthday Special to Be Seen on KOAM-TV." Joplin *Globe*, *Showtime* 18 May 1969: 9

"'Pogo' Birthday Special to Enliven Television Sunday Evening on NBC." Idaho *State Journal*, 16 May 1969: 2

"Pogo to End 26-Year Silence." Hagerstown *Herald-Mail*, 17 May 1969: 1-TV

"Pupil Punishment Ruling Splits Education Groups." Publication unknown, 21 Apr. 1977

WEBPAGES:

salon.com/books/int/2001/03/12/juster/print.html

newsfromme.com/archives/2009_11_15.html

americanrhetoric.com/speeches/newtonminow.htm

INDEX

1001 Arabian Nights 14
5,000 Fingers of Dr. T, The 24
ABC 12, 14, 17, 36, 38, 39
Action for Children's Television (ACT) 36
Adventures of the Road-Runner, The 8, 10-12, 26, 28, 33, 49
Alcala, Alfredo 42
Ambro, Hal 17
Angel Puss 43
Arioli, Don 36, 41, 42, 43, 49
Avery, Tex 8, 36
Baloo the Bear 41
Barrier, Barrier 4, 23
Bear That Wasn't, The 22, 23
Beck, Jerry 4, 9, 282
Bell, Carl 4, 14, 17
Bell Labs Science. 17
Bemidji (Minnesota) *Pioneer* 7, 282
Berenstain, Stan and Jan 38
Bien, Walter N. 16, 17
Blanc, Mel 17
Boyhood Daze 9
Bradbury, Ray 26, 36
Bugs Bunny 9, 10, 42, 44
Bugs Bunny Show, The 10
Bugs Bunny/Road Runner Movie, The 42
Bugs Bunny's Bustin' Out All Over 42
Bugs Bunny's Looney Christmas Tales 42
Burns, Stan 36
Buttons, Red 14
Capra, Frank 24
Caulfield 29, 30
Charlie and Otto 30-32
Chicago Tribune–New York News Syndicate 38, 42
Christmas Carol, A 36, 38, 39, 209
Chuck Amuck 7, 43, 282
Claude Cat 9
Clifton 12, 50
Condoms are Safe 41
Connecticut Yankee in King Arthur's Court, A 42, 44
Crawford (comic strip) 7, 8, 12, 14, 42-44, 48-49, 82-193

Cricket in Times Square, A 43
Curiosity Shop, The 36, 38, 41, 42, 282
Daffy Duck 9, 42, 44
Daffy Duck's Thanks-for-Giving Special 42
DeGuard, Philip 9, 17
Deitch, Gene 16
DePatie 25, 42
DePatie-Freleng Enterprises 25, 42
Dern, Marian (see Jones)
Dick Tracy (cartoon) 14
Disney, Walt 8, 17, 41,
Disney Studios 17, 22, 25, 36, 39, 41
Don Coyote and Sancho Plazma 33
Don Morgan 4, 14, 16, 26, 44
Dot and the Line, The 18, 22, 23
Dover Boys of Pimento University, The 9
Dr. Seuss's How the Grinch Stole Christmas 7, 24, 25, 43
Duck Amuck 7
Duck Dodgers in the 24½ Century 9
Duck, Rabbit, Duck 9
Earth Creatures 44, 46, 49
Eisner, Michael 36
Federal Communications Commission (FCC) 36
Fiddler's Green 32-35
Filmation Associates *16*
Flip the Frog 8
Foray, June 17, 25
Foster, Don 44
Friedwald, Will 9
From A to Z-Z-Z-Z 9, 43
Garland, Judy 14
Gay Pur-ee 14
Geisel, Ted 23-26, 35
Gillette "Foamy" 16, 17
Goldman, Les 14, 16, 17, 24
Goulet, Robert 14
Grant, John 38
Hanna-Barbera 9, 17, 26
Harris, Ken 9, 14, 38
Harris, Julian 49
Hart, Johnny 38, 42
Here Comes Crawford (1969 TV

proposal) 26, 28-36, 48-50, 234-281
Horton Hears a Who 25
Hubie and Bertie 9
Idaho State *Journal* 25, 282
Iwerks, Ub 8
Jimmy Penis and Vicki Vulva 41
Jones, Charles Martin (Chuck)
    Academy Awards 7, 9, 18, 23, 36, 38, 43
    early life and career 8-10, 43
    first feature film 18-23
    photographs 6, 14, 15, 19-21, 23-25, 37, 40,
    return to Warners Bros. characters 42
    starts own studio 14-16
    VP of Children's Programming at ABC 36
Jones, Dorothy Webster 8, 14, 36, 38, 42, 48
Jones, Marian Dern 4, 42
Jungle Book 39, 41
Juster, Norton 18, 19, 22, 26, 282
Karloff, Boris 24
Kausen, Craig 42
Kausen, Todd 101
Kausler, Mark 4, 14, 39, 48
Kaye, Danny 9
Keaton, Buster 17, 32, 33
Kelly, Selby 25
Kelly, Walt 25, 36, 44, 209
Kerkorian, Kirk 26
Ketcham, Hank 38
Kimball, Ward 25
Kipling, Rudyard 10, 39, 41, 43
Levitow, Abe 9, 14, 17, 18, 21, 22, 36, 38
Maurice Noble 9, 12, 17, 18, 282
Lazarus, Mell 38
Looney Tunes 8-10, 14, 17, 18, 28, 29, 36, 42, 43-44
Lynde, Stan 42
Maltese, Michael 9, 17
Marc Anthony 9
Markes, Larry 36
Marmer, Mike 36

Marvin the Martian 9
Merrie Melodies 8, 9, 43
MGM and MGM Animation/Visual Arts 9, 16-18, 22, 23, 25-29, 36, 38, 44
Michel, Don 4, 44, 48, 82
Mighty Hunters 43
Minnow, Newton N. 36
Monahan, David 18
Morgan, Don 4, 14, 16, 26, 44, 282
Mowgli 10, 39, 41, 43
Mowgli's Brothers 39, 41, 43
Mr. Magoo 14, 16
National Film Board of Canada 36, 41
NBC 25, 26, 36
New York *Daily News* 7
New York Mets 26
Night Watchman, The 43
Noble, Maurice 9, 12, 17, 18, 22, 282
Off to See the Wizard 17
One Froggy Evening 9
Pal, George 36
Partch, Virgil "VIP" 38
Patrick, Butch 18, 19, 21, 22
Peale, Noman Vincent 50
Pent-House Mouse 17
Pepé Le Pew 7, 9
Phantom Tollbooth, The 10, 18, 19, 21 22, 36, 43
Phi Beta Pogo 25, 282
Phillips, Arnold 10-12, 28
Phillips, Irving 38
Phillips, Ralph 9-12, 14, 18, 22, 26, 28, 33, 43, 49, 50
Pogo 25, 43, 44, 209, 282
Pogo Special Birthday Special, The 25, 43
Private Snafu 24
Pumpkin Who Couldn't Smile, The 42, 50
Rabbit of Seville 9
Rabbit Seasoning 9
Raggedy Ann 42, 44
Raggedy Ann and Andy in the Great Santa Claus Caper 42

Raggedy Ann and Andy in the Pumpkin Who Couldn't Smile 42
Ray, Tom 14
Reed, Robert 4, 38, 42, 44, 48
Rick O'Shay 42
Rikki-Tikki-Tavi 39, 43
Road Runner & Coyote 7, 9-12, 14, 26, 42
Robin Hood Makes Good 43
Sabella, Paul 49
Scheimer, Lou 16
Schlesinger, Leon 8, 9, 14, 43
Selden, George 39
Sesame Street 16, 42
Seuss, Dr. 23-26, 35
SIB Productions 16, 17
Sutherland, Hal 16
Tashlin, Frank 9, 22, 23, 26, 282
Termite Terrace 8, 14, 22
Thompson, Richard 9, 14
Thompson, Steve 25, 282
Tom & Jerry 9, 16, 17, 18, 36
Tower Twelve 14-17, 26, 32, 36, 39
Towsley, Don 17
Tremaine, Les 25
Twain, Mark 18, 32, 44, 50
United Artists 14
United Productions of America 14, 16
Unscratchables, The 26, 27
Untouchables, The 27
Van Citters, Darrell 4, 14, 282
Vaughan, Lloyd 9
Very Merry Cricket, A 39
Warner Bros. Studio 8-10, 12, 14, 16, 17, 38, 41-44
Warner, Jack 14
Washam, Ben 9, 14, 17
Webster, Dorothy (see Jones)
What's Opera, Doc? 7
White Seal, The 39, 41, 43
Williams, Richard 36, 38
Willie Whopper 8
Yankee Doodle Cricket 39
Zagreb Studios 36

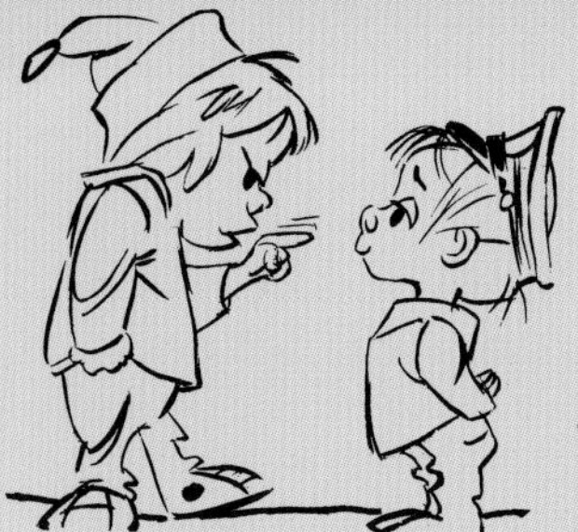

The Great American Comics

FROM IDW AND THE LIBRARY OF AMERICAN COMICS

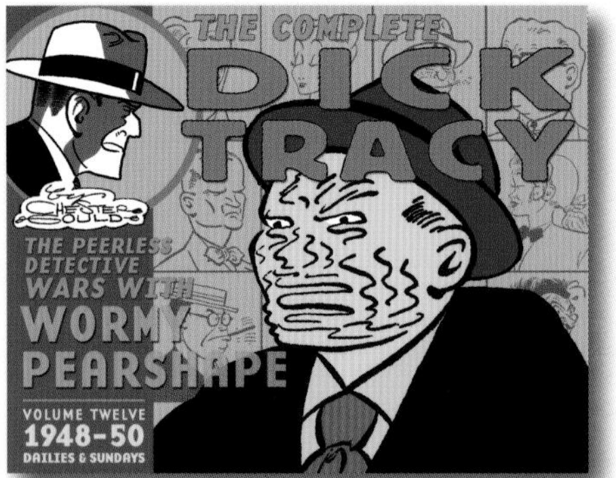

THE COMPLETE
DICK TRACY
THE PEERLESS DETECTIVE WARS WITH WORMY PEARSHAPE
VOLUME TWELVE
1948–50
DAILIES & SUNDAYS

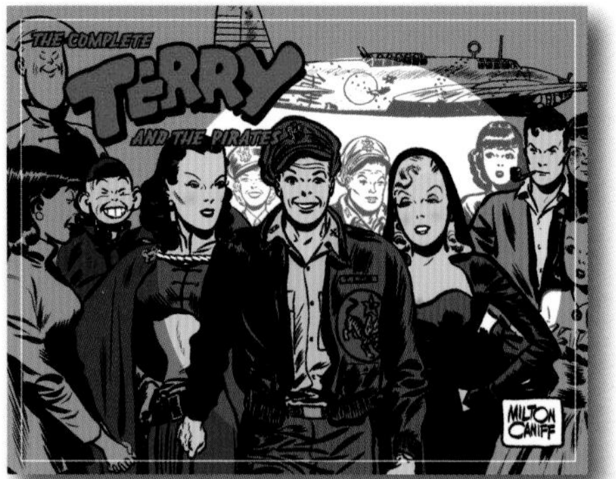

THE COMPLETE
TERRY AND THE PIRATES
MILTON CANIFF

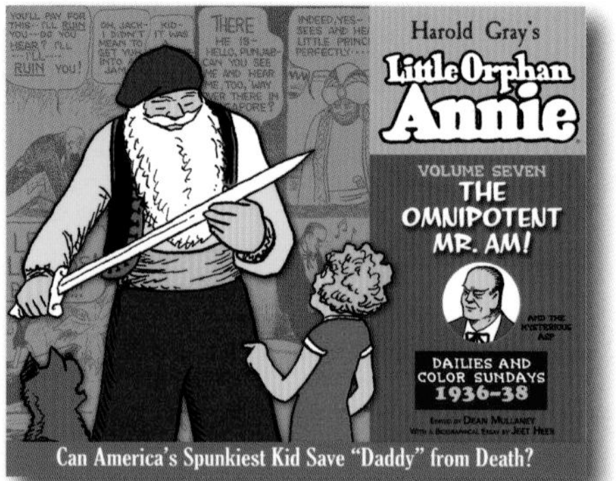

Harold Gray's
Little Orphan Annie
VOLUME SEVEN
THE OMNIPOTENT MR. AM!
DAILIES AND COLOR SUNDAYS
1936–38
Can America's Spunkiest Kid Save "Daddy" from Death?

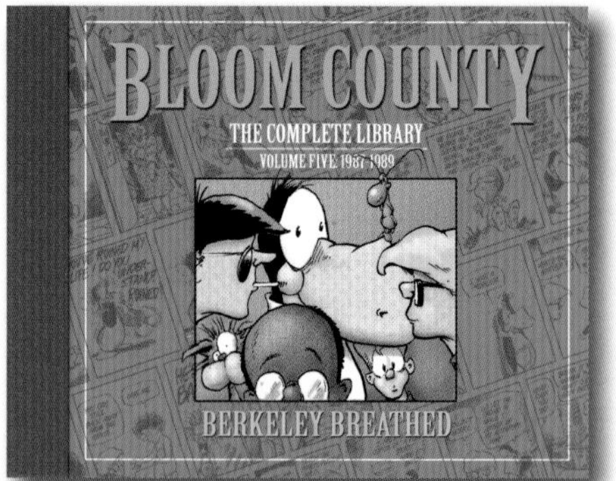

BLOOM COUNTY
THE COMPLETE LIBRARY
VOLUME FIVE 1987–1989
BERKELEY BREATHED

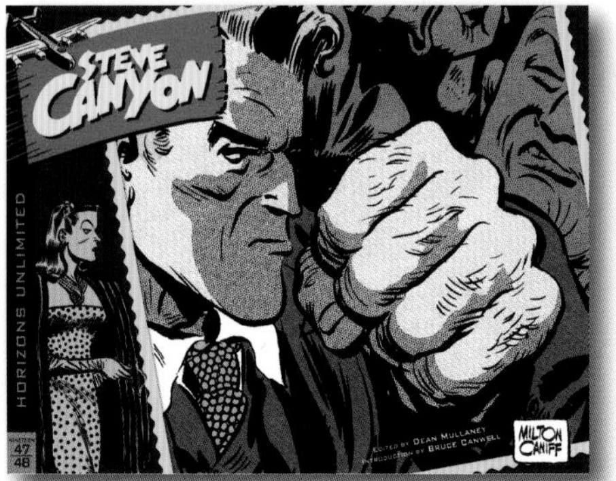

STEVE CANYON
HORIZONS UNLIMITED
MILTON CANIFF

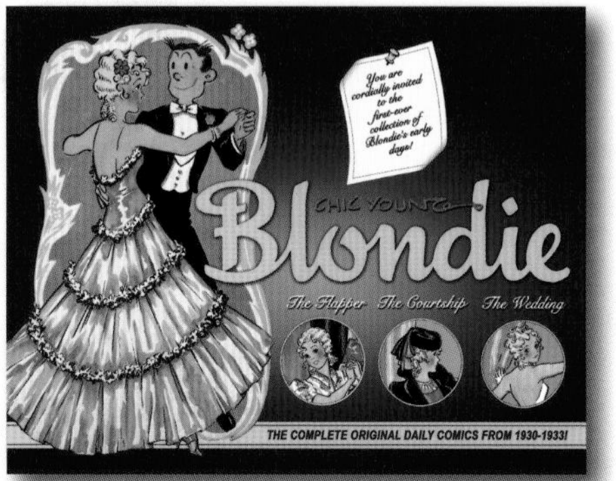

You are cordially invited to the first-ever collection of Blondie's early days!
CHIC YOUNG'S
Blondie
The Flapper The Courtship The Wedding
THE COMPLETE ORIGINAL DAILY COMICS FROM 1930-1933!

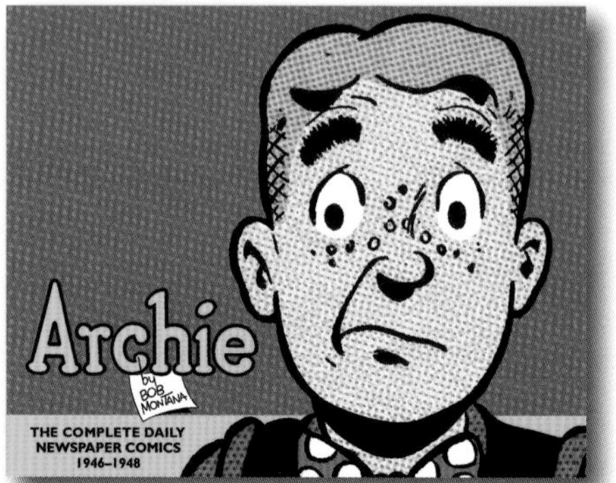

Archie
BY BOB MONTANA
THE COMPLETE DAILY NEWSPAPER COMICS
1946–1948

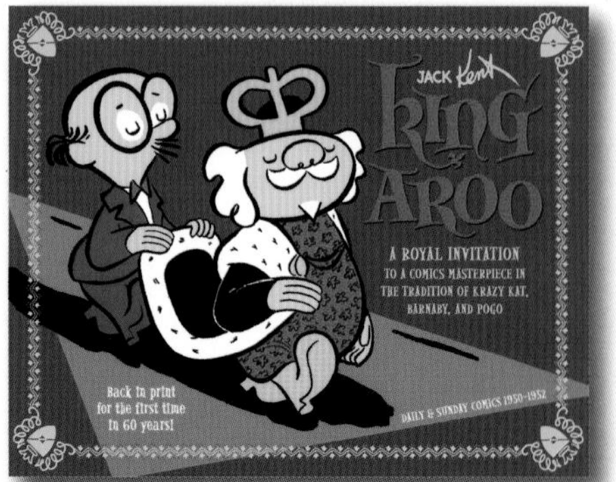

JACK KENT
King Aroo
A ROYAL INVITATION TO A COMICS MASTERPIECE IN THE TRADITION OF KRAZY KAT, BARNABY, AND POGO
Back in print for the first time in 60 years!

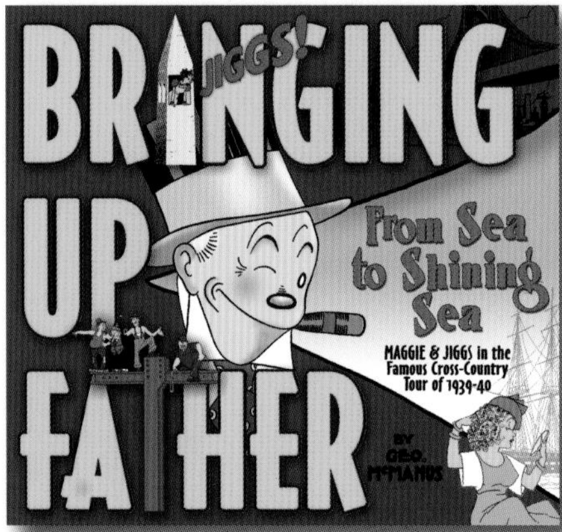

BRINGING UP FATHER
JIGGS!
From Sea to Shining Sea
MAGGIE & JIGGS in the Famous Cross-Country Tour of 1939-40
BY GEO. McMANUS

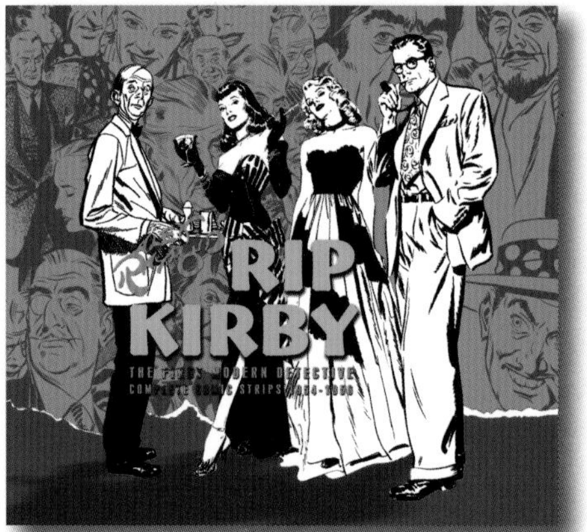

RIP KIRBY

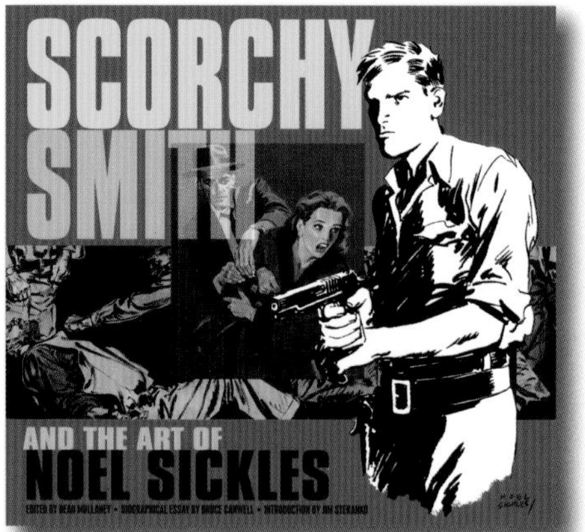

SCORCHY SMITH
AND THE ART OF
NOEL SICKLES

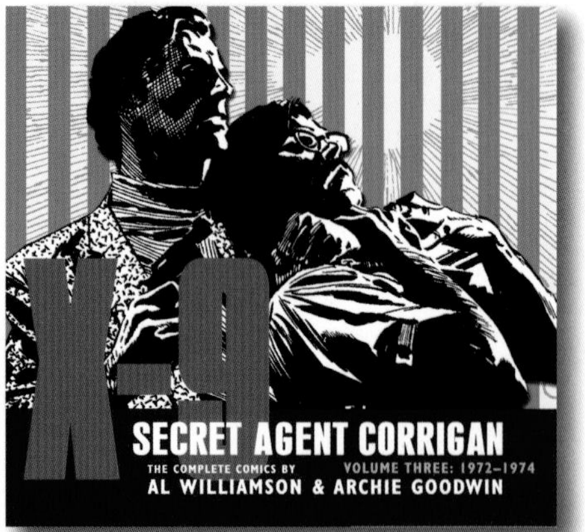

X-9
SECRET AGENT CORRIGAN
THE COMPLETE COMICS BY
VOLUME THREE: 1972–1974
AL WILLIAMSON & ARCHIE GOODWIN

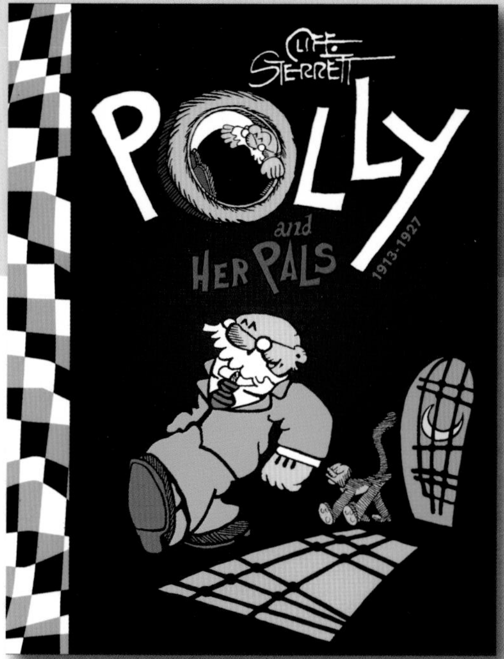
Cliff Sterrett
POLLY
and
HER PALS
1913-1927

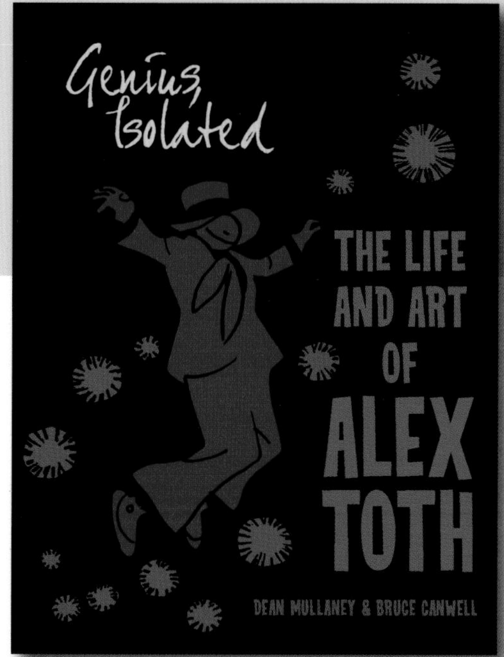
Genius, Isolated
THE LIFE AND ART OF ALEX TOTH
DEAN MULLANEY & BRUCE CANWELL

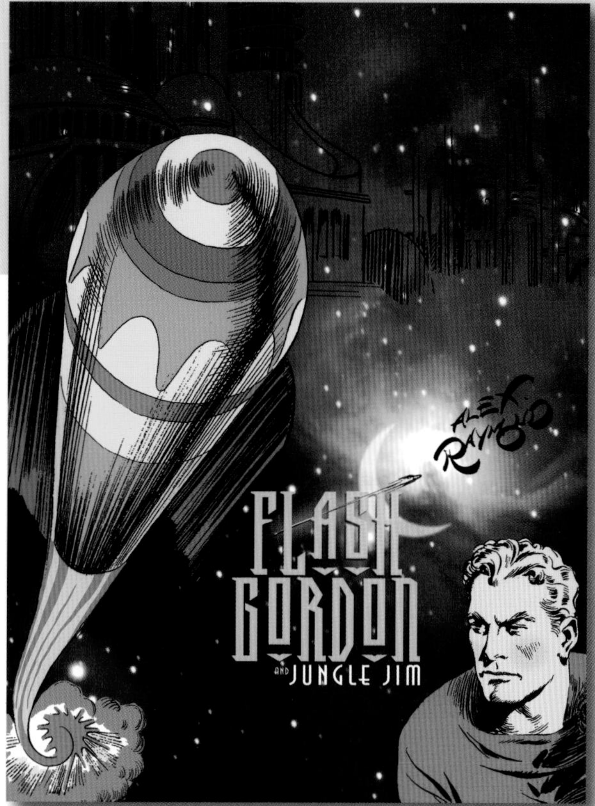
ALEX RAYMOND
FLASH GORDON
AND JUNGLE JIM

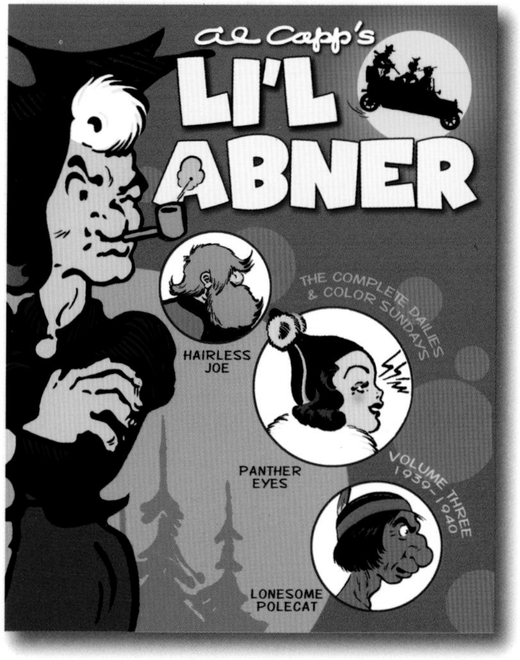
Al Capp's
LI'L ABNER
THE COMPLETE DAILIES & COLOR SUNDAYS
HAIRLESS JOE
PANTHER EYES
VOLUME THREE 1939-1940
LONESOME POLECAT

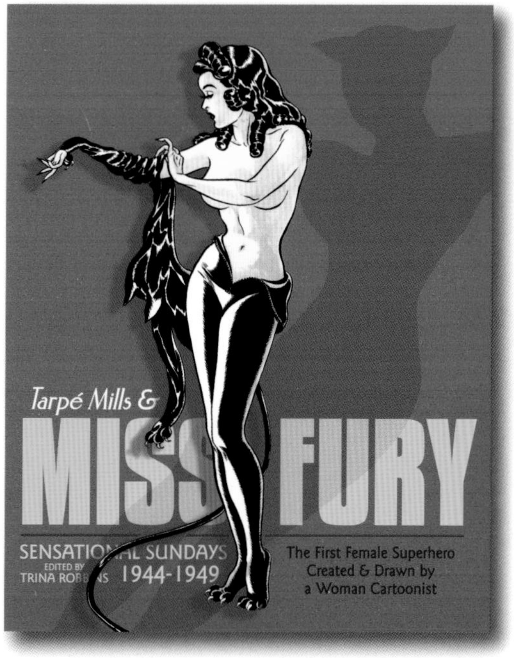
Tarpé Mills &
MISS FURY
SENSATIONAL SUNDAYS
EDITED BY TRINA ROBBINS
1944-1949
The First Female Superhero Created & Drawn by a Woman Cartoonist

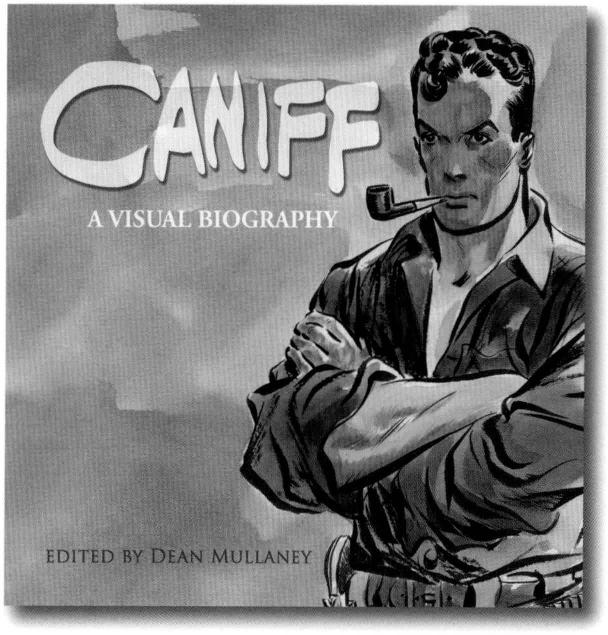
CANIFF
A VISUAL BIOGRAPHY
EDITED BY DEAN MULLANEY

For those interested in exploring the breadth of comic strip and comic book history, we are fortunate to have, among others, two comprehensive university library resources. We highly recommend them:

MICHIGAN STATE UNIVERSITY'S COMIC ART COLLECTION
comics.lib.msu.edu

THE OHIO STATE UNIVERSITY BILLY IRELAND CARTOON LIBRARY & MUSEUM
cartoons.osu.edu

We invite you to visit us online at
LibraryofAmericanComics.com

THE LIBRARY OF AMERICAN COMICS

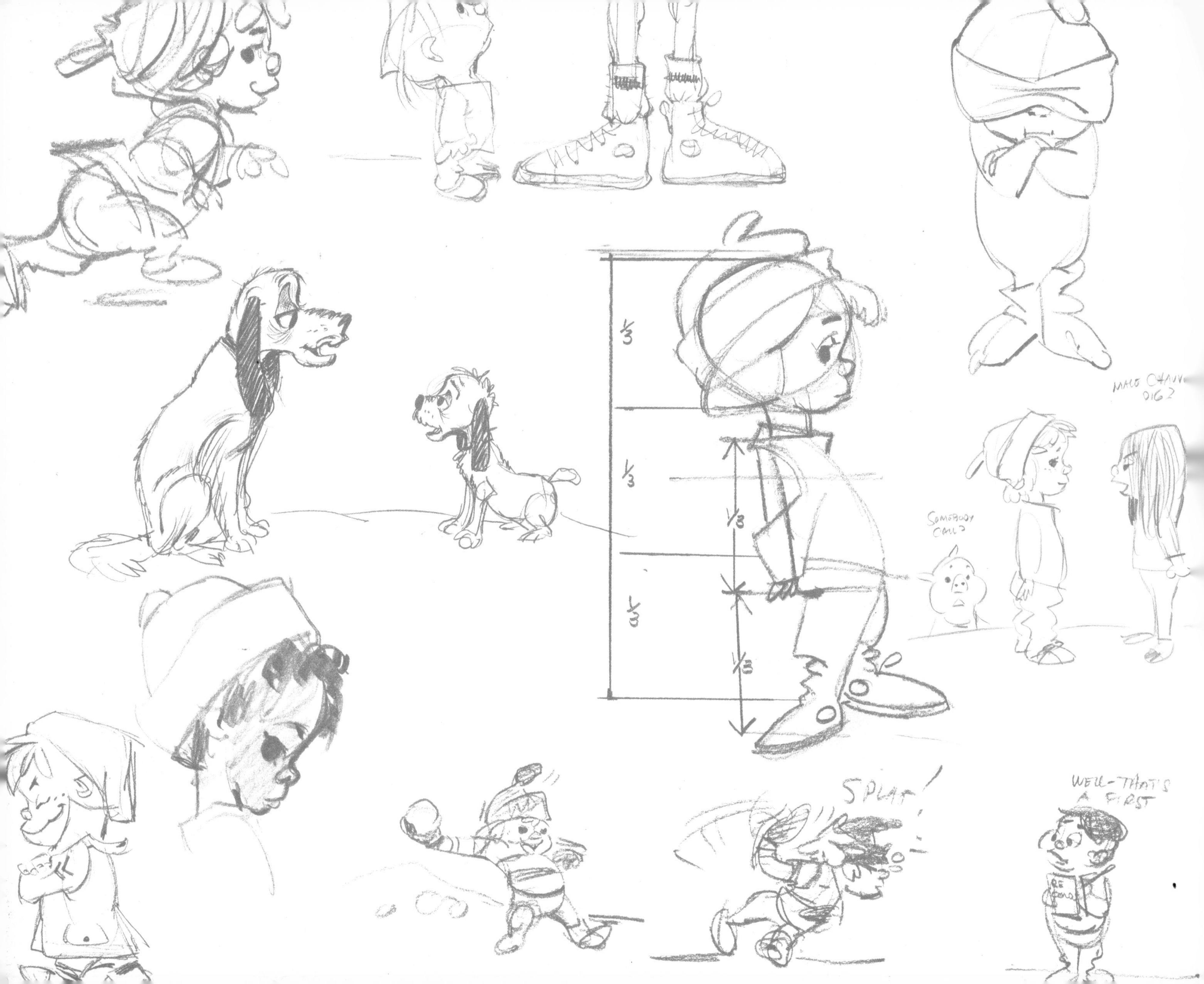
1/3
1/3
1/3
1/3
1/3
SOMEBODY CALL?
SPLAT!
WELL-THAT'S A FIRST